TAKING SIDES

Clashing Views on

Psychological Issues

SEVENTEENTH EDITION, EXPANDED

TAKING SIDES

Clashing Views on

Psychological Issues

SEVENTEENTH EDITION, EXPANDED

Selected, Edited, and with Introductions by

Brent Slife
Brigham Young University

The **McGraw·Hill** Companies

TAKING SIDES: CLASHING VIEWS ON PSYCHOLOGICAL ISSUES, SEVENTEENTH EDITION, EXPANDED

Published by McGraw-Hill, a business unit of The McGraw-Hill Companies, Inc., 1221 Avenue of the Americas, New York, NY 10020. Copyright © 2013 by The McGraw-Hill Companies, Inc. All rights reserved. Previous edition(s) © 2010, 2008, and 2006. Printed in the United States of America. No part of this publication may be reproduced or distributed in any form or by any means, or stored in a database or retrieval system, without the prior written consent of The McGraw-Hill Companies, Inc., including, but not limited to, in any network or other electronic storage or transmission, or broadcast for distance learning.

Some ancillaries, including electronic and print components, may not be available to customers outside the United States.

Taking Sides® is a registered trademark of the McGraw-Hill Companies, Inc.
Taking Sides is published by the **Contemporary Learning Series** group within the McGraw-Hill Higher Education division.

This book is printed on acid-free paper.

1 2 3 4 5 6 7 8 9 0 DOC/DOC 1 0 9 8 7 6 5 4 3 2

MHID: 0-07-805051-0
ISBN: 978-0-07-805051-0
ISSN: 1098-5409

Managing Editor: *Larry Loeppke*
Senior Developmental Editor: *Jade Benedict*
Permissions Coordinator: *Rita Hingtgen*
Marketing Director: *Adam Kloza*
Marketing Manager: *Nathan Edwards*
Project Manager: *Jessica Portz*
Cover Designer: *Studio Montage, St. Louis, MO*
Buyer: *Jennifer Pickel*
Media Project Manager: *Sridevi Palani*

Compositor: MPS Limited
Cover Image: © *Brand X Pictures/Getty Images RF*

www.mhhe.com

Editors/Academic Advisory Board

Members of the Academic Advisory Board are instrumental in the final selection of articles for each edition of *Taking Sides*. Their review of articles for content, level, and appropriateness provides critical direction to the editors and staff. We think that you will find their careful consideration well reflected in this volume.

TAKING SIDES: Clashing Views on PSYCHOLOGICAL ISSUES

Seventeenth Edition, Expanded

EDITOR

Brent Slife
Brigham Young University

ACADEMIC ADVISORY BOARD MEMBERS

Editors/Academic Advisory Board continued

Preface

Critical-thinking skills are a significant component of a meaningful education, and this book is specifically designed to stimulate critical thinking and initiate lively and informed dialogue on psychological issues. In this book I present 36 selections, arranged in pro and con pairs, that address a total of 18 different controversial issues in psychology. The opposing views demonstrate that even experts can derive conflicting conclusions and opinions from the same body of information.

A dialogue approach to learning is certainly not new. The Ancient Greek philosopher Socrates engaged in it with his students some 2,400 years ago. His point-counterpoint procedure was termed a *dialectic*. Although Socrates and his companions hoped eventually to know the "truth" by this method, they did not see the dialectic as having a predetermined end. There were no right answers to know or facts to memorize. The emphasis in this learning method is on how to evaluate information—on developing reasoning skills.

It is in this dialectical spirit that *Taking Sides: Clashing Views on Psychological Issues* was originally compiled, and it has guided me through this 17th edition as well. To encourage and stimulate discussion and to focus the debates in this volume, each issue is expressed in terms of a single question that is answered with two different points of view. But certainly the reader should not feel confined to adopt only one or the other of the positions presented. Readers' positions may fall between the views expressed or totally outside them, and I encourage readers to fashion their own conclusions.

Some of the questions raised in this volume go to the very heart of what psychology as a discipline is all about and the methods and manner in which psychologists work. Others address newly emerging concerns. In choosing readings I was guided by the following criteria: the readings had to be understandable to newcomers to psychology, they had to have academic substance, and they had to express markedly different points of view.

Plan of the book   Each issue in this volume has an issue *introduction*, which defines each author's position and sets the stage for debate. Also provided is a set of point-counterpoint statements that pertain to the issue and that should help to get the dialogue off the ground. Each issue concludes with *challenge questions* to provoke further examination of the issue. The introduction and challenge questions are designed to assist the reader in achieving a critical and informed view on important psychological issues. Also, at the beginning of each part is a list of Internet site addresses (URLs) that should prove useful as starting points for further research. At the back of the book is a listing of all the contributors to this volume, which gives information on the psychologists, psychiatrists, philosophers, professors, and social critics whose views are debated here.

In the interest of space, the reference lists of many of the original articles have been omitted or severely curtailed. However, all references for this edition can be accessed on the website at www.mhhe.com/cls for further investigations into these issues.

Changes to this edition This edition entails considerable revision. There are four completely new issues in this edition. Also new is a re-work of the units and issues within those units.

A word to the instructor An *Instructor's Resource Guide with Test Questions* (multiple-choice and essay) is available through the publisher for the instructor using *Taking Sides* in the classroom. A general guidebook, *Using Taking Sides in the Classroom*, which discusses methods and techniques for integrating the pro-con approach into any classroom setting, is also available. An online version of *Using Taking Sides in the Classroom* and a correspondence service for *Taking Sides* adopters can be found at www.mhhe.com/cls.

Taking Sides: Clashing Views in Psychological Issues is only one title in the Taking Sides series. If you are interested in seeing the table of contents for any of the other titles, please visit the Taking Sides website at www.mhhe.com/cls.

Acknowledgments In working on this revision I received useful suggestions from many of the users of the previous edition, and I was able to incorporate many of their recommendations for new issues and new readings.

In addition, special thanks to the McGraw-Hill staff for their support and perspective.

Brent Slife
Brigham Young University

Contents In Brief

UNIT 1 Biological Issues   1

Issue 1. Is Addiction a Brain Disease? 2

Issue 2. Is Homosexuality Biologically Based? 13

Issue 3. Is Evolution a Good Explanation for Psychological Concepts? 33

UNIT 2 Research Issues   57

Issue 4. Is American Psychological Research Generalizable to Other Cultures? 58

Issue 5. Are Traditional Empirical Methods Sufficient to Provide Evidence for Psychological Practice? 68

Issue 6. Does Teaching Scientific Determinism Lead to Bad Behavior? 90

UNIT 3 Development Issues   113

Issue 7. Are Today's Youth More Self-Centered Than Previous Generations? 114

Issue 8. Do Online Friendships Hurt Adolescent Development? 134

UNIT 4 Cognitive–Emotional Issues   155

Issue 9. Can Positive Psychology Make Us Happier? 156

Issue 10. Is Emotional Intelligence Valid? 178

UNIT 5 Mental Health Issues   201

Issue 11. Does an Elective Abortion Lead to Negative Psychological Effects? 202

Issue 12. Is Attention-Deficit Hyperactivity Disorder (ADHD) a Real Disorder? 223

Issue 13. Does Facebook Have Generally Positive Psychological Effects? 245

UNIT 6 Psychotherapy Issues   265

Issue 14. Are All Psychotherapies Equally Effective? 266

Issue 15. Should Therapists Be Eclectic? 287

UNIT 7 Social Issues   313

Issue 16. Should Psychologists Abstain from Involvement in Coercive Interrogations? 314

Issue 17. Does the Evidence Support Evolutionary Accounts of Female Mating Preferences? 329

Issue 18. Can Sex Be Addictive? 356

Issue 19. Does Birth Order Predict Intelligence? 371

Issue 20. Is the Need for Social Enhancement Universal Across Cultures? 392

Contents

Preface   vii

Correlation Guide   xvii

Topic Guide   xx

Introduction   xxii

UNIT 1   BIOLOGICAL ISSUES   1

Issue 1.   Is Addiction a Brain Disease?   2

YES: **National Institute on Drug Abuse,** from "The Science of Addiction," *Drugs, Brain, and Behavior: The Science of Addiction,* rev. ed. (*National Institutes of Health,* 2007)   *4*

NO: **Sally Satel and Scott O. Lilienfeld,** from "Singing the Brain Disease Blues," *AJOB Neuroscience* (January 2010)   *9*

A publication from the National Institute on Drug Abuse argues that addiction is a brain disease and that scientific information is available about the nature, prevention, and treatment of this disease. Psychiatrist Sally Satel and psychologist Scott O. Lilienfeld object to the brain disease characterization of drug addiction, asserting that addiction is an activity whose course can be altered by its foreseeable consequences.

Issue 2.   Is Homosexuality Biologically Based?   13

YES: **Qazi Rahman,** from "The Neurodevelopment of Human Sexual Orientation," *Neuroscience & Biobehavioral Reviews* (October 2005)   *15*

NO: **Stanton L. Jones and Alex W. Kwee,** from "Scientific Research, Homosexuality, and the Church's Moral Debate: An Update," *Journal of Psychology and Christianity* (Winter 2005)   *21*

Professor of psychobiology Qazi Rahman claims that the current research on the biology of homosexuality supports prenatal biological determination and refutes learning models of sexual orientation. Professor of psychology Stanton L. Jones and clinical psychologist Alex W. Kwee claim the current research on the biology of homosexuality provides no firm evidence for biological causation and leaves room for learning models of sexual orientation.

Issue 3.   Is Evolution a Good Explanation
for Psychological Concepts?   33

YES: **Glenn Geher,** from "Evolutionary Psychology Is Not Evil! (. . . And Here's Why . . .)," *Psychological Topics* (December 2006)   *35*

NO: **Edwin E. Gantt and Brent S. Melling,** from "Evolutionary Psychology Isn't Evil, It's Just Not Any Good" (An Original Essay Written for This Volume, 2009)   *46*

Evolutionary psychologist Glenn Geher maintains that evolution provides the best meta-theory for explaining and understanding human psychology. Theoretical psychologists Edwin Gantt and Brent Melling argue that an evolutionary account of psychology omits many important and good things about humans.

UNIT 2 RESEARCH ISSUES 57

Issue 4. Is American Psychological Research Generalizable to Other Cultures? 58

YES: Gerald J. Haeffel, Erik D. Thiessen, Matthew W. Campbell, Michael P. Kaschak, and Nicole M. McNeil, from "Theory, Not Cultural Context, Will Advance American Psychology," *American Psychologist* (September 2009) *60*

NO: Jeffrey J. Arnett, from "The Neglected 95%, a Challenge to Psychology's Philosophy of Science," *American Psychologist* (September 2009) *64*

Haeffel and his colleagues believe that psychological studies of American people often generalize to people of other cultures, especially when basic processes are being studied. Jeffrey Arnett, psychological research professor, argues that culture is central to the functioning of humans and thus to psychological findings.

Issue 5. Are Traditional Empirical Methods Sufficient to Provide Evidence for Psychological Practice? 68

YES: APA Presidential Task Force on Evidence-Based Practice, from "Report of the 2005 Presidential Task Force on Evidence-Based Practice," *American Psychologist* (May/June 2006) *70*

NO: Brent D. Slife and Dennis C. Wendt, from "The Next Step in the Evidence-Based Practice Movement," APA Convention Presentation (August 2006) *81*

The APA Presidential Task Force on Evidence-Based Practice assumes that a variety of traditional empirical methods is sufficient to provide evidence for psychological practices. Psychologist Brent D. Slife and researcher Dennis C. Wendt contend that traditional empirical methods are guided by a single philosophy that limits the diversity of methods.

Issue 6. Does Teaching Scientific Determinism Lead to Bad Behavior? 90

YES: Kathleen D. Vohs and Jonathan W. Schooler, from "The Value of Believing in Free Will: Encouraging a Belief in Determinism Increases Cheating," *Psychological Science* (vol. 19, no. 1, 2008) *92*

NO: Eddy Nahmias, from "Why 'Willusionism' Leads to 'Bad Results': Comments on Baumeister, Crescioni, and Alquist," *Neuroethics* (July 31, 2009) *102*

Marketing professor Kathleen Vohs and psychology professor Jonathan Schooler attempt to demonstrate that a scientific belief in determinism (that humans lack free will) leads to a host of bad behaviors such as lying, cheating, and stealing. Eddy Nahmias, a philosopher with the Neuroscience Institute at Georgia State University, counters the claim that such scientific beliefs cause bad behavior by arguing that laypersons fail to understand what scientists are actually saying about determinism.

UNIT 3   DEVELOPMENT ISSUES   113

Issue 7.   Are Today's Youth More Self-Centered Than Previous Generations?   114

YES: **Jean M. Twenge, Sara Konrath, Joshua D. Foster, W. Keith Campbell, and Brad J. Bushman**, from "Egos Inflating Over Time: A Cross-Temporal Meta-Analysis of the Narcissistic Personality Inventory," *Journal of Personality* (August 2008)   *116*

NO: **Kali H. Trzesniewski, M. Brent Donnellan, and Richard W. Robins**, from "Do Today's Young People Really Think They Are So Extraordinary? An Examination of Secular Trends in Narcissism and Self-Enhancement," *Psychological Science* (February 2008)   *124*

Psychologist Jean Twenge and colleagues argue that the evidence suggests that young people are more egocentric than the previous generation. Professor Kali Trzesniewski and colleagues maintain that the evidence shows there is no change in the over-all level of narcissism since the previous generation.

Issue 8.   Do Online Friendships Hurt Adolescent Development?   134

YES: **Lauren Donchi and Susan Moore**, from "It's a Boy Thing: The Role of the Internet in Young People's Psychological Wellbeing," *Behavior Change* (vol. 21, no. 2, 2004)   *136*

NO: **Patti M. Valkenburg and Jochen Peter**, from "Online Communication and Adolescent Well-Being: Testing the Stimulation Versus the Displacement Hypothesis," *Journal of Computer-Mediated Communication* (vol. 12, issue 4, 2007)   *144*

Psychologists Lauren Donchi and Susan Moore report that adolescent males who rate online friendships higher than face-to-face friendships are more likely to be lonely and experience low self-esteem. Professors of communication Patti M. Valkenburg and Jochen Peter maintain that online relationships actually *enhance* an adolescent's face-to-face peer relations and psychological wellbeing.

UNIT 4   COGNITIVE–EMOTIONAL ISSUES   155

Issue 9.   Can Positive Psychology Make Us Happier?   156

YES: **Julia K. Boehm and Sonja Lyubomirsky**, from "The Promise of Sustainable Happiness," in *The Oxford Handbook of Positive Psychology*, 2nd ed. (Oxford University Press, 2009)   *158*

NO: **Laurel C. Newman and Randy J. Larsen**, from "How Much of Our Happiness Is Within Our Control?" An original article written for this text (2009)   *171*

Health researcher Julia Boehm and psychologist Sonja Lyubomirsky argue that empirical research has established that people can use multiadaptive strategies to increase their levels of happiness. Psychologists Laurel Newman and Randy Larsen challenge the external validity and sustainability of the effects of these strategies, arguing that most of what influences our long-term happiness is outside our control.

Issue 10.   Is Emotional Intelligence Valid?   178

YES: **John D. Mayer, Peter Salovey, and David R. Caruso,** from "Emotional Intelligence: New Ability or Eclectic Traits?" *American Psychologist* (September 2008)   *180*

NO: **Edwin A. Locke,** from "Why Emotional Intelligence Is an Invalid Concept," *Journal of Organizational Behavior* (January 2005)   *192*

Psychologists John Mayer, Peter Salovey, and David Caruso maintain that some individuals have a greater emotional intelligence (EI), a greater capacity than others to carry out sophisticated information processing about emotions. Social science professor Edwin A. Locke argues that "emotional intelligence" is not a form of intellectual ability.

UNIT 5   MENTAL HEALTH ISSUES   201

Issue 11.   Does an Elective Abortion Lead to Negative Psychological Effects?   202

YES: **Priscilla K. Coleman, Catherine T. Coyle, Martha Shuping, and Vincent M. Rue,** from "Induced Abortion and Anxiety, Mood, and Substance Abuse Disorders: Isolating the Effects of Abortion in the National Comorbidity Survey," *Journal of Psychiatric Research* (May 2009)   *204*

NO: **Julia Renee Steinberg and Nancy F. Russo,** from "Abortion and Anxiety: What's the Relationship," *Social Science & Medicine* (July 2008)   *213*

Associate Professor Priscilla K. Coleman and colleagues argue that the evidence suggests that abortion is causal to psychological problems. Researchers Julia R. Steinberg and Nancy F. Russo counter that other factors, common to women who abort, are responsible for later psychological problems.

Issue 12.   Is Attention-Deficit Hyperactivity Disorder (ADHD) a Real Disorder?   223

YES: **National Institute of Mental Health,** from *Attention Deficit Hyperactivity Disorder* (NIH Publication No. 3572, 2006)   *225*

NO: **Rogers H. Wright,** from "Attention Deficit Hyperactivity Disorder: What It Is and What It Is Not," in Rogers H. Wright and Nicholas A. Cummings, eds., *Destructive Trends in Mental Health: The Well Intentioned Path to Harm* (Routledge, 2005)   *234*

The National Institute of Mental Health asserts that ADHD is a real disorder that merits special consideration and treatment. Psychologist Rogers H. Wright argues that ADHD is not a real disorder, but rather a "fad diagnosis" that has resulted in the misdiagnosis and overmedication of children.

Issue 13.   Does Facebook Have Generally Positive Psychological Effects?   245

YES: **Amy L. Gonzales and Jeffery T. Hancock,** from "Mirror, Mirror on My Facebook Wall: Effects of Exposure to Facebook on Self-Esteem," *Cyberspcyhology, Behavior, and Social Networking* (January/February 2011)   *248*

NO: **Gwenn Schurgin O'Keeffe, Kathleen Clarke-Pearson, and Council on Communications and Media,** from "Clinical Report—The Impact of Social Media on Children, Adolescents, and Families," *Pediatrics* (April 2011)   *256*

Social scientists Amy Gonzales and Jeffery Hancock present empirical research suggesting that selective self-presentation, such as Facebook profiles, enhances self-esteem. Pediatricians Gwenn Schurgin O'Keeffe and Kathleen Clarke-Pearson caution that inappropriate use of online social networks like Facebook may pose dangers to adolescents, such as isolation and depression.

UNIT 6   PSYCHOTHERAPY ISSUES   265

Issue 14.   Are All Psychotherapies Equally Effective?   266

YES: **Benjamin Hansen,** from "The Dodo Manifesto," *Australian and New Zealand Journal of Family Therapy* (December 2005)   *268*

NO: **Jedidiah Siev, Jonathan D. Huppert, and Dianne L. Chambless,** from "The Dodo Bird, Treatment Technique, and Disseminating Empirically Supported Treatments," *The Behavioral Therapist* (April 2009)   *277*

Psychologist Benjamin Hansen agrees that psychotherapeutic techniques clearly differ among the various approaches, but he argues that all such psychotherapy techniques produce similar outcomes. Psychologists Jedidiah Siev, Jonathan Huppert, and Dianne Chambless assert that outcomes among the various psychotherapies differ primarily because one technique or therapy is better than another.

Issue 15.   Should Therapists Be Eclectic?   287

YES: **Jean A. Carter,** from "Theoretical Pluralism and Technical Eclecticism," in Carol D. Goodheart, Alan E. Kazdin, Robert J. Sternberg, eds., *Evidence-Based Psychotherapy: Where Practice and Research Meet* (APA, 2006)   *289*

NO: **Don MacDonald and Marcia Webb,** from "Toward Conceptual Clarity with Psychotherapeutic Theories," *Journal of Psychology and Christianity* (Spring 2006)   *300*

Counseling psychologist Jean Carter insists that the continued improvement and effectiveness of psychotherapy requires that techniques and theories include the different approaches of psychological theory and practice through an eclectic approach. Professors of psychotherapy Don MacDonald and Marcia Webb contend that eclecticism creates an unsystematic theoretical center for psychological ideas and methods that ultimately limits overall therapeutic effectiveness.

UNIT 7   SOCIAL ISSUES   313

Issue 16.   Should Psychologists Abstain from Involvement in Coercive Interrogations?   314

YES: **Mark Costanza, Ellen Gerrity, and M. Brinton Lykes,** from "Psychologists and the Use of Torture in Interrogations." *Analyses of Social Issues and Public Policy* (December 2007)   *316*

NO: **Kirk M. Hubbard,** from "Psychologists and Interrogations: What's Torture Got to Do with It?" *Analyses of Social Issues and Public Policy* (December 2007)   *324*

Psychologists Mark Costanzo, Ellen Gerrity, and M. Brinton Lykes assert that all psychologists should be banned from any involvement in interrogations that involve torture or other unethical forms of coercion. Psychologist and intelligence consultant Kirk M. Hubbard argues that a ban on a psychologist's involvement in coercive interrogations would overly restrict the ways in which psychologists can ethically contribute to their country's intelligence needs.

Issue 17.   Does the Evidence Support Evolutionary Accounts of Female Mating Preferences?   329

YES: **David M. Buss,** from *Evolutionary Psychology: The New Science of the Mind,* 3rd ed. (Allyn and Bacon, 2008)   *331*

NO: **David J. Buller,** from *Adapting Minds: Evolutionary Psychology and the Persistent Quest for Human Nature* (MIT Press, 2005)   *341*

Professor of psychology David M. Buss contends that the research data indicate an evolved female preference for high-status, resource-possessing males. Philosopher of science David J. Buller argues that the research data support several alternative explanations for Buss's findings.

Issue 18.   Can Sex Be Addictive?   356

YES: **Patrick Carnes,** from "Understanding Sexual Addiction," *SIECUS Report* (June/July 2003)   *358*

NO: **Lawrence A. Siegel and Richard M. Siegel,** from "Sex Addiction: Recovering from a Shady Concept," An Original Essay Written for *Taking Sides: Human Sexuality,* 10th ed. (2007)   *363*

Sexual addiction expert Patrick J. Carnes argues not only that sex can be addictive but that sex can be as addictive as drugs, alcohol, or any other chemical substance. Sex therapists Lawrence A. Siegel and Richard M. Siegel believe that while some sexual behaviors might be dysfunctional, calling those behaviors "addictive" confuses a moralistic ideology with a scientific fact.

Issue 19.   Does Birth Order Predict Intelligence?   371

YES: **R. B. Zajonc and Frank J. Sulloway,** from "The Confluence Model: Birth Order as a Within-Family or Between-Family Dynamic?" *Personality and Social Psychology Bulletin* (vol. 33, no. 9, pp. 1187–1194, 2007)   *374*

NO: Aaron L. Wichman, Joseph Lee Rodgers, and Robert C. MacCallum, from "Birth Order Has No Effect on Intelligence: A Reply and Extension of Previous Findings," *Personality and Social Psychology Bulletin* (vol. 33, no. 9, pp. 1195–1200, 2007)   *384*

R. B. Zajonc (deceased), professor of psychology at Stanford University, and Frank J. Sulloway, adjunct professor in the Department of Psychology at the University of California, Berkeley, maintain that due to available resources, earlier-born children have higher IQ. Aaron L. Wichman, assistant professor of psychology at Western Kentucky University, Joseph Lee Rodgers, professor of psychology at the University of Oklahoma, and Robert C. MacCallum, professor of psychology at the University of North Carolina–Chapel Hill, argue that the birth-order effect on intelligence does not hold when comparing siblings within a single family.

Issue 20.   Is the Need for Social Enhancement Universal Across Cultures?   392

YES: Constantine Sedikides, Lowell Gaertner, and Jack L. Vevea, from "Inclusion of Theory-Relevant Moderators Yield the Same Conclusions as Sedikides, Gaertner, and Vevea (2005): A Meta-analytical Reply to Heine, Kitayama, and Hamamura (2007)," *Asian Journal of Social Psychology* (vol. 10, no. 2, pp. 59–67, 2007). doi: 10.1111/j.1467-839X.2007.00212.x   *395*

NO: Steven J. Heine, Shinobu Kitayama, and Takeshi Hamamura, from "Inclusion of Additional Studies Yields Different Conclusions: Comment on Sedikides, Gaertner, and Vevea (2005), *Journal of Personality and Social Psychology*," *Asian Journal of Social Psychology* (vol. 10, no. 2, pp. 49–58, 2007). doi: 10:1111/j.1467-839X.2007.00211.x   *404*

Constantine Sedikides, director of the Center for Research on Self and Identity at the University of Southampton, England; Lowell Gaertner, professor of psychology at the University of Tennessee, Knoxville; and Jack L. Vevea, associate professor of quantitative psychology at the University of California, Merced, maintain that all people, regardless of culture, positively inflate self-ratings on dimensions important to themselves. Steven J. Heine, professor of psychology at the University of British Columbia; Shinobu Kitayama, professor of psychology at the University of Michigan; and Takeshi Hamamura, assistant professor of psychology at the Chinese University of Hong Kong, argue that people of interdependent cultures inflate positive self-ratings less than those of independent cultures.

Contributors   416

Correlation Guide

The *Taking Sides* series presents current issues in a debate-style format designed to stimulate student interest and develop critical-thinking skills. Each issue is thoughtfully framed with an issue summary, an issue introduction with points and counterpoints, and challenge questions. The pro and con essays—selected for their liveliness and substance—represent the arguments of leading scholars and commentators in their fields.

Taking Sides: Clashing Views on Psychological Issues, 17/e, Expanded is an easy-to-use reader that presents issues on important topics such as *homosexuality, addiction, online friendships,* and *positive psychology*. For more information on *Taking Sides* and other *McGraw-Hill Contemporary Learning Series* titles, visit www.mhhe.com/cls.

This convenient guide matches the issues in **Taking Sides: Psychological Issues, 17/e, Expanded** with the corresponding chapters in three of our best-selling McGraw-Hill psychology textbooks by Feldman, Lahey, and Feist/Rosenberg.

Taking Sides: Psychological Issues, 17/e	Psychology and Your Life, 2/e by Feldman	Psychology: An Introduction, 11/e by Lahey	Psychology: Perspectives & Connections, 2/e by Feist/Rosenberg
Issue 1: Is Addiction a Brain Disease?	**Chapter 2:** Neuroscience and Behavior **Chapter 7:** Motivation and Emotion	**Chapter 3:** Biological Foundations in Behavior **Chapter 14:** Abnormal Behavior	**Chapter 3:** The Biology of Behavior **Chapter 16:** Treatment of Psychological Disorders
Issue 2: Is Homosexuality Biologically Based?	**Chapter 8:** Development **Chapter 9:** Personality and Individual Differences	**Chapter 3:** Biological Foundations in Behavior **Chapter 4:** Interplay of Nature and Nurture	**Chapter 5:** Human Development
Issue 3: Is Evolution a Good Explanation for Psychological Concepts?	**Chapter 1:** Introduction to Psychology **Chapter 8:** Development **Chapter 9:** Personality and Individual Differences	**Chapter 1:** Introduction to Psychology **Chapter 2:** Research Methods in Psychology **Chapter 3:** Biological Foundations in Behavior **Chapter 10:** Developmental Psychology	**Chapter 1:** Introduction to Psychology **Chapter 2:** Conducting Research in Psychology **Chapter 3:** The Biology of Behavior **Chapter 13:** Personality: The Uniqueness of the Individual
Issue 4: Is American Psychological Research Generalizable to Other Cultures?	**Chapter 1:** Introduction to Psychology	**Chapter 2:** Research Methods in Psychology	**Chapter 1:** Introduction to Psychology **Chapter 2:** Conducting Research in Psychology

(Continued)

Taking Sides: Psychological Issues, 17/e	Psychology and Your Life, 2/e by Feldman	Psychology: An Introduction, 11/e by Lahey	Psychology: Perspectives & Connections, 2/e by Feist/Rosenberg
Issue 5: Are Traditional Empirical Methods Sufficient to Provide Evidence for Psychological Practice?	**Chapter 1:** Introduction to Psychology **Chapter 11:** Treatment of Psychological Disorders	**Chapter 1:** Introduction to Psychology **Chapter 2:** Research Methods in Psychology	**Chapter 1:** Introduction to Psychology **Chapter 2:** Conducting Research in Psychology
Issue 6: Does Teaching Scientific Determinism Lead to Bad Behavior?	**Chapter 9:** Personality and Individual Differences **Chapter 10:** Psychological Disorders **Chapter 12:** Social Psychology	**Chapter 14:** Abnormal Behavior	**Chapter 3:** The Biology of Behavior **Chapter 8:** Learning **Chapter 14:** Social Behavior
Issue 7: Are Today's Youth More Self-Centered Than Previous Generations?	**Chapter 7:** Motivation and Emotion **Chapter 8:** Development **Chapter 9:** Personality and Individual Differences **Chapter 12:** Social Psychology	**Chapter 11:** Motivation and Emotion **Chapter 12:** Personality	**Chapter 11:** Motivation and Emotion **Chapter 13:** Personality: The Uniqueness of the Individual **Chapter 14:** Social Behavior
Issue 8: Do Online Friendships Hurt Adolescent Development?	**Chapter 8:** Development **Chapter 9:** Personality and Individual Differences **Chapter 12:** Social Psychology	**Chapter 16:** Social Psychology	**Chapter 5:** Human Development **Chapter 11:** Motivation and Emotion **Chapter 14:** Social Behavior **Chapter 15:** Psychological Disorders
Issue 9: Can Positive Psychology Make Us Happier?	**Chapter 2:** Neuroscience and Behavior **Chapter 7:** Motivation and Emotion **Chapter 8:** Development **Chapter 9:** Personality and Individual Differences **Chapter 12:** Social Psychology	**Chapter 10:** Developmental Psychology **Chapter 11:** Motivation and Emotion **Chapter 12:** Personality	**Chapter 5:** Human Development **Chapter 11:** Motivation and Emotion **Chapter 12:** Stress and Health **Chapter 13:** Personality: The Uniqueness of the Individual
Issue 10: Is Emotional Intelligence Valid?	**Chapter 2:** Neuroscience and Behavior **Chapter 7:** Motivation and Emotion	**Chapter 9:** Cognition, Language, and Intelligence **Chapter 11:** Motivation and Emotion	**Chapter 10:** Intelligence, Problem Solving, and Creativity **Chapter 11:** Motivation and Emotion
Issue 11: Does an Elective Abortion Lead to Negative Psychological Effects?	**Chapter 2:** Neuroscience and Behavior **Chapter 7:** Motivation and Emotion **Chapter 12:** Social Psychology	**Chapter 3:** Biological Foundations in Behavior **Chapter 11:** Motivation and Emotion **Chapter 16:** Social Psychology	**Chapter 3:** The Biology of Behavior **Chapter 11:** Motivation and Emotion **Chapter 14:** Social Behavior

Taking Sides: Psychological Issues, 17/e	Psychology and Your Life, 2/e by Feldman	Psychology: An Introduction, 11/e by Lahey	Psychology: Perspectives & Connections, 2/e by Feist/Rosenberg
Issue 12: Is Attention-Deficit Hyperactivity Disorder (ADHD) a Real Disorder?	**Chapter 2:** Neuroscience and Behavior **Chapter 8:** Development **Chapter 10:** Psychological Disorders **Chapter 12:** Social Psychology	**Chapter 3:** Biological Foundations in Behavior **Chapter 10:** Developmental Psychology **Chapter 14:** Abnormal Behavior **Chapter 15:** Therapies **Chapter 16:** Social Psychology	**Chapter 3:** The Biology of Behavior **Chapter 8:** Learning **Chapter 14:** Social Behavior **Chapter 15:** Psychological Disorders **Chapter 16:** Treatment of Psychological Disorders
Issue 13: Does Facebook Have Generally Positive Psychological Effects?	**Chapter 12:** Social Psychology	**Chapter 16:** Social Psychology	**Chapter 11:** Motivation and Emotion **Chapter 14:** Social Behavior **Chapter 15:** Psychological Disorders
Issue 14: Are All Psychotherapies Equally Effective?	**Chapter 11:** Treatment of Psychological Disorders	**Chapter 15:** Therapies	**Chapter 16:** Treatment of Psychological Disorders
Issue 15: Should Therapists Be Eclectic?	**Chapter 11:** Treatment of Psychological Disorders	**Chapter 15:** Therapies	**Chapter 16:** Treatment of Psychological Disorders
Issue 16: Should Psychologists Abstain from Involvement in Coercive Interrogations?	**Chapter 11:** Treatment of Psychological Disorders	**Chapter 15:** Therapies	**Chapter 16:** Treatment of Psychological Disorders
Issue 17: Does the Evidence Support Evolutionary Accounts of Female Mating Preferences?	**Chapter 2:** Neuroscience and Behavior **Chapter 7:** Motivation and Emotion **Chapter 8:** Development **Chapter 12:** Social Psychology	**Chapter 3:** Biological Foundations in Behavior **Chapter 11:** Motivation and Emotion **Chapter 16:** Social Psychology	**Chapter 3:** The Biology of Behavior **Chapter 5:** Human Development **Chapter 11:** Motivation and Emotion **Chapter 14:** Social Behavior
Issue 18: Can Sex Be Addictive?	**Chapter 2:** Neuroscience and Behavior **Chapter 7:** Motivation and Emotion **Chapter 12:** Social Psychology	**Chapter 11:** Motivation and Emotion **Chapter 14:** Abnormal Behavior **Chapter 16:** Social Psychology	**Chapter 11:** Motivation and Emotion **Chapter 14:** Social Behavior **Chapter 15:** Psychological Disorders
Issue 19: Does Birth Order Predict Intelligence?	**Chapter 8:** Development	**Chapter 3:** Biological Foundations in Behavior	**Chapter 3:** The Biology of Behavior **Chapter 5:** Human Development
Issue 20: Is the Need for Social Enhancement Universal Across Cultures?	**Chapter 12:** Social Psychology	**Chapter 16:** Social Psychology	**Chapter 14:** Social Behavior

Topic Guide

This topic guide suggests how the selections in this book relate to the subjects covered in your course. You may want to use the topics listed on these pages to search the Web more easily.

All the articles that relate to each topic are listed below the bold-faced term.

Addiction

1. Is Addiction a Brain Disease?
18. Can Sex Be Addictive?

Attention Deficit Disorder/ Attention Deficit Hyperactivity Disorder

12. Is Attention-Deficit Hyperactivity Disorder (ADHD) a Real Disorder?

Behavior

6. Does Teaching Scientific Determinism Lead to Bad Behavior?
18. Can Sex Be Addictive?

Birth Order

19. Does Birth Order Predict Intelligence?

Brain and Neuroscience

2. Is Homosexuality Biologically Based?
1. Is Addiction a Brain Disease?

Culture

2. Is Homosexuality Biologically Based?
4. Is American Psychological Research Generalizable to Other Cultures?
7. Are Today's Youth More Self-Centered Than Previous Generations?
20. Is the Need for Social Enhancement Universal Across Cultures?

Development

8. Do Online Friendships Hurt Adolescent Development?

Emotions

9. Can Positive Psychology Make Us Happier?
10. Is Emotional Intelligence Valid?

Emotional Intelligence

10. Is Emotional Intelligence Valid?

Evolution/Evolutionary Psychology

3. Is Evolution a Good Explanation for Psychological Concepts?
17. Does the Evidence Support Evolutionary Accounts of Female Mating Preferences?

False Confessions

16. Should Psychologists Abstain from Involvement in Coercive Interrogations?

Gender

8. Do Online Friendships Hurt Adolescent Development?
17. Does the Evidence Support Evolutionary Accounts of Female Mating Preferences?

Happiness

9. Can Positive Psychology Make Us Happier?

Health

11. Does an Elective Abortion Lead to Negative Psychological Effects?

Intelligence

19. Does Birth Order Predict Intelligence?

Internet

8. Do Online Friendships Hurt Adolescent Development?
13. Does Facebook Have Generally Positive Psychological Effects?

Morality

16. Should Psychologists Abstain from Involvement in Coercive Interrogations?

Personality

15. Should Therapists Be Eclectic?

Positive Psychology

9. Can Positive Psychology Make Us Happier?
13. Does Facebook Have Generally Positive Psychological Effects?

Psychological Disorders

11. Does an Elective Abortion Lead to Negative Psychological Effects?
12. Is Attention-Deficit Hyperactivity Disorder (ADHD) a Real Disorder?

Psychotherapy/Psychological Treatment/Intervention

14. Are All Psychotherapies Equally Effective?
15. Should Therapists Be Eclectic?

Research Issues

4. Is American Psychological Research Generalizable to Other Cultures?
5. Are Traditional Empirical Methods Sufficient to Provide Evidence for Psychological Practice?
6. Does Teaching Scientific Determinism Lead to Bad Behavior?

Self-control

18. Can Sex Be Addictive?

Social Behaviors

7. Are Today's Youth More Self-Centered Than Previous Generations?
8. Do Online Friendships Hurt Adolescent Development?
13. Does Facebook Have Generally Positive Psychological Effects?
20. Is the Need for Social Enhancement Universal Across Cultures?

Stress

11. Does an Elective Abortion Lead to Negative Psychological Effects?

Introduction

Why does psychology need a *Taking Sides* book? The expression "taking sides" implies that there are "controversial psychological issues," as the book title states. But how can there be controversial issues in a discipline that considers itself a science? Controversial issues would seem inherent in such disciplines as philosophy and religion, but wouldn't the issues of psychology be resolved by science—by finding out what is true and false through psychology's empirical methods? If so, are the "controversial issues" presented in this book only *temporary* issues waiting for empirical resolution? And if they are only temporary, why learn or argue about them? Why "take a side"?

As this introduction will argue, there are all sorts of reasons and opportunities to take a side in psychology. Scientific findings are not only decided by data—the information produced by scientific research—but they are also decided by theoretical allegiances, industry loyalties, and philosophical assumptions that are not themselves driven or resolved by data. These allegiances and assumptions allow for and even spawn controversial issues. Indeed, they form what some call the "disguised ideologies" of science (Bernstein, 1983; Richardson, Fowers, and Guignon, 1999): implicit worldviews or philosophies that guide what variables to select for research, what methods to use in these investigations, and what sense to make of the resulting data. As we will see, these are just a few of the many places in psychological research where the researcher's bias or ideology, and thus "controversial issues," can come into play.

Some may hold that the problem of bias affects only the "soft" sciences. They may believe that "hard" sciences, such as physics and chemistry, have essentially eliminated biases and ideologies. However, as we will show, both soft and hard sciences are subject to these ideologies and controversial issues. Indeed, one of the recent conclusions of physics is that the observer's "frame of reference" always affects what is observed (Einstein, 1990; Heisenberg, 1958; Wolf, 1981). In this introduction, we will point to dramatic examples of systematic biases in both types of sciences, showing how some of the most important research—research about health treatment—is substantially driven by factors outside the data per se.

Even so, some scientists will argue that these biases are miscarriages of science, that science conducted correctly would have no systematic ideologies. As we will attempt to describe, however, nothing could be further from the truth, because the scientific method is itself based on a philosophy. It is itself based on a broad ideology in this sense. This is not to say that science is *only* bias or that science is worthless. Indeed, we will argue that science is one of the best tools we have for helping to resolve controversial issues. The main point of this introduction is that ideologies, biases, and "issues" are *never* avoided entirely and, indeed, play a *necessary* role in science. We believe this role is all the more reason to become aware of psychology's controversial issues, think them through, and, yes, even take a well-reasoned and well-informed "side."

Allegiance Effects in the Soft Sciences

Many examples of systematic bias in psychology exist (Slife, Reber, and Richardson, 2005), but Luborsky's theoretical (or ideological) "allegiance" is surely one of the more striking and significant (Luborsky, Diguer, Seligman, and colleagues, 1999; Luborsky and Barrett, in press). It is striking because theoretical allegiance is such an impressive predictor of psychological research, forecasting an unprecedented two-thirds of the variability in treatment outcomes, with correlations as high as 0.85 (Luborsky and Barrett, in press). We say "unprecedented" because correlations in psychology are rarely this high. Theoretical allegiance is also significant because it concerns the pivotal question: Which psychological treatment is best? In other words, this particular systematic bias is involved in deciding what actually works in psychology.

The term *allegiance* refers to a person's conscious or unconscious loyalty or commitment to a particular ideal, philosophy, or organization. In research on psychotherapy, Luborsky views theoretical allegiance as the degree of a researcher's loyalty to a specific theory of behavior change. The most common theories of psychotherapy, and thus types of theoretical loyalty, are the broad categories of dynamic, cognitive, behavioral, and pharmacological. Luborsky and Barrett (in press) essentially showed that a researcher's preference for one of these broad categories—as rated most accurately through reprints, self-ratings, and colleague ratings—correlates with the therapy found to be the best in the researcher's comparison of several therapies. In other words, whatever therapies or ideas researchers favor *before* their investigation are, with few exceptions, what the researchers "find" their results favoring *after* the investigation.

Luborsky found this correlation through "meta-analyses." Instead of a conventional analysis of one particular study, a meta-analysis is usually an analysis of many studies—an analysis of many conventional analyses. To understand what Luborsky's meta-analysis means, consider an example. Let us say that a particular researcher favors a certain theoretical approach, such as behavioral, and sets up a study comparing behavioral and pharmacological therapies. Luborsky's analysis indicates that this study will probably favor behavioral therapies over pharmacological, even though the two might *really* be equivalent in effectiveness. According to Luborsky, "treatment benefits, as evidenced in comparative trials, are so influenced by the researcher's theoretical allegiance that in many comparisons differences between treatments lessen or become negligible when the influence of allegiance is considered" (Luborsky and Barrett, in press, p. 355).

Therefore, if we know the theoretical orientation of the researcher, we can predict with considerable accuracy the outcome of an empirical comparison among the various treatment approaches—without even making the comparison! Theoretical allegiance, in this sense, is a clear bias or ideology that is not being corrected by what is really happening in the treatment comparison.

Theoretical allegiances are occurring in spite of the controls instituted for subjective biases in these elaborate research designs. Although Luborsky believes that such allegiances should be controlled, conventional scientific methods are not currently doing so. In short, there are "controversial issues" that are not currently being resolved by the data. Also, as we will see (in the "What Is Happening?" section following), scientific research is conducted in a way that will never eliminate or resolve all the controversial issues.

Allegiance Effects in the Hard Sciences

Is this also true in the hard sciences, or do they avoid the ideas and ideologies that lead to controversial issues? As mentioned, physics has long recognized Heisenberg's (1958) "uncertainty principle" and Einstein's (1990) relativity of the "inertial frame of reference" as just two of the ways in which the observer is assumed to have an important impact on the observed (Bohm, 1980; Wolf, 1981). However, the hard sciences also have meta-analyses that are similar to Luborsky's. Findings in medicine, for example, parallel those we have just described in psychology. Here, *theoretical* allegiance is less of an issue, but *industry* allegiance is widely acknowledged as a potent bias in medical research (Bhandari and colleagues, 2004; Kjaergard and Als-Nielson, 2002; Lexchin and colleagues, 2003). Industry allegiance refers to the high correlations between the industry sponsor of research and the pro-industry outcome of this research.

Healy (1999), for instance, suggests that much of our current conception of the effectiveness of antidepressants is molded more by the marketing imperatives of the pharmaceutical industry than by the scientific findings. There is certainly no dispute that the pharmaceutical industry is the largest funder of medical research in North America, and this, as Valenstein (1998) notes, is "overwhelmingly true" for research on psychiatric drugs (p. 187). Indeed, Valenstein claims that these companies are unlikely to fund researchers who have been negative about drug effectiveness. Still, it is one thing to point to this industry's massive funding efforts and profit motives, and quite another to claim that industry allegiance biases investigators. Is there evidence for this latter claim?

In fact, editorials in five different prestigious medical journals have all pointed to evidence that pharmaceutical funding has tainted the objectivity of these studies (Greenberg, 2001). Freemantle, Anderson, and Young (2000), for example, have recently shown in a meta-analysis of comparative studies that a sponsor's funding is the best predictor of whether studies will show the sponsor's drug to be effective. Similarly, Friedberg and colleagues (1999) have shown empirically that company-supported studies are more likely to report efficacy for the company's product than are independent studies of the same product. Bhandari and colleagues (2004) even report this effect for surgical interventions. Stern and Simes (1997) also found considerable evidence that studies that do not reflect positively on antidepressants are less likely to be published. Moncrieff (2001) reports that the problem of publication bias is even more pronounced with recent SSRI antidepressants because the majority of trials have been conducted by the pharmaceutical industry, which has no obligation to publish negative results and may see little advantage in doing so.

What Is Happening?

What is happening in the soft and hard sciences to produce these "allegiance" effects, either theoretical or industrial? There are issues, such as allegiance, that data never seem to determine or decide definitively. This suggests that some issues require old-fashioned discussion and debate among those in the discipline. It also indicates that scientific experiments alone will not always suffice. Why? Why can't data alone decide all the discipline's "controversial issues"? One of the primary reasons is a concept called *underdetermination,* which means that research data never *completely* determine the interpretation made of that data (Curd and Cover, 1998; Slife and Williams, 1995). The researcher always has a limited choice (within the parameters of the data) about which interpretation to use.

To begin to understand why this is true, consider that any set of data is meaningless without some interpretive framework for that data. In other words, a researcher must *add* his or her own organization or interpretation to the data for the results of any study to be meaningful findings. Even a quick scan of a (typical) data set reveals a bewildering array of numbers, especially if this scan lacks the researcher's explanation as to what specific categories of data and statistical results *mean* (or how they should be interpreted). (For an example, see Slife and Williams, 1995, pp. 5–6.) Researchers will often claim to "see" meanings in their data; this is not because the data *inherently* "mean" something, but because the researcher *already* has an interpretive framework, consciously or unconsciously, for the data in mind.

It is important to recognize that the interpretation selected must "fit" the data for the interpretation to be viable. In other words, not just any interpretation will do; meaningful interpretations must make sense of *all* the data. Nevertheless, more than one interpretation of all the data is always possible, with some potentially dramatic differences in these interpretations. This is what *underdetermination* means. (Please see Curd and Cover, 1998, and Slife and Williams, 1995, pp. 185–187, for the more technical considerations of this conception.) In this sense, a study's "findings" are never *merely* the data, because the data are not meaningful findings until the researcher organizes or interprets the data, allowing for systems of ideas, and thus "controversial issues," to enter the research picture.

Actually, data interpretation is just one of the many places where biases can creep into scientific research. Consider how researchers have all sorts of "subjective" choice points in their studies: first—what to study (what variables are crucial), second—how to study the variables (what operationalization and method design to use), third—how to analyze the study (what assumptions are met and statistics used), fourth—what the statistical results really mean (what interpretation to use), and fifth—what limits the study has (what study problems might impede certain interpretations). These choice points mean that subjective factors, such as allegiance, are inevitably part of any research study. Researchers, knowingly or unknowingly, are favoring their own ideologies through the decisions they make at these choice points. Part of the purpose of *Taking Sides* books, then, is to reveal and discuss these ideologies and to help students become aware of their impact on the discipline.

Science as Ideology

Many scientists will argue that influential ideological factors are not a necessary part of science—that the allegiance effects of psychology and medicine are examples of bad research. They may believe that good science occurs when all the systematic biases, and thus disguised ideologies, have been eliminated or controlled. However, as mentioned earlier, science itself is based on a broad ideology (or philosophy) about how science should be conducted. Moreover, this broad ideology could not itself have been scientifically derived because one would need the ideology (before its derivation) to conduct the scientific investigations to derive it. In short, *there is no empirical evidence for the philosophy of empiricism that underlies the scientific method.* Some may claim that this philosophy has been successful, but this is only a claim or an opinion, not a scientific fact. Even if we were to endorse this claim, which we would, it does not minimize the broad ideology of this philosophy of science, along with the biases and values it promotes.

Perhaps the most obvious bias or value of the philosophy of empiricism is the observability value. Because this philosophy assumes that sensory experience is the only really knowable experience, traditional science has based its doctrine of knowing on the sensory experience of vision or observability. For many students, this valuing of observability will not seem like a value (Slife, 2008). These students may have unknowingly (no pun intended) accepted this philosophy as their own, without critically examining it. In this case, the doctrine of observability will seem more like an axiom than a value.

To be a value rather than an axiom, observability must indicate not only what particular things have merit or worth but also what alternative things *could* be valued (Slife, 2008). Regarding the worth issue, it is probably obvious that traditional empiricism values, and thus selects, observable phenomena as having more merit or worth than nonobservable phenomena for scientific purposes. Perhaps the bigger hurdle for appreciating the value-ladenness of observability is understanding the possibility of alternatives—in this sense, the possibility of knowing *non*observables. Here, we could ask the empiricists if their doctrine of observability is itself observable. In other words, is the idea that "only the sensory can be known" *itself* observable? And if it is not, how then do we know that this idea is correct? Given that empiricists do not observe this idea, and given that they hold it to be correct, there must be other ways of knowing things than by observability.

We can at this point describe other philosophies (or epistemologies) of knowing that assert that many unobservable experiences are knowable, such as the feelings we have for someone or the thoughts we have about something. With the feelings of love, for example, we can surely observe someone who is "in love"—hugging and kissing or any specified observable factor (in research, these are called *operationalizations*). However, we would rarely assume that the feeling of love and these observables are identical. Hugs and kisses can occur without this feeling, and this feeling can occur without hugs and kisses. Therefore, studies of hugs and kisses (or any specified observable) are *not* studies of love. At the risk of noting the obvious, studies of observables are not studies of nonobservables. They may be studies of observables that are associated with nonobservables, but then if we cannot know the nonobservable, how can we know what is associated with them?

For this reason, traditional scientific methods selectively attend to, and thus value, one particular aspect of the world—observables over nonobservables. Indeed, this is part of the reason qualitative research methods were formulated and have become increasingly popular in psychology and other disciplines. They claim that they can investigate nonobservable experiences that are not strictly observable, such as meaning and emotion (cf. Denzin and Lincoln, 2000). If this is true, knowing nonobservables is possible, and the value-ladenness of only attending to observables is clear. Again, some may insist that only observables can be known, but this insistence is not itself a scientific claim because it cannot be decided through scientific observation (Slife, Wiggins, and Graham, 2005). It is a philosophical claim about how knowing occurs and is thus subject to comparison with other philosophical claims about knowing (other epistemologies).

Observability is not the only value of traditional scientific methods. Many of the customs and traditions of how one conducts and is supposed to conduct research originate from similarly unproven values and assumptions, including reductionism (Yanchar, 2005), instrumentalism (Richardson, 2005), naturalism (Richards and Bergin, 2005), and positivism (Slife and Williams, 1995). Indeed, the journal *Counseling and Values* (2008) devoted an entire issue to the topic of the values and assumptions of psychology's scientific methods, which are the hidden roots of some of today's "controversial issues."

The lesson here is that many values and unproven ideas are *inherent* in the system of science itself. Before a method is even formulated, the persons formulating the method must make assumptions about the world in which the method would be successful. The world cannot be known through the method, because the method has not been invented yet. Consequently, the assumptions and values used for its formulation have to be speculations and guesswork to some degree—in short, values and assumptions that are not themselves scientifically proven (Slife, 2008). Again, this does not make science wrong or bad. Indeed, these scientific values and assumptions have made science what it is, including any perceived effectiveness it has.

Still, the perceived effectiveness of the scientific enterprise does not mean that we can forget about these values. They are still unproven values, after all, and as such they can be either problematic or helpful, depending on the context in which they are used. As we described, they may be useful for observable aspects of the world but not so useful for nonobservable aspects of the world. In this sense, there will always be "controversial issues" in any scientific enterprise, hard or soft. Some will be resolved by data, but some will require other means of examination and debate.

Application to the Issues of This Book

The issues of this book are a wide assortment of both types: "empirical questions," which are primarily decided by research, and "philosophical questions," which are primarily decided by discussion and consensus or theoretical examination in relation to disciplinary values. Psychologists typically have the most skills in resolving empirical or research issues. They have been trained since their undergraduate days with multiple courses, such as "research methods" and "statistics," all in support of resolving empirical or research questions.

Psychologists are rarely as adept at philosophical questions, even though these questions pervade the discipline (as we have shown). Indeed, many psychologists may despair at such questions because they associate philosophy with irresolvable issues—issues that seem interminable. We have sympathy for this attitude, yet we need to be careful not to "throw the baby out with the bathwater." In other words, just because there are seemingly interminable problems in philosophy does not mean that decisions and judgments cannot be made about the philosophical issues of a discipline such as psychology.[1] Many decisions and judgments have, of course, already been made. Otherwise, we would not have a philosophy that guides our science or a set of values that guides our ethics. As the issues of this book indicate, however, not all of these values and assumptions have been decided. Moreover, there is a case to be made that even the decided values should be continually explicated and reevaluated, as new research arenas and topics come to the fore.

Let us close this introduction, then, by pointing explicitly to how such philosophical issues may rear their ugly heads in a discipline such as psychology, and thus in this book. One way to categorize these issues is in terms of the *production* of research and the *outcome* of research. The first involves the many ways in which controversial ideas can enter the conducting of psychological investigations, whereas the second entails the many ways in which controversial ideas can enter the interpretation of a study's data or a program of research.

In the first case, controversial issues can arise when researchers have an allegiance or agenda in formulating and conducting their programs of research. This agenda does not have to be conscious, because loyalties can be influential—political or sociological, theoretical or organizational—whether or not they are known or articulated. They can influence what researchers consider important to study, along with the design, operational and analysis of the study. All these phases of a study, as we have just described, are choice points for researchers that allow for agendas to be revealed and loyalties to be identified. It would thus be important for students of "controversial issues" to try to discern these loyalties and agendas in the production of data. That is the reason there is often no substitute for studying the studies themselves.

Controversial issues can also result from interpretations of the existing data and studies. Perhaps the most striking example of this involves two sets of scholars—each well-trained and each looking at essentially the same data—coming to dramatically different conclusions. First, as we have noted, they can interpret the same data in two different ways (through the *underdetermination* of the data). Second, these interpretive frameworks can also lead researchers to weigh different sets of data differently. Although one set of investigators views certain studies as pivotal, another set considers the same studies deeply problematic, and thus gives them far less weight. In both cases, the interpretive framework of the researchers is part of the reason they "take the side" they do.

---

[1]Likewise, we should not "throw out" the achievements of science just because they are not totally objective.

There is no doubt that the data of the studies are important. Nevertheless, there is also no doubt that the sides taken and the interpretations made are not solely data driven.

Conclusion

The bottom line is that no science can avoid controversial issues. As long as humans are involved *as* scientists, allegiances and biases will be factors. There are just too many choice points for a scientist's ideologies, known or unknown, to seep into the methods employed. Truth be told, human beings are also the inventors and formulators of the methods of science. This means not only that these methods embody the biases and assumptions of the original inventors but also that subsequent changes in the philosophies that guide science will also stem from biased humans. In this sense, we will never be rid of controversial issues. Our job, then, is to expose them, discuss them, and take a well-informed "side" with respect to them.

References

Bernstein, R. J. (1983). *Beyond objectivism and relativism.* Philadelphia: University of Pennsylvania Press.

Bhandari, M. et al. (2004). Association between industry fundings and statistically significant pro-industry findings in medical and surgical randomized trials. *Journal of the Canadian Medical Association, 170,* 477–480.

Bohm, D. (1980). *Wholeness and the implicate order.* London: Routledge & Kegan Paul.

Curd, M., & Cover, J. A. (1998). *Philosophy of science: The central issues.* New York: W. W. Norton & Company.

Denzin, N. K., & Lincoln, Y. S. (Eds.). (2000). *Handbook of qualitative methods.* Thousand Oaks, CA: Sage.

Einstein, A. (1961/1990). Relativity: The special and general theory. Translated by Robert W. Larson. In M. Adler (Ed.), *Great books of the Western world.* Chicago: University of Chicago Press.

Freemantle, N., Anderson, I. M., & Young, P. (2000). Predictive value of pharmacological activity for the relative efficacy of antidepressant drugs: Meta-regression analysis. *British Journal of Psychiatry, 177,* 292–302.

Friedberg, M., Saffran, B., Stinson, T. J., Nelson, W., & Bennett, C. L. (1999). Evaluation of conflict of interest in economic analyses of new drugs used in oncology. *Journal of the American Medical Association, 282,* 1453–1457.

Greenberg, R. (2001). Qualms about balms: Perspectives on antidepressants. *Journal of Nervous and Mental Disease, 189*(5), 296–298.

Greenberg, R. P., Bornstein, R. F., Greenberg, M. D., & Fisher, S. (1992). A meta-analysis of antidepressant outcome under "blinder" conditions. *Journal of Consulting & Clinical Psychology, 60,* 664–669.

Healy, D. (1999). The three faces of the antidepressants: A critical commentary on the clinical-economic context of diagnoses. *Journal of Nervous and Mental Disorder, 187,* 174–180.

Heiman, G. W. (1995). *Research methods in psychology.* Boston: Houghton-Mifflin.

Heisenberg, W. (1958). *Physics and philosophy: The revolution of modern science.* New York: Harper Books.

Kjaergard, L. L., & Als-Nielson, B. (2002). Association between competing interests and authors' concluions: Epidemiological study of randomised clinical trials published in the *BMJ*. *British Journal of Medicine, 325,* 249–253.

Lexchin, J., Bero, L. A., Djulbegovic, B., & Clark, O. (2003). Pharmaceutical industry sponsorship and research outcome and quality: Systematic review. *British Medical Journal, 326,* 1167–1170.

Luborsky, L. B., & Barrett, M. S. (in press). Theoretical allegiance.

Luborsky, L., Diguer, L., Seligman, D. A., Rosenthal, R., Krause, E. D., Johnson, S., Halperin, G., Bishop, M., Berman, J. S., & Schweizer, E. (1999). The researcher's own therapy allegiances: A "wild card" in comparisons of treatment efficacy. *Clinical Psychology: Science and Practice, 6,* 95–132.

Moncrieff, J. (2001). Are antidepressants overrated? A review of methodological problems in antidepressant trials. *The Journal of Nervous and Mental Disease, 189,* 288–295.

Richardson, F. (2005). Psychotherapy and modern dilemmas. In B. Slife, J. Reber, & F. Richardson, (Eds.), *Critical thinking about psychology: Hidden assumptions and plausible alternatives* (pp. 17–38). Washington, DC.: American Psychological Association Press.

Richards, P. S., & Bergin, A. E. (2005). *A spiritual strategy for counseling and psychotherapy* (2nd ed.). Washington, DC: American Psychological Association.

Richardson, F., Fowers, B., & Guignon, C. (1999). *Re-envisioning psychology: Moral dimensions of theory and practice.* San Francisco, CA: Jossey-Bass.

Slife, B. D. (2008). A primer of the values implicit in counseling research. *Counseling and Values, 53* (1), 8–21.

Slife, B. D., Reber, J., & Richardson, F. (2005). *Critical thinking about psychology: Hidden assumptions and plausible alternatives.* Washington, DC.: American Psychological Association Press.

Slife, B. D., Wiggins, B. J., & Graham, J. T. (2005). Avoiding an EST monopoly: Toward a pluralism of methods and philosophies. *Journal of Contemporary Psychotherapy, 35,* 83–97.

Slife, B. D., & Williams, R. N. (1995). *What's behind the research? Discovering hidden assumptions in the behavioral sciences.* Thousand Oaks, CA: Sage.

Stern, J. M., & Simes, R. J. (1997). Publication bias: Evidence of delayed publication in a cohort study of clinical research projects. *British Medical Journal, 315,* 640–645.

Valenstein, E. S. (1998). *Blaming the brain: The truth about drugs and mental health.* New York: Free Press.

Wolf, F. A. (1981). *Taking the quantum leap.* San Francisco: Harper-Row.

Yanchar, S. (2005). A contextualist alternative to cognitive psychology. In B. Slife, J. Reber, & F. Richardson (Eds.), *Critical thinking about psychology: Hidden assumptions and plausible alternatives* (pp. 171–186). Washington, DC: American Psychological Association Press.

Internet References . . .

National Institute on Drug Abuse

This is the National Institute on Drug Abuse website. It has all sorts of well-written and well-researched articles on various forms of drug addiction.

www.nida.nih.gov/scienceofaddiction/

Addiction Journal

This site is devoted to the journal, *Addiction*, as well as the Society for the Study of Addiction to Alcohol and Other Drugs.

www.addictionjournal.org/

Wikipedia—Homosexuality

Wikipedia is not always the most scholarly of reference sources, but this particular site is not only fairly balanced but also brimming with good references.

http://en.wikipedia.org/wiki/Homosexuality

Evolutionary Psychology Journal

This is the site for a respected journal on evolutionary psychology.

www.epjournal.net/

Stanford Encyclopedia of Philosophy

This reference source is an excellent and balanced source for evolutionary psychology and its critique.

http://plato.stanford.edu/entries/evolutionary-psychology/

Biological Issues

*O*ur biology is obviously a fundamental influence on behavior, one of the most important subject matters of psychology. But can we take biology's influence too far? Is it the basis or determinant for all behaviors, or is there room for personal decision making that is not completely forced by our biology? These are just some of the questions that arise in trying to understand behaviors such as addiction and homosexuality. Do people have a choice about their homosexual or addictive behaviors, or are they forced by their brain chemistry or genes to behave the way they do? Evolutionary theory is a prominent biological approach to explaining not only species changes but also social changes. Could it be another valid approach to understanding the biological influences in such behaviors as addiction and homosexuality?

- Is Addiction a Brain Disease?
- Is Homosexuality Biologically Based?
- Is Evolution a Good Explanation for Psychological Concepts?

ISSUE 1

Is Addiction a Brain Disease?

YES: National Institute on Drug Abuse, from "The Science of Addiction," *Drugs, Brain, and Behavior: The Science of Addiction,* rev. ed. (*National Institutes of Health,* 2007)

NO: Sally Satel and Scott O. Lilienfeld, from "Singing the Brain Disease Blues," *AJOB Neuroscience* (January 2010)

ISSUE SUMMARY

YES: A publication from the National Institute on Drug Abuse argues that addiction is a brain disease and that scientific information is available about the nature, prevention, and treatment of this disease.

NO: Psychiatrist Sally Satel and psychologist Scott O. Lilienfeld object to the brain disease characterization of drug addiction, asserting that addiction is an activity whose course can be altered by its foreseeable consequences.

Have you ever heard people say that they are addicted to chocolate? What do they mean by the term "addicted"? Do they mean that they merely like chocolate a lot, and so they exercise their free will to choose to eat it whenever they can? In this sense, they mean that they can stop eating chocolate whenever they want, without any problem. Or, do they mean by "addicted" that there is some chemical in the chocolate that forces their brains to crave it? In this latter sense, their will power is so greatly diminished that they cannot stop eating it, even if they wanted to.

These two positions, one where cravings can be overcome by will power and one where cravings are irresistible, form two important sides of a more serious debate about addiction. Are there drugs, such as alcohol or cocaine, that cause users to lose control over their desires and actions? In other words, the addict is a victim of the drug and is forced to want more of it. If so, then addiction treatment would focus more on medical or biological interventions (e.g., other drugs), because the addicts themselves cannot be counted on to help with their own recovery. On the other hand, if addicts are themselves involved in some way, such as through their own possibly misguided decision making, then psychological interventions should also be considered.

As it happens, the YES article describes the position of the National Institute for Drug Abuse, which appears to take the more biological understanding of addiction, sometimes known as the "disease model." For this organization, it is quite clear that drug addiction is "considered a brain disease because drugs change the brain—they change its structure and how it works." The obvious implication of this brain disease model of addiction is that these changes of brain structure hijack the person's self-control. Even though the initial decision to take drugs may be "mostly voluntary" (a decision that the person is not forced to make), "when drug abuse takes over, a person's ability to exert self-control can become seriously impaired." In other words, the drug's effects on the brain can force the person to exhibit addictive behaviors.

Psychiatrist Sally Satel and psychologist Scott O. Lilienfeld reject this characterization of all addictions, including drug addictions. They do not dispute that repeated use of certain drugs can produce brain changes. However, they do doubt that a person's will and decision-making ability are suddenly lost as a result of these changes. The loss of a person's will and decision-making ability would mean that addicts are totally helpless and incapable of contributing to their own treatment, which Sally Satel and Scott Lilienfeld dispute. Moreover, the brain disease model of addiction would imply that the most effective intervention for addicts is exclusively medical or biological. Sally Satel and Scott O. Lilienfeld note that research indicates many incentive programs, which facilitate different decisions on the part of addicts, have also been shown to be effective.

POINT	COUNTERPOINT
• Drug addiction is a brain disease because repeated use and abuse of drugs changes the brain.	• The brain disease model of addiction makes medical treatment the only viable approach to addiction.
• Drug addiction alters brain pleasure centers, so that normal happiness requires higher and more frequent drugs.	• Even if pleasure centers were altered, this does not mean that willpower (denying pleasures) is absent.
• Brain imaging studies show changes in the brain that are critical to judgment, decision making, and behavior control.	• Psychological research indicates that addiction can be altered by the addict's awareness of foreseeable consequences and choice to do otherwise.
• The risk for becoming an addict is greatly dependent on one's biology, such as gender or ethnicity.	• The risk for becoming an addict is also influenced by the pattern of one's life choices and discipline.
• The preponderance of research indicates neurological effects of repeated drug use.	• The popularity of the brain disease model obscures other important understandings and treatments of addiction.

The Science of Addiction

Drug Abuse and Addiction

What Is Drug Addiction?

Addiction is defined as a chronic, relapsing brain disease that is character-ized by compulsive drug seeking and use, despite harmful consequences. It is considered a brain disease because drugs change the brain—they change its structure and how it works. These brain changes can be long lasting, and can lead to the harmful behaviors seen in people who abuse drugs.

Is Continued Drug Abuse a Voluntary Behavior?

The initial decision to take drugs is mostly voluntary. However, when drug abuse takes over, a person's ability to exert self control can become seriously impaired. Brain imaging studies from drug-addicted individuals show physi-cal changes in areas of the brain that are critical to judgment, decision mak-ing, learning and memory, and behavior control. Scientists believe that these changes alter the way the brain works, and may help explain the compulsive and destructive behaviors of addiction.

Why Do Some People Become Addicted to Drugs, While Others Do Not?

As with any other disease, vulnerability to addiction differs from person to per-son. In general, the more risk factors an individual has, the greater the chance that taking drugs will lead to abuse and addiction. "Protective" factors reduce a person's risk of developing addiction.

What Factors Determine If a Person Will Become Addicted?

No single factor determines whether a person will become addicted to drugs. The overall risk for addiction is impacted by the biological makeup of the individual—it can even be influenced by gender or ethnicity, his or her devel-opmental stage, and the surrounding social environment (e.g., conditions at home, at school, and in the neighborhood).

Published by *National Institutes of Health*, NIH Pub no. 07-5605, April 2007, pp. 5, 7–8, 10, 15–20.

Which Biological Factors Increase Risk of Addiction?

Scientists estimate that genetic factors account for between 40 and 60 percent of a person's vulnerability to addiction, including the effects of environment on gene expression and function. Adolescents and individuals with mental disorders are at greater risk of drug abuse and addiction than the general population.

The Brain Continues to Develop into Adulthood and Undergoes Dramatic Changes During Adolescence

One of the brain areas still maturing during adolescence is the prefrontal cortex—the part of the brain that enables us to assess situations, make sound decisions, and keep our emotions and desires under control. The fact that this critical part of an adolescent's brain is still a work-in-progress puts them at increased risk for poor decisions (such as trying drugs or continued abuse). Thus, introducing drugs while the brain is still developing may have profound and long-lasting consequences.

Drugs and the Brain

Introducing the Human Brain

The human brain is the most complex organ in the body. This three-pound mass of gray and white matter sits at the center of all human activity—you need it to drive a car, to enjoy a meal, to breathe, to create an artistic masterpiece, and to enjoy everyday activities. In brief, the brain regulates your basic body functions; enables you to interpret and respond to everything you experience, and shapes your thoughts, emotions, and behavior.

The brain is made up of many parts that all work together as a team. Different parts of the brain are responsible for coordinating and performing specific functions. Drugs can alter important brain areas that are necessary for life-sustaining functions and can drive the compulsive drug abuse that marks addiction. Brain areas affected by drug abuse—

- *The brain stem* controls basic functions critical to life, such as heart rate, breathing, and sleeping.
- *The limbic system* contains the brain's reward circuit—it links together a number of brain structures that control and regulate our ability to feel pleasure. Feeling pleasure motivates us to repeat behaviors such as eating—actions that are critical to our existence. The limbic system is activated when we perform these activities—and also by drugs of abuse. In addition, the limbic system is responsible for our perception of other emotions, both positive and negative, which explains the mood-altering properties of many drugs.
- *The cerebral cortex* is divided into areas that control specific functions. Different areas process information from our senses, enabling us to see, feel, hear, and taste. The front part of the cortex, the frontal cortex or forebrain, is the thinking center of the brain; it powers our ability to think, plan, solve problems, and make decisions.

How Does the Brain Communicate?

The brain is a communications center consisting of billions of neurons, or nerve cells. Networks of neurons pass messages back and forth to different structures within the brain, the spinal column, and the peripheral nervous system. These nerve networks coordinate and regulate everything we feel, think, and do.

- *Neuron to Neuron*
  Each nerve cell in the brain sends and receives messages in the form of electrical impulses. Once a cell receives and processes a message, it sends it on to other neurons.
- *Neurotransmitters—The Brain's Chemical Messengers*
  The messages are carried between neurons by chemicals called neurotransmitters. (They transmit messages between neurons.)
- *Receptors—The Brain's Chemical Receivers*
  The neurotransmitter attaches to a specialized site on the receiving cell called a receptor. A neurotransmitter and its receptor operate like a "key and lock," an exquisitely specific mechanism that ensures that each receptor will forward the appropriate message only after interacting with the right kind of neurotransmitter.
- *Transporters—The Brain's Chemical Recyclers*
  Located on the cell that releases the neurotransmitter, transporters recycle these neurotransmitters (i.e., bring them back into the cell that released them), thereby shutting off the signal between neurons.

How Do Drugs Work in the Brain?

Drugs are chemicals. They work in the brain by tapping into the brain's communication system and interfering with the way nerve cells normally send, receive, and process information. Some drugs, such as marijuana and heroin, can activate neurons because their chemical structure mimics that of a natural neurotransmitter. This similarity in structure "fools" receptors and allows the drugs to lock onto and activate the nerve cells. Although these drugs mimic brain chemicals, they don't activate nerve cells in the same way as a natural neurotransmitter, and they lead to abnormal messages being transmitted through the network.

Other drugs, such as amphetamine or cocaine, can cause the nerve cells to release abnormally large amounts of natural neurotransmitters or prevent the normal recycling of these brain chemicals. This disruption produces a greatly amplified message, ultimately disrupting communication channels. The difference in effect can be described as the difference between someone whispering into your ear and someone shouting into a microphone.

How Do Drugs Work in the Brain to Produce Pleasure?

All drugs of abuse directly or indirectly target the brain's reward system by flooding the circuit with dopamine. Dopamine is a neurotransmitter present in regions of the brain that regulate movement, emotion, cognition, motivation, and feelings of pleasure. The overstimulation of this system, which rewards our natural behaviors, produces the euphoric effects sought by people who abuse drugs and teaches them to repeat the behavior.

How Does Stimulation of the Brain's Pleasure Circuit Teach Us to Keep Taking Drugs?

Our brains are wired to ensure that we will repeat life-sustaining activities by associating those activities with pleasure or reward. Whenever this reward circuit is activated, the brain notes that something important is happening that needs to be remembered, and teaches us to do it again and again, without thinking about it. Because drugs of abuse stimulate the same circuit, we learn to abuse drugs in the same way.

Why Are Drugs More Addictive Than Natural Rewards?

When some drugs of abuse are taken, they can release 2 to 10 times the amount of dopamine that natural rewards do. In some cases, this occurs almost immediately (as when drugs are smoked or injected), and the effects can last much longer than those produced by natural rewards. The resulting effects on the brain's pleasure circuit dwarfs those produced by naturally rewarding behaviors such as eating and sex. The effect of such a powerful reward strongly motivates people to take drugs again and again. This is why scientists sometimes say that drug abuse is something we learn to do very, very well.

What Happens to Your Brain If You Keep Taking Drugs?

Just as we turn down the volume on a radio that is too loud, the brain adjusts to the overwhelming surges in dopamine (and other neurotransmitters) by producing less dopamine or by reducing the number of receptors that can receive and transmit signals. As a result, dopamine's impact on the reward circuit of a drug abuser's brain can become abnormally low, and the ability to experience any pleasure is reduced. This is why the abuser eventually feels flat, lifeless, and depressed, and is unable to enjoy things that previously brought them pleasure. Now, they need to take drugs just to bring their dopamine function back up to normal. And, they must take larger amounts of the drug than they first did to create the dopamine high—an effect known as tolerance.

How Does Long-Term Drug Taking Affect Brain Circuits?

We know that the same sort of mechanisms involved in the development of tolerance can eventually lead to profound changes in neurons and brain circuits, with the potential to severely compromise the long-term health of the brain. For example, glutamate is another neurotransmitter that influences the reward circuit and the ability to learn. When the optimal concentration of glutamate is altered by drug abuse, the brain attempts to compensate for this change, which can cause impairment in cognitive function. Similarly, long-term drug abuse can trigger adaptations in habit or nonconscious memory systems.

Conditioning is one example of this type of learning, whereby environmental cues become associated with the drug experience and can trigger uncontrollable cravings if the individual is later exposed to these cues, even without the drug itself being available. This learned "reflex" is extremely robust and can emerge even after many years of abstinence.

What Other Brain Changes Occur with Abuse?

Chronic exposure to drugs of abuse disrupts the way critical brain structures interact to control behavior—behavior specifically related to drug abuse. Just as continued abuse may lead to tolerance or the need for higher drug dosages to produce an effect, it may also lead to addiction, which can drive an abuser to seek out and take drugs compulsively. Drug addiction erodes a person's self-control and ability to make sound decisions, while sending intense impulses to take drugs.

Sally Satel and Scott O. Lilienfeld  **NO**

Singing the Brain Disease Blues

Well over a decade ago, the National Institute on Drug Abuse began advancing the idea that addiction is a "brain disease." Over the years, the concept has become orthodoxy—a dubious achievement that has justifiably prompted Buchman and his colleagues (2010) to call for a more nuanced perspective on addiction. In this peer commentary we challenge the validity of the brain disease model of addiction and discuss its adverse implications for treatment.

Let us begin with the concept of brain disease. "That addiction is tied to changes in brain structure and function is what makes it, fundamentally, a brain disease," wrote a former director of the National Institute on Drug Abuse in a seminal 1997 *Science* article (Leshner 1997). What does this statement really mean? Surely, drugs operate at the level of the brain (Hyman 2007). No dispute there. Regular, heavy use of alcohol, nicotine, heroin, cocaine, and other substances produces brain changes (reward centers are "hijacked," as it is commonly put) that, in turn, influence the urge to use drugs and the struggle to quit. Brain-related differences among users influence the rapidity with which they develop addiction, their subjective experience of the drug, the potency of their craving, and the severity of their withdrawal symptoms.

That said, why should this make addiction a brain disease as opposed to, say, a molecular disease, a psychological disease, or a sociocultural disease? All are equally valid perspectives for different purposes. As psychologist Nick Heather wisely asserted, "Addiction can be defined in any way the definer thinks fit. . . . The crucial issue is how useful the definition is for specific purposes" (Heather 1998). So, for example, if one's purpose is to investigate dopamine circuitry, then viewing addiction as as brain-based phenomenon makes sense. But if one's purpose is providing psychosocial treatment and devising policy, then the "neurocentric" view doesn't help much.

The mechanical simplicity of the "brain disease" rhetoric has a seductive appeal that obscures the considerable degree of choice in addiction, as Buchman and colleagues note. Consider the daily routine of addicts. They rarely spend all of their time in the throes of an intense neurochemical siege. Most heroin addicts, for example, perform some kind of gainful work between administrations of the drug. In the days between binges, cocaine addicts make many decisions that have nothing to do with drug-seeking. Should they try to find a different job? Kick that freeloading cousin off their couch? Attend a Narcotics Anonymous

From *AJOB Neuroscience*, January, 2010, pp. 46–47. Copyright © 2010 by Taylor & Francis Journals. Reprinted by permission.

meeting, enter treatment if they have private insurance, or register at a public clinic if they don't? These decisions are often based on personal meaning. Many autobiographical accounts by former addicts reveal that they were startled into quitting by a spasm of self-reproach (Lawford 2008): "My God, I almost robbed someone!" or "What kind of mother am I?"

Most important, knotty philosophical issues of free will versus determinism aside, addiction is an activity whose course can be altered by its foreseeable consequences. No amount of reinforcement or punishment can alter the course of an entirely autonomous biological condition. Imagine bribing an Alzheimer's patient to keep her dementia from worsening, or threatening to impose a penalty on her if it did. It won't work. But incentives do work in addicted patients, as clinical trials of a strategy called "contingency management" show. The standard trial compares addicts who know they will receive a reward for submitting drug-free urines with matched addicts not offered rewards (Silverman et al. 2001). In general, the groups that are eligible to be rewarded with, for example, cash, gift certificates, or services are about two to three times more likely to turn in drug-free urines compared with similar counterparts who were not able to work for such incentives. In drug courts (a jail-diversion treatment program for nonviolent drug offenders), offenders are sanctioned for continued drug use (perhaps a night or two in jail) and rewarded for cooperation with the program. The judge holds the person, not his or her brain, accountable for setbacks and progress.

Even without formal incentives or sanctions, users perform their own mental calculations all the time. Repetitive drug use is reduced or stopped altogether when the adverse consequences of drug use exceed its rewards. An addict might reason, for example, "Heroin quells my psychic pain and soothes withdrawal, but it is costing my family too much." In a choice model, according to psychologist Gene Heyman (2009), addiction is the triumph of feel-good local decisions ("I'll use today") over punishing global anxieties ("I don't want to be an addict tomorrow"). As the relative value of costs and benefits of addiction change over time (yes, benefits: people use drugs and maintain addictions for psychological reasons—a reality obfuscated by the brain disease model), users become less ambivalent about quitting.

Whether powered by changes in meaning or incentives, the capacity for self-governance is the key to the most promising treatments for addiction. This fact is often obscured, however, by a semantic glitch whereby the state of "addiction" is taken to mean that the desire to use is unmalleable and beyond the reach of environmental contingencies. In circular fashion, then, addicted individuals are believed to be helpless to change their behavior. And, if so, it is wrong to expect them to respond to sanctions.

This was the destructive logic employed by the opponents of Proposition 36 in California, a 2001 referendum on the state's jail diversion program for nonviolent drug offenders (Urada et al. 2008). They prevailed and within a few years treatment program staff began clamoring for permission to use modest penalties and incentives—without them, the staff had no leverage. Similarly, drug courts and probationary programs have been hampered by ideological resistance to imposing consequences for positive urine tests because, after all, victims of a brain disease cannot be held accountable for their behavior; what's more, they are "supposed" to relapse.

The brain disease model implies erroneously that the brain is necessarily the most important and useful level of analysis for understanding and treating addiction. Like Buchman and colleagues, we believe that it is far more productive to view addiction as a behavior that operates on several levels, ranging from molecular function and structure to brain physiology to psychology to psychosocial environment and social relations (see also Kendler 2005; Lilienfeld 2007). The lower levels of explanation, particularly the brain, are merely among them—and not necessarily the most informative for practical purposes. Indeed, an "eliminative" or "greedy" (to use philosopher Daniel Dennett's apt term) reductionistic view—which posits that lower levels of analysis render higher levels superfluous—leads to ambivalence about the importance of holding addicts accountable and, in turn, undermines the most effective behavioral treatments available (Dennett 1995). Fortunately for addicts, their behavior can be modified by contingencies. Official rhetoric does them a disservice when it implies they are merely helpless victims of their own hijacked brains.

All references for articles included in *Taking Sides: Clashing Views on Psychological Issues, 17/e* can be found on the Web at http://www.mhhe.com/cls.

CHALLENGE QUESTIONS

Is Addiction a Brain Disease?

1. Describe the implications of these two positions (discussed in the introduction) on addiction for actually treating the addict. Which would you prefer if you were addicted, and why?
2. Explain how the old free will/determinism controversy is vitally involved in this debate about addiction. In other words, how does the notion that human nature entails a freedom of will lead to one position and the notion that human nature is controlled by its biological makeup and its environmental programming lead to the other?
3. Satel and Lilienfeld hold that drugs can change brains and yet still allow for some modicum of self-control. Describe the reasons for your agreement or disagreement. Is there empirical evidence that might have some import for your position?
4. In your view, is it possible for one's biology to predispose someone to addiction and yet retain his or her ability to resist it? Describe the reasons for your agreement or disagreement.
5. If the repeated use of chemicals in drugs alters one's brain chemistry, what could this imply about the repeated use of chemicals in prescribed drugs, and even food additives?

Suggested Readings

Heyman, G. M. (2009). *Addiction: A disorder of choice.* Cambridge: Harvard University Press.

Hoffman, J. (2007). *Addiction: Why can't they just stop? New knowledge. New treatments. New hope.* Emmaus, PA: Rodale Books.

Mate, G. (2010). *In the realm of hungry ghosts: Close encounters with addiction.* Berkeley, CA: North Atlantic Books.

Nace, E. P., & Tinsley, J. A. (2007). *Patients with substance abuse problems: Effective identification, diagnosis, and treatment.* New York: W.W. Norton.

Vale, P.H. (2010). Addiction—and rational choice theory. *International Journal of Consumer Studies, 34*(1), 38–45.

ISSUE 2

Is Homosexuality Biologically Based?

YES: Qazi Rahman, from "The Neurodevelopment of Human Sexual Orientation," *Neuroscience & Biobehavioral Reviews* (October 2005)

NO: Stanton L. Jones and Alex W. Kwee, from "Scientific Research, Homosexuality, and the Church's Moral Debate: An Update," *Journal of Psychology and Christianity* (Winter 2005)

ISSUE SUMMARY

YES: Professor of Psychobiology Qazi Rahman claims that the current research on the biology of homosexuality supports prenatal biological determination and refutes learning models of sexual orientation

NO: Professor of Psychology Stanton L. Jones and Clinical Psychologist Alex W. Kwee claim the current research on the biology of homosexuality provides no firm evidence for biological causation and leaves room for learning models of sexual orientation.

Many of the so-called "culture wars" in the United States have been fought over the issue of homosexuality. On one side of this "war" are those who claim that homosexuality is a moral issue, perhaps even a "sin." Yet, for this to be a moral issue, homosexuals would have to have some measure of control over or even a choice of their sexual orientation. Do they have such control? If this orientation is biologically determined, whether at birth or later, the control or choice necessary for sexual preference to be a "moral issue" would seem to be unavailable. If, on the other hand, homosexuals have made choices that lead them learn to "prefer" (choose) a certain type of sexual orientation, then a moral understanding of homosexuality could be justified.

Only relatively recently have psychologists and neuroscientists begun to conduct scientific research to address these issues. One of the earliest of these researchers, neuroscientist Simon LeVay, a self-declared gay person, found dramatic brain differences between gay and straight men. This investigation led many to speculate that sexual orientation was completely biological. Indeed, other scientific findings have been reported, especially as sensationalized by the media, that would seem to have confirmed this speculation. Do we now have enough evidence to conclude that homosexuality is completely biologically based? Can we omit the role of learning factors in homosexuality all together?

One of the foremost researchers in this area, Dr. Qazi Rahman, answers these questions in the first article by reviewing research on the neurodevelopment of human sexual orientation. He claims the research supports the proposal that homosexuality is biologically determined, even before birth. In support of his claim, he cites evidence from twin-studies, genetic scanning, brain structure studies, and the fraternal birth order effect. He even refutes the idea that learning plays a role in the development of homosexuality by arguing that the theories which attempt to explain sexual orientation through cultural socialization, either by authority figures or peers, are simply "not supported."

In the second selection, on the other hand, noted psychologists Stanton Jones and Alex Kwee review much of the same research on the biology of homosexuality but come to very different conclusions. In discussing relevant twin studies, for example, they point to methodological weaknesses and side with one of the original studies' researchers that there is "no statistically significant indication of genetic influence on sexual orientation." While they agree that the research points to a correlation between biology and homosexuality, they contend that there is still no evidence of the cause of this correlation, whether learning from the environment or "hard-wiring" of the brain. They argue that there is still plenty of room for a learning model in the development of homosexuality by citing a recent study about the influence of parental socialization on homosexuality.

POINT	COUNTERPOINT
• Evidence from twin-studies points to a genetically heritable homosexuality.	• Twin-studies suffer from methodological weaknesses that call into question the genetic influence on sexual orientation.
• Genetic scanning shows that homosexuality is correlated with several genes.	• Findings based on genetic scanning are ambiguous.
• The maternal immune theory is well established because it relies on the very reliable fraternal birth order effect.	• The maternal immune theory relies on disputed findings regarding the fraternal birth order effect.
• The fraternal birth order effect is accounted for in the prenatal environment.	• The fraternal birth order effect can be accounted for in the postnatal social environment.
• Brain structures differ between homosexual and heterosexual men.	• Brain structure difference could be the effect rather than the cause of homosexuality.
• Research shows that learning plays no appreciable role in the development of sexual orientation.	• Research shows that learning plays a role in the development of sexual orientation.

YES

Qazi Rahman

The Neurodevelopment of Human Sexual Orientation

1. Introduction

Sexual orientation refers to a dispositional sexual attraction towards persons of the opposite sex or same sex. Sexual orientation appears 'dispositional' in that it comprises a target selection and preference mechanism sensitive to gender, motivational approach behaviours towards the preferred target, and internal cognitive processes biased towards the preferred target (such as sexual fantasies). In contrast, sexual orientation does not appear to be a matter of conscious self-labelling or past sexual activity because these are subject to contingent social pressures, such as the presence of linguistic descriptors and visible sexual minorities within an individual's culture, and the availability of preferred sexual partners. Therefore, in human investigations, sexual orientation is often assessed using self-report measures of 'sexual feelings' (i.e. sexual attraction and sexual fantasies) rather than self-labelling or past hetero- or homosexual activity.

Sexual orientation appears to be a dichotomous trait in males, with very few individuals demonstrating an intermediate (i.e. 'bisexual') preference. This is borne out by fine-grained analyses of self-reported heterosexual and homosexual orientation prevalence rates (using measures of sexual feelings) in population-level samples, and work on physiological genital arousal patterns (e.g. using penile plethysmography) in response to viewing preferred and non-preferred sexual imagery. Both lines of evidence consistently demonstrate a bimodal sexual orientation among men—heterosexual or homosexual, but rarely 'bisexual'. This is less so in the case among women. For example, Chivers et al. demonstrated a 'bisexual' genital arousal pattern among both heterosexual and lesbian women, suggesting a decoupling of self-reported sexual feelings (which appears broadly bimodal) from peripheral sexual arousal in women.

If sexual orientation among humans is a mostly bimodal trait, this implicates a canalization of development along a sex-typical route (heterosexual) or a sex-atypical (homosexual) route. Statistical taxometric procedures have confirmed this by demonstrating that latent taxa (i.e. non-arbitrary natural classes) underlie an opposite-sex, or same-sex, orientation in both men and women.

From *Neuroscience & Biobehavioral Reviews*, vol. 29, no. 7, October 2005, pp. 1057–1058, 1060, 1062, 1063 (excerpts). Copyright © 2005 by Elsevier Ltd. Reprinted by permission via Rightslink.

Less well established are the factors that may be responsible for this 'shunting' of sexual orientation along two routes (the edges of which are fuzzier in women). These factors are the subject of the remaining discussion and it is suggested that they probably operate neurodevelopmentally before birth.

2. Behavioural and Molecular Genetics

A natural starting point for the neurodevelopment of physiological and behavioural traits must begin with the genetic level of investigation. Several family and twin studies provide clear evidence for a genetic component to both male and female sexual orientation. Family studies, using a range of ascertainment strategies, show increased rate of homosexuality among relatives of homosexual probands. There is also evidence for elevated maternal line transmission of male homosexuality, suggestive of X linkage, but other studies have not found such elevation relative to paternal transmission. Among females, transmission is complex, comprising autosomal and sex-linked routes. Twin studies in both community and population-level samples report moderate heritability estimates, the remaining variance being mopped up by non-shared environmental factors. Early attempts to map specific genetic loci responsible for sexual orientation using family pedigree linkage methods led to the discovery of markers on the Xq28 chromosomal region, with one subsequent replication limiting the effect to males only. However, there is at least one independent study which produced null findings, while a recent genome wide scan revealed no Xq28 linkage in a new sample of families but identified putative additional chromosomal sites (on 7q36, 8pl2 and 10q26) which now require denser mapping investigations. These studies are limited by factors such as the unclear maternal versus paternal line transmission effects, possible autosomal transmission and measurement issues. Two candidate gene studies which explored the putative hormonal pathways in the neurodevelopment of sexual orientation (see Section 3): one on the androgen receptor gene and another on aromatase (CYP19A1) both produced null findings. . . .

3. The Fraternal Birth Order Effect and Maternal Immunity

The maternal immunity hypothesis is certainly the most revolutionary neurodevelopmental model of human sexual orientation. Empirically, it rests on one very reliable finding—the fraternal birth order effect (FBO): that is, homosexual men have a greater number of older brothers than heterosexual men do (and relative to any other category of sibling), in diverse community and population-level samples, and as early as they can be reliably surveyed. The estimated odds of being homosexual increase by around 33% with each older brother, and statistical modelling using epidemiological procedures suggest that approximately 1 in 7 homosexual men may owe their sexual orientation to the FBO effect. It has been suggested that the remaining proportions of homosexual men may owe their sexual orientation to other causes, such as differential prenatal androgen levels. Homosexual and heterosexual women do not differ in sibling sex composition or their birth order, thus any neurodevelopmental explanation for the FBO effect is limited to males. Importantly, recent work has demonstrated that homosexual males with older brothers have significantly lower birth weights compared to heterosexual males with older brothers. As birth weight is undeniably prenatally determined, some common developmental factor operating before birth must underlie FBO and sexual orientation among human males.

Specifically, investigators have proposed a role for the progressive immunization of some mothers to male-linked antigens produced by carrying each succeeding male foetus. That is, the maternal immune system 'sees' male-specific antigens as 'non-self' and begins producing antibodies against them. One possible group of antigens are the Y-linked minor histocompatibility antigens, specifically *H–Y*. The accumulating H–Y antibodies may divert male-typical sexual differentiation of the foetal brain, leading the individual to be sexually attracted to males. For example, male-specific antibodies may bind to, and inactivate, male-differentiating receptors located on the surface of foetal neurons thus preventing the morphogenesis of masculinized sexual preferences.

The maternal immunity theory is consistent with a number of observations: the number of older sisters is irrelevant to sexual orientation in later born males; the H–Y antigen is expressed by male foetuses only and thus the maternal immune system 'remembers' the number of males carried previously and may modulate its response; and H–Y antigens are strongly represented in neural tissue. Nonetheless, there is no data specifying a role for these particular antigens in sexual preferences among humans. There are several alternative candidate antigens to H–Y, including the distinct Y-linked protein families' *protocadherin* and *neuroligin,* both of which have been found in humans. These cell adhesion proteins are thought to influence cell–cell communication during early male-specific brain morphogenesis and may have male-typical behavioural consequences. Consistent with these studies is neurogenetic evidence for the direct transcription of Y-linked sex determination genes *SRY* and *ZFY* in the male human brain (including hypothalamus). The maternal immunity model may also explain the link between birth weight and sexual preferences: mouse models show that maternal immunization to male-derived antigens can affect foetal weight. Furthermore, male mice whose mothers are immunized to H–Y prior to pregnancy show reduced male-typical consummatory sexual behaviour towards receptive females.

The maternal immunity model implicitly relies on a non-hormonal immunologic neurodevelopmental explanation and thus cannot immediately explain the hyper-male features (e.g. 2D:4D and AEPs) associated with male homosexuality. It is possible that male-specific antibodies may interact with sexual differentiation processes controlled by sex hormones or be completely independent of them—this is unknown as yet. . . .

4. Neural Circuitry

Neurodevelopmental mechanisms must wire neural circuits differently in those with same-sex attractions from those with opposite-sex attractions, but we still know very little about this circuitry. The first indication for neural correlates of sexual partner preference came from Simon LeVay autopsy study of the third interstitial nucleus of the anterior hypothalamus (INAH-3) which he found to be smaller in homosexual men than in presumed heterosexual men, and indistinguishable from presumed heterosexual women. Another study found a non-significant trend for a female-typical INAH-3 among homosexual men (and confirmed the heterosexual sex difference), but this was not evidenced the main sexually dimorphic parameter reported by this study (the total number of neurons). This preceding finding is noteworthy as a prediction from the prenatal androgen theory would be that a parameter which shows significant sexual dimorphism should also demonstrate within-sex variation attributable to sexual orientation. A conservative conclusion regarding these data is that while INAH-3 is larger in heterosexual men than in heterosexual women, and possibly smaller in homosexual men, structurally speaking this within-sex difference may not be very large at all.

One recent positron emission tomography study has demonstrated stronger hypothalamic response to serotonergic challenge in heterosexual than in homosexual men, and neuroimaging studies comparing heterosexual men and women while viewing preferred sexual imagery show significantly greater hypothalamic activation in heterosexual men. These findings, coupled with the anatomical findings described earlier, could be taken to suggest that there is a functionally distinct anterior hypothalamic substrate to sexual attraction towards women. This supposition is further supported by mammalian lesion models of the preoptic area (POA) of the anterior hypothalamus showing reduced appetitive responses towards female by male animals. Nevertheless, investigations comparing heterosexual and homosexual women are needed to support a role for this region in sexual preference towards females among humans.

While animal models point to a role for prenatal androgens in producing sexual variation in hypothalamic regions, a similar relationship in humans is unclear. One study found no sexual-orientation-related differences in the distribution of androgen receptors in sexually dimorphic hypothalamic regions. However, one animal model often overlooked by scientists may provide some guidance. Some males of certain species of sheep show an exclusive same-sex preference, and also how reduced aromatase activity and smaller ovine sexually dimorphic nuclei (a possible homolog to the human INAH-3) compared to female-oriented sheep. A role for aromatized metabolites of testosterone in underscoring possible hypothalamic variation related to human sexual orientation requires further study in light of these findings. Moreover, putative sexual orientation differences in aromatase activity in human males may go some way to explaining the 'mosaic' profile of hypo- and hyper-masculinized traits described earlier. For example, a reduction in aromatase activity in homosexual compared to heterosexual men (predicted from the Roselli findings) may lead to reduced availability of aromatized testosterone (i.e. estradiol) which typically masculinizes the male mammalian brain. This may lead to hypo-masculinized hypothalamic circuitry and yet leave excess non-aromatized testosterone to hyper-masculinize additional androgen sensitive traits (e.g. 2D:4D) through other metabolic pathways, such as 5-alpha reductase. Note, one mitigating piece of evidence with respect to these suggestions is the null finding of DuPree et al. regarding sexual-orientation-related variation in the aromatase gene. . . .

5. Is There a Role for Learning in the Development of Human Sexual Orientation?

The role of learning in the development of human sexual orientation has been the subject of much debate and controversy, most likely because it is erroneously believed to result in particular socio-political consequences associated with homosexuality. While data are a little thin on the ground, several lines of evidence mitigate the involvement of learning mechanisms. In animal models, there are documented effects of conditioning on sexual arousal, approach behaviour, sexual performance and strength of sexual preference towards opposite-sex targets, but no robust demonstrations of learning in the organization of same-sex preferences among males. Interestingly, one study in female rats demonstrated that the volume of the sexually dimorphic nucleus of the preoptic region was increased (male-typical) by testosterone administration coupled with same-sex sexual experience. This suggests that sexual experience may interact with steroid exposure to shape sexual partner preferences in females.

In humans, the extent of childhood or adolescent homosexual versus heterosexual activity does not appear to relate to eventual adult sexual orientation. Documented evidence regarding the situational or cultural 'initiation' of juvenile males into extensive same-sex experience (for example, in single-sex public schools in Britain or the obligatory homosexual activity required of young males in the Sambia tribe of New Guinea) does not result in elevated homosexuality in adulthood.

An alternative explanation for the FBO effect is that sexual interaction with older brothers during critical windows of sexual development predisposes towards a homosexual orientation. Studies in national probability samples show that sibling sex-play does not underscore the link between FBO and male sexual orientation, and that the sexual attraction component of sexual orientation, but not sexual activity, are best predicted by frequency of older brothers. In further support, same-sex play between pairs of gay brothers is also unrelated to adult homosexual attraction.

Perhaps parent–child interactions influence the sexual orientation of children? An informative test here is to examine the sexuality of children of homosexual parents because this type of familial dynamic could promote same-sex preferences through observational learning mechanisms. However, evidence from retrospective and prospective studies provides no support for this supposition. Nonetheless, one must bear in mind that if parental behaviour does determine offspring sexual orientation, it could be equally common in homosexual and heterosexual parents.

While a role for learning factors can never be entirely omitted, it is perplexing that several of the key routes by which these could have their effect, such as through sexual experience during childhood or adolescence, or through parental socialization, are not supported. Almost certainly the expression of homosexual *behaviour* has varied over time and across cultures, but there is little reason to think that dispositional homosexuality varies greatly cross-culturally or even historically. . . .

**Stanton L. Jones and
Alex W. Kwee**

 **NO**

Scientific Research, Homosexuality, and the Church's Moral Debate: An Update

Etiological Research

Significant new research on etiology has emerged in six areas: 1) behavioral genetics; 2) genetic scanning, 3) human brain structure studies, 4) studies of "gay sheep" and "gay fruit flies," 5) fraternal birth order research, and 6) familial structure impact.

Behavioral Genetics

Bailey's behavioral genetics studies of sexual orientation in twins and other siblings seemed to provide solid evidence of a substantial degree of genetic influence on formation of homosexual orientation. Jones and Yarhouse criticized these studies severely, most importantly on the grounds that both studies were making population estimates of the degree of genetic influence on sexual orientation on *potentially biased samples,* samples recruited from advertisements in gay publications and hence potentially biased by differential volunteerism by subjects inclined to favor a genetic hypothesis for the causation of their orientation. Later research by Bailey and other associates with a truly representative sample of twins drawn from the Australian Twin Registry in fact refuted the earlier findings by failing to find a significant genetic effect in the causation of homosexual orientation.

Not included in our review was a major behavioral genetics study paralleling the work of Bailey: Kendler, Thornton, Gilman, and Kessler. This study is remarkable in two ways. First, it replicates almost exactly the findings of the earlier Bailey studies in reporting relatively strong probandwise concordances for homosexual monozygotic twins. Kendler et al. report their findings as pairwise concordances, but when the simple conversions to probandwise concordances are done, Kendler et al.'s 48% probandwise concordance for males and females together (reported as a 31.6% pairwise concordance) is remarkably similar to Bailey's reports of probandwise concordances of 52% for men and 48% for women.

From *Journal of Psychology and Christianity (JPC),* vol. 24, no. 4, Winter 2005, pp. 304–307, 308–312 (excerpts). Copyright © 2005 by Christian Association for Psychological Studies, Inc – CAPS. Reprinted by permission.

Second, the Kendler et al. study is also remarkably similar to the earlier Bailey studies in its methodological weaknesses. Trumpeted as a study correcting the "unrepresentative and potentially biased samples" of the Bailey studies by using a "more representative sample," specifically a "U. S. national probability sample" (p. 1843), this study appears actually to suffer all of the original problems of volunteer sample bias of the 1991 and 1993 Bailey studies. Further, the methodological problems give every sign of compounding one upon the next. The description of the methodology is confusing: Kendler et al. state that their sample comes from a MacArthur Foundation study of 3,032 representatively chosen respondents, but then they note that since this sample produced too few twins and almost no homosexual twins (as would be expected), they turned to a different sample of 50,000 households that searched for twins, and here the clear sampling problems begin: 14.8% of the households reported a twin among the siblings, but only 60% gave permission to contact the twin. There was further erosion of the sample as only 20.6% of the twins agreed to participate if the initial contact was with another family member, compared to 60.4% if the initial contact was a twin him- or herself (and given the lower likelihood of an initial contact being with a twin, this suggests a low response rate for twins overall). Yet further erosion may have occurred at the next step of seeking contact information of all siblings in the family; the write-up is confusing on this point. With all these potential sampling problems, it is then quite striking that the absolute number of identical/monozygotic twin pairs concordant for homosexuality were only 6 (out of a total of 19 pairs where at least one twin was "non-heterosexual"). With such a small absolute number of monozygotic twin pairs concordant for homosexuality, the smallest bias in the assembly of the sample would introduce problems in data interpretation; loss of just two concordant twin pairs would have wiped out the findings. It is remarkable that Kendler et al. give no explicit attention to these problems. Thus, we must regard this new study, promoted by some as a replication of Bailey's original 1991 and 1993 studies, as having the same fatal flaws as those earlier studies and as rightly superseded by Bailey's report in 2000 that there is no statistically significant indication of genetic influence on sexual orientation.

Genetic Scanning

Mustanski et al. reported on a "full genome scan of sexual orientation in men" (p. 272). This is the third study of genetics and homosexuality to emerge from the laboratory of the associates of Dean Hamer, and this study utilized 146 families; 73 families previously studied by either Hamer, Hu, Magnuson, Hu, and Pattatucci or Hu et al., and 73 new families not previously studied. The same sample limitations are present in these studies as were discussed in Jones and Yarhouse (pp. 79–83). If these studies were attempting to establish population estimates, these would constitute biased samples, but because they explicitly state that they are looking for genetic factors in a subpopulation of homosexual men predetermined to be more likely to manifest genetic factors, these are limitations and not methodological weaknesses. They obtained their sample through "advertisements in local and national homophile publications" and the "sole inclusion criterion was the presence of at least two self-acknowledged gay male siblings" (p. 273), a rare occurrence indeed.

Two findings are worth noting. First, the Mustanski et al. study continued the pattern of failing to replicate the original 1993 Hamer finding of an Xq28 region of the X chromosome being linked to male homosexuality, this despite somewhat heroic statistical focus in this study. This is yet another blow to the credibility of their original findings.

Second, while media outlets headlined the Mustanski et al. study as having found genes linked to homosexuality on chromosomes 7, 8, and 10, this is precisely what they did *not* find, but rather "we found one region of near significance and two regions close to the criteria for suggestive linkage" (p. 273). None of their findings, in other words, achieved statistical significance. It is hard to tell whether these findings represent a cluster of near false positives that will fail future replication, or clues that will lead to more fine-grained and statistically significant findings. If the latter, these genetic segments may be neither necessary nor sufficient to cause homosexual orientation, and may either contribute to the causation of the orientation directly or indirectly. This is an intriguing but ambiguous report.

Human Brain Structure Studies

New brain research allows us to expand the reported findings on the relationship of brain structure to sexual orientation, and to correct one element of our prior presentation of the data in this complex field. We duplicate [here] . . . (Table 1) part of the table summarizing brain findings from pages 68–69 of Jones and Yarhouse.

Table 1

Summary of Brain Differences by Biological Sex and Sexual Orientation

Study	INAH1	Brain INAH2	Region INAH3	INAH4
Swaab & Fliers (1985)	HetM > HetF			
Swaab & Hoffman (1988)	HetM = HomM; (HetM & HomM) > HetF			
Allen et al. (1989)	HetM = HetF	HetM > HetF	HetM > HetF	HetM = HetF
LeVay (1991)	HetM = HetF	HetM = HetF	HetM > (HetF & HomM)	HetM = HetF
Byne et al. (2000)	HetM = HetF	HetM = HetF	HetM > HetF	HetM = HetF
Byne et al. (2001)	HetM = HetF	HetM = HetF	HetM > HetF	HetM = HetF
			HetM = HomM in number of neurons	

HetM = heterosexual males; HetF = heterosexual females; HomM = homosexual males.

Our correction is to recategorize in Table 1 the findings of Swaab and Hoffman from our listing, following the original report, as from the SDNH or sexually differentiated nucleus of the hypothalamus to a finding reporting on the INAH1 or interstitial nucleus of the hypothalamus, area 1. The review of Byne et al. pointed out that the SDNH *is* the INAH1; Swaab's 1988 report was an extension of his earlier work and not an exploration of a new area. The new work of Byne et al. continued the pattern of refuting Swaab's reported findings.

The new findings reporting on brain structure and sexual orientation (summarized in Table 1) come from the respected laboratory of William Byne and his colleagues. We cited Byne heavily in our critique of the famous Simon LeVay studies of brain differences in the INAH3 region. Byne et al. replicated the previous findings of sexual dimorphism (male-female differences) in INAH3, and thus it is now safe to say that this is a stable finding. Further, Byne and his team have refined the analysis to be able to say, based on their 2000 study, that the INAH3 size difference by sex "was attributable to a sex difference in neuronal number and not in neuronal size or density." Simply put, the INAH3 area in women is, on average, smaller than it is in men, and this is because women have fewer neurons in this area, and *not* because their neurons are smaller or less dense.

This makes the findings of Byne et al. on sexual orientation yet more curious; they found the size (specifically, volume) of the INAH3s of homosexual males to be intermediate (to a statistically nonsignificant degree) between heterosexual males and heterosexual females. In other words, the volume of the INAH3s was, on average, between the average volumes of heterosexual males and heterosexual females such that the differences did not achieve statistical significance in comparison to either heterosexual males or females. Hence, "Sexual orientation cannot be reliably predicted on the basis of INAH3 volume alone." Further, and to complicate things more, they found that the nonsignificant difference noted between homosexual and heterosexual males was *not* attributable (as it was for the male-female difference) to numbers of neurons, as homosexual and heterosexual males were found to have comparable neuronal counts. So, there may be a difference between homosexual and heterosexual males, but if there is, it is not the same type of difference as that between males and females.

To complicate the analysis even further, Byne et al. point out that these differences, if they exist, are not proof of prenatal, biological determination of sexual orientation. While it is possible that differences in INHA3 may be strongly influenced by prenatal hormones, "In addition, sex related differences may also emerge later in development as the neurons that survive become part of functional circuits" (p. 91). Specifically, the difference in volume could be attributed to "a reduction in neuropil within the INAH3 in the homosexual group" (p. 91) as a result of "postnatal experience." In other words, if there are brain structure differences between homosexuals and heterosexuals, they could as well be the result rather than the cause of sexual behavior and sexual preference. (The same conclusion about directionality of causation can be drawn about the new study showing activation of sexual brain centers in response to female pheromones by male heterosexuals, and to male pheromones by female heterosexuals *and* male homosexuals. The authors themselves point out that these brain activations could be the result of learning as well as evidence of the "hard-wiring" of the brain.) . . .

Second, and in a rare admission for those advancing biological explanations of sexual orientation, Roselli et al. admit that the direction of causation is at this time completely unclear, in the process echoing the possible causal role of postnatal experience mentioned by Byne et al. above:

> However, the existing data do not reveal which is established first—oSDN size or mate preference. One might assume that the neural structure is determined first and that this, in turn, guides the development of sexual partner preference. However, it is equally possible that some other factors(s), including social influences or learned associations, might shape sexual partner preference first. Then, once a sexual partner preference is established, the continued experiences and/or behaviors associated with a given preference might affect the size of the oSDN. (p. 241)

A new study released in June, 2005 has ignited the latest frenzy about biological causation of sexual orientation. In response to this study, the president of the Human Rights Campaign ("the largest national lesbian, gay, bisexual and transgender political organization") stated that "Science is closing the door on right-wing distortions. . . . The growing body of scientific evidence continues to refute the opponents of equality who maintain that sexual orientation is a 'choice.'" Chairman of the Case Western Reserve University Department of Biochemistry Michael Weiss expressed for the *New York Times* his hope that this study "will take the discussion about sexual preferences out of the realm of morality and put it into the realm of science." Both quotes epitomize the over-interpretation and illogic of those anxious to press findings from science to moral conclusions.

The new study appears to be a strong piece of scientific research that will have important implications for our understanding of the biological bases of sexual behavior. The researchers generated a gene fragment (the *"fruitless (fru)"* allele) that was "constitutively spliced in either the male or the female mode" in the chromosomes of the opposite sex (i.e., male fruit flies had the allele inserted in a female mode and female fruit flies had the allele inserted in a male mode) with dramatic effects: "Forcing female splicing in the male results in a loss of male courtship behavior and orientation, confirming that male-specific splicing of *fru* is indeed essential for male behavior. More dramatically, females in which *fru* is spliced in the male mode behave as if they were males: they court other females" (p. 786). The results reported were indeed powerful; the behavioral distinctions in the modified fruit flies were almost unequivocal.

The authors of this study were reasonably circumspect in their report of the implications of their findings, though others were not as noted before. Three issues deserve attention. First, as in our discussion of "gay sheep," the differences between human and animal (or insect) mating patterns are enormous, and those differences limit application to the human situation. Demir and Dickson noted that male courtship of the female fruit fly is highly scripted, "largely a fixed-action pattern" (p. 785). The finding that the normal, almost robotic mating patterns of this creature are hard-wired is hardly surprising; in contrast, the enormous complexity of human sexual and romantic response indicates that such a finding will be challenging to apply to the human condition. Further, the interpretation that this study establishes a genetic base for "sexual orientation" in fruit flies is careless; the study rather finds genetic determination (to some degree) of an entire pattern of mating/reproductive behavior. The genetic control of mating behavior in this study is of something both more and less than sexual orientation as experienced by humans.

Second, we have plenty of existing data to indicate that no such encompassing genetic determination of sexual behavior exists in humans. The behavior genetics evidence of sexual orientation (see the earlier discussion of the Kendler et al. study) provides strong evidence that genetic factors provide (at most) incomplete determination of sexual orientation, even if genetic factors are part of a multivariant causal array.

Third, we must question the following claim of the authors:

> Thus, male-specific splicing of *fru* is both necessary and *sufficient* [emphasis added] to specify male courtship behavior and sexual orientation. A complex innate behavior is thus specified by the action of a single gene, demonstrating that behavioral switch genes do indeed exist and identifying *fru* as one such gene.

Strictly understood, the authors appear to be claiming that the presence of *fru* elicits, *necessarily and sufficiently,* stereotypical male courtship by males of female fruit flies, but a famous study from a decade before falsifies the sufficiency of *fru* causation. Zhang and Odenwald reported on genetic alterations in male fruit flies which produced "homosexual behavior" in the altered fruit flies. This study too resulted in many tabloid headlines heralding the creation of a "homosexual gene." Media reports failed to cite the other curious finding of the study: when genetically normal or "straight" fruit flies were introduced into the habitat of the "gay" flies without females present, the normal (genetically unaltered) male flies began engaging in the same type of "homosexual" behavior as the genetically altered flies. In other words, genetically normal ("straight") flies began to act like homosexual flies because of their *social environment.* Thus, in a most biological experiment, evidence of environmental ("psychological") influence emerged once again. So if the authors of the 2005 study are claiming that the presence of *fru* elicits (is sufficient to produce) stereotypical male courtship, that claim was falsified a decade before by the finding that normal male fruit flies (presumably with intact *fru* alleles), when exposed to certain social contexts ("gay" flies), engage in behavior that violates the stereotypical male courtship of females; other conditions—specifically, *social* conditions—are also sufficient to elicit homosexual behavior in fruit flies.

Together, these three issues suggest that, as powerful as the recent findings about fruit flies are, interpretive caution in application to humans is indicated.

Fraternal Birth Order Research

The fraternal birth order studies by Ray Blanchard, Anthony Bogaert, and various other researchers purport to show that sexual orientation in men correlates with an individual's number of older brothers. Specifically, it is claimed that male homosexuals tend to be born later in their sibships than male heterosexuals, and that male homosexuality is statistically (and causally) related to the number of older biological brothers (but not sisters) in the family. This purported relationship within the fraternal birth order is such that each additional older brother, it is claimed, increases the odds of homosexuality by 33%, and for gay men with approximately 2.5 older brothers, older brothers equal all the other causes of homosexuality combined.

Blanchard, Bogaert, and others advance the so-called maternal immune hypothesis to explain the fraternal birth order effect. According to this hypothesis, some mothers progressively produce, in response to each succeeding male fetus, antibodies to a substance called the H-Y antigen, which is produced by male fetuses and foreign to female bodies. The maternally produced anti-H-Y antibodies are thought to be passed on to the male fetus, preventing the fetal brain from developing in a male typical pattern, thereby causing the affected sons to develop homosexual orientations in later life. So much hyperbole surrounds the maternal immune causal hypothesis that it appears the assumption is simply being made that the fraternal birth order effect itself is indisputable when, in fact, it is not. We will direct the bulk of our critical attention to the birth order phenomenon. The maternal immune theory underlying the phenomenon can be quite readily dispatched at this point by stating that no direct evidence has ever been found for it, and so it remains purely speculative.

The major flaw of the fraternal birth order research is that the main studies were conducted on nonrepresentative samples. For example, one of the "landmark" studies that demonstrated the birth order effect recruited its sample from the 1994 Toronto Gay Pride Parade and several LGBT community organizations. Nonrepresentative samples are known to be vulnerable to a variety of selection biases. For instance, perhaps later-born gay men were overrepresented in this sample because they were more apt to be "out and proud," participate in Gay Pride events, and affiliate with overtly LGBT groups. If later born siblings tend to be less conventional and more rebellious as some research shows, later-born gay men, accordingly, may be less gender conforming and more likely to flaunt their sexual orientation. This may have resulted in an overrepresentation of later-born gay men and an underrepresentation of earlier-born gay men at Gay Pride events and within LGBT groups, which naturally exaggerated the fraternal birth order effect in this sample. This is just one of several possible selection biases which may have flawed Blanchard and Bogaert's sample.

To his credit, Bogaert attempted to correct for the methodological flaw of selection bias by examining national probability samples in the United States and Britain respectively. His study yielded a finding of fraternal birth order effects in both samples. While this may appear to replicate initial research results, we must question the size of the effects given the large samples involved—over 1,700 subjects in each of the samples. Bogaert did not clearly report the effect sizes he found. It is well known that using large enough samples, even small differences can be found to be statistically significant. Since statistical signifi-cance is a function of both sample size and effect size, and we really care about the effect size (and not merely that it is non-zero), Bogaert's findings are quite unhelpful.

In an even more recent study, Bogaert and Cairney attempted to answer the question of whether there is a fraternal birth order and parental age interac-tion effect in the prediction of sexual orientation. The researchers examined two samples—a U.S. national probability sample, and the flawed Canadian sample which we discussed above. The study based on the U.S. sample found an inter-action, but the data was so flawed—and acknowledged to be so by the authors themselves—that we cannot possibly take its conclusion seriously. Specifically, the preexisting U.S. data allowed for only an examination of absolute (not fra-ternal) birth order, surmised sexual orientation from behavior alone, and did not separate biological from non-biological siblings. The conclusion was counterin-tuitive in that while a positive association between (absolute) birth order and the likelihood of homosexuality was found, this association was weakened and in fact *reversed* with increasing maternal age. We believe that this conclusion high-lights the problem of bias when researchers attempt to find putative phenomena in data to support a cherished theory. If one is trying to establish a link between maternal age and homosexuality, it seems counterintuitive that the likelihood of homosexuality weakens or is reversed with increasing maternal age. Of course, if there is no relationship between sexual orientation and maternal age (which we suspect), a finding of *any* relationship is probably spurious and a methodologi-cal artifact. The researchers acknowledge the counterintuitiveness of their result by stating that they "know of no evidence of a stronger maternal reaction [to the H-Y antigen] in younger (versus older) mothers" (p. 32), betraying their bias towards a theory for which no direct evidence has ever been established, and then calling for new research.

Turning to the Canadian sample, Bogaert and Cairney found a Parental Age x Birth Order interaction. Their weighted analysis (giving larger families a greater impact on the results) revealed that this interaction was carried by a Mother's Age x Older Sisters effect. This finding actually *undermines* the frater-nal birth order theory because it provides some evidence that homosexuality is independent of the fraternal birth order effect. The authors acknowledge but downplay this, calling instead for the gathering of new data.

Other studies have falsified the fraternal birth order effect or showed no support for the maternal immune hypothesis. Using an enormous and nation-ally representative sample of adolescents that we discuss fully below, Bearman and Brückner found "no evidence for a speculative evolutionary model of homosexual preference" (i.e., the older-brother findings; p. 1199).

Despite various methodological problems with the fraternal birth order research, we concede that the evidence as a whole points to some sort of relationship between the number of older brothers and homosexuality. As responsible scientists, we should approach this body of research critically but not ignore the fact that it consistently shows some link between sexual orientation and fraternal but not sororal birth order. Research may well identify some pathway by which some men develop a stable same-sex attraction that is linked to their placement in the birth order. However, those who argue that the maternal immunosensitivity theory explains the fraternal birth order effect run into the problem of having to show that the same hypothesis does not underlie pedophilia, sexual violence, and other forms of sexual deviancy. While Blanchard, Bogaert, and other researchers deny any link between fraternal birth order and pedophilia, or they believe that any such link exists only for pedophiles who are homosexual, other studies have demonstrated a link between fraternal birth order and general (pedophilic and non-pedophilic) sexual offending, raising the possibility that homosexuality shares a common pathway with some forms of sexual deviance.

Research has not clearly established what this pathway is. One of the most natural but politically divisive speculations, which cautiously raises its head in the literature now and then, is that childhood sexualization and abuse has some causative relationship to homosexuality and pedophilia. This speculation is logical in relation to the fraternal birth order effect because younger brothers with higher fraternal birth order indices may have a higher probability of being victimized sexually by older brothers or otherwise experiencing same-sex sexualization. Preadolescent sexualization and abuse underlie the post-natal learning theory of homosexuality and pedophilia, which most recently has been supported by James in his review of several major studies. However plausible this theory appears, it is based on inferences from other studies and the direct empirical evidence for it is extremely weak.

Familial Structure Impact

A particularly powerful study challenging all of the major paradigms asserting biological determination of sexual orientation, and of the claim that there is no meaningful evidence of psychological/experiential causation of orientation, was recently published. Bearman and Brückner reported on analyses of an enormous database of almost 30,000 sexuality interviews with adolescents, with fascinating findings on the determinants of same-sex attraction for males (they found no evidence of significant determinants for females). Their summary of their findings merits citation in full:

> The findings presented here confirm some findings from previous research and stand in marked contrast to most previous research in a number of respects. First, we find no evidence for intrauterine transfer of hormone effects on social behavior. Second, we find no support for genetic influences on same-sex preference net of social structural

Table 2

Core Findings of Bearman & Brückner

Relationship (Subject is a . . .)	% Reporting Same-Sex Attraction	N (all males)
Opposite Sex Dizygotic Twin	16.8%	185
Same Sex Dizygotic Twin	9.8%	276
Same Sex Monozygotic Twin	9.9%	262
Opposite Sex Full Sibling	7.3%	427
Same Sex Full Sibling	7.9%	596
Other (adopted non-related; half-sibling)	10.6%	832

constraints. Third, we find no evidence for a speculative evolutionary model of homosexual preference. Finally, we find substantial indirect evidence in support of a socialization model at the individual level. (p. 1199)

Their second conclusion is a direct reference to the types of genetic influence posited by Bailey and others; the third conclusion a direct reference to the "older-brother" findings of Blanchard, Bogaert and others. But not only do their findings contradict other research, a new finding of socialization effects on same-sex attraction emerge from their data (see Table 2).

Bearman and Brückner found a single family constellation arrangement that significantly increased the likelihood that an adolescent male would report same-sex attraction, and that was when the adolescent male was a dizygotic (fraternal) twin whose co-twin is a sister (what they call "male opposite-sex twins"); in this arrangement, occurrence of same-sex attraction more than doubled over the base-rate of 7% to 8%: "we show that adolescent male opposite-sex twins are *twice as likely* as expected to report same-sex attraction, and that the pattern of concordance (similarity across pairs) of same-sex preference for sibling pairs does not suggest genetic influence independent of the social context" (p. 1181). They advance a socialization hypothesis to explain this finding, specifically proposing that sexual attraction is an outgrowth of gender socialization, and that no arrangement presents as much a challenge to parents to gender socialization than for a boy to be born simultaneous with a girl co-twin. In other words, they suggest that the parental task of accomplishing effective solidification of male sexual identity is challenged by parents having to handle a mixed-sex twin pair. The result of the diminished effectiveness of sexual identity formation in boys on average is the increased probability of same-sex attraction in the group of boys with twin sisters.

Bearman and Brückner go on to explore in their data the possibility that there could be a hormonal explanation for this finding: "Our data falsify the hormonal transfer hypothesis [i.e., the hypothesis posited to explain the fraternal birth order phenomenon], by isolating a single condition that eliminates the OS effect we observe—the presence of an older same-sex sibling" (p. 1181). Put simply, they found their effect disappeared when the boy with the twin sister was born into a family where there was already an older brother, an effect they attributed to the family already having grown accustomed to the process of establishing the sexual identity of a boy child; parents appear to be able to better handle the special challenges of a mixed-sex twin pair when they have already had some practice with an older brother. They firmly suggest that their "results support the hypothesis that less gendered socialization in early childhood and preadolescence shapes subsequent same-sex romantic preferences" (p. 1181). At a moment in time when it is common for many to deny that any firm evidence exists for the influence of non-biological causes on sexual orientation, these are remarkable findings (perhaps especially when the presence of an older brother decreases rather than increases the likelihood of homosexual orientation). . . .

CHALLENGE QUESTIONS

Is Homosexuality Biologically Based?

1. Is homosexuality a product of biology or learning? Support your claims with research evidence.
2. Many argue that if it were proven that homosexuality is biologically based, discrimination against homosexuals would decrease. Support this argument with research on discrimination and prejudice.
3. In Rahman's review of the research, he believes the evidence clearly points to a biological, prenatal based homosexuality. On the other hand, Jones and Kwee find the same research to be ambiguous and flawed. In fact, they interpret much of the same findings as evidence of a postnatal, learned homosexuality. What would convince you to take one side or the other? Provide reasons for your position.
4. Read the section from Rahman's Controversial book *Born Gay* (co-authored with Glenn Wilson) about treating homosexuality. Also, find the full Jones and Kwee article and read the section entitled "Treatment Outcome Research." Each argues opposing viewpoints on the malleability of sexual orientation. Do you believe sexual orientation can be changed? Should we pursue such a research question?
5. Stanton Jones, the first author of the second article, has recently co-authored a book entitled, "Ex-Gays?" In this book, he reports a complex research study that he argues is an indicator that homosexuals can change their sexual orientation. If this is true, what would this finding mean for the possibility of biological determination of sexual orientation?

ISSUE 3

Is Evolution a Good Explanation for Psychological Concepts?

YES: **Glenn Geher,** from "Evolutionary Psychology Is Not Evil! (. . . And Here's Why . . .)" *Psychological Topics* (December 2006)

NO: **Edwin E. Gantt and Brent S. Melling**, from "Evolutionary Psychology Isn't Evil, It's Just Not Any Good," (An Original Essay Written for This Volume, 2009)

ISSUE SUMMARY

YES: Evolutionary psychologist Glenn Geher maintains that evolution provides the best meta-theory for explaining and understanding human psychology.

NO: Theoretical psychologists Edwin Gantt and Brent Melling argue that an evolutionary account of psychology omits many important and good things about humans.

Given the wide-spread success of evolutionary explanations in biology, many psychologists have suggested that these explanations can adequately and powerfully explain psychological and social behavior. Evolutionary Psychology (EP) has become an increasingly recognized field, with numerous programs and institutes dedicated to researching its explanations. However, EP is not without its critics. Going beyond methodological issues (see issue 4 of this *Taking Sides* volume), those who are uncomfortable with EP argue that its philosophical assumptions ultimately deny important aspects of humanity, such as morality and personal responsibility. In response, evolutionary psychologists often observe that "evolution is not evil . . ."

There's little argument that evolutionary explanations have been useful, and not "evil," in the biological sciences. Still, there is considerable debate about whether such an explanation can account for all facets of human experience and behavior. Can it explain, for example, the human sense of morality? Some scholars have held that morality itself is evolutionarily derived, with our own innate sense of rightness and goodness evolved from what is evolutionarily effective and efficient. On the other hand, critics argue that such a stance confuses morality with biology and that morality involves much more than can be explained by biological mechanisms.

The author of the first article, Glenn Geher, disagrees. As the Director of the Evolutionary Studies Program at the State University of New York at New Paltz, he argues that the best way to understand all psychological phenomena is to borrow evolutionary explanations from the biological sciences. EP makes the "modest" claim, according to Geher, that "minds are on the same footing as bodies where . . . natural selection is concerned." He maintains that evolutionary explanations do no harm, because they do not deny important human meanings or morality. Critics who see EP as "sexist, racist, [or] eugenicist" are misinformed about the point of EP. Evolutionary psychology merely tries to explain human behavior, not prescribe what humans *should* do.

Psychological researchers Edwin Gantt and Brent Melling argue that evolutionary psychology is not as innocent as it seems and, in fact, has major negative implications for the study of human behavior. They suggest that EP has a number of implicit biases that distort the world of human meaning but are rarely discussed in the EP literature. Despite claims to the contrary, for example, Gantt and Melling argue that EP presumes humans have no real choices about their behaviors, and thus no personal responsibility for them. For this reason and others, Gantt and Melling prompt caution in wholeheartedly accepting the latest scientific "facts" of EP. They note, instead, that scientific history is littered with "obvious facts that are later found to be not only questionable but on occasion outright false and misleading" (e.g., phlogiston, phrenology). Gantt and Melling conclude that such misleading facts and assumptions ultimately undermine the efforts of evolutionary psychologists to promote neutrality and morality.

POINT

- Critics have unreasonable or outmoded biases against Evolutionary Psychology (EP).
- EP research is objective and shows the world as it is.
- Evolutionary psychology is not evil.
- EP is a powerful tool for understanding all aspects of psychology.

COUNTERPOINT

- Rational, thoughtful individuals can have serious issues with Evolutionary Psychology (EP).
- EP has implicit biases that skew how researchers understand their data.
- EP denies the possibility of good or evil.
- EP cannot account for many important aspects of human psychology.

YES

Glenn Geher

Evolutionary Psychology Is Not Evil! (. . . and Here's Why . . .)

Abstract

Evolutionary psychology has faced 'implacable hostility' (Dawkins, 2005) from a number of intellectual fronts. Critics of evolutionary psychology have tried to paint this perspective variously as reductionist and overly deterministic, at best, and as sexist, racist, and downright evil at worst. The current paper argues that all psychological frameworks which assume that human beings are the result of the organic evolutionary forces of natural and sexual selection are, essentially, evolutionary in nature (regardless of whether they traditionally fall under the label of evolutionary psychology). In other words, the perspective presented here argues that all psychology is evolutionary psychology. Two specific mis-characterizations of evolutionary psychology ((a) that it is eugenicist in nature and (b) that it is a fully non-situationist, immutable perspective on behavior) are addressed here with an eye toward elaborating on how these distorted conceptions of evolutionary psychology are non-constructive and non-progressive. A final section focuses on how the social sciences in general could benefit from being evolutionized.

"Evolutionary psychology (is) . . . subject to a level of implacable hostility which seems far out of proportion to anything even sober reason or common politeness might sanction."

If you are a modern scholar of human behavior who uses evolutionary theory to help guide your research and, accordingly, label yourself an evolutionary psychologist (as I do), you may find Dawkins' aforementioned quote as capturing the essence of how evolutionary psychology (EP) is perceived in many modern academic circles. In fact, based on my experiences, this quote captures the current state of affairs regarding EP in the broader landscape of academia in general so well that it is actually a bit unsettling.

Worded another way, this implacable hostility seems to result from scholars across disparate disciplines who conceptualize EP as downright evil. EP is often framed as evil by all sorts of people for all sorts of reasons. In terms of purely academic critiques, EP is often framed as overly deterministic and

From *Psychological Topics (Psihologijske teme)*, vol. 15, no. 2, December 2006, pp. 181–189, 194–197 (excerpts). Copyright © 2006 by Psychological Topics. Reprinted by permission of the Faculty of Arts & Sciences, University of Rijeka, Croatia.

reductionistic while social critics of EP with more applied concerns paint EP as a sexist, racist, and even eugenicist doctrine designed with a hidden political agenda that should serve the status quo by, presumably, justifying such amoral acts as sexual harassment, murder, and war.

An unfortunate outcome regarding the current state of affairs pertains to the fact that EP is attacked from people holding political perspectives that span the spectrum of ideologies. Fundamentalist Christians, who necessarily reject ideas that are premised on evolution as an accepted theory of speciation, reject EP simply due to its reliance on evolutionary theory. This ideological hurdle is by no means small: A recent survey found that 87% of United States citizens do not believe that evolutionary forces in general (and natural selection, in particular), unaided by a supernatural deity, are responsible for human origins. Such individuals, whose numbers are, simply, daunting, are likely to reject EP as a sustainable perspective on any aspect of human functioning.

However, in addition to the resistance to EP presented by fundamentalist religious individuals, there is, in effect, a new kind of creationist, so to speak, rooted in secular intellectualism. These so-called new creationists are, in fact, very different from fundamentalist Christians in their ideological foundation. The new creationists may be conceptualized as academics and scholars who study varied aspects of human affairs from the perspective of the Standard Social Science Model, a model for understanding human behavior which is largely premised on the notion of the blank slate. The SSSM essentially conceives of human psychology as qualitatively different from the psychology of all other species. The SSSM presumes that there is no basic human nature—that the mind (and its corresponding physiological substrates) are fully malleable based on environmental stimuli and that all behavioral and psychological aspects of people are the result of experiences with environmental stimuli across ontogenetic time.

This denial of human nature, which is prevalent in many of the social sciences, has come to serve as the only politically acceptable paradigm in much of academia. Champions of this perspective are often more critical of EP than are adherents of fundamentalist Christianity. From the perspective of the SSSM, EP is problematic largely because its basic premises focus on understanding the nature of human nature.

For instance, consider David Buss' work which revolves around understanding sex-differentiated mating strategies in humans from an evolutionary perspective. Research by Buss and his colleagues has documented many basic sex differences in the psychology of human mating. Several different studies, using varied methods, have replicated Buss' basic finding that men desire more lifetime sexual partners than do women. Buss' evolution-based explanation of these findings is rooted in Trivers' parental investment theory which suggests that males and females should differ in their mating tactics as a result of fundamentally different costs faced by each sex associated with bearing and raising children across the evolution of our species. From this perspective, women in our ancestral past who were driven to pursue short-term sexual strategies would have, on average, had less reproductive success compared with males pursuing similarly promiscuous strategies. A result of this sex-specific differential reproduction associated with variability in promiscuity over deep time would have led to sex-specific mating strategies (favoring promiscuity in males over females).

Critics of EP who may be thought to represent new creationism have tried hard to argue that findings which demonstrate such sex differences in mating strategies are based on flawed research. Further, such critics argue that even if such phenomena as sex differences in number of sex partners desired have been documented via sound research, these findings are best understood as resulting completely from environmental conditions during ontogenetic time. In other words, the SSSM perspective argues that all differences between the sexes in number of sexual partners desired results from males and females learning different messages about sexuality across their lifetimes. In short, this perspective argues that this phenomenon does not reflect basic and natural differences between male and female mating psychology—it only reflects differences in socialization between the sexes (differences that exist, in varying degrees, across human cultures).

Adherents of the SSSM perspective argue that appealing to evolutionarily shaped differences between the psychologies of men and women to explain something such as universal sex differences in desire for multiple sex partners is an inherently sexist approach. In short, these new creationists believe that any appeals to an evolutionarily shaped human nature to explain psychological phenomena (regardless of how well the said phenomena are documented) imply that human behavior is highly constrained by our nature, is genetically determined, and is, in effect, immutable. As such, adherents of the SSSM feel something of an obligation to fight EP, as they believe they are fighting an intellectual doctrine which sees human behavior as largely immutable and which ultimately provides a scholarly rationale for the status quo (which inherently treats people unfairly).

From the SSSM perspective, EP paints a picture of humans as fully under the control of genes. Further, the SSSM perspective sees EP as a doctrine that endorses all aspects of the status quo related to sexism. As seen through the lens of the SSSM, all phenomena documented by evolutionary psychologists and, subsequently, framed as resulting from evolutionary forces, are implicitly endorsed by evolutionary psychologists. As such, phenomena such as male promiscuity, filicide, rape, murder, and war are seen, from the SSSM perspective, as phenomena that are, essentially, supported, condoned, and, perhaps, encouraged by evolutionary psychologists as they are phenomena that evolutionary psychologists have studied from an evolutionary perspective and have tried to explain in terms of the nature of human nature.

Let me go on the record saying that I am very uncomfortable (on both moral and intellectual grounds) with any perspective that sees humans as fully incapable of choosing their own behaviors. Further, I am ardently opposed to sexism—ardently opposed to the idea that men and women (and boys and girls) should be treated differently by rules created by a society and should be given different opportunities within a society. I am, further, from a personal standpoint, not someone who encourages males to engage in promiscuous behavior and not someone who supports men who fly into violent jealous rages with females as targets of their anger and aggression. Additionally, I am strongly opposed to war, murder, rape, and filicide. I would feel a moral obligation to reject outright any doctrine which is inconsistent with these fundamental aspects of my belief system. In sum, I would see such a doctrine as downright evil.

So herein lies the problem, a problem which, as I see it, is largely one of perspective. If EP were the kind of intellectual doctrine that I describe in the prior paragraph, then it would be a morally disturbing framework. However, as several scholars have argued before me, EP is simply not such a doctrine. In the remainder of this paper, I argue that EP is the following:

A. A basic intellectual framework for understanding all psychological phenomena
B. A set of principles which, at its core, simply asserts that the human nervous system and resultant behavior are ultimately products of organic evolutionary processes
C. One of the most situationist/contextualist perspectives that exists within psychology writ large
D. A perspective that has the potential to serve as an underlying meta-theory to guide all the behavioral sciences in the future.

Evolutionary Psychology Is Not Evil

In engaging in the thought exercise of trying to empathize with academics who characterize EP as downright evil, I have concluded that the problem seems to lie largely in the naturalistic fallacy. Often, when people hear that some phenomenon is being framed as part of our nature, shaped by evolutionary forces across thousands of generations, they infer that the scientists who are documenting said evolutionarily shaped quality see this quality as something about us that should be the case. In other words, for instance, if one hears Daly, Wilson, and Weghorst argue that male sexual jealousy, and violence that has been directed toward countless women as a result of such jealousy, may be part of our evolutionary heritage, one may infer that these authors are arguing that men should show marked, intense, and emotional jealousy when faced with cheating partners and, further, that they should use violence against women as a solution to such problems.

Of course, Daly et al. believe nothing of the kind. Documenting that something is part of our nature is not synonymous with arguing that it should be condoned by society. Similarly, when David Buss argues that natural selection has shaped patterns of homicide and murder in a non-random way, such that our ancestors were most likely to murder when murder was likely to have increased the possibility of passing on genes of the murderer (i.e., under conditions in which murder had fitness benefits), he is not arguing that murder is good and/or that society should support murder. He is, rather, using evolutionary theory, the most powerful intellectual framework that exists in the life sciences, to help understand behaviors that are of high relevance to the functioning of society.

In sum, the naturalistic fallacy corresponds to conflating phenomena that naturally are with phenomena that should be. As evolutionary psychologists are charged with the task of understanding the nature of human psychological processes, they are at particular risk of having their work mis-characterized by others who are employing the reasoning that typifies the naturalistic fallacy. Further, for someone who is conflating some findings and ideas from EP with statements by evolutionary psychologists regarding how things should be, EP is likely to come across as appearing morally deficient and, yes, perhaps even evil!

What Evolutionary Psychology Is

While there are different brands of EP, with some variability in basic assertions, EP is, in its most basic form, simply an understanding of behavior that is guided by evolutionary theory. In the words of Richard Dawkins: "The central claim . . . (that evolutionary psychologists) . . . are making is not an extraordinary one. It amounts to the exceedingly modest assertion that minds are on the same footing as bodies where Darwinian natural selection is concerned."

As such, EP is an explanatory framework that has implications for understanding all psychological phenomena. It essentially conceptualizes humans as products of natural selection—thereby not conceiving of our species as somehow immune from the laws that govern the natural world. It is a humbling perspective in some respects.

In any case, this perspective is monistic at its core; it conceives of human behavior as resulting from the nervous system—including the brain—which was, according to this perspective (and to most modern scientists who study psychological phenomena), shaped by evolutionary processes such as natural selection.

If the nervous system were shaped by natural selection, then individual humans with certain neuronal qualities in our ancestral past (e.g., those with features of the autonomic nervous system) were more likely to survive and reproduce compared with conspecifics (other humans) with nervous systems that were less likely to ultimately lead to reproduction.

Ancestral humans with features of the autonomic nervous system were more likely to respond optimally to immediate threatening stimuli in requisite situations (e.g., running from a predator). Thus, they were more likely to survive than others with less advanced autonomic nervous systems. A simple logical truth is that being more likely to survive necessarily increases the likelihood of reproduction (corpses are not very good at successfully mating). As such, this (partly) genetically shaped feature of human anatomy (with integral implications for human behavior), the autonomic nervous system, was 'naturally selected' and has thereby come to typify our species.

This same reasoning applies to all domains of psychology. Human behavioral patterns are part of the natural world—and human beings are living organisms that have come about by evolutionary processes. As such, attempts

Table 1

Web-Based Resources that Provide Basic Information about Evolutionary Psychology

1. Syllabus from Glenn Geher's section of Evolutionary Psychology taught at SUNY New Paltz:
   http://www.newpaltz.edu/~geherg/classes/fall08/syl307r.doc
2. The website for the international Evolutionary Studies (EvoS) Consortium:
   http://www.evostudies.org
3. Information on the Evolutionary Studies Program at the State University of New York at New Paltz http://www.newpaltz.edu/EvoS
4. Information on the Evolutionary Studies Program at Binghamton University http://evolution.binghamton.edu/evos/ directed by David Sloan Wilson (http://evolution.binghamton.edu/dswilson/)
5. Ed Hagen's Chapter on Controversies Surrounding Evolutionary Psychology (published in David Buss' Handbook of Evolutionary Psychology)
   http://itb.biologie.hu-berlin.de/%7Ehagen/papers/Controversies.pdf
6. Leda Cosmides and John Tooby's Introduction to the Field of Evolutionary Psychology
   http://www.psych.ucsb.edu/research/cep/primer.html
7. Ed Hagen's "Frequently Asked Questions about Evolutionary Psychology (e.g., "Is Evolutionary Psychology Sexist?")"
   http://www.anth.ucsb.edu/projects/human/evpsychfaq.html
8. Russil Durant and Bruce Ellis's Introduction to Evolutionary Psychology
   http://media.wiley.com/product_data/excerpt/38/04713840/0471384038.pdf
9. Human Behavior and Evolution Society page introducing the field:
   http://www.hbes.com/intro_to_field.htm
10. Personal Accounts about Applying for Academic Jobs While Branded as an Evolutionary Psychologist
    http://human-nature.com/ep/articles/ep02160173.html

at understanding such basic aspects of the human experience—mind and behavior—without understanding the broad evolutionary factors that have given rise to our species and, ultimately, to our psychology, is, from the perspective of EP, simply misguided. We can do better in understanding human psychology by understanding the nuances of evolutionary principles.

From my perspective, these are the basic ideas of EP. Note that I provide a list of resources (mostly developed by others; see Table 1) to introduce the reader to this field from various angles that fall under the general umbrella of EP. In sum, EP is simply a framework for understanding human behavior that has the capacity to unite all areas of psychology more so than any other paradigm that has existed in the history of psychology as a discipline. It is not driven by ideology; it is driven by the basic scientific motive of increasing understanding of the natural world.

Evolutionary Psychology Mischaracterized as an Immutable, Hyper-Dispositionist, Non-Situationist Perspective

One of the beliefs that many people tend to hold about EP is that it is a non-situationist doctrine, suggesting that organisms have just a few immutable, invariant ways of responding which are under the direct control of genes.

This portrait of EP is simply inaccurate. EP posits that species-typical psychological design features with some heritable component have been shaped by natural and sexual selection. Often, many (but not all) evolutionary psychologists will conceive of such design features as adaptations. In any case, such adaptations are rarely understood by evolutionary psychologists as being context-independent.

Evolutionary psychologists and biologists make an important distinction between non-conditional and conditional strategies that describe the phenotypes of different organisms. A classic example of a non-conditional, folly genetically determined (and immutable) strategy is found in male sunfish, which come in two varieties. The first variety includes large males who have the ability to acquire sufficient territories in intra-sexual competition. The second variety includes smaller, sneakier males, who are nearly indiscernible from females and who do not elicit aggressive responses from territory-holding males. While territory-holding males reproduce by honestly attracting females, sneaker males use a somewhat dishonest strategy: they blast their gametes after a female has released her eggs in a large male's territory, thereby using deception as a tool for reproduction. It turns out that the differences between these kinds of males is attributable to genetic differences. As such, the strategies employed are non-conditional.

The notion of conditional strategies, on the other hand, corresponds to situations in which an organism modifies its strategy *vis a vis* variability in situational factors. For instance, male tree frogs use strategies similar to the male sunfish when it comes to mating. Sometimes, a male will carve out a territory and croak loudly. At other times, a male will hide near a territory-holding male and try to mate with females that are attracted to the croaking, territory-holding male. Importantly, in this species, males have been documented to show strategic pluralism; they modify their choice of strategy depending on the nature of such situational factors as the number of male territory-holders at a given time.

The use of a variety of strategies by male wood frogs does not suggest that their repertoire of mating behaviors is somehow outside the bounds of natural law or that these strategies are not designed with for 'purpose' of reproduction. Clearly, these mating strategies are related to optimal reproduction, a fact that speaks to their selection by evolutionary processes. As such, evolutionary geneticists and evolutionary psychologists have come to apply evolutionary reasoning to our understanding of mixed behavioral strategies that are highly context-sensitive.

In fact, modern-day EP is an extraordinarily situationist perspective. Consider, for instance, evolutionary informed research on homicide and familial violence. All of the most highly cited work in this area focuses on situational factors that underlie family violence. For instance, Daly and Wilson's often-cited work on violence toward children is all about contextual factors that covary with this atrocious act. Simply, the presence of a step-parent in a household has been shown to be the primary contextual factor that predicts fatal violence toward children. Another contextual factor that Daly and Wilson document as having a significant relationship with such violence has to do with the age of a given child (another contextual factor). In fact, their research, which is, in this regard, very prototypical of much work in EP overall, is all about contextual factors that underlie behaviors.

Consider, as another example, research on factors that predict promiscu-ous behavior on the part of women. Evolutionary psychologists have uncov-ered such important contextual factors as localized sex ratios, ovulation cycles, a woman's age, and the presence of children from prior mateships—each such contextual factor serving as an important statistical predictor of female pro-miscuity. In short, EP is, in fact, a highly situationist perspective, generally conceiving of human behavioral strategies as being extremely flexible and as falling within the realm of this general idea of strategic pluralism.

EP does not conceptualize humans as genetically guided automatons whose conscious decision-making processes are irrelevant or non-existent. Rather, this perspective sees humans as capable of extraordinary conscious decision-making. Further, with its roots in strategic pluralism, EP is situation-ist at its core. Importantly, EP has lessons to provide regarding the nature of situationism as an epistemological doctrine. While situationism in the social sciences is often framed as conceiving of human behavior as highly under the influence of situational influences (both small and large), this generic brand of situationism has generally been framed in a manner that is devoid of any insights into how important psychological design features have been ulti-mately shaped by evolutionary forces for the purpose of reproduction.

The kind of situationism that characterizes modern-day EP may be thought of as a sort of evolutionary situationism. This particular brand of sit-uationism suggests that while human behavior is largely under the control of situational influences, the particular situational factors that should mat-ter most in affecting behavior are ones that bear directly on factors associ-ated with survival and reproductive success. As such, Daly and Wilson did not document just any factors that underlie familial violence—they specifically uncovered the role of step-parenting, a situational factor with clear and theo-retically predictable relevance to issues tied to genetic fitness (from a strictly genetic-fitness perspective, a step-child shares no genes with a step-parent, and is, thus, costly).

Given the tremendous potential for EP to inform the search for contex-tual factors that underlie human psychological outcomes, this idea of evolu-tionary situationism has the potential to create extraordinary bridges between traditional social psychology and EP. . . .

The Future of Evolutionary Psychology

Evolutionary psychology has proven extremely powerful in (a) providing coherent explanations for many basic human behavioral patterns, (b) generat-ing new research questions that simply would not be on the radar screen with-out EP as a guiding framework, and (c) generating novel findings about what it means to be human.

In terms of providing coherent explanations for basic psychological processes, consider Ekman and Friesen's landmark work demonstrating the universal nature of emotional expression. The evolutionary reasoning that these authors draw upon, arguing, essentially, that emotional-expression abilities must have been positively selected for across the evolution of our species due to the fitness-related benefits of such abilities, provides an extremely useful and coherent framework for understanding human emotion in general. I am fully confident that it is very much in the interest of all the behavioral sciences to ultimately support efforts designed to understand human behavioral patterns in light of our evolutionary history.

In generating novel research questions, consider Haselton and Miller's research demonstrating that women are particularly attracted to indices of creativity in potential mates during peaks in their ovulatory cycles. This research is excessively rooted in evolutionary ideas. First, the general idea that female mating psychology should vary as a function of variability in fertility across the ovulatory cycle is an idea that only makes sense when we think of psychological processes as being designed for the purposes of successfully reproducing. Additionally, the fact that this research focuses on attraction to indices of creative intelligence is rooted in Miller's theory of higher-order human cognitive abilities (such as creative intelligence) as having resulted from sexual selection pressures across evolutionary time and as serving the function of affording individuals benefits in the domain of intrasexual competition. Again, without guidance from EP, which suggests that basic psychological processes likely serve a reproductive function, the questions addressed in this research simply never would have made it onto the radar screen.

Just as EP allows novel questions to be asked, it allows such questions to be answered, thereby providing the world with all kinds of discoveries regarding our nature. While research in the domain of adaptations to ovulation strongly demonstrates several novel findings regarding human mating behavior, such research only provides the tip of the iceberg when it comes to novel findings obtained by evolutionary psychologists. In fact, evolutionary psychologists are responsible for uncovering novel findings across the entire range of psychological phenomena such as the inter-play between mating and homicide, the neuropsychological substrates underlying the detection of individuals who cheat in social-exchange situations the phenomenology of stranger anxiety experienced by babies, and the nature of altruistic tendencies across species.

(For a reader interested in reading more about the scientific utility of EP across the modern landscape of the behavioral sciences, I strongly recommend Ketelaar and Ellis' paper which conceives of EP as a meta-theory that guides research in a coherent manner and a paper by Schmitt and Pilcher which provides a model regarding the thorough methodology employed by evolutionary psychologists when they are at their best in trying to uncover human nature.)

In light of the powerful nature of EP in generating new questions and findings, I believe, strongly, that psychology writ large can only reach its potential by incorporating an evolutionary perspective across all its areas. Further, I believe that there is reason for optimism regarding the future of EP and the future of an evolutionarily informed psychology in general. Consider, for example, a recent analysis of articles published in a leading journal in the behavioral sciences, Behavioral and Brain Sciences, which revealed that more than 30% of articles published in the last decade include evolution in the title or as a keyword. These findings suggest that evolution is, in fact, making its way into the behavioral sciences.

However, with that said, an analysis regarding the education of the authors of these evolutionarily informed articles tells a different story. When authors of these articles were interviewed about their education, they generally reported being self-taught with regard to evolutionary principles. Such an effect is consistent with the portrait of academic institutions as less than fully embracing of the incorporation of evolution into the realm of human behavior.

Taken together, the different ideas presented in this section paint a variegated picture with regard to the inclusion of evolution into the behavioral sciences. On the one hand, a great deal of research on the evolutionary origins of human behavior and psychological processes is being conducted. This research is leading to novel findings regarding topics that cut across all areas within psychology. On the other hand, EP is a target of hostility from adherents of multiple political and ideological perspectives. Such implacable hostility emanates from characterizations of EP as overly deterministic, reductionistic, sexist, racist, and, simply, evil.

Importantly, there are several critiques of EP that are reasonable and that should be addressed. For instance, Panksepp and Panksepp, argue that evolutionary psychologists could improve their work by taking a less modularistic approach, working more closely on neurological substrates of behavior, and paying more attention to research regarding the neuroplasticity which seems to characterize much of the human brain. To be fair to these critics (and to others), I strongly believe that EP is not perfect and this approach to psychology has room for improvement. However, I see no reason to throw the baby out with the bath water. As Dawkins writes regarding recent critiques of EP: "Some individual evolutionary psychologists need to clean up their methodological act. Maybe many do. But that is true of scientists in all fields."

In short, EP has proven itself as having extraordinary abilities to (a) yield novel ways of thinking about who we are and to (b) generate new findings that shed light on the depths of our minds. While this approach may not be perfect, and while certain studies conducted under the general banner of EP may need improvement, the overall approach to understanding human behavior—focusing on understanding how basic psychological processes ultimately bear on issues tied to reproductive success—has an enormous capacity to improve our understanding of ourselves. I urge psychological researchers and students to go down the path of evolutionary enlightenment so as to allow psychology to realize its full potential—ultimately allowing our discipline to best help people deal with the many problems associated with what it means to be human.

Conclusion

My intellectual passions permeate my teaching and my research. After learning about applications of evolutionary theory to issues regarding behavior in Benjamin Sachs' Animal Behavior course in 1990 at the University of Connecticut, I came to see the evolutionary informed approach to psychology as the most coherent and powerful framework for understanding behavior across species (including *Homo Sapiens*). This intellectual approach to understanding psychology has permeated my teaching and my research since that time.

As stated prior, I do not believe that all EP is perfect. In the future, evolutionary approaches to psychology will surely benefit from better understanding the interrelationship between cultural and genetic forces that underlie behavior, studying the nature of neuroplasticity from an evolutionary perspective, teasing apart psychological qualities that were shaped for survival versus reproductive purposes, and addressing the interplay between behaviors that emerge in an ontogenetic timescale versus behaviors that are the result of thousands of generations of selection across our phylogenetic history. Further, I am certain that other improvements to an evolutionary approach to psychology are out there!

However—my student Warren Greig tells me that I need to be less apologetic when it comes to my passion for EP. And, as usual, he is right. As such, I end by making some simple points. First, EP is not an inherently evil approach to understanding human behavior. It is not overly immutable in its portrait of humans. It is, alternatively, one of the most situationistic/contextualistic doctrines that exists regarding human behavior. EP is not the new eugenics. In fact, EP and eugenics have virtually no commonalities whatsoever.

Evolutionary psychology is an extraordinarily coherent framework for understanding virtually all of human psychology. Its basic assumptions, suggesting (a) that fundamental human psychological processes were shaped by evolutionary forces and that (b) such psychological processes and behavioral patterns can be best understood in light of such evolutionary forces, are as solid and reasonable as the theory of evolution itself. Acknowledging this point is sure to benefit all work conducted in the realm of psychology.

Edwin E. Gantt and
Brent S. Melling

 **NO**

Evolutionary Psychology Isn't Evil, It's Just Not Any Good

"... If there is a sure road to intellectual atrophy, it is paved with the complacent certainty that one's critics are deluded."

It is hard not to be amused when one hears advocates of evolutionary psychology (EP), such as Richard Dawkins, Daniel Dennett, and Glenn Geher, grumble that so many people take issue with their ideas. After all, couldn't one reasonably suspect that such firm believers in the universal truth of evolution would welcome the opportunity to see how their theories fare in the cutthroat competitive marketplace of ideas? Academics, red in tooth and claw, and all that? Certainly, if the theories of EP are true, they are strong enough to take on all comers and prove their hardiness by adapting to the challenges of lesser ideas. In the end, isn't that what evolutionary theory is all about anyway?

Oddly, most evolutionary psychologists seem to prefer to short-circuit critique instead of welcoming it, declaring critical examination to be off-limits at the outset. When not casting aspersions on critics by claiming they can only be motivated by unscientific or religious impulses, they treat objections to EP as though they were wholesale rejections of well-established Darwinian principles in biology. While this may be a clever debating move, and might win you a few points with the high school debating club, it is nonetheless pure sophistry and unworthy of the serious intellectual examination that science demands. Still, since Geher begins his defense of EP by chiding the motives of any who might venture a critique, it is important to be very clear at the outset here about what our response is NOT. What we have to say here is NOT some fundamentalist Christian rejection of evolutionary biology or Darwin's theories of natural selection. Neither is this article motivated by some desire to defend Creationism, Young Earth Theology, or Intelligent Design Theory. Although some of the controversies presently surrounding Darwinism in biology and its Intelligent Design rivals are thought-provoking, those issues are not our issues. The fact is that it is possible to be a strident and thoughtful critic of EP and have no commitment whatsoever to a religious worldview, fundamentalist or otherwise.

Additionally, this paper is in no way a defense of what evolutionary psychologists (EPs) like to call the "Standard Social Science Model (SSSM)" or "Secular Creationism." Indeed, despite all of the bluster to the contrary by folks like Geher, Steven Pinker, and others, it is hard to imagine that there is anyone in contemporary psychology who would defend what these people claim that advocates of the SSSM believe, especially given that "no serious figure embraces that view since, perhaps, John Watson in the early twentieth century." This "rhetoric of exclusion," whereby "whomever is not for the program is against Darwin," clearly owes more to hidebound dogmatism than it does to open-minded, scientific thinking.

What, then, is our purpose here? It is simply this: We seek to engage in a critical scientific and philosophical reflection about fundamental concepts in the social sciences, as well as consider of some of the implications of taking EP seriously. In short, what we propose to do here is a brief bit of critical thinking about some of the assumptions, implications, and claims of EP. We aim to show that EP is not nearly as coherent, obvious, or harmless as its defenders suggest.

Rhetoric, Values, and Ideology

In addition to the rhetoric of exclusion, EPs often employ the rhetoric of objectivism. Although there are various ways in which the term "objectivism" is defined, we will use it to refer to the assumption that one's methods are value-neutral and unbiased and, thus, that one's reporting of research findings is the reporting of objective facts about the world rather than particular interpretations of it. As is often the case in scientific research, the findings of EP researchers are usually presented as being objective in nature, the products of a value-neutral and unbiased mode of inquiry. For example, Geher offers up the research findings of many of his colleagues in order to support his contention about the significant contributions that EP is making to the study of human nature. While citing supporting research is necessary, it is important to note the language that Geher employs in so doing. Like other evolutionary psychologists, he frequently states that EP research has "documented" or is "demonstrating" some fact about human nature and the evolution of behavior. This rhetorical strategy helps paint a mental picture in which psychologists like Geher are engaged in simply observing the world of human behavior and documenting the facts of such behavior—facts that would be obvious to any rational being using the scientific method and not blinded by personal ambition, cultural shortsightedness, or religious bigotry. Likewise, when Geher maintains that EP is not "driven by ideology; it is driven by the basic scientific motive of increasing understanding of the natural world," he is invoking the authority of objectivism to persuade us that we can have confidence both in both his own claims and that of his EP colleagues because such claims are free of the self-serving and biasing influences of values and ideologies.

Unfortunately, Geher's confident assurances to the contrary, EP is inescapably undergird with a variety of biases, values, and ideological commitments that serve not only to direct and shape EP's study of human behavior, but also provide the conceptual framework from within which data is interpreted. There are at least three such biases that often go unexamined or unacknowledged by EP theorists and researchers: objectivism, materialism, and instrumentalism. The first of these—objectivism—has already been discussed above in terms of its role in the rhetoric employed by advocates of EP. Objectivism is not just a rhetorical strategy, but is also a particular value—though rarely admitted as such. Objectivism is a bias not only in holding that the results of scientific research are value-neutral and free of the taint of human bias, but also in suggesting that the results of scientific investigation *ought to be* free of such flaws. Ironically, this claim that science "ought" to be objective to be good science is itself a subjective preference (or value) regarding how research-ers should go about conducting their science and is not the only valid or pos-sible perspective.

Likewise, materialism is a commonly taken-for-granted assumption in the natural and social sciences, particularly among EPs. Materialism is the notion that matter is the only reality and that everything, including thought, feeling, mind, and will, can be exhaustively explained in terms of matter and physical phenomena. This stance is not an incontrovertible fact of the uni-verse conclusively demonstrated by scientific investigation but an assumption about the nature of reality that itself cannot be proven or disproven, especially by a materialist science that begins by assuming that materialism is true. In other words, materialism is a sort of faith, or set of beliefs and ideas that one assumes to be true but for which there is not—nor ever can be—conclusive proof. It is, in this way, clearly an ideology and not a demonstrated fact of the universe. Thus, EPs prefer materialist accounts of human behavior, not because such accounts have been *proven* in any way to be the best, the tru-est, or the most rational ones available, but rather because materialism is the ideology they have come to endorse for philosophical, theological, and/or cultural reasons.

Finally, EP accounts of human behavior assume instrumentalism, or the idea that all behavior is governed by some manner of calculative means-ends rationale, whereby any given behavior is best understood as just a means to attaining some other goal. In the case of EP, the ultimate goal or end toward which all behavior is striving is, of course, reproductive success. In fact, as Richard Dawkins has argued, from the EP perspective we are really just "sur-vival machines" designed by our genes over eons of evolutionary history to ensure that these genes are able to continue on into future generations. "Their preservation," says Dawkins, "is the ultimate rationale for our existence." Thus, Geher speaks of "mating tactics" and "sexual strategies" and asserts that car-ing for step-children is "costly" because such children share no genes with the step-parent. Similarly, Robert Wright, another ardent advocate of EP, argues that "beneath the thoughts and feelings and temperamental differences mar-riage counselors spend their time sensitively assessing are the stratagems of the genes—cold hard equations composed of simple variables: social status, age of spouse, number of children, their ages, outside romantic opportunities, and so on." Nonetheless, even though EPs are strident and vocal in their assertion that all human behavior can be explained in terms of means-ends calculation, such claims are not based on any indisputable or documented fact but on certain philosophical assumptions about human nature and what constitutes the ultimate good in life. Even though instrumentalist assumptions may be so widely held in modern Western culture as to seem obvious, it is still the case that instrumental reasoning reflects a particular set of values arising from a particular ideology.

What the Data Says

Although their commitment to objectivism leads EPs to present their research findings as though the data is obvious and can only be explained from an evolutionary perspective, it is simply not the case that data ever speaks for itself. Data must always be interpreted in some way. Scientists must always provide some meaningful context within which particular findings can be understood and rendered sensible. Indeed, some authors have shown that not only does one's data require interpretation to be meaningful, but one's chosen method of investigation itself reflects an interpretation of the world that directs researchers to particular ways of making sense of one's data. Thus, no one is surprised when a feminist interprets an event as evidence of gender inequality, or by a Marxist who interprets the same event as the result of class-struggle. So we shouldn't be surprised when an evolutionary psychologist interprets the same event as a product of natural selection. None of these theorists use their particular explanatory framework because there is inherently more factual evidence for them—it is the framework itself that determines what counts as evidence and how it is to be interpreted. Thus, a feminist theorist will tend to see all situations as providing evidence of feminist assumptions, a Marxist will tend to see confirmation of Marxist assumptions, and an EP will tend to see evidence of evolutionary processes at work.

While most contemporary philosophers of science recognize that the interpretation of data requires an assumed framework, many EPs seem to think that their interpretive framework—or "meta-theory"—is inherently better because it is more parsimonious, more rational, or can explain all of the empirical data. What they seem to fail to realize is that all other reasonably sophisticated meta-theories can do the same. The ability to explain psychological phenomena by means of concepts borrowed from evolutionary biology is not testament to the fact that such explanations are true, only that evolution is a sophisticated and encompassing worldview—but, then again, so are many others.

Thus, while Geher cites the work of David Buss on mate-age selection as empirical proof that females select older men due the imperatives of natural selection, what is actually being offered is a particular way of interpreting the data at hand. Other interpretations are not only possible but viable. For example, rather than evidence of natural selection's instrumental operation for reproductive advantage, it could be that the age differential in mate-selection might reflect that women typically mature earlier than men and are more socially and verbally inclined. Thus, the observed age differences might simply reflect women's efforts to assure themselves of more socially skilled, verbally expressive, and interesting companions. Likewise, Geher offers up Daly and Wilson's research on domestic violence to demonstrate what has come to be known as the Cinderella Effect. Namely that children living with step-parents are about 100 times more likely to be fatally abused because natural selection shaped humans to take better care of our biological offspring than children with whom we do not share genes. Here too, alternative explanations are available that account for the data and are rationally defensible. A child is only going to be living with a stepparent if there has been some significant emotional, economic, and/or social disturbance of the family in the first place. Therefore, the social and relational problems that have contributed to the break-up of the original family are likely to continue with parents and children into subsequent family arrangements. It should be apparent that one need not invoke some powerful underlying genetic recognition and selection process to make adequate sense of this particular situation (for additional examples of alternative interpretations of EP research findings).

These examples of data reinterpretation aren't just interesting and clever intellectual exercises. Rather, we feel that they are important illustrations of critically reflecting on scientific knowledge claims, especially in terms of how data is interpreted and reported, for the history of science is replete with examples of researchers discovering and reporting presumably obvious facts that are later found to be not only questionable but on occasion outright false and misleading (e.g., phlogiston, phrenology, the geocentric theory of the universe, the Meckel-Serres Law, and classical Newtonian physics). The proper conduct of science requires, we believe, humility and continual critical self-reflection, not the dogmatic and repetitious assertion that one has found once and for all the indisputable truth of life, the universe, and everything.

Reductionism and Determinism

Another guiding ideology of EP is monism—the idea that all of reality is of the same kind, subject to the same rules and laws. The advantage to this position is that it avoids some of the tricky issues inherent in "the mind-body problem" (e.g., how do minds and bodies interact, how can mind be observed or measured, etc.). By starting from the assumption that "minds are on the same footing as bodies where Darwinian natural selection is concerned," EPs hope to sidestep the problem of how something seemingly immaterial, such as a thought or an emotion can have an effect on the material world. The way evolutionary psychologists achieve this monism, however, is by reducing one side of our experience (i.e., the immaterial side of minds, thoughts, and emotions) to another side of our experience (i.e., the material side of genes, brains, and bodies). As Geher states, the evolutionary perspective fundamentally "conceives of human behavior as resulting from the nervous system." In such a scheme, what we experience as immaterial (like feelings of love) is seen to be really nothing more than an expression of complicated physical realities (e.g., elevated hormones, particular neuronal firings, genetic tendencies and environmental conditions). Instead of integrating the immaterial and material into a meaningful whole, however, one facet of human experience is simply explained away by reducing it down to another. The end result of this sort of approach is not monism, but rather a "one-sided dualism" in which important but less easily or accurately measured features of the mind (i.e., thoughts, intentions, emotions, etc.) are ignored or discounted so that attention can be solely focused on the precisely measurable features of the brain such as synaptic activity and neurotransmitter levels. Unfortunately for EP, however, simply ignoring or discounting the essential nature of mental phenomena does little to actually explain how such things might arise out of one's genes or nervous system in the first place. After all, while a well-functioning nervous system may certainly be something that is necessary for having thoughts, making choices, and experiencing emotions, this does not mean that the nervous system is the only thing that one has to attend to when trying to make sense of where our thoughts, choices, and feelings come from or what they mean.

Unfortunately, this reductionism perpetuates the problems that evolutionary psychologists typically seek to avoid—a loss of meaning, morality, and choice. All of these things—though intangible in nature—are nonetheless real phenomena common to human experience that cannot be easily dismissed. By reducing mind to brain, however, EPs ultimately reduce the rich meanings of our lives and relationships into the merely mechanical happenings of our bodies. Instead of being human persons capable of making genuine choices, we become, as the novelist Terry Bisson once famously wrote, "Thinking meat! Conscious meat! Loving meat! Dreaming meat! The meat is the whole deal!" If we take EP seriously, our values and ethics are ultimately really nothing more than the chance result of a complicated interaction of genetic survival mechanisms and environmental happenstance. What is morally good in life, what is worthy and right is simply whatever increases our likelihood to survive, or at least pass on our genetic material to subsequent generations.

Evolutionary psychologists often protest these sorts of criticisms, arguing that they do not reduce all human activity to biology because other factors—such as culture and personal disposition—play a significant role in how our genetic predispositions are realized. However, when accounting for the origins of culture and its variations, EP ultimately falls back on biological reductionism. As Geher states, genetic shaping by natural selection (determinism) "applies to all domains of psychology" and any account that does not see how "the broad evolutionary factors that have given rise to our species and, ultimately, to our psychology, is . . . simply misguided." According to EP, culture is itself a product of natural selection and exists primarily to provide particular mating rituals that will help to ensure genetic fitness in our offspring. So, if complex social and cultural behaviors are part of the natural world and not immune from the laws that govern it, then it is hard to believe defenders of EP when they say that human beings are not determined by their biology. Granted, it is not a direct genetic determinism where "behavior is controlled exclusively by genes, with little or no role for environmental influence." But, such assurances provide little comfort in the face of EP's contention that our behavior is controlled *mutually* by our genes AND the cultural forces that genetic selection has produced. So, if Geher and other EPs are, in fact, "uncomfortable (on both moral and intellectual grounds) with any perspective that sees humans as fully incapable of choosing their own behaviors," then perhaps it is time for them to be a little more uncomfortable with evolutionary psychology's conception of human nature.

The Problem of Nihilism

Possibly the most troubling problem inherent to an EP approach is that it is fundamentally nihilistic. Nihilism is the notion that life is, at its root, without ultimate meaning or purpose, and that the genuine moral distinctions between good and bad, right and wrong, cannot be rationally defended. If all human behavior is just the causal outcome of the unthinking, undirected, mechanical processes of natural selection, then human actions are no longer meaningful in any real sense. In other words, if our behavior is something that is determined for us by something beyond of our control or active participation, then what we do or think or feel does not possess any intrinsic meaning.

For example, consider the day-long motion of blades of grass as they slowly bend and change position relative to the location of the sun. As a fundamentally biological and determined event, this phenomenon is simply what it is, and has no intrinsic meaning. Granted, a golfer might attribute meaning to the "lean of the grass" while preparing to make a putt, but this attribution of meaning is merely subjective and, as such, does not reflect any real meaning in the events of the natural world taking place there on the green. Of course, if the golfer's subjective meaning is itself just the causal product of something going on in her brain, then that too would lack any genuine meaning and be basically the same as what is taking place with the grass. Only if there is the genuine possibility that a given event could be otherwise than it is does it make any sense to consider it to be genuinely meaningful (as opposed to merely subjectively meaningful).

Thus, if to be human is to be nothing more than a "gigantic lumbering robot" whose sole purpose for existing is the preservation of our genes, the meaning of our lives, our loves, our friends and families seems quite hollow. Sure, we may experience ourselves as being deeply in love with our spouse but such feelings are simply "illusions" caused by particularly complex biochemistry striving to get our body motivated enough to find a suitable mate for replicating our genes. All this romantic fuss is just so much clever claptrap meant to manipulate suitable others into sticking around long enough for successful reproduction. If EP is correct on this point, and matter is all that matters, then in the end nothing else about us *really* matters at all.

Given their commitment to objectivity, EP is typically presented as nothing more than an account of the "is" of human behavior. Advocates of EP, such as Geher, passionately reject any suggestion that their theories of human nature have anything whatsoever to say about how human behavior "ought" to be, claiming that such criticism simply reflects the naturalistic fallacy. However, if one of the most basic claims of EP is true (i.e., human nature is the causal product of material events and natural laws), and culture is itself just a byproduct of evolutionary forces acting on material events (i.e., brain function and genetic selection), then it makes little sense to say that there are any legitimate "oughts" in the world at all. If culture "originates in, is transmitted by, and is propagated through mental mechanisms that evolved through natural selection," and evolution through natural selection is fundamentally a purposeless, random process reliant on the chance interplay of natural events, then the "oughts" we experience and which constitute our cultural moral norms are really just accidental developments in the long march of human evolutionary history. If our fundamental sensibilities of right and wrong, good and evil are such accidents, then it makes no more sense to argue that murder or rape or theft is morally wrong than it does to claim that elephants should have smaller trunks or longer tusks. Unless morality is ultimately grounded in something a bit more solid and trustworthy than contingent evolutionary history, it is impossible to maintain that any particular way of life is really better or more meaningful than any other.

In closing, after all that has been said so far, one cannot help but wonder whether EP is ultimately not only an enemy of meaning and morality, but also of science and reason. A basic claim of EP—and one with which we have taken repeated issue in this brief essay—is materialism, or the notion that at the root of all of our thoughts and ideas there are really just the happenstance events of the brain and the genes. This truly startling claim has become so commonplace in our modern world that it's deeply disturbing implications for not only how we understand ourselves but also how we understand science typically go entirely unnoticed. We have tried to explore a few of those implications throughout this piece. There is, however, one last implication of this line of thinking that we would like mention before concluding.

Because of its fundamental commitment to materialism and determinism, EP claims that all of our thoughts, feelings, and behaviors are rooted in unthinking, non-rational, non-caring processes and causes aimed solely at ensuring successful reproduction. Therefore, because the driving purpose behind evolution is reproduction, not rationality, we cannot assume that the fruits of evolution, including human thought and culture, reflect the rise of anything inherently rational. Natural selection's fundamental aim, after all, is not to shape a human mind capable of producing true beliefs but to produce a mind whose beliefs motivate us toward reproductively advantageous behaviors, whether those beliefs are true or not. As Churchland, a prominent advocate of EP, has stated:

> "Looked at from an evolutionary point of view, the principle function of nervous systems is to enable the organism to move appropriately. Boiled down to essentials, a nervous system enables the organism to succeed in the four F's: feeding, fleeing, fighting, and reproducing. The principle chore of nervous systems is to get the body parts where they should be in order that the organism may survive. . . . Truth, whatever that is, definitely takes the hindmost."

There is more than a little irony in such a confident pronouncement, especially when the one making it is doing so in the name of scientific progress and truth. For, if our thoughts are simply the results of our biochemistry moving us toward reproduction, then the thought "evolutionary psychology is the best way to understand people" is itself not a rationally defensible or inherently true thought. Rather, it is simply something our brains make us think and say so that we might impress other reproductively viable members of our species in order to get them to mate with us.

The irony doesn't end here, though, for whether you accept the notion that evolutionary psychological theories of human behavior are true or reject them as pseudoscientific fables depends entirely on which genes are influencing your current neurological interactions with the environment AND NOT on whether you have been or could ever be persuaded by reasoned argument and the convincing power of truth. To put it another way, if EP is true, then the only reason anyone would advocate it is because (anyone, they) must do so given their evolutionary history and the particular mental mechanisms that their genes have provided them. Likewise, critics of the theory are only critics because they don't happen to possess the appropriate "evolutionary psychology is true" thought generating brain functions or genes. So much for reason, so much for science, so much for truth!

Ultimately, then, if EP is the "basic intellectual framework for understanding all psychological phenomena," as Geher argues, then natural selection is also the undergirding explanation for all of the activities and ideas of scientific researchers. The theories and conclusions of these scientists, including the evolutionary psychologist, are nothing more than the results of complex interactions between meaningless arrangements of matter and, as such, provide no assurance that they accurately reflect the truth of things. Indeed, if what Geher asserts is true, then his own scientific article is to be explained as really just an elaborate manipulation of his readers by his genes to maximize their chances of reproductive success. If EP is taken to its logical conclusion, then, there is nothing left of truth, meaning or morality in *any* human phenomenon, let alone the phenomenon of generating a scientific theory like EP and writing an article about it. In the end, we can't help but conclude that Geher is correct when he states that EP isn't evil—because from the EP perspective there is ultimately no such thing as good or evil, right or wrong, meaning or reason or truth. So, while its own perspective guarantees that EP cannot be evil, it also makes a pretty strong case that it isn't any good.

CHALLENGE QUESTIONS

Is Evolution a Good Explanation for Psychological Concepts?

1. A major contention between these two positions is the objectivity of EP. Are evolutionary accounts of human behavior unbiased in their explanations? Should they be?
2. The authors of both articles agree that evolution is not evil, but for different reasons. What are these reasons? Do the articles differ about the "goodness" of EP? Why or why not?
3. Geher claims that EP works well for all aspects of psychology. How well does it account for the claims of humanistic or existential psychologists? If EP has trouble accounting for these claims, then what might this suggest about these schools of psychology? What does it suggest for EP?
4. What results have we gained from EP research? What would Gantt and Melling say about these results?
5. Geher suggests that EP is monism because the mind is governed by the same natural processes as the body. However, Gantt and Melling accuse this position of being a type of dualism. Which do you feel is correct on this issue, and why?
6. Geher suggests that EP is not overly deterministic because it takes account of environment and circumstance. Does this avoid the charge of determinism (i.e., all so-called human choices are determined by other factors and thus the person really has no true options)?

Internet References . . .

Journal of Cross-Cultural Psychology

This is a site for the *Journal of Cross-Cultural Psychology.*

http://jcc.sagepub.com/

Cultural Psychology Links

This is a site that provides links of other sites on cultural psychology.

http://www.socialpsychology.org/cultural.htm

Psychology Research Issues

This site's home page offers a wealth of information about different research issues in psychology. This particular link provides access to different papers that discuss the empirically supported treatment (EST) movement.

http://www.academyprojects.org/est.htm

Encyclopedia on Science and Religion

This web site is a portion of the *Encyclopedia on Science and Religion*, which provides an overview of the issue along with other links.

http://www.enotes.com/science-religion-encyclopedia/determinism

Research Issues

*R*esearch methods are the means by which psychologists test their ideas. Yet, the way that psychologists conduct their research and interpret their findings is sometimes the subject of controversy. When, for example, are the findings sufficient to support a particular conclusion? Psychological practices, such as psychotherapy, are complicated phenomena, involving not only observable behaviors, the typical province of empirical methods, but also less observable client and therapist meanings. Also, how generalizable are such findings to other cultures? If American researchers dominate the research on a given topic, how applicable are these findings to other cultures, with different customs and social traditions? And what about specific research assumptions, such as scientific determinism, the notion that all things, including humans, are determined by causal forces outside their control? Could these assumptions, when taught to psychology students, affect them in unexpected ways?

- Is American Psychological Research Generalizable to Other Cultures?
- Are Traditional Empirical Methods Sufficient to Provide Evidence for Psychological Practice?
- Does Teaching Scientific Determinism Lead to Bad Behavior?

ISSUE 4

Is American Psychological Research Generalizable to Other Cultures?

YES: Gerald J. Haeffel, Erik D. Thiessen, Matthew W. Campbell, Michael P. Kaschak, and Nicole M. McNeil, from "Theory, Not Cultural Context, Will Advance American Psychology," *American Psychologist* (September 2009)

NO: Jeffrey J. Arnett, from "The Neglected 95%, a Challenge to Psychology's Philosophy of Science," *American Psychologist* (September 2009)

ISSUE SUMMARY

YES: Haeffel and his colleagues believe that psychological studies of American people often generalize to people of other cultures, especially when basic processes are being studied.

NO: Jeffrey Arnett, psychological research professor, argues that culture is central to the functioning of humans and thus to psychological findings.

We live in a multicultural world, with important and substantial difference among cultures. Unfortunately, however, traditional psychological research has focused almost exclusively on a narrow portion of this multicultural world. Specifically, the majority of academic psychological investigations have been conducted using undergraduate American college students as participants (and generally those enrolled in psychology courses). While there are some variations within this subpopulation, college students are typically more homogenous than the wider population in categories like socioeconomic status, education, ethnicity, age, and values.

The major concern with studying such a narrow segment of the wider multicultural world is the question of *generalizability*—do studies of American college students actually tell us much about other populations in other circumstances? If they do not, then the findings of such research would not count as general knowledge. These findings would be viewed as more local, and thus not necessarily applicable to other populations. The primary issue in the generalizability question is whether contextual and cultural factors are *vital* to understanding humans. Are these factors merely "add-ons," and humans are essentially the same the world over? If so, investigations of *any* humans, including American college students, tell us what is essential about all other humans. Alternatively, if situational and ethnic factors are required to understand the functioning of humans, then humans are not such interchangeable parts.

In the first article, Haeffel and his colleagues believe that concerns about the generalizability of American psychology are overstated. Although they agree that cultural factors are a valid concern for some research topics, such as gender roles and family structure, they consider these factors less relevant to "basic human processes," processes that are universal to all humans, such as perception and cognition. Haeffel and his colleagues also dispute the notion that these basic processes have no real-world implications. They cite several examples, which they believe illustrate the critical role of basic research, including the recent development of cognitive behavioral therapy from basic research on cognition. Science mainly progresses, they argue, on the basis of falsifiable theories that deal with core psychological processes. Cultural factors are important for understanding the particular manifestations of these universals, but these factors do not prevent the generalizability of research on these basic processes.

Psychological researcher Jeffrey Arnett argues that psychological investigations must become dramatically less American to truly make progress in understanding humans. By Arnett's calculations, psychologists conduct research on less than 5 percent of the world's population, and this selective group does *not* automatically represent the other 95 percent. Therefore, as Dr. Arnett maintains, we should be more cautious about assuming the generalizability of psychological findings. Psychologists should do more to train investigators in multicultural issues; rigorous hypothesis testing alone is not sufficient to advance psychological knowledge. Only by broadening psychology's cultural horizons will the research become ecologically valid and truly contribute to an understanding of how people live their lives.

POINT	COUNTERPOINT
• Psychology should not focus primarily on culture and diversity issues	• Psychology should step up its recognition and promotion of multicultural awareness, especially in research.
• Science progresses by rigorously testing falsifiable theories that include universals.	• Understanding cultural context is essential to the advancement of psychological science.
• Humans around the world have the same basic psychological processes.	• The ways in which humans meaningfully carry out their activities are particular to their context.
• The careful control of variables through the scientific method will answer the basic questions of psychology.	• Laboratory control cannot answer many important questions about human nature, development, and experience.

YES

Gerald J. Haeffel et al.

Theory, Not Cultural Context, Will Advance American Psychology

In his recent article, "The Neglected 95%: Why American Psychology Needs to Become Less American," Arnett (October 2008) provided a thought-provoking analysis of the current state of psychology. He made two primary arguments: (a) Psychological research using American samples cannot generalize to the rest of the world, and (b) psychology's emphasis on basic processes should be replaced by an emphasis on context and culture. We agree with the author's call for greater attention to issues of context. However, we[1] fundamentally disagree with his position on issues related to generalizability and basic research. The goal of this comment is to provide a critical evaluation of Arnett's primary arguments as well as to offer alternative strategies for facilitating scientific progress on cultural and diversity issues.

Generalizability

Arnett's (2008) first argument is that American psychology does not represent people everywhere, and thus, its findings are not generalizable. This argument is a variation of the well-known "college sophomore problem." The argument is as follows: Research findings from a select sample such as college sophomores (or Americans, in this case) will not apply to other samples. This is a valid concern, and clearly there are situations in which research on select samples may not generalize. However, the problem of generalizability is often overstated. Studies using one sample of humans (e.g., Americans) often generalize to other samples of humans (e.g., Spaniards), particularly when basic processes[2] are being studied (e.g., Anderson, Lindsay, & Bushman, 1999). The results of studies investigating a wide range of psychological phenomena, including personality, information processing, aggression, and mental illness, tend to hold in a variety of contexts and with a variety of participant samples (see Stanovich, 2007, for review). The consistency of research findings across contexts and samples should not be surprising given that all humans, whether they live in America or a developing country, share a common genome, brain organization, and capacity for cognition, perception, and emotion.

The college sophomore problem is not new, and it is not clear that Arnett's (2008) discussion advances our understanding of the issue. His case is based largely on "straw man" arguments. He provided numerous examples of

From *American Psychologist,* vol. 64, no. 6, September 2009, pp. 570–571. Copyright © 2009 by American Psychological Association. Reprinted by permission via Rightslink.

when differences between Americans and other samples would be expected, including gender roles, marital relations, family structure, and the nature of formal education. Although subjectively compelling, these examples do not address the issue of the generalizability of research on *basic processes*. The existence of cultural variation does not imply that there are no universals worth studying. The same basic process can generate different products depending on the structure of the environment in which that process operates. It is not enough to show that American culture is different from other cultures. This fact is not disputed. The critical question is what these differences mean for human psychology. That is, what do cultural differences (e.g., gender roles, family structure, formal mathematical skills) say about the basic human processes (e.g., perception, cognition, emotion) that played a role in the development of those differences?

Basic Research

Arnett's (2008) second argument is that psychological research should focus on culture and diversity rather than on basic processes. He went so far as to state, "At a time when there are numerous daunting international problems that psychological science could address, such as religious fundamentalism, terrorism, international ecological crises, war, the HIV pandemic, and growing poverty, the main thrust in American psychology continues to be a research focus on processes and principles that goes forward as if none of these issues existed" (p. 612). This statement demonstrates a fundamental misunderstanding about basic research. His statement is akin to asking why medical research continues to focus on growing stem cells when there are more daunting problems such as Alzheimer's and Parkinson's disease. Basic research in psychology has clear implications for real-world issues. For example, research on information processing and behavioral activation has led to the creation of highly effective treatments (e.g., cognitive behavior therapy) for disorders such as depression and anxiety. Similarly, research on early experience with binocular vision (e.g., Banks, Aslin, & Letson, 1975) demonstrated the critical need for early (as opposed to delayed) detection and treatment of conditions that cause abnormal binocular experience such as esotropia. In addition, research on obedience (e.g., the Milgram studies and Zimbardo's prison experiment) has important implications for understanding the sometimes atrocious behavior of humans (e.g., Abu Ghraib, terrorism, Nazi war crimes). These are just a few of many examples that illustrate the critical role of basic research (both human and animal[3]) in understanding, and creating solutions for, real-world issues.

Cultural Context—Where's the Theory?

Arnett's (2008) argument against basic research raises fundamental questions about how to define science (i.e., the problem of demarcation) and how to evaluate scientific progress. Following Arnett's reasoning, science is defined by its applicability to real-world problems, sample representativeness, and the use of nonexperimental designs. Thus, he concluded that psychological science is "incomplete" because of its focus on basic processes, American samples, and experimental designs. In contrast to Arnett, we subscribe to a philosophy of science described by philosophers such as Popper and Meehl. According to Popper (1959), science is characterized by the falsification of theories. If a theory is falsifiable, it is by definition scientific. Popper's definition of science does not depend on whether the work is basic or applied. It does not depend on the type of research design one uses (longitudinal, cross-sectional, experimental, quasi-experimental, etc). It does not depend on the sample (e.g., American or Nigerian). Science is characterized by testing and falsifying theories (Meehl, 1978).

In light of this philosophy, it is unclear why research on cultural context should be considered more scientifically progressive than research on basic processes. In fact, Arnett's (2008) description of cultural research raises concerns that it could actually slow progress in psychology. His vision of cultural psychology does not invoke theory or the importance of having testable hypotheses. Rather, cultural psychology appears to be exploratory and descriptive in nature. Will cultural psychology simply be an anecdotal record of cultural differences or a collection of replication studies? Will 100% of the world's population have to be studied before psychology can be considered a "complete science?" Arnett failed to provide any information about how cultural psychology will progress as a science.

From a philosophy of science perspective, Arnett's (2008) distinction between cultural context and basic processes is a false dichotomy. The problem with human psychology is not its focus on basic processes rather than cultural context; it is the lack of strong falsifiable theories (Meehl, 1978). Cultural context cannot exist in a vacuum isolated from basic processes such as cognition, perception, language, and so forth. If cultural research is to take hold in psychology, then it must be theory driven and integrated into work on basic processes. It is not enough to surmise that different cultures may lead to different outcomes. Researchers need to specify the conditions for when they would and would not expect culture to affect basic processes and behaviors.

Cultural context can serve an important purpose in psychological science: It will enable us to test hypotheses about which features of human behavior are acquired through experience and which are basic (or innate). Basic processes are mechanisms via which humans—and other animals—are able to respond adaptively to typical environments; however, these processes can be distinguished from another kind of adaptation, acquired associations or strategies (such as reading), which vary across situations and cultures. Within this framework, cultural adaptations can be thought to arise from the operation of basic processes, such as learning.[4] For example, at one time it was thought that language was acquired solely through imitation of and reinforcement by models within one's sociocultural context (e.g., Skinner's, 1957, *Verbal Behavior*), until Chomsky's synthesis of cross-cultural linguistic variation revealed important similarities across cultures, suggesting that language acquisition also depends on a more basic structure or process that all humans share. Similarly, conventional wisdom suggests that abstract mathematical concepts are learned through years of formal education and training; however, studies of hunter-gatherer cultures (e.g., the Pirahã; Gordon, 2004) and even of nonhuman animals (e.g., monkeys, rats, pigeons; Gallistel & Gelman, 2000) have shown that we all share a common system for representing the abstract concept of number. In clinical psychology, many assume that eating disorders such as anorexia nervosa and bulimia nervosa share a common genetic etiology. However, recent research suggests that the genetic diathesis for bulimia nervosa may exhibit greater pathoplasticity cross-culturally than the diathesis for anorexia nervosa; this finding indicates distinct etiologies for these disorders (Keel & Klump, 2003). These examples highlight the importance of using cultural context to test theories about basic and acquired human behavior.

Conclusion

Focusing on cultural context *rather* than basic processes is not going to advance American psychology, or psychology in general. Neither [is] having students travel abroad or take anthropology classes (as recommended by Arnett), in and of themselves. Rather, science will advance by developing and testing theories. We believe that psychological science can benefit most by using differences in culture and context to develop and test novel hypotheses about basic human processes.

Notes

1. The authors of this commentary represent a broad cross-section of psychological science including clinical, developmental, biological, and cognitive areas.

2. By basic processes, we mean those psychological or biological processes that are shared by all humans at appropriate developmental levels (e.g., cognition, perception, learning, brain organization, genome).

3. In addition to basic research on humans, there is also a large body of animal research to consider. For example, Michael Davis's research delineating the neural basis of fear and anxiety in rats led to the creation of a cognitive enhancer (D-cycloserine), which is currently being used to treat Iraq veterans with posttraumatic stress disorder (Davis, Myers, Ressler, & Rothbaum, 2005). Similarly, Michael Meaney's (2001) research on maternal care and gene expression in rats has tremendous implications for understanding of human attachment, stress reactivity, and even developmental disorders such as autism.

4. Note that this formulation of the purpose of cross-cultural psychology differs markedly from Arnett's (2008), which espouses cultural representativeness as a goal unto itself.

All references for articles included in *Taking Sides: Clashing Views on Psychological Issues, 17/e* can be found on the Web at http://www.mhhe.com/cls.

Jeffrey Jensen Arnett  **NO**

The Neglected 95%, a Challenge to Psychology's Philosophy of Science

My goal in writing "The Neglected 95%: Why American Psychology Needs to Become Less American" (Arnett, October 2008) was to fuel a conversation in psychology about whether American psychological research should become more reflective of how human beings in different cultures around the world experience their lives. I am pleased to see that many of my colleagues have taken up this conversation, as represented in the four comments [in] *American Psychologist* . . . [published in September 2009]. The four comments were well chosen in that they represent quite different reactions to my article. Two of the comments were generally in support of my thesis that American psychology is too narrow culturally, and sought to provide additional information on the issues I raised. The other two comments were in opposition to my thesis and presented the grounds for their opposition. In this rejoinder I address the issues raised in [the second of the] opposing comments. Following this, I address the more general problem that cuts across the comments: American psychology's dominant philosophy of science. . . .

What Is Science? What Is Scientific Progress?

The most extensive of the four commentaries is the one offered by Haeffel, Thiessen, Campbell, Kaschak, and McNeil . . . [September 2009, *American Psychologist*], who took the position that "Theory, Not Cultural Context, Will Advance American Psychology" (p. 570). Their main goal was to defend the value of research on basic processes (e.g., cognition, perception, learning) and question the value of culturally diverse research.

Haeffel et al. (2009) are on shaky ground from the beginning. They showed the limits of their perceptions in asserting that "the problem of generalizability is often overstated" (p. 570), offering in support of this statement the assertion "Studies using one sample of humans (e.g., Americans) often generalize to other samples of humans (e.g., Spaniards)" (p. 570). Even adding Spaniards to Americans (and throwing in Canadians for good measure) still makes for less than 5% of the world's population. Psychologists are far too quick to jump from one study of Americans and one study of Spaniards to a declaration of a universal psychological principle. It is not the problem of generalizability that is overstated but the research findings of psychologists based on a tiny and unusual segment of humanity.

From *American Psychologist*, vol. 64, no. 6, September 2009, pp. 571–572, 573–574 (excerpts). Copyright © 2009 by American Psychological Association. Reprinted by permission via Rightslink.

There may be an effective case to be made for the value of psychological research on basic processes, but Haeffel and colleagues (2009) did not make it.[1] They claimed that I suffer from a "fundamental misunderstanding about basic research" and that my position is "akin to asking why medical research continues to focus on growing stem cells when there are more daunting problems such as Alzheimer's and Parkinson's disease" (p. 570). If only the connection between psychological research on basic processes and real-world human problems were as clear as the relation between stem cell research and diseases like Alzheimer's and Parkinson's! The relation between stem cell research and treatments for Alzheimer's and Parkinson's disease is evident even to the nonscientist. The relation between basic research in psychology and real human problems is far less clear even to a research psychologist. There may be value in psychological research on basic processes, especially when the results are linked to cultural contexts, as Haeffel et al. suggested. It is just that research on basic processes alone is not enough for a science of humanity. This approach to research leaves out too much about cultural beliefs, cultural practices, and social relations.

Haeffel et al. (2009) accurately identified the heart of the difference between my perspective and theirs as a divergence in views of "how to define science . . . and how to evaluate scientific progress" (p. 570). They hold to a philosophy of science they attribute to Popper (1959) and Meehl (1978): "If a theory is falsifiable, it is by definition scientific" (Haeffel et al., 2009, p. 570). To some extent, I agree with this view. Certainly testing falsifiable hypotheses is one part of psychological science. However, restricting research to falsifiable theories alone is far too narrow a view of psychology as a human science. A focus on falsifiable theories narrows psychology's intellectual and scientific scope mainly to the laboratory, where experimental situations can be carefully controlled. The problem with this focus is that laboratory studies are often ecologically invalid and have little relation to how people actually live and how they experience their lives. There are many aspects of human development, behavior, and experience that are worth investigating even if they cannot be reduced to falsifiable theories (Rogoff, 2003). Psychology needs to get over its "physics envy" and adapt its methods and theoretical approaches to its uniquely human topic, in all its cultural complexity and diversity, rather than endlessly and fruitlessly aping the natural sciences.

Toward a Broader Philosophy of Our Human Science

The four comments on my article (Arnett, 2008) are diverse, but together they suggest a need for a reexamination of psychology's dominant philosophy of science. Even the two comments that were sympathetic to my thesis did not fully grasp the crux of the problem. Both assumed that a cultural understanding of human psychology could be attained through cross-cultural research, not realizing how transporting American-based theories and methods to other cultures might result in missing the most distinctive and essential features of those cultures. The two opposing comments represented well the traditional approach to psychological research, with its confident assurance that progress in psychology is best served by following the model of the natural sciences, investigating basic processes in search of universal laws, with limited or no attention to that distracting variable, cultural context, that actually means the most to how people behave, how they function psychologically, and how they understand and interpret their lives.

I advocate a broader, more intellectually vibrant and inclusive philosophy of science. The goal of the human sciences should not be simply the pursuit of universal laws and the falsification of theories—no matter how dull or trivial the theory, no matter how little relation the theory has to how people experience life outside the laboratory. The goal of the human sciences should be to use the tools of the scientific method to illuminate our understanding of human behavior, human functioning, and human development. The tools of the scientific method in psychology should be construed broadly to include not just laboratory tasks but any systematic investigation of human phenomena. In this philosophy of science, the structured interview and the ethnography are no less legitimate as tools of the scientific method than are the laboratory or the questionnaire. Many diverse methods are welcome, and all contribute valuable pieces to the mosaic that makes up a full understanding of humanity.

That mosaic is still missing many large and essential pieces, over a century after psychology was first established as a field. However, many research psychologists are working daily to fill it in, using a wide range of theories and methods (Jensen, 2010). What we need now in American psychology is not a narrowing of theories and methods to those that seem best to mimic the methods of the natural sciences, but a wider range of new, creative theories and methods, synthesizing cultural perspectives from all over the world, that will broaden our understanding of the endlessly fascinating human experience.

Note

1. Haeffel et al. (2009) claimed, "Basic research in psychology has clear implications for real-world issues" (p. 570), but the examples they provided fall flat. Research on information processing and behavioral activation has not "led to the creation of highly effective treatments (e.g., cognitive behavior therapy) for disorders such as depression and anxiety" (p. 570). Cognitive behavior therapy was developed in the 1950s and 1960s by Albert Ellis and Aaron Beck, and its roots are in ancient Greek philosophy, not basic research on information processing and behavioral activation. To find an example of basic research related to any of the problems I suggested that psychology should address (e.g., religious fundamentalism, terrorism, international ecological crises, war), the authors are forced to go back half a century to Milgram's obedience studies and Zimbardo's prison experiment. I agree about the value of the Milgram and Zimbardo studies, and I regard it as a great pity that psychological research today is rarely as creative in its methods as those studies were. As for research on "abnormal binocular experience such as esotropia" (p. 570), this seems more in the realm of optometry than psychology.

All references for articles included in *Taking Sides: Clashing Views on Psychological Issues, 17/e* can be found on the Web at http://www.mhhe.com/cls.

CHALLENGE QUESTIONS

Is American Psychological Research Generalizable to Other Cultures?

1. Arnett accuses psychology of "physics envy" and suggests psychology should develop methods that better reflect the unique nature of humans. Why does he make this accusation, and what sorts of methods might be considered in this development?
2. Haeffel and colleagues make a distinction between "basic research" and the cross-cultural studies suggested by Arnett. What are the advantages and disadvantages of basic research compared to culturally sensitive studies? From your perspective, which is more needed in psychology, and why do you hold this position?
3. Why is generalizability such an important issue for some psychologists? Are there disadvantages to increasing generalizability through greater experimental control?
4. Both articles in this issue are written by scholars at American universities. How might their own cultural perspective inform or limit their view of this issue?
5. A central question debated in these two articles is what counts as scientific progress and understanding. What are the different understandings of these authors on the issue of progress, and how does this understanding impact their respective arguments?

ISSUE 5

Are Traditional Empirical Methods Sufficient to Provide Evidence for Psychological Practice?

YES: APA Presidential Task Force on Evidence-Based Practice, from "Report of the 2005 Presidential Task Force on Evidence-Based Practice," *American Psychologist* (May/June 2006)

NO: Brent D. Slife and Dennis C. Wendt, from "The Next Step in the Evidence-Based Practice Movement," APA Convention Presentation (August 2006)

ISSUE SUMMARY

YES: The APA Presidential Task Force on Evidence-Based Practice assumes that a variety of traditional empirical methods is sufficient to provide evidence for psychological practices.

NO: Psychologist Brent D. Slife and researcher Dennis C. Wendt contend that traditional empirical methods are guided by a single philosophy that limits the diversity of methods.

$\mathbf{I}$magine that one of your family members needs to see a therapist for a severe depression. Of the two therapists available, the first therapist's practices are supported by evidence obtained through traditional scientific methods. The second therapist's practices are not. The latter's practices could be equally effective or even more effective than the first therapist's practices, but we do not know. Which therapist would you choose for this member of your family?

Most people would readily choose therapists who have scientific evidence for their interventions. They think of psychotherapy much like they think of medicine, with treatments that have stood the test of science. Just as physicians can provide evidence that pain relievers actually relieve pain, so too psychologists hope to provide evidence that their practices deliver their desired results. Because not all psychological treatments come with evidence to support their use, some psychologists worry that some treatments could actually do more harm than good. It is with this potential harm in mind that many psychologists banded together to establish empirically supported treatments (ESTs). The goal was to establish a list of ESTs for specific psychological disorders. Those involved in this movement (various task forces from different divisions of the American Psychological Association) initially stressed the use of randomized clinical (or controlled) trials (RCTs)—a specific type of research design—to be sure that the scientific examination of these treatments was rigorous and thorough.

In the first article of this issue, however, the APA Presidential Task Force on Evidence-Based Practice questions whether too much emphasis has been placed on RCT research designs. This Task Force affirms the need for empirically based evidence in psychology but tries to reframe the notion of evidence-based practice so that a diversity of empirical methods, including correlational and even case study methods, are considered important for producing evidence. The Task Force calls for objectivity in gathering all forms of evidence. In fact, it still considers RCTs the most rigorous type of objective method. However, it also acknowledges that other empirical approaches to gathering information and evidence can and do have their place in deciding psychology's evidence-based practices.

In the second selection, psychologist Brent D. Slife and researcher Dennis Wendt applaud the APA Task Force for taking important steps in the right direction. Nevertheless, they argue that the Task Force's statement is "ultimately and fundamentally inadequate." The Task Force correctly champions the objectivity and diversity of methods and evidence, in their view, but they contend that the Task Force is not objective and diverse enough. They claim that just as the EST movement restricted the gathering of evidence to a single method (RCTs), the Task Force's suggestions assume, but never justify, that evidence-based practice should be restricted to a single *epistemology* of method. They acknowledge that many psychologists view this empirical epistemology as not affecting the outcome of research, but they note that most practices that are considered evidence-based fit the biases of the philosophy of empiricism.

POINT

- Psychological treatments should be supported by evidence.
- Evidence should include RCTs as well as other empirical methods.

- Evidence should be both objective and diverse.
- Evidence should not be limited to a single method (RCT).

COUNTERPOINT

- Not all psychologists agree on what qualifies as evidence.
- Traditional empirical methods are not the only methods by which evidence can be obtained.
- Including only the "empirical" is neither objective nor diverse.
- Evidence should not be limited to a single methodology.

Report of the 2005 Presidential Task Force on Evidence-Based Practice[1]

From the very first conceptions of applied psychology as articulated by Lightner Witmer, who formed the first psychological clinic in 1896, psychologists have been deeply and uniquely associated with an evidence-based approach to patient care. As Witmer pointed out, "the pure and the applied sciences advance in a single front. What retards the progress of one retards the progress of the other; what fosters one fosters the other." As early as 1947 the idea that doctoral psychologists should be trained as both scientists and practitioners became the American Psychological Association (APA) policy. Early practitioners such as Frederick C. Thorne articulated the methods by which psychological practitioners integrate science into their practice by . . . "increasing the application of the experimental approach to the individual case into the clinician's own experience." Thus, psychologists have been on the forefront of the development of evidence-based practice for decades.

Evidence-based practice in psychology is therefore consistent with the past twenty years of work in evidence-based medicine, which advocated for improved patient outcomes by informing clinical practice with relevant research. Sackett and colleagues describe evidence-based medicine as "the conscientious, explicit, and judicious use of current best evidence in making decisions about the care of individual patients." The use and misuse of evidence-based principles in the practice of health care has affected the dissemination of health care funds, but not always to the benefit of the patient. Therefore, psychologists, whose training is grounded in empirical methods, have an important role to play in the continuing development of evidence-based practice and its focus on improving patient care.

One approach to implementing evidence-based practice in health care systems has been through the development of guidelines for best practice. During

[1]This document was received by the American Psychological Association (APA) Council of Representatives during its meeting of August, 2005. The report represents the conclusions of the Task Force and does not represent the official policy of the American Psychological Association. The Task Force wishes to thank John R. Weisz, PhD, ABPP for his assistance in drafting portions of this report related to children and youth. The Task Force also thanks James Mitchell and Omar Rehman, APA Professional Development interns, for their assistance throughout the work of the Task Force.

From *American Psychologist,* vol. 61, issue 4, May/June 2006, pp. 271–285 (excerpts). Copyright © 2006 by American Psychological Association. Reprinted by permission via Rightslink.

the early part of the evidence-based practice movement, APA recognized the importance of a comprehensive approach to the conceptualization of guidelines. APA also recognized the risk that guidelines might be used inappropriately by commercial health care organizations not intimately familiar with the scientific basis of practice to dictate specific forms of treatment and restrict patient access to care. In 1992, APA formed a joint task force of the Board of Scientific Affairs (BSA), the Board of Professional Affairs (BPA), and the Committee for the Advancement of Professional Practice (CAPP). The document developed by this task force—the *Template for Developing Guidelines: Interventions for Mental Disorders and Psychosocial Aspects of Physical Disorders* (Template)—was approved by the APA Council of Representatives in 1995 (APA, 1995). The Template described the variety of evidence that should be considered in developing guidelines, and cautioned that any emerging clinical practice guidelines should be based on careful systematic weighing of research data and clinical expertise. . . .

Although the goal was to identify treatments with evidence for efficacy comparable to the evidence for the efficacy of medications, and hence to highlight the contribution of psychological treatments, the Division 12 Task Force report sparked a decade of both enthusiasm and controversy. The report increased recognition of demonstrably effective psychological treatments among the public, policymakers, and training programs. At the same time, many psychologists raised concerns about the exclusive focus on brief, manualized treatments; the emphasis on specific treatment effects as opposed to common factors that account for much of the variance in outcomes across disorders; and the applicability to a diverse range of patients varying in comorbidity, personality, race, ethnicity, and culture.

In response, several groups of psychologists, including other divisions of APA, offered additional frameworks for integrating the available research evidence. In 1999, APA Division 29 (Psychotherapy) established a task force to identify, operationalize, and disseminate information on empirically supported therapy relationships, given the powerful association between outcome and aspects of the therapeutic relationship such as the therapeutic alliance. Division 17 (Counseling Psychology) also undertook an examination of empirically supported treatments in counseling psychology. The Society of Behavioral Medicine, which is not a part of APA but which has significantly overlapping membership, has recently published criteria for examining the evidence base for behavioral medicine interventions. As of this writing, we are aware that task forces have been appointed to examine related issues by a large number of APA divisions concerned with practice issues. . . .

Definition

Based on its review of the literature and its deliberations, the Task Force agreed on the following definition:

> Evidence-based practice in psychology (EBPP) is the integration of the best available research with clinical expertise in the context of patient characteristics, culture, and preferences.

This definition of EBPP closely parallels the definition of evidence-based practice adopted by the Institute of Medicine as adapted from Sackett and colleagues: "Evidence-based practice is the integration of best research evidence with clinical expertise and patient values." Psychology builds on the IOM definition by deepening the examination of clinical expertise and broadening the consideration of patient characteristics. The purpose of EBPP is to promote effective psychological practice and enhance public health by applying empirically supported principles of psychological assessment, case formulation, therapeutic relationship, and intervention.

Psychological practice entails many types of interventions, in multiple settings, for a wide variety of potential patients. In this document, *intervention* refers to all direct services rendered by health care psychologists, including assessment, diagnosis, prevention, treatment, psychotherapy, and consultation. As is the case with most discussions of evidence-based practice, we focus on treatment. The same general principles apply to psychological assessment, which is essential to effective treatment. The settings include but are not limited to hospitals, clinics, independent practices, schools, military, public health, rehabilitation institutes, primary care, counseling centers, and nursing homes.

To be consistent with discussions of evidence-based practice in other areas of health care, we use the term *patient* in this document to refer to the child, adolescent, adult, older adult, couple, family, group, organization, community, or other populations receiving psychological services. However, we recognize that in many situations there are important and valid reasons for using such terms as *client, consumer,* or *person* in place of patient to describe the recipients of services. Further, psychologists target a variety of problems, including but not restricted to mental health, academic, vocational, relational, health, community, and other problems, in their professional practice.

It is important to clarify the relation between EBPP and ESTs (empirically supported treatments). EBPP is the more comprehensive concept. ESTs start with a treatment and ask whether it works for a certain disorder or problem under specified circumstances. EBPP starts with the patient and asks what research evidence (including relevant results from RCTs) will assist the psychologist to achieve the best outcome. In addition, ESTs are specific psychological treatments that have been shown to be efficacious in controlled clinical trials, whereas EBPP encompasses a broader range of clinical activities (e.g., psychological assessment, case formulation, therapy relationships). As such, EBPP articulates a decision making process for integrating multiple streams of research evidence, including but not limited to RCTs, into the intervention process.

The following sections explore in greater detail the three major components of this definition—best available research, clinical expertise, and patient characteristics—and their integration.

Best Available Research Evidence

A sizeable body of scientific evidence drawn from a variety of research designs and methodologies attests to the effectiveness of psychological practices. The research literature on the effect of psychological interventions indicates that these interventions are safe and effective for a large number of children and youth, adults and older adults across a wide range of psychological, addictive, health, and relational problems. More recent research indicates that compared to alternative approaches, such as medications, psychological treatments are particularly enduring. Further, research demonstrates that psychotherapy can and often does pay for itself in terms of medical costs offset, increased productivity, and life satisfaction.

Psychologists possess distinctive strengths in designing, conducting, and interpreting research studies that can guide evidence-based practice. Moreover, psychology—as a science and as a profession—is distinctive in combining scientific commitment with an emphasis on human relationships and individual differences. As such, psychology can help develop, broaden, and improve the research base for evidence-based practice.

There is broad consensus that psychological practice needs to be based on evidence, and that research needs to balance internal and external validity. Research will not always address all practice needs. Major issues in integrating research in day-to-day practice include: a) the relative weight to place on different research methods; b) the representativeness of research samples; c) whether research results should guide practice at the level of principles of change, intervention strategies, or specific protocols; d) the generalizability and transportability of treatments supported in controlled research to clinical practice settings; e) the extent to which judgments can be made about treatments of choice when the number and duration of treatments tested has been limited; and f) the degree to which the results of efficacy and effectiveness research can be generalized from primarily white samples to minority and marginalized populations. Nevertheless, research on practice has made progress in investigating these issues and is providing research evidence that is more responsive to day-to-day practice. There is sufficient consensus to move forward with the principles of EBPP.

Meta-analytic investigations since the 1970s have shown that most therapeutic practices in widespread clinical use are generally effective for treating a range of problems. In fact, the effect sizes for psychological interventions for children, adults and older adults rival, or exceed, those of widely accepted medical treatments. It is important not to assume that interventions that have not yet been studied in controlled trials are ineffective. Specific interventions that have not been subjected to systematic empirical testing for specific problems cannot be assumed to be either effective or ineffective; they are simply untested to date. Nonetheless, good practice and science call for the timely testing of psychological practices in a way that adequately operationalizes them using appropriate scientific methodology. Widely used psychological practices as well as innovations developed in the field or laboratory should be rigorously evaluated and barriers to conducting this research should be identified and addressed.

Multiple Types of Research Evidence

Best research evidence refers to scientific results related to intervention strategies, assessment, clinical problems, and patient populations in laboratory and field settings as well as to clinically relevant results of basic research in psychology and related fields. APA endorses multiple types of research evidence (e.g., efficacy, effectiveness, cost-effectiveness, cost-benefit, epidemiological, treatment utilization studies) that contribute to effective psychological practice.

Multiple research designs contribute to evidence-based practice, and different research designs are better suited to address different types of questions. These include:

- Clinical observation (including individual case studies) and basic psychological science are valuable sources of innovations and hypotheses (the context of scientific discovery).
- Qualitative research can be used to describe the subjective lived experience of people, including participants in psychotherapy.
- Systematic case studies are particularly useful when aggregated as in the form of practice research networks for comparing individual patients to others with similar characteristics.
- Single case experimental designs are particularly useful for establishing causal relationships in the context of an individual.
- Public health and ethnographic research are especially useful for tracking the availability, utilization, and acceptance of mental health treatments as well as suggesting ways of altering them to maximize their utility in a given social context.
- Process-outcome studies are especially valuable for identifying mechanisms of change.
- Studies of interventions as delivered in naturalistic settings (effectiveness research) are well suited for assessing the ecological validity of treatments.
- Randomized clinical trials and their logical equivalents (efficacy research) are the standard for drawing causal inferences about the effects of interventions (context of scientific verification).
- Meta-analysis is a systematic means to synthesize results from multiple studies, test hypotheses, and quantitatively estimate the size of effects.

With respect to evaluating research on specific interventions, current APA policy identifies two widely accepted dimensions. As stated in the *Criteria for Evaluating Treatment Guidelines,* "The first dimension is *treatment efficacy,* the systematic and scientific evaluation of whether a treatment works. The second dimension is *clinical utility,* the applicability, feasibility, and usefulness of the intervention in the local or specific setting where it is to be offered. This dimension also includes determination of the generalizability of an intervention whose efficacy has been established." Types of research evidence with regard to intervention research in ascending order as to their contribution to conclusions about efficacy include: clinical opinion, observation, and consensus among recognized experts representing the range of use in the field (Criterion 2.1); systematized clinical observation (Criterion 2.2); and sophisticated empirical methodologies, including quasi experiments and randomized controlled experiments or their logical equivalents (Criterion 2.3). Among sophisticated empirical methodologies, "randomized controlled experiments represent a more stringent way to evaluate treatment efficacy because they are the most effective way to rule out threats to internal validity in a single experiment."

Evidence on clinical utility is also crucial. As per established APA policy, at a minimum this includes attention to generality of effects across varying and diverse patients, therapists and settings and the interaction of these factors, the robustness of treatments across various modes of delivery, the feasibility with which treatments can be delivered to patients in real world settings, and the cost associated with treatments.

Evidence-based practice requires that psychologists recognize the strengths and limitations of evidence obtained from different types of research. Research has shown that the treatment method, the individual psychologist, the treatment relationship, and the patient are all vital contributors to the success of psychological practice. Comprehensive evidence-based practice will consider all of these determinants and their optimal combinations. Psychological practice is a complex relational and technical enterprise that requires clinical and research attention to multiple, interacting sources of treatment effectiveness. There remain many disorders, problem constellations, and clinical situations for which empirical data are sparse. In such instances, clinicians use their best clinical judgment and knowledge of the best available research evidence to develop coherent treatment strategies. Researchers and practitioners should join together to ensure that the research available on psychological practice is both clinically relevant and internally valid. . . .

Clinical Expertise[2]

Clinical expertise is essential for identifying and integrating the best research evidence with clinical data (e.g., information about the patient obtained over the course of treatment) in the context of the patient's characteristics and preferences to deliver services that have the highest probability of achieving the goals of therapy. Psychologists are trained as scientists as well as practitioners. An advantage of psychological training is that it fosters a clinical expertise informed by scientific expertise, allowing the psychologist to understand and integrate scientific literature as well as to frame and test hypotheses and interventions in practice as a "local clinical scientist."

Cognitive scientists have found consistent evidence of enduring and significant differences between experts and novices undertaking complex tasks in several domains. Experts recognize meaningful patterns and disregard irrelevant information, acquire extensive knowledge and organize it in ways that reflect a deep understanding of their domain, organize their knowledge using functional rather than descriptive features, retrieve knowledge relevant to the task at hand fluidly and automatically, adapt to new situations, self-monitor

---

[2]As it is used in this report, clinical expertise refers to competence attained by psychologists through education, training, and experience resulting in effective practice; clinical expertise is not meant to refer to extraordinary performance that might characterize an elite group (e.g., the top two percent) of clinicians.

their knowledge and performance, know when their knowledge is inadequate, continue to learn, and generally attain outcomes commensurate with their expertise.

However, experts are not infallible. All humans are prone to errors and biases. Some of these stem from cognitive strategies and heuristics that are generally adaptive and efficient. Others stem from emotional reactions, which generally guide adaptive behavior as well but can also lead to biased or motivated reasoning. Whenever psychologists involved in research or practice move from observations to inferences and generalizations, there is inherent risk for idiosyncratic interpretations, overgeneralizations, confirmatory biases, and similar errors in judgment. Integral to clinical expertise is an awareness of the limits of one's knowledge and skills and attention to the heuristics and biases—both cognitive and affective—that can affect clinical judgment. Mechanisms such as consultation and systematic feedback from the patient can mitigate some of these biases.

The individual therapist has a substantial impact on outcomes, both in clinical trials and in practice settings. The fact that treatment outcomes are systematically related to the provider of the treatment (above and beyond the type of treatment) provides strong evidence for the importance of understanding expertise in clinical practice as a way of enhancing patient outcomes. . . .

Patient Characteristics, Culture, and Preferences

Normative data on "what works for whom" provide essential guides to effective practice. Nevertheless, psychological services are most likely to be effective when responsive to the patient's specific problems, strengths, personality, sociocultural context, and preferences. Psychology's long history of studying individual differences and developmental change, and its growing empirical literature related to human diversity (including culture[3] and psychotherapy), place it in a strong position to identify effective ways of integrating research and clinical expertise with an understanding of patient characteristics essential to EBPP. EBPP involves consideration of patients' values, religious beliefs, worldviews, goals, and preferences for treatment with the psychologist's experience and understanding of the available research.

Several questions frame current debates about the role of patient characteristics in EBPP. The first regards the extent to which cross-diagnostic patient characteristics, such as personality traits or constellations, moderate the impact of empirically tested interventions. A second, related question concerns the extent to which social factors and cultural differences necessitate different

---

[3]Culture, in this context, is understood to encompass a broad array of phenomena (such as shared values, history, knowledge, rituals, and customs) that often result in a shared sense of identity. Racial and ethnic groups may have a shared culture, but those personal characteristics are not the only characteristics that define cultural groups (e.g., deaf culture, inner-city culture). Culture is a multifaceted construct, and cultural factors cannot be understood in isolation from social, class and personal characteristics that make each patient unique.

forms of treatment or whether interventions widely tested in majority populations can be readily adapted for patients with different ethnic or sociocultural backgrounds. A third question concerns maximizing the extent to which widely used interventions adequately attend to developmental considerations, both for children and adolescents and for older adults. A fourth question is the extent to which variable clinical presentations, such as comorbidity and polysymptomatic presentations, moderate the impact of interventions. Underlying all of these questions is the issue of how best to approach the treatment of patients whose characteristics (e.g., gender, gender identity, ethnicity, race, social class, disability status, sexual orientation) and problems (e.g., comorbidity) may differ from those of samples studied in research. This is a matter of active discussion in the field and there is increasing research attention to the generalizability and transportability of psychological interventions.

Available data indicate that a variety of patient-related variables influence outcomes, many of which are cross-diagnostic characteristics such as functional status, readiness to change, and level of social support. Other patient characteristics are essential to consider in forming and maintaining a treatment relationship and in implementing specific interventions. These include but are not limited to a) variations in presenting problems or disorders, etiology, concurrent symptoms or syndromes, and behavior; b) chronological age, developmental status, developmental history, and life stage; c) sociocultural and familial factors (e.g., gender, gender identity, ethnicity, race, social class, religion, disability status, family structure, and sexual orientation); d) current environmental context, stressors (e.g., unemployment or recent life event), and social factors (e.g., institutional racism and health care disparities); and e) personal preferences, values, and preferences related to treatment (e.g., goals, beliefs, worldviews, and treatment expectations). Available research on both patient matching and treatment failures in clinical trials of even highly efficacious interventions suggests that different strategies and relationships may prove better suited for different populations.

Many presenting symptoms—for example, depression, anxiety, school failure, bingeing and purging—are similar across patients. However, symptoms or disorders that are phenotypically similar are often heterogeneous with respect to etiology, prognosis, and the psychological processes that create or maintain them. Moreover, most patients present with multiple symptoms or syndromes rather than a single, discrete disorder. The presence of concurrent conditions may moderate treatment response, and interventions intended to treat one symptom often affect others. An emerging body of research also suggests that personality variables underlie many psychiatric syndromes and account for a substantial part of the comorbidity among syndromes widely documented in research. Psychologists must attend to the individual person to make the complex choices necessary to conceptualize, prioritize, and treat multiple symptoms. It is important to know the person who has the disorder in addition to knowing the disorder the person has.

EBPP also requires attention to factors related to the patient's development and life-stage. An enormous body of research exists on developmental processes (e.g., attachment, socialization, and cognitive, social-cognitive, gender, moral, and emotional development) that are essential in understanding adult psychopathology and particularly in treating children, adolescents, families, and older adults.

Evidence-based practice in psychology requires attention to many other patient characteristics, such as gender, gender identity, culture, ethnicity, race, age, family context, religious beliefs, and sexual orientation. These variables shape personality, values, worldviews, relationships, psychopathology, and attitudes toward treatment. A wide range of relevant research literature can inform psychological practice, including ethnography, cross-cultural psychology, psychological anthropology, and cultural psychotherapy. Culture influences not only the nature and expression of psychopathology but also the patient's understanding of psychological and physical health and illness. Cultural values and beliefs and social factors such as implicit racial biases also influence patterns of seeking, using, and receiving help; presentation and reporting of symptoms, fears and expectations about treatment; and desired outcomes. Psychologists also understand and reflect upon the ways their own characteristics, values, and context interact with those of the patient.

Race as a social construct is a way of grouping people into categories on the basis of perceived physical attributes, ancestry, and other factors. Race is also more broadly associated with power, status, and opportunity. In Western cultures, European or white "race" confers advantage and opportunity, even as improved social attitudes and public policies have reinforced social equality. Race is thus an interpersonal and political process with significant implications for clinical practice and health care quality. Patients and clinicians may "belong" to racial groups, as they choose to self-identify, but the importance of race in clinical practice is relational, rather than solely a patient or clinician attribute. Considerable evidence from many fields suggests that racial power differentials between clinicians and their patients, as well as systemic biases and implicit stereotypes based on race or ethnicity, contribute to the inequitable care that patients of color receive across health care services. Clinicians must carefully consider the impact of race, ethnicity, and culture on the treatment process, relationship, and outcome.

The patient's social and environmental context, including recent and chronic stressors, is also important in case formulation and treatment planning. Sociocultural and familial factors, social class, and broader social, economic, and situational factors (e.g., unemployment, family disruption, lack of insurance, recent losses, prejudice, or immigration status) can have an enormous influence on mental health, adaptive functioning, treatment seeking, and patient resources (psychological, social, and financial).

Psychotherapy is a collaborative enterprise, in which patients and clinicians negotiate ways of working together that are mutually agreeable and likely to lead to positive outcomes. Thus, patient values and preferences (e.g., goals, beliefs, and preferred modes of treatment) are a central component of EBPP. Patients can have strong preferences for types of treatment and desired outcomes, and these preferences are influenced by both their cultural context and individual factors. One role of the psychologist is to ensure that patients understand the costs and benefits of different practices and choices. Evidence-based practice in psychology seeks to maximize patient choice among effective alternative interventions. Effective practice requires balancing patient preferences and the psychologist's judgment, based on available evidence and clinical expertise, to determine the most appropriate treatment. . . .

Conclusions

Evidence-based practice in psychology is the integration of the best available research with clinical expertise in the context of patient characteristics, culture, and preferences. The purpose of EBPP is to promote effective psychological practice and enhance public health by applying empirically supported principles of psychological assessment, case formulation, therapeutic relationship, and intervention. Much has been learned over the past century from basic and applied psychological research as well as from observations and hypotheses developed in clinical practice. Many strategies for working with patients have emerged and been refined through the kind of trial and error and clinical hypothesis generation and testing that constitute the most scientific aspect of clinical practice. Yet clinical hypothesis testing has its limits, hence the need to integrate clinical expertise with best available research.

Perhaps the central message of this task force report, and one of the most heartening aspects of the process that led to it, is the consensus achieved among a diverse group of scientists, clinicians, and scientist-clinicians from multiple perspectives that EBPP requires an appreciation of the value of multiple sources of scientific evidence. In a given clinical circumstance, psychologists of good faith and good judgment may disagree about how best to weight different forms of evidence; over time, we presume that systematic and broad empirical inquiry—in the laboratory and in the clinic—will point the way toward best practice in integrating best evidence. What this document reflects, however, is a reassertion of what psychologists have known for a century: that the scientific method is a way of thinking and observing systematically and is the best tool we have for learning about what works for whom.

Clinical decisions should be made in collaboration with the patient, based on the best clinically relevant evidence, and with consideration for the probable costs, benefits, and available resources and options. It is the treating psychologist who makes the ultimate judgment regarding a particular intervention or treatment plan. The involvement of an active, informed patient is generally crucial to the success of psychological services. Treatment decisions should never be made by untrained persons unfamiliar with the specifics of the case.

The treating psychologist determines the applicability of research conclusions to a particular patient. Individual patients may require decisions and interventions not directly addressed by the available research. The application of research evidence to a given patient always involves probabilistic inferences. Therefore, ongoing monitoring of patient progress and adjustment of treatment as needed are essential to EBPP.

Moreover, psychologists must attend to a range of outcomes that may sometimes suggest one strategy and sometimes another and to the strengths and limitations of available research vis-à-vis these different ways of measuring success. Psychological outcomes may include not only symptom relief and prevention of future symptomatic episodes but also quality of life, adaptive functioning in work and relationships, ability to make satisfying life choices, personality change, and other goals arrived at in collaboration between patient and clinician.

EBPP is a means to enhance the delivery of services to patients within an atmosphere of mutual respect, open communication, and collaboration among all stakeholders, including practitioners, researchers, patients, health care managers, and policy-makers. Our goal in this document, and in the deliberations of the Task Force that led to it, was to set both an agenda and a tone for the next steps in the evolution of EBPP.

Brent D. Slife and
Dennis C. Wendt

 **NO**

The Next Step in the Evidence-Based Practice Movement

Nearly everyone agrees that psychological practice should be informed by evidence (Westen & Bradley, 2005, p. 266; Norcross, Beutler, & Levant, 2006, p. 7). However, there is considerable disagreement about what qualifies as evidence (e.g., Reed, 2006; Kihlstrom, 2006; Messer, 2006; Westen, 2006; Stirman & DeRubeis, 2006). This disagreement is not a simple scientific dispute to be resolved in the laboratory, but rather a "culture war" between different worldviews (Messer, 2004, p. 580). As Carol Tavris (2003) put it, this "war" involves "deeply held beliefs, political passions, views of human nature and the nature of knowledge, and—as all wars ultimately involve—money, territory, and livelihoods" (as qtd. in Norcross et al., p. 8).

How does one address a cultural battle of deeply held worldviews and political passions? We believe the approaches that have tried to address it so far in psychology have been well-intended and even headed in the right direction, but are ultimately and fundamentally inadequate. We will first describe what we consider the two major steps in this regard, beginning with the empirically supported treatment (EST) movement, which still has considerable energy in the discipline, and then moving to the "common factors" approach, which recently culminated in a policy regarding evidence-based practice (EBP) in psychology from the American Psychological Association (APA, 2006). We specifically focus on the latter, extolling its goals, but noting their distinct lack of fulfillment. We then offer what seems to us the logical extension of these first two steps—what could be called "objective methodological pluralism" in the spirit of one of our discipline's founding parents, William James (1902/1985; 1907/1975).

The First Step: The EST Movement

Psychology's first step in addressing this evidence controversy involved a succession of APA Division 12 (Clinical) task forces. Beginning in 1993, these task forces have "constructed and elaborated a list of empirically supported, manualized psychological interventions for specific disorders" (Norcross et al., 2006, p. 5). In other words, this first step assumed that the battle of worldviews would be resolved through rigorous scientific evidence. "Rigorous evidence," in this case, was idealized as the randomized clinical (or controlled) trial (RCT), widely esteemed as the gold standard of evidence in medicine. The advantages of this step were obvious. Third-party payers were familiar with this gold standard from medicine, and many psychologists believed that an EST list would provide a clear-cut index of "proven" treatments, not to mention greater respect from medicine.

Unfortunately, this seemingly rigorous, clear-cut approach has manifested more than a few problems (Westen & Bradley, 2005; Messer, 2004). Much like the testing movement in education, where teachers found themselves "teaching to the test," psychologists found their practices being shaped by the RCT "test." The critics of the RCT showed how professional practices were conforming, consciously or unconsciously, to the RCT worldview in order to make the EST list. In other words, the practices being studied tended to accommodate the particular RCT perspective on treatments, therapists, and patients.

With regard to treatments, this medical-model worldview of the RCT is biased toward "packaged" treatments for well-defined, compartmentalized disorders (e.g., Bohart, O'Hara, & Leitner, 1998). This model of treatment took its cues from the pharmaceutical industry, where "one must specify the treatment and make sure it is being applied correctly" (p. 143). According to this model, every patient would receive the same thing, and it is this thing, not the therapist or patient, that is considered the agent of change. Critics have argued that this view of treatment undermined many types of therapy, such as humanistic or psychodynamic therapies, in which "treatment" does not entail a manualized set of principles (e.g., Bohart et al.; Safran, 2001).

A related argument against this packaged view of treatment concerned the role of therapists. The assumptions or worldview of the RCT, these critics contended, turned the therapist into an interchangeable part, discounting the importance of the therapist's distinctive personality, practical wisdom, and unique relationship with the patient. Many researchers have worried, to use the words of Allen Bergin (1997), that the RCT manualization of treatments turned therapists into "cookie cutters" and researchers into "mechanotropes" (pp. 85–86). This worry has been validated by research suggesting that manualization often hinders important therapeutic factors, such as the therapeutic alliance and the therapist's genuineness, creativity, motivation, and emotional involvement (Duncan & Miller, 2006; Piper & Ogrodniczuk, 1999).

Third, critics have noted that the biases of RCTs shaped one's view of the patient, assuming that researchers and clinicians work with pure patient pathologies only. According to this argument, RCTs are limited to patients with textbook symptoms of a single DSM disorder; thus, their results "may apply only to a narrow and homogeneous group of patients" (Butcher, Mineka, & Hooley, 2004, p. 563). This limitation is no small problem, critics have warned, because the vast majority of U.S. patients are not pathologically "pure" in this narrow RCT sense. Rather, they are co- or "multi"-morbid in the sense that they are an amalgam of disorders (Morrison, Bradley, & Westen, 2003; Westen & Bradley, 2005). The prevalence of these "messy" patients is corroborated by the 35%–70% exclusion rates of RCTs for major disorders (Morrison et al., p. 110).

The common theme behind the above criticisms is that the biases of the EST movement stem from its narrow framework for validating evidence. Thus, it is not mere coincidence, critics have argued, that therapies that exemplify this type of treatment (e.g., behavioral or cognitive-behavioral treatments) are the most frequently listed as ESTs (Messer, 2004). The exclusion of other types of therapy (e.g., humanistic and psychodynamic therapies) has prompted critics to contend that the EST movement constitutes a methodological bias toward behavioral and cognitive-behavioral therapies (e.g., Slife, Wiggins, & Graham; Messer, 2004). If this first step has taught psychologists anything, it has taught that what the evidence seems to say has a great deal to do with what one considers evidence.

The Second Step: The Common Factors Movement

The second step—the common factors movement—was, in part, an attempt to learn from the shortcomings of the EST movement. Common factors advocates have argued that a focus on specific, "packaged" treatments for specific disorders is a narrow way of conceptualizing psychological research and practice (e.g., Westen & Bradley, 2005; Bohart et al., 1998). An alternative approach is to discover and validate factors of therapeutic change that are common across treatments. In this way, responsibility for change is not just attributed to the treatment, as in ESTs. Change is considered the result of a dynamic relationship among the "common factors" of therapy, which include the therapist, patient, and technique (APA, 2006, p. 275).

A common factors approach is especially appealing to the majority of practitioners, who consider themselves eclectics or integrationists. Its popularity has helped it to play a significant role in shaping APA's (2006) new policy statement on evidence-based practice. For this policy statement, evidence was liberalized not only to include studies of therapist and patient variables but also to include other methods than RCTs for conducting these studies (pp. 274–75). The main guideposts for selecting these methods, according to the underlying rationale of the APA policy, were their objectivity and their diversity. Methods should be *objective* to prevent the intrusion of human error and bias that would distort the findings (p. 276), and they should be *diverse* to prevent the shaping of practice that a focus on only one method might produce, such as the problems created by RCTs (pp. 272–74).

The problem, from our perspective, is that the APA culmination of this common factors approach is not objective and diverse enough. In other words, we applaud the goals but criticize the implementation. The APA policy is a clear step forward, in our view, but its conceptions of objectivity and diversity are inadequate. As we will attempt to show, this inadequacy means that the lessons of the EST movement have not been sufficiently learned. Recall that this first step restricted itself to a single ideal of evidence, the RCT, and thus disallowed any true diversity of methods. Recall also that several biases resulted from this restriction, obviating objectivity and shaping practice even before investigation. As we will argue, this same lack of diversity and objectivity has continued into the second approach to the evidence controversy.

Our basic criticism is this: Just as an EST framework uncritically restricts acceptable evidence to a *single method* ideal (the RCT), so does the APA policy uncritically restrict acceptable evidence to a *single epistemology.* By "epistemology" we mean the philosophy of knowing that provides the logic and guides the conduct of a group of methods (Slife & Williams, 1995). Although the EST framework is biased toward a certain *method,* the common factors framework is biased toward a certain *methodology—*a narrow brand of *empiricism.*

According to this empiricist epistemology, "we can only know, or know best, those aspects of our experience that are sensory" (Slife, Wiggins, & Graham, 2005, p. 84). This narrow conception of empiricism is fairly traditional in psychology. More liberal usages of empiricism differ substantially, such as William James' radical empiricism. James' empiricism encompasses "the whole of experience," including *non*-sensory experiences such as thoughts, emotions, and even spiritual experiences (James, 1902/1985; 1907/1975). Still, psychologists have interpreted the natural sciences to be grounded in the narrow empiricism. Historically, psychologists have wanted to be both rigorously scientific and comparable to medicine, leading them to embrace the narrower empiricism. As we will attempt to show, however, this restriction to a single epistemology is not based on evidence. Analogous to the EST restriction to a single method, the APA policy merely assumes and never justifies empiricism as the only appropriate epistemology for evidence-based practice, in spite of other promising epistemologies.

The reason for this lack of justification seems clear. Throughout much of the history of psychology, empiricism has been mistakenly understood not as a *particular* philosophy of science, but as a *non*-philosophy that makes reality transparent. Analogous to the way in which many EST proponents view RCTs, empiricism is not *a* way to understand evidence, but *the* way. Consequently, nowhere in the APA policy or its underlying report is a rationale provided for a commitment to empirical research, and nowhere is a consideration given for even the possibility of a "non-empirical" contribution to evidence-based practice.

This equation of evidence with empiricism is directly parallel to the EST movement's equation of evidence with RCT findings. Just as Westen and Bradley (2005) noted that "EBP > EST" (p. 271), we note that EBP > empirical. After all, there is no empirical evidence for empiricism, or for RCTs, for that matter. Both sets of methods spring from the human invention of philosophers and other humanists. Moses did not descend Mt. Sinai with the Ten Commandments in one hand and the principles of science in the other. Moreover, these principles could not have been scientifically derived, because one would need the principles (before their derivation) to conduct the scientific investigations to derive them.

Indeed, the irony of this epistemology's popularity is that many observers of psychology have long considered empiricism to be deeply problematic for psychological research. Again, the parallel to the dominance of RCTs is striking. Just as the majority of real-world patients, therapists, and treatments were perceived to defy RCT categories, so too the majority of real-world phenomena can be perceived to defy empirical categories. Indeed, many of the common factors for evidence-based practice are not, strictly speaking, empirical at all.

Rather, they are experiences and meanings that are not sensory, and thus not observable, in nature (Slife et al., 2005, p. 88).

Consider, for example, the efforts of APA Division 29 (Psychotherapy) to provide empirical support for therapy relationships, such as therapeutic alliance and group cohesion (Norcross, 2001; APA, 2006, p. 272). Although patients and therapists probably experience this alliance and cohesion, these relationships literally never fall on their retinas. The people involved in these relationships are observable in this sense, to be sure, but the "betweenness" of these relations—the actual alliance or cohesion themselves—never are. Their unobservability means, according to the method requirements of empiricism, that they must be operationalized, or made observable. Thus, it is not surprising, given its commitment to a narrow empiricism, that the APA policy report presumes that operationalization is a requirement of method (p. 274).

The problem with this requirement, however, is that any specified operationalization, such as a patient's feelings about the relationship (e.g., Norcross, 2002), can occur without the therapeutic alliance, and any such alliance can occur without the specified operationalization. The upshot is that the construct (e.g., alliance) and the operationalization are two different things, yet the operationalization is the only thing studied in traditional research. Moreover, one can never know empirically the relation between the construct and its operationalization because pivotal aspects of this relation—the construct and relation itself—are never observable. Thus, APA's policy runs the risk of making psychotherapy research a compendium of operationalizations without any knowledge of how they relate to what psychologists want to study.

Problems such as these are the reason that alternative philosophies of science, such as qualitative methods, were formulated. Many qualitative methods were specifically formulated to investigate unobservable, but experienced, meanings of the world (Denzin & Lincoln, 2000; Patton, 1990; Slife & Gantt, 1999). The existence of this alternative philosophy of science implies another problem with the unjustified empiricist framework of the APA policy report—it runs roughshod over alternative frameworks, such as qualitative methods. Although the policy includes qualitative research on its list of acceptable methods (APA, p. 274), it fails to understand and value qualitative research as a different philosophy of science.

A clear indication of this failure is the use of the word "subjective" when the report describes the purpose of qualitative research (p. 274). In the midst of a report that extols "objective" inquiry, relegating only qualitative methods to the "subjective" is second-class citizenship, at best. More importantly, this relegation only makes sense within an empiricist framework. In non-empiricist philosophies, such as those underlying many qualitative methods, the notions of "objective" and "subjective" are largely irrelevant because most non-empiricist conceptions of science do not assume the dualism of a subjective and objective realm (Slife, 2005).

The bottom line is that a common factors approach to the evidence controversy is a clear advancement of the EBP project, but it is not an unqualified advance. Indeed, it recapitulates some of the same problems that it is attempting to correct. In both the EST and the common factors approaches, criteria for what is evidence shape not only the studies conducted but also the practices considered supported. Indeed, we would contend there is no method or methodology that is not ultimately biased in this regard. As philosophers of science have long taught, all methods of investigation must make assumptions about the world *before* it is investigated (Curd & Cover, 1998). The question remains, however, whether there can be a framework for understanding evidence that does not *automatically* shape practice before it is investigated.

Presaging the Next Step: The Ideas of William James

The answer, we believe, is "yes," and we do not have to reinvent the wheel to formulate this alternative. One of the intellectual parents of our discipline, William James, has already pointed the way. Consequently, we will first briefly describe three of James' pivotal ideas: his radical empiricism, his pluralism, and his pragmatism. Then, we will apply these ideas to the evidence-based practice issue, deriving our alternative to the current monopoly of empiricism—objective methodological pluralism.

James was actually quite critical of what psychologists consider empirical today. As mentioned above, his radical empiricism embraces the whole of experience, including non-sensory experiences such as thoughts, emotions, and spiritual experiences (James, 1902/1985; 1907/1975). His position implies, as he explicitly recognizes, that there are several epistemologies of investigation ("ways of knowing") rather than just one. As James (1909/1977) put it, "nothing includes everything" (p. 145). In other words, no philosophy of science is sufficient to understand everything.

Psychology needs, instead, a *pluralism* of such philosophies, which is the second of James's ideas and an intriguing way to actualize APA's desire for diversity. In other words, we not only need a diversity of methods, which the APA report (2006) clearly concedes (p. 274), we also need a diversity of *methodologies* or philosophies underlying these methods. It is not coincidental, in this regard, that James (1902/1985) used qualitative methods to investigate spiritual meanings in his famous work, *Varieties of Religious Experiences.* His pluralism of methods dictated that he should not change or operationalize his phenomena of study to fit the method, but that he should change his method to best illuminate the phenomena—spiritual phenomena, in this case.

This approach to method implies the third of James's ideas—his pragmatism. According to James:

> Rationalism sticks to logic and . . . empiricism sticks to the external senses. Pragmatism is willing to take anything, to follow either logic or the senses and to count the humblest and most personal of experiences. [Pragmatism] will count mystical experiences if they have practical consequences. (James, 1907/1975, p. 61)

As James implies, the heart of pragmatism is the notion that one should never approach the study or understanding of anything with fixed schemes and methods. There is too much danger that the method will distort understanding of the phenomena being studied. This is not to say that one can or should approach such phenomena without some method or interpretive framework. Yet this framework does not have to be cast in stone; psychologists should allow the phenomenon itself to guide the methods we choose to study it.

This pragmatism may sound complicated, but it is not significantly different from what good carpenters do at every job—they let the task dictate the tools they use. They have a pluralism of tools or methods, rather than just one, because many tasks cannot be done with just one tool, such as a hammer. Moreover, not every carpentry job can be "operationalized" into a set of "nails." As Dupré (1993) and others (e.g., Feyerabend, 1975; Viney, 2004) have noted, this pragmatism is the informal meta-method of physics, where the object of study is the primary consideration, and the method of studying it is a secondary consideration.

By contrast, APA's version of evidence-based practice is method-driven rather than object-driven. That is to say, psychologists have decided the logic of their investigation before they even consider what they are studying. If the object of study does not fit this logic, they have no choice but to modify it to fit this logic through operationalization. For example, an unobservable feeling, such as sadness, becomes operationalized as an observable behavior, such as crying.

The irony of this familiar research practice is that psychologists are driven more by an unrecognized and unexamined philosophy of science, as manifested through their methods, than by the objects they are studying. Indeed, they are changing their object of study—from sadness to crying—to accommodate this philosophy. We believe that this accommodation is contrary to good science, where everything including the philosophies that ground one's methods, should be subject to examination and comparison.

The Next Step: Objective Methodological Pluralism

This description of James' three pivotal ideas—his radical empiricism, pluralism, and pragmatism—sets the stage for our proposal on evidence-based practice: "objective methodological pluralism." First, this pluralism assumes a broader empiricism, in the spirit of James. To value only sensory experiences, as does the conventional empiricist, is to affirm a value that is itself unproven and non-empirical. There simply is no conceptual or empirical necessity to value only the sensory. We recognize that many would claim the success of this value in science, but we also recognize that no scientific comparison between such philosophical values has occurred. These claims of success, then, are merely opinion, uninformed by scientific findings.

In practical terms, this move from conventional empiricism to radical empiricism means that alternative methods, such as qualitative methods, are no longer second class citizens. They are no longer "subjective" and experimental methods considered "objective," because all methods ultimately depend on experiences of one sort or another. This creates more of a level playing field for methods—a pluralism—and allows for an even-handed assessment of each method's advantages and disadvantages.

Unlike the APA policy's conception, the criteria of this assessment are not already controlled by one, unexamined philosophy of science. They are guided, instead, by the object of one's study. This is the reason for the term "objective" in our alternative, *objective* methodological pluralism. Methods, we believe, should be driven not by some philosophy of method that is deemed to be correct *before* the object of study has even been considered. Methods should be driven by consideration of the objects themselves.

This consideration is itself evaluated pragmatically, in terms of the practical differences it makes in the lives of patients. As James realized, any evaluation of practical significance begs the question of "significant to what?" In other words, any methodological pluralism requires thoughtful disciplinary discussion of the moral issues of psychology, a discussion that has begun in a limited way in positive psychology (Seligman, 2002): What is the good life for a patient? When is a life truly flourishing? Such questions cannot be derived from the "is" of research; they must be discussed as the "ought" that guides this research and determines what practical significance really means.

Obviously, much remains to be worked out with a Jamesian pluralism. Still, we believe that this particular "working out" is not only possible but also necessary. The monopoly and problems of empiricism—the lessons of our first two steps in the evidence controversy—do not go away with a rejection of this pluralism. This is the reason we titled this article "the next step"—the difficulties with empiricism and APA's desire for diversity lead us logically, we believe, to this next general step. Admittedly, this kind of pluralism is a challenging prospect. Still, if carpenters can do it in a less complex enterprise, surely psychologists can. In any case, it is high time that psychologists face up to the challenge, because ignoring it will not make it go away.

All references for articles included in *Taking Sides: Clashing Views on Psychological Issues, 17/e* can be found on the Web at http://www.mhhe.com/cls.

CHALLENGE QUESTIONS

Are Traditional Empirical Methods Sufficient to Provide Evidence for Psychological Practice?

1. The label "objective" is typically used only in reference to empirical evidence. Why is this typical, and what would Slife and Wendt say about this practice?

2. The APA Task Force bases its definition of evidence-based practice on a conception formulated by the Institute of Medicine. Find out what this definition is and form your own informed opinion about its relevance or irrelevance to psychotherapy. Support your answer.

3. Many people think they would feel safer if their therapist used practices that have been validated by science. Explain what it is about science that leads people to feel this way.

4. William James is known as the father of American psychology. Why do you think the APA has largely neglected to take his pluralism into consideration?

5. Slife and Wendt believe that the methods of psychology (and any other science, for that matter) are based on and guided by philosophies, yet few psychology texts discuss these philosophies. Why do you feel that this is the case, and is the absence of this discussion justified?

ISSUE 6

Does Teaching Scientific Determinism Lead to Bad Behavior?

YES: **Kathleen D. Vohs and Jonathan W. Schooler,** from "The Value of Believing in Free Will: Encouraging a Belief in Determinism Increases Cheating," *Psychological Science* (vol. 19, no. 1, 2008)

NO: **Eddy Nahmias,** from "Why 'Willusionism' Leads to 'Bad Results': Comments on Baumeister, Crescioni, and Alquist," *Neuroethics* (July 31, 2009)

ISSUE SUMMARY

YES: Marketing professor Kathleen Vohs and psychology professor Jonathan Schooler attempt to demonstrate that a scientific belief in determinism (that humans lack free will) leads to a host of bad behaviors such as lying, cheating, and stealing.

NO: Eddy Nahmias, a philosopher with the Neuroscience Institute at Georgia State University, counters the claim that such scientific beliefs cause bad behavior by arguing that laypersons fail to understand what scientists are actually saying about determinism.

Have you ever wondered why you sometimes do "bad" things, even if you think you should not? Psychological researchers have long attempted to understand what leads individuals to "immoral" behavior. Previous work on the subject has pointed to factors such as social pressure (Zimbardo, 2007), authority figures (Milgram, 1963), and self-interest (Levitt and Dubner, 2009). Among the most important factors considered responsible for bad behavior are certain cognitive processes such as thoughts, intentions, or beliefs. Recently, one particular belief has become the subject of considerable study and debate—belief in determinism or the lack of human free will.

Although the issue of free will is not new to psychology, recent scholarly publications have distanced themselves from debating about whether humans actually *possess* a free will and instead have sought to understand what the consequences of this belief might be. In other words, does believing in free will lead to better outcomes, such as job success and prosocial behavior?

Conversely, is the belief that historical and environmental factors completely determine our actions an important impetus for our bad behavior? In other words, if psychologists advocate for a deterministic position, might they inadvertently encourage immorality?

Vohs and Schooler suggest that this just might be the case. In "The Value of Believing in Free Will," they argue that exposure to deterministic statements and ideas causes subjects to lie, cheat, and steal more than counterparts who are exposed to free will or neutral statements. They conducted two research studies that seemed to show that college students' behavior was negatively affected by exposure to a deterministic message from a notable scientist. They further argued that this message affected *belief* in free will, which mediated the cheating behavior.

Eddy Nahmias sees the issue differently. He does not directly dispute the results of the studies by Kathleen D. Vohs and Jonathan W. Schooler or those of other researchers who have claimed that disbelief in free will leads to bad behavior. However, he argues that what is happening is a misunderstanding between philosophers, scientists, and the general population. Although scientists may say that humans do not possess free will, they do not mean by this that humans "lack the powers of rational choice and self-control." Still, Eddy Nahmias argues, this is precisely what laypersons understand from those statements. He attributes the "bad results" (e.g., increased cheating) not to scientists' disbelief in free will, but to misunderstandings about what scientists mean about determinism.

References

Levitt, S. D., and Dubner, S. J. (2009). *Freakonomics: A rogue economist explores the hidden side of everything.* New York: Harper Perennial.

Milgram, S. (1963). Behavioral study of obedience. *Journal of Abnormal and Social Psychology, 67*(4), 371–378.

Zimbardo, P. (2007). *The Lucifer effect: How good people turn evil.* New York: Random House.

POINT	COUNTERPOINT
• Scientific ideas about determinism are incompatible with free will.	• Beliefs about free will and determinism are not mutually exclusive.
• Reducing morality to brain chemistry may lower personal responsibility.	• Neurological determinism can be compatible with personal responsibility.
• Belief in scientific determinism leads to bad behavior.	• Belief in fatalism leads to "bad results."
• Advocating a deterministic worldview undermines moral behavior.	• Scientists need to be more careful in explaining their worldview as it does not undermine moral behavior.
• Whether or not free will exists, it is valuable to *believe* that it does.	• What is valuable to believe in is what actually exists, our powers of rationality.

YES

Kathleen D. Vohs and
Jonathan W. Schooler

The Value of Believing in Free Will: Encouraging a Belief in Determinism Increases Cheating

> We are always ready to take refuge in a belief in determinism if this
> freedom weighs upon us or if we need an excuse. (Sartre, 1943/1956,
> pp. 78–79)

The belief that one determines one's own outcomes is strong and pervasive. In a massive survey of people in 36 countries, more than 70% agreed with the statement that their fate is in their own hands (International Social Survey Programme, 1998). Yet the view from the scientific community is that behavior is caused by genes underlying personality dispositions, brain mechanisms, or features of the environment (e.g., Bargh, 2006; Crick, 1994; Pinker, 2002). There is reason to think that scientists' sentiment is spreading to nonscientists. For example, the news magazine *The Economist* recently ran the headline, "Free to Choose? Modern Neuroscience Is Eroding the Idea of Free Will" ("Free to Choose?" 2006). What would happen if people came to believe that their behavior is the inexorable product of a causal chain set into motion without their own volition? Would people carry on, selves and behavior unperturbed, or, as Sartre suggested, might the adoption of a deterministic worldview serve as an excuse for untoward behaviors?

It is well established that changing people's sense of responsibility can change their behavior. For example, invoking a sense of personal accountability causes people to modify their behavior to better align with their attitudes (Harmon-Jones & Mills, 1999). Believing that outcomes are based on an inborn trait, rather than effort, also influences behavior. For instance, Mueller and Dweck (1998) observed 10-year-old children who were told that they had been successful on an initial task either as the result of their intelligence or through their hard work. In a second round, all the children encountered a task that was well beyond their performance level (i.e., they failed at it). When the children were given yet a third task, those who thought their earlier success was due to their intelligence put forth less effort and reported lower enjoyment than those who thought their initial success was due to their own effort. The authors concluded that the former children's belief that their performance was linked to

From *Psychological Science*, vol. 19, no. 1, 2008, pp. 49–54. Copyright © 2008 by Sage
Publications—Journals. Reprinted by permission via Rightslink.

their intelligence indicated to them that achieving a high score on the difficult problems in the second round was beyond their ability. Hence, faring poorly (on an admittedly difficult task) indicated to children in the intelligence condition that they were simply not smart enough for the task, which in turn led them to stop trying to perform well and to like the task less.

If reducing people's sense of control also reduces the amount of effort they put toward improving their performance, then advocating a deterministic worldview that dismisses individual causation may similarly promote undesirable behavior. In this vein, Peale (1989) bemoaned how quickly and consistently deviant behavior is tagged a "disease," a label that obviates personal responsibility for its occurrence. As a recent *Washington Post* article on neuroscience and moral behavior put it succinctly, "Reducing morality and immorality to brain chemistry—rather than free will—might diminish the importance of personal responsibility" (Vedantam, 2007, p. A01).

Although some people have speculated about the societal risks that might result from adopting a viewpoint that denies personal responsibility for actions, this hypothesis has not been explored empirically. In the two experiments reported here, we manipulated beliefs related to free will and measured their influence on morality as manifested in cheating behavior. We hypothesized that participants induced to believe that human behavior is under the control of predetermined forces would cheat more than would participants not led to believe that behavior is predetermined. Our experimental results supported this hypothesis.

Experiment 1
Method

Participants
Participants were 30 undergraduates (13 females, 17 males).

Procedure
Participants came to the lab individually. First, according to the condition to which they were randomly assigned, they read one of two passages from *The Astonishing Hypothesis,* a book written by Francis Crick (1994), the Nobel-prize-winning scientist. In the *anti-free-will* condition, participants read statements claiming that rational, high-minded people—including, according to Crick, most scientists—now recognize that actual free will is an illusion, and also claiming that the idea of free will is a side effect of the architecture of the mind. In the *control* condition, participants read a passage from a chapter on consciousness, which did not discuss free will. After reading their assigned material, participants completed the Free Will and Determinism scale (FWD; Paulhus & Margesson, 1994) and the Positive and Negative Affectivity Schedule (PANAS; Watson, Clark, & Tellegen, 1988), which we used to assess whether the reading manipulation affected their beliefs and mood.

Subsequently, participants were given a computer-based mental-arithmetic task (von Hippel, Lakin, & Shakarchi, 2005) in which they were asked to calculate the answers to 20 problems (e.g., $1 + 8 + 18 - 12 + 19 - 7 + 17 - 2 + 8 - 4 = ?$), presented individually. They were told that the computer had a programming glitch and the correct answer would appear on the screen while they were attempting to solve each problem, but that they could stop the answer from being displayed by pressing the space bar after the problem appeared. Furthermore, participants were told that although the experimenter would not know whether they had pressed the space bar, they should try to solve the problems honestly, on their own. In actuality, the computer had been rigged not only to show the answers, but also to record the number of space-bar presses. The dependent measure of cheating was the number of times participants pressed the space bar to prevent the answer from appearing. Afterward, participants were debriefed and thanked for their participation.

Results

Scores on the FWD Scale

We first checked to see whether participants' beliefs about free will were affected by the excerpts they read (anti-free-will vs. control condition). As expected, scores on the Free Will sub-scale of the FWD scale showed that participants in the anti-free-will condition reported weaker free-will beliefs ($M = 13.6$, $SD = 2.66$) than participants in the control condition ($M = 16.8$, $SD = 2.67$), $t(28) = 3.28$, $p < .01$. Scores on the other three subscales of the FWD scale (Fate, Scientific Causation, and Chance) did not differ as a function of condition, $ts < 1$.

Cheating

We first recoded the dependent measure by subtracting the number of space-bar presses from 20, so that higher scores indicated more cheating. Analysis of the main dependent measure, degree of cheating, revealed that, as predicted, participants cheated more frequently after reading the anti-free-will essay ($M = 14.00$, $SD = 4.17$) than after reading the control essay ($M = 9.67$, $SD = 5.58$), $t(28) = 3.04$, $p < .01$.

Does Rejecting the Idea of Free Will Lead to Cheating?

To test our hypothesis that cheating would increase after participants were persuaded that free will does not exist, we first calculated the correlation between scores on the Free Will subscale and cheating behavior. As expected, we found a strong negative relationship, $r(30) = -.53$, such that weaker endorsement of the notion that personal behavior is determined by one's own will was associated with more instances of cheating.

We next performed a mediation analysis to test our prediction that degree of belief in free will would determine degree of cheating. Using analysis of covariance (ANCOVA), we found support for this hypothesis: When Free Will subscale scores were entered as a predictor of cheating alongside experimental condition, the effect of condition failed to predict cheating, $F < 1$, whereas the effect of free-will beliefs remained significant, $F(1, 27) = 7.81$, $p < .01$.

Ancillary Measure: Mood
To ensure that the essays did not inadvertently alter participants' moods, we assessed positive and negative emotions using the PANAS. Mood did not differ between conditions, $ts < 1.35$, $ps > .19$.

Experiment 2

In Experiment 1, participants cheated more frequently on a simple arithmetic task after reading an essay that refuted the notion of free will than after reading a neutral essay. Moreover, reading the anti-free-will essay reduced participants' belief in free will, a change that accounted for the impact of the essay on cheating behavior.

Although the evidence in Experiment 1 is strong statistically, the way in which cheating was operationalized clouds interpretation of the results. Recall that cheating behavior was measured by the number of instances in which participants allowed answers to math questions to appear when they were supposed to be calculating the answers mentally. Although this is a well-validated method of assessing cheating (von Hippel et al., 2005), note that simply doing nothing is coded as cheating. Hence, the anti-free-will essay may have induced passivity generally, rather than immoral behavior specifically. Although participants were instructed to press the space bar to avoid receiving the answers, their failure to do so—counted as cheating—may not have been deliberately unethical.

Experiment 2 addressed this limitation by using a task that required active behavior in order to cheat (Mazar, Amir, & Ariely, 2007) and that made clear the moral ramifications of an infraction. We also included a condition intended to strengthen free-will beliefs so that we could systematically test our hypothesis about the relation between strength of free-will beliefs and moral behavior. Finally, to bolster confidence in the interpretation of our results, we added conditions in which we obtained participants' scores on the task when they could not cheat.

Method

Participants
Participants were 122 undergraduates (46 females, 75 males, 1 participant who did not specify gender). Data from 3 participants were unusable: One participant was a friend of the experimenter, and in two cases in which participants had the opportunity to cheat, only 1 person arrived at the experiment, which meant that a sense of anonymity was absent (see the next paragraph).

Procedure
Participants were randomly assigned to one of five conditions, in three of which cheating was possible. In the cheating-possible conditions (namely, the free-will, determinism, and neutral conditions), participants arrived at the laboratory in groups of 2 to 5, but were immediately shown to individual carrels,

where they performed all tasks individually. This arrangement promoted a sense of anonymity, which was relevant for the cheating opportunity. In the two noncheating conditions, participants reported to the laboratory individually and were not given an opportunity to cheat.

In the cheating-possible conditions, participants first completed a task, similar to one used by Velten (1968), that involved reading and considering a series of statements meant to change beliefs or feelings. Participants were given a booklet of 15 statements (1 per page) and were asked to think about each statement for 1 min before turning the page. A tape-recorded voice indicated when to turn the page.

Belief in free will was manipulated by varying the content of the statements. In the *free-will* condition, participants read statements such as, "I am able to override the genetic and environmental factors that sometimes influence my behavior," and "Avoiding temptation requires that I exert my free will." In the *determinism* condition, participants read statements such as, "A belief in free will contradicts the known fact that the universe is governed by lawful principles of science," and "Ultimately, we are biological computers—designed by evolution, built through genetics, and programmed by the environment." In the *neutral* condition, participants read statements such as, "Sugar cane and sugar beets are grown in 112 countries." The neutral statements came from Velten's (1968) original method, whereas we created the free-will and determinism statements. After participants read and pondered all of the statements, they completed the FWD scale (Paulhus & Margesson, 1994) and the PANAS (Watson et al., 1988).

We then orchestrated an opportunity to cheat (e.g., Mazar et al., 2007). Participants were given a set of 15 reading-comprehension, mathematical, and logic and reasoning problems taken from the Graduate Record Examination practice tests. This type of task has been used previously to present subjects with a challenging but solvable set of problems (Schmeichel, Vohs, & Baumeister, 2003). Participants were told that the experimenter was investigating people's enjoyment of tasks when they receive feedback and rewards for performance, and hence that they would receive $1 for each problem they solved correctly.

At this point, the experimenter looked at her cellular telephone and announced that she had suddenly realized she had a meeting to attend. She indicated that participants should work for a maximum of 15 min, and then score their own problems and pay themselves $1 for each correct answer. The experimenter motioned to several answer sheets and a manila envelope containing $1 coins. She told participants to use the mechanical shredder to shred their answer sheets because she did not have permission to keep the sheets. The experimenter left the room but waited outside to debrief participants as they exited. Although this procedure did not allow us to determine individual participants' scores on the task or the amount of money each participant paid him- or herself, we were able to calculate the average payment per participant, and this average served as a proxy for each participant's number of correct answers.

Two comparison conditions, labeled *baseline experimenter-scored* and *determinism experimenter-scored,* enabled us to measure veridically the number of questions that participants answered correctly (i.e., when participants were not in the self-scoring, self-payment situation). In the baseline experimenter-scored condition, participants simply completed the cognitive problems, which the experimenter scored; participants then received $1 for each correct answer. We did not ask participants in this condition to complete the FWD scale so as not to activate the concept of free will. In the determinism experimenter-scored condition, we gave participants the determinism statements and then the logic problems. The experimenter scored the problems and paid participants $1 for each correct answer. This comparison condition allowed us to assess whether reading the scientific-sounding determinism statements had the incidental effect of aiding in solving the logic problems.

Thus, there were three comparison conditions we could use to examine the effects of the determinism and free-will manipulations on cheating: a neutral condition, in which participants were allowed to cheat but were not exposed to statements that might change their beliefs about free will; a baseline experimenter-scored condition, in which participants' true scores on the cognitive task were calculated without any manipulation; and a determinism experimenter-scored condition, in which participants read deterministic statements but were not allowed to cheat, so that their true scores on the problem set were known.

Results

Scores on the FWD Scale
Participants in the free-will, determinism, and neutral conditions completed the FWD scale so that we could check whether the manipulations in the statement-reading task had been effective. Scores on the Free Will subscale differed as a function of condition, $F(2, 70) = 17.03$, $p < .01$. A planned contrast revealed that participants in the free-will condition reported stronger beliefs in free will ($M = 23.09$, $SD = 6.42$) than did participants in the neutral condition ($M = 20.04$, $SD = 3.76$), $t(70) = 12.54$, $p < .01$. A second planned contrast showed that participants in the determinism condition reported weaker beliefs in free will ($M = 15.56$, $SD = 2.79$) than did participants in the neutral condition, $t(70) = 3.52$, $p < .01$.

The manipulations also affected endorsement of statements on the Scientific Causation subscale, $F(2, 70) = 5.85$, $p < .01$. Specific contrasts showed that participants in the determinism condition had higher scores ($M = 23.14$, $SD = 2.69$) than those in the neutral and free-will conditions (neutral: $M = 20.40$, $SD = 3.40$; free will: $M = 20.78$, $SD = 3.21$), $t(70) = 2.98$, $p < .01$. Scores on the Fate and Chance subscales were unaffected by the manipulations, $Fs < 0.2$, $ps > .30$.

Assessment of Cheating Behavior
In three conditions, participants paid themselves after scoring (and shredding) their own answer sheets, whereas in two additional conditions, the experimenter paid participants according to their actual performance.

Hence, to assess cheating behavior, we compared payments in the self-paid, cheating-possible groups with payments in the experimenter-scored groups. Recall that we did not have participants' answer sheets in the three self-paid conditions; therefore, we divided the number of $1 coins taken by each group by the number of group members to arrive at an average self-payment. These group averages, along with the known payments in the baseline experimenter-scored and determinism experimenter-scored conditions, were subjected to an analysis of variance, which showed a significant effect of condition, $F(4, 114) = 5.68$, $p < .01$. Planned contrasts revealed that participants who had read the determinism statements and who were allowed to pay themselves for correct answers walked away with more money than the others, $t(114) = 4.48$, $p < .01$ (see Figure 1). None of the other groups differed from each other, $ts < 1$.

Did Changing Beliefs About Free Will Change Cheating Behavior?
To test our hypothesis that discouraging a belief in free will would lead to cheating, we first calculated the correlation between scores on the Free Will subscale and average payments. As expected, we found a strong negative relationship, $r(71) = -.47$, indicating that the more participants endorsed statements of free will, the less they paid themselves (on average) for the self-scored cognitive test.

Next, we performed a mediation analysis to assess our prediction that free-will beliefs determine cheating. In an ANCOVA in which Free Will scores and condition were entered as predictors of cheating, the effect of condition failed to predict cheating behavior, $F < 1$, whereas the effect of free-will beliefs remained significant, $t(67) = 10.72$, $p < .01$.

Ancillary Measure: Mood
To ensure that the statements did not inadvertently alter participants' moods, we assessed positive and negative emotions using the PANAS. There were no differences as a function of condition, $Fs < 1$.

General Discussion

In two experiments, we found that weakening free-will beliefs reliably increased cheating. We measured cheating in Experiment 1 using a passive cheating opportunity. To avoid cheating, participants had to actively prevent the answer to an arithmetic problem from appearing on the computer screen. This scenario is perhaps akin to accidentally receiving too much change from a store clerk but not returning the extra money. In Experiment 2, we measured active cheating. We found that when participants were allowed to pay themselves for each correct answer on a difficult cognitive test, those who read statements promoting a deterministic worldview paid themselves more (in effect, claimed to have answered more items correctly) than did those who read other kinds of statements; moreover, participants who read deterministic statements and who paid

Figure 1

Mean amount of money, in dollars, that participants received in the five conditions in Experiment 2. Participants in the free-will, neutral, and determinism conditions paid themselves $1 for each answer they claimed to have solved. Participants in the two experimenter-scored conditions were paid according to the true number of solutions. Error bars show standard errors.

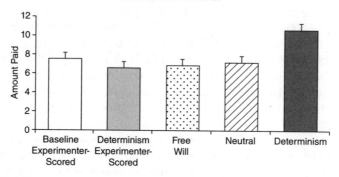

themselves gave themselves more money than was earned by participants who were paid for their true performance.

One limitation of Experiment 2 is that we did not measure the amount of money that each individual took, but rather assessed the total amount of money taken by each group overall. However, this aspect of the procedure had the advantage of allowing participants in the cheating-possible conditions to not only score but also shred their own tests, which was crucial to establishing the anonymity necessary to measure active cheating in the lab. It is possible that only 1 or 2 participants in each group cheated, and that the remainder took their fair share of money (or less). With this procedure, we cannot be sure.

What we do know is that the average take-home pay was far greater for participants in the determinism condition than for participants in any of the other four conditions, including two additional conditions in which participants scored and shredded their own tests. Note, too, that participants who read deterministic statements claimed to have solved more problems correctly than participants who read the same deterministic statements but whose true scores on the logic task were known.

The fact that brief exposure to a message asserting that there is no such thing as free will can increase both passive and active cheating raises the concern that advocating a deterministic worldview could undermine moral behavior. The data from the experiments reported here are consistent with this hypothesis. Reading deterministic statements decreased people's self-reported belief in free will, and this change accounted for heightened cheating. Although people appear to have a tacit, default belief in free will (as evidenced both by participants' default responses on the Free Will subscale and by the lack of a difference in cheating behavior between the free-will and neutral conditions in Experiment 2), participants' views on this topic were in fact quite pliable. Indeed, brief exposure to messages arguing against free will was sufficient to alter participants' views (and consequent actions).

The present findings raise the genuine concern that widespread encouragement of a deterministic worldview may have the inadvertent consequence of encouraging cheating behavior. Consistent with this view are recent trends suggesting both a decrease in beliefs in personal control and an increase in cheating. A recent meta-analysis that took into account cohort effects (Twenge, Zhange, & Im, 2004) revealed substantial changes in Locus of Control scores from the 1960s to the 1990s. The Locus of Control scale (Rotter, 1966) assesses lay beliefs about whether internal (personal) or external (situational) factors are responsible for one's outcomes in life (Rotter, 1966). People's belief that they do not control their own outcomes (external locus of control) jumped more than three quarters of a standard deviation over the decades Twenge et al. studied.

With respect to cheating, reports from the academic realm indicate that levels of cheating have increased recently. One scientist who has been tracking cheating across several decades has found that self-reports of cheating have increased (Schab, 1991). The percentage of students who admitted that they had used a "cheat sheet" on an exam rose from 34% in 1969 to 68% in 1989. Other types of cheating have risen as well (e.g., allowing other students to copy work and lifting statements from printed material; Schab, 1991). There are numerous reasons why self-reported cheating might have increased in recent years. However, the concurrent decrease in belief in an internal locus of control, in combination with our findings, raises the ominous possibility that reduced belief in free will may contribute to an increase in cheating.

Although the study reported here raises concerns about the possible impact of deterministic views on moral behavior, it is important not to over-interpret our findings. Our experiments measured only modest forms of ethical behavior, and whether or not free-will beliefs have the same effect on more significant moral and ethical infractions is unknown. In addition, a deterministic viewpoint may have a host of possible consequences, and only some of these may be unfavorable. For example, adopting the view that behavior is a consequence of environmental and genetic factors could encourage compassion for the mentally ill and discourage retribution in legal contexts (Greene & Cohen, 2004). A deterministic outlook may also enhance people's sensitivity to the subtle influences known to affect their goals and actions (Bargh, 2006).

It is also crucial to emphasize that the findings reported here do not speak to the larger issue of whether free will actually exists. It is possible that free will is an illusion that nevertheless offers some functionality. It may be that a necessary cost of public awareness regarding the science of human behavior will be the dampening of certain beliefs about personal agency (Wegner, 2002). Conversely, it may prove possible to integrate a genuine sense of free will into scientific accounts of human behavior (see Baumeister, 2010; Dennett, 2003; Kane, 1996; Shariff, Schooler, & Vohs, 2008). Although the concept of free will remains scientifically in question, our results point to a significant value in believing that free will exists.

If exposure to deterministic messages increases the likelihood of unethical actions, then identifying approaches for insulating the public against this danger becomes imperative. Ultimately, in order to oppose the unfavorable consequences of deterministic sentiments, the field must first develop a deeper understanding of why dismissing free will leads to amoral behavior. Does the belief that forces outside the self determine behavior drain the motivation to resist the temptation to cheat, inducing a "why bother?" mentality (cf. Baumeister & Vohs, 2007)? Much as thoughts of death and meaninglessness can induce existential angst that can lead to ignoble behaviors (e.g., Arndt, Greenberg, & Solomon, 1997; Heine, Proulx, & Vohs, 2006), doubting one's free will may undermine the sense of self as agent. Or, perhaps, denying free will simply provides the ultimate excuse to behave as one likes.

All references for articles included in *Taking Sides: Clashing Views on Psychological Issues, 17/e* can be found on the Web at http://www.mhhe.com/cls.

Eddy Nahmias

 **NO**

Why 'Willusionism' Leads to 'Bad Results': Comments on Baumeister, Crescioni, and Alquist

Roy Baumeister, A. William Crescioni, and Jessica Alquist [1] are appropriately modest about what psychology can contribute to debates about free will, not because they don't have much to contribute to those debates—they do. Rather, they understand that it is not obvious how people do, or should, understand the concept of free will and that, in part because of this, scientific discoveries can inform debates about free will only to the extent that we are clear about which conception of free will is at issue. Baumeister et al. offer us a particular conception of free will that is naturalistic and useful. Useful because scientific discoveries about human decision-making and self-control, such as those offered in the research they discuss, can help to *explain* how such free will works, what its limits are, and even how it might be developed. Many other scientists work with a conception of free will that is non-naturalistic. With that conception in mind, they suggest that scientific discoveries about human decision-making *explain away* free will, suggesting that it is an illusion.

Rather than use Baumeister et al.'s article as a target of my criticisms, I will instead draw on its main points in order to develop some criticisms against these other scientists who suggest they are showing that free will is an illusion. By considering the different ways philosophers, scientists, and lay-persons understand free will, we can see why such scientific claims about free will may have significant ethical and social ramifications. I will argue that scientists' claims that humans lack free will are ambiguous: to the extent they are justified, they are, for the most part, harmless, but they also lend themselves to unjustified interpretations that are potentially harmful.

Imagine that scientists say that they have discovered that free will is an illusion and that the media report it widely. How would people react to such news? It would depend, of course, on whether people believed it was true and on what they take free will to mean. Most people tend to believe what science says it has *discovered* (after all, you can't discover something false any more than you can *know* something false), so let's suppose most people would accept the scientists' claims and the media's reports. Indeed, Baumeister et al. give us reason to think that people are susceptible to believing such claims about free will since they found that people's behavior changes when they read such

From *Neuroethics*, vol. 4, no. 1, July 31, 2009, pp. 17–24. Copyright © 2011 by Springer Science and Business Media. Reprinted by permission via Rightslink.

claims. And their behavior changes for the *worse*. For instance, subjects who read a series of sentences, such as "Science has demonstrated that free will is an illusion," are less likely to be helpful and more likely to be aggressive than those who read neutral sentences or sentences affirming that we have free will [2]. Furthermore, Vohs and Schooler [3] found that people are more likely to cheat and steal when they read such sentences or when they read a passage by a famous scientist, Francis Crick, asserting that humans lack free will. I will call these findings that people behave *worse* when they are told that they lack free will the 'bad results'.

These 'bad results' of diminished belief in free will should trouble us since the scientists' claims and the media's reports are not entirely fictional. Scientists such as Benjamin Libet [4], Daniel Wegner [5], John Bargh [6], Mark Hallet [7], Joshua Greene & Jonathan Cohen [8], and Sue Pockett [9] have suggested that their own and others' research in neuroscience and psychology threatens the existence of human free will. For instance, Bargh concludes, "this strong feeling [of free will] is an illusion, just as much as we experience the sun moving through the sky, when in fact it is we who are doing the moving" ([6]: 148–9). Wegner's *The Illusion of Conscious Will* concludes: "It seems we are agents. It seems we cause what we do. . . . It is sobering and ultimately accurate to call all this an illusion" ([5]: 341–342). And Joshua Greene & Jonathan Cohen assert: "Free will, as we ordinarily understand it, is an illusion" ([8]: 1783). Meanwhile, media reports are disseminating (sometimes exaggerating) these claims. For instance, a recent *ScienceNews* article reports, "'Free will' is not the defining feature of humanness, modern neuroscience implies, but is rather an illusion that endures only because biochemical complexity conceals the mechanisms of decision making" (12/6/08). And novelist Tom Wolfe says, "The bottom line of neuroscience is that . . . your idea that you have a soul or even a self, much less free will, is just an illusion" (*NYTimes* 6/2/02). I'll label the claim that science is showing that free will is an illusion 'willusionism'.

If the 'bad results' are replicated and extended to show that these 'willusionist' claims about free will have significant adverse effects on people's behavior—not to mention their self-conception—this would raise a troublesome (neuroethical) question: Should academic and political resources be used to attempt to contain the dissemination of willusionist claims? As someone who would be loathe to advocate any such response, I am hopeful that there is a better alternative—to correct the willusionists' claims. The sense of 'free will' they are using when they claim it is an illusion is ambiguous, and how willusionism is interpreted depends on how ordinary people understand free will. I will argue that the best explanation for the 'bad results' is that people interpret willusionism in ways that the evidence does not justify.

First, let's set up the conceptual landscape, drawing on Alfred Mele's helpful commentary here [10]. Mele reminds us that philosophers debating the relationship between free will and determinism have developed two conceptions of the powers required for free action. *Incompatibilists* about free will and determinism suggest that free and responsible agency requires 'libertarian powers'. These powers involve, at a minimum, indeterministic 'gaps' at appropriate places in the process of human decision-making, and often an extra power of agents to initiate causal processes without being caused to do so ('agent causation'). On the other hand, *compatibilists* about free will and determinism argue that free will does not require these libertarian powers (LPs); rather, 'compatibilist powers' (CPs) suffice for free action and morally responsible agency. CPs typically include the sort of cognitive and volitional capacities that Baumeister et al. identify with free will, things like self-control, rational choice, and planning. For instance, CPs might include an agent's capacities to consider alternatives for action and her competing desires to perform them, to form preferences about which of them offer good reasons for action, and to control her actions in light of her considered reasons. These sorts of psychological capacities are compatible with the truth of determinism and, more generally, with a naturalistic understanding of human decision-making and behavior. That is, even if these psychological capacities are manifested in accord with causal (even deterministic) laws, they may still play an essential causal role in the way agents act; indeed, the laws may need to *account for* the role of these compatibilist powers in our actions rather than undermining them. (I have, of course, condensed thousands of pages of philosophical theorizing about LPs and CPs into these oversimplified descriptions.)

The questions I want to focus on are: (1) When scientists and the media say free will is an illusion, which powers (LPs or CPs) are they talking about? And (2) when ordinary people think about free will, which powers are *they* thinking about? Considering these questions will allow us to examine how people's interpretations of willusionists' claims (a) may be different from what the willusionists mean and (b) may influence people's behavior in the negative ways suggested by Baumeister et al.'s and Vohs and Schooler's 'bad results'.

I think the answer to the first question is that willusionist scientists typically think of free will in terms of libertarian powers (LPs). They tend to take 'determinism' as equivalent to 'naturalism' or 'physicalism'— the view that every event in our universe, including human decisions and actions, is governed by natural laws.[1] And they tend to assume that free will is obviously incompatible with this sort of naturalism, in some cases because they seem to associate LPs with consciousness and to assume consciousness cannot be naturalized. Neuroscientist Read Montague puts it starkly: "Free will is the idea that we make choices and have thoughts independent of anything remotely resembling a physical process. Free will is the close cousin to the idea of the soul—the concept that 'you', your thoughts and feelings, derive from an entity that is separate and distinct from the physical mechanisms that make up your body. . . . Consequently, the idea of free will is not even in principle within reach of scientific description" ([11]: R584). Benjamin Libet similarly assumes that free will requires that "conscious decisions can proceed to some degree independently of natural determinism [. . . i.e.,] natural laws that govern the activities of nerve cells in the brain" ([4]: 55).[2]

These scientists also tend to assume that ordinary people understand free will in the same way. For instance, Joshua Greene and Jonathan Cohen write, "intuitive free will . . . requires the rejection of determinism and an implicit commitment to some kind of magical mental causation" ([8]: 1780).[3] Finally, willusionists often assume that the consensus among philosophers is that free will is incompatible with determinism (and naturalism), even though the majority of philosophers are compatibilists and even more develop theories of free will designed to be compatible with naturalism.[4] Hence, willusionists seem to assume that free will requires LPs, and then they take their research to provide reasons to doubt that we have LPs. After all, if one assumes LPs are non-natural powers, "not even in principle within reach of scientific description," then the more that the cognitive sciences can offer complete explanations of human decision-making, the more they seem to suggest that free will is an illusion. Notice, however, what will be important below: scientific evidence suggesting that humans do not have (non-natural) LPs says nothing about whether humans have (natural) CPs.

But do ordinary people associate free will with LPs or CPs? The answer is complex. Research on 'folk intuitions' that my co-authors and I have carried out suggests that most people think that free will and moral responsibility are *compatible* with determinism—e.g., with our decisions being completely caused by prior events or being predictable in accord with natural laws [13, 14]. On the other hand, most people think that free will is threatened by a fully reductionistic account of human decision-making in terms of neural processes, one that suggests to people that conscious mental states do not play a proper role in causing our actions [15]. I conclude from such data that most people associate free will primarily with CPs, though they also tend to think such powers are inconsistent with the reductionistic framework sometimes suggested by neuroscience and psychology. Nonetheless, some people also seem to believe that free will requires indeterminism, and some—perhaps especially in the Judeo-Christian tradition—also believe that free will requires non-natural powers (e.g., a non-physical soul that is not 'constrained' by the laws of the physical world). I should note, however, that my work suggests that this dualist view of free will appears to be less pervasive than some philosophers and scientists seem to think. Baumeister et al.'s research on ordinary people's judgments of free vs. unfree actions also suggests that people take CPs to be important components of free will in that they pick out free actions as those that involve conscious reflection, resisting temptation, and resisting external influences.

What are we to make of these different views about free will that vary both *among* individuals and perhaps also *within* individuals? One possibility is that there are two entirely distinct concepts of free will, one which involves LPs and one which involves CPs. If so, perhaps different people use the concept 'free will' to refer to different capacities, or perhaps individuals apply the concept in different ways in different contexts. (Theorists could *stipulate* that only one of these concepts should be used to refer to (real) free will, but they should then motivate this revision of ordinary people's understanding of free will.) Another possibility is that many people understand free will to require both CPs and LPs. I suspect that some people who believe this do so because they believe that LPs are required for CPs—perhaps they cannot conceive of how a non-dualist understanding of the human mind could explain consciousness or rationality. However, given the way I have described these powers (and the way Baumeister et al. describe CPs), this belief is *mistaken*—we can have CPs without LPs. The upshot is that the existing evidence suggests that people's conception of 'free will' clearly involves CPs, though some people also think free will involves LPs, and some in the latter group might think this only because they mistakenly think CPs require LPs. That's complicated, but suffice it to say that it looks like CPs are more central to ordinary people's conception of free will than LPs.

If so, what happens when people who hold such views read claims that science is discovering that free will is an illusion? Again, it depends on what the scientists are claiming, how nuanced their claims are, and how people interpret them. I have argued that the willusionists are usually not very nuanced about these claims (e.g., [16]). As indicated above, they generally seem to think of free will in terms of non-natural LPs, and they argue that scientific accounts of human decision-making show that we lack such powers. Sometimes, however, the scientists suggest they are showing that humans lack CPs as well, in some cases because they seem to think CPs require LPs. For instance, when psychologists like Bargh and Wegner argue that conscious processes play no causal role in action, they are unclear about whether they take this to mean that humans lack LPs or CPs or both. To the extent they mean to be providing evidence that humans entirely lack CPs, their claims are highly contentious and, I believe, false. The relevant research has *not* shown that conscious reasoning and intention-formation have no significant causal effects on what we decide to do or how we act (see [16–18]). On the contrary, Baumeister et al. and others (e.g., [19]) are helping to *explain* the psychological processes involved in CPs— e.g., self-control, conscious reasoning, and 'implementation intentions'—and their efficacy in action. And neuroscientific research is poised to elucidate the neurobiological processes that underlie these psychological processes. It may be that humans' capacities for rational deliberation and self-control are more *limited* than we tend to think—for instance, Baumeister et al. point out that willpower appears to be a limited resource, and research in social psychology suggests that our reported reasons for action are sometimes merely post-hoc rationalizations. But there is an important difference between saying free will is an illusion and saying free will is hard work.

Regardless of my claims about what the scientists have actually discovered about LPs or CPs, when they claim we lack free will, they tend *not* to make clear distinctions between LPs and CPs in order to clarify which of these they are challenging. And when ordinary people read such claims, it is unlikely they finish this uncompleted task and parse out exactly which powers they are purportedly losing and which they may be retaining. This leads to a problematic outcome:

1. If people believe that free will involves both libertarian powers and compatibilist powers (and especially if they believe that it involves primarily or only CPs), and
2. if scientists and the media inform people that free will is an illusion, and
3. if neither they nor ordinary people are clear about what is meant by 'free will' or exactly which powers are in question, then
4. *people may very well come to doubt that they have CPs.*

This conclusion allows us to see more clearly the connection between the willusionist claims about free will and the 'bad results' and to see the potential danger of scientists and the media claiming that free will is an illusion.

I've provided some reasons to think that (1), (2), and (3) are plausible. Now let's consider (4): What would people think if they started to question their compatibilist powers, such as rational choice and willpower—and how might their behavior change? They would likely think that their efforts to deliberate about what would be best to do were inconsequential and that their efforts to do what they think best were insignificant. They might think that what they end up doing is caused by forces that bypass conscious reasoning and decisions. Even if the willusionist claims simply percolate below the surface, they might lead people to make fewer or weaker attempts to deliberate about what to do and to exert willpower. For instance, people may engage in less counterfactual reasoning about alternatives for action, and they may not try very hard to be helpful or honest or nice. Put simply, if people are told they have no free will, they might interpret this to mean they lack willpower, and believing *that* might lead them to exert less willpower to do the more difficult (but more appropriate) thing to do.

I think this is the most plausible explanation for the 'bad results' from Baumeister et al. and Vohs and Schooler. People read that Nobel laureate Francis Crick is discovering that "Who you are is nothing but a pack of neurons" such that "although we *appear* to have free will, in fact, our choices have already been predetermined for us and we cannot change that" [3], and it seeps in enough to make them believe that nothing they try to do can change anything. They internalize this fatalistic view that suggests one's conscious decisions and efforts make no difference to what ends up happening. And since people do not think of themselves as being just "a pack of neurons," when they are then told that their neurons cause everything they do, they are likely to think that their conscious mind or self plays no role in what they do. Or people read the sentence, "Everything a person does is a direct consequence of their environment and genetic makeup" [2], and it leads them to think that their actions are *directly* caused by these forces, without their conscious deliberations or efforts (their CPs) playing any real role in what they do. Indeed, most of the no-free-will primes in these studies emphasize the idea that our actions are caused by our genes and the environment or by brain processes (e.g., "All behavior is determined by brain activity, which in turn is determined by a combination of environmental and genetic factors"). None of them mention any role for conscious deliberation or any other mental processes (except the one that says "Our mental activities are exclusively the product of physical processes"). It would be natural to read these reductionistic claims as suggesting that we have limited or no CPs, that our conscious deliberations and efforts of self-control are *bypassed* by processes over which we have no control (see [15]). And such reductionistic claims permeate the willusionist literature.

It is crucial to remember, however, that lacking LPs does *not* entail that our conscious decisions and our efforts make no difference to what we do, nor does determinism (or naturalism) entail such fatalism. It may be that some people *think* that lacking LPs has this consequence, but if so, they are confusing their

CPs with their LPs. Indeed, one danger of willusionist claims is that, like some of the willusionists, people do not properly distinguish CPs from LPs.

Of course, another possibility is that the 'bad results' occur because people are reading the no-freewill primes to mean that humans lack LPs. How would this story go? It could be that many people are committed to the more general belief that they (their souls) are not part of the natural world, and claims to the contrary lead them to question the legitimacy of morality (or the meaning of life, etc.), which then leads them to act less morally. If so, the trouble runs deeper than claims about free will. And we should predict similar 'bad results' from primes that discuss this more general naturalistic picture but do not specifically mention free will. Again, there is nothing about naturalism that properly threatens CPs, but it may be difficult for some people to see this. For those who *do* see this distinction, we should predict that any claims about naturalism that do *not* challenge CPs will *not* have 'bad results'. Indeed, this prediction is borne out, at least as far as I can tell: compatibilists and 'hard determinists' (who believe we do not have LPs but we do have CPs) do not behave any worse than non-naturalists who believe we do have LPs.

The moral of my story is that it would be much worse to lose compatibilist powers than libertarian powers. Indeed, some (like me) think that 'losing' LPs is to lose something we never had and never needed in order to have free will or to be morally responsible agents. But it is very hard to imagine someone who would not be troubled by the prospect that humans lack CPs—that the *apparent* impact that our conscious deliberations, rational choices, and efforts have on our behavior is, as a matter of fact, illusory. (It's a bit hard to imagine how to even make sense of that possibility.)

If my interpretation of the 'bad results' is on track, then willusionist claims are problematic because the negative effects they have on people's behavior are based on a false claim (that we lack CPs), or on a claim that is too easily interpreted as this false claim. The more significant claim is not that we lack LPs but that we lack CPs, yet the scientists are *not* showing that we have no CPs. Of course, the claim that science is showing that we lack LPs would still have an impact on many people's self-conception. However, if these people came to understand that lacking non-natural libertarian powers does *not* mean we lack the powers of rational choice, self-control, etc., then they would likely come to accept that they still have most of what they already thought free will was good for. And like the people who *already* believe that our minds are not super-natural and that free will involves CPs rather than LPs, they would probably not react by becoming more selfish or aggressive or dishonest.

Let me conclude by emphasizing that nothing I have said here suggests that scientific discoveries about the human mind are irrelevant to debates about free will. Quite the contrary. Baumeister et al. offer us some excellent models of how such discoveries can be relevant (indeed, the willusionist scientists also carry out excellent research that is highly relevant to debates about free will, if not always in the ways they suggest). Such discoveries may inform us that human free will is more limited than we tend to think—which I believe would be more significant than the potential discovery that the physical laws are deterministic. Our compatibilist powers may not be as extensive as we believe or hope they are (e.g., as Baumeister et al. suggest, self-control, deliberation, and conscious decision-making all draw on the same limited resources). But this information, properly understood, should not lead to the 'bad results' if, as I have suggested, these results derive from the fatalistic attitude that it doesn't really matter how we deliberate or how hard we try. If anything, information about the limitations of our CPs should encourage us to *try harder* (and more efficiently). Such information can open up opportunities for us to learn (and teach) strategies to strengthen free will (e.g., Baumeister suggests willpower is like a muscle that can be built up with practice) and to use our rational capacities more effectively (e.g., to understand when conditions are more or less ideal for making rational choices). Science has not shown that free will is an illusion. But it may be showing that exercising free will can be hard work.

Notes

1. This is a mistake, since naturalism does *not* entail determinism (e.g., quantum mechanics may be indeterministic and its indeterministic interactions may 'percolate up' to affect macro-level events). Furthermore, determinism, as philosophers use the term, does not seem to entail naturalism either, or if it does, it certainly does not entail a reductionistic view that suggests that conscious mental states have no causal role in action.

2. And Sue Pockett writes that "in order to believe in the existence of a libertarian free will [LPs], one must necessarily be a fullblown dualist with regard to the nature of consciousness—that is to say, one must regard consciousness as being a non-physical phenomenon" ([9]: 282).

3. And John Bargh writes, "Free will may be defined as an agent's ability to act on the world by its own volition, independently of purely physical (as opposed to metaphysical) causes and prior states of the world. The *folk notion of free will* is laden with the concept of a soul, a non-physical, unfettered, internal source of choice-making—in other words, an uncaused causer" ("The Will is Caused, not 'Free'" *Psychology Today* blog 6/23/09, my italics).

4. For instance, Robert Kane's libertarian account of free will requires indeterminism but not agent causation in part because he wants to offer an account that "might show how such freedom could exist in the natural order" ([12]: 106). Kane's view, then, is roughly that free will requires CPs plus indeterminism in the right places, though not the dualistic aspect of LPs.

All references for articles included in *Taking Sides: Clashing Views on Psychological Issues, 17/e* can be found on the Web at http://www.mhhe.com/cls.

CHALLENGE QUESTIONS

Does Teaching Scientific Determinism Lead to Bad Behavior?

1. If teaching determinism does lead to bad behavior (as Vohs and Schooler contend), what, if anything, should be changed about our scientific education?
2. Nahmias suggests that it is not belief in scientific principles that leads to bad behavior, but the sort of fatalism that suggests humans lack any powers of reason and control. Is this distinction valid? Might bad behavior still result from belief in determinism even if scientists were clearer on its specific implications? Why or why not?
3. Vohs and Schooler claim not to be making any claims as to whether or not free will actually exists, yet the crux of their (and most) scientific experiments is that their independent variable (statements about determinism) *caused* participants to act in a certain way. In other words, the experimental environment was responsible for behavior, not participants' free will. How might this sort of subtle deterministic language affect reader's moral behaviors?
4. Nahmias emphasizes the difference between compatibilist powers and libertarian powers of free will, arguing that one is compatible with scientific naturalism while the other is not. However, many scholars still debate the issue. Can free will be understood naturalistically? Why or why not?
5. Many people who believe the same things still act differently. For example, there might be free will deniers who regularly lie and free will deniers who regularly tell the truth. What else may be valid causes of bad behavior? How might these causes interact with differing beliefs?

Internet References . . .

Adolescent Egocentrism

This site has many links to the similar psychological construct of adolescent egocentrism.

**http://tweenparenting.about.com/od/behaviordiscipline/a/
AdolescentEgocentrism.htm**

Psychology Today

This Web site is a more balanced account from *Psychology Today*, with links to several points of view on the issue of the self-centeredness of youth.

**http://www.psychologytoday.com/blog/what-the-wild-things-are/201006/
are-today-s-youth-even-more-self-absorbed-and-less-caring-gener**

American Academy of Child & Adolescent Psychiatry

This is an authoritative site on adolescent development from the American Academy of Child & Adolescent Psychiatry.

**http://aacap.org/page.ww?name=Normal+Adolescent+Development+Part+
I&section=Facts+for+Families**

Development Issues

*T*he objective of most developmental psychologists is to document the course of physical, social, and cognitive changes over the entire span of our lives. But what has the greatest influence on human development? Some have said that today's youth have been raised with such material affluence and parental indulgence that they have learned to become self-centered rather than other-centered. Is that true? Moreover, the amount of time spent online has led some psychological researchers to be curious about the effect of digital social connections, such as online friendships, on development. How are these online friendships affecting today's youth? Are they different from the youth of a generation ago?

- Are Today's Youth More Self-Centered Than Previous Generations?
- Do Online Friendships Hurt Adolescent Development?

ISSUE 7

Are Today's Youth More Self-Centered Than Previous Generations?

YES: Jean M. Twenge, Sara Konrath, Joshua D. Foster, W. Keith Campbell, and Brad J. Bushman, from "Egos Inflating Over Time: A Cross-Temporal Meta-Analysis of the Narcissistic Personality Inventory," *Journal of Personality* (August 2008)

NO: Kali H. Trzesniewski, M. Brent Donnellan, and Richard W. Robins, from "Do Today's Young People Really Think They Are So Extraordinary? An Examination of Secular Trends in Narcissism and Self-Enhancement," *Psychological Science* (February 2008)

ISSUE SUMMARY

YES: Psychologist Jean Twenge and colleagues argue that the evidence suggests that young people are more egocentric than the previous generation.

NO: Professor Kali Trzesniewski and colleagues maintain that the evidence shows there is no change in the over-all level of narcissism since the previous generation.

It is not uncommon to hear complaints about the current generation of young people. Recent accusations suggest modern youth are increasingly materialistic and even selfish. For example, a Pew Research Center report from 2007 labeled today's college population as the "Look at Me" generation. Many observers suggest that the positive self-esteem movement has gone too far in encouraging children to have their own sense of worth. However, other commentators disagree, noting that there is a healthy amount of self-focus and that older generations have always complained about their younger counterparts.

Psychological investigators are attempting to provide some answers to this controversy. A common tool in this research is the Narcissistic Personality Inventory (NPI), which attempts to measure various non-clinical levels of narcissistic tendencies such as superiority, vanity, and entitlement. It accomplishes this through a number of forced-choice items (e.g., "I am going to be a great person" or "I hope I am going to be successful" answered yes or no). Because the

NPI has been around for several decades, it has been used to measure the narcissism of several populations across relatively long periods of time.

In the first article, Dr. Jean Twenge and her colleagues use such measurements to argue that there has been a dramatic increase in the level of college-aged narcissism in the last 20 years. With a meta-analysis of 85 studies, they evaluated data from over 16,000 American college students who took the NPI between 1979–2006. They found NPI scores increasing by a third of a standard deviation, with two-thirds of recent college students scoring significantly higher than earlier students. They conclude that their results are consistent with beliefs that modern America is increasing in individualism and related traits, such as self-esteem and narcissism. They call for further research into the causes of this increased narcissism. Yet, they suggest that grade inflation, the self-esteem movement, and the proliferation of personal technological devices have all contributed.

Kali Trzesniewksi M. Brent Donnellan, and Richard Robins disagree. They acknowledge several valid criticisms of the self-esteem movement but argue that broadly labeling the current generation as more narcissistic is premature, at best. They conducted their own study of modern college students and found no evidence of an increase in levels of narcissism or self-enhancement since 1988. They maintain that their conclusions are more accurate than previous studies because they avoided several important method problems that have plagued previous research. Furthermore, the authors make use of the NPI's sub-scales to suggest that socially toxic aspects of narcissism, such as superiority, are decreasing, while benign traits, such as self-sufficiency, are increasing.

POINT

- Narcissism has increased in the past three decades
- Americans are increasingly individualistic
- An increase in narcissism is a bad thing
- An education that tries to promote self-esteem might have a negative impact

COUNTERPOINT

- Narcissism has not increased in the last generation
- Americans have increased some types of individualism but not others
- An increase in narcissism has some positive features
- Even if narcissism has increased, there is not sufficient evidence to blame the self-esteem movement

YES

Jean M. Twenge et al.

Egos Inflating Over Time: A Cross-Temporal Meta-Analysis of the Narcissistic Personality Inventory

It is common for older people to complain about "kids these days," describing the younger generation as self-centered, entitled, arrogant, and/or disrespectful. As a bromide set in a particular time, it is difficult to tell whether these perceptions are a function of age (maybe younger people are more self-centered than older people simply because they are young) or of generation (maybe the younger generation actually is more self-centered than the older generation was at the same age). It is also possible that older people will complain about the younger generation even if young people are actually less self-centered than they were when they were young themselves.

To study generational change scientifically, it is necessary to separate the effects of generation from age and to measure traits using psychometrically sound questionnaires. This is best accomplished through the time-lag method, which analyzes samples of people of the same age at different points in time. For example, college students from the 1980s can be compared with college students from the 1990s and 2000s. All samples are of the same age, but are from different generations (otherwise known as *birth cohorts*). Birth cohort is a useful proxy for the sociocultural environment of different time periods. For example, children growing up in the 1970s were exposed to a fundamentally different culture than children growing up in the 1990s. The logic underlying this approach is similar to that used to assess the self-conceptions and personality traits of individuals across different world regions, except that individual differences between birth cohorts (instead of cultural groups) are assessed. In support of this idea, several previous studies have found strong birth cohort differences in characteristics such as anxiety, self-esteem, locus of control, and sexual behavior. These studies used meta-analysis to locate samples of college students and children who completed the same psychological questionnaires at different points in historical time. The correlation between mean scores and the year the data were collected were then analyzed, using a method known as cross-temporal meta-analysis.

The present study uses cross-temporal meta-analysis to examine changes in scores on the Narcissistic Personality Inventory, or NPI. The NPI is the

From *Journal of Personality*, vol. 76, no. 4, August 2008. Copyright © 2008 by the Jean M. Twenge, Sara Konrath, Joshua D. Foster, W. Keith Campbell, and Brad J. Bushmans. Reprinted by permission of Wiley-Blackwell via Rightslink.

most widely used measure of narcissistic personality in the general population. The NPI is not designed as a clinical instrument for measuring narcissistic personality disorder (NPD), and there is no cut-off score for clinically high narcissism. Narcissism is characterized first and foremost by a positive and inflated view of the self, especially on agentic traits (e.g., power, importance, physical attractiveness). Second, narcissism is associated with social extraversion, although people high in narcissism have relatively little interest in forming warm, emotionally intimate bonds with others. Third, narcissism involves a wide range of self-regulation efforts aimed at enhancing the self. These efforts can range from attention seeking and taking credit from others to seeking high-status romantic partners and opportunities to achieve public glory. Those high in narcissism also lash out with aggression when they are rejected or insulted. Many of these behaviors can potentially be explained by the link between narcissism and impulsivity. In a sense, narcissism can be conceptualized as a self-regulating system, where self-esteem and enhancement are sought through a variety of social means but with little regard for the consequences borne by others.

The NPI is ideal for a cross-temporal meta-analysis assessing changes in narcissism. First, it is reliable, well validated, and widely used. Second, the NPI is somewhat protected from social desirability influences through its use of forced-choice dyads, and, perhaps as a result, is not correlated with measures of social desirability. For each of the 40 forced-choice dyads on the NPI, participants choose either the narcissistic response (e.g., "I can live my life anyway I want to") or the non-narcissistic response (e.g., "People can't always live their lives in terms of what they want"). The 40 items are summed together. Higher scores indicate higher levels of narcissism.

Previous Literature

Most previous studies suggest that narcissistic traits should increase with the generations. Several authors have argued that American culture has increasingly emphasized individualism. Perhaps as a result, previous cross-temporal meta-analyses demonstrate a clear rise in individualistic traits. Between the 1970s and the 1990s, both college men and women scored higher on the agentic traits measured by the Bem Sex Role Inventory M scale, such as "independent," "individualistic, particular to me," and "leadership ability." College women and—on some scales—college men scored higher on assertiveness measures between the 1970s and the 1990s, and both sexes increased in extraversion. College students scored higher on the Rosenberg Self-Esteem Scale between the 1960s and the 1990s, and children scored higher on the Coopersmith Self-Esteem Inventory between the 1980s and the 1990s. Agentic traits, assertiveness, extraversion, and self-esteem are all positively correlated with narcissism. A study of changes in personality with age development shows that younger cohorts increase with age more than older cohorts in social dominance but also in agreeableness and conscientiousness over the young adulthood years between 18 and 40. . . .

Although most evidence points to increases in narcissism over the generations, an alternative model suggests a decrease in narcissism. Generational theorists Howe and Strauss describe Baby Boomers (in college early 1960s to early 1980s) as inner fixated and self-absorbed; they specifically use the word "narcissistic" in their description. In contrast, they portray Generation X (in college mid-1980s to late-1990s), as "lacking ego strength" and having "low self-esteem." Finally, they describe the "Millennials" (in college early 2000s to late 2010s, sometimes called "GenY") as outer-fixated, group-oriented, and civically responsible. "Are they self-absorbed? No. They're cooperative team players," say Howe and Strauss. They continue, "Individualism and the search for inner fulfillment are all the rage for many Boomer adults, but less so for their kids, [who are] not as eager to grow up putting self ahead of community the way their parents did." However, these descriptions are not based on empirical data collection. Although Strauss and Howe's portrayal of generations includes many traits that are not related to narcissism, the descriptions above suggest that Baby Boomers should be the highest in narcissism, GenXers the lowest, and "Millennials" either just as low or even lower (as Strauss and Howe specifically say that they are *not* self-absorbed). Thus, their characterization of generations suggests that narcissism decreased among college students between the 1980s and the 2000s, or, at the very least, stayed steady after the Baby Boomers left college in the mid-1980s.

Overview

This article presents a cross-temporal meta-analysis of American college students' responses to the 40-item, forced-choice version of the NPI. This analysis will examine the correlation between NPI mean scores and the year the data were collected, showing how narcissism levels have changed over the generations. . . .

Method

Literature Search

Studies were primarily located using the Web of Knowledge citation index. The Web of Knowledge is an extensive database, including virtually all journals in the social sciences, biological and physical sciences, and medicine. We searched the citation index for articles that cited one of the original sources of the NPI. We also gathered unpublished means by posting a message to the Society for Personality and Social Psychology Listserv (spsp-discuss@stolaf.edu) asking for NPI means that fit the criteria outlined below, and we included unpublished means from our labs.

Inclusion Rules

Possible data points for the analysis were included or excluded on the basis of specific inclusion rules. To be included in the analysis, a study had to meet the following criteria: (a) participants were undergraduates at conventional 4-year institutions (e.g., not 2-year colleges, not military academies); (b) participants were attending college in the United States; (c) means were reported for unselected groups of students, not those chosen for scoring high or low on the NPI or another measure or singled out for being maladjusted, clients at a counseling center, and so on; (d) samples were not more than 79% female or 79% male; and (e) the study used the 40-item forced-choice version of the NPI. The 40-item forced-choice version is by far the most common version of the NPI used by researchers, so it yielded the most data. Other versions of the NPI include different items and produce different means; one of the requirements of cross-temporal meta-analysis is that the means are from the same measure so they can be directly compared across time. In addition, the 40-item NPI is more internally reliable than other versions; when Raskin and Terry created the 40-item scale, they eliminated the 14 items from the original 54-item scale that did not correlate with the scale's primary factors. . . .

Data Analytic Strategy

We analyzed how NPI scores have changed over time, primarily by examining correlations between mean scores and year of data collection. As in previous cross-temporal meta-analyses, means were weighted by the sample size of each study to provide better estimates of the population mean. We performed our analyses using SPSS, and the βs reported are standardized to allow for easier interpretation.

To calculate the magnitude of change in NPI scores, we used the regression equations and the averaged standard deviation (SD) of the individual samples. To compute the mean scores for specific years (e.g., 1982 or 2006), we used the regression equation from the statistical output (used to draw the regression line). The regression equation follows the algebraic formula $y = Bx + C$, where B = the unstandardized regression coefficient, x = the year, C = the constant or intercept, and y = the predicted mean NPI score. This formula yielded the position of the regression line (the mean NPI score, on the Y axis) for particular years. We obtained the average standard deviation (SD) by averaging the within-sample SDs reported in the data sources; thus this reflects the average variance of the measure in a sample of individuals. It is important to note that this method avoids the ecological fallacy, also known as *alerting correlations*. The ecological fallacy occurs when the magnitude of change is calculated using the variation in mean scores rather than the variation within a population of individuals. This exaggerates the magnitude of the effect, because mean scores do not differ as much as individual scores. The method used here, in contrast, uses the standard deviation of the individual studies to capture the variance of the scale among a population of individuals.

Results

American college students score progressively higher on narcissism between the early 1980s and 2006. There is a significant and positive correlation between NPI scores and year of data collection when weighted by sample size (β = .53, p <.001, k = 85). Thus, more recent generations report more narcissistic traits. The regression equation (NPI mean = 0.09293 × year − 169.128) yields a score of 15.06 for 1982 and 17.29 for 2006. The average *SD* reported for the individual samples (from the articles we collected) is 6.86. Thus NPI scores increased 0.33 standard deviation from the early 1980s to 2006. This is a small-to-medium effect size (between .20 and .50) by Cohen's guidelines.

Converting the *SD* change to percentile scores is also informative. If the average student in the early 1980s scored at the 50th percentile of the distribution, the average student in 2006 scored at the 65th percentile (assuming a normal curve). In other words, almost two-thirds of recent college students are above the mean 1979–1985 narcissism score, a 30% increase (65 out of 100 in 2006, compared to 50 out of 100 in 1979–1985).

If we assume that the NPI still has a normal distribution, this shift in the mean score means that there are now more college students at the top end of the original distribution. For example, 24% of 2006 college students score 1 *SD* above the 1979–1985 narcissism mean, compared to 15% during that original data collection. (One *SD* above the 1979–1985 is a score of 22, representing someone who answers the clear majority of items—22 out of 40—in a narcissistic direction.) It is also interesting to note how recent means compare to data collected on a sample of celebrities such as movie stars, reality TV winners, and famous musicians. This celebrity sample had a mean NPI score of 17.84, not much higher than the 2006 regression equation mean of 17.29. Thus, recent college students approach celebrities in their levels of narcissism. . . .

Discussion

A meta-analysis of 85 samples of American college students shows a systematic increase in scores on the Narcissistic Personality Inventory. The shift in scores means that the average college student now endorses about two more narcissism items than his or her predecessors did in the early 1980s. Although the effect size for the shift is statistically moderate rather than large (one-third of a standard deviation), it is larger than the effect of violent video games on aggression and most racial differences in self-esteem. The generational shift over 25 years is also twice as large as the current sex difference in narcissism; thus generation is a better predictor of narcissism scores than gender.

These data are consistent with theories positing an increase in individualism in American society and with previous studies finding generational increases in other individualistic traits such as self-esteem and agency. The most recent college students score about the same on the NPI as a sample of celebrities. The change is linear and steady, with the correlation significant when the analysis is limited to certain years only. It also appears that women are driving the increase in narcissism, consistent with the finding that the generational increase in agentic traits and assertiveness was stronger for women.

We were unable to analyze changes in specific subscales of the NPI, as very few researchers reported NPI means broken down by subscale. Thus, we do not know if only certain facets of narcissism are increasing among American college students, or if the change is evenly distributed across them. In addition, we do not know how the increase in narcissism is related to the previously documented rise in self-esteem. The rise in narcissism could be directly related to increases in self-esteem, or there could have been an increase in narcissistic traits independent of self-esteem.

Correlates of Narcissism

Is this rise in narcissism a bad thing? As measured by the NPI, narcissism is linked to a range of positive emotional outcomes, including self-esteem, positive affect, extraversion, and life satisfaction. Narcissism is associated with other benefits to the self as well, such as short-term (but not long-term) likeability, enhanced performance on public evaluation tasks including being selected for reality television, short-term victories in competitive tasks, and emergent (though not successful) leadership. Narcissism also has many costs to the self, such as distorted judgments of one's abilities, risky decision making, potential addictive disorders including alcohol abuse, compulsive shopping, and pathological gambling. Many of the costs of narcissism are borne by other people. These include troubled romantic relationships, aggression, assault, white collar crime, and rapidly depleting common resources. In sum, narcissism is associated with benefits to the individual that are primarily affective and most evident in the short term, but the costs of narcissism are paid by others and, eventually, by the individual as well. . . . Thus the implications of the rise in narcissism may be positive in the short term for individuals, but negative for other people, for society, and for the individual in the long term.

Many of the correlates of narcissism are also on the upswing, although we cannot be certain if they are directly tied to the rise in narcissism. Several positive personality traits correlated with narcissism have increased over the same time period, including self-esteem, agentic traits, extraversion and assertiveness. Behaviors and attitudes have also shifted in a direction consistent with a rise in narcissism. There is a trend among college students toward "hooking up" rather than having sex within committed relationships. Materialism has increased: 74% of college freshmen in 2004 cited "being very well-off financially" as an important life goal, compared to only 45% in 1967. In a 2006 survey, 81% of 18- to 25-year-olds said that getting rich was among their generation's most important goals; 64% named it as the most important goal of all. In addition, 51% said that becoming famous was among their generation's important goals. In contrast, only 30% chose helping others who need help, and only 10% named becoming more spiritual. . . .

Future Research: The Uncertain Causes of Narcissism

The relationship between personality and culture is likely reciprocal, with societal changes driving increases in narcissism and vice versa. What societal trends may have led to the increased narcissism we found? We can speculate on several of these, although a great deal of future work needs to be done on the causes of narcissism. Schools and media activities may have promoted an increase in narcissism. Children in some preschools sing a song with the lyrics, "I am special/I am special/Look at me . . . ," and many television shows for children emphasize positive self-feelings and specialness. Future research should examine whether school and media programs intended to raise self-esteem also raise narcissism. Grade inflation may also play a role: In 1980, only 27% of college freshmen reported earning an A average in high school, but by 2004 almost half (48%) reported a high school A average. However, the amount of studying has actually declined (33% of American college freshmen in 2003 reported studying 6 or more hours a week during their last year of high school, compared to 47% in 1987), as has performance on tests like the SAT. Future research should determine whether grade inflation builds narcissism.

Finally, future research should examine whether current technology is related to narcissistic traits. Devices such as iPods and Tivo allow people to listen to music and watch television in their own individual ways, and web-sites such as MySpace and YouTube (whose slogan is "Broadcast yourself) permit self-promotion far beyond that allowed by traditional media. These trends motivated *Time* magazine to declare that the 2006 Person of the Year was "You," complete with a mirror on the cover. Most of the increase in narcissism occurred before the wide use of such technology, so these shifts— even if they do play a role—did not cause the initial upswing in narcissism scores. Instead, the rise in narcissism may have influenced the ways people use technology.

Limitations

The present study provides the most comprehensive examination to date of generational change in narcissistic personality traits. Even so, it is not without its limitations. Any analysis of self-report data is potentially limited by socially desirable responding. However, the NPI is not significantly correlated with social desirability. In addition, there have not been concomitant changes in socially desirable responding, which did not change during this time period. This makes it very unlikely that changes in socially desirable responding account for the present results.

This study also limits its conclusions to American society and genera-tions, partially because there is not much data available over time from other countries. Americans score higher on narcissism than people from other world regions. Future analyses might determine if narcissism is also increasing in other cultures or if this cultural trend is limited to the United States. . . .

This study also cannot determine whether the change in narcissism is a purely generational effect or a time-period effect. As with any time-lag study including people of only one age group, we cannot know if those in other age groups also changed. It is possible that both younger and older Americans became more narcissistic from the 1980s to the 2000s. It is also possible that older Americans did not change at all or even became less narcissistic. Given the relative stability of social dominance after young adulthood, as well as cross-sectional research showing lower narcissism scores in older adults, it seems likely that much of the shift is a generational rather than a time-period effect.

Kali H. Trzesniewski, M. Brent
Donnellan, and Richard W. Robins

 **NO**

Do Today's Young People Really Think They Are So Extraordinary?

An Examination of Secular Trends in Narcissism and Self-Enhancement

Several decades ago, California State Congressman John Vasconcellos, who referred to himself as the "Johnny Appleseed of self-esteem," spearheaded a movement to create school programs designed to improve self-esteem. This movement came under attack almost immediately and continues to be attacked today. Although well-designed self-esteem interventions can have positive effects on children's outcomes, the Vasconcellos-inspired school programs often lacked precise implementation and grounding in research. Many of these programs seemed to emphasize feeling good over achieving, giving awards and good grades to all students even in the absence of real achievements. Similarly, American culture is stereotyped as being overly focused on seeking high self-esteem at all costs. As a result, there is widespread concern that the American "feel good culture" and the self-esteem programs it spawned have inadvertently produced a generation of young narcissists.

Most notably, Twenge has characterized Americans born in the 1970s, 1980s, and 1990s as "Generation Me," a label selected to capture their purported tendency to be more egotistical, entitled, and overconfident than previous generations, presumably because they grew up in this "culture of self-worth." Media reports based on Twenge, Konrath, Foster, Campbell, and Bushman's forthcoming analysis of generational changes in average scores on the Narcissistic Personality Inventory have further disseminated the idea that America's youth are increasingly narcissistic. Coverage of this work has been widespread, appearing in high-profile media outlets such as the *Atlantic Monthly*, *CBS News*, and *National Public Radio* as well as in major newspapers such as the *Boston Globe*, the *Los Angeles Times*, and the *Washington Post*.

The purpose of this report is to examine the evidence for the claim that today's young people are more self-centered and self-aggrandizing than young people of previous generations. We analyzed secular changes in narcissism using large samples of undergraduate students from northern California, the geographic epicenter of the self-esteem movement. In addition, we examined secular changes in one prominent manifestation of narcissism,

From *Psychological Science*, vol. 19, no. 2, February 2008, pp. 181–187. Copyright © 2008 by the Association for Psychological Science. Reprinted by permission of Wiley-Blackwell.

self-enhancement (i.e., the tendency to hold unrealistically positive beliefs about the self), using data from the college-student samples and from the Monitoring the Future project, a large national probability study of high school seniors conducted annually since 1976.

Why might narcissism and self-enhancement be increasing in recent generations? A number of social commentators have noted a shift in American culture from communitarian values and strong social ties toward an emphasis on individualism and the pursuit of one's own needs. These social values are thought to shape individual personality characteristics. As noted by Lasch, "Every society reproduces its culture—its norms, its underlying assumptions, its modes of organizing experience—in the individual, in the form of personality" (p. 76). It is difficult to devise models that explain the processes through which broad societal trends affect personality. However, identifying changes in personality associated with birth cohort is an important first step.

Unfortunately, identifying cohort effects is empirically challenging. One approach, pioneered by Twenge and her colleagues, is to conduct a cross-temporal meta-analysis in which changes in average personality scores are examined as a function of date of data collection. Using this methodology, Twenge et al. found that the average NPI score has increased steadily in college students since the scale was first administered in 1982. Although this is an important application of meta-analytic techniques, the results are nonetheless constrained by limitations in the sampling procedures used in the original studies. The college-student samples included in the meta-analysis were mostly small and perhaps subject to selection biases; thus, we believe that it is informative to examine secular trends in narcissism and self-enhancement in large samples of prescreening data and in a nationally representative sample.

In the present study, we tested the hypothesis that narcissism levels are increasing by comparing mean scores on the NPI using data collected on college students in the 1980s, 1990s, and 2000s. The NPI was designed to assess personality characteristics associated with the clinical definition of narcissistic personality disorder in the third edition of the *Diagnostic and Statistical Manual of Mental Disorders*. These attributes include a grandiose sense of importance, a preoccupation with power and success, exhibitionism, arrogance, exploitativeness, and a sense of entitlement. The NPI is the most widely used and well-validated measure of subclinical levels of narcissism and has been shown to predict psychologists' ratings of narcissism. Thus, the NPI provides one of the best ways to measure whether or not today's college students exhibit more narcissistic tendencies than previous generations. To complement our analysis of secular trends in the NPI, we also examined trends in self-enhancement, a construct that is associated with narcissism. We operationalized self-enhancement as the discrepancy between participants' ratings of their intelligence and more objective indicators of their intellectual ability (SAT scores and grade point average, or GPA). If young people have been getting more narcissistic over the past three decades, then the degree to which they overestimate their ability should have been increasing as well.

Method

Narcissism

We used data drawn from mass testing sessions of introductory psychology students conducted at the University of California, Davis and Berkeley campuses, in 1996 and annually from 2002 to 2007. We restricted the analyses to the 25,849 students between 18 and 24 years of age (Mdn = 19, SD = 1.40) who completed the 40-item forced-choice version of the NPI (alpha reliability ranged from .84 to .85 across years). We selected students who were of traditional college age to provide a cleaner test of the cohort-effect hypothesis. The sample was 66.3% female; 39.7% were Asian American, 30.9% were Caucasian, 2.2% were African American, 9.4% were Hispanic, and 17.8% were of mixed or other races or did not state their ethnic background. To extend our test of secular trends, we compared means from the 1990s and 2000s with means first published by Raskin and Terry; these means were based on 1,018 participants (52.5% female) who completed the NPI between 1979 and 1985.

Self-Enhancement

To track secular trends in self-enhancement, we used data from two sources. First, in the mass testing sessions conducted at the University of California between 2003 and 2007 (self-enhancement data were not available in the 1996 and 2002 assessments), students were asked to "rate your intelligence compared to the general population," using a scale ranging from 1 (*bottom 5%*) to 10 (*top 5%*). To gauge self-enhancement, we computed the degree to which self-perceived intelligence was higher than objective indicators of academic ability (SAT scores and college GPA). Specifically, we conducted multiple regression analyses (using data from all assessment years, i.e., from 2003 through 2007) in which each indicator of ability was regressed on the self-ratings of intelligence and the unstandardized residuals were retained. Because the two resulting self-enhancement indices— one based on SAT scores and the other based on GPA—were almost perfectly correlated (r = .90), we computed a single combined index by entering both academic criteria simultaneously into a multiple regression predicting self-rated intelligence and then saving the unstandardized residuals. Positive values indicate self-enhancement (i.e., overestimation by the self), and negative values indicate self-diminishment (i.e., underestimation by the self). Residual scores have been widely used to assess self-enhancement. In this sample, self-enhancement correlated .27 with NPI score, a finding consistent with previous research.

Second, we examined long-term trends in self-enhancement using data from the Monitoring the Future project, a very large national probability study of high school seniors conducted annually since 1976 (total N across the 30 years used in these analyses = 410,527; 50.7% female . . .). Every year from 1976 to 2006, high school seniors were asked, "How intelligent do you think you are compared to others your own age?" This item was rated from 1 (*far below average*) to 7 (*far above average*). To assess self-enhancement bias, we used an unstandardized residual score (computed via regression using data from all years) reflecting the discrepancy between self-perceived intelligence and high school grades; standardized-test scores were not available in the Monitoring the Future data, but given the .90 correlation between self-enhancement based on grades and self-enhancement based on SAT scores in the University of California data, it is unlikely that the secular trends would have been different if test scores had been used as a criterion instead of grades. Because of privacy issues associated with publicly available data, ethnicity was coded as White or non-White (83.4% White).

Results

Secular Trends in Narcissism

Table 1 shows the means and standard deviations by year of data collection for the full-scale NPI. Given the large sample sizes, we focus on effect sizes rather than significance levels. We discuss all effects that meet or surpass Cohen's guideline of a small effect (i.e., an r of .10 or a d of 0.20).

Year of data collection (from 1996 to 2007) was uncorrelated with full-scale NPI score ($r = .01$). Given the lack of time trend in these data, we computed the average score on the NPI for all participants from 1996 through 2007 and compared this aggregate score to that reported by Raskin and Terry. This comparison provides a direct test of the cohort hypothesis because it compares Generation Me (i.e., members of our sample were all born after 1971) with previous generations (i.e., participants in Raskin and Terry's study were all born before 1969). As Table 1 shows, there was a very small difference ($d = -0.06$) between NPI means computed in our data (Generation Me) and in Raskin and Terry's original data. To further illustrate the effects, we standardized all NPI scores from 1996 through 2007 to Raskin and Terry's mean and standard deviation. . . . [All] of the means from 1996 through 2007 were slightly below Raskin and Terry's average (e.g., the largest standardized difference was −0.10, for scores in 2002, $N = 3,117$). Thus, we found no evidence for a secular increase in NPI scores among college students from the 1980s to the 2000s, and if anything, we found weak support for a secular decline.

Gender, ethnicity, and age did not moderate the time trend (none of the interaction terms accounted for more than 0.1% of the variance), although we did find some main effects. Men ($M = 0.41$) had higher narcissism scores than women ($M = 0.37$; $d = 0.24$), and Caucasians ($M = 0.39$) had higher narcissism scores than Asian Americans ($M = 0.34$; $d = 0.29$). Age was uncorrelated with NPI scores in this age-restricted sample ($r = .01$).

It is possible that specific aspects of narcissism have increased over time while others have decreased, producing no aggregate change at the full-scale level. However, an examination of time trends from 1996 to 2007 for NPI subscales created by Emmons and by Raskin and Terry (1988) provided no evidence for changes in specific aspects of narcissism ($r = -.01–.02$ for correlations between subscale scores and year of data collection). Nonetheless, we found a few differences when comparing the subscale means for 1996 through

Table 1

Mean Full-Scale and Subscale Scores on the Narcissistic Personality Inventory (NPI) by Year of Data Collection

Year	N	Full NPI	Subscale						
			Authority	Exhibitionism	Superiority	Entitlement	Exploitiveness	Self-Sufficiency	Vanity
1982[a]	1,018	0.39(0.17)	0.52(0.27)	0.32(0.25)	0.51(0.27)	0.28(0.23)	0.29(0.34)	0.35(0.25)	0.46(0.36)
1996	670	0.38(0.17)	0.51(0.29)	0.27(0.27)	0.44(0.28)	0.32(0.25)	0.33(0.27)	0.41(0.25)	0.39(0.35)
2002	3,117	0.37(0.17)	0.49(0.28)	0.27(0.25)	0.41(0.28)	0.30(0.24)	0.31(0.26)	0.41(0.25)	0.37(0.35)
2003	4,820	0.38(0.17)	0.50(0.29)	0.28(0.25)	0.41(0.28)	0.31(0.24)	0.32(0.27)	0.41(0.24)	0.38(0.35)
2004	4,770	0.38(0.17)	0.50(0.28)	0.28(0.25)	0.40(0.28)	0.32(0.24)	0.32(0.27)	0.41(0.25)	0.39(0.36)
2005	4,434	0.38(0.17)	0.51(0.29)	0.28(0.25)	0.41(0.28)	0.32(0.24)	0.33(0.27)	0.41(0.24)	0.39(0.35)
2006	4,974	0.38(0.17)	0.50(0.28)	0.28(0.25)	0.42(0.28)	0.32(0.25)	0.32(0.27)	0.41(0.24)	0.39(0.35)
2007	3,064	0.39(0.18)	0.51(0.28)	0.29(0.26)	0.43(0.28)	0.32(0.24)	0.33(0.27)	0.42(0.24)	0.39(0.35)
α	—	.84	.75	.65	.54	.48	.53	.42	.62
d[b]	—	-0.06	-0.07	-0.16	-0.36	0.17	0.10	0.24	-0.20
		(-0.15 to 0.04)	(-0.17 to 0.02)	(-0.25 to -0.07)	(-0.45 to -0.26)	(0.07 to 0.26)	(0.02 to 0.20)	(0.16 to 0.34)	(-0.29 to -0.11)

Note. For each year, standard deviations are given in parentheses.
[a]The data in this row were obtained from Raskin and Terry (1988); means and standard deviations were converted from sums to scale means. The data were collected from 1979 to 1985, so 1982 is the average year of data collection. [b]This row presents the standardized difference between the mean score in 1996 through 2007 and Raskin and Terry's (1998) mean score for 1979 through 1985. A positive value indicates that the mean was higher in 1996 through 2007. The numbers in parentheses are 95% confidence intervals.

2007 with subscale means from 1979 through 1985 reported by Raskin and Terry. As Table 1 shows, scores on four subscales decreased (Authority, Exhibitionism, Superiority, and Vanity), and scores on three increased (Entitlement, Exploitiveness, and Self-Sufficiency), although the largest effect size was a decline of only a third of a standard deviation in Superiority.

Secular Trends in Self-Enhancement

We found no evidence that self-enhancement changed over time in either sample; the correlation (r) between self-enhancement and year of data collection was $-.02$ and $-.03$, respectively, for the University of California sample (2003–2007) and the Monitoring the Future sample (1976–2006). Moreover, neither gender nor ethnic group moderated the time trend (neither of the interaction terms accounted for more than 0.1% of the variance in either sample). Results were similar to those for narcissism in that men self-enhanced more than women in both the college sample ($Ms = 0.27$ vs. -0.14, $d = 0.39$) and the high school sample ($Ms = 0.19$ vs. -0.18, $d = 0.36$) and that Caucasian college students ($M = 0.22$) reported higher levels of self-enhancement than Asian college students ($M = -0.24$; $d = 0.46$). However, in the high school sample, non-Caucasians ($M = 0.12$) and Caucasians ($M = 0.00$) did not differ in self-enhancement ($d = 0.12$).

Discussion

The goal of this study was to investigate secular changes in narcissism and self-enhancement using large samples of northern Californian college students and a nationally representative sample of high school students from the Monitoring the Future study. California is regarded as the home of the self-esteem movement, so data from universities in this state are particularly useful given recent claims about the negative impact of the culture of self-worth. Contrary to previous research and media reports, this study yielded no evidence that levels of narcissism have increased since Raskin and Terry first published their 40-item forced-choice version of the NPI. Likewise, we found no evidence that self-enhancement, defined as inflated perceptions of intelligence, has increased over the past 30 years. Thus, today's youth seem to be no more narcissistic and self-aggrandizing than previous generations.

Indeed, the means for the NPI from our sample closely resemble the means from a large Internet sample. In the latter sample, the average NPI score for Americans ages 20 to 24 was 15.58 ($N = 775$; J. Foster, personal communication, April 5, 2007) and in our sample, the mean NPI score for students ages 20 to 24 was 15.23 ($N = 10,491$). In addition, the mean reported by Foster et al. is very close to the average of 15.55 reported by Raskin and Terry. Thus, both our data and the Internet data collected by Foster et al. fail to show a robust secular trend toward increases in narcissism in young people over the past few decades.

Why do our findings differ from those of Twenge et al.? First, our NPI results are based on large prescreening samples, and our self-enhancement findings are based on a nationally representative sample, whereas the findings of

Twenge et al. are meta-analytic results based on aggregated data from comparatively small samples of college students (median $N = 126$, range = 24–1,182). Aggregating means from small convenience studies of college students might not be the best strategy for making inferences about birth cohorts because students choose to participate in studies on the basis of titles and descriptions that might appeal to their individual characteristics, including narcissism. In contrast, we used data from large mass testing sessions, which makes our NPI samples considerably larger than those of most individual studies of college students (our average annual sample size was 3,692) and makes the possibility of selection effects less of a concern. Moreover, the Monitoring the Future results are based on a representative sampling of high school students, a sampling procedure that is particularly well suited for evaluating claims about secular increases in self-enhancement.

Indeed, we believe that issues of sampling are paramount when making generalizations about entire birth cohorts. Researchers who are interested in making point estimates of particular attitudes often pay careful attention to sampling procedures. Most college-student samples are generated using non-probability sampling techniques. As noted by Pedhazur and Schmelkin, "the incontrovertible fact is that, in non-probability sampling, it is not possible to estimate sampling errors. Therefore, validity of inferences to a population cannot be ascertained" (p. 321). To be sure, pooling together convenience samples of college students will never lead to estimates that can be defended as representative of an entire population of college students, let alone members of an entire birth cohort. That is, no amount of aggregation will circumvent the limitations of convenience sampling.

A second reason why our results differ from those of Twenge et al. is that cross-temporal meta-analyses yield ecological coefficients, which are calculated using summary statistics (e.g., sample means) rather than individual data points. As Rosenthal, Rosnow, and Rubin noted, "correlations based on aggregated data (e.g., group means) can be dramatically larger or smaller (even in the opposite direction) than correlations based on individual scores" (p. 2). We examined this issue by comparing the correlation between year of data collection and self-enhancement based on the full Monitoring the Future sample with the alerting correlation based on the mean self-enhancement score for each year (i.e., the data in Table 2). As reported in the Results section, the correlation based on the full sample was −.03; in contrast, the alerting correlation was −.57. Similarly, using the college-student data from 1996 to 2007, we compared the individual-level correlation between year of data collection and NPI score with the altering correlation for the mean scores reported in Table 1. The individual-level correlation was .01, whereas the alerting correlation was .40; likewise, the individual-level correlations ranged from .00 to .01 across Raskin and Terry's NPI subscales, whereas the alerting correlations ranged from −.41 (Superiority) to .82 (Exhibitionism). These often dramatic differences are consistent with the methodological literature, which indicates that alerting correlations overestimate individual effects in most behavioral research. Thus, the cross-temporal meta-analytic approach may amplify effects that are trivial from a psychological perspective.

Table 2

Mean Self-Enhancement by Year of Data Collection

Year	/V	Mean (SD)
1976	14,277	−0.06 (0.95)
1977	15,638	−0.03 (0.97)
1978	15,877	0.00 (0.96)
1979	14,141	−0.01 (0.96)
1980	14,056	0.07 (0.99)
1981	15,611	0.06 (0.99)
1982	15,704	0.04 (0.99)
1983	14,514	0.03 (0.99)
1984	14,026	0.03 (1.00)
1985	14,096	0.03 (1.00)
1986	13,631	0.03 (1.01)
1987	14,390	0.07 (1.01)
1988	14,571	0.06 (1.03)
1989	14,785	0.03 (1.04)
1990	11,285	0.03 (1.03)
1991	13,462	0.04 (1.04)
1992	13,845	0.01 (1.06)
1993	13,913	−0.01 (1.06)
1994	13,096	−0.02 (1.08)
1995	10,647	0.02 (1.06)
1996	11,917	0.05 (1.07)
1997	12,728	0.00 (1.09)
1998	12,627	0.01 (1.09)
1999	11,347	−0.01 (1.09)
2000	10,218	−0.02 (1.10)
2001	10,390	−0.06 (1.09)
2002	10,258	−0.08 (1.09)
2003	11,718	−0.10 (1.08)
2004	11,957	−0.11 (1.07)
2005	11,966	−0.08 (1.09)
2006	13,836	−0.08 (1.08)
d^a	—	−0.06 (−0.08 to −0.04)

[a]This row presents the standardized difference between the mean for 2004 through 2006 and the mean for 1976 through 1978. The negative value indicates that the latter mean was higher. The numbers in parentheses are the 95% confidence interval.

A third issue to consider is that the NPI measures multiple facets of narcissism, and temporal changes at the facet level may not always map onto temporal changes in the full-scale score. Emmons showed that subscales of the NPI can have distinct external correlates, some of which might be considered psychologically adaptive. Similarly, Konrath, Bushman, and Campbell reported that the NPI Entitlement subscale is a better predictor of laboratory-based measures of aggression than the full scale is, which suggests that not all of the narcissistic tendencies assessed by the NPI are equally destructive. The most important concern, however, is that because the NPI assesses a number of constructs, it is unclear how to precisely interpret any changes in the summary score. A secular change in the NPI might signal changes in socially toxic traits (e.g., entitlement), socially noxious traits (e.g., vanity), or simply relatively benign traits (e.g., leadership). Our results illustrate this point: The largest increase was found for the seemingly benign trait of self-sufficiency, and the largest decrease was found for the seemingly socially toxic trait of superiority.

This study has several limitations. First, although we used large samples of college students to evaluate secular changes in narcissism, our large samples are not likely representative of the entire U.S. population of 18- to 24-year-olds. Indeed, students at 4-year colleges represent only 24% of the population ages 18 to 24. Moreover, it is unknown how students in psychology courses differ in psychological characteristics from other college students. Nonetheless, these two concerns are mitigated to some extent by the fact that we also failed to find a secular trend in self-enhancement in a representative sample of high school students. Thus, we failed to find evidence of a secular trend in self-enhancement using both representative and convenience samples. Second, we did not have an ideal proxy measure for intelligence to assess self-enhancement in the high school sample. However, this concern is ameliorated by the fact that the results were similar to those based on SAT scores in the college-student sample, which is not surprising because in the latter sample, the correlation between self-enhancement based on grades and self-enhancement based on test scores was .90. Thus, the strengths and limitations of our data sets are quite complementary, and the results converge in showing few indications of secular change in self-enhancement.

Finally, some of the findings we report are based on null results. However, null results can be critical in science when they counter a predicted effect and when they are based on large samples, which rules out concerns of a lack of power to detect predicted effects. The lack of a clear trend toward increasing narcissism directly addresses recent claims of secular increases in narcissism that have received a great deal of attention in the media, as shown by Jimmy Carter's response in *Rolling Stone* magazine. The degree of empirical support for claims of increasing narcissism among this generation of young American adults has important implications for how this generation is viewed by others and how young adults view themselves.

We believe that great care needs to be exercised when making broad generalizations about cohort-related increases in narcissism. We were unable to find evidence that either narcissism or the closely related construct of self-enhancement has increased over the past three decades. Moreover, even if we had found evidence for a secular increase in narcissism, placing the blame on the self-esteem movement would seem to go well beyond the data, especially when there is evidence that well-designed and well-implemented self-esteem programs are effective interventions for youth with certain problems. Our view is that the research findings concerning generational differences should be based on well-established results and presented to the public with a good degree of caution given the inherent complexities involved in studying cohort effects.

Acknowledgments—The first and second authors contributed equally to this article; the ordering of authorship was arbitrary. We thank Rob Ackerman, Kim Assad, Portia Dyrenforth, Richard Lucas, and Ed Witt for helpful comments on an earlier draft of this article.

CHALLENGE QUESTIONS

Are Today's Youth More Self-Centered Than Previous Generations?

1. The researchers on both sides of this issue used the same measurement tool (the NPI) but came to very different conclusions. Why might this be?
2. If today's youth really are more narcissistic, is this a bad thing? What might be the consequences of such a shift, and what, if anything, should be done to alter it?
3. What are the implications of these two positions for the self-esteem movement? Given the disagreement on the issue, what should we do about teaching self-esteem?
4. How does your own perceptions of your self affect your views of this issue? Would your position be different if you were not included in the population accused of being more narcissistic? Does caring about this issue suggest you are narcissistic?
5. Do you consider some Internet sites, for example, MySpace, Facebook, and YouTube as self-centering sites? What are the implications of their proliferation?

ISSUE 8

Do Online Friendships Hurt Adolescent Development?

YES: Lauren Donchi and Susan Moore, from "It's a Boy Thing: The Role of the Internet in Young People's Psychological Wellbeing," *Behavior Change* (vol. 21, no. 2, 2004)

NO: Patti M. Valkenburg and Jochen Peter, from "Online Communication and Adolescent Well-Being: Testing the Stimulation Versus the Displacement Hypothesis," *Journal of Computer-Mediated Communication* (vol. 12, issue 4, 2007)

ISSUE SUMMARY

YES: Psychologists Lauren Donchi and Susan Moore report that adolescent males who rate online friendships higher than face-to-face friendships are more likely to be lonely and experience low self-esteem.

NO: Professors of communication Patti M. Valkenburg and Jochen Peter maintain that online relationships actually *enhance* an adolescent's face-to-face peer relations and psychological wellbeing.

Although virtually non-existent a generation ago, the Internet has rapidly become a staple of modern life. The Internet is used to shop, watch television, conduct investigations, hold business meetings, and even perform remote surgeries. Perhaps one of the most common uses of the Internet is personal communication (e-mails, text messages, blogs, etc). Social networking sites, in which users can share content and communicate with friends, have experienced an exponential rise in popularity, with sites such as Facebook.com (which only opened to the public in September 2006) boasting over 200 million active users.

A significant factor in this networking boom has been the increasing online presence of adolescent users. A 2005 Pew Report found that over 87% of American teenagers had regular access to the Internet. Along with this increase in access, some lawmakers and parents have expressed concern with the possible detrimental effects of excessive online activity. While highly publicized cases have focused on Internet-related suicides and sex crimes, there is a broader concern over the social development of teenagers who seem to spend more and more time in the virtual world and less time in the "real" world.

In their article, Donchi and Moore review a number of research reports detailing the negative psychological effects of adolescent Internet use. They specifically examine studies of loneliness, the number of online and offline friends, and the quality of friendships; they conclude that "all well-being measures were negatively related to Internet focus." They also note a "gender effect," meaning that these negative effects appear to be more pronounced for males than for females. Consequently, they argue that online relationships cannot adequately substitute for offline face-to-face friendships in promoting social-emotional development in teenage boys.

Valkenburg and Peter, in the second article, make the distinction between online activities that *stimulate* offline relationships and those that *displace* them. The latter activities mean that time spent online is time spent away from developing meaningful human connections (displacing them). On the other hand, the authors suggest that there are many online activities—such as instant messaging (IM), e-mail, and chat rooms—that enhance an adolescent's offline relationships. They report a study that examines several hypotheses related to these two ways of interacting online. They conclude that online activity benefits offline peer development, at least for direct communication, such as IM. As they put it, "Internet communication is positively related to [an adolescent's] well being."

POINT

- Internet use can psychologically impair adolescent development.
- Time spent with online friends displaces offline relationships.
- Gender is an important variable influencing the effect of the Internet.

- Time online negatively affects both social and emotional measures (e.g., loneliness).

COUNTERPOINT

- Online friends do not damage psychological wellbeing.
- Online friendships enhance offline relationships.
- Type of online activity is an important variable influencing the effect of the Internet.
- Internet involvement increases intimate self-disclosure, helping teens foster trust and caring.

YES

Lauren Donchi and
Susan Moore

It's a Boy Thing: The Role of the Internet in Young People's Psychological Wellbeing

In Australia, 37% of all households currently have Internet access and this percentage is continuing to rise (Australian Bureau of Statistics, 2001). However, while the majority of Australians (61%) have some access to the Internet, the largest single grouping of users is teenage children. Males, particularly younger males, are more frequent users than females, although Odell, Korgen, Schumacher and Delucchi (2000) argue that the gender gap is closing quickly. Given these statistics, it would not be surprising to hear that the Internet has a marked effect on social life. . . .

One way to assess the relationships between social wellbeing and Internet use among young people is to examine the role that online and offline (face-to-face) friendships play in the alleviation of loneliness and the maintenance or development of self-esteem. . . . While it is well known that friendship is important to wellbeing, is this importance specific to face-to-face friends? . . .

Another variable of importance in examining wellbeing in Internet-use relationships is the actual time spent online. Longer amounts of time could be interpreted as relatively antisocial, and may reduce possibilities for social learning and social reinforcement in 'real-life' situations. On the other hand, if the time is spent engaged in Internet relationships, social learning and social rewards may still be available. Thus, in this study, we investigated the associations between time spent on the Internet (in different pursuits including personal communication, entertainment and information-seeking), number and importance of online and offline friendships, and social wellbeing.

This study focuses on Internet use and social relationships of young people in the 15 to 21 years age group, . . . a time in which friendship and peer-group belongingness is particularly salient to psychosocial development. . . . Peer interactions present opportunities for adolescents to develop the social competencies and social skills required for participation in adult society. Research affirms that peer friendships are important for maintaining psychological health and that peer-relationship difficulties are likely to be a source of stress to young people that leads to feelings of loneliness (Demir & Tarhan, 2001; Parkhurst & Asher, 1992). . . .

While adolescent social relations typically take place in face-to-face settings the introduction of communication applications on the Internet (e.g., email, chatrooms, Usenet newsgroups), . . . has led to the suggestion that Internet networks may also function as important social networks for users. Some support for this view is provided by Parks and Floyd (1996), who . . . found that nearly two-thirds of respondents had formed personal relationships with people they had met via an Internet newsgroup. . . . Further, a study by the Pew Internet and American Life Project (2001) . . . found that Internet communication was an essential feature of young people's social lives and had partially replaced face-to-face interactions. So while the Internet enables people to form online social networks, whether these online friendships can provide a substitute for face-to-face friendships in assisting development towards social maturity and psychological wellbeing is an open question. . . .

Disturbing signs that the Internet fosters loneliness in users first emerged in a longitudinal study conducted by Kraut and colleagues (Kraut et al., 1998; Kraut & Mukopadhyay, 1999) . . . [who] found that after controlling for initial-outcome variables, greater use of the Internet was associated with increased loneliness. They also found that teenagers used the Internet for more hours than adults and increases in Internet use were associated with larger increases in loneliness for teenagers than for adults. These findings were somewhat controversial, and the study was criticized for methodological reasons (small sample; no control group without access to the Internet). . . .

Since the publication of Kraut et al.'s (1998) . . . study that claimed 'using the Internet adversely affects psychological wellbeing' (p. 1028), social scientists have shown . . . interest in the Internet. However, much of the available research . . . has produced mixed results.

Some research has substantiated claims that Internet use is associated with reduced psychological wellbeing. For example, Armstrong, Phillips and Saling (2000) examined Internet use and self-esteem levels . . . [and found] that more time spent on the Internet was associated with lower self-esteem.

[On the other hand, a] recent longitudinal study conducted by Shaw and Gant (2002) [investigating] Internet use, loneliness and self-esteem . . . found that over the course of the study, during which subjects chatted anonymously on the Internet, participants' loneliness decreased and self-esteem increased.

Other research has [also] shed doubt on the association between Internet use and psychological wellbeing. Gross, Juvonen and Gable (2002) found that time online was not associated with loneliness. They surveyed 130 adolescents between the ages of 11 and 13 years. . . . Kraut and colleagues (2002) [in] . . . a second longitudinal study . . . found no overall relationship between Internet use and loneliness or self-esteem. However, they [did report] that Internet use was associated with better outcomes for extroverts (i.e., decreased loneliness and increased self-esteem) and worse outcomes for introverts (i.e., increased loneliness and decreased self-esteem). Hence in [their] study, individual characteristics served as important moderating variables between Internet use and psychological wellbeing. . . . In sum, while much research has studied the relationship between Internet use and psychological wellbeing, the available data is equivocal.

One reason for the mixed findings regarding Internet use and loneliness may be that while evidence points to the importance of employing a multidimensional concept of loneliness, there is little available research which links more complex conceptions of loneliness to Internet use. Most studies have employed the UCLA Loneliness Scale, which has come to be viewed as the standard scale to assess loneliness, measuring it as a global construct. One exception was Weiss (1973), who distinguished between emotional loneliness and social loneliness. Emotional loneliness is characterised by a feeling of abandonment, emptiness and apprehension due to the absence of a close, intimate attachment. Social loneliness refers to the feeling of boredom and marginality due to the lack of belonging to a social network or community. Weiss argues that relief from emotional loneliness requires the formation of an attachment relationship that promotes a sense of emotional security, whereas remediation from social loneliness requires being accepted as a member of a friendship network that provides a sense of social integration.

The association between Internet use and Weiss's (1973) bimodal theory of loneliness was examined by Moody (2001), who compared 166 university students' self-reported Internet use to their social and emotional loneliness and to their friendship networks both on the Internet and on a face-to-face basis. Moody developed the Social Network Scale to assess the latter. His findings revealed that while students who spent more time on the Internet communicating with friends were likely to have higher rates of emotional loneliness, they were less like to experience social loneliness than those who spent less time on the Internet communicating with friends. Moody concluded that the psychological effects of Internet use are more complex than previous studies have indicated. His findings suggest that by limiting the face-to-face component of social interaction, emotional loneliness might occur despite high Internet use, providing some individuals with a sense of social integration and thus lowered social loneliness.

Following Moody's (2001) lead, the present study employed Weiss's (1973) distinction between emotional and social loneliness in studying the associations between Internet use, social networks and psychological wellbeing. Furthermore, in keeping with previous research, global loneliness (as measured by the UCLA scale) and self-esteem were also used as measures of psychological wellbeing. The study distinguished between time spent on different activities on the Internet, and used measures of social networks which included, but were not limited to, number of friends. . . . In short, this study examined the relationships between wellbeing, time spent on the Internet, and social networks, including online and offline (face-to-face) networks. Patterns of relationships were examined separately for the sexes because of previous research suggesting differences in the ways young men and young women use the Internet, even though differences in the amount of time spent on the Internet by males and females are closing (Odell et al., 2000).

Method

Participants

There were 336 participants, aged 15 to 21 years in the sample (114 males and 222 females). This included 110 [secondary school students (mean age 16.16) and] 226 university-based [students (mean age 18.55)]. . . .

Materials

The questionnaire consisted of sections designed to measure demographic variables (gender, age, education level), Internet use, social networks, loneliness and self-esteem.

Measuring Internet use   In order to assess the amount of time young people spend on the Internet on an average day, respondents were presented with a list of Internet activities. Thirteen of the activities related to three categories of Internet use: interpersonal communication (4 items; e.g., 'visiting chat rooms'), entertainment (5 items; e.g., 'searching for things of personal interest') and information (4 items; e.g., 'finding articles and references'). For each Internet activity, participants were asked to indicate in minutes the time spent on each activity 'on an average day'. . . .

Measuring social networks   Respondents use of the Internet and face-to face relations for communicating with friends was measured using the 12-item Social Network Scale (Moody, 2001). . . . Respondents were asked to indicate how well each item described them on a 5-point Likert scale. . . .

In order to assess the number of friends young people regularly communicate with on the Internet and on a face-to-face basis, participants were asked to answer two questions: 'How many friends do you talk to regularly on the Internet?' and 'How many friends do you talk to regularly on a face-to-face basis?'

Measuring loneliness   The UCLA Loneliness Scale was used to measure loneliness conceptualized as a global, unidimensional construct. . . . The 20-item scale has 10 descriptive feelings of loneliness and 10 descriptive feelings of satisfaction with social relationships. . . .

[The] . . . 10-item Emotional and Social Loneliness Scale . . . was used to measure loneliness conceptualized as a multidimensional construct. The scale comprises two 5-item subscales that distinguish between emotional loneliness (e.g., 'I don't have a special love relationship') and social loneliness (e.g., 'Mostly, everyone around me seems like a stranger'). . . .

Measuring self-esteem   The measure used to obtain an assessment of self-esteem was Form A of the 16-item Texas Social Behaviour Inventory. . . .

Results

Gender Differences in Internet Use

. . . Males and females spent similar lengths of time on the Internet on an average day engaged in personal communication: female mean—65.4 minutes, male mean—68.7 minutes; and information-seeking: female mean—56.5 minutes, male mean—59.1 minutes. However, males spent significantly longer using the Internet for entertainment on an average day, in fact, about twice as much time as females: female mean—63.9 minutes, male mean—121.6 minutes. . . . In addition, males said they had more regular Internet friends than females. . . . For face-to-face regular friendships the trend was reversed, with females indicating more friendships. . . . The sexes did not differ on the importance they attached to either Internet or face-to-face friendships.

Relationships between Online and Face-to-Face Friendships

. . . The numbers of friends on- and offline were positively associated for both sexes; the more friends in one domain, the more in the other (they may indeed be an overlapping set). An interesting gender difference occurred for the scales measuring perceived importance of the two domains; for females these two scales were unrelated, suggesting that online and offline networks were not developed at the expense of one another. For males, these two scales were negatively associated, suggesting that the young men in this study tended to emphasise one domain over the other.

Network Group Differences on Wellbeing

The number of regular face-to-face friends (face-to-face friends) and number of regularly-communicated-with online friends (online friends) were divided at their respective medians into high and low face-to-face and high and low online friendship groups. A four-way multivariate analysis of variance was conducted with gender (male, female), education level (school university), face-to-face friendship group (high, low) and online friendship group (high, low) as the independent variables. The dependent variables were the four measures of wellbeing: general loneliness (UCLA loneliness score), social loneliness, emotional loneliness and self-esteem.

The main effects of gender . . . and face-to-face friendship group . . . were significant; other main effects did not show significant group differences. . . .

Males were significantly more socially lonely than females, . . . and males were also significantly more emotionally lonely than females. . . . The trends for the males in the sample to have lower self-esteem and score higher on the UCLA loneliness scale than females were not statistically significant.

Not surprisingly, face-to-face friendship group was also related to the wellbeing measures. Specifically, those with more face-to-face friends had higher self-esteem than those in the low face-to-face friendship group. . . . The high friendship group was also less socially lonely, . . . and less generally lonely on the UCLA scale than the low face-to-face friendship group. . . .

There were gender-by-friendship group interactions for both online and face-to-face friendship groups. . . . [Females] with more online friends were higher on self-esteem and lower on loneliness than females with fewer online friends, but . . . the opposite was true for males. Higher numbers of online regular friendships seemed to militate against self-esteem and be related to greater loneliness for males. . . .

For face-to-face friendships, the effects on wellbeing were in the same direction for males and females, but they were stronger for males. [Those] with more face-to-face friendships were higher on self-esteem and less lonely, with males showing greater extremes of loneliness and low self-esteem than females, and wellbeing as more strongly associated with face-to-face friendships for males than for females.

Predicting Wellbeing from Number of Friends (On- and Offline), Social Network Importance (On- and Offline) and Time Spent on the Internet

Regressions were conducted (separately for males and females) to assess whether the set of variables including number of online and face-to-face friends, perceived importance of online and face-to-face networks and time spent on the Internet predicted wellbeing (self-esteem and 3 measures of loneliness). None of the potential predictor variables were correlated at greater than 6. . . . Correlations . . . showed a pattern for girls of significant positive correlations between wellbeing and face-to-face friendship indicators, and weak or nonsignificant correlations between wellbeing and online friendship indicators. There were no significant correlations between time spent on the Internet and wellbeing for girls. For boys, the correlations between wellbeing and face-to-face friendship indicators were significant and positive and between wellbeing and both time spent on the Internet and online friendship indicators were significant and negative. . . .

The regressions show a similar pattern of findings to the MANOVA, in the sense that the results for males suggest a greater implication of Internet use in loneliness and lower self-esteem. While the importance associated with face-to-face friendships and, to some extent, the number of face-to-face friends were the strongest predictors of loneliness and self-esteem, online relationship activity was also consistently associated with well being for males, but in a negative direction. In other words, young men who rated their online friendship networks as very important were more likely to have lower self-esteem and to be lonely. None of the measures of the time spent online (for communication, entertainment or information-related activities) were significant predictors of wellbeing.

Discussion

The present study supported previous research suggesting that young males would spend more time on the Internet on an average day than young females (Kraut & Mukopadhyay, 1999; Odell et al., 2000). Both sexes indicated that they spent large amounts of time with this medium, three hours per day for girls and four for boys. While these times may have been overestimated due to the form of measurement used (assessing minutes per average day across several categories of activity), they do suggest some cause for concern. The gender gap had closed for the Internet activities of personal communication and information-seeking, but was still very much in evidence for Internet entertainment, an activity on which boys spent about two hours per day—twice as long as the girls. In addition, boys had more Internet friends and fewer face-to-face friends than girls, although the total friendship numbers were equal. Boys who ascribed high importance to their Internet friends tended to estimate their face-to-face networks as less important, while girls rated the importance of their Internet and face-to-face friendships similarly. The picture that emerges is of young people spending long hours at the computer, with boys in particular limiting their time for face-to-face interactions and, to some extent, discounting these. Time available for offline activities is thus reduced, particularly for boys. How do these findings relate to wellbeing?

Young people reported that the number of face-to-face friendships were clearly related to wellbeing, with more friends associated with higher self-esteem and lower social and general loneliness. These effects were stronger for boys, indicating that offline friends were particularly important as markers of wellbeing for them. In addition, while online friendships were associated with better wellbeing for girls, the opposite was true for boys. Higher numbers of regular online friendships amongst boys were related to lower self-esteem and greater loneliness. In the regressions, offline friendship number and perceived importance positively predicted wellbeing for both sexes, while online friendship number and importance negatively predicted wellbeing for boys only. These effects of friendship patterns swamped any relationships between wellbeing and time spent online.

Thus, the answer to the question of whether online social interactions can substitute for (or enhance) offline face-to-face friendships for young people during adolescence and early adulthood appears to be a definite 'no' for boys. There is a great deal of evidence that peer relations play an important role in promoting adolescent and youth social–emotional development, act as a buffer against loneliness and enhance self-esteem (e.g., Demir & Tarhan, 2001; Parkhurst & Asher, 1992). This study suggests a need for young men to experience a significant proportion of these peer relationships in the real-world domain. Those young men who strongly emphasise the importance of their online relationships may be cutting off options for psychosocial development through the give and take of face-to-face friendships. This may be a result of lack of social confidence and poor social skills leading to avoidance of real-world friendships with all their difficulties. Or it may be that the nature of Internet relationships (e.g., possibilities for anonymity and role-playing, reduced need to 'work at' friendships) can undermine skills needed in face-to-face relationships. Or, more simply, online friendships may reduce time available for offline friendships which appear to have a greater potential to relate positively to wellbeing. Kraut and colleagues (1998) speculated that negative effects of Internet use could result from both the displacement of social activities and of strong ties. According to this view, the time an individual spends online might interrupt or replace time they had previously spent engaged in real-life social activities. Furthermore, by using the Internet, an individual may be substituting their better real-life relationships or 'strong ties', which are thought to lead to better psychological outcomes, for artificial online relationships or 'weak ties.'

Girls, on the other hand, seem to have developed mechanisms by which their online activity does not interfere with offline friendships, and may even enhance it. For girls, more friendships either on- or offline related to positive indicators of wellbeing. This may relate in part to the fact that girls spend less time on the Internet altogether. In addition, when they do access the Internet, around one-third of this time is devoted to personal communication activities, some of which may involve relating to friends who are substantially of the face-to-face type. Boys, on the other hand, spend only about one-quarter of their time in such activities, preferring to engage in Internet entertainment, games and so on, which have a greater potential to be socially isolating.

It has been suggested that the lack of clarity in the literature to date regarding the association between wellbeing and Internet use may relate to issues surrounding the measurement of wellbeing (Moody, 2001). We used 4 measures and, in particular, were able to test out Moody's (2001) idea that time spent on the Internet communicating with friends would be related to higher emotional, but not higher social, loneliness. This was not the case. In fact, all wellbeing measures were negatively related to Internet focus (time spent on the Internet, Internet friendships, and their perceived importance) for boys. For girls, the relationships between Internet activity and measures of loneliness were weakly negative or nonexistent. Thus boys appear to be disadvantaged both socially and emotionally by their reliance on Internet friendships, while social and emotional advantage is associated with online and offline friendships for girls, and offline friendships for both sexes. . . .

All references for articles included in *Taking Sides: Clashing Views on Psychological Issues, 17/e* can be found on the Web at http://www.mhhe.com/cls.

Patti M. Valkenburg
and Jochen Peter

 **NO**

Online Communication and Adolescent Well-Being: Testing the Stimulation Versus the Displacement Hypothesis

Introduction

Opportunities for adolescents to form and maintain relationships on the Internet have multiplied in the past few years. Not only has the use of Instant Messaging (IM) increased tremendously, but Internet-based chatrooms and social networking sites are also rapidly gaining prominence as venues for the formation and maintenance of personal relationships. In recent years, the function of the Internet has changed considerably for adolescents. Whereas in the 1990s they used the Internet primarily for entertainment, at present they predominantly use it for interpersonal communication (Gross, 2004).

The rapid emergence of the Internet as a communication venue for adolescents has been accompanied by diametrically opposed views about its social consequences. Some authors believe that online communication hinders adolescents' well-being because it displaces valuable time that could be spent with existing friends. . . . Adherents of this displacement hypothesis assume that the Internet motivates adolescents to form online contacts with strangers rather than to maintain friendships with their offline peers. Because online contacts are seen as superficial weak-tie relationships that lack feelings of affection and commitment, the Internet is believed to reduce the quality of adolescents' existing friendships and, thereby, their well-being.

Conversely, other authors suggest that online communication may enhance the quality of adolescents' existing friendships and, thus, their well-being. Adherents of this stimulation hypothesis argue that more recent online communication technologies, such as IM, encourage communication with existing friends (Bryant, Sanders-Jackson, & Smallwood, 2006). Much of the time adolescents spend alone with computers is actually used to keep up existing friendships (Gross, 2004; Valkenburg & Peter, 2007). If adolescents use the Internet primarily to maintain contacts with their existing friends, the prerequisite for a displacement effect is not fulfilled. . . .

From *Journal of Computer-Mediated Communication*, vol. 12, issue 4, 2007, pp. 1169–1182 (excerpts). Copyright © 2007 by International Communication Association. Reprinted by permission of Wiley-Blackwell and Patti M. Valkenburg and Jochen Peter.

Several studies have investigated the effect of Internet use on the quality of existing relationships and well-being. Some of these studies used depression or loneliness measures as indicators of well-being; others employed measures of life-satisfaction or positive/negative affect. The studies have provided mixed results: Some have yielded results in agreement with the displacement hypothesis. Others have produced results in support of the stimulation hypothesis. . . .

At least one omission in earlier research may contribute to the inconsistent findings regarding the Internet-well-being relationship. Most research to date has been descriptive or exploratory in nature. The studies investigate direct linear relationships between Internet use and one or more dependent variables, such as social involvement, depression, or loneliness. Hardly any research has been based on a-priori explanatory hypotheses regarding *how* Internet use is related to well-being. More importantly, there is no research that contrasts opposing explanatory hypotheses in the same study. . . .

The main aim of this study is to fill the gap in earlier research and pit the predictions of the displacement hypothesis against those of the stimulation hypothesis. By empirically studying the validity of the processes proposed by the two hypotheses, we hope to improve theory formation and contribute to a more profound understanding of the social consequences of the Internet. In fact, the two hypotheses are based on the same two mediators. Both hypotheses state that online communication affects adolescents' well-being through its influence on (1) their time spent with existing friends and (2) the quality of these friendships. However, the displacement hypothesis assumes a negative effect from online communication on time spent with existing friends, whereas the stimulation hypothesis predicts a positive relationship between these two variables. The two opposing hypotheses are stated below.

H1a: Online communication will reduce time spent with existing friends.
H1b: Online communication will enhance time spent with existing friends.

. . . Neither hypothesis predicts a direct relationship between online communication and well-being. Rather, both suggest that the influence of online communication on well-being will be mediated by the quality of friendships. There is general agreement that the quality of friendships is an important predictor of well-being. Quality friendships can form a powerful buffer against potential stressors in adolescence (Hartup, 2000), and adolescents with high-quality friendships are often more socially competent and happier than adolescents without such friendships. Based on these considerations, we hypothesize that if online communication influences well-being, it will be through its influence on the quality of existing friendships. Our second hypothesis, . . . therefore states:

H2: Adolescents' quality of friendships will positively predict their well-being and act as a mediator between online communication and well-being.

However, the relationship between online communication and the quality of friendships may also not be direct. Both the displacement and stimulation hypotheses assume that time spent with existing friends acts as a mediator between online communication and the quality of friendships. Based on these assumptions, we hypothesize an indirect relationship between online communication and the quality of friendships, via the time spent with existing friends:

> **H3:** Adolescents' time spent with friends will predict the quality of their friendships and act as a mediator between online communication and the quality of friendships.

Type of Online Communication: IM Versus Chat

In earlier Internet effects studies, the independent variable Internet use has often been treated as a one-dimensional concept. This may be another important reason why the findings of these studies are so mixed. Many studies only employed a measure of daily or weekly time spent on the Internet and did not distinguish between different types of Internet use, such as surfing or online communication. . . .

It is quite possible that daily time spent on the Internet does not affect one's well-being, whereas certain types of Internet use do have such an effect. In this study, we focus on the type of Internet use that is theoretically most likely to influence well-being and the quality of existing friendships: online communication. We believe that if the Internet influences well-being, it will be through its potential to alter the nature of social interaction through the use of online communication technologies. In this study, well-being is defined as happiness or a positive evaluation of one's life in general (Diener, Suh, Lucas, & Smith, 1999).

Online communication in itself is a multidimensional concept. We focus on two types of communication that are often used by adolescents. IM and chat in public chatrooms. Both types of online communication are synchronous and often used for private communication. However, they differ in several respects. First, whereas chat in a public chatroom is often based on anonymous communication between unacquainted partners, IM mostly involves non-anonymous communication between acquainted partners (Valkenburg & Peter, 2007). Second, whereas chat is more often used to *form* relationships, IM is typically used to *maintain* relationships (Grinter & Palen, 2004). Although there is no previous research on the social consequences of IM versus chat, it is entirely possible that these two types of online communication differ in their potential to influence the quality of existing friendships and well-being. . . . The second aim of our study is to investigate the differential effects of IM versus chat on well-being and the two mediating variables. Because previous research does not allow us to formulate a hypothesis regarding these differential effects of different types of online communication, our research question asks:

> **RQ1:** How do the causal predictions of the displacement and stimulation hypothesis differ for IM and chat in a public chatroom?

Method

Sample

In December 2005, an online survey was conducted among 1,210 Dutch adolescents between 10 and 17 years of age (53% girls, 47% boys). Sampling and fieldwork were done by Qrius, a market research company in Amsterdam, the Netherlands. . . . The sample was representative of Dutch children and adolescents who use the Internet in terms of age, gender, and education. . . . Adolescents were notified that the study would be about Internet and well-being and that they could stop participation at any time they wished. . . . Completing the questionnaire took about 15–20 minutes.

We preferred an online interviewing mode to more traditional modes of interviewing, such as face-to-face or telephone interviews. There is consistent research evidence that both adolescents and adults report sensitive behaviors more easily in computer-mediated interviewing modes than in non-computer-mediated modes. . . . Therefore, the response patterns in our study may have benefited from our choice of a computer-mediated interviewing mode as far as more intimate issues, such as the quality of friendships and well-being, are concerned.

Measures

IM Use

We measured adolescents' IM use with four questions: (a) "On *weekdays* (Monday to and including Friday), how many days do you usually use IM?" (b) "On the *weekdays* (Monday to and including Friday) that you use IM, how long do you then usually use it?" (c) "During *weekends* (Saturday and Sunday), how many days do you usually use IM?" The response options were: (1) *Only on Saturday;* (2) *Only on Sunday;* (3) *On both days;* and (4) *I do not use IM on the weekends.* If respondents selected response options 1 to 3 in the question on IM weekend use, they were asked the following question for Saturday and/ or Sunday: (d) "On a Saturday (a Sunday), how long do you usually use IM?" Respondents' IM use per week was calculated by multiplying the number of days per week that they used IM (range 0 through 7) by the number of minutes they used it on each day. . . . The mean time spent with IM per week was 15 hours and 15 minutes (SD = 21 hours and 10 minutes).

Chat Use

We measured respondents' chat use in the same way as their IM use. Using the same four questions, we asked the respondents to evaluate how much time per week they used chat in public chatrooms. The mean time spent with chat per week was 1 hour and 23 minutes (SD = 7 hours and 30 minutes).

Time Spent with Friends

Time spent with existing friends was measured with three items that were adopted from the companionship subscale of Buhrmester's (1990) Network of Relationship Inventory. We first asked respondents to think of the friends they know from their offline environment, such as from school and the neighborhood. Then we asked them three questions: (a) "How often do you meet with one or more of these friends?," (b) "How often do you and these friends go to places and do things together?," and (c) "How often do you go out and have fun with one or more of these friends?" Response options ranged from 1 (*never*) to 9 (*several times a day*). The three items loaded on one factor, which explained 69% of the variance (Cronbach's alpha = .76, M = 5.78; SD =1.65).

Quality of Friendships

The quality of existing friendships was measured with the relationship satisfaction (three items), approval (three items), and support (three items) subscales of Buhrmester's (1990) Network of Relationship Inventory. We asked respondents to think of the friends they know from their offline environment, such as from school and the neighborhood. Example items were: (1) "How often are you happy with your relationship with these friends?" (satisfaction), "How often do these friends praise you for the kind of person you are?" (approval), and (3) "How often do you turn to these friends for support with personal problems?" Response options ranged from 1 (*never*) to 5 (*always*). The nine items were averaged to form a quality of friendship scale (Cronbach's alpha = .93; M = 3.44; SD = 0.72).

Well-Being

We used the five-item satisfaction with life scale developed by Diener, Emmons, Larsen, and Griffin (1985). Examples of items of this scale are "I am satisfied with my life" and "In most ways my life is close to my ideal." Response categories ranged from 1 (*agree entirely*) to 5 (*disagree entirely*) and were reversely coded. Cronbach's alpha for the scale was .88, which is comparable to the alpha of .87 reported by Diener et al. (1985).

Results

Time Spent with IM and Chat

Respondents spent significantly more time per day on IM than on chat. Specifically, they spent on average two hours and 11 minutes per day on IM and on average 12 minutes per day on chat. This greater amount of time spent on IM suggests that if any effect of the Internet is to be expected, it will occur through the use of IM. However, to verify this claim, we test the separate effects of IM and chat in the subsequent analyses.

Online Communication with Existing Friends

We also investigated the assumption in this and earlier studies that IM is most often used to communicate with existing friends, whereas chat in a public chatroom is more often used to communicate with strangers. This assumption was supported. Ninety-one percent of the respondents indicated that they "often" to "always" used IM to communicate with existing friends. Thirty-seven percent of the respondents indicated that they "often" to "always" used chat to communicate with existing friends.

Pitting the Displacement Hypothesis against the Stimulation Hypothesis

Following the displacement and stimulation hypothesis, we did not assume a direct relationship between online communication and well-being. Rather, we expected that the direct relationship between online communication would be mediated by the time spent with existing friends and the quality of these friendships. . . . In line with our expectations, neither IM nor chat use was directly related to well-being. However, the results do suggest a mediated positive effect of IM use and, to a lesser extent, a positive mediated effect of chat use on well-being through the time spent with friends and the quality of friendships.

We used a formal mediation analysis to test our hypotheses. In recent years, several approaches to examining indirect or mediated effects have been discussed. The most widely used approach is the causal steps approach developed by Judd and Kenny (1981). . . . The causal steps approach has recently been criticized, first because it does not provide a statistical test of the size of the indirect effects, and second because the requirement that there must be a significant direct association between the independent and dependent variable is considered too restrictive.

The problems inherent in the causal steps approach are solved in the intervening variable approach proposed by MacKinnon and his colleagues (MacKinnon, Lockwood et al., 2002), which was used in the present study. The first step in this approach is to run a regression analysis with the independent variable predicting the mediator. The second step is to estimate the effect of the mediator on the dependent variable, after controlling for the independent variable. However, because we hypothesized that two (rather than one) intervening variables would mediate the effect of online communication on well-being, we used a four-step procedure to test for mediation.

In the first step, the independent variable (online communication) predicted the first intervening variable (time spent with friends). In the second step, the first intervening variable (time spent with friends) predicted the second intervening variable (quality of friendships), while controlling for the independent variable (online communication). In the third step, the first intervening variable (time spent with friends) predicted the second intervening variable (quality of friendships), and in the fourth and final step, the second intervening variable (quality of friendships) predicted well-being, while controlling for the first intervening variable (time spent with friends). . . .

The first mediation analysis shows that time spent with IM was positively related ($\beta = .15$, $p < .001$) to the time spent with existing friends, a result which supports the stimulation hypothesis and our H1b. The opposite displacement hypothesis expressed in H1a, which predicted a negative path between these two variables, was not supported. The regression analysis showed that time spent with chat was not significantly related to time spent with friends ($\beta = .02$, n.s.). This implies that the first condition for mediation was not met in the case of time spent with chat. In other words, the causal predictions of the two hypotheses (H1a and H1b) only applied to IM, but not to chat. Therefore, the subsequent mediation analyses were only conducted for time spent with IM.

Our second hypothesis stated that the quality of friendships would positively predict well-being and act as mediator between time spent with friends and well-being. This hypothesis was supported. . . . The second mediation analysis shows that the quality of friendships significantly predicted well-being ($\beta = .16$, $p < .001$), even when the first mediating variable (time spent with friends) was controlled. The fact that time spent with friends remained a significant predictor ($\beta = .13$, $p < .001$) of well-being when the quality of friendship was controlled indicates that the mediation of quality of friendship was only partial. Finally, in support of our third hypothesis time spent with friends acted as a full mediator between time spent with IM and the quality of friendships. . . .

We tested the significance of the indirect effects by means of a formula developed by Sobel (1982). If the Sobel test leads to the critical z-value of 1.96, the mediator carries the influence of the independent variable to the dependent variable. . . . The z-value for the first mediation analysis was 5.03, $p = .001$; the z-value for the second mediation analysis was 4.98, $p = .001$. These significant z-values indicate that both the time spent with friends and the quality of friendships are valid underlying mechanisms through which the effect of IM on well-being can be explained.

Discussion

The aim of this study was to test the validity of two opposing explanatory hypotheses on the effect of online communication on well-being: the displacement hypothesis and the stimulation hypothesis. Both hypotheses assume that online communication affects adolescents' well-being through its influence on their time spent with existing friends and the quality of those friendships. However, the displacement hypothesis assumes a negative effect from online communication to time spent with existing friends, whereas the stimulation hypothesis predicts a positive relationship between these variables.

We used formal mediation analyses to test the validity of the two mediating variables. Our results were more in line with the stimulation hypothesis than with the displacement hypothesis. We found that time spent with IM was positively related to the time spent with existing friends. In addition, the quality of friendships positively predicted well-being and acted as a first mediator between time spent with IM and well-being. Finally, we found that time spent with friends mediated the effect of time spent with IM on the quality of friendships.

However, the positive effects of our study held only for the time spent with IM and not for time spent with chat in a public chatroom. IM and chat seem to have very different functions for adolescents. In line with earlier studies, we found that the majority of adolescents use IM to talk with their existing friends. Chat in a public chatroom is less often used by adolescents. However, when utilized, adolescents primarily seem to chat with strangers. It is important for future research to differentiate between the uses of online communication technologies. . . .

Overall, our study suggests that Internet communication is positively related to the time spent with friends and the quality of existing adolescent friendships, and, via this route, to their well-being. These positive effects may be attributed to two important structural characteristics of online communication: its controllability and its reduced cues. . . . Studies have shown that these characteristics of online communication may encourage intimate self-disclosure (e.g., Valkenburg & Peter, 2007), especially when adolescents perceive these characteristics of Internet communication as important (Valkenburg & Peter, 2007). Because intimate self-disclosure is an important predictor of reciprocal liking, caring, and trust, Internet-enhanced intimate self-disclosure may be responsible for a potential increase in the quality of adolescents' friendships. . . .

All references for articles included in *Taking Sides: Clashing Views on Psychological Issues, 17/e* can be found on the Web at http://www.mhhe.com/cls.

CHALLENGE QUESTIONS

Do Online Friendships Hurt Adolescent Development?

1. Both articles focus on general wellbeing and developmental issues related to online activity. How might their findings be related to the more sensationalized instances of online activity gone bad (e.g., teen suicide over MySpace.com messages, "sexting," and predatory activity)?
2. Why might Donchi and Moore have found a gender effect? What other "gender factors" may be involved in the differences between male and female approaches to friendship?
3. If Donchi and Moore are right about the negative effects of online usage of teens, what should be done to avoid these effects? If Valkenburg and Peter are correct, how can positive Internet usage be promoted? Is there a way to do both?
4. What developmental differences do the "Internet" youth of today face that their parents and grandparents did not face?
5. What in your view are the advantages and disadvantages of social networking sites (i.e. MySpace, Facebook, and YouTube)? Should there be restrictions placed on teen activity on such sites, or should they be entitled to the same access as adults? What are the pros and cons of your position?

Internet References . . .

University of Pennsylvania

This is the site of the Positive Psychology Center at the University of Pennsylvania.

http://www.ppc.sas.upenn.edu/

Psychology Today

This is the site for Psychology Today, with several links on positive psychology and happiness.

http://www.psychologytoday.com/basics/positive-psychology

About.com

This site provides several important links to the concept of emotional intelligence.

http://psychology.about.com/od/personalitydevelopment/ a/emotionalintell.htm

Consortium for Research on Emotional Intelligence

This site is a helpful source of research information on emotional intelligence from the Consortium for Research on Emotional Intelligence in Organizations.

http://www.eiconsortium.org/

Cognitive–Emotional Issues

*A*long with behavior, our cognitive and emotional abilities are of vital interests to psychologists. Many people, for example, are concerned with a particular emotion—how to become and remain happy. Could psychological research on the factors that facilitate and maintain well-being help us to be happier? What about emotions in general? Is there a skill or sensitivity regarding emotions that is akin to intelligence? Are some people better than others at empathizing, reading emotions, or knowing how to manipulate them?

- Can Positive Psychology Make Us Happier?
- Is Emotional Intelligence Valid?

ISSUE 9

Can Positive Psychology Make Us Happier?

YES: Julia K. Boehm and Sonja Lyubomirsky, from "The Promise of Sustainable Happiness." In *The Oxford Handbook of Positive Psychology*, 2nd ed. (Oxford University Press, 2009)

NO: Laurel C. Newman and Randy J. Larsen, from "How Much of Our Happiness Is Within Our Control?" An original article written for this text (2009)

ISSUE SUMMARY

YES: Health researcher Julia Boehm and psychologist Sonja Lyubomirsky argue that empirical research has established that people can use multiadaptive strategies to increase their levels of happiness.

NO: Psychologists Laurel Newman and Randy Larsen challenge the external validity and sustainability of the effects of these strategies, arguing that most of what influences our long-term happiness is outside our control.

Who wants to be happy? Or perhaps the empirical question is, how *can* we be happy? The U.S. *Declaration of Independence* lists the pursuit of happiness as an unalienable right, but no psychological researcher was around in 1776 to teach U.S. citizens how best to pursue it. Nor is the quest for happiness an exclusively U.S. business; the country Bhutan, for instance, has a Gross National Happiness (GNH) index to help guide government policy. Still, in the Western world of psychological research, Maslow's hierarchy of needs seems to be at play. In Maslow's hierarchy, we must satisfy our most basic needs (e.g., hunger) before we can concern ourselves with higher level needs, such as happiness and flourishing. If this is true, then only the more affluent countries, those that have satisfied their citizens' more basic needs, can even afford to ask the happiness question.

With this affluence, the positive psychology movement has risen during the last decade with the study of human flourishing as its major aim. Its focus on examining and nurturing what is best in humans is grounded in Ancient Greek philosophies and more recent humanistic psychological theories, such as that of Carl Rogers. Recently, happiness has become a popular emphasis of the movement, with a host of psychological researchers attempting to answer many important questions. Is happiness biologically based? Is it environmental? How much is under our personal control? Sonja Lyubomirsky's early book described research that she contended would achieve lasting happiness, but many critics examined her results with skepticism. Is the research now substantial enough for psychologists to finally tell people how they can become happy?

Julia Boehm and Sonja Lyubomirsky seem to think so. In the YES article, they argue that there are individual differences in "hedonic adaptation," a term that means people return to previous happiness levels after positive or negative events. Julia Boehm and Sonja Lyubomirsky believe that these differences imply that some people enhance and sustain their own happiness by strategizing the way they construe the world, make decisions, and self-reflect. They hold that genes determine about half of personal happiness, and circumstances may account for another 10 percent, but the other 40 percent may be within individual control. They contend that less happy people can not only learn strategies (e.g., doing acts of kindness, expressing gratitude, and visualizing best possible selves), but also apply these strategies to increase their levels of happiness. Indeed, psychological studies seem to show that careful interventions can be effective in facilitating happiness.

Laurel Newman and Randy Larsen believe that psychologists should be cautious before making public announcements about how we can make ourselves happier. For them, psychologists are misleading when they say that 40 percent of happiness is within our control. Although Laurel Newman and Randy Larsen agree that roughly half of the difference in happiness scores (within a group) may be attributed to genetics, they also believe that most life-changing events (those that affect happiness) are out of a person's control. This means, perhaps most importantly, that strategies and techniques for increasing happiness are not likely to endure, because people have a surprising tendency to return to preexisting levels of happiness after good and bad events have produced temporary changes in happiness levels. Moreover, Laurel Newman and Randy Larsen contend that the experimental effects of the most oft-cited happiness interventions are at best weak and require very specific circumstances to produce any effect.

POINT

- According to some models, 40 percent of happiness may be within our control.
- Circumstantial factors do not adequately explain different levels of happiness.
- Studies with happiness-inducing strategies show people can increase their levels of happiness.
- Individual differences in adaptation show that people can use strategies to help themselves stay happy, even after a less-than-happy event.

COUNTERPOINT

- Heritability estimates describe variations in groups and do not apply to individuals.
- A variety of environmental variables predict happiness, and many of them are uncontrollable.
- These strategies have weak statistical effects that show up only under very specific circumstances.
- People adapt quickly to negative and positive changes, returning to previous levels of happiness.

YES

Julia K. Boehm and
Sonja Lyubomirsky

The Promise of Sustainable Happiness

"How to gain, how to keep, how to recover happiness is in fact for most men at all times the secret motive of all they do, and of all they are willing to endure."

—William James

The quest for ever-greater happiness has existed since antiquity. Interest has not abated in today's society, whose preoccupation with becoming happier is evident in countless books and magazine articles promising the secret to a happy life. Indeed, the pursuit of happiness is not without reward, as empirical support is accumulating for the notion that happiness promotes multiple successful life outcomes (including superior health, higher income, and stronger relationships). Nonetheless, conflicting evidence raises questions about whether it is even possible for people to realize and then sustain meaningful changes in well-being.

In this chapter, we examine several issues with respect to sustainable happiness. To begin, we describe what happy and unhappy people are like, paying particular attention to the strategies that chronically happy people appear to use to foster and preserve their well-being. Next, we address some of the scientific community's reservations and uncertainties with respect to the possibility of sustainably increasing happiness. Finally, we review evidence suggesting that people can indeed learn strategies to achieve durable increases in well-being.

What Are Happy and Unhappy People Like?

Why are some people happier than others? Is it due to their marital status or the salary they earn? Is it because of the experiences they have or the culture they grow up in? Hundreds of empirical articles to date have examined how these and other so-called "objective" circumstances relate to happiness. Surprising to many laypeople, such objective factors (including marriage, age, sex, culture, income, and life events) explain relatively little variation in people's levels of well-being.

Given that circumstantial factors do not tell a satisfactory story to account for the differences between happy and unhappy people, one must look elsewhere to understand them. We propose that happy and unhappy individuals[1] differ considerably in their *subjective experience and construal* of the world. In other words, happy people are inclined to perceive and interpret their environment differently from their less happy peers. This construal theory prompts us to explore how an individual's thoughts, behaviors, and motivations can explain her happiness over and above the mere objective circumstances of her life. A growing body of research suggests that happy people successfully enhance and maintain their happiness through the use of multiple adaptive strategies vis-à-vis construal of themselves and others, social comparison, decision making, and self-reflection.

Construal

Indeed, research suggests that happy individuals tend to view the world relatively more positively and in a happiness-promoting way. For example, when describing their previous life experiences, self-nominated happy people retrospectively evaluated the experiences as more pleasant at both the time of occurrence and when recalling them. Unhappy people, however, evaluated their past life events relatively unfavorably at both time points. Interestingly, objective judges did not rate the events described by happy people as inherently more positive than those described by unhappy people, suggesting that happy and unhappy people experience similar events but interpret them differently. Further supporting this finding, when participants were asked to evaluate hypothetical situations, dispositionally happy people rated the situations more positively compared with their less happy peers, even after current mood was controlled.

Self-nominated chronically happy people also have been found to use a positive perspective when evaluating themselves and others. For example, in one study, students interacted with a female stranger in the laboratory and were then asked to evaluate her personality. Happy students rated the stranger more positively, and expressed a stronger interest in becoming friends with her, compared with unhappy students. Furthermore, happy people tend to judge almost everything about themselves and their lives favorably, including their friendships, recreation, self-esteem, energy levels, and purpose in life.

Social Comparison

At its most basic level, the general finding from the social comparison domain is that happy people are less sensitive to feedback about other people's performances, even when that feedback is unfavorable. An illustrative study from our laboratory involved participants solving anagrams in the presence of a confederate who was performing the same task either much quicker or much slower. When exposed to a slower confederate, all participants (regardless of how happy they were) reacted the same way to the experience—that is, performing the task bolstered confidence in their skills. In the presence of a faster confederate, however, happy students did not change their judgments of how good they were at the task, but unhappy participants derogated their own skills. This finding supports the argument that the self-perceptions of happy individuals are relatively invulnerable to social comparisons.

In another study, students were asked to "teach" a lesson about conflict resolution to a hypothetical audience of children while presumably being evaluated by experts. After this teaching task, participants were supplied with an expert evaluation of their own—and a peer's—teaching performance. The results showed that happy people responded to the situation in a predictable and adaptive manner—they reported more positive emotions when told that their performance was excellent (even when a peer had done even better) than when told that their performance was poor (even when a peer had done even worse). Unhappy people's reactions, by contrast, were surprising and even dysfunctional. They reported more positive emotions after receiving a *negative* expert evaluation (accompanied by news that a peer had done even worse) than after receiving a positive expert evaluation (accompanied by news that a peer had done even better). Again, this suggests that happy people's emotions and self-regard are much less impacted by comparisons with others than those of their unhappy peers.

Happy individuals' inclinations to deemphasize social comparison feedback have been observed in a group context as well. For example, in one study, students competed in 4-person groups (or "teams") in a relay race involving word puzzles. The announcement of the winning team—or their individual rank on their team—did not influence happy participants' moods. In contrast, unhappy participants showed depressed moods after their team supposedly lost, and bolstered moods after learning that they had individually placed 1st on their losing team. The results of this study suggest that unhappy students are more responsive to both group and individual information, particularly in "failure" situations. Whereas unhappy people use individual ranking information (i.e., 1st place on their team) to buffer against unfavorable group comparisons (i.e., their team's underperformance), happy people do not appear to need such a buffer.

Decision Making

Besides using different strategies in the social comparison domain, happy and unhappy people also respond distinctively when making decisions. For example, empirical evidence suggests that happy and unhappy individuals show divergent responses to both inconsequential decisions (e.g., selecting a dessert) and momentous ones (e.g., selecting a college). Happy people tend to be more satisfied with all of their available options (including the option they eventually choose) and only express dissatisfaction in situations when their sense of self is threatened. For example, when self-reported happy students were asked to rate the attractiveness of several desserts before and after learning which dessert they would get to keep, they increased their liking for the dessert they got and didn't change their liking for the dessert they couldn't get. This seems to be an adaptive strategy. In contrast, unhappy students found the option they were given to be minimally acceptable (derogating that dessert after learning they could keep it), and the forgone options to be even worse.

Similar patterns have been observed for happy and unhappy people facing a more significant decision-making situation—namely, the choice of a university. After being accepted by individual colleges, self-described happy students boosted their liking and judgments of those colleges. To protect themselves, however, these happy students decreased their overall ratings of the colleges that had rejected them. This dissonance reduction presumably allowed the happy participants to maintain positive feelings and self-regard. By contrast, unhappy participants did not use the same strategy to maintain positivity; instead, they (maladaptively) maintained their liking for the colleges that had rejected them.

Happy and unhappy people also differ in how they make decisions in the face of many options. Research suggests that happy individuals are relatively more likely to "satisfice"—namely, to be satisfied with an option that is merely "good enough," without concern for alternative, potentially better options. Unhappy individuals, by contrast, are more likely to "maximize" their options—that is, they seek to make the absolute best choice. Although maximizers' decisions may ultimately produce objectively superior results (e.g., a more lucrative job), maximizers experience greater regret and diminished well-being relative to satisficers. The maximizing tendencies of unhappy individuals may thus serve to reinforce their unhappiness.

Intrusive Dwelling

Happy people are much less likely than their unhappier peers to excessively self-reflect and dwell upon themselves. For example, in several studies, unhappy students led to believe that they had failed at a verbal task experienced negative affect and intrusive negative thoughts, which interfered with their concentration and impaired their performance on a subsequent intellectually demanding test. These findings suggest that unhappy people engage in negative (and maladaptive) dwelling more so than do happy people, and their excessive dwelling not only makes them feel bad, but brings about significant detrimental outcomes. Notably, another study revealed that manipulating a person's focus of attention (i.e., reflecting versus distracting) could eliminate the differences between the cognitive strategies and processes shown by happy and unhappy individuals. This finding hints at a critical mechanism underlying differences between happy and unhappy people—namely, that one could "turn" a happy person into an unhappy one by instructing her to ruminate about herself. Conversely, one could make an unhappy person "look like" a happy person by directing his attention away from himself.

The way that people consider their past life events also may differentially impact happiness. A recent set of studies in the U.S. and Israel examined the relationship between well-being and two different thought perspectives that can be used to consider autobiographical experiences—namely, "endowing" (or reflecting on) life events versus "contrasting" them with the present. Happy people are relatively more likely to report endowing (or savoring) past positive life experiences and contrasting negative life experiences (i.e., considering how much better off they are today), whereas unhappy people are relatively more likely to report endowing (or ruminating about) negative experiences and contrasting positive experiences (i.e., considering how much worse off they are today). This evidence suggests that happy people's strategies of processing life events serve to prolong and preserve positive emotions, whereas the strategies of unhappy individuals serve to dampen the inherent positivity associated with positive events and to enhance the negative affect associated with negative events.

Can Less Happy People Learn Strategies to Achieve Sustainable Happiness?

Our current understanding of the differences between chronically happy and unhappy people suggests that happy people think and behave in ways that reinforce their happiness. Given these findings, is it possible for unhappy people to learn deliberate strategies to achieve ever-greater well-being? Evidence suggests that in naturalistic settings people do try to become happier. For example, college students report a variety of strategies that they use to increase happiness, including social affiliation, pursuing goals, engaging in leisure activities, participating in religion, and "direct" attempts (e.g., act happy, smile). Although some of these techniques—especially social affiliation and direct attempts—are positively correlated with happiness, it is unclear whether such strategies *cause* increases in happiness or whether already happy people are simply more likely to practice them.

Sources of Pessimism Regarding Happiness Change

Doubts about the possibility of increasing and maintaining happiness have dominated the area of well-being and personality. To begin with, twin and adoption studies suggest that genetics account for approximately 50% of the variation present in well-being. For example, Tellegen and colleagues investigated the well-being of identical and fraternal twins who had been raised together or apart. The happiness levels of the identical twin pairs were strongly correlated, and this correlation was equally high regardless of whether such twins had grown up under the same roof ($r = .58$) or miles apart ($r = .48$). Pairs of fraternal twins, however, showed much smaller correlations between their levels of well-being, even when they shared the same upbringing and household ($rs = .23$ vs. $.18$). Longitudinal studies of changes in well-being over time bolster these data even further. For example, although positive and negative life experiences have been shown to increase or decrease happiness in the short-term, people apparently rapidly return to their happiness baselines. These lines of evidence indicate that each person may have a unique set point for happiness that is genetically determined and immune to influence.

Another concern regarding sustainable changes in well-being is rooted in the concept of hedonic adaptation. Brickman and Campbell argued that after positive or negative life experiences, people quickly become accustomed to their new conditions and eventually return to their baseline happiness. This notion of a "hedonic treadmill" suggests that people adapt to circumstantial changes, especially positive ones. Many people still believe, however, that an incredibly exciting experience or major positive life change, such as winning the lottery, would make them considerably happier. In fact, a study comparing lottery winners and people who experienced no sudden windfall demonstrated that the lottery winners were no happier—and even appeared to obtain less pleasure from daily activities—than did non-winners. This suggests that hedonic adaptation is another potent barrier to sustainably increasing well-being.

A final source of pessimism about the possibility of real change in happiness is the strong association between happiness and personality. Personality traits are characterized by their relatively fixed nature and lack of variation across time. Thus, some researchers conceptualize happiness as part of a person's stable personality and, by extension, as a construct that is unlikely to undergo meaningful change.

The Sustainable Happiness Model

In their model of the primary determinants of happiness, Lyubomirsky, Sheldon, and Schkade challenge these reservations, and offer an optimistic perspective regarding the possibility of creating sustainable increases in happiness. According to their model, chronic happiness, or the happiness one shows during a specific period in life, is influenced by three factors—one's set point, one's life circumstances, and the intentional activities in which one engages. As mentioned, the set point is thought to account for approximately 50% of the variance in individual differences in chronic happiness. Unfortunately, however, because the set point is "set" or fixed, it is resistant to change. Given its relative inflexibility, the set point is unlikely to be a fruitful direction to pursue increases in happiness.

Counter to many lay notions of well-being, a person's circumstances generally account for only about 10% of individual differences in chronic happiness. Life circumstances include such factors as a person's national or cultural region, demographics (e.g., gender, ethnicity), personal experiences (e.g., past traumas and triumphs), and life status variables (e.g., marital status, education level, health, and income). Given that such circumstances are relatively constant, they are more susceptible to adaptation and, hence, have comparatively little impact on happiness. Thus, circumstantial factors also do not appear to be a promising route through which to achieve sustainable well-being.

Interestingly, however, although the average person easily adapts to positive changes in her life, like getting married, winning the lottery, or acquiring sharper vision, individual differences have been found in degrees of adaptation. For example, in a study of reactions to marriage, some newlyweds reported substantial boosts in life satisfaction after the wedding and remained very satisfied even years later, while others rapidly returned to their baseline happiness and others still actually became less happy and stayed relatively unhappy. These findings suggest that people vary in how they *intentionally behave* in response to changing circumstances—for example, the extent to which they might express gratitude to their marriage partner, put effort into cultivating their relationship, or savor positive experiences together.

The most promising factor for affecting change in chronic happiness then, is the approximate 40% portion represented by intentional activity. Characterized by committed and effortful acts in which people choose to engage, intentional activities can be behavioral (e.g., practicing random acts of kindness), cognitive (e.g., expressing gratitude), or motivational (e.g., pursuing intrinsic significant life goals). The benefits of intentional activities are that they are naturally variable and tend to have beginning and ending points (i.e., they are episodic). These two characteristics alone have the potential to work against adaptation. That is, it is much more difficult to adapt to something that is continuously changing (i.e., the activities that one pursues) than to something that is relatively constant (i.e., one's circumstances and situations).

Supporting this argument, when people were asked to rate various aspects of recent positive changes in their activities (e.g., starting a new fitness program) versus positive changes in their circumstances (e.g., moving to a nicer apartment), they described their activity-based changes as more "variable" and less prone to adaptation. Furthermore, activity-based changes predicted well-being both 6 and 12 weeks after the start of the study, whereas circumstance-based changes only predicted well-being at 6 weeks. It appears that by the 12th week of the study, students had already adapted to their circumstantial changes, but not to their intentional activities.

Using Intentional Activities as the Basis of Happiness Interventions

Preliminary evidence suggests that happiness interventions involving intentional activities can be effective in increasing and sustaining happiness. One of the first researchers to teach volitional strategies to increase happiness was Fordyce. Fordyce taught his "14 Fundamentals" of happiness (e.g., socializing, practicing optimism, being present-oriented, reducing negativity, and not worrying) to different classrooms of students. Across seven studies, students who were taught the happiness-increasing strategies demonstrated increases in happiness compared with students who received no training.

Fordyce's pioneering studies provide preliminary evidence that people have the potential to increase their short-term happiness through "training" programs. Extending this work, we have examined in depth several intentional happiness-enhancing activities in the laboratory, and have sought to identify significant moderators and mediators of their effectiveness.

Committing Acts of Kindness

A randomized controlled intervention from our laboratory involved a behavioral intentional activity—in a 10-week experiment, participants were invited to regularly practice random acts of kindness. Engaging in kind acts (e.g., holding the door open for a stranger or doing a roommate's dishes) was thought to impact happiness for a variety of reasons, including bolstered self-regard, positive social interactions, and charitable feelings towards others and the community at large. In this study, happiness was measured at baseline, mid-intervention, immediately post-intervention, and one month later. Additionally, two variables were manipulated: 1) the frequency with which participants practiced acts of kindness (either three or nine times each week) and 2) the variety with which participants practiced acts of kindness (either varying their kind acts or repeating the same acts weekly). Finally, a control group merely listed events from the past week.

Interestingly, the frequency with which kind acts were performed had no bearing on subsequent well-being. The variety of the kind acts, however, influenced the extent to which participants became happier. Those who were asked to perform a wide variety of kind acts revealed an upward trajectory for happiness, even through the 1-month follow-up. By contrast, the control group showed no changes in their happiness throughout the 14 weeks of the study, and those not given the opportunity to vary their kind acts actually became less happy midway through the intervention, before eventually rebounding to their baseline happiness level at the follow-up assessment.

In another kindness intervention from our laboratory, students were asked to perform five acts of kindness per week over the course of 6 weeks, and those five acts had to be done either within a single day (e.g., all on Monday), or across the week. In this study, happiness levels increased for students performing acts of kindness, but only for those who performed all of their kind acts in a single day. Perhaps when kind acts were spread throughout the week, the effect of each kind act was dispersed, such that participants did not differentiate between their normal (and presumably habitually kind) behavior and the kindnesses prompted by this intervention. Taken together, our two kindness interventions suggest that not only can happiness be boosted by behavioral intentional activities, but that both the timing and variety of performing such intentional activities significantly moderates their impact on well-being.

Expressing Gratitude

Another intervention from our laboratory—one examining the effect of expressing gratitude (or "counting one's blessings") on changes in well-being—conceptually replicated the kindness studies. Being grateful was predicted to bolster happiness because it promotes the savoring of positive events and situations, and may counteract hedonic adaptation by allowing people to see the good in their life rather than taking it for granted. In this study, which was modeled after Emmons and McCullough, participants were asked to keep gratitude journals once a week, three times a week, or not at all (a no-treatment control). In their journals, participants wrote down up to five things for which they were grateful in the past week. The "blessings" recounted included relatively significant things (e.g., health, parents), as well as more trivial ones (e.g., AOL instant messenger).

Well-being was measured both before and after the gratitude manipulation. Corroborating the results of our 6-week kindness study, the role of optimal timing again proved decisive. Accordingly, increases in well-being were observed only in participants who counted their blessings once a week rather than three times a week. This finding provides further evidence supporting the argument that not only can an intentional activity successfully increase happiness, but that the way that activity is implemented is critical.

Visualizing Best Possible Selves

Sheldon and Lyubomirsky investigated yet another intentional activity that might be effective at elevating happiness—namely, the practice of visualizing and writing about one's best possible selves (BPS). This 4-week intervention also included a gratitude condition (in which participants counted their blessings) and a control condition (in which they recalled daily events). In the BPS condition, participants were encouraged to consider desired future images of themselves. King had previously demonstrated that writing about one's best future selves—a process that presumably enhances optimism and helps integrate one's priorities and life goals—is related to boosts in well-being. Results of our 4-week intervention indicated that participants in both experimental conditions reported increased positive feelings immediately after the intervention; however, these increases were statistically significant only among those who visualized best possible selves.

Processing Happy Life Experiences

Another series of happiness intervention studies focused on the way that people consider positive life experiences. We hypothesized that systematically analyzing and structuring one's thoughts and feelings associated with the happiest moments in life would reduce some of the inherent joy associated with such experiences. In contrast, re-experiencing or savoring such moments (without attempting to find meaning or organization in them) was expected to preserve positive emotions and generally increase happiness. Two experiments tested these ideas using Pennebaker's expressive writing paradigm. In the first study, participants were asked to write about their life experiences (versus talk into a tape recorder or think privately about them) for 15 minutes on each of 3 days. The findings revealed that those who thought about their happiest event reported higher life satisfaction relative to those who talked or wrote about it.

In the second study, participants wrote or thought about their happiest day by either systematically analyzing or repetitively replaying it. The combination of writing and analysis was expected to be the most detrimental to well-being, whereas thinking and replaying was expected to be the most beneficial to well-being. Indeed, those participants who repetitively replayed their happiest day while thinking about it showed increases in positive emotions 4 weeks after the study was over, when compared with the other groups. In sum, the evidence suggests that, when considering the happiest moments in one's life, strategies that involve systematic, planful integration and structuring (e.g., the processes naturally engendered by writing or talking) may diminish the accompanying positive emotions. A successful happiness-increasing strategy, by contrast, involves replaying or reliving positive life events as though rewinding a videotape.

Current and Future Directions

An important caveat to the happiness intervention research conducted to this date is that participants practicing a particular happiness-enhancing activity have not yet been followed in the long term. To be sure, a complete investigation of the sustainable impact of activity-based interventions on happiness must use a longitudinal perspective (i.e., assessing well-being many months and even years post intervention). Although some studies have measured happiness 6 months, 9 months, and even 18 months later, it is unclear whether participants were still engaging in their assigned exercises for that period of time. Indeed, after the prescribed intervention period—when researchers are not encouraging, let alone enforcing, participants to practice their happiness-inducing activity—participants may or may not continue with the activity on their own accord. The committed effort shown by those who use happiness-enhancing strategies should be systematically measured and tested for the extent to which it moderates the effectiveness of strategy enactment.

Empirical evidence suggests, for example, that the participants likely to show long-term benefits of a happiness intervention are those who continue to implement and integrate the intervention activity into their lives, even after the active intervention period has ended. For example, in our study that asked students to either express gratitude or visualize their best futures, positive affect was predicted 4 weeks later by *continued performance* of the intervention activity. Furthermore, those students who found the happiness-enhancing activity rewarding were the most likely to practice it. Similarly, a recent intervention study from our laboratory revealed that the well-being benefits of engaging in a happiness-inducing exercise (either gratitude or optimism) accrued only to those participants who were motivated to become happier, and this effect was in evidence even 9 months later. More to the point, 3 months after completing our intervention, participants who were still practicing their previously assigned exercise reported greater increases in well-being relative to others.

Future researchers also might find it valuable to investigate a variety of specific intentional activities that serve to enhance and sustain well-being. Fordyce proposed as many as 14 different strategies to increase happiness, and dozens of other candidates undoubtedly exist. Thus far, only a subset of strategies has been tested experimentally (e.g., expressing gratitude, imagining best possible selves, practicing kind acts, adjusting cognitive perspective). Although additional happiness exercises have been examined in web-based interventions (e.g., applying personal strengths or thinking positively, the investigation of specific intervention strategies in a controlled laboratory setting is critical, as it allows the testing of theory-based hypotheses about how and why a particular strategy "works."

The variety of questions that controlled laboratory studies can address include the role of variables that potentially moderate the effectiveness of any particular happiness-enhancing strategy. Exploring such moderators may be crucial to understanding the relationship between intentional activities and subsequent well-being. Several moderators, described briefly here, already have begun to be examined (e.g., timing, variety, effort), but many others are untested or unknown. For example, one important moderator to consider in future studies is the "fit" between a person and an appropriate intentional activity—that is, the notion that not every activity is likely to benefit every person. Supporting the critical role of fit, preliminary findings reveal that individuals who report a relatively high degree of fit with the activity they practice (i.e., performing it for self-determined reasons) report bigger gains in happiness.

Happiness interventions also may be more effective when the participant has the support of close others. When training for a marathon, runners who are part of a "team" have others to provide encouragement and to share both the challenges and rewards of their endeavor. As a result, runners with emotional and tangible support are likely to be more successful than those training alone. Likewise, people practicing strategies to enhance well-being are also likely to benefit from social support.

Another important moderator to consider is culture. The individualist notion of personal happiness distinctive to North America and Europe actually may run counter to the values and prescriptives of collectivist nations. Indeed, the pursuit of happiness in general—or specific strategies in particular—may not be as accepted or well-supported in non-Western cultures. Thus, cultural differences are critical to recognize when evaluating the effectiveness of well-being interventions. Indeed, the results of a recent study support the intriguing idea that foreign-born Asian Americans may benefit less—and differently—from practicing grateful and optimistic thinking than their Anglo-American peers.

Happiness in the Spotlight

This review of the sustainable well-being literature illustrates positive psychology's increasing focus on the causes, correlates, variations, and consequences of happiness. Why has happiness rapidly emerged into the scientific spotlight? Throughout the history of Western individualist societies, both laypeople and intellectuals alike have been preoccupied with attaining greater well-being. Indeed, people in a wide array of cultures report the pursuit of happiness as one of their most meaningful, desirable, and significant life goals. It is not surprising then that happiness should become a topic of tremendous research interest. Furthermore, whereas earlier thinkers, lacking in the proper scientific tools, could only philosophize about the nature and roots of happiness, advances in assessment and methodology have enabled current researchers to investigate subjective well-being with greater confidence and increased precision. Finally, as ever more people around the globe, and especially in the West, have their basic needs met, they have begun to enjoy the "luxury" of focusing on psychological fulfillment—that is, on psychological well-being rather than only on material well-being. And, for those with non-essential wealth, there may be a dawning recognition that material consumption—possessing the latest gadget or living in the grandest house—is not rewarding in and of itself.

Are there any costs to devoting energy and resources to the scientific study of well-being? We believe the costs are avoidable and few. Certainly, a single-minded obsession with the pursuit of happiness may obscure or preclude other important goals or activities for the individual—activities that may be "right," virtuous, or moral, but not happiness-inducing. Furthermore, although many characteristics of happy individuals help them achieve success in many areas of life, some of their characteristics (e.g., reliance on heuristics or diminished attention to the self) may be detrimental in certain contexts. In sum, happiness may be a necessary condition of the good life—a healthy, well-lived life—but it is not a sufficient condition. Other concerns should motivate people too, like cultivating self-acceptance and nourishing strong social relationships. Then again, it is notable that many, if not most, important, worthy, and socially desirable life activities, which sometimes appear to be incongruent with the pursuit of happiness—like caring for a sick family member, cramming for the MCATs, or turning the other cheek—can all be used as strategies to ultimately enhance well-being.

Concluding Remarks

"Man is the artificer of his own happiness."

– Henry David Thoreau

We have reviewed a number of cognitive, judgmental, and behavioral strategies that happy people use to maintain their high levels of well-being and have suggested that less happy people can strive successfully to be happier by learning a variety of effortful, happiness-enhancing strategies and implementing them with determination and commitment. Lyubomirsky, Sheldon, and Schkade's model of the determinants of happiness suggests that, despite historical sources of pessimism regarding change in well-being, people *can* become sustainably happier by practicing intentional activities—but only with concerted effort and under optimal conditions. We believe that hedonic adaptation to positive changes in people's lives is one of the most significant barriers to happiness. The intentional activities described here, and likely many others, can work to inhibit, counteract, or slow down the adaptation process.

Although empirical validation of our model is in the preliminary stage, increasing evidence suggests that engaging in purposeful activities leads to meaningful changes in well-being. Future researchers would do well to consider not only what strategies may successfully enhance happiness, but also under what conditions intentional activities are most effective.

Future Questions

1. Besides happiness, what other outcomes related to the "good life" might be affected by the practice of intentional activities?
2. Which additional intentional activities might serve to enhance happiness?

3. Would certain strategies to increase happiness be more effective in a collectivist versus an individualist culture?
4. Although the variable and episodic nature of intentional activities may serve to counteract adaptation, could people grow accustomed to a certain level of positivity in their lives and hence need more positive experiences just to maintain the same level of well-being?
5. Are activities to increase happiness more effective for happy people (who presumably already implement similar strategies in their daily lives) or unhappy people (who presumably have more to gain in happiness)? Are some strategies a better fit for one group versus the other?

Note

1. In the majority of the studies reported here, happy and unhappy people were identified using a median or quartile split on the widely used 4-item Subjective Happiness Scale. In other words, those scoring in the top half (or quarter) of the happiness distribution were classified as chronically happy, whereas those in the bottom half (or quarter) were classified as chronically unhappy.

Laurel C. Newman and
Randy J. Larsen

 **NO**

How Much of Our Happiness Is Within Our Control?

In reviewing articles for the "no" side of this issue, there were several individual perspectives on why we psychologists should take caution before announcing to the public that we know how to make people happier. However, there was no culminating piece containing the variety of lines of logic and research that inspire this warning. Thus, the purpose of this piece is not to insist that we have absolutely zero control over our own happiness. Rather, it is to summarize the evidence suggesting that we have much less control over it than positive psychologists typically espouse.

1. **The heritability of happiness:** In 1989, a group of researchers began a wildly ambitious and comprehensive study of twins called the Minnesota Twin Family study. They used comparisons of identical twins, fraternal twins, and other family members to determine the proportion of the variation in the public's happiness scores that is caused by genetic factors, which is called the *heritability* of happiness. In 1996, two of the researchers (David Lykken and Auke Tellegen) published a paper reporting that the heritability is around .50, which means about half of the variability we see in the population's happiness scores is caused by people's genes, and about half by other things. Most psychologists would concede that a person cannot change his or her genes, so it follows that at least one major cause of happiness lies outside of our control.

2. **The hedonic treadmill:** In 1978, Brickman, Coates, and Janoff-Bulman published a well-cited study showing that people who had befallen great fortune (lottery winners) or great tragedy (recent paraplegics) returned to their preexisting levels of happiness within a year following the event. A re-analysis of the data from the study showed that the paraplegics' level of happiness really never fully returned to baseline. Nevertheless, follow-up research has been done on the topic, and most psychologists agree that people do adapt emotionally to most of the good and bad events in life and have a surprising tendency to remain very near their preexisting level of happiness despite life's slings and arrows. This has been called the "hedonic treadmill theory" because no matter how fast or slow people "run," they stay in the same place (emotionally, of course). This is good news because it means we have the capacity to adapt to the inevitable

An original essay written for this volume.

tragedies and problems of life, but it is also bad news because, for most people, it precludes ever attaining everlasting bliss.

The two points made thus far comprise the portion of this "no we cannot make ourselves happier" argument that is generally accepted, and even pointed out, by most positive psychologists. The points that follow may be viewed as more controversial.

3. **The famous 40 percent:** Sonja Lyubomirsky is most often cited by positive psychologists and the media as the person who has cracked the happiness code and made the fruits available to all. In her book, *The How of Happiness: A New Approach to Getting the Life You Want,* she summarizes the research showing that happiness is 50 percent heritable and 10 percent due to well-studied demographic variables. She claims *that means* the remaining 40 percent of happiness is within our control. To illustrate this concept, the cover of her book contains a pie with 40 percent removed and the claim, "this much happiness—up to 40 percent—is within your power to change." Her book has been touted by many as scientific evidence of great news: We have a surprisingly high level of control over our own happiness. There are a few problems with this conclusion, though.

   a. She misuses heritability estimates. Heritability estimates estimate the proportion of individual differences, or variation, in scores *among a group of people* that can be attributed to their genes. They describe variation in a group, and cannot be applied to any individual person.[1] There are undoubtedly people whose happiness lies largely within their control, and others who suffer from life circumstances that will likely cause lasting and inescapable misery. It is the job of positive psychologists to study these sorts of distinctions rather than making the misleading claim that everyone has an equal capacity for increasing his or her happiness.

   b. Even if the 40 percent estimate were valid (which, as I just explained, it isn't), it is not accurate to claim that whatever portion of our happiness is not due to genetics and not due to as-of-yet carefully studied demographic variables is by default within our control. That 40 percent estimate would simply include *everything else*—everything besides genes and the demographic variables that have been carefully studied. That leaves room for many situational and personality variables that likely have a strong impact on our emotional state. Home foreclosures, lost jobs, unfaithful spouses, chronic illness, unplanned pregnancies, miscarriages, broken down cars and other daily hassles, work/life conflict, marital discord—the list is practically endless of things that would be included in that "everything else" portion, and the very important question remains as to which of those variables matter most, and to what extent those variables are actually within our control.

   c. The evidence for the effectiveness of existing happiness interventions is shaky and unclear. Several positive psychologists have their own prescriptions for how to increase one's own happiness.

These prescriptions are generally based on scientific research,[2] and most involve happiness exercises you can do easily at home to boost your happiness. There are currently two lines of research that have received the most attention that claim to increase happiness. In her book, Sonja Lyubomirsky describes exercises such as a *gratitude exercise* (wherein you contemplate 5 things you are grateful for at the end of each week), committing regular acts of kindness toward others, and distracting yourself when things are going badly rather than ruminating. Seligman and colleagues have tested 5 similar strategies and found scattered effects with 3 of them (though they also found temporary effects with an unconvincing placebo exercise). Although these interventions are often referred to by positive psychologists as promising evidence that we can boost our own happiness, the actual effects of these interventions are unimpressive. Though Lyubomirsky's book does not include actual data from her studies, a careful reading of the original journal articles reporting her results shows that many of the strategies have weak, improperly derived, or even unreported statistical effects that only show up at all under a very specific set of circumstances. Her 2005 paper is most commonly cited as scientific evidence that happiness-boosting interventions can work. However, in the actual paper, the *gratitude exercise* only mattered for people who did it once per week (not three times per week) and the *acts of kindness* exercise only mattered for people who did 5 acts of kindness all in one day for 6 weeks straight (not people who spread the acts out). Additionally, I use the term "mattered" rather than "worked" because the data were not reported in the article, nor were the results of any statistical tests.[3] Indeed, Boehm and Lyubomirsky's chapter in the *Handbook of Positive Psychology* reviews 8 studies, each testing several of what they call successful activities for increasing happiness. But the whole of the chapter contains mention of only one statistically significant result. The situation is surprisingly bleak considering the methodological features of her studies that should stack the results in her favor.[6] Nevertheless, her book has been translated into 11 languages and she is cited by positive psychologists and the media alike as having uncovered lasting keys to happiness. Several crucial questions remain: Do these exercises really increase happiness at all? If, so what boundary conditions are necessary for them to work? Are they ineffective for some people, and can they even have drawbacks?[4] Will any boost to happiness resulting from these exercises be long-lasting?[5] Given what we know about the hedonic treadmill, and given that emotional adaptation is even faster for good events than for bad ones, it seems likely that any benefits that people might gain from these interventions would dissipate quickly over time.

4. **The trouble with the denominator:** It might be surprising to most people to learn that personality psychologists have found that positive and negative affect (PA and NA) are independent of each other. This means the people who experience the most positive emotions are not necessarily the people who experience the least negative

emotions. Furthermore, most psychologists accept the proposition that our subjective well-being is defined, in emotional terms, as our ratio of positive to negative affect. So to make a person happier, you could increase the numerator (PA) *or* decrease the denominator (NA). Unfortunately, there is also a well-documented pattern of findings across various subfields of psychology that "bad is stronger than good." Bad events have a deeper and longer lasting impact on us emotionally than good events. This is called the *negativity bias*, and it is interpreted by most as having an evolutionary purpose: avoiding threats helps us survive; relishing accomplishments does not. What all this suggests is that people would get more bang for their buck by trying to eliminate the causes of negative emotion in their lives than by trying to increase the positive. This has been pointed out in the positive psychology literature,[7] but it remains largely ignored or even dismissed by most positive psychologists, as their "declaration of independence" depends on their determination to focus on increasing the positive and not dwelling on the negative. To make matters worse, while bad is stronger than good, it also seems evident that many key sources of negative affect (such as those listed in paragraph 3b) are largely if not fully outside of people's control. Indeed, Diener and colleagues recently stressed the need for a *revised adaptation (hedonic treadmill) theory* based on results from a large longitudinal study investigating whether or not people's life satisfaction levels are stable across time. They concluded that most people's were largely stable (which fits with hedonic treadmill theory), but that a portion of people (about 25 percent) have more fluctuating levels of life satisfaction. What variables did they find have a significant and lasting impact on life satisfaction? Unemployment and widowhood (both negative and outside of our control) had the strongest effects, with divorce having significant but smaller effects (an event most people view as negative and often outside of their control). It was in this article that they pointed out that paraplegics and other disabled people (again, negative and outside of their control) actually do not return fully to baseline. The lottery winners did not gain any lasting happiness from their wins (a positive event outside of their control). In fact, almost all the data cited in their review shows that, though life satisfaction may fluctuate, it seems to be lastingly influenced primarily by events that are negative and outside of our control. Another comprehensive study by Diener and colleagues compared well-being data from large samples of people from 55 nations and found that subjective well-being was higher among people who lived in nations that were wealthier, individualistic, and that protected their citizens' human rights. Few people in countries that lack these characteristics are there by choice.

There is some debate as well among psychologists as to whether we *should* be trying to increase happiness in the American public, most of whom report being pretty happy already. That is an issue for another day. The question here is, *if* we concede that boosting happiness is a worthwhile goal to pursue for psychologists, to what extent is doing so *possible*? Careful research has shown that happiness is by no means predetermined or "fixed" by genetics. Psychologists have uncovered a variety of environmental variables that predict (correlate with or cause) happiness. However, we must not confuse prediction with control. Nobody chooses to become a widow, be confined to a wheelchair, live in an impoverished nation, or lose their job. Many of the most influential environmental variables in our lives are every bit as uncontrollable as our genes.

In the field of psychology, unbridled enthusiasm often gives way to skepticism, and this is a good thing for the field. Psychology has a long history of demonstrating that people like to be in control of their surroundings, and they like to be happy. It comes as no surprise that they would embrace the finding that they are in control of making themselves happy. But the job of psychologists is to make claims based on objective interpretation of scientific evidence. Objective interpretation seems to point more to the idea that most of what influences our happiness in large and lasting ways lies outside the realm of the controllable.

Notes

1. See Diener, 2008, for a lengthier explanation of this concept.

2. Psychologists agree that any finding in the field of psychology as well as any claims for treatment or intervention must be based on scientific research, so this is a good thing. However, claiming that one's opinions are based on scientific research has become somewhat of a free pass to say whatever you want as long as there is at least some trend in your data that is consistent with your theory. Most psychologists are not going to take the time to sift through the details of others' (often unpublished) data and publish purposeful criticisms of others' work, and most laypersons do not have the skills to judge the quality of research. Therefore, whether or not the quality and results of the research actually warrant the claims being made is a question that often goes unchecked.

3. The results were described by bar graphs, which showed increases in well-being of .4 points for the acts of kindness exercise and .15 points (identical to the magnitude of change for the control group, incidentally) for the gratitude exercise. However, because there was no information on the scale or its end points and no statistical analyses were presented, it is impossible to judge what these values mean. One can only assume the results were not statistically significant, in which case it is misleading to refer to this article as evidence that these two activities increase happiness.

4. For example, the advice to stop ruminating probably has a lot of cash value for a chronic ruminator, but for most normal, well-adjusted people, ruminating can signal to us that we need to do something about a problem in our environment. Indeed, evolutionary and personality psychologists agree that negative emotions exist because they serve a purpose. Stifling the emotion, though more affectively pleasant, may not always be in our best interest.

5. Occasionally, researchers do conduct follow-up studies several months down the road. When they do, they often find mixed success, meaning

that people are still a little happier who engaged in some of the exercises, but people who completed other exercises have returned to baseline (if they ever budged at all).

6. For example, lack of a convincing placebo control group (even though there is evidence that placebos have an effect in these types of studies), multiple measures of happiness and subjective well-being as dependent variables (which increases the overall probability of finding a significant result due to chance), and instructions telling participants that the researchers *expect* the exercises to boost people's moods (which can influence participants' responses).

7. Larsen and Prizmic estimate that bad events impact us about 3.14 times as strongly as good events.

CHALLENGE QUESTIONS

Can Positive Psychology Make Us Happier?

1. Imagine you are an unhappy person who wishes to become happier. How would each of these viewpoints influence your decision of whether or not to seek therapy? What might you expect from therapy in each case?
2. Which of these viewpoints do you agree with most? How does your choice make a difference in how you, as a hypothetical therapist, might address an unhappy client's needs?
3. Larsen and Newman say psychologists should take caution before making public announcements about how we can make ourselves happier. What might result from a lack of caution?
4. Psychologists debate whether or not we should try to increase happiness in the American public. What arguments might either side make?
5. Given that people usually adapt emotionally to good and bad events in life (e.g., their previous happiness levels return), how would you study why unemployment, widowhood, and other circumstances seem to durably lower happiness levels?

ISSUE 10

Is Emotional Intelligence Valid?

YES: John D. Mayer, Peter Salovey, and David R. Caruso, from "Emotional Intelligence: New Ability or Eclectic Traits?" *American Psychologist* (September 2008)

NO: Edwin A. Locke, from "Why Emotional Intelligence Is an Invalid Concept," *Journal of Organizational Behavior* (January 2005)

ISSUE SUMMARY

YES: Psychologists John Mayer, Peter Salovey, and David Caruso maintain that some individuals have a greater emotional intelligence (EI), a greater capacity than others to carry out sophisticated information processing about emotions.

NO: Social science professor Edwin A. Locke argues that "emotional intelligence" is not a form of intellectual ability.

Do you have a friend who seems to get along with everyone? Is it simply a phenomenon of personality, or do some individuals possess a type of intelligence that facilitates this social skill? Could there be a social or emotional intelligence apart from that measured by standard intelligence tests? From as early as the 1920s, psychologists such as Thorndike, Wechsler, and Gardner have sought to explain performance outcomes that could not be explained by traditional intelligence models. The term emotional intelligence (EI) was coined as early as 1966 to account for some of that unexplained portion, but it was not until the 1990s that psychologists developed models and tests for measuring EI. After *Time Magazine* ran a 1996 cover story on EI, the term became a buzzword in the popular media and among professionals, some of whom assert that EI may be more important to business success than standard intelligence.

The concept has taken on a life of its own since Harvard psychologist Daniel Goleman's 1995 book on EI promised to redefine what it means to be smart. Seminars and books appeared advising leaders about the importance of EI in the workplace, and some psychologists attempted to incorporate EI into their models of intelligence. However, many other psychologists disagreed. Apart from the confusion of what exactly EI means, some researchers insisted that the original definition of EI is not a true form of intelligence but rather a matter of awareness and introspection. They argued that intelligence factors have to be part of a single, general mental ability.

In the YES article, John Mayer, Peter Salovey, and David Caruso concede that the popularization of EI has led to considerable confusion as to what EI is or should be. They argue, however, that their own scientific conception of EI qualifies as a valid intelligence because it refers to a mental ability that may exist apart from general intelligence or personality. Further, EI reliably and uniquely predicts behaviors, such as the ability to maintain positive personal commitments. They note that individuals high in EI have a differentiated ability to comprehend and use emotions to benefit themselves and others. Even when personality traits are controlled, EI measurements can predict deviancy and problem behaviors.

In the NO article, Edwin Locke argues that the concept of EI departs from scientific rationality in that its many definitions and claims render it unintelligible. He contends that the purpose behind theories of multiple intelligence, such as EI, is political rather than scientific because EI redefines what it means to be intelligent so that everybody is intelligent. Further, the claim that individuals high in EI can reason with emotion is contradictory; instead, he argues that one simply applies standard intelligence to emotional information. What EI models claim to predict, according to Locke, belongs to an introspective skill or a personality trait, not an intellectual ability.

POINT

- The earliest model of EI was in some respects overly broad and therefore interpreted incorrectly.
- Emotions are signals that convey information, so one can use them to facilitate thinking.
- Measures of EI significantly increase the prediction of standard intelligence tests.
- Whereas emotional knowledge (the *information* that EI operates on) can be learned easily, EI is a stable aptitude not easily learned.

COUNTERPOINT

- Most definitions are so all-inclusive that they make the concept unintelligible.
- One cannot reason with emotion. Reason and emotion are two distinct processes.
- What is termed emotional intelligence is simply intelligence applied to emotions.
- Discriminating between emotions is a learned skill, just as is detecting a given emotion.

YES

John D. Mayer, Peter Salovey, and David R. Caruso

Emotional Intelligence: New Ability or Eclectic Traits?

The notion that there is an emotional intelligence (EI) began as a tentative proposal (Mayer, DiPaolo, & Salovey, 1990; Salovey & Mayer, 1990). The original idea was that some individuals possess the ability to reason about and use emotions to enhance thought more effectively than others. Since 1990, EI has grown into a small industry of publication, testing, education, and consulting (Matthews, Roberts, & Zeidner, 2004; Matthews, Zeidner, & Roberts, 2002). Matthews et al. (2002) have outlined the dramatic growth of the psychological literature concerning an EI. Yet the apparent size of the field dwarfs what we regard as relevant scientific research in the area. In fact, one commentator recently argued that EI is an invalid concept in part because it is defined in too many ways (Locke, 2005, p. 425).

The original definition of EI conceptualized it as a set of interrelated abilities (Mayer & Salovey, 1997; Salovey & Mayer, 1990). Yet other investigators have described EI as an eclectic mix of traits, many dispositional, such as happiness, self-esteem, optimism, and self-management, rather than as ability based (Bar-On, 2004; Boyatzis & Sala, 2004; Petrides & Furnham, 2001; Tett, Fox, & Wang, 2005). This alternative approach to the concept—the use of the term to designate eclectic mixes of traits—has led to considerable confusion and misunderstandings as to what an EI is or should be (Daus & Ashkanasy, 2003; Gohm, 2004; Mayer, 2006). Many features, such as self-esteem, included in these models do not directly concern emotion or intelligence or their intersection (Matthews et al., 2004, p. 185). We agree with many of our colleagues who have noted that the term *emotional intelligence* is now employed to cover too many things—too many different traits, too many different concepts (Landy, 2005; Murphy & Sideman, 2006; Zeidner, Roberts, & Matthews, 2004). "These models," wrote Daus and Ashkanasy (2003, pp. 69–70), "have done more harm than good regarding establishing emotional intelligence as a legitimate, empirical construct with incremental validity potential." In this article, we explore these key criticisms of the field, contrasting what we believe to be a meaningful theory of EI with models describing it as a mix of traits.

Our principal claim is that a valid EI concept can be distinguished from other approaches. This valid conception of EI includes the ability to engage in sophisticated information processing about one's own and others' emotions and the ability to use this information as a guide to thinking and behavior. That

From *American Psychologist*, September 2008, pp. 63, 503–517. Copyright © 2008 by American Psychological Association. Reprinted by permission via Rightslink.

is, individuals high in EI pay attention to, use, understand, and manage emotions, and these skills serve adaptive functions that potentially benefit themselves and others (Mayer, Salovey, & Caruso, 2004; Salovey & Grewal, 2005). As we use the term, *emotional intelligence* is an instance of a standard intelligence that can enrich the discussion of human capacities (Mayer, Salovey, Caruso, & Sitarenios, 2001).

The deeper question raised by Locke's (2005) and others' assertions that EI has become overgeneral is "How does one decide something ought or ought not to be called emotional intelligence?" To address this question, in the first section of this article, The Schism in the Field, we examine the central conception of EI and the current confusion in the field. In the second section, The Four-Branch Model of EI, we further describe our approach to EI. In the third section, The Significance of EI, we examine the various reasons why EI is important as a discrete variable. Finally, in the Discussion and Recommendations section, we consider how the term *emotional intelligence* has come to be so misused and the steps that can be taken to improve terminology and research in the area.

The Schism in the Field
Initial Ideas

Our initial view of EI was that it consists of a group of related mental abilities. For example, we first defined EI as "the ability to monitor one's own and others' feelings and emotions, to discriminate among them and to use this information to guide one's thinking and actions" (Salovey & Mayer, 1990, p. 189). An empirical companion piece operationalized aspects of EI as an ability: Participants examined a set of colors, faces, and designs and had to identify each one's emotional content (Mayer et al., 1990). In a subsequent editorial in the journal *Intelligence*, we discussed the difference between traits such as extraversion, self-confidence, and EI, noting,

> Although a trait such as extraversion may depend on social skill, or result in it, [it] is a . . . preference rather than an ability. Knowing what another person feels, in contrast, is a mental ability. Such knowledge may stem from *g*, or be somewhat independent of it. The way in which we have defined emotional intelligence—as involving a series of mental abilities— qualifies it as a form of intelligence. (Mayer & Salovey, 1993, p. 435) . . .

External Factors

A journalistic rendering of EI created and also complicated the popular understanding of it. Goleman's (1995) best-selling book *Emotional Intelligence* began with the early version of our EI model but mixed in many other personality traits including persistence, zeal, self-control, character as a whole, and other positive attributes. The book received extensive coverage in the press, including a cover story in *Time* magazine (Gibbs, 1995). Because the book included, in part, the theory we developed, some investigators wrongly believed that we endorsed this complex and, at times, haphazard composite of attributes as an interpretation of EI.

The journalistic version became the public face of EI and attracted further attention, in part, perhaps, owing to its extraordinary claims. Goleman (1995, p. 34) wrote of EI's importance that "what data exist, suggest it can be as powerful, and at times more powerful, than IQ." A few years later, Goleman (1998a, p. 94) remarked that "nearly 90% of the difference" between star performers at work and average ones was due to EI. Although these ideas appeared in trade books and magazine and newspaper articles, they influenced scientific articles as well. For example, one refereed journal article noted that "EI accounts for over 85% of outstanding performance in top leaders" and "EI—not IQ—predicts top performance" (Watkin, 2000, p. 89). Our own work never made such claims, and we actively critiqued them (Mayer, 1999; Mayer & Cobb, 2000; Mayer & Salovey, 1997; Mayer, Salovey, & Caruso, 2000). More recently, Goleman (2005, p. xiii) wrote that others who believed that EI predicts huge proportions of success had misunderstood his 1995 book.

The Advent of Mixed Models

With EI defined in the public mind as a variety of positive attributes, subsequent approaches continued to expand the concept. One defined EI quite broadly as, "an array of noncognitive capabilities, competencies, and skills that influence one's ability to succeed in coping with environmental demands and pressures" (Bar-On, 1997, p. 14). Although the model included emotion-related qualities such as emotional self-awareness and empathy, into the mix were added many additional qualities, including reality testing, assertiveness, self-regard, and self-actualization. It was this mixing in of related and unrelated attributes that led us to call these *mixed models* of EI (Mayer et al., 2000). A second mixed model of EI included such qualities as trustworthiness, adaptability, innovation, communication, and team capabilities as emotional competencies (Goleman, 1998b). The additions of this model led to the characterization of such an approach as "preposterously all-encompassing" (Locke, 2005, p. 428).

Still another research team defined a trait EI as referring to "a constellation of *behavioral dispositions* and *self-perceptions* concerning one's ability to recognize, process, and utilize emotion-laden information. It encompasses . . . empathy, impulsivity, and assertiveness as well as elements of social intelligence . . . and personal intelligence" (Petrides & Furnham, 2003, p. 278). At this point, the pattern is clear: A large number of personality traits are amassed, mixed in with a few socioemotional abilities, and the model is called one of EI or trait EI. (The "trait" designation is particularly confusing, as *trait* is typically defined as a distinguishing quality, or an inherited characteristic, and could apply to any EI model.) Generally speaking, these models include little or no justification for why certain traits are included and others are not, or why, for that matter, certain emotional abilities are included and others are not, except for an occasional mention that the attributes have been chosen because they are most likely to predict success (e.g., Bar-On, 1997).

Such approaches are disappointing from a theoretical and construct validity standpoint, and they are scientifically challenging in that, with so many independent qualities, it is hard to identify a global theme to these lists of attributes. There is, however, an alternative to such a state of (what we see as) disorganization. We believe that our four-branch model of emotional intelligence, for example, provides one conceptually coherent approach (Mayer & Salovey, 1997). It is to this model that we turn next.

The Four-Branch Model of EI

General Introduction to EI

Intelligence Considered

It is possible to develop a coherent approach to the concept of EI. In order to describe an EI, we need first to define intelligence. From the beginning of intelligence theorizing and testing, debates have raged regarding not only the nature of intelligence but also how many intelligences exist (Neisser et al., 1996). However, even the fiercest of g theorists, those proposing that intelligence is best described as consisting of a single, general mental ability factor, allow for the existence of more specific ability factors (e.g., Carroll, 1993).

Intelligences can be divided up in different ways, for example, according to whether they address crystallized (memory-dependent) or fluid (process-dependent) abilities or, alternatively, according to the type of information that is their focus. The approach that divides intelligences into information areas, for example, yields a verbal/propositional intelligence that deals with words and logic and a spatial intelligence that deals with arranging and rotating objects in space, among others. Analogously, an EI would address (a) the capacity to reason with and about emotions and/or (b) the contribution of the emotions system to enhancing intelligence.

One longstanding grouping of intelligences divides them into verbal/propositional and perceptual/organizational areas (e.g., Kaufman, 2000). For decades, researchers have searched for an elusive third intelligence, believing that these two core intelligences by themselves were insufficient to describe individual differences in mental abilities (Walker & Foley, 1973; Wechsler, 1943). In 1920, Thorndike (p. 228) suggested the existence of a social intelligence, which involved "the ability to understand and manage men and women, boys and girls—to act wisely in human relations" (see also Bureau of Personnel Administration, 1930; Thorndike & Stein, 1937). Social intelligence began to be investigated, although it had vocal critics—whose criticisms may have impeded the field's growth (Cronbach, 1960).

None of the proposed earlier intelligences, however, explicitly concerned an EI—reasoning validly about emotions and then using emotions in the reasoning process. By the early 1980s, there was a greater openness to the idea of specific (or multiple) intelligences (Gardner, 1983; Guilford, 1959; Sternberg, 1985), and at the same time, research in emotions was blossoming. Ekman (1973) and others had resurrected Darwin's ideas that some types of emotional information—for example, human facial expressions of certain emotions—are universal; others examined how events lead to cognitive appraisals that in turn generate emotions (Dyer, 1983; Roseman, 1984; Scherer, 1993; Sloman & Croucher, 1981; Smith & Ellsworth, 1985).

Perhaps the elusive intelligence that could complement the traditional dichotomy of verbal/propositional and perceptual/organizational might be one of EI. An EI, after all, when compared with social intelligence, arguably could have a more distinct brain locus in the limbic system and its cortical projections (Damasio, 1994; LeDoux, 2000; MacLean, 1973; TenHouten, Hoppe, Bogen, & Walter, 1985). An initial theory of EI developed these ideas along with a first demonstration study to indicate how aspects of it might be measured (Mayer et al., 1990; Salovey & Mayer, 1990).

Emotions as Signals

To describe convincingly what it means to reason with emotions, however, one must understand their informational content. Initially, some people express surprise that emotions convey information at all. Emotions often are viewed as irrational, will-o'-the-wisp states—even pathological in their arbitrariness (Young, 1943). Although this does describe the operation of emotion at times, it is far from a complete picture of a normal, functioning emotion system.

. . . [T]here is compelling evidence that many emotion meanings are in large part universal—and play a key role in helping people to understand their own and others' actions (e.g., Dyer, 1983; Ekman, 1973).

By the 1990s, the significance of emotions and their meanings were better appreciated and were increasingly studied empirically. The functional role of emotions as communication signals became widely accepted, although further issues remain to be explored, such as the meanings of affective dimensions and how social influences may modify emotional expression (Averill, 1992; Barrett & Russell, 1999). . . .

EI and the Four-Branch Model

Emotional abilities can be thought of as falling along a continuum from those that are relatively lower level, in the sense of carrying out fundamental, discrete psychological functions, to those that are more developmentally complex and operate in the service of personal self-management and goals. Crucial among lower level, fundamental skills is the capacity to perceive emotions accurately. Higher level skills include, for example, the capacity to manage emotions properly. These skills can be arranged in a rough hierarchy of four branches (these branches refer to a treelike diagram; Mayer & Salovey, 1997). These include the abilities to (a) perceive emotions in oneself and others accurately, (b) use emotions to facilitate thinking, (c) understand emotions, emotional language, and the signals conveyed by emotions, and (d) manage emotions so as to attain specific goals (Mayer & Salovey, 1997). . . .

Measuring EI

Ability Measures of EI

Individual differences exist in each of these four processes. For example, some people are more accurate in initially perceiving how each individual . . . might be feeling, recognizing their feelings from faces and postures. Such individual differences can be measured. Each ability area of our four-branch model of

EI can be operationalized formally as a set of to-be-solved problems, and test takers' responses can be checked against a criterion of correctness. There are a number of ability-based scales of emotional perception (Archer, Costanzo, & Akert, 2001; Matsumoto, LeRoux, & Wilson-Cohn, 2000), emotional identification and understanding (Geher, Warner, & Brown, 2001), and emotional integrative complexity (Lane, Quinlan, Schwartz, Walker, & Zeitlin, 1990).

One measure that spans these areas is the Mayer-Salovey-Caruso Emotional Intelligence Test (MSCEIT). It consists of eight tasks, two for each of the four branches of our EI model (Mayer, Caruso, & Salovey, 1999; Mayer, Salovey, & Caruso, 2002; Mayer, Salovey, Caruso, & Sitarenios, 2003). For example, Perceiving Emotions is assessed by asking participants to identify emotions in pictures of faces, in one task, and in photographs and artwork, in another. . . .

Theory of the Measurement of EI
There are two powerful theoretical reasons why only such a clearly focused, ability-based approach can best measure EI. First, intelligences most generally are defined as mental abilities, and measuring mental abilities involves asking test takers relevant questions and then evaluating their answers against a criterion of correctness (e.g., Carroll, 1993). The MSCEIT expert scoring system identified correct answers by using the pooled responses of 21 emotions researchers (Mayer et al., 2003). . . .

Key Findings Concerning EI and Other Psychological Traits
If, as we claim, EI involves a unique source of variation that reflects a new intelligence, then it should exhibit some overlap with other intelligence scales. Studies indicate that EI, as measured by the MSCEIT and its precursor test the Multifactor Emotional Intelligence Scale (MEIS), correlates about .35 or so with verbal intelligence, and lower with perceptual/organizational IQ (Ciarrochi, Chan, & Caputi, 2000; Mayer et al., 1999). Most of the overlap with verbal intelligence is accounted for by the third branch of the MSCEIT, Understanding Emotions.

EI also should be relatively independent of more traditional personality scales. To test this, one can correlate scales of EI with the Big Five personality traits. The Big Five traits are Extraversion–Introversion, Neuroticism–Stability, Openness–Closedness, Agreeableness–Disagreeableness, and Conscientiousness–Carelessness. Each of the Big Five traits can be divided into more specific traits. For example, one approach to the Big Five divides Extraversion–Introversion into such facets as gregariousness, assertiveness, and warmth (Costa & McCrae, 1992). The Big Five represents a good starting point for frequently studied personality dimensions, although some traits arguably are not measured by the Big Five (e.g., educated–uneducated, diplomatic–humorous, religious–unreligious; Saucier & Goldberg, 1998).

EI, defined here as an ability, should have minimal correlations with Big Five traits such as Extraversion or Neuroticism: Whether or not people are sociable or emotional, they can be smart about emotions. We did predict that EI would have a modest relation to Openness, as Openness often correlates with intelligences (Mayer & Salovey, 1993). The scale correlated .25 with Openness and .28 with Agreeableness, a trait that includes empathic and interpersonally sensitive content, and had lower correlations with the rest (Brackett & Mayer, 2003). . . .

A number of observers and commentators on the field have expressed reservations about whether such tests are adequate measures of EI and whether they predict important outcomes (e.g., Brody, 2004; Oatley, 2004; Zeidner, Matthews, & Roberts, 2001). The recent *Annual Review of Psychology* examination of EI and its measurement covers such concerns in greater detail and summarizes many of the central, continuing issues (Mayer et al., 2008). To date, however, we believe that ability scales provide the best benchmark for this new construct, although existing scales still have room for substantial improvement.

The Significance of EI

General Considerations of the Validity of an EI Measure

We recognize that the MSCEIT has important limitations (see, e.g., our Recommendation 5 below), and yet we consider it among the better and most widely used of the valid measures available. As such, we focus on it in this section. The measurement issues surrounding EI are elements of broader questions: Is a measure such as the MSCEIT a valid assessment of EI? And can a test such as the MSCEIT account for new variance in important outcomes? In the mid-20th century, psychologists believed that such questions about validity could be answered on the basis of findings from key correlational and experimental studies of the test itself (e.g., Barley, 1962). . . .

Thus far, the measurement evidence tends to favor the ability-based EI approach described here over other research alternatives (such as dismissing EI or using mixed models). Valid approaches to EI can be divided into two central areas: specific-ability approaches, such as the study of accurate emotional perception, and integrative models of EI, one example of which is the four-branch model and the MSCEIT (see Mayer et al., 2008, for other measures). Drawing on revised criteria for test validity (AERA, APA, & NCME, 1999), a research team (including one of the present authors) surveyed such EI measures and concluded that tests based either on specific or integrative ability approaches to measurement exhibited generally good evidence for their validity. Tests based on mixed models, by contrast, did not adequately measure EI (Mayer et al., 2008). . . .

EI and Understanding Feelings

Higher EI does appear to promote better attention to physical and mental processes relevant to clinical outcomes. For example, people higher in some EI skills are more accurate in detecting variations in their own heartbeat—an emotion-related physiological response (Schneider, Lyons, & Williams, 2005). Higher EI individuals also are better able to recognize and reason about the emotional consequences of events. For example, higher EI individuals are more accurate in affective forecasting—that is, in predicting how they will feel at some point in the future in response to an event, such as the outcome of a U.S. presidential election (Dunn et al., 2007).

EI and Subjective Symptoms

Abilities such as affective forecasting are important, for example, because psychotherapy patients from a wide diversity of backgrounds seek help with the hope of gaining insight into their feelings and motives (Evans, Acosta, & Yamamoto, 1986; Noble, Douglas, & Newman, 1999). If EI increases an individual's attention to and accuracy about his or her feelings under various conditions, this could, in turn, minimize the individual's psychiatric symptoms. David (2005) examined EI and psychiatric distress on the Symptom Checklist–90–Revised (SCL-90-R). The higher a person's EI, the lower their reports of symptoms on the Positive Symptom Total ($r = -.38$), including, for example, fewer headaches and less trouble concentrating. Scores on the Symptom Distress Index, which measures symptom intensity, also declined as EI rose ($r = -.22$). After she controlled for the Big Five personality dimensions, EI still accounted for between 1% and 6% of the variance in SCL-90-R scales—supporting the incremental validity of EI. Other reports have indicated that, for example, those diagnosed with dysthymia have lower EI scores than other psychiatric groups (Lizeretti, Oberst, Chamarro, & Farriols, 2006).

EI and Understanding Social Relationships

Many psychotherapy clients hope to improve what have become problematic social behaviors and relationships (Evans et al., 1986; Noble et al., 1999). Research on EI indicates that people with high EI tend to be more socially competent, to have better quality relationships, and to be viewed as more interpersonally sensitive than those lower in EI (Brackett et al., 2006; Brackett, Warner, & Bosco, 2005; Lopes et al., 2004; Lopes, Salovey, Côté, & Beers, 2005; Lopes, Salovey, & Straus, 2003). Many associations between EI and these kinds of variables remain significant even after one controls for the influence of traditional personality variables and general intelligence on the measured outcome.

In one study of friendships, the relationship between EI and participants' engagement in destructive responses to life events experienced by their friends was often significant, even after the researchers controlled for the Big Five, psychological well-being, empathy, life satisfaction, and Verbal SAT scores, but for men only (Brackett et al., 2006); MSCEIT correlations ranged from $-.02$ to $-.33$.

Although the findings described above were based on self-evaluated outcome criteria, similar findings have come from observer reports of the same individuals. For example, judges' positive ratings of a videotaped "getting acquainted" social interaction were predicted by the MSCEIT, although again, only for men and not for women. Ratings of the ability to work well with others as well as overall judged social competence correlated .53 and .51, respectively, with EI. The authors noted that significant correlations remained after they partialed out the Big Five (Brackett et al., 2006).

Just as higher EI predicts better social outcomes, lower EI predicts interpersonal conflict and maladjustment. Teenagers lower in EI were rated as more aggressive than others and tended to engage in more conflictual behavior than their higher EI peers in two small-sample studies (Mayer, Perkins, Caruso, & Salovey, 2001; Rubin, 1999). Lower EI also predicted greater drug and alcohol abuse. For example, levels of drug and alcohol use are related to lower EI among males (Brackett, Mayer, & Warner, 2004). Inner-city adolescents' smoking is also related to their EI (Trinidad & Johnson, 2002).

EI and Understanding Work Relationships

High EI correlates with better relationships in business settings as well. Managers higher in EI are better able to cultivate productive working relationships with others and to demonstrate greater personal integrity according to multirater feedback (Rosete & Ciarrochi, 2005). EI also predicts the extent to which managers engage in behaviors that are supportive of the goals of the organization, according to the ratings of their supervisors (Côté & Miners, 2006). In one study, 38 manufacturing supervisors' managerial performance was evaluated by their 1,258 employees. Total EI correlated .39 with these managerial performance ratings, with the strongest relations for the ability to perceive emotions and to use emotions (Kerr, Garvin, & Heaton, 2006). . . .

Discussion and Recommendations

EI as a Valid and Significant New Concept

In this article, we have argued that there exists a valid and conceptually important new variable for investigators and practitioners. EI can be defined as an intelligence that explains important variance in an individual's problem solving and social relationships. Yet the acceptance of the construct is threatened less by its critics, perhaps, than by those who are so enthusiastic about it as to apply the term indiscriminately to a variety of traditional personality variables (as pointed out by Daus & Ashkanasy, 2003, and Murphy & Sideman, 2006).

Why Do Some Investigators and Practitioners Use the Term Emotional Intelligence Overly Broadly?

Expansion of the Emotional and Cognitive Areas of Thinking

Why are traits such as the need for achievement, self-control, and social effectiveness (let alone character and leveraging diversity) sometimes referred to as EI? Perhaps one contributing cause is a lack of perspective on personality as a whole. Psychology needs good overviews of the central areas of mental function—models that define personality's major areas. Yet few such overviews reached any level of currency or consensus in the psychology of the 1980s and 1990s. Hilgard (1980) indicated that psychology is thrown out of balance by the absence of such models. Indeed, the cognitive revolution of the 1960s and 1970s (Miller, 2003), followed by the intense interest in affective (emotional) sciences in the 1980s and 1990s (e.g., Barsade, Brief, & Spataro, 2003), contributed to a sense that cognitive and emotional systems were dominant aspects of the whole of personality. Many psychologists and other investigators began to refer to cognition, affect, and behavior, as though they provided complete coverage of the study of mental life (e.g., Thompson & Fine, 1999). In that impoverished context, the term emotional intelligence could be mistaken as a label for much of mental processing. In fact, however, the three-legged stool of cognition, affect, and behavior underemphasizes such areas of personality as representations of the self, motivation, and self-control processes; more comprehensive models have since been proposed (Mayer, 2003, 2005; McAd-ams & Pals, 2006). . . .

Our Viewpoint

We agree with a number of observers of this area of study that the term emotional intelligence is used in too all-inclusive a fashion and in too many different ways (Landy, 2005; Locke, 2005; Matthews et al., 2004; Murphy, 2006). Referring in particular to the broadened definitions of EI, Locke (2005) remarked, "What does EI . . . not include?" (p. 428). We believe that there is a valid EI concept. However, we certainly agree that there is widespread misuse of the term to apply to concepts that simply are not concerned with emotion or intelligence or their intersection. The misuses of the term are, to us, invalid in that they attempt to overthrow or subvert the standard scientific language in psychology, with no apparent rationale for doing so. Other investigators similarly have pointed out that it is important to distinguish between valid and invalid uses of the concept (Daus & Ashkanasy, 2005; Gohm, 2004); to date, however, this message has not been heeded as we believe it should be.

Recommendations

. . . Those investigators interested in EI increasingly are asking for clarification of what is and is not legitimate work in the field. Murphy and Sideman (2006, p. 296) put it as a need to "succeed in separating the valid work from the hype." One central concern of ours (and of others), here and elsewhere, has been to distinguish better from poorer approaches to EI.

From our perspective, renaming the Big Five and other classic personality traits as "emotional intelligence" reflects a lack of understanding of personality theory and undermines good scientific practice. It obscures the meaning of EI, and EI is an important enough new construct as to make that unfortunate and problematic. Only when researchers revert to using the term to refer to its legitimate meaning within the conceptual, scientific network can it be taken seriously (AERA, APA, & NCME, 1999; Cronbach & Meehl, 1955). There are a good number of researchers who understand this and who have used the term consistently in a meaningful fashion. As for the others, one of our reasons for writing this article is to convince them of the common sense of using the current personality terminology. On a very practical level, it is often impossible to evaluate a journal article purporting to study EI on the basis of keywords or the abstract: The study may examine well-being, assertiveness, self-perceptions of emotional abilities, or actual abilities.

We have provided an overview of EI in particular with an eye to helping distinguish EI from other more traditional personality variables. We have attempted to make it clearer than before where EI begins and ends and where other personality approaches pick up. Much of the mixed-model research on EI (sometimes called EQ), can be described by what Lakatos (1968, cited in G. T. Smith, 2005, p. 401) referred to as a "degenerating research program," which consists of a series of defensive shifts in terminology and hypotheses "unlikely to yield new knowledge or understanding."

We realize that the recommendations below may be obvious to many, even to those who have not read our article. To be as clear as we can be, however, we propose a set of simple recommendations that we believe will help to safeguard the field and foster its progress.

Recommendation 1

In our opinion, the journalistic popularizations of EI frequently employ inadequate and overly broad definitions of EI, implausible claims, and misunderstandings of the concepts and research more generally. We urge researchers and practitioners alike to refer to the scientific literature on emotions, intelligence, and emotional intelligence to guide their thinking. Simply put, researchers need to cite the research literature rather than journalistic renderings of scientific concepts, which serve a different purpose.

Recommendation 2

Referring to the diverse approaches to EI, one research group observed, "It is precisely because of this heterogeneity that we need clear conceptualization and definition" (Zeidner et al., 2004, p. 247). To restore clarity to the study of EI, we recommend that the term *emotional intelligence* be limited to abilities at the intersection between emotions and intelligence—specifically limited to the set of abilities involved in reasoning about emotions and using emotions to enhance reasoning.

Recommendation 3

We recommend that those interested in EI refocus on research relevant to the ability conception of EI. This includes studies using emotional knowledge measures, emotional facial recognition ability, levels of emotional awareness, emerging research on emotional self-regulation, and related areas (e.g., Elfen-bein & Ambady, 2002b; Izard et al., 2001; Lane et al., 1990; Mayer et al., 2003; Nowicki & Mitchell, 1998).

Recommendation 4

We recommend that groups of widely studied personality traits, including motives such as the need for achievement, self-related concepts such as self-control, emotional traits such as happiness, and social styles such as assertiveness should be called what they are, rather than being mixed together in haphazard-seeming assortments and named emotional intelligence.

Recommendation 5

Much remains unknown about EI (Matthews, Zeidner, & Roberts, 2007). Our final recommendation is that, following the clearer terminology and conceptions above, good theorizing and research on EI continue until more is known about the concept and about human mental abilities more generally. Enough has been learned to indicate that EI is a promising area for study but also that significant gaps in knowledge remain. For example, there needs to be greater attention to issues of culture and gender and their impact on theories of EI and the measurement of EI. Further progress in the measurement of EI generally also is required. Applications of EI must be conducted with much greater attention to the research literature, be grounded in good theory, and reject outlandish claims. . . .

In this article, we hope to have separated this EI from other constructs that may be important in their own right but are ill-labeled as *emotional intelligence*. By clarifying our model and discussing some of the confusion in the area, we hope to encourage researchers and practitioners to distinguish EI from other domains of study. Such distinctions will help pave the way for a healthier, more convincing, and better understood EI, one that best can serve the discipline of psychology and other fields.

All references for articles included in *Taking Sides: Clashing Views on Psychological Issues,* **17/e can be found on the Web at http://www.mhhe.com/cls.**

Edwin A. Locke  **NO**

Why Emotional Intelligence Is an Invalid Concept

Summary In this paper I argue that the concept of emotional intelligence (EI) is invalid both because it is not a form of intelligence and because it is defined so broadly and inclusively that it has no intelligible meaning. I distinguish the so-called concept of EI from actual intelligence and from rationality. I identify the actual relation between reason and emotion. I reveal the fundamental inadequacy of the concept of EI when applied to leadership. Finally, I suggest some alternatives to the EI concept. Copyright © 2005 John Wiley & Sons, Ltd.

The concept of intelligence refers to one's ability to form and grasp concepts, especially higher-level or more abstract concepts. The observations on which the concept of intelligence is formed are that some people are simply able to 'get' things better than others; that is, they are able to make connections, see implications, reason deductively and inductively, grasp complexity, understand the meaning of ideas, etc., better than other people. Motivation obviously plays a role in understanding concepts and can partly compensate for low ability, but even highly motivated people differ in intellectual ability. Those who are better able to grasp higher-level concepts are better able to handle complex tasks and jobs.

Intelligence must be clearly distinguished from rationality. Whereas intelligence refers to one's *capacity* to grasp abstractions, rationality refers to how one actually *uses* one's mind. A rational individual takes facts seriously and uses thinking and logic to reach conclusions. A person can be very intelligent and yet very irrational (cf. many modern philosophers; Ghate & Locke, 2003). For example, a person's thinking may be dominated by emotions, and they may not distinguish between what they feel and what they can demonstrate to be true.

The concept of emotional intelligence (EI) was introduced by Salovey and Mayer (1990), although related ideas such as 'social intelligence' had been introduced by earlier writers—originally by E. L. Thorndike. Salovey and Mayer (1990, p. 189) defined emotional intelligence as *'the ability to monitor one's own and others' feelings and emotions, to discriminate among them and to use this information to guide one's thinking and actions.'* (Note: definitions of EI are constantly

From *Journal of Organizational Behavior*, vol. 26, no. 4, June 2005, pp. 425–431. Copyright © 2005 by John Wiley & Sons. Reprinted by permission via Rightslink.

changing, an issue I will return to later.) There are several problems with this definition. First, the ability to monitor one's emotions does not require any special degree or type of intelligence. Monitoring one's emotions is basically a matter of where one chooses to focus one's attention, outwards at the external world or inward at the contents and processes of one's own consciousness. (This claim obviously implies that people have volitional control over focusing their minds. For a detailed discussion and defense of the claim that people possess volition or free will, see Binswanger, 1991; and Peikoff, 1991.) Focusing inwards involves introspection. Similarly, the ability to read the emotions of others is not necessarily an issue of intelligence. It could simply be a matter of paying attention to others and being aware of one's own emotions so that one can empathize with others. For example, if one is unaware, due to defensiveness, that one can feel fear, one will not be able to empathize with fear in others.

Second, discriminating between emotions is a learned skill, just as is detecting a given emotion. A highly intelligent person may be better able to make very subtle distinctions between similar emotions (e.g., jealousy and envy), but for basic emotions (e.g., love, anger, fear, desire) it just a matter of focusing inwards so as to develop one's introspective skill.

Third, whether one *uses* one's knowledge in everyday action is not an issue of intelligence per se. Many factors may come into play here. Among them are rationality (vs. emotionalism), being in (vs. out of) focus, integrity (including courage in the face of opposition), and the nature of one's purpose. In sum, the definition of EI indicates that it is really some combination of assorted habits, skills and/or choices rather than an issue of intelligence.

It is simply arbitrary to attach the word 'intelligence' to assorted habits or skills, as Howard Gardner and EI advocates do, on the alleged grounds that there are multiple types of intelligences. This extension of the term simply destroys the meaning of the concept—which, in fact, is the hidden agenda of the advocates of multiple intelligences. The ultimate motive is egalitarianism: redefining what it means to be intelligent so that everyone will, in some form, be equal in intelligence to everyone else. The agenda here is not scientific but political. However, arbitrary redefinitions do not change reality. Some people actually are more intelligent, in terms of their ability to grasp concepts, than others, but this ability is not necessarily reflected in every skill that people choose to develop. If one wants to group a set of related phenomena into a single concept, there must be a conceptually identified, common element among them. Otherwise, the concept has no clear meaning.

As another case in point, consider how Salovey and Mayer, in the same article cited above (Salovery & Mayer, 1990, p. 190), expand their conceptualization of EI. It is said to include the appraisal and expression of emotions in the self, both verbal and non-verbal; the appraisal and identification of emotions in others through non-verbal identification and empathy; the regulation of emotions in oneself and in others; and the utilization of emotions so as to engage in flexible planning, creative thinking, direction of attention, and motivation.

Observe that the concept of EI has now become so broad and the components so variegated that no one concept could possibl[y] encompass or integrate all of them, no matter what the concept was called; it is no longer even an intelligible concept. What is the common or integrating element in a concept that includes: introspection about emotions, emotional expression, non-verbal communication with others, empathy, self-regulation, planning, creative thinking and the direction of attention? There is none.

Following Salovey and Mayer, Daniel Goleman (1995) popularized the concept of EI. According to Goleman, EI involves self-motivation and persistence; skill at introspection; delay of gratification; self-control of impulses, moods and emotions; empathy; and social skills (the ability to make friends). These elements overlap considerably with those of Salovey and Mayer and are equally un-integratible by means of a single concept. Most of the actions involved actually require the use of reason.

To add to the confusion, in another article, Mayer (1999, p. 50) defines EI as, 'the capacity to reason with emotion in four areas: to perceive emotion, to integrate it in thought, to understand it and to manage it'. The fundamental problem here is that one cannot 'reason with emotion'. This is a contradiction in terms. Reason and emotion are two very different cognitive processes, and they perform very different psychological functions. To reason means to observe reality starting with the material provided by the senses, to integrate, without contradiction, sensory material into concepts and concepts into principles. Reason is the means of gaining and validating one's knowledge. It is a volitional process guided by the conscious mind.

In contrast, emotions entail an automatic process based on subconsciously held knowledge and values. Emotions reflect one's stored beliefs about objects, people or situations, and one's subconscious appraisal of them based on one's values. Emotions are the form in which one experiences automatized value judgments (Peikoff, 1991). Every emotion reflects a specific type of value judgment. For example, fear is the automatic response to the judgment of a physical threat. Anger is the response to the judgment that a wrong has been done to you or valued others. Joy is the result of having achieved some important value. Desire results from appraising some object that one does not possess or some person who one does not yet have a relationship with as a positive value.

Because emotions are automatic and based on subconsciously stored beliefs and values, they cannot be assumed to be valid assessments of reality. One's beliefs might be wrong; one's values might be irrational. Emotions—automatic productions of the subconscious mind—are not tools of knowledge. The psychological function of emotions is not to know the world but to make automatic evaluations and motivate action. Emotions contain, as part of the experience, felt action tendencies. Positive emotions entail the felt tendency to approach, possess, or retain the appraised object; negative emotions entail the felt tendency to flee, harm, or destroy the appraised object. This does not mean, however, that emotions have to be acted on. Through the power of reason we can decide whether action in a given case is appropriate or not and, if appropriate, what action is most suitable given the total situation.

One cannot, therefore, 'reason with emotion'; one can only reason about it. It is through reason that one identifies what emotion one is experiencing, discovers the beliefs and values that gave rise to it, and decides what action, if any, to take on the face of it. It is also through reason, which, as noted earlier, is an active, volitional process, that one determines whether the beliefs behind an emotion are valid and if the values that underlie it are rational. Reason also enables one to reprogram the subconscious so that the automatized appraisals (beliefs, values) that give rise to specific emotions are changed. Further, reason is used to identify defense mechanisms which may distort or prevent one from experiencing emotions, and thus stultify their motivating power.

Reason is also the key to self-regulation, not only of one's emotions in the sense described above, but also of one's life in general. Regulating one's life requires being purposeful, which means setting long-range goals and identifying plans which will enable one to achieve them. This process is not divorced from emotions, since one has to identify what one wants (e.g., in one's career, in romance) before setting a goal to pursue it, but reason must be used to identify one's desires and ensure that they are rational if one is to achieve one's long-range goals. In short, reason, the volitional, active part of one's mind, has to be in charge or one is left at the mercy of the emotions of the moment.

Some EI advocates might agree with all this and argue that EI, despite the definitions usually given, *really* means being intelligent *about* emotions, that is, recognizing their nature and proper function, their relationship to reason, and the need for introspection. If this is what EI advocates mean by their concept, then what they are actually referring to is not another form or type of intelligence but *intelligence (the ability to grasp abstractions) applied to a particular life domain*: emotions. Intelligence, of course, can be applied to any of thousands of life domains, but it does not follow that there are thousands of types of intelligences. If we want to talk about how well a person has *mastered* a certain domain, we already have a word for it: skill.

There is one more aspect to the EI story. In a later book, *Primal Leadership*, Goleman, Boyatzis, and McKee (2002) take EI theory a step further, into the realm of leadership. Effective leadership traits which they claim to be based on EI include:

- Objective self-assessment
- Self-confidence and self-esteem
- Moral character (e.g., honesty and integrity)
- Adaptability and flexibility
- Achievement motivation
- Initiative and self-efficacy
- Organizational awareness (e.g., of organizational politics)
- Customer service
- The use of persuasion tactics
- Developing the ability of followers
- Initiating change
- Conflict management
- Team building
- The use of humor

Goleman et al. (2002) also argue that EI includes the use [of] any or all of the six following leadership styles:

- Visionary
- Coaching
- Affiliative
- Democratic
- Pacesetting
- Commanding

The question one must ask here is, given that leadership based on EI allegedly encompasses such a long list of characteristics that people have associated with effective leadership, what does EI *not* include? One thing is missing from the list: actual intelligence!

In addition to making the concept of EI–leadership preposterously all-encompassing, Goleman et al. (2002, p. ix) seriously misconstrue what organizational leadership involves. They claim that 'The fundamental task of leaders is to create good feelings in those they lead'. This is simply not true. The function of organizations is to attain goals; in the case of private organizations the goal is long-term profitability. Organizations, other than psychotherapy clinics, are not in the 'feel-good' business. Employee morale is important, but as a means to an end not as an end in itself divorced from effectiveness.

It ironic that Goleman et al's EI approach to leadership, despite its long list of elements, omits any discussion of the *intellectual* aspects of leadership—aspects which are critical to organizational success, including business success. These aspects require the leaders of profit-making organizations to focus not inwards but outwards, at the business environment. For example, does the leader know or understand:

- Where the company should be heading?
- The role of the different corporate functions?
- The big picture? (Is there an integrating vision?)
- How to fit the different parts and processes of the organization together?
- The strategic and technological environments?
- How to attain a competitive advantage?
- How to achieve cash flow?
- How to prioritize?
- How to balance the short term with the long term?
- How to judge talent when hiring and promoting?
- How to build a culture?
- How to formulate and enforce core values?

Note that performing these very complex tasks requires, among other qualities, *actual* intelligence. Making oneself or other people feel good will not substitute for intellectual deficiencies. Good leadership requires consistent rational thinking by a mind that is able to grasp and integrate all the facts needed to make the business succeed.

Michael Dell (1999, p. 206) makes an important observation regarding the relation of emotions and knowledge:

> there are countless successful companies that are thriving now despite the fact that they started with little more than passion and a good idea. There are also many that failed, for the very same reason. The difference is that the thriving companies gathered the knowledge that gave them a substantial edge over their competition, which they used to improve their execution . . . those that didn't simply didn't make it.

Leadership is not primarily about making people feel good; it's about knowing what you are doing and knowing what to do.

Conclusion

Despite the insuperable problems with the various definitions of EI, there is no denying the importance of one element of EI in human life: introspection. Introspection is a very important human skill; it involves identifying the contents and processes of one's own mind. It is only through introspection that one can monitor such things as one's degree of focus, one's defensive reactions, and one's emotional responses and their causes. Such monitoring has important implications for self-esteem and mental health.

Given their emphasis on introspection, it is ironic that advocates of EI show virtually no understanding of the actual nature of emotions. For example, while granting that emotions entail impulses to action, Goleman's (1995) discussion of their causes is confined almost entirely to neurophysiology, especially brain structure. But psychology cannot be reduced to neurophysiology (Bandura, 1997); ideas do not have the same attributes as neurons. Especially unfortunate—and mistaken (see Peikoff, 1991)—is his claim that, like a Frankenstein monster, we have an innate mind–body dichotomy, two clashing brains, one rational and one emotional. This is reminiscent of Freud's arbitrary division of the personality into opposing parts (id, ego and superego)—a notion which originated with Plato.

What is the error here? If EI advocates actually used introspection themselves, they would observe that emotions, as noted earlier, are the product of subconscious ideas—stored knowledge about the objects and automatic value appraisals based on that knowledge. Thus there is no inherent clash between reason and emotion (Peikoff, 1991). As noted, it is through reason that we are able to acquire the knowledge and the values which cause our emotions. It is through reason that we can identify and, through reprogramming, change our emotions. It is through reason that we have the power to decide whether and how to act in the face of emotions. Emotions obviously have a neurophysiological aspect, but brain structure does not determine the content of our knowledge nor of our values. Nor does it determine whether and how we use our reason, since reasoning is a volitional process (Binswanger, 1991).

EI's extension into the field of leadership is even more unfortunate. By asserting that leadership is an emotional process, Goleman denigrates the very critical role played by rational thinking and actual intelligence in the leadership process. Given all the add-ons to the concept proposed by Goleman et al. (2002), any associations between leadership effectives and an EI scale that included these add-ons would be meaningless.

What, then, are we to conclude about EI?

1. The definition of the concept is constantly changing.
2. Most definitions are so all-inclusive as to make the concept unintelligible.
3. One definition (e.g., reasoning with emotion) involves a contradiction.
4. There is no such thing as actual emotional intelligence, although intelligence can be applied to emotions as well as to other life domains.

A more productive approach to the EI concept might be to replace it with the concept of introspective skill. (This would be a prerequisite to emotional self-regulation.) Alternatively, it might be asked whether EI could be relabeled and redefined as a personality trait—possibly, provided it was (re)defined intelligibly and that it was differentiated from skills and from traits that have already been identified (e.g., empathy). However, it is not at all clear at this point what such a trait would be called.

Ayn Rand (1975, p. 77) stated that 'Definitions are the guardians of rationality, the first line of defense against the chaos of mental disintegration.' With respect to the concept of EI, not to mention many other concept[s] in psychology and management (Locke, 2003), we are more in need of rational guardians tha[n] ever.

All references for articles included in *Taking Sides: Clashing Views on Psychological Issues,* 17/e can be found on the Web at http://www.mhhe.com/cls.

CHALLENGE QUESTIONS

Is Emotional Intelligence Valid?

1. Consider Locke's statement that the ultimate motive for advocates of multiple intelligence is egalitarianism. If EI is accepted as intelligence, what real-life changes might take place toward egalitarianism?
2. What is the difference between personality and emotional intelligence? How would you devise tests to measure one while excluding the other?
3. Consider people you know who seem to handle social situations well. Do they differ from others in ability, or is it simply a difference in personality? If ability, does it correlate positively with other abilities? Support your answers.
4. How might the motives of each of these authors be considered political?
5. What social benefits, if any, might result from restricting the scientific definition to the traditional model of a single type of intelligence?

Internet References . . .

Elective Abortion

This Web site has been established for the sole purpose of collecting data concerning the *effects of elective abortion* on men and women.

http://www.menandabortion.info/l0-research.html

American Association of Pro-Life Obstetricians and Gynecologists

This site has important links to the "yes" side of the issue on the psychological effects of elective abortion from the American Association of Pro-Life Obstetricians and Gynecologists.

http://www.aaplog.org/about-2/

The National Institute for Mental Health

This is a good, general-topic site for links to the attention-deficit hyperactivity disorder issue from the National Institute for Mental Health.

http://www.nimh.nih.gov/health/publications/attention-deficit-hyperactivity-disorder/complete-index.shtml

Children and Adults with Attention Deficit/Hyperactivity Disorder (CHADD)

This Web site provides a more experiential understanding of attention-deficit hyperactivity disorder from the organization of Children and Adults with Attention Deficit/Hyperactivity Disorder.

http://www.chadd.org/

Mental Health Issues

A *mental disorder is often defined as a pattern of thinking or behavior that is either disruptive to others or harmful to the person with the disorder. This definition seems straightforward, yet there is considerable debate about whether some disorders truly exist. For example, does a child's disruptive behavior and short attention span unquestionably warrant that he or she be diagnosed with attention-deficit hyperactive disorder (ADHD)? When does "curiosity" and "fidgetiness" become pathological and warrant medication? When, also, are life events, such as elective abortions, considered sufficiently traumatic that they can cause mental health issues, such as posttraumatic stress disorder?*

- Does an Elective Abortion Lead to Negative Psychological Effects?
- Is Attention-Deficit Hyperactivity Disorder (ADHD) a Real Disorder?
- Does Facebook Have Generally Positive Psychological Effects?

ISSUE 11

Does an Elective Abortion Lead to Negative Psychological Effects?

YES: Priscilla K. Coleman, Catherine T. Coyle, Martha Shuping, and Vincent M. Rue, from "Induced Abortion and Anxiety, Mood, and Substance Abuse Disorders: Isolating the Effects of Abortion in the National Comorbidity Survey," *Journal of Psychiatric Research* (May 2009)

NO: Julia Renee Steinberg and Nancy F. Russo, from "Abortion and Anxiety: What's the Relationship," *Social Science & Medicine* (July 2008)

ISSUE SUMMARY

YES: Associate Professor Priscilla K. Coleman and colleagues argue that the evidence suggests that abortion is causal to psychological problems.

NO: Researchers Julia R. Steinberg and Nancy F. Russo counter that other factors, common to women who abort, are responsible for later psychological problems.

The practice of abortion is one of the most widely debated issues in the public sphere. Mere discussion has not seemed to resolve the problems. Would objective studies from psychology help to address the contentious issues surrounding the abortion debate? A recent (2008) task force from the American Psychological Association was especially commissioned to help answer this question. The task force produced a detailed, 91-page report summarizing the psychological literature on the subject.

As this report clarifies, the area of abortion that psychologists have primarily studied is the potential for negative emotional and mental effects on women who terminate their pregnancy. If women who abort are more likely to experience depression and anxiety later in life, as several national surveys appear to indicate, does it necessarily follow that abortion is the *cause* of these psychological problems, or could other factors influence both the likelihood of abortion and negative mental health? Prominent researchers have argued both approaches.

In the first article, authors Coleman, Coyle, Shuping, and Rue seem to argue that abortion leads directly to important psychological problems. They collected data from a nationally representative study (National Comorbidity Survey). Even after accounting for personal, situational, and demographic variables, they found that abortion was related to an increased risk for mental health problems such as panic attacks, agoraphobia, posttraumatic stress disorder (PTSD), and major depression. These authors also found an increased risk for drug abuse among women who underwent an abortion. They concluded that abortion is implicated in between 4.3 and 16.6 percent of these disorders. In addition, they suggested that abortion negatively impacts more mental health outcomes than many other impactful life events such as rape, abuse, and neglect.

In contrast, Steinberg and Russo performed their own analysis of the national data, including the data from National Comorbidity Survey, and came to quite a different conclusion—that abortion cannot be held responsible for negative psychological consequences. They argue that analyses and conclusions, such as those of Coleman and her coauthors, fail to take into account the specific life histories of the women involved in abortion, such as their experience with violence. Steinberg and Russo also believe that many such studies fail to control for important factors such as number of pregnancies, intentions to get pregnant, and prior abortions. They conclude that most of the apparent connection between abortion and anxiety disorders could be attributed to other factors such as violence in the lives of aborting women.

POINT

- Abortion can be considered a trauma.

- When removing the effect of other factors, abortion has a significant relationship to anxiety disorders.

- There is sufficient evidence to conclude that abortion is at least partially responsible for poor mental health outcomes.
- More research is needed to understand the particular ways in which abortion contributes to anxiety.

COUNTERPOINT

- Abortion is often confounded with other life events associated with trauma.
- When removing the effect of other factors, abortion does not have a significant relationship to anxiety disorders.
- There is not sufficient evidence to conclude that abortions rather than life events are responsible for negative outcomes.
- More research is needed to understand how factors other than abortion are responsible for increased anxiety.

YES

Priscilla K. Coleman et al.

Induced Abortion and Anxiety, Mood, and Substance Abuse Disorders: Isolating the Effects of Abortion in the National Comorbidity Survey

1. Introduction

Does induced abortion carry the potential to adversely affect the psychological well-being of women? This seemingly straightforward question is complicated by a number of characteristics inherent in the variables of interest as well as external factors surrounding investigative efforts. Diverse personal, relational, situational, and cultural forces converge in every woman's decision to abort and adjustment afterwards is likewise embedded in a multifaceted context rendering it difficult to tease out effects of the procedure. The private, sensitive, and frequently distressing nature of the abortion experience also introduces challenges to data collection with many women declining to participate or dropping out mid-study resulting in potentially skewed results. Finally, as a topic of academic study with bearing on a divisive social issue that engenders strong emotion, the socio-political views of researchers, reviewers, and journal editors may compromise objectivity in data collection, analysis, interpretation, and publication.

Despite these obstacles, the international literature pertaining to abortion as a predictor of adverse mental health outcomes has grown considerably in the past several decades and the rigor of the published studies has increased. Bradshaw and Slade, authors of an extensive review of published studies on abortion and emotional experiences, concluded "There has been increasing understanding of abortion as a potential trauma" (p. 929) and "The quality of studies has improved, although there are still some methodological weaknesses" (p. 929). In a review by Thorp et al. employing strict inclusion criteria related to sample size and length of time before follow-up, the researchers concluded that induced abortion increased the risk for "mood disorders substantial enough to provoke attempts of self-harm." (p. 67).

Employment of national data sets with reproductive history and mental health variables collected for broad investigative purposes greatly minimizes

From *Journal of Psychiatric Research*, vol. 43, issue 8, May 2009, pp. 770–773, 775–776 (refs. omitted). Copyright © 2009 by Elsevier Inc. Reprinted by permission via Rightslink.

the potential for bias in data collection and low consent-to-participate rates which might otherwise compromise research on abortion. Large government funded data collection efforts have the benefit of employing professionally trained researchers or clinicians who are blind to the hypotheses of potential studies generated from the data. Further, the integrity and utility of data are maximized when trained professionals interview respondents to determine if they have experienced the symptoms of various disorders. Large-scale, national data sets also typically contain numerous personal and family history background variables that can be conveniently used as control variables.

Unfortunately the number of studies employing large representative samples with controls for third variables likely to be related to both the choice to abort and to the development of mental health problems remains rather small or non-existent for some disorders. Nevertheless, there are studies with nationally representative samples and a variety of controls for extraneous variables indicating an induced abortion puts women at risk for depression. Only one of these studies incorporated a comprehensive measure of mental health problems, leading to insight regarding the likelihood that women who have an abortion will develop an actual diagnosable psychological disorder.

There are a few studies employing national samples that have failed to detect significant associations between abortion and subsequent mental health. However, in the Gilchrist et al. study, very few controls were applied for confounding third variables. As a result, the comparison groups may very well have differed systematically with regard to income, relationship quality including exposure to domestic violence, social support, and other potentially critical factors. The attrition rate in this study was very high and there were additional methodological shortcomings. In the Schmiege and Russo study central analyses lacked controls for variables identified as significant predictors of abortion (higher education, income, and smaller family size). Without the controls, the delivery group, which was associated with lower education and income and larger families, had more depression variance erroneously attributed to pregnancy resolution.

In a recently published qualitative paper by Goodwin and Ogden, the authors concluded that "women's responses to their abortion do not always follow the suggested reactions of grief, but are varied and located within the personal and social context" (p. 231). This reality underscores the necessity of employing sufficient controls for confounding variables. All the large-scale studies described above controlled for an assortment of basic demographic variables including age, marital status, social support, number of children, and education. Many of these studies also included control variables indicative of pre-abortion mental health. However, a handful of very recent studies have gone a step beyond and included experiential variables that may be related to the choice to abort and to mental health outcomes. Among the variables in this latter category are relationship problems and childhood or adult history of physical and/or sexual abuse.

There is ample evidence indicating adverse interpersonal experiences, particularly abuse of various forms, predisposes individuals to emotional problems and mental illness. Women who experience intimate partner violence are also more likely to abort compared to women who were not victimized, necessitating the advent of controls for these personal history variables in studies of abortion and mental health.

No existing studies of abortion and mental health have included all the above categories of potential third variables in addition to incorporating variables suggestive of other sources of significant stress in women's lives. One obvious factor that should be controlled is history of miscarriage or stillbirth as non-voluntary forms of perinatal loss have been linked with mental health problems including anxiety and depression. Miscarriages are common, with estimates ranging from 25% to 43% of women experiencing at least one in their lifetime, underscoring the need to collect data on involuntary perinatal loss and control for it in research on the mental health effects of abortion. Serious accidents or life threatening illnesses, chronic health problems, heavy familial demands, and difficulty paying bills are relatively common stressors that should be controlled as well. Social support is another variable that may differ systematically based on abortion choice and/or mental health status and there is research indicating that women who have a strong support system are less likely to be harmed by an abortion.

The purpose of the current study was to explore associations between abortion history and a wide range of anxiety (panic disorder, panic attacks, PTSD, agoraphobia), mood (bipolar disorder, mania, major depression), and substance abuse disorders (alcohol and drug abuse and dependence) using a nationally representative sample. In line with current research trends, the present study incorporates controls for 22 personal history and sociodemographic characteristics. Data from the national comorbidity survey were selected because the data base provides the most comprehensive epidemiological data on the prevalence of psychological disorders in the US. Given that most of the previously reviewed large-scale studies employing a variety of controls have detected an independent contribution of abortion to a variety of mental health concerns, abortion was hypothesized to have a similar effect with the present survey data, which employed more comprehensive assessments and a more expansive list of controls.

A few of the diagnoses examined herein have not been actively explored in the previous literature on abortion and mental health and inclusion will expand the range of outcomes that have been investigated. Although only one study has identified an association between abortion history and bipolar disorder an extensive literature review conducted by Alloy et al. revealed that individuals with bipolar disorder often experience an increase in stressful events before the onset and recurrences of mood episodes. Similarly no studies to date have examined a potential link between abortion and panic attacks or panic disorder, yet panic disorder is twice as common in women compared to men and research indicates a history of psychosocial stressors including trauma in many who experience panic episodes.

Most of the diagnoses examined in this report have been identified as significant correlates of abortion; however, the effects have not been isolated effectively due to insufficient controls for third variables. In the context of surveying and controlling for potential third variables, this study has the added benefit of providing useful data regarding the magnitude of a large number of individual and situational predictors of several different mental disorders. Oftentimes when the available evidence pertaining to abortion and mental health is debated, there is an assumption that the correlational evidence could likely be explained away by uncontrolled third variables. For example, some may argue it is not the abortion per se, but exposure to intimate partner violence that is behind both the abortion choice and ensuing mental health struggles. Quantification of these risks should bring some clarity to the debate.

2. Method

2.1. Data Source

The national comorbidity survey (NCS) is widely recognized as the first nationally representative survey of mental health in the United States. The general purpose of the NCS was to study the prevalence and correlates of DSM III-R disorders and service utilization trends for these disorders. The structured psychiatric interviews were administered by the Survey Research Center at the Universiry of Michigan (UM), Ann Arbor, between September 14, 1990 and February 6, 1992.

2.2. Participants

The NCS employed a stratified, multi-stage area probability sample of individuals between the ages of 15 and 54 years who represented the non-institutionalized civilian population in the 48 coterminous United States. A response rate of 82.6% was achieved with a total of 8098 respondents participating in the survey. The NCS data relevant to this study include the following: a Diagnostic Interview administered to the entire study sample ($n = 8098$) and a Risk Assessment Interview administered to a subsample ($n = 5877$). Several of the study variables including abortion history and other potential risk factors for the various disorders were only assessed in the subsample. The current sample was therefore confined to the subsample and included all women for whom there were data available on all variables of interest: 399 women who had either one (77%) or more (23%) abortions and 2650 women who did not report an abortion. The average age for the first abortion was 21.8 (SD = 5.49) years with first abortion age spanning 14–37 years.

2.3. Procedure

The NCS employed 158 interviewers with an average of 5 years of prior experience interviewing at the Survey Research Center. Diagnoses were based on a modified version of the Composite International Diagnostic Interview (the UM-CIDI), developed at the University of Michigan and based on the diagnostic criteria of the DSM-III-R. The NCS interviewers went through an intensive training program in the use of the UM-CIDI.

In addition to interview responses, a series of indicator variables for psychiatric diagnoses were created by the staff. These are referred to as "DXDM variables" and were employed as the dependent variables in the current study. Some of these variables were created from items in the Diagnostic interview while others were created from items in the Risk Assessment Interview. The psychiatric illnesses were assessed as "present" or "absent" at the time of data collection providing assurance that in most cases, the abortion preceded the diagnosis.

Abortion history served as the independent variable in the current study. Twenty two different demographic, history, and personal/situational variables operated as control variables in the logistic regression analyses performed to assess independent contributions of abortion history to mental disorders from those most frequently linked to abortion in previous research (anxiety, mood, and substance abuse). The choice of control variables was driven by the literature reviewed previously indicating factors likely to predict the choice to abort and/or mental health problems.

Deriving accurate results from the NCS requires application of correct sample weights. In this study, necessary weighting was conducted as advised by the NCS authors in order to achieve nationally representative results.

3. Results

. . . Significance tests (chi-square for dichotomous variables and t-tests for continuous dependent variables) revealed differences between women with and without abortion experience relative to marital status, race, number of residents in the respondent's household, employment status, educational attainment, feelings of being worthy/equal to others, history of miscarriage/stillbirth, rape, having been sexually molested in childhood, physically attacked in adulthood, and having experienced a life threatening accident. No differences were observed between the two groups relative to the degree to which the respondent relies on relatives for problems, the frequency with which relatives make demands on the respondent, number of children, having been physically abused as a child, another terrible experience, difficulty paying bills, and health problems.

. . . For every disorder, the abortion group had a higher frequency that was statistically significant. The disorders with the highest frequencies across both groups were alcohol abuse and drug abuse "with or without dependence" and major depression. Lower frequencies were obtained for bipolar disorder and mania.

. . . A series of 15 logistic regression analyses with one mental health outcome operating as the criterion variable in each model were conducted. In each analysis the 22 control variables . . . were entered into the equation. What is reported . . . for every mental health diagnosis is the strength of each significant predictor after the effects of all other predictors were removed. For the induced abortion variable both adjusted and unadjusted effects are provided. For 12 out of 15 of the mental health outcomes examined, abortion made a significant contribution independent of all control variables. For the anxiety disorders, which included panic disorder, panic attacks, PTSD, agoraphobia with or without panic disorder, agoraphobia without panic disorder, a history of abortion when compared to no history was associated with [a] 111%, 44%, 59%, 95%, and a 93% increased risk, respectively. With regard to substance abuse disorders, an induced abortion was associated with a 120%, 145%, 79%, 126% increased risk for alcohol abuse with or without dependence, alcohol dependence, drug abuse with or without dependence, and drug dependence, respectively. Finally, for the mood disorders, the experience of an abortion increased risk of developing bipolar disorder by 167%, major depression without hierarchy by 45% and major depression with hierarchy by 48%. The term "hierarchy" was applied to indicate that the condition was not better accounted for by another disorder.

The abortion variable made a significant independent contribution to more mental health outcomes than a history of rape, sexual abuse in childhood, physical assault in adulthood, physical abuse in childhood, and neglect which contributed to between four and ten different diagnoses. Other variables that made significant contributions to several disorders included age, the respondent's family making frequent demands, health problems, experiencing a life threatening accident, race, lower income, feeling less worthy than others, religion, difficulty paying bills, employment, number of children with the majority of effects showing fewer children was a risk factor, more people in the household, miscarriage/stillbirth, experiencing other terrible life events, marital status, and education. The tendency to feel as though one could not rely on family for problems was only associated with one outcome. . . .

Population attributable risk (PAR) percentages were calculated for each mental health problem. In order to calculate PAR when employing a retrospective design, population exposure must be estimated and odds ratios employed. The adjusted odds ratios . . . which reflect controls for the 22 potential third variables were used. . . . Abortion accounted for between 4.3% and 16.6% of the incidence of the various disorders in the population for which the procedure made an independent contribution.

4. Discussion

The results of this study revealed that women who have aborted are at a higher risk for a variety of mental health problems including anxiety (panic attacks, panic disorder, agoraphobia, PTSD), mood (bipolar disorder, major depression with and without hierarchy), and substance abuse disorders when compared to women without a history of abortion after controls were instituted for a wide range of personal, situational, and demographic factors. As noted above there were a number of demographic and personal history variables that differed systematically between women who had aborted and those who had not. In general, women with an abortion history were more likely to be older, more highly educated, black, separated, divorced, or widowed, live in smaller households, to have been working, to have reported a personal history of more sexual trauma in childhood and adulthood, and they identified more unusually stressful events in adulthood (miscarriage, having been physically attacked, and life threatening accident). Controlling for these variables is an essential design feature of studies pertaining to the mental health correlates of voluntary termination. Consider for example, one of these factors, history of miscarriage/stillbirth. In this study the abortion group when compared to the no abortion group was considerably more likely to have experienced a non-voluntary loss (31% versus 18.7%) and very few previous studies have included this control. The effects of miscarriage/stillbirth are well documented with approximately 25% likely to suffer from persistent, serious psychological problems. With the variance associated with miscarriages/stillbirths and the number of children statistically removed, the groups in the present study were effectively equated relative to reproductive history. Interestingly non-voluntary losses only had an independent effect on 4 of the 15 psychiatric illnesses examined (drug abuse with or without dependence, drug dependence, mania, and depression without hierarchy).

What is most notable in this study is that abortion contributed significant independent effects to numerous mental health problems above and beyond a variety of other traumatizing and stressful life experiences. The strongest effects based on the attributable risks indicated that abortion is responsible for more than 10% of the population incidence of alcohol dependence, alcohol abuse, drug dependence, panic disorder, agoraphobia, and bipolar disorder in the population. Lower percentages were identified for 6 additional diagnoses.

Of the 15 disorders examined the only diagnoses not significantly associated with abortion after removing the effects of confounding variables were alcohol and drug abuse without dependence and mania. The mania diagnosis had fewer than 15 cases in each group, far too few to have confidence in the results. A lack of effects for alcohol or drug abuse without dependence is not surprising in that people periodically abuse substances for widely varying reasons including boredom, rebelliousness, curiosity, recreation, etc. without dependency and substance dependence is more likely to be related to emotional difficulties.

The linkages between abortion and substance abuse/dependence, major depression, bipolar disorder, and PTSD add to the existing body of literature. However, no previous studies have identified links between abortion and panic disorder, panic attacks, and agoraphobia. Some studies have identified biochemical similarities between PTSD and panic disorder, indirectly suggesting related processes may be involved in the associations between abortion and PTSD and between abortion and other anxiety disorders. Taylor and Arnow found that in adults the onset of most panic disorders begins with a spontaneous panic attack within six months of [a] major stressful event. If women experience the abortion as a trauma, the event may trigger a psychological and/or physiological process that culminates in an anxiety disorder. More research is needed to understand the precise process mechanisms linking abortion with various anxiety disorders. Both the abortion and no abortion groups had higher than average rates of trauma of various forms and this may explain the relatively high proportion of women who met criteria for PTSD and other diagnoses.

There are several limitations of this research. Due to data constraints the subsample reported here included only 37.6% of the full NCS. Further, the NCS data do not include a variable related to pregnancy intendedness/wantedness, therefore it was not possible to compare women who aborted to women who carried an unintended/unwanted pregnancy to term. Although on the surface this may seem like an ideal control group to employ when examining the mental health effects of abortion, the utility of the intendedness and wanted-ness variables becomes nebulous when examined more closely. According to Finer and Henshaw, "women's pregnancy intentions cannot always be accurately ascertained or neatly dichotomized." (p. 95). Santelli et al. also concluded: "traditional measures of pregnancy intentions did not readily predict a woman's choice to continue or abort the pregnancy." (p. 2009). Pregnancies that are aborted may have been initially intended by one or both partners and pregnancies that are initially unintended may become wanted as the pregnancy progresses. Moreover, after controlling for maternal age, education, marital status, number of people residing with the respondent, trimester in which prenatal care was sought, number of prior births, and all forms of reproductive loss, Coleman et al. found that experiencing an unwanted pregnancy was not related to excessive drug or alcohol consumption. Similarly, Joyce et al. reported that associations between pregnancy wantedness and negative maternal behaviors like substance abuse tend to be minimal after controlling for a comprehensive set of socio-demographic variables.

Most women are likely to experience a variety of reproductive events encompassing multiple pregnancies that continue or are terminated voluntarily or involuntarily with each characterized by distinct levels of intendedness over the course of their lives. Statistically controlling for all reproductive events may be the optimal method given the complex reproductive histories of most women. Controlling only for the intendedness of one pregnancy that is the focus of a study provides no assurance that the proportion of women in the abortion vs. delivery group is equivalent in terms of the intendedness and/or resolution of past or subsequent pregnancies. Future research might however address the mental health trajectories of women with varying combinations of wanted and unwanted pregnancies continued and terminated over an extended period of time. In this way, assessing both positive and negative aspects of a pregnancy in a woman's life might also provide improved understanding of these complex interrelationships.

The problem of women concealing a past abortion which plagues most studies on this topic was also potentially operative here. Additional limitations, the most important of which is probably recall error, are also obviously associated with retrospective data collection. Further, the results provided did not identify the percentage of women with an abortion history who may have suffered from more than one diagnosis. The data pertaining to the number of women who experience post-abortion mental health problems may be somewhat inflated by the failure to account for multiple diagnoses in one individual.

The strengths of this study included the use of a reasonably large nationally representative sample, quantification of risks, professional data collection, well-developed measures of numerous mental disorders examined as correlates of abortion history, and employment of a broad set of control variables. Research with these methodological features is essential to the process of clarifying the mental health risks unique to abortion.

Future research is needed to shed light on mediating mechanisms linking abortion to various disorders and to decipher the characteristics of women most prone to developing a particular mental health problem. For example, women who have considered their options thoroughly yet remained ambivalent about an abortion based on personal beliefs and/or moral or religious proscriptions may become particularly prone to anxiety or depression when social support is lacking. Or alternatively, women who go through an abortion without much thought or difficulty initially may later find themselves battling a substance abuse problem as a way of numbing thoughts or feelings that emerge in the months or years following an abortion.

The topic of abortion and mental health has been vastly understudied and the progress of research in this area was stalled for a number of years as the literature contained a great deal of conflicting data regarding the basic question of whether or not abortion increases risk for mental health problems. The academic debate was fueled by socio-political agendas that impeded and at times contaminated scientific efforts. Recent years have however ushered in large scale, methodologically sophisticated studies, some of which were reviewed in the introduction segment of this article. These studies have now clearly established an increased risk for a variety of mental health problems in conjunction with abortion. To fully understand the documented risks and move toward developing professional therapy protocols for addressing mental health needs prior to, during, and in the years following an abortion, research efforts need to move beyond dated battles and become devoted to achieving a more substantive understanding of the meaning of abortion in women's lives.

Julia Renee Steinberg
and Nancy F. Russo

Abortion and Anxiety:
What's the Relationship?

$\mathbf{A}$bortion is a common life circumstance for women, with an estimated 1 in 5 women experiencing at least 1 abortion in their lifetime. Recently, concerns have been raised about the impact of having an abortion on women's risk for anxiety as well as other mental health outcomes. A number of researchers have reported an association between pregnancy outcome and anxiety.

Compared to men, women have higher rates of anxiety. Given that an estimated 43% of females will experience at least one anxiety disorder in their lifetime, it is not surprising that some women who have had an abortion also report having anxiety symptoms. The questions addressed here are do women who have abortions have higher rates of anxiety than other women, and if so, how might this abortion–anxiety relationship be understood?

Answering these questions is difficult because abortion is confounded with many life events that have been associated with negative mental health outcomes, in particular unintended pregnancy. An estimated 92% of the pregnancies ending in abortion are unintended, compared to 31% of all births. Differences between women who have an abortion and other groups of women must be interpreted in light of this fact. One way to address the association of pregnancy outcome and pregnancy intention is to examine pregnancy outcome among groups of women who have had unintended pregnancies. Another is to control for experiences that are associated with anxiety and with unintended pregnancy or abortion. In this article we use both strategies and present two studies that examine the relationship of abortion to anxiety symptoms and disorders. Our goal is to ascertain whether the relationship of abortion to anxiety can be explained by pre-existing anxiety, violence exposure, and other relevant covariates.

Abortion and Anxiety

Several studies have examined the relationship between abortion and anxiety in samples of patients as well as non-patients. Although some women do experience post-abortion anxiety, the prevalence of post-abortion anxiety is low, and generally lower than that found pre-abortion. For instance, Lowenstein et al. found that women's anxiety significantly declined after having an abortion. In a review of the post-1990 literature on abortion and mental health, Bradshaw and Slade concluded that most studies found a decrease in anxiety

From *Social Science & Medicine*, vol. 67, no. 2, July 2008, pp. 238–251 (excerpts; no refs.). Copyright © 2008 by Elsevier Science Ltd. Reprinted by permission via Rightslink.

or distress after having an abortion. More recently, however, two studies have been used as evidence that abortion increases risk for subsequent anxiety. . . .

Several factors limit the conclusions of the Fergusson et al. study, however. First, it did not have an appropriate comparison group of women who delivered an unintended pregnancy. Second, small numbers precluded conducting prospective analyses specifically on anxiety or separating out the 21.6% of the sample who reported having multiple abortions. Third, the data were not broken out by specific disorder. Unfortunately the pathways from abortion to anxiety disorder may differ depending on the disorder, and the definition of anxiety disorder used in the study encompassed generalized anxiety disorder, social anxiety disorder, specific phobia, panic disorder, and agoraphobia. Finally, New Zealand's legal requirements use mental health grounds for screening women who have abortions. These laws require that women must first be referred to two certifying specialist consultants who must agree that (1) the pregnancy would seriously harm the life, physical or mental health of the woman or baby; or (2) the pregnancy is the result of incest; or (3) the woman is severely mentally handicapped. An abortion will also be considered on the basis of age, or when the pregnancy is the result of rape. Given that mentally healthy women are less able to obtain abortions in this legal context, it is not surprising to find higher rates of mental disorders in the abortion group. Thus, the Fergusson et al. study does not provide strong evidence for an abortion–anxiety relationship.

Violence, Unintended Pregnancy, and Anxiety

A substantial body of research has established that the rates of violence in the lives of women who have unintended pregnancies—whether or not those pregnancies end in abortion—are higher than rates for other women.

For instance, of 39,348 women in 14 states, Goodwin et al. found that among mothers of newborns, women with unintended pregnancies were 2.5 times more likely to experience physical abuse compared to women whose pregnancies were intended. Additionally, in a meta-analysis of the relation of intimate partner violence and sexual health, Coker found that intimate partner violence was associated with unwanted pregnancy in 3 of 4 studies. Intimate partner violence was associated with abortion in 6 of 8 studies that addressed this association. Two studies also noted an association between abortion and both physical and sexual abuse. Finally, in a multi-national population-based study of 10 countries, Garcia-Moreno, Jansen, Ellsberg, Heise, and Watts found that in 8 of the countries, compared to women who had not experienced violence, women who had experienced some violence in their lives were more likely to have had an abortion. Hence, research consistently finds a relationship of violence with unintended pregnancy, whether terminating in delivery or abortion.

There is also empirical research to support the relation of violence and anxiety. First, violence is a known cause of post-traumatic stress disorder. Second, studies show that both childhood sexual and physical abuse are associated with anxiety disorders such as post-traumatic stress disorder (PTSD) or generalized anxiety disorder. Given violence is strongly and consistently related to both abortion and anxiety, controlling for violence when investigating the relationship of abortion and anxiety is warranted. . . .

In summary, previous research suggests an association between abortion and anxiety, but assessment of anxiety symptoms vs. a specific diagnosis (GAD, social anxiety, PTSD) is lacking. We hypothesize that the relation of anxiety symptoms or disorders and abortion can be explained by pre-pregnancy anxiety and the higher rates of violence in the lives of women who have abortions.

The Case of Multiple Abortions

Most sexually active women are at risk for having an unintended pregnancy, with the risk for more than one such pregnancies increasing over her lifetime. However, researchers have found that the more severe the adversity in childhood, the greater the likelihood of unintended pregnancy. Further, there is evidence that a history of childhood physical or sexual abuse is associated with repeat abortion, which is an indicator of repeated unintended pregnancy. Thus, we hypothesize that the experience of repeat abortions is related to higher rates of violence in women's lives, which in turn puts a woman at greater risk for anxiety. . . .

Study 1: The National Survey of Family Growth (NSFG)

. . .

Results

Do women who terminate a first pregnancy have significantly higher rates of experiencing anxiety symptoms (EAS) compared to women who deliver a first pregnancy?

The answer is yes. . . . The results from logistic regression analyses . . . used first pregnancy outcome to predict subsequent anxiety symptoms among *unintended first pregnancies* and among *all first pregnancies*, respectively, with no covariates controlled. For this model, in both samples pregnancy outcome was significant, with abortion found to be associated with a greater likelihood of having subsequent anxiety symptoms.

To what extent are differences in post-pregnancy rates of anxiety symptoms explained by pre-pregnancy anxiety symptoms, rape experience, and demographic characteristics known to co-vary with anxiety and abortion?

Controlling for pre-pregnancy anxiety symptoms, rape experience, and the other covariates was sufficient to explain the relationship of pregnancy outcome to anxiety symptoms; abortion was no longer found to be associated with increased risk for anxiety symptoms in either sample. . . .

Is there a significant relationship of abortion status (0, 1, or repeat abortion) to rates of anxiety symptoms after first pregnancy?

The answer is a qualified no. . . . [In women with post-pregnancy anxiety symptoms and whoever experienced rape], post-pregnancy anxiety symptoms increased with levels of abortion status, the difference in prevalence of anxiety symptoms between women having repeat (2 or more) abortions and 1 abortion is not statistically significant. Specifically, in this model where no covariates are controlled, logistic regression analyses found that women who reported having repeat abortions were significantly more likely to be identified as having anxiety symptoms than those who reported 0 abortions (*unintended first pregnancies:* $t = 3.48$, $p = 0.001$; *all first pregnancy:* $t = 4.74$, $p < 0.0005$), but not significantly more so than women who reported 1 abortion (*unintended first pregnancies:* $t = 1.40$, $p = 0.16$; *all first pregnancy:* $t = 1.70$, $p = 0.09$). Women who reported experiencing 1 abortion were also significantly more likely to be identified as having anxiety symptoms than those who reported experiencing 0 abortions (*unintended first pregnancies:* $t = 2.58$, $p = 0.01$; *all first pregnancy:* $t = 4.04$, $p < 0.0005$). . . .

Discussion

The finding that women who terminated a first pregnancy had a greater likelihood of subsequent anxiety symptoms than women who delivered a first pregnancy—regardless of intention—is congruent with previous research that has reported an association between abortion and anxiety when relevant variables are not controlled. One contribution of this study is to show that this relation can be accounted for by other factors, particularly pre-pregnancy anxiety and violence. Similar to Major et al.'s findings, for both samples, the strongest predictor of post-pregnancy anxiety was the occurrence of pre-pregnancy anxiety. No relation between abortion on the first pregnancy and anxiety symptoms was found in either NSFG sample when pre-pregnancy anxiety, rape experience, and other relevant covariates were controlled. The significant and independent contributions of pre-pregnancy anxiety symptoms and rape experience to post-pregnancy anxiety symptoms suggest that a more fruitful line of investigation would be to focus on understanding both the pathways of pre-existing conditions and violence exposure to pregnancy outcome among women.

The findings with regard to repeat abortion are problematic due to the lack of information about the timing of the predictor and outcome variables. For women having 1 abortion that occurred on their first pregnancy event, we could assess when anxiety occurred relative to that abortion. However, for women who had abortions after their first pregnancy event, we do not know the timing of those abortions with respect to post-pregnancy anxiety. Consequently, a thorough examination of the relationship of repeat abortion status to anxiety was beyond the scope of this study. Thus, in interpreting our findings with regard to repeat abortions, it must be kept in mind that lack of information about timing of the relevant variables makes speculation about causal inferences particularly inappropriate.

Keeping these caveats in mind, we can say that women who reported having repeat abortions were more likely to experience rape at some time in their lives, as predicted, and were more likely to have higher rates of anxiety symptoms than women who reported 0 abortions, even when covariates were controlled. Similarly, women who experienced 1 vs. 0 abortions were more likely to experience anxiety symptoms, even when controlling for the study variables. However, the fact that the non-significant difference between women who reported repeat abortions compared to women reporting 1 abortion emerged as significant when covariates were controlled suggests that more needs to be known about the women's characteristics to understand what is going on, and that general statements about the relation of "abortion" to mental health are not sufficiently informative to inform clinical practice or public policy. In particular, future research is needed to learn more about how women who have repeat abortions differ in experience from women who report 1 abortion, and how both groups differ from women who report 0 abortion[s].

The ability to identify pregnancy intention in the NSFG provided an opportunity to examine the extent to which pregnancy intention contributes independently to variation in post-pregnancy anxiety symptoms beyond that associated with pre-pregnancy anxiety and pregnancy outcome (abortion vs. delivery). The finding that pregnancy intention continued to make an independent contribution to post-pregnancy anxiety when the other 2 variables were controlled underscores the importance of controlling for pregnancy intention in studies seeking to understand the relation of abortion to mental health. If a study reports a significant correlation between abortion and a mental health outcome such as anxiety, even if pre-existing mental health factors are carefully controlled, unless pregnancy intention is also controlled the explanation for that correlation is problematic.

In addition to limitations common to retrospective survey research, the major limitations of this particular study include limited assessment of exposure to violence and the inability to define a clinically diagnosed anxiety disorder. Moreover, we determined that among all women, the lifetime prevalence of the variable used to assess generalized anxiety symptoms in the NSFG was more than twice as high (14.8%) as the lifetime prevalence for women in the NCS, a population survey in which a clinical diagnosis of GAD was assessed (6.6%). Thus, it is likely that the anxiety symptoms in the NSFG were reflecting more than generalized anxiety. It may be that effects of pregnancy outcome may emerge for specific clinically diagnosed anxiety disorders. To investigate this possibility, as well as to provide a more thorough examination of the relation of violence exposure to pregnancy outcome, we examined the relation of abortion to selected anxiety disorders using data from the National Comorbidity Survey.

Study 2: The National Comorbidity Survey (NCS)

. . .

Results and Discussion

Do women who terminate a first pregnancy have significantly higher rates of experiencing anxiety disorder, social anxiety, or PTSD compared to women who deliver a first pregnancy?

The answer is no. [In the study,] although the rates of anxiety disorder and social anxiety were higher in the delivery group and the rate of PTSD was higher in the abortion group, these differences were not statistically significant; thus, only the first model is presented.

For the first model we conducted logistic regression analyses with outcome of first pregnancy (abortion vs. delivery) predicting subsequent anxiety disorder, social anxiety, and PTSD, respectively. In contrast to NSFG results, first pregnancy outcome was not related to anxiety disorder, social anxiety, or PTSD. In other words, in the NSFG there was an association between anxiety symptoms and abortion on the first pregnancy that was subsequently explained by the presence of covariates. In the NCS data, however, there was no such association to be explained.

Is there a significant relationship of abortion status (0, 1, or repeat abortion) to rates of each disorder after first pregnancy?

The answer depends on the disorder. . . . For generalized anxiety disorder, the answer is no. There is no relation between first pregnancy outcome and subsequent generalized anxiety disorder. For social anxiety and PTSD, the answer is yes, but the relationships differ for each disorder.

Specifically, in parallel to the approach to the NSFG analyses, a series of logistic regressions were conducted to determine the relationship of abortion status to generalized anxiety disorder, social anxiety, and PTSD. When no covariates were controlled, no relationship of abortion status to generalized anxiety disorder was found, but abortion status was related to rates of social anxiety and PTSD after first pregnancy. . . . Women who reported repeat (2 or more) abortions had higher rates of social anxiety than those who reported 0 abortions, but the difference was not statistically significant ($p < 0.09$). However, they were significantly more likely to have social anxiety than those who reported 1 abortion ($p = 0.008$). Further, . . . women who had repeat abortions were significantly more likely to have PTSD than those who reported 0 abortions, but not 1 abortion. Women who reported 1 abortion did not differ significantly from women who reported 0 abortions with regard to rates of social anxiety or PTSD, respectively (social anxiety: $t = -1.01$, $p = 0.32$; PTSD: $t = 0.70$, $p = 0.49$).

To what extent is the relationship of multiple abortions to anxiety disorder explained by pre-pregnancy anxiety disorder, violence exposure, and demographic characteristics known to co-vary with anxiety and abortion?

Given the limited assessment of violence exposure in the NSFG, we were particularly interested in investigating whether relations found between abortion status and anxiety disorder could be explained with a more thorough assessment of violence exposure. Logistic regression analyses revealed that women who experienced repeat abortion were more likely to be exposed to certain forms of violence than other women. . . . Compared to women who reported having 0 abortions, women who reported having multiple abortions were significantly more likely to report experiencing rape ($t = 3.765$, $p < 0.01$) or any type of violence ($t = 2.360$, $p < 0.05$), being held captive/kidnapped/ threatened with a weapon ($t = 3.367$, $p < 0.01$), or being physically attacked ($t = 4.539$, $p < 0.0005$). They were more likely to report experiencing molestation, but the difference did not achieve conventional levels of statistical significance ($t = 1.961$, $p = 0.057$). They were equally likely to report experiencing child physical abuse ($t = 0.516$, $p = 0.609$).

Compared to women who had 1 abortion, women who reported having multiple abortions were significantly more likely to report being physically attacked ($t = 2.847$, $p < 0.01$). Although not statistically reliable, they were also more likely to report being held captive/kidnapped/threatened with a weapon ($t = 1.910$, $p < 0.08$). They were equally likely to report experiencing rape ($t = 1.346$, $p = 0.136$), molestation ($t = 0.349$, $p = 0.729$), child physical abuse ($t = 0.640$, $p = 0.526$), or any type of violence ($t = 0.489$, $p = 0.628$).

Compared to women who reported 0 abortions, women who had 1 abortion were significantly more likely to report experiencing any type of violence ($t = 2.161$, $p = 0.036$). . . .

Specifically, women who experienced repeated, 1, or 0 abortions were all equally likely be identified as having PTSD ($ts < 0.47$, $ps > 0.63$) and social anxiety ($ts < 1.57$, $ps > 0.12$). However, women who were raped, kidnapped/held captive/threatened with a weapon or physically attacked and those with PTSD before their pregnancy were significantly more likely to have PTSD; and women who had social anxiety before their pregnancy were more likely to have social anxiety afterwards.

Thus, no evidence was found in the NCS data for the claim that abortion on the first pregnancy leads to higher risk for any of the anxiety diagnoses studied, even though it was not possible to control for unintended pregnancy. This finding underscores the importance of careful assessment of outcome variables if an accurate portrait of women's post-abortion mental health is to be developed. The strengths of this study lie in its assessment of multiple forms of violence and the measurement of 3 clinical anxiety disorders. It shares a number of problems with Study 1, however (described below), and wantedness of pregnancy was not assessed.

General Discussion

In both the NSFG and the NCS, two samples that are representative of the United States, we found that women who have abortions on their first pregnancy are more likely to experience violence in their lives, congruent with other research finding an association between violence and abortion. The results also provide additional documentation of the association between violence exposure and anxiety outcomes in the lives of women regardless of pregnancy outcome.

Moreover, the congruence of the findings in the 2 separate studies provides strong support for our hypothesis that confounding factors, including pre-existing anxiety and violence exposure, can explain the abortion–anxiety relationship. The differences in the pattern of findings are informative for interpreting contradictions across studies as well, for they establish that the findings regarding the relation of abortion and mental health will depend on type of violence exposure controlled (e.g., rape vs. physical attack) and clinical significance of the outcome variable (i.e., general symptoms vs. a diagnosis) and warrant limitations on generalization.

The results do not support the use of abortion history as a marker for identifying patients at risk for GAD—women who terminated their first pregnancy were not at higher risk for having an actual diagnosis of GAD. Indeed, such a practice is ill-advised given that being raped, physically attacked, and held captive/threatened with a weapon remained significant predictors of PTSD when pregnancy outcome and other covariates were in the model. . . .

Limitations

. . . The use of these national data sets to study the relationship of abortion and anxiety disorders (and other measured mental health outcomes) has several limitations in addition to the standard problems associated with retrospective self-report methods, including underreporting of stigmatized conditions and unreliability of memory for timing of events. The length of time from the woman's first pregnancy outcome to the onset of anxiety symptoms (in the NSFG) or to the diagnosis of anxiety disorders (in the NCS) varied from 1 to 6 months to 20 years later. In addition to the standard issues related to reliability of memory, personal (divorce, infertility) and societal (e.g., rising influence of fundamentalist religions, stigmatization of abortion) events that occur subsequent to first pregnancy outcome (and that were not assessed in the survey) may differentially affect anxiety experience or alter the meaning and memory of women who chose to deliver vs. terminate a previous pregnancy. . . .

Whether or not pregnancy intention is controlled, it should be remembered that research on pregnancy outcome, even when prospective and longitudinal, cannot determine that abortion is the *cause* of psychological disorder. This limitation is inherent in abortion outcome research because it is unethical to randomly assign women to the conditions of conceiving and then terminating vs. delivering an unintended pregnancy.

Conclusion

The body of findings reported here suggests that the associations between abortion and anxiety reported previously in the literature may be explained by the fact that in previous research the outcome variable was not a specific clinical anxiety diagnosis, pre-pregnancy anxiety was not controlled, or that women who have unintended pregnancies have higher rates of violence exposure in their lives than women who have intended pregnancies. More theory-based research based on complex models and directed towards understanding the interrelationship among violence, unintended pregnancy, pregnancy outcome (abortion vs. delivery), and mental health is needed. For research having the goal of creating a body of knowledge that will be useful in providing informed consent to women seeking abortion, pregnancy intention should serve as a defining variable in the creation of comparison groups.

Meanwhile, given the lack of evidence that abortion increases risk for anxiety disorder, emphasizing abortion as a marker or screening factor may itself be harmful because focusing on abortion may distract attention from factors that do. The women who experience violence—regardless of pregnancy outcome—are the ones who are at higher risk and who need assistance. It is important that clinicians explore the effects of violence in women's lives to avoid mis-attribution of the negative mental health outcomes of victimization to having an abortion. To do otherwise may be to impede full exploration and understanding of the origins of women's mental health problems and prolong their psychological distress.

CHALLENGE QUESTIONS

Does an Elective Abortion Lead to Negative Psychological Effects?

1. Given that only correlating data can be collected on this topic (it being unethical to randomly assign women to either pregnancy or abortion conditions), what are the method limitations for any research on abortion? How do these limitations hinder psychological researchers from settling the abortion debate?
2. Both articles agree that more research on this issue needs to be done. In your view, what type of research is needed and why?
3. The studies presented here used similar data sets, similar methods of analysis, and similar demographic controls. What, then, could account for their opposite conclusions? (Hint: Read the introduction to this book.)
4. How should psychological research impact public decision making and national laws? Can psychology contribute to a public debate if it has disagreements on the conclusions of its data? If so, how can it best make a contribution?
5. Both of these articles look exclusively at the impact of abortion on women. What would you hypothesize might be the impact of an abortion on the man who fathered the fetus? How might a woman's decision to abort (or not) impact her family and other relations? How might the answers to these questions influence the research conclusions on abortion and anxiety?

ISSUE 12

Is Attention-Deficit Hyperactivity Disorder (ADHD) a Real Disorder?

YES: National Institute of Mental Health, from *Attention Deficit Hyperactivity Disorder* (NIH Publication No. 3572, 2006)

NO: Rogers H. Wright, from "Attention Deficit Hyperactivity Disorder: What It Is and What It Is Not," in Rogers H. Wright and Nicholas A. Cummings, eds., *Destructive Trends in Mental Health: The Well Intentioned Path to Harm* (Routledge, 2005)

ISSUE SUMMARY

YES: The National Institute of Mental Health asserts that ADHD is a real disorder that merits special consideration and treatment.

NO: Psychologist Rogers H. Wright argues that ADHD is not a real disorder, but rather a "fad diagnosis" that has resulted in the misdiagnosis and overmedication of children.

Diagnosis presents considerable challenges for mental health professionals. The *Diagnostic and Statistical Manual (DSM),* now in its fourth edition, defines widely recognized disorders in terms of clusters of symptoms that typically characterize these disorders. Because mental disorders are usually defined in terms of symptoms, there has been significant room for debate as to which groupings of symptoms constitute legitimate disorders that merit professional attention. Indeed, through its multiple revisions the *DSM* has added some disorders, redefined others, and set aside yet others as these diagnostic debates have shifted the ways we understand mental disorders.

Attention-Deficit Hypractivity Disorder, or ADHD, has been a particularly controversial diagnosis from the time it first appeared in the *DSM-III* nearly 30 years ago. Parents, teachers, psychologists, legislators, and even celebrities have debated not only whether ADHD is a real disorder but also whether the pharmacological treatments that are frequently prescribed are appropriate. Some people worry that we are pathologizing behaviors that are normal and typical of young children (e.g., curiosity, exploration, fidgetiness). Others worry that dismissing the diagnosis and leaving affected children untreated will place these children at a social, academic, and emotional disadvantage.

In the first selection, the National Institute of Mental Health (NIMH) argues that ADHD is a neurologically-based disorder that affects 3–5% of school-age children. According to the NIMH, we can all be occasionally distracted, impulsive, and hyperactive. However, the scientists at the NIMH assert that children with ADHD struggle not only with these sorts of behaviors in greater frequency and intensity but also in a manner that is inappropriate for their age group. Moreover, the NIMH argues that there are treatments, which typically should include medicine, that will prevent greater problems in a child's later life.

In the second article, psychologist Rogers H. Wright contends that ADHD is not a real disorder, but rather a "fad diagnosis." According to Wright, there are a number of complex reasons why a child may show distractibility and/or hyperactivity other than ADHD. Wright discusses how stress and fatigue in children can produce these symptoms as well as neurological and/or emotional problems. Wright argues that the diagnosis of ADHD can distract mental health professionals from assessing for these other possible causes of distractibility and hyperactivity, leading to misdiagnosis and inappropriate treatments.

POINT

- There is mounting research evidence that ADHD is a diagnosable disorder that is neurologically based and strongly linked to genetics.
- Hyperactivity and distractibility are common among all children, but these symptoms are more pervasive and inappropriate in children with ADHD.
- ADHD can be diagnosed by assessing whether a person's behavior matches the criteria indicated by the DSM-IV-TR for ADHD.

- Research suggests that the best treatments for ADHD should include medication as part of their regimen.

COUNTERPOINT

- ADHD is a "fad diagnosis" that does not exist, like other similar diagnoses that have come and gone.

- Even when symptoms are more pervasive and inappropriate, these are more often signs of excessive fatigue or stress.

- The cluster of symptoms attributed to ADHD leads mental health professionals to treat a diverse group of people as having a single problem that requires a single solution.

- Pharmaceutical treatments for ADHD can create problems and are often unnecessary when the true cause of symptoms is understood.

**National Institute of
Mental Health**

Attention Deficit
Hyperactivity Disorder

Attention Deficit Hyperactivity Disorder (ADHD) is a condition that becomes apparent in some children in the preschool and early school years. It is hard for these children to control their behavior and/or pay attention. It is estimated that between 3 and 5 percent of children have attention deficit hyperactivity disorder (ADHD), or approximately 2 million children in the United States. This means that in a classroom of 25 to 30 children, it is likely that at least one will have ADHD.

A child with ADHD faces a difficult but not insurmountable task ahead. In order to achieve his or her full potential, he or she should receive help, guidance, and understanding from parents, guidance counselors, and the public education system.

Symptoms

The principle characteristics of ADHD are inattention, hyperactivity, and impulsivity. These symptoms appear early in a child's life. Because many normal children may have these symptoms, but at a low level, or the symptoms may be caused by another disorder, it is important that the child receive a thorough examination and appropriate diagnosis by a well qualified professional. Symptoms of ADHD will appear over the course of many months, often with the symptoms of impulsiveness and hyperactivity preceding those of inattention that may not emerge for a year or more. Different symptoms may appear in different settings, depending on the demands the situation may pose for the child's self-control. A child who "can't sit still" or is otherwise disruptive will be noticeable in school, but the inattentive daydreamer may be overlooked. The impulsive child who acts before thinking may be considered just a "discipline problem," while the child who is passive or sluggish may be viewed as merely unmotivated. Yet both may have different types of ADHD. All children are sometimes restless, sometimes act without thinking, sometimes daydream the time away. When the child's hyperactivity, distractibility, poor concentration, or impulsivity begin to affect performance in school, social relationships with other children, or behavior at home, ADHD may be suspected. But because the symptoms vary so much across settings, ADHD is not easy to diagnose. This is especially true when inattentiveness is the primary symptom.

From *National Institute of Mental Health,* NIH Publication No. 3572, 2006. Published by The National Institute of Mental Health. www.nimh.nih.gov

According to the most recent version of the Diagnostic and Statistical Manual of Mental Disorder (DSM-IV-TR), there are three patterns of behavior that indicate ADHD. People with ADHD may show several signs of being consistently inattentive. They may have a pattern of being hyperactive and impulsive far more than others of their age. Or they may show all three types of behavior. This means that there are three subtypes of ADHD recognized by professionals. These are the predominantly hyperactive-impulsive type (that does not show significant inattention); the predominantly inattentive type (that does not show significant hyperactive-impulsive behavior) sometimes called ADD—an outdated term for this entire disorder; and the combined type (that displays both inattentive and hyperactive-impulsive symptoms).

Hyperactivity-Impulsivity

Some signs of hyperactivity-impulsivity are:

- Feeling restless, often fidgeting with hands or feet, or squirming while seated
- Running, climbing, or leaving a seat in situations where sitting or quiet behavior is expected
- Blurting out answers before hearing the whole question
- Having difficulty waiting in line or taking turns.

Inattention

The DSM-IV-TR gives these signs of inattention.

- Often becoming easily distracted by irrelevant sights and sounds
- Often failing to pay attention to details and making careless mistakes
- Rarely following instructions carefully and completely losing or forgetting things like toys, or pencils, books, and tools needed for a task
- Often skipping from one uncompleted activity to another.

Is It Really ADHD?

Not everyone who is overly hyperactive, inattentive, or impulsive has ADHD. Since most people sometimes blurt out things they didn't mean to say, or jump from one task to another, or become disorganized and forgetful, how can specialists tell if the problem is ADHD?

Because everyone shows some of these behaviors at times, the diagnosis requires that such behavior be demonstrated to a degree that is inappropriate for the person's age. The diagnostic guidelines also contain specific requirements for determining when the symptoms indicate ADHD. The behaviors must appear early in life, before age 7, and continue for at least 6 months. Above all, the behaviors must create a real handicap in at least two areas of a person's life such as in the schoolroom, on the playground, at home, in the community, or in social settings. So someone who shows some symptoms but whose schoolwork or friendships are not impaired by these behaviors would not be diagnosed with ADHD. Nor would a child who seems overly active on the playground but functions well elsewhere receive an ADHD diagnosis.

To assess whether a child has ADHD, specialists consider several critical questions: Are these behaviors excessive, long-term, and pervasive? That is, do they occur more often than in other children the same age? Are they a continuous problem, not just a response to a temporary situation? Do the behaviors occur in several settings or only in one specific place like the playground or in the schoolroom? The person's pattern of behavior is compared against a set of criteria and characteristics of the disorder as listed in the DSM-IV-TR.

Diagnosis
Professionals Who Make the Diagnosis

If ADHD is suspected, to whom can the family turn? What kinds of specialists do they need?

Ideally, the diagnosis should be made by a professional in your area with training in ADHD or in the diagnosis of mental disorders. Child psychiatrists and psychologists, developmental/behavioral pediatricians, or behavioral neurologists are those most often trained in differential diagnosis. Clinical social workers may also have such training. The family can start by talking with the child's pediatrician or their family doctor. Some pediatricians may do the assessment themselves, but often they refer the family to an appropriate mental health specialist they know and trust. In addition, state and local agencies that serve families and children . . . can help identify appropriate specialists.

Within each specialty, individual doctors and mental health professionals differ in their experiences with ADHD. So in selecting a specialist, it's important to find someone with specific training and experience in diagnosing and treating the disorder.

Whatever the specialist's expertise, his or her first task is to gather information that will rule out other possible reasons for the child's behavior. Among possible causes of ADHD-like behavior are the following:

- A sudden change in the child's life—the death of a parent or grandparent; parents' divorce; a parent's job loss.
- Undetected seizures, such as in petit mal or temporal lobe seizures
- A middle ear infection that causes intermittent hearing problems
- Medical disorders that may affect brain functioning
- Underachievement caused by learning disability
- Anxiety or depression

Next the specialist gathers information on the child's ongoing behavior in order to compare these behaviors to the symptoms and diagnostic criteria listed in the DSM-IV-TR. This also involves talking with the child and, if possible, observing the child in class and other settings.

The child's teachers, past and present, are asked to rate their observations of the child's behavior on standardized evaluation forms, known as behavior rating scales, to compare the child's behavior to that of other children the same age.

The specialist interviews the child's teachers and parents, and may contact other people who know the child well, such as coaches or baby-sitters. Parents are asked to describe their child's behavior in a variety of situations. They may also fill out a rating scale to indicate how severe and frequent the behaviors seem to be.

In most cases, the child will be evaluated for social adjustment and mental health. Tests of intelligence and learning achievement may be given to see if the child has a learning disability and whether the disability is in one or more subjects.

The specialist then pieces together a profile of the child's behavior.

A correct diagnosis often resolves confusion about the reasons for the child's problems that lets parents and child move forward in their lives with more accurate information on what is wrong and what can be done to help. Once the disorder is diagnosed, the child and family can begin to receive whatever combination of educational, medical, and emotional help they need. This may include providing recommendations to school staff, seeking out a more appropriate classroom setting, selecting the right medication, and helping parents to manage their child's behavior.

What Causes ADHD?

One of the first questions a parent will have is "Why? What went wrong?" "Did I do something to cause this?" There is little compelling evidence at this time that ADHD can arise purely from social factors or child-rearing methods. Most substantiated causes appear to fall in the realm of neurobiology and genetics. This is not to say that environmental factors may not influence the severity of the disorder, and especially the degree of impairment and suffering the child may experience, but that such factors do not seem to give rise to the condition by themselves.

The parents' focus should be on looking forward and finding the best possible way to help their child. Scientists are studying causes in an effort to identify better ways to treat, and perhaps someday, to prevent ADHD. They are finding more and more evidence that ADHD does not stem from home environment, but from biological causes. Knowing this can remove a huge burden of guilt from parents who might blame themselves for their child's behavior.

Genetics.   Attention disorders often run in families, so there are likely to be genetic influences. Studies indicate that 25 percent of the close relatives in the families of ADHD children also have ADHD, whereas the rate is about 5 percent in the general population. Many studies of twins now show that a strong genetic influence exists in the disorder.

Researchers continue to study the genetic contribution to ADHD and to identify the genes that cause a person to be susceptible to ADHD. Since its inception in 1999, the Attention-Deficit Hyperactivity Disorder Molecular

Genetics Network has served as a way for researchers to share findings regarding possible genetic influences on ADHD.

Recent Studies on Causes of ADHD.   Some knowledge of the structure of the brain is helpful in understanding the research scientists are doing in searching for a physical basis for attention deficit hyperactivity disorder. One part of the brain that scientists have focused on in their search is the frontal lobes of the cerebrum. The frontal lobes allow us to solve problems, plan ahead, understand the behavior of others, and restrain our impulses. The two frontal lobes, the right and the left, communicate with each other through the corpus callosum, (nerve fibers that connect the right and left frontal lobes).

The basal ganglia are the interconnected gray masses deep in the cerebral hemisphere that serve as the connection between the cerebrum and the cerebellum and, with the cerebellum are responsible for motor coordination. The cerebellum is divided into three parts. The middle part is called the vermis.

All of these parts of the brain have been studied through the use of various methods for seeing into or imaging the brain. These methods include functional magnetic resonance imaging (fMRI), positron emission tomography (PET), and single photon emission computed tomography (SPECT). The main or central psychological deficits in those with ADHD have been linked through these studies. By 2002 the researchers in the NIMH Child Psychiatry Branch had studied 152 boys and girls with ADHD, matched with 139 age- and gender-matched controls without ADHD. The children were scanned at least twice, some as many as four times over a decade. As a group, the ADHD children showed 3–4 percent smaller brain volumes in all regions—the frontal lobes, temporal gray matter, caudate nucleus, and cerebellum.

This study also showed that the ADHD children who were on medication had a white matter volume that did not differ from that of controls. Those never-medicated patients had an abnormally small volume of white matter. The white matter consists of fibers that establish long-distance connections between brain regions. It normally thickens as a child grows older and the brain matures.

The Treatment of ADHD

Every family wants to determine what treatment will be most effective for their child. This question needs to be answered by each family in consultation with their health care professional. To help families make this important decision, the National Institute of Mental Health (NIMH) has funded many studies of treatments for ADHD and has conducted the most intensive study ever undertaken for evaluating the treatment of this disorder. This study is known as the Multimodal Treatment Study of Children with Attention Deficit Hyperactivity Disorder (MTA).

The MTA study included 579 (95–98 at each of 6 treatment sites) elementary school boys and girls with ADHD, randomly assigning them to one of four treatment programs: (1) medication management alone; (2) behavioral treatment alone; (3) a combination of both; or (4) routine community care.

In each of the study sites, three groups were treated for the first 14 months in a specified protocol and the fourth group was referred for community treatment of the parents' choosing. All of the children were reassessed regularly throughout the study period. An essential part of the program was the cooperation of the schools, including principals and teachers. Both teachers and parents rated the children on hyperactivity, impulsivity, and inattention, and symptoms of anxiety and depression, as well as social skills.

The children in two groups (medication management alone and the combination treatment) were seen monthly for one-half hour at each medication visit. During the treatment visits, the prescribing physician spoke with the parent, met with the child, and sought to determine any concerns that the family might have regarding the medication or the child's ADHD-related difficulties. The physicians, in addition, sought input from the teachers on a monthly basis. The physicians in the medication-only group did not provide behavioral therapy but did advise the parents when necessary concerning any problems the child might have.

In the behavior treatment-only group, families met up to 35 times with a behavior therapist, mostly in group sessions. These therapists also made repeated visits to schools to consult with children's teachers and to supervise a special aide assigned to each child in the group. In addition, children attended a special 8-week summer treatment program where they worked on academic, social, and sports skills, and where intensive behavioral therapy was delivered to assist children in improving their behavior.

Children in the combined therapy group received both treatments, that is, all the same assistance that the medication-only received, as well as all of the behavior therapy treatments.

In routine community care, the children saw the community-treatment doctor of their parents' choice one to two times per year for short periods of time. Also, the community-treatment doctor did not have any interaction with the teachers.

The results of the study indicated that long-term combination treatments and the medication-management alone were superior to intensive behavioral treatment and routine community treatment. And in some areas—anxiety, academic performance, oppositionality, parent-child relations, and social skills—the combined treatment was usually superior. Another advantage of combined treatment was that children could be successfully treated with lower doses of medicine, compared with the medication-only group.

Medications

For decades, medications have been used to treat the symptoms of ADHD.

The medications that seem to be the most effective are a class of drugs known as stimulants.

Some people get better results from one medication, some from another. It is important to work with the prescribing physician to find the right medication and the right dosage. For many people, the stimulants dramatically reduce their hyperactivity and impulsivity and improve their ability to focus, work, and learn. The medications may also improve physical coordination, such as that needed in handwriting and in sports.

The stimulant drugs, when used with medical supervision, are usually considered quite safe. . . . [T]o date there is no convincing evidence that stimulant medications, when used for treatment of ADHD, cause drug abuse or dependence. A review of all long-term studies on stimulant medication and substance abuse, conducted by researchers at Massachusetts General Hospital and Harvard Medical School, found that teenagers with ADHD who remained on their medication during the teen years had a lower likelihood of substance use or abuse than did ADHD adolescents who were not taking medications.

The stimulant drugs come in long- and short-term forms. The newer sustained-release stimulants can be taken before school and are long-lasting so that the child does not need to go to the school nurse every day for a pill. The doctor can discuss with the parents the child's needs and decide which preparation to use and whether the child needs to take the medicine during school hours only or in the evening and weekends too.

About one out of ten children is not helped by a stimulant medication. Other types of medication may be used if stimulants don't work or if the ADHD occurs with another disorder. Antidepressants and other medications can help control accompanying depression or anxiety.

Side Effects of the Medications

Most side effects of the stimulant medications are minor and are usually related to the dosage of the medication being taken. Higher doses produce more side effects. The most common side effects are decreased appetite, insomnia, increased anxiety and/or irritability. Some children report mild stomach aches or headaches.

When a child's schoolwork and behavior improve soon after starting medication, the child, parents, and teachers tend to applaud the drug for causing the sudden changes. Unfortunately, when people see such immediate improvement, they often think medication is all that's needed. But medications don't cure ADHD; they only control the symptoms on the day they are taken. Although the medications help the child pay better attention and complete school work, they can't increase knowledge or improve academic skills. The medications help the child to use those skills he or she already possesses.

Behavioral therapy, emotional counseling, and practical support will help ADHD children cope with everyday problems and feel better about themselves.

Facts to Remember about Medication for ADHD
- Medications for ADHD help many children focus and be more successful at school, home, and play. Avoiding negative experiences now may actually help prevent addictions and other emotional problems later.
- About 80 percent of children who need medication for ADHD still need it as teenagers. Over 50 percent need medication as adults.

The Family and the ADHD Child

Medication can help the ADHD child in everyday life. He or she may be better able to control some of the behavior problems that have led to trouble with parents and siblings. But it takes time to undo the frustration, blame, and anger that may have gone on for so long. Both parents and children may need special help to develop techniques for managing the patterns of behavior. In such cases, mental health professionals can counsel the child and the family, helping them to develop new skills, attitudes, and ways of relating to each other. In individual counseling, the therapist helps children with ADHD learn to feel better about themselves. The therapist can also help them to identify and build on their strengths, cope with daily problems, and control their attention and aggression. Sometimes only the child with ADHD needs counseling support. But in many cases, because the problem affects the family as a whole, the entire family may need help. The therapist assists the family in finding better ways to handle the disruptive behaviors and promote change. If the child is young, most of the therapist's work is with the parents, teaching them techniques for coping with and improving their child's behavior.

Several intervention approaches are available. Knowing something about the various types of interventions makes it easier for families to choose a therapist that is right for their needs.

Psychotherapy works to help people with ADHD to like and accept themselves despite their disorder. It does not address the symptoms or underlying causes of the disorder. In psychotherapy, patients talk with the therapist about upsetting thoughts and feelings, explore self-defeating patterns of behavior, and learn alternative ways to handle their emotions. As they talk, the therapist tries to help them understand how they can change or better cope with their disorder.

Behavioral therapy (BT) helps people develop more effective ways to work on immediate issues. Rather than helping the child understand his or her feelings and actions, it helps directly in changing their thinking and coping and thus may lead to changes in behavior. The support might be practical assistance, like help in organizing tasks or schoolwork or dealing with emotionally charged events. Or the support might be in self-monitoring one's own behavior and giving self-praise or rewards for acting in a desired way such as controlling anger or thinking before acting.

Social skills training can also help children learn new behaviors. In social skills training, the therapist discusses and models appropriate behaviors important in developing and maintaining social relationships, like waiting for a turn, sharing toys, asking for help, or responding to teasing, then gives children a chance to practice. For example, a child might learn to "read" other people's facial expression and tone of voice in order to respond appropriately. Social skills training helps the child to develop better ways to play and work with other children.

Attention Deficit Hyperactivity Disorder in Adults

Attention Deficit Hyperactivity Disorder is a highly publicized childhood disorder that affects approximately 3 to 5 percent of all children. What is much less well known is the probability that, of children who have ADHD, many will still have it as adults. Several studies done in recent years estimate that between 30 percent and 70 percent of children with ADHD continue to exhibit symptoms in the adult years.

Typically, adults with ADHD are unaware that they have this disorder—they often just feel that it's impossible to get organized, to stick to a job, to keep an appointment. The everyday tasks of getting up, getting dressed and ready for the day's work, getting to work on time, and being productive on the job can be major challenges for the ADHD adult.

Diagnosing ADHD in an Adult

Diagnosing an adult with ADHD is not easy. Many times, when a child is diagnosed with the disorder, a parent will recognize that he or she has many of the same symptoms the child has and, for the first time, will begin to understand some of the traits that have given him or her trouble for years—distractability, impulsivity, restlessness. Other adults will seek professional help for depression or anxiety and will find out that the root cause of some of their emotional problems is ADHD. They may have a history of school failures or problems at work. Often they have been involved in frequent automobile accidents.

To be diagnosed with ADHD, an adult must have childhood-onset, persistent, and current symptoms. The accuracy of the diagnosis of adult ADHD is of utmost importance and should be made by a clinician with expertise in the area of attention dysfunction. For an accurate diagnosis, a history of the patient's childhood behavior, together with an interview with his life partner, a parent, close friend or other close associate, will be needed. A physical examination and psychological tests should also be given. Comorbidity with other conditions may exist such as specific learning disabilities, anxiety, or affective disorders.

A correct diagnosis of ADHD can bring a sense of relief. The individual has brought into adulthood many negative perceptions of himself that may have led to low esteem. Now he can begin to understand why he has some of his problems and can begin to face them.

Rogers H. Wright  **NO**

Attention Deficit Hyperactivity Disorder: What It Is and What It Is Not

It is almost axiomatic in the mental health field that fads will occur in the "diagnosis" and treatment of various types of behavioral aberrations, some of which border on being mere discomforts. Although the same faddism exists to some degree in physical medicine, its appearance is not nearly as blatant, perhaps in part because physical medicine is more soundly grounded in the physical sciences than are diagnoses in the mental health field. These fads spill over into the general culture, where direct marketing often takes place. One has to spend only a brief period in front of a television set during prime time to discover ADHD (Attention Deficit Hyperactivity Disorder), SAD (Social Anxiety Disorder), or IBS (Irritable Bowl Syndrome). Even when purporting to be informational, these are more or less disguised commercials, inasmuch as they posit a cure that varies with the drug manufacturer sponsoring the television ad.

The other certainty is that these "diagnoses" will fall from usage as other fads emerge, as was the case a decade or so ago with the disappearance of a once-common designation for what is now sometimes called ADHD. That passing fad was known as minimal brain syndrome (MBS) and/or food disorder (ostensibly from red dye or other food additives). From this author's perspective, these fad "diagnoses" don't really exist. Other writers in this volume (e.g., Cummings, Rosemond, and Wright) have commented on the slipperiness of these "diagnoses"—that is, the elevation of a symptom and/or its description to the level of a disorder or syndrome—and the concomitant tendency to over-medicate for these nonexistent maladies.

Children and ADHD

Certainly, there are deficiencies of attention and hyperactivity, but such behavioral aberrancies are most often indicative of a transitory state or condition within the organism. They are not in and of themselves indicative of a "disorder." Every parent has noticed, particularly with younger children, that toward the end of an especially exciting and fatiguing day children are literally

From *Destructive Trends In Mental Health: The Well Intentioned Path To Harm* (Routledge 2005) pp. 129–141. Copyright © 2005 by Taylor & Francis Books, Inc. Reprinted by permission of Taylor & Francis Books, Inc. via the Copyright Clearance Center.

"ricocheting off the walls." Although this behavior may in the broadest sense be classifiable as hyperactivity, it is generally pathognomonic of nothing more than excessive fatigue, for which the treatment of choice is a good night's sleep. Distractibility (attention deficit) is a frequent concomitant of excessive fatigue, particularly with children under five years of age, and can even be seen in adults if fatigue levels are extreme or if stress is prolonged. However, such "symptoms" in these contexts do not rise to the level of a treatable disorder.

Conversely, when distractibility and/or hyperactivity characterize the child's everyday behavior (especially if accompanied by factors such as delayed development, learning difficulties, impaired motor skills, and impaired judgment), they may be indicative of either a neurological disorder or of developing emotional difficulties. However, after nearly fifty years of diagnosing and treating several thousand such problems, it is my considered judgment that the distractibility and hyperactivity seen in such children is not the same as the distractibility and hyperactivity in children currently diagnosed as having ADHD. Furthermore, the hyperactivity/distractibility seen in the non-ADHD children described above is qualitatively and quantitatively different, depending on whether it is caused by incipient emotional maldevelopment (functional; i.e., nonorganic) or whether it is due to neurological involvement.

It is also notable that most children whose distractibility and/or hyperactivity is occasioned by emotional distress do not show either the kind or degree of learning disability, delayed genetic development, poor judgment, and impaired motor skills that are seen in children whose "distractibility/hyperactivity" is occasioned by neurological involvement. Only in children with the severest forms of emotional disturbance does one see the kind of developmental delays and impaired behavioral controls that are more reflective of neurological involvement (or what was known as MBS until the ADHD fad took hold). Differentiating the child with actual neurological involvement from the child that has emotionally based distractibility is neither simple nor easy to do, especially if the behavioral (as opposed to neurological) involvement is severe.

A major and profound disservice occasioned by the current fad of elevating nonspecific symptoms such as anxiety and hyperactivity to the level of a syndrome or disorder and then diagnosing ADD/ADHD is that we lump together individuals with very different needs and very different problems. We then attempt to treat the problem(s) with a single entity, resulting in a one-pill-fits-all response. It is also unfortunately the case that many mental health providers (e.g., child psychiatrists, child psychologists, child social workers), as well as many general care practitioners (e.g., pediatricians and internists), are not competent to make such discriminations alone. Therefore, it follows that such practitioners are not trained and equipped to provide ongoing care, even when an appropriate diagnosis has been made.

To add to an already complicated situation, the symptom picture in children tends to change with time and maturation. Children with neurological involvement typically tend to improve spontaneously over time, so that the symptoms of distractibility and hyperactivity often represent diminished components in the clinical picture. Conversely, children whose distractibility and hyperactivity are emotionally determined typically have symptoms that tend to intensify or be accompanied/replaced by even more dramatic indices of emotional distress.

Management of Children Exhibiting "ADHD" According to Etiology

It is apparent that somewhat superficially similar presenting complaints (i.e., distractibility and hyperactivity) may reflect two very different causative factors, and that the successful treatment and management of the complaint should vary according to the underlying causation. Neurological damage can stem from a number of causative factors during pregnancy or the birth process, and a successful remedial program may require the combined knowledge of the child's pediatrician, a neuropsychologist specializing in the diagnosis and treatment of children, and a child neurologist. In these cases appropriate medication for the child is often very helpful.

Psychotherapy for the child (particularly younger children) is, in this writer's experience, largely a waste of time. On the other hand, remedial training in visual perception, motor activities, visual—motor integration, spatial relations, numerical skills, and reading and writing may be crucial in alleviating or at least diminishing the impact of symptoms. Deficits in these skills can be major contributors to the hyperactivity and distractibility so frequently identified with such children. Counseling and psychotherapeutic work with the parents is very important and should always be a part of an integrated therapeutic program. Such children need to be followed by an attending pediatrician, a child neurologist, a child neuropsychologist, and an educational therapist, bearing in mind that treatment needs change throughout the span of remediation. For example, medication levels and regimens may need to be adjusted, and training programs will constantly need to be revised or elaborated.

It is also noteworthy that so-called tranquilizing medication with these children typically produces an adverse effect. This writer remembers a situation that occurred early in his practice, a case he has used repeatedly to alert fledgling clinicians to the importance of a comprehensive initial evaluation and ongoing supervision in the development of neurologically involved children.

John, a two-and-a-half-year-old boy, was referred by his pediatrician for evaluation of extreme hyperactivity, distractibility, and mild developmental delay. The psychological evaluation elicited evidence of visual perceptual impairment in a context of impaired visual motor integration, a finding suggestive of an irritative focus in the parietal-occipital areas of the brain. This finding was later corroborated by a child neurologist, and John was placed on dilantin and phenobarbital. A developmental training program was instituted, and the parents began participation in a group specifically designed for the parents of brain-injured children. Over the next couple of years, the patient's progress was excellent, and his development and learning difficulties were singularly diminished. The parents were comfortable with John's progress and with their ability to manage it, so they decided to have a long-wanted additional child. In the meantime, the father's work necessitated moving to another location, leading to a change of obstetrician and pediatrician.

The second pregnancy proceeded uneventfully and eventuated in the birth of a second boy. Shortly after the mother returned home with the new infant, John began to regress, exhibiting a number of prior symptoms such as hyperactivity and distractibility, as well as problems in behavioral control. The new pediatrician referred the family to a child psychiatrist, who promptly placed John on a tranquilizer. Shortly thereafter, John's academic performance began to deteriorate dramatically, and his school counseled the parents about the possibility that he had been promoted too rapidly and "could not handle work at this grade level."

At this point, the parents again contacted this writer, primarily out of concern for John's diminished academic performance. Because it had been more than two years since John had been formally evaluated, I advised the parents that another comprehensive evaluation was indicated. The parents agreed, and a full diagnostic battery was administered to John, the results of which were then compared to his prior performance. It immediately became apparent that he was not functioning at grade level, and that the overall level of his functioning had deteriorated dramatically.

In his initial evaluation, John's functional level had been in the Bright Normal range (i.e., overall IQ of 110 to 119), whereas his current functioning placed him at the Borderline Mentally Retarded level (IQ below 60). The history revealed nothing of significance other than the behavioral regression after the birth of the sibling and the introduction of the new medication. I advised the parents that I thought the child was being erroneously medicated, with consequent diminution of his intellectual efficiency, and that the supposition could be tested by asking the attending child psychiatrist to diminish John's medication to see if the child's performance improved.

The attending child psychiatrist was quite upset by the recommendations and the implications thereof and threatened to sue me for "practicing medicine without a license." I informed the physician that I was not practicing medicine but rather neuropsychology, along with deductive reasoning known as "common sense," which we could test by appropriately reducing John's dosage level for a month and then retesting him. Faced with the alternative of a legal action for slander or libel for having accused this neuropsychologist of a felony, the child psychiatrist agreed.

Upon retesting a month later, the child's performance level had returned to Bright Normal, and his academic performance and behavior in school had improved dramatically. By this time approximately six to eight months had elapsed since the birth of the sibling, and John had become accustomed to his new brother. All concerned agreed that the medication had not been helpful and that the child should continue for another three to six months without medication. Subsequent contact with the parents some six months later indicated that John was doing well at school. The parents were quite comfortable with the behavioral management skills they had learned, which enabled them to handle a child with an underlying neurological handicap.

As noted earlier, the marked distractibility and/or hyperactivity in children with neurological involvement tends to diminish through adolescence, especially after puberty, as do many of the other symptoms. As a consequence, these children present a very different clinical picture in adolescence and adult-hood. Typically, they are characterized by impulsivity, at times poor judgment, and excessive fatigability. It is generally only under the circumstances of extreme fatigue (or other stress) that one will see fairly dramatic degrees of distractibility and hyperactivity. Thus, an appropriate diagnosis leading to productive interven-tion is difficult to make.

Conversely, children who exhibit the symptoms of distractibility and hyperactivity on an emotional basis typically do not show the diminution of symptomatology with increasing age. In fact, the symptoms may intensify and/or be replaced by even more dramatic symptoms, especially during puberty and adolescence. It should also be emphasized that the kind of distractibility and hyperactivity exhibited by the emotionally disturbed youngster is very different in quality and quantity from that of a youngster whose hyperactivity and dis-tractibility has a neurological basis. Unfortunately, it is also frequently the case that a youngster with a neurological handicap may have significant emotional problems overlaying the basic neurological problems, making diagnosis even more complicated. But the overriding problem confronting parents today is the misdiagnosis of emotionally-based symptoms that brings the recommendation of unwarranted medication.

In the largest study of its kind, Cummings and Wiggins retrospectively examined the records of 168,113 children and adolescents who had been referred and treated over a four-year period in a national behavioral health provider operating in thirty-nine states. Before beginning treatment, sixty-one percent of the males and twenty-three percent of the females were taking psychotropic medication for ADD/ADHD by a psychiatrist, a pediatrician, or a primary care physician. Most of them lived in a single-parent home, and lacked an effective father figure or were subjected to negative and frequently abusive male role models. Behavioral interventions included a compassion-ate but firm male therapist and the introduction of positive male role models (e.g., fathers, Big Brothers, coaches, Sunday school teachers, etc.) into the child's life. Counseling focused on helping parents understand what consti-tutes the behavior of a normal boy.

After an average of nearly eleven treatments with the parent and approx-imately six with the child, the percentage of boys on medication was reduced from sixty-one percent to eleven percent, and the percentage of girls on medi-cation went from twenty-three percent to two percent. These dramatic results occurred despite very strict requirements for discontinuing the medication, which seems to point to an alarming overdiagnosis and overmedication of ADD/ADHD and greater efficacy of behavioral interventions than is generally believed to be the case by the mental health community.

Adult ADHD

The wholesale invasion of ADHD in childhood and adolescence is accompa-nied by a concurrent explosion of such diagnoses into adulthood. One can-not watch television without being bombarded by the direct marketing that asks: "Do you find it difficult to finish a task at work? Do you frequently find yourself daydreaming or distracted? You may be suffering from ADD. Consult your physician or WebMD." Of course, adult ADD exists; children with real ADD will grow into adulthood. But the symptoms described in this aggressive TV marketing are more reflective of boredom, the mid-day blahs, job dissatisfaction, or stress than a syndrome or disorder requiring treatment.

Unfortunately, treatment interventions focused primarily on medication and based on such ethereal and universal symptoms promise an instant "cure" for the patient who now does not have to confront possible unhappiness or stress. Such simple solutions also find great favor with the insurers and HMOs that look for the cheapest treatment. Persons exhibiting "symptoms" are more likely to benefit from a variety of behavioral interventions ranging from vocational counseling for job dissatisfaction and marital counseling for an unhappy marriage, to psychotherapy for underlying emotional stress, anxiety, or depression. Such interventions tend to be time-consuming and costly, with the consequence that the patients may inadvertently ally themselves with managed care companies devoted to the principle that the least expensive treatment is the treatment of choice.

Distractibility and hyperactivity of the type that we have called the "real ADHD" does exist in adults. However, in general, symptoms are much more subtle and, in many if not most cases, overshadowed by other symptoms. Thus, if mentioned at all, distractibility and hyperactivity are rarely significant presenting complaints. Such things as poor judgment, behavioral difficulties, forgetting, difficulties in reading/calculating, and getting lost are typically pre-eminent in the adult patient's presenting complaints. These usually become apparent in adulthood after an accident, strokes (CVA), infections of the brain, and other such events. The very drama of the causative factor typically makes the diagnosis apparent, and treatment providers are "tuned in" to anticipate sequellae secondary to neurological damage: intellectual and/or judgmental deficits, behavioral change, impulsivity, and motor impairment.

It should be emphasized that hyperactivity and distractibility, although present, are less dramatic symptoms that are understandably of less concern to the patient. Furthermore, they often diminish rapidly in the first eighteen months following the neurological event. Even then, the major constellation of symptoms may not be sufficiently dramatic to alert attending medical personnel as to the primary cause of the patient's complaints. This is particularly true of contrecoup lesions occurring most frequently in auto accidents.

Although circumstances resulting in contrecoup damage are frequent and often missed, there are also other, even more significant, types of neurological involvement that may also pass unnoticed. These include early-onset Alzheimer's disease beginning at age fifty and cerebral toxicity resulting from inappropriate medication in the elderly, which is usually misdiagnosed as incipient Alzheimer's. Expectation can unfortunately contribute not only to a misdiagnosis, but also failure to order tests that might elicit the underlying condition. In addition, the converse may infrequently occur: Neurological involvement may be anticipated but is not demonstrable and does not exist. Three illustrative cases follow.

Case 1

Bill, a young construction worker, received notice of his imminent induction into the armed services. Right after lunch on a Friday afternoon, a large section of 2 × 4 lumber dropped from the second story of a work site, striking him butt-first in the right anterior temporal region of the head. He was unconscious for a short period of time, quickly recovered consciousness, and showed no apparent ill effects from the blow. He refused hospitalization, and was taken by his employer to his home.

On the following Monday, Bill phoned his employer saying that he was still "not feeling too good," and given the imminence of his induction into the Army, he "was just going to goof off" until he was "called up." The employer had no further contact with Bill, who was inducted into the Army, where he almost immediately began to have difficulty, primarily of a behavioral type. Throughout his basic training, he tended to be impulsive and to use poor judgment, and he was constantly getting into fights with his companions. He barely made it through training and was shipped overseas where he was assigned to a unit whose primary duty was guard duty.

Throughout his training and his subsequent duty assignment, Bill was a frequent attendee at sick call with consistent complaints of headache, earning him the reputation of "goof-off." His military career was terminated shortly after an apparently unprovoked attack on the officer in charge of the guard detail to which Bill was assigned. After a short detention in the stockade, he was discharged from the Army. His headaches and impulsivity continued into civilian life and prompted Bill to seek medical assistance through the Veterans Administration. The VA clinic's case study included neurological screening tests that were strongly suggestive of brain involvement. Consequently, he was given a full psychological work-up, which revealed intellectual impairment attendant to temporal lobe damage.

Subsequent neurological and encephalographic studies were consistent with the neuropsychological conclusions, and indicated a major focus in the anterior temporal area of the brain. A careful and detailed history was taken, and the incident of the blow to the head was elicited. This case suggests that even though Bill refused hospitalization, because of the severity of the blow it would have been prudent for the employer to insist on a thorough evaluation.

Case 2

James, a man in his late forties, was the son of a Southern sharecropper. Upon graduation from high school, he attended the Tuskegee Institute for a short period before he was drafted into the armed forces. James had a productive military career and upon his discharge moved to California, got married, and proceeded to raise his family. He had trained himself as a finish carpenter and cabinetmaker. His work was highly regarded, and his annual income was well above the average for his field. One of his three children was a college graduate, a second was well along in college, and the third was graduating from high school. James owned his own home and enjoyed a fine reputation as a contributing citizen of his community.

While at work installing a complicated newel post and banister, James became disoriented and tumbled from a stair landing, falling some five feet and landing primarily on his head and shoulders but experiencing no apparent loss of consciousness. He was taken to a hospital for evaluation but was released with no significant findings. Almost immediately thereafter, he began to have difficulty at work. He would become disoriented, could not tell left from right, and made frequent mistakes in measuring, sawing, and fitting even simple elements. Before the accident he seldom if ever missed work, but now he became a frequent absentee. The quality of his work deteriorated and his income plummeted. He sought medical advice and was given a small stipend under the Workers Compensation program.

Over several weeks, he demonstrated no progress, and the attending neurologist and neurosurgeon referred him for neuropsychodiagnostic evaluation as a possible malingerer. The neuropsychologist noted that James' current status was completely at odds with his prior history, and not at all consistent with malingering. For example, the evaluation revealed that this highly skilled cabinetmaker, to his embarrassment, could no longer answer the question, "How many inches are there in two and a half feet?" The neuropsychological finding of pervasive occipital-parietal involvement was subsequently corroborated by electroencephalographic study.

Case 3

An airline captain driving along Wilshire Boulevard in Los Angeles lost consciousness when he experienced a spontaneous cerebral hemorrhage. He was immediately taken to a nearby major hospital where he received immediate and continuing care. Subsequently, a subdural hematoma developed, requiring surgical intervention. The captain recovered and showed no clinically significant signs of neurological involvement. An immediate post-recovery issue was the possibility of being returned to flight status. The attending neurosurgeon referred the patient for a comprehensive neuropsychological evaluation that found no indication of residual neurological deficit. Consequently, the neuropsychologist and the attending neurosurgeon recommended return to flight status.

In summary, in none of the foregoing situations was attention deficit or hyperactivity a significant presenting complaint, although the presence of both was clinically demonstrable at various times in the posttraumatic period. Yet the failure to recognize their presence would not have had a negative impact on treatment planning and or management in any of the three cases. Conversely, if excessive focus on the possible "attention deficits and/or hyperactivity disorder" dictated the nature of the therapeutic intervention, a significant disservice to each of these patients would have resulted.

Traditionally when distractibility and/or hyperactivity are prominent parts of the presenting complaint, the mental health provider directs diagnostic energies toward ascertaining the underlying source of these dysphoric experiences. The distractibility and hyperactivity would have been viewed as secondary symptoms to be tolerated, if possible, until the resolution of the underlying problem resulted in their alleviation. In situations where the symptoms were so extreme as to be significantly debilitating, the mental health provider might reluctantly attempt to provide some symptom relief. However, in such cases this was done with the certain knowledge that it was an expedient, and was not addressing causation.

Times have changed dramatically, reflecting the interaction of a number of factors such as competition and cost controls. With the emergence of a plethora of mental health service providers, psychiatry opted to "remedicalize," essentially abandoning what it refers to as "talk therapy" in favor of medicating question-able syndromes and disorders. Psychology, pushed by its academic wing, could never decide what level of training was sufficient for independent mental health service delivery (i.e., master's versus doctoral degrees), and graduate-level train-ing programs began to turn out hordes of master's-level providers in counseling, social work, education, and school psychology.

Meanwhile, the inclusion of mental health benefits in pre-paid health pro-grams broadened consumption and brought about managed care as a means of reducing consumption of all kinds of health services, including behavioral health services. When the American public's impatience with time-consuming processes is added to managed care's limiting of services in the context of a glut of mental health providers the scene is set for considerable mischief. Add to this brew the fact that psychiatry holds a virtual medication-prescribing monopoly in mental health and that drug manufacturers are constantly developing and mar-keting new magic pills, it all adds up to an environment that encourages the "dis-covery" of yet another syndrome or disorder for which treatment is necessary.

Summary

When hyperactivity and/or distractibility is truly one of the presenting symp-toms, it is indicative of a complex situation that warrants extensive and thought-ful evaluation, and, more often than not, complex and comprehensive treatment planning from the perspective of a variety of specialists. In situations where the attention deficit and/or hyperactivity reflects problems in parenting, chemother-apeutic intervention for the child is likely to be, at best, no more than palliative and, at worse, may succeed in considerably complicating the situation. In this writer's experience, chemotherapeutic intervention for emotionally disturbed children is a last resort and of minimal value in addressing the overall problem. Psychotherapeutic intervention with the parents, which may or may not include the child, is more often than not the treatment of choice. This is a judgment that is best made only after exhaustive study by pediatrics, psychology, neurol-ogy, and perhaps, last of all, psychiatry, which so often seems all too eager to overmedicate. . . .

Where the presenting complaints of hyperactivity and distractibility are in a context of delayed development, excessive fatigability, learning defi-cits, and other such signs, the complexity of the diagnostic problem is sub-stantially increased. In such circumstances, it is absolutely not in the child's best interest to limit the diagnostic evaluation to a single specialty. With the increasing evidence that neurological involvement can follow any number of prenatal and postnatal exposures, wise and caring parents will insist on a comprehensive evaluation by specialists in pediatrics, child neurology, and child neuropsychology. More often than not, if medication is indicated, it will be of a type quite different than what is used in the management of so-called ADHD.

Furthermore, treatment intervention and case management will likely involve skilled educational training of the specialized type developed for use with the brain-injured child. In the case of a friendly pediatrician, a concerned psychologist, or a caring child psychiatrist, any or all attempting unilaterally to diagnose and/or manage the treatment regimen, the concerned and caring parent is well advised to promptly seek additional opinions. For a comprehensive description of the type of evaluation that is most productive in the management of children of this kind.

CHALLENGE QUESTIONS

Is Attention-Deficit Hyperactivity Disorder (ADHD) a Real Disorder?

1. According to these authors, how does normal distractibility differ from disordered distractibility? What motivations might some people have to label normal distractibility as a disorder?
2. Wright argues that medication can often create problems whereas NIMH suggests that medication might be necessary to treat ADHD. What are the risks and benefits of pharmacological treatment? What are the risks and benefits of eschewing pharmacological treatment?
3. Based on your readings, do you believe that ADHD is a real disorder? Why or why not? What does it mean if ADHD is or is not a real disorder?
4. There are many people involved in the question of ADHD's legitimacy as a disorder, including children themselves, parents, doctors, psychologists, politicians, and the media. Who should decide whether ADHD is a real disorder? Might any of these groups have motives that could bias them toward one conclusion or the other?

ISSUE 13

Does Facebook Have Generally Positive Psychological Effects?

YES: Amy L. Gonzales and Jeffery T. Hancock, from "Mirror, Mirror on My Facebook Wall: Effects of Exposure to Facebook on Self-Esteem," *Cyberspcyhology, Behavior, and Social Networking* (January/February 2011)

NO: Gwenn Schurgin O'Keeffe, Kathleen Clarke-Pearson, and Council on Communications and Media, from "Clinical Report—The Impact of Social Media on Children, Adolescents, and Families," *Pediatrics* (April 2011)

ISSUE SUMMARY

YES: Social scientists Amy Gonzales and Jeffery Hancock present empirical research suggesting that selective self-presentation, such as Facebook profiles, enhances self-esteem.

NO: Pediatricians Gwenn Schurgin O'Keeffe and Kathleen Clarke-Pearson caution that inappropriate use of online social networks like Facebook may pose dangers to adolescents, such as isolation and depression.

Walk into a computer lab on any college campus and you will find multiple students editing their own Facebook profiles or reading the profiles of others. Especially among teens and young adults, Facebook has established itself as a tool for self-expression and managing social relationships. How could it be so amazingly popular if it did not have many positive effects? Surely those who participate in Facebook expect new and better relationships as well as a greater or different sense of intimacy, not to mention helpful information and just plain entertainment!

On the other hand, thoughtful observers have also raised some concerns. The relative novelty and the dramatic increase in the popularity of such social media have given rise to a host of psychological questions. Do users become isolated from the real world, or do they make more social connections? Does the relative anonymity of the participant increase antisocial behavior? The sheer popularity of Facebook has precipitated hundreds of studies and articles in an attempt to answer these questions. Some studies have raised concerns that Internet use may promote loneliness and depression (Kraut et al., 1998; Melville, 2010), while others have suggested that Internet use decreases loneliness and depression (Shaw and Gant, 2002). How do we make sense of this amalgam of findings?

Social science researchers Amy Gonzales and Jeffrey Hancock present the results of an empirical study to test the effects of using Facebook on self-esteem. They approach the study using two opposing theories. Although one of the theories postulates that self-esteem decreases when people are prompted to view themselves, another theory suggests that self-esteem increases when people view an *ideal* version of the self. Because Facebook users select the ways they present themselves, their profiles may contain only ideal images and messages. Amy Gonzales and Jeffrey Hancock thus contend that looking at one's own Facebook profile may actually raise self-esteem. In fact, the researchers found that participants who viewed their profiles scored higher on a self-esteem scale than those who did not view their profiles. Further, those who actively edited their profiles scored still higher. Amy Gonzales and Jeffrey Hancock conclude that because Facebook provides multiple ways to selectively present the optimal self, it can positively influence self-esteem.

Gwenn Schurgin O'Keeffe and Kathleen Clarke-Pearson caution that although using social media may have benefits, most adults do not realize how often adolescents are at risk online. For example, cyberbullying is common and may lead to serious psychosocial outcomes, such as depression, anxiety, isolation, and even suicide. Further, teens who have engaged in sexting (sending or receiving sexually explicit media through digital devices) have been suspended from school or criminally charged, and victims of such activity also suffer emotional distress. Gwenn Schurgin O'Keefe and Kathleen Clarke-Pearson also argue that adolescents have limited self-regulating capacity, which makes them vulnerable to the advertising that is directed specifically at them on social networking sites. Moreover, adolescents may put their future reputations at risk by posting inappropriate messages and images. Considering all these risks, adults need to be aware of and supervise the online activity of preadolescents and adolescents.

References

Kraut, R., Patterson, M., & Lundmark, V. (1998). Internet paradox: A social technology that reduces social involvement and psychological well-being? *American Psychologist, 53,* 1017–1031.

Melville, K. (2010). Facebook use associated with depression. *Science A Go Go.* Retrieved May 26, 2011, from http://www.scienceagogo.com/news/20100102231001data_trunc_sys.shtml.

Shaw, L.H., Gant, L.M. (2002). In defense of the Internet: The relationship between Internet communication and depression, loneliness, self-esteem, and perceived social support. *CyberPsychology & Behavior, 5,* 157–171.

POINT

- Study participants using Facebook scored higher than control groups on the Rosenburg Self-Esteem Scale.
- People with low self-esteem may benefit from Facebook social opportunities.
- Although the nonedited view of the self may decrease self-esteem, selective self-exposure to one's Facebook profile enhances self-esteem.
- Facebook provides multiple ways to selectively present and view the *optimal* self, thus increasing the likelihood of self-esteem.

COUNTERPOINT

- A depressed child is likely to be depressed online as well, with parents less aware of the online situation.
- Due to a child's limited capacity for self-regulation, peer pressure on social media sites may have influence on views of social norms.
- Peer-to-peer cyberbullying, the most common social media risk for teens, can lead to many negative effects.
- Those who suffer from Facebook depression may turn to risky sites that promote self-destructive behaviors.

YES

Amy L. Gonzales and
Jeffrey T. Hancock

Mirror, Mirror on My Facebook Wall: Effects of Exposure to Facebook on Self-Esteem

Abstract

Contrasting hypotheses were posed to test the effect of Facebook exposure on self-esteem. Objective Self-Awareness (OSA) from social psychology and the Hyperpersonal Model from computer-mediated communication were used to argue that Facebook would either diminish or enhance self-esteem respectively. The results revealed that, in contrast to previous work on OSA, becoming self-aware by viewing one's own Facebook profile enhances self-esteem rather than diminishes it. Participants that updated their profiles and viewed their own profiles during the experiment also reported greater self-esteem, which lends additional support to the Hyperpersonal Model. These findings suggest that *selective self-presentation* in digital media, which leads to intensified relationship formation, also influences impressions of the self.

Introduction

Over a decade ago, Internet use was thought to promote negative psychosocial well-being, including depression and loneliness.[1] Having attracted attention in and out of the research community, these findings prompted researchers to take a more nuanced look at the relationship between Internet use and psychosocial health,[2,3] at times finding evidence that Internet use could be beneficial.[3,4] The present study extends this research by examining the effects of the social-networking site Facebook (http://facebook.com), which represents a popular new form of Internet communication, on self-esteem.

Previous work has addressed the role of Facebook and the ability to socialize, and the role that socializing online plays in supporting self-esteem and various forms of social capital.[5,6] For example, one recent study found that Facebook can enhance "social self-esteem," measured as perceptions of one's physical appearance, close relationships, and romantic appeal, especially when users received positive feedback from Facebook friends.[5] Also, individuals with low self-esteem may see particularly positive benefits from the social opportunities provided by Facebook.[6]

From *Cyberpsychology, Behavior and Social Networking*, January/February 2011, pp. 79–83.

The effect of Facebook exposure on general self-esteem has not been explored. Yet Facebook, and other social-network sites, have the potential to affect temporary states of self-esteem. Social-network sites are designed to share information about the self with others, including likes/dislikes, hobbies, and personal musings via "wall posts," and "status updates." This information could make people aware of their own limitations and shortcomings, which would lower self-esteem,[7] or it could be that this information represents selective and therefore positively biased aspects of the self, which might raise self-esteem.[8] Does Facebook operate on self-esteem in the same way non-digital information does, by decreasing self-esteem? Or does the opportunity to present more positive information about the self while filtering negative information mean that reviewing one's own Facebook site enhances self-esteem? The following piece examines these questions, by exploring the theoretical predictions of Objective Self-Awareness (OSA) theory[9] and the Hyperpersonal Model.[8]

Objective Self-awareness

One theoretical approach relevant to the effects of social-networking sites on self-esteem is OSA theory, one of the first experimentally tested psychological theories of the self. The theory assumes that humans experience the self as both subject and object.[9] For example, the self as subject is found in daily experiences of life (e.g., waiting for the bus, eating lunch, watching TV[10]). In those experiences the self is an active participant in life and is not self-conscious. However, people become the "object of [their] own consciousness" when they focus attention on the self,[9(p2)] which can have both positive and negative effects.

In a state of objective self-awareness, Duval and Wicklund[9] claim that people are prone to self-evaluations based on broader social standards and norms. This usually results in a greater sense of humility, or downgraded ratings of self, and increased pro-social behavior. For example, people report feeling greater responsibility for social injustice,[11] or are less likely to take an extra helping of candy without being observed.[12] On the other hand, because most people often fall short of social standards when self-awareness is heightened, positive affect and self-esteem typically decrease when people are exposed to objective self-awareness stimuli.[13]

The stimuli used to evoke objective self-awareness is most commonly a mirror,[13] although other stimuli include images of the self,[14] audio feedback,[15] having a video camera pointed at participants,[16] or having participants write autobiographical information.[11] These stimuli cause people to view themselves as they believe others do, even if they are not immediately under observation. Exposure to these stimuli is what leads to pro-social behavior and decreases in self-esteem.

Given that social-networking profiles include information about the self similar to the type of information that is used to prompt objective self-awareness (e.g., photos, autobiographical information), viewing one's profile should prompt a downgrading of self-esteem according to OSA theory. That is, viewing one's Facebook profile should negatively affect one's self-esteem.

Furthermore, research in computer-mediated communication has found that information online is often over-interpreted relative to the same information provided offline,[17] leading to exaggerated or stereotyped impressions.[18] Is it possible that this same process could occur for impressions of the self? If Facebook acts on self-esteem in the same way as previous OSA stimuli, only to a more extreme degree, one prediction is:

> H1: Exposure to one's Facebook site will have a more negative effect on self-esteem than traditional objective self-awareness stimuli (e.g., mirror).

Selective Self-presentation

A second relevant theoretical approach to understanding effects of Facebook use is the Hyperpersonal Model.[8] Walther posits that affordances of the Internet allow users to *selectively self-present* themselves in asynchronous media. People can take their time when posting information about themselves, carefully selecting what aspects they would like to emphasize. Evidence of selective self-presentation is found in a variety of Internet spaces, including e-mails,[19] discussion boards,[20] and online dating Web sites.[21,22]

In addition to evidence that online self-presentations are especially positive presentations, recent research in computer-mediated communication (CMC) suggests that online self-presentations can become integrated into how we view ourselves, especially when the presentations take place in a public, digital space.[23] This phenomenon, known as *identity shift*, demonstrates that self-presentations enacted in online space can impact users' self-concepts.

Self-presentations online can be optimized through selective self-presentation, and online self-presentation affects attitudes about the self. Facebook profiles may provide sufficiently positively biased stimuli to counter the traditional effects of objective self-awareness, and instead prompt a positive change in self-esteem. From this perspective, the hyperpersonal prediction of exposure to Facebook is:

> H2: Exposure to one's Facebook site will have a more positive effect on self-esteem than a control condition or traditional self-awareness stimuli (e.g., mirror).

Furthermore, if exposure to one's own Facebook profile increases self-esteem due to selective self-presentation, then behaviors associated with selective self-presentation should correlate with changes in self-esteem. For example, because self-stimuli are most likely to be on one's own profile page, we would expect that participants who only view their own profile page would report higher self-esteem than participants who view other profiles within Facebook. Thus:

> H3: Participants who exclusively examine only their own profile will report higher self-esteem than participants who view other profiles in addition to their own profiles.

Finally, selective self-presentation should be reflected primarily in editing of one's online self-presentation, according to Walther.[8] That is, the ability to edit one's self-presentation after the fact is a unique attribute of asynchronous, text-based communication. Thus, according to the Hyperpersonal Model, we predict that:

> H4: Participants who make changes to their profile during the experiment will report higher self-esteem than participants who do not.

Each of these predictions is tested in the following study, comparing the effect of viewing one's Facebook site, viewing one's own image in a mirror, and being in a control condition on self-reported self-esteem.

Methods

Participants

A total of 63 students (16 males, 47 females) from a large, Northeastern university participated in this study for extra credit. The study consisted of three conditions: exposure to a mirror, exposure to one's own Facebook site, and a control condition in which participants used the same room without any treatment. Participants were randomly assigned to one of the three conditions, with a total of 21 participants taking part in each of the three conditions.

Procedure

Each participant was told that the study was designed to examine "people's attitudes about themselves after exploring different Internet sites." People in both offline conditions were told that they were in a control condition, and thus would not be online. In the online condition, participants were asked to examine their own Facebook site.

In the Facebook stimulus condition, after logging on to Facebook, participants were instructed to click on the "Profile" tab after the experimenter left the room. The profile page contains the primary source of information on an individual user. Participants were told to look through any of the tabs on that page (Wall posts, Photos, Info, Boxes). Participants were given no specific instructions about making changes to their profile during the study. In addition to the main profile photo, the profile page has information on recent activity on Facebook sent to and from the site owner, personal demographic information, photos, and quizzes completed by the site owner. After being on Facebook for 3 minutes, the experimenter returned with a survey. Participants were instructed to keep the profile page open while completing the questionnaire.

Participants in the offline conditions were taken to the same small computer cubicle used in the online condition. In the objective self-awareness stimulus condition, a mirror was placed against the computer screen. To reduce suspicion of the mirror, they were also told that the cubicle was being used for another experiment and that they should not move anything. Other items were laid about the room in all conditions (e.g., intercoms, a television) in order to enhance the perception that the room was being used for another experiment. Participants were given a survey of questions, which were answered while being exposed to their own reflection in the mirror.

In the offline control condition, participants sat in the same room as participants in the previously mentioned two conditions, but without the mirror present and without the computer screen turned on. Participants were left with the survey and given instructions to buzz the experimenter when they had finished completing the survey. In all conditions, experimenters returned to collect the survey, and participants were then debriefed and probed for suspicion or failure to comply with instruction.

Measures

Self-esteem
Self-esteem was measured using the Rosenburg Self-Esteem scale,[24] in which 10 items were used to assess self-esteem (α = 0.82). Half of the items were reverse coded. Responses were scored on a 4-point scale, ranging from "strongly agree" to "strongly disagree." Although this scale is generally used to measure trait self-esteem, as mentioned above, previous studies of objective self-awareness have used this measure to capture temporary changes in self-esteem due to awareness-enhancing stimuli.[7]

Selective Self-presentation
In order to examine behaviors predicted by the Hyperpersonal Model, we asked participants in the Facebook condition about their behavior while they were on Facebook. Questions included, "Did you leave your profile at any time during the study?" (1 = "yes," 2 = "no"), and "Did you change your profile while you were on the Web site?" (1 = "yes," 2 = "no").

Results

To establish that the objective self-awareness stimuli had an effect on self-esteem, an analysis of variance (ANOVA) was first performed. Gender was also included in the model as a covariate, given previous research suggesting that gender may predict differences in self-esteem.[25] The following analyses all reflect significant differences using two-tailed tests of significance, unless otherwise noted. Indeed, the stimuli did have an effect on self-esteem, $F(1, 59) = 4.47$, $p = 0.02$, $\eta^2 = 0.13$. However, gender was not a significant predictor of self-esteem, $F(1, 60) = 0.94$, $p = 0.34$. This finding reveals that self-reported self-esteem did vary by condition.

To test the hypothesis that Facebook had a more negative effect on self-esteem than traditional objective self-awareness stimulus (H1), a linear contrast analysis was performed with a weight 0 assigned to the traditional objective self-awareness stimulus condition (i.e., mirror, $M = 2.97$, $SD = 0.51$), a weight of -1 assigned to the Facebook condition ($M = 3.35$, $SD = 0.37$), and a weight of 1 assigned to the control condition ($M = 3.23$, $SD = 0.40$). The results of this test were not significant, $F(1, 60) = 0.95$, $p = 0.33$.

To test the opposing hypothesis that Facebook has a positive impact on self-esteem (H2), a different linear contrast analysis was performed. A contrast weight of −1 was assigned to the traditional objective self-awareness stimuli condition, 0 was assigned to the control condition, and +1 was assigned to the Facebook condition. This contrast analysis was significant, $F(1, 59) = 8.60$, $p < 0.01$, $\eta^2 = 0.13$, demonstrating support for H2 and suggesting that Facebook has a positive effect on self-esteem relative to a traditional objective self-awareness stimulus.

Given that viewing Facebook enhanced self-esteem, is there additional evidence that the process of selective self-presentation was responsible for influencing self-esteem? Our first method of testing this question included examining whether participants who exclusively viewed their own profile reported having higher self-esteem than participants who also viewed the profiles of others. An ordinary least squares (OLS) regression of self-esteem on viewing behavior (self-only profile vs. self and other profiles) and gender revealed a significant effect on viewing behavior, $b = 0.40$, $p = 0.03$ (one-tailed, 1 = "yes," 2 = "no"), indicating that participants who left their profile during the study reported lower self-esteem than those participants who exclusively viewed their own profile site, supporting H3. The relationship between gender and self-esteem was not significant, $b = 0.33$, $p = 0.12$ (1 = female, 2 = male).

Finally, we expected that changes to any part of the profile (i.e., status, photo, etc.) during the study would increase participant self-esteem (H4), as editing is a primary means of optimizing self-presentation, according to the Hyperpersonal Model.[8] We tested this hypothesis using OLS regression, and once again included gender in the analysis. In support of this hypothesis, participants who changed their profile during the study reported higher self-esteem than those who did not change their profile, $b = -0.53$, $p = 0.01$, (1 = "yes," 2 = "no"). These data suggest that, because asynchronous social-network profiles allow for added time and energy to construct positive self-presentations, profiles contain information that prompts positive, rather than negative, effects on self-esteem. Men reported having greater self-esteem than women after controlling for the likelihood that participants changed their profile, $b = 0.45$, $p = 0.03$. However, this result cannot be fairly interpreted due to the very small number of men (17 women, 4 men).

Discussion

This study was designed to test the effects of exposure to Facebook on self-esteem relative to traditional self-awareness enhancing stimuli, such as a mirror or photo of oneself. The study suggests that selective self-presentation, afforded by digitally mediated environments can have a positive influence on self-esteem.

These findings are in contrast to predictions from OSA theory, which posits that stimuli that prompt self-awareness (e.g., mirror, photo, autobiographical information) activate discrepancies between oneself and social standards,[9] and consequently lower self-esteem.[13,15] Instead, the results demonstrate that exposure to information presented on one's Facebook profile enhances self-esteem, especially when a person edits information about the self, or *selectively self-presents*. These findings are consistent with Walther's Hyperpersonal Model[8] and suggest that the process of selective self-presentation, which takes place in mediated spaces due to increased time for creating a self-presentation, makes Facebook a unique awareness-enhancing stimuli.

This study is a preliminary step toward understanding how selective self-presentation processes, which have been previously discussed in the context of interpersonal impression formation,[19,20,22] may also influence impressions of the self. Whereas a non-edited view of the self (i.e., mirror) is likely to decrease self-esteem, these findings suggest that the extra care involved in digital self-presentations may actually improve self-esteem. By allowing people to present preferred or positive information about the self, Facebook is a unique source of self-awareness stimuli in that it enhances awareness of the optimal self. This finding is consistent with previous work that has found that digital self-presentations can shape self-assessments.[23] In this case, however, the findings are striking because they contradict previous work on the negative effect of self-awareness enhancing information on self-assessments.

Previous work examining self-esteem suggests that consistency between the actual and the ideal self is an important factor in understanding how information can affect self-esteem.[26] Although participant perceptions between the actual and ideal self were not measured, it is possible that Facebook activates the ideal self. Future research on implications of self-evaluations on self-esteem is needed to test this possibility.

Facebook may also be unique in that the public nature of the site may contribute to objective self-awareness. In previous work, autobiographical information or photos have prompted objective self-awareness.[11,14,15] We tested OSA in Facebook because these features are present there. However, Facebook is a public site, which should also remind users of self-evaluation. In this case, the same information that is prompting OSA is *actually* viewed and evaluated by others as well. Further work is necessary to determine whether public Internet audiences alone may stimulate OSA. In this case, we can only speculate that the high visibility of one's Facebook profile further adds to a sense of objective self-awareness. The difference is that that while Facebook may prime awareness of an audience and self-evaluation, it is a more optimal self that is being evaluated. Thus the effect of self-esteem is positive rather than negative.

Limitations

An important limitation of this study was our failure to account for the effect of the number of Facebook friends on self-esteem. As previous research has demonstrated, the social opportunities in Facebook contribute to an enhanced feeling of social competence.[5,6] We cannot rule out the possibility that reminders of one's social connections are partially responsible for the increase in self-esteem. On the other hand, social connection does not seem to be completely responsible for this effect. Changes to one's profile and attention to one's profile (vs. others' profiles) have a positive effect on self-esteem, which suggests that selective self-presentation is a factor in shaping the resultant self-reports of self-esteem.

Another limitation is that we cannot know the long-term implications of using Facebook on self-esteem from a single study. The measure of self-esteem used in this study is generally used as a measure of stable self-esteem, but has been used on other occasions to measure temporary shifts in self-esteem.[7,13,15] Though difficult to perform in an experimental setting, research that examines long-term effects of social-network sites, such as Facebook, would be valuable. Also, incorporating pre- and post-test measures of self-esteem and other relevant psychological measures would be useful in future work.

The focus in the present study is on Facebook, although we make arguments about social-network sites in general regarding their effect on self-esteem. While future research will be required to extend these findings beyond Facebook, the Facebook interface has several advantages over other sites, such as MySpace (http://myspace.com), including a more uniform layout and the sheer popularity of the site. Given that every person must view their own site, the increased uniformity and popularity of Facebook made it a useful starting point for examining digital self-awareness stimuli and self-esteem.

Finally, participants in the offline conditions did not have the same 3-minute lapse between coming into the room and completing the questionnaire as participants in the Facebook condition. We were concerned, however, that including a filler task would potentially introduce an additional and unintended manipulation into the study. It seems unlikely that the time lapse alone was part of the reason for the different ratings of self-esteem, but to be sure, future research will need to account for this effect by providing an appropriate filler task for participants in the non-digital environments.

Conclusion

The Internet has not created new motivation for self-presentation, but provides new tools to implement such motives. The negative effects of objective self-awareness on self-esteem originated from work in the early 1970s.[9,13–15] Social-networking sites, a product of the 21st century, provide new access to the self as an object. By providing multiple opportunities for selective self-presentation—through photos, personal details, and witty comments—social-networking sites exemplify how modern technology sometimes forces us to reconsider previously understood psychological processes. Theoretical development can benefit from expanding on previous "offline" theories by incorporating an understanding of how media may alter social processes.

All references for articles included in *Taking Sides: Clashing Views on Psychological Issues, 17/e* can be found on the Web at http://www.mhhe.com/cls.

Gwenn Schurgin O'Keeffe et al.

 **NO**

Clinical Report—The Impact of Social Media on Children, Adolescents, and Families

Abstract

Using social media Web sites is among the most common activity of today's children and adolescents. Any Web site that allows social interaction is considered a social media site, including social networking sites such as Facebook, MySpace, and Twitter; gaming sites and virtual worlds such as Club Penguin, Second Life, and the Sims; video sites such as YouTube; and blogs. Such sites offer today's youth a portal for entertainment and communication and have grown exponentially in recent years. For this reason, it is important that parents become aware of the nature of social media sites, given that not all of them are healthy environments for children and adolescents. Pediatricians are in a unique position to help families understand these sites and to encourage healthy use and urge parents to monitor for potential problems with cyberbullying, "Facebook depression," sexting, and exposure to inappropriate content. *Pediatrics* 2011;127:800–804

Social Media Use by Tweens and Teens

Engaging in various forms of social media is a routine activity that research has shown to benefit children and adolescents by enhancing communication, social connection, and even technical skills.[1] Social media sites such as Facebook and MySpace offer multiple daily opportunities for connecting with friends, classmates, and people with shared interests. During the last 5 years, the number of preadolescents and adolescents using such sites has increased dramatically. According to a recent poll, 22% of teenagers log on to their favorite social media site more than 10 times a day, and more than half of adolescents log on to a social media site more than once a day.[2] Seventy-five percent of teenagers now own cell phones, and 25% use them for social media, 54% use them for texting, and 24% use them for instant messaging.[3] Thus, a large part of this generation's social and emotional development is occurring while on the Internet and on cell phones.

From *Pediatrics*, vol. 127, no. 4, April 2011, pp. 800–804. Copyright © 2011 by American Academy of Pediatrics. Reprinted by permission.

Because of their limited capacity for self-regulation and susceptibility to peer pressure, children and adolescents are at some risk as they navigate and experiment with social media. Recent research indicates that there are frequent online expressions of offline behaviors, such as bullying, clique-forming, and sexual experimentation,[4] that have introduced problems such as cyberbullying,[5] privacy issues, and "sexting."[6] Other problems that merit awareness include Internet addiction and concurrent sleep deprivation.[7]

Many parents today use technology incredibly well and feel comfortable and capable with the programs and online venues that their children and adolescents are using. Nevertheless, some parents may find it difficult to relate to their digitally savvy youngsters online for several reasons. Such parents may lack a basic understanding of these new forms of socialization, which are integral to their children's lives.[8] They frequently do not have the technical abilities or time needed to keep pace with their children in the ever-changing Internet landscape.[8] In addition, these parents often lack a basic understanding that kids' online lives are an extension of their offline lives. The end result is often a knowledge and technical skill gap between parents and youth, which creates a disconnect in how these parents and youth participate in the online world together.[9]

Benefits of Children and Adolescents Using Social Media

Socialization and Communication

Social media sites allow teens to accomplish online many of the tasks that are important to them offline: staying connected with friends and family, making new friends, sharing pictures, and exchanging ideas. Social media participation also can offer adolescents deeper benefits that extend into their view of self, community, and the world, including[1,10]:

1. opportunities for community engagement through raising money for charity and volunteering for local events, including political and philanthropic events;
2. enhancement of individual and collective creativity through development and sharing of artistic and musical endeavors;
3. growth of ideas from the creation of blogs, podcasts, videos, and gaming sites;
4. expansion of one's online connections through shared interests to include others from more diverse backgrounds (such communication is an important step for all adolescents and affords the opportunity for respect, tolerance, and increased discourse about personal and global issues); and
5. fostering of one's individual identity and unique social skills.[11]

Enhanced Learning Opportunities

Middle and high school students are using social media to connect with one another on homework and group projects.[11] For example, Facebook and similar social media programs allow students to gather outside of class to collaborate and exchange ideas about assignments. Some schools successfully use blogs as teaching tools,[12] which has the benefit of reinforcing skills in English, written expression, and creativity.

Accessing Health Information

Adolescents are finding that they can access online information about their health concerns easily and anonymously. Excellent health resources are increasingly available to youth on a variety of topics of interest to this population, such as sexually transmitted infections, stress reduction, and signs of depression. Adolescents with chronic illnesses can access Web sites through which they can develop supportive networks of people with similar conditions.[13] The mobile technologies that teens use daily, namely cell phones, instant messaging, and text messaging, have already produced multiple improvements in their health care, such as increased medication adherence, better disease understanding, and fewer missed appointments.[14] Given that the new social media venues all have mobile applications, teenagers will have enhanced opportunities to learn about their health issues and communicate with their doctors. However, because of their young age, adolescents can encounter inaccuracies during these searches and require parental involvement to be sure they are using reliable online resources, interpreting the information correctly, and not becoming overwhelmed by the information they are reading. Encouraging parents to ask about their children's and adolescents' online searches can help facilitate not only discovery of this information but discussion on these topics.

Risks of Youth Using Social Media

Using social media becomes a risk to adolescents more often than most adults realize. Most risks fall into the following categories: peer-to-peer; inappropriate content; lack of understanding of online privacy issues; and outside influences of third-party advertising groups.

Cyberbullying and Online Harassment

Cyberbullying is deliberately using digital media to communicate false, embarrassing, or hostile information about another person. It is the most common online risk for all teens and is a peer-to-peer risk.

Although "online harassment" is often used interchangeably with the term "cyberbullying," it is actually a different entity. Current data suggest that online harassment is not as common as offline harassment,[15] and participation in social networking sites does not put most children at risk of online harassment.[16] On the other hand, cyberbullying is quite common, can occur to any young person online, and can cause profound psychosocial outcomes including depression, anxiety, severe isolation, and, tragically, suicide.[17]

Sexting

Sexting can be defined as "sending, receiving, or forwarding sexually explicit messages, photographs, or images via cell phone, computer, or other digital devices."[18] Many of these images become distributed rapidly via cell phones or the Internet. This phenomenon does occur among the teen population; a recent survey revealed that 20% of teens have sent or posted nude or seminude photographs or videos of themselves.[19] Some teens who have engaged in sexting have been threatened or charged with felony child pornography charges, although some states have started characterizing such behaviors as juvenile-law misdemeanors.[20,21] Additional consequences include school suspension for perpetrators and emotional distress with accompanying mental health conditions for victims. In many circumstances, however, the sexting incident is not shared beyond a small peer group or a couple and is not found to be distressing at all.[4]

Facebook Depression

Researchers have proposed a new phenomenon called "Facebook depression," defined as depression that develops when preteens and teens spend a great deal of time on social media sites, such as Facebook, and then begin to exhibit classic symptoms of depression.[22-27] Acceptance by and contact with peers is an important element of adolescent life. The intensity of the online world is thought to be a factor that may trigger depression in some adolescents. As with offline depression, preadolescents and adolescents who suffer from Facebook depression are at risk for social isolation and sometimes turn to risky Internet sites and blogs for "help" that may promote substance abuse, unsafe sexual practices, or aggressive or self-destructive behaviors.

Privacy Concerns and the Digital Footprint

The main risk to preadolescents and adolescents online today are risks from each other, risks of improper use of technology, lack of privacy, sharing too much information, or posting false information about themselves or others.[28] These types of behavior put their privacy at risk.

When Internet users visit various Web sites, they can leave behind evidence of which sites they have visited. This collective, ongoing record of one's Web activity is called the "digital footprint." One of the biggest threats to young people on social media sites is to their digital footprint and future reputations. Preadolescents and adolescents who lack an awareness of privacy issues often post inappropriate messages, pictures, and videos without understanding that "what goes online stays online."[8] As a result, future jobs and college acceptance may be put into jeopardy by inexperienced and rash clicks of the mouse. Indiscriminate Internet activity also can make children and teenagers easier for marketers and fraudsters to target.

Influence of Advertisements on Buying

Many social media sites display multiple advertisements such as banner ads, behavior ads (ads that target people on the basis of their Web-browsing behavior), and demographic-based ads (ads that target people on the basis of a specific factor such as age, gender, education, marital status, etc) that influence not only the buying tendencies of preadolescents and adolescents but also their views of what is normal. It is particularly important for parents to be aware of the behavioral ads, because they are common on social media sites and operate by gathering information on the person using a site and then targeting that person's profile to influence purchasing decisions. Such powerful influences start as soon as children begin to go online and post.[29] Many online venues are now prohibiting ads on sites where children and adolescents are participating. It is important to educate parents, children, and adolescents about this practice so that children can develop into media-literate consumers and understand how advertisements can easily manipulate them.

On Too Young: Mixed Messages from Parents and the Law

Many parents are aware that 13 years is the minimum age for most social media sites but do not understand why. There are 2 major reasons. First, 13 years is the age set by Congress in the Children's Online Privacy Protection Act (COPPA), which prohibits Web sites from collecting information on children younger than 13 years without parental permission. Second, the official terms of service for many popular sites now mirror the COPPA regulations and state that 13 years is the minimum age to sign up and have a profile. This is the minimum age to sign on to sites such as Facebook and MySpace. There are many sites for preadolescents and younger children that do not have such an age restriction, such as Disney sites, Club Penguin, and others.

It is important that parents evaluate the sites on which their child wishes to participate to be sure that the site is appropriate for that child's age. For sites without age stipulations, however, there is room for negotiation, and parents should evaluate the situation via active conversation with their preadolescents and adolescents.

In general, if a Web site specifies a minimum age for use in its terms of service, the American Academy of Pediatrics (AAP) encourages that age to be respected. Falsifying age has become common practice by some preadolescents and some parents. Parents must be thoughtful about this practice to be sure that they are not sending mixed messages about lying and that online safety is always the main message being emphasized.

The Role of Pediatricians

Pediatricians are in a unique position to educate families about both the complexities of the digital world and the challenging social and health issues that online youth experience by encouraging families to face the core issues of bullying, popularity and status, depression and social anxiety, risk-taking, and sexual development. Pediatricians can help parents understand that what is happening online is an extension of these underlying issues and that parents can be most helpful if they understand the core issues and have strategies for dealing with them whether they take place online, offline, or, increasingly, both.

Some specific ways in which pediatricians can assist parents include:

1. Advise parents to talk to their children and adolescents about their online use and the specific issues that today's online kids face.
2. Advise parents to work on their own participation gap in their homes by becoming better educated about the many technologies their youngsters are using.
3. Discuss with families the need for a family online-use plan that involves regular family meetings to discuss online topics and checks of privacy settings and online profiles for inappropriate posts. The emphasis should be on citizenship and healthy behavior and not punitive action, unless truly warranted.
4. Discuss with parents the importance of supervising online activities via active participation and communication, as opposed to remote monitoring with a "net-nanny" program (software used to monitor the Internet in the absence of parents).

In addition, the AAP encourages all pediatricians to increase their knowledge of digital technology so that they can have a more educated frame of reference for the tools their patients and families are using, which will aid in providing timely anticipatory media guidance as well as diagnosing media-related issues should they arise.

To assist families in discussing the more challenging issues that kids face online, pediatricians can provide families with reputable online resources, including "Social Media and Sexting Tips" from the AAP (www.aap.org/advocacy/releases/june09socialmedia.htm),[30] the AAP Internet safety site (http://safetynet.aap.org),[31] and the AAP public education site, Healthy Children.org (www.healthychildren.org/english/search/pages/results.aspx?Type=Keyword&Keyword=Internet+safety),[32] and encourage parents to discuss these resources with their children. Pediatricians with Web sites or blogs may wish to create a section with resources for parents and children about these issues and may suggest a list of or links to social media sites that are appropriate for the different age groups. In this way, pediatricians can support the efforts of parents to engage and educate youth to be responsible, sensible, and respectful digital citizens.

All references for articles included in *Taking Sides: Clashing Views on Psychological Issues, 17/e* can be found on the Web at http://www.mhhe.com/cls.

CHALLENGE QUESTIONS

Does Facebook Have Generally Positive Psychological Effects?

1. Gonzales and Hancock used the Rosenburg Self-Esteem Scale to measure levels of self-esteem. If you were to take the 10-question survey, would you expect it to be a valid measure of your self-esteem? Explain your answer.
2. Gonzales and Hancock look at Facebook in terms of self-conceptualization. Should this be the basis on which the positive psychological effects of using Facebook are evaluated? Explain your answer.
3. O'Keeffe and Clarke-Pearson cite the limited capacity for self-regulation in children and adolescents as a risk factor in their use of online social media. What is this capacity and what actions might lessen the risk?
4. Considering your own experience with Facebook, do you think O'Keeffe and Clarke-Pearson's concerns about resultant depression are founded? Support your answer.
5. How would you conduct a study to refute the claim that advertisements on social media sites have a powerful influence on the buying behavior of adolescents?

Internet References . . .

Psychology Today

This *Psychology Today* site has a somewhat balanced article with helpful links to various aspects of the social media controversy.

**http://www.psychologytoday.com/blog/positively-media/201102/
the-psychology-social-media-fuels-social-change**

Society for Psychotherapy Research

This is the site for the Society for Psychotherapy Research, a helpful source of authoritative information pertinent to the recent research on psychotherapy.

http://www.psychotherapyresearch.org/

Counseling and Psychotherapy Research Journal

This site provides helpful links to recent psychotherapy research in association with *Counseling and Psychotherapy Research*.

http://www.cprjournal.com/

Wikipedia

Although Wikipedia is not a typical scholarly resource, this particular article has helpful information and links to other sites.

http://en.wikipedia.org/wiki/Integrative_psychotherapy

Psychotherapy Issues

*M*any *psychologists specialize in treating the mental, emotional, and behavioral difficulties of life and living. Yet, there is considerable debate about what difficulties should be treated and how therapy should be conducted. Should difficulties in dealing with Facebook, for example, be treated, or is Facebook a primarily positive social influence? Also, are all types of therapy equally effective, or is there psychological evidence that some therapeutic techniques are more effective than others? What about therapist training? Should therapists specialize in particular approaches and theories of psychotherapy, or should they be more eclectic and train to be ready to administer all approaches and theories for the life problem at hand?*

- Are All Psychotherapies Equally Effective?
- Should Therapists Be Eclectic?

ISSUE 14

Are All Psychotherapies Equally Effective?

YES: Benjamin Hansen, from "The Dodo Manifesto," *Australian and New Zealand Journal of Family Therapy* (December 2005)

NO: Jedidiah Siev, Jonathan D. Huppert, and Dianne L. Chambless, from "The Dodo Bird, Treatment Technique, and Disseminating Empirically Supported Treatments," *The Behavioral Therapist* (April 2009)

ISSUE SUMMARY

YES: Psychologist Benjamin Hansen agrees that psychotherapeutic techniques clearly differ among the various approaches, but he argues that all such psychotherapy techniques produce similar outcomes.

NO: Psychologists Jedidiah Siev, Jonathan Huppert, and Dianne Chambless assert that outcomes among the various psychotherapies differ primarily because one technique or therapy is better than another.

Have you or a member of your family ever considered psychotherapy? If so, you may have wondered how you would select the best therapist. Are some therapists better than others? Are some techniques or theories better than others? Will just any therapist or technique do? These kinds of concerns have led psychologists to investigate the effectiveness of various elements of psychotherapy. They attempt to examine not only which of these elements—therapists, techniques, and even the clients themselves—are the most influential but also whether certain types of psychotherapy theories are more effective than other theories in relation to these elements.

Most researchers have concluded that the different elements of therapy do come together to prompt positive changes. However, some disagree on the specific features that make one therapy more effective than another. One camp of researchers believes that all psychotherapy techniques are essentially equal in their effectiveness. This position is sometimes called the *Dodo hypothesis*, because the Dodo bird in *Alice's Adventures in Wonderland* arranged a race in which all the contestants won, and "all must have prizes." In other words, all the different therapy techniques "won" or are equally effective, so the differential effects of psychotherapy must be due to other factors (sometimes called "common factors"), such as client relationship and therapist skill. The other camp, by contrast, believes that therapeutic techniques are crucial to any effective therapy. In fact, for psychologists who oppose the Dodo hypothesis, technique is pivotal because it often interacts with common factors to produce therapeutic change.

In the YES article, Benjamin Hansen is clearly from the first researcher camp. He affirms that the Dodo hypothesis is correct: no one type of therapy is superior to any other. He agrees that psychotherapy is generally helpful to those who receive it, but he believes that there is ample empirical evidence to suggest that those positive effects occur for a variety of patients and disorders irrespective of technique. Those therapists who believe that a particular technique is better than another only do so because they are biased toward a favored theoretical position. He argues, instead, that therapists should rely on a common factors approach to achieve successful therapy results.

By contrast, in the NO article, Jedidiah Siev, Jonathan Huppert, and Dianne Chambless argue that research on the Dodo hypothesis conceals significant differences in treatment outcomes for therapies and techniques. From their perspective, such research is aggregated from so many different populations, disorders, and treatments that it cannot make comparisons on particular treatments for specific disorders. Yet, this is what consumers and therapists most need—information about which therapy or technique is most effective for specific problems under certain circumstances. Jedidiah Siev, Jonathan Huppert, and Dianne Chambless do not deny the significance of "common factors," but they also do not believe that this significance eliminates the importance of therapy strategies. Indeed, it is in the interaction of these factors and these techniques that the greatest effectiveness is achieved.

POINT

- Effects of psychotherapy are due to common factors rather than specific techniques.
- Meta-analyses provide evidence that particular treatments do not significantly differ.
- Therapies are equally effective because all forms share similar technical components.
- Because no one technique is better than another, more therapy options are available to treat distressed persons.

COUNTERPOINT

- Specific techniques interact with and influence common factors to produce the general effects of psychotherapy.
- Meta-analyses confound too many variables to discern specific treatment superiorities.
- Techniques among therapies differ enough to produce different results.

- The disorder should dictate what technique is used. No psychotherapy can be superior for all disorders and all contexts.

YES

Benjamin Hansen

The Dodo Manifesto

There is currently a very strong move in healthcare toward 'outcomes', 'evidence-based practice' and 'standardised treatments'. This appears to be inspired by escalating costs. In such an environment, evidential (rhetorical?) lightweights like family therapy will struggle to compete with interventions such as CBT and medication. Do we have anything real to worry about?

The Dodo Hypothesis and Comparative Studies of Psychotherapy

The Dodo hypothesis originated with the psychologist Saul Rosenzweig in 1936. Rosenzweig published a paper about 'implicit common factors' in psychotherapy. He speculated that the efficacy of all forms of psychotherapy was similar, and that the success of psychotherapy was due to factors such as the therapeutic relationship and aspects of the patient's and therapist's personalities rather than specific techniques. Rosenzweig was reminded of an episode from *Alice's Adventures in Wonderland* where the somewhat deranged Dodo bird organises a race in which the contestants start from different points on the course and at different times. After a while, the Dodo decides that the race is over. When asked who won the race the Dodo declares that 'everybody won, and all must have prizes'.

Some of the earliest empirical support for the Dodo hypothesis came in the late 1950s from the work of the psychiatrist Jerome Frank. Frank conducted research that compared weekly individual therapy, weekly group therapy and fortnightly supportive therapy (1/2 hour) for depressed patients. He found no difference between the conditions with regard to the relief of distress (Frank & Frank, 1993).

In 1975, Luborsky, Singer and Luborsky published an influential paper titled 'Comparative Studies of Psychotherapies: Is It True That Everyone Has Won and All Must Have Prizes?' These authors conducted a review of the available research literature and concluded that psychotherapy was an effective treatment, all psychotherapies were similarly efficacious, and medications were more efficacious than psychotherapy.

From *Australian and New Zealand Journal of Family Therapy*, vol. 26, no. 4, December 2005, pp. 210–218. Copyright © 2005 by Australian and New Zealand Journal of Family Therapy. Reprinted by permission.

In 1977, Smith and Glass published the first meta-analysis of psycho-therapy outcomes. This technique, pioneered by Glass, enabled the statistical coding and analysis of a host of relevant variables. The technique was a significant improvement on the subjective reviews of the past, and meta-analysis did much to establish the credibility of psychotherapy as a bona fide treatment for psychological distress (Wampold, 2001). Smith (1982) provided an overview of the original work and some subsequent refinements. The average effect size for psychotherapy was found to be 0.85, a large effect. This meant that the average person who received psychotherapy was better off than 80% of those who did not, assuming that the benefits of psycho-therapy were normally distributed. This positive effect held across the spectrum of client variables and disorders. Smith found no significant differences between the various types of psychotherapy, and no significant differences between the efficacies of psychotherapy and medication. Furthermore, she discovered no correlation between therapist effectiveness and their qualifications and experience. These findings have been replicated in more recent meta-analyses (Wampold et al., 1997; Wampold, 2001; Elliott, 2002). Shad-ish et al. (1995) provided an overview of meta-analytic findings specific to marital and family therapy (MFT). Essentially the news is the same. MFT works. Only modest differences emerge between orientations with regard to outcomes. MFT does not appear to be any more effective than individual therapies.

The National Institute of Mental Health (NIMH) Treatment of Depression Collaborative Research Program compared the efficacy of cognitive behaviour therapy (CBT), interpersonal therapy (IPT), the tricyclic antidepressant Imi-pramine plus clinical management, and a placebo pill plus clinical management. Elkin (1994) reported on the general effectiveness of the treatments. Overall 24% of patients fully recovered from their depression by the end of the 16-week treatment period and stayed well throughout the 18-month follow-up period. The percentages of patients who recovered and stayed well in each of the conditions were CBT (30%), IPT (26%), placebo (20%), and Imipramine (19%).

The findings reported above are derived from efficacy studies—evaluations of psychotherapy in controlled (to varying degrees) conditions. Seligman (1995) reviewed and summarised the findings of the 'Consumer Reports' survey on psychotherapy. This was an effectiveness study; that is, an evaluation of the usefulness of psychotherapy as it is practised in the real world. The survey revealed that psychotherapy generally appeared to be very beneficial to its recipients, but no one treatment was more effective than any other. Other findings were that long-term therapy was more beneficial than short-term treatment; medication did not enhance the benefits of psychotherapy; psychologists, psychiatrists and social workers were equally effective practitioners of psychotherapy, while marriage counsellors and family GPs were not as effective as mental-health professionals. These results were recently replicated in Germany (Hartmann & Zepf, 2003).

But Wait, There's More . . .

Much of the empirical support for the Dodo hypothesis comes from comparative studies of psychotherapy, but data from client, process and component studies are also supportive. For example Sotsky et al. (1991) reviewed data from the NIMH Treatment of Depression Collaborative Research Program in order to determine which patients might benefit most from particular treatments. They found that the least cognitively impaired subjects appeared to respond most favourably to CBT. Ilardi and Craighead (1994) looked at process data and found that most of the improvement that occurs during the course of cognitive therapy for depression occurs before any cognitive restructuring has begun. And, closer to home, Walsh (2004) conducted a study that involved 100 families who underwent structural family therapy. He found that the type of intervention used was not related to outcome. Structural family therapy apparently does not change family structure. Ahn and Wampold (2001) conducted a meta-analysis of component studies. They found that the key components of various treatment packages appear to add virtually nothing to the effectiveness of therapy.

Further support for the Dodo hypothesis comes from studies of therapist effects vs. treatment effects. Kim (2003) reviewed the data produced by the NIMH Treatment of Depression Collaborative Research Program in order to evaluate therapist effects against treatment effects. Kim found that 12.4% of the outcome variance at termination between the CBT and IPT conditions was due to therapist effects. Treatment effects accounted for 0% of the variance. Huppert et al. (2001) also found that therapist effects were very significant vis-à-vis treatment effects in a study that looked at the treatment of panic disorder. Interestingly, both of these studies involved manualised treatments. It thus appears unlikely that psychotherapy can ever truly be standardised.

The Dodo hypothesis is also supported by studies in which the effectiveness of trained and untrained therapists is compared. Trained therapists would presumably have a better grasp of technique than untrained therapists, and if technique is truly important, be more effective than untrained therapists. The most infamous study in this area is that published by Strupp and Hadley in 1979. The study compared the psychotherapeutic potency of very experienced psychologists and psychiatrists (average length of experience, 23 years) to college professors without a relevant professional background but who appeared to be able to form understanding relationships. The subjects were male college students who exhibited symptoms of mild depression and anxiety. On average, the subjects treated by the professors showed as much improvement as the subjects treated by the professionals. This study, however, raises some concerns. One problem was that the professionals were assigned harder cases. However, the general finding is far from unique. For example, Leonard Bickman's (1999) review concluded that the available evidence did not support the utility of experience or higher degree programs for psychotherapists. In a more recent review, Atkins and Christensen (2001) reached the same conclusion. One review by Stein and Lambert (1995) found a modest effect for training, but the evidence was indirectly derived from the reviewed studies, and the authors concluded their review with a comment about the overall paucity of supporting evidence for graduate training.

CBT Equals Supertherapy?

A key issue in the literature is the relatively large effect sizes often attributed to cognitive and behavioural therapies. Some researchers have attributed such findings to allegiance effects (Smith, 1982; Miller et al., 1997; Wampold, 2001). Others, such as Eysenck (1994), say that this is all nonsense and maintain that cognitive and behavioural treatments are actually much better than the rest. A known tendency toward bias occurs in comparative trials of psychotherapy. This is apparently in the direction of the theoretical orientation of the first senior author (Denman, 1993). Luborsky et al. (1999) assessed that 69% of the variance in outcomes in comparative studies of psychotherapy was due to allegiance effects.

It is hard, however, to prove bias objectively. Robert Matthews' (2004) article about parapsychology provides an interesting parallel. Matthews reported on a number of studies that showed strong evidence for ESP. He was not interested in exploring whether or not ESP existed, but rather looked at the fact that scientific data had little impact on the opinions of believers and non-believers alike. Believers felt that positive data confirmed the obvious—ESP was real. Nonbelievers felt that data must have been contaminated or fraudulently produced because ESP does not exist. Matthews suggested that empirical evidence does not carry as much weight as we often assume, because the data around effects are construed through philosophical frameworks that are inherently subjective.

In any case, one does not have to look hard to find studies that suggest that CBT is nothing special. For example, Parker, Roy & Eyers (2003) concluded in a recent review that the superiority of CBT to other psychotherapies as a treatment for depression had not been proven. Shear et al. (1994) directly compared CBT to nonprescriptive counselling as a treatment for panic disorder. They found that both interventions were equivalently helpful. And, in a relatively rare instance of a specific finding in a comparative study of psychotherapies, McIntosh et al. (2005) found that nonspecific supportive clinical management was significantly superior to CBT and IPT as a treatment for anorexia nervosa. Another specific finding, very relevant to family therapists, came about through the London Depression Intervention Trial. This study compared systemic therapy, CBT and antidepressant medications for depression. Systemic therapy was clearly the most efficacious treatment (Jones & Asen, 2000). . . .

What Are the Common Factors in Psychotherapy?

We don't really know. Empirically what has been established is that specific effects account for, at best, 8% of outcomes, general effects account for 70%, and the remaining 22% is unexplained but may have something to do with client characteristics (Wampold, 2001).

Frank & Frank (1993) suggested four factors common to all forms of psychotherapy. First, a relationship between the patient and the helper such that the patient had confidence in the helper's competence and desire to help. Second, the therapy took place in a setting designated by society as a place of healing. The setting also offered advantages such as safety and confidentiality. Third, a rationale was offered for the patient's distress that contained the possibility of resolution. Fourth, a task was prescribed by the therapist's rationale or theory that required some sacrifice or effort on the part of the patient. These factors invoked a placebo response. In essence, psychotherapy enhanced the patient's morale and this, in effect, could lead to snowballing changes in the patient's attitudes and behaviour.

Following the above model, it would appear that seeing a psychotherapist is little different to seeing a shaman in another culture. Perhaps you are feeling poorly. You go to see the Great Healer at her Sacred Tent. The healer tells you that you have offended the gods. She hands you a big stick and tells you that you need to take on a bear to make up for it. You narrowly survive your encounter with the bear and soon after start to feel better.

There is some empirical support for the view that psychotherapy is a placebo treatment. Baskin et al. (2003) conducted a meta-analysis of the structural equivalence of placebo controls in psychotherapy. They found that when placebo conditions are structurally equivalent to treatment conditions—that is, same number and duration of sessions, same format of therapy and equivalently trained therapists—the effects of active treatments above placebo appear to be negligible.

One the most popular common-factor models was proposed by Miller, Duncan and Hubble (1997). These authors suggested that the effectiveness of psychotherapy was due to a set of factors—extratherapeutic (40% of any change that occurs), therapeutic relationship (30%), placebo effects (15%) and technique (15%). The percentages in this model obviously involve some guesswork, but the components have substantial empirical support. Extratherapeutic factors refer to client characteristics and chance events. The therapeutic relationship is the most well-supported common factor (Lambert & Barley, 2001). As an aside, it is interesting to note that the therapeutic relationship appears to impact significantly on the efficacy of drug treatments as well (Krupnick et al., 1996). Placebo effects refer to hope and expectancy. Technique is important in the sense that it provides structure. Unstructured therapy is highly correlated with poor outcomes. This model seems to reflect the literature on common factors pretty well.

Sprenkle and Blow (2004) suggested that family therapists had largely ignored common-factors research. This was apparently due to the discipline's proud 'maverick' tradition. The authors also noted, importantly, that family therapy is uniquely complex in that we have to apply common factors to families rather than individuals. Thus, for example, family therapists need to build and maintain a number of therapeutic alliances at any one time.

On the Other Hand . . .

Responses could be made to the Dodo hypothesis. The most salient would likely be that most of the research done tests psychotherapies against each other across broad heterogeneous groups. This means that average effect sizes may be quite meaningless. Parker et al. (2003) make this point in relation to research on CBT as a treatment for depression. Subjects are put into categories that are based on severity rather than aetiology. Treatments are assessed in terms of their universal impact. This means little chance of any specific effects being noted. The authors draw an analogy with oncology—cancers are not classified as belonging to groups such as major cancer, minor cancer or sub-clinical cancer and neither chemotherapy nor surgery is used as a universal treatment.

In addition to obfuscating potentially very important differences among clients, there is also the reliability problem with psychiatric diagnoses. Kutchins and Kirk (1998) cited an impressive array of evidence to the effect that this issue surfaces even when trained and experienced assessors are used. These authors reported that in DSM field trials, professionals were often unable to agree on the category of disorder from which a particular patient suffered, let alone a specific diagnosis. A number of diagnoses also have validity issues. Here is an example relevant to those of us who work with children and youth— 'conduct disorder'. Lambert et al. (2001) found that the diagnostic criteria for conduct disorder had only slightly more internal consistency than symptoms chosen at random from the DSM-IV.

And another problem. How many unique manoeuvres are there in psychotherapy? Miller et al. (1997) suggest a tendency for the proponents of the various schools of psychotherapy to highlight the differences among 'brands'. These authors use solution-focused brief therapy and Narrative therapy as an example. A number of therapeutic moves are common to both approaches but different language is used, and this suggests differences in content. In a study that has dire implications for comparative studies of psychotherapy, Ablon and Jones (2002) looked at data from the NIMH Treatment of Depression Collaborative Research Program. They had hypothesised that manualised psychotherapy regimens in controlled trials overlap considerably in process and technique. When they compared prototypical regimens for IPT and CBT with transcripts from the NIMH study's IPT and CBT conditions they found significant overlap, and indeed therapists in both conditions appeared to be doing CBT. Have we been comparing Coke to Pepsi and puzzling over findings that they both appear to be fizzy cola drinks?

Some authors have suggested that all forms of psychotherapy share effective technical components. Eysenck (1994) suggested that behavioural interventions (relaxation, modelling, suggestion, flooding with response prevention, and so on) were responsible for all of the benefit of psychotherapy, as well as spontaneous remission and placebo responses to psychotherapy. These techniques were sometimes inadvertently used by nonbehavioural therapists.

Gibney (2003) proposed that the essence of all psychotherapy was 'double description'. Gibney's idea was not a response to the Dodo hypothesis, but it is relevant. Double description is about drawing distinctions—comparing one version of events with other possibilities. The idea comes from Gregory Bateson's (1972) observation that the defining quality of mind is the ability to take multiple perspectives. Gibney suggested that the various schools of psychotherapy offered alternate, novel descriptions of the client's issues and thus established contexts in which new ways of thinking and behaving could develop. This is a poetic explanation that may contain some truth.

A third problem with the data that substantiates the Dodo hypothesis is that most of it comes from efficacy studies—subjects usually have one uncomplicated diagnosis, treatment regimens are manualised, supervision is intense and so on. This is, of course, exactly how psychotherapy is not usually practised in the real world. So how relevant is the information from such studies?

Sexton, Ridley and Kleiner (2004) have been highly critical of the idea of grounding MFT practice and research in common factors. These authors made the point, probably correctly, that the so-called common factors are not clearly defined identities and are 'decontextualised'—they are not tied to the process of therapy. Sexton et al. suggested that a common-factors approach is old hat and somewhat primitive. They maintained that family therapists can now draw upon a variety of theoretically sound and well-validated models in the marketplace. Sexton is in fact a developer of one such product—Functional Family Therapy (see Sexton & Alexander, 2003).

What Does it All Mean?

The good thing about science is that it often reveals 'truths' that are not readily apparent. For example, the fact that matter and energy are the same thing is surprising. The fact that the book of life is written in an alphabet of only four letters is also surprising. However, to draw upon the 40-30-15-15 model described above, for example, it is not surprising to find that clients have lives outside of therapy that may impact very significantly on their well-being. It is not surprising that treating clients with sensitivity and respect is helpful. It is not surprising that hope is helpful. It is not surprising that taking a structured approach to solving client's problems is more helpful than just having a chat. Further to this list of not surprising revelations—it is not surprising that these factors would take precedence over the technical aspects of therapy. The utility of a supportive relationship and some hope to a distressed person is patently obvious. And because psychotherapy is conducted *with* intelligent, autonomous human beings rather than *on* inert mechanisms, factors such as the therapeutic relationship will determine the utility of any technical procedures because they will determine the participation of the client in therapy. So it would appear that after more than 40 years of research into psychotherapy, we have arrived at commonsense. And we cannot even say for sure that technical factors have no specific effects, because of significant flaws in the way the basic concepts have been operationalised in efficacy trials.

In my view, the current state of affairs reflects an obsession in Western culture that was originally inspired by Isaac Newton. Prior to Newton, most people had existed in a state of resigned bafflement about the apparendy discontinuous vastness that was the universe.

Newton's genius was to unite a collection of previously disparate phenomena with a few simple 'laws'. Since that time, it has been on for young and old, with generations of thinkers trying to duplicate the great man's feat within their own fields of expertise. Sadly, those of us who work within the 'mind sciences' have been given the short end of the stick. We work with inordinately complex, invisible, indivisible and often inferred entities that elude simple quantification. As a result our 'science' often does not turn out very well. What it all means is this—the positivistic paradigm is not a good paradigm through which to legitimise the practice of family therapy, or any form of psychotherapy for that matter. It has obviously been very useful in other fields, but much less so here.

I am not suggesting that we abandon research, but it may be more useful for family therapists to justify their practice with hard results rather than flashy rhetoric. I am sure that we can all cite very successful psychotherapeutic interventions with our clients. The psychologist Daniel Fishman (1999) has pointed out that while universal solutions do not appear to have adequately met many human problems, there are a plethora of smaller, local, contextual examples of successful interventions. Fishman suggested a pragmatic approach where psychotherapists and professionals in related fields direct their efforts toward addressing the specific concerns of clients by the most appropriate means available. Such interventions could be incorporated into a database of case studies through which future practice could be informed. (Given the concerns about bias in the outcomes literature, it may be appropriate for future efficacy trials to be run by neutral parties or perhaps teams of ideologically opposed researchers such as psychoanalysts and radical behaviourists.) Fishman's approach seems sensible in light of the Dodo hypothesis. Indeed, it was the approach followed by one of family therapy's folkheroes—Milton Erickson. Erickson's approach was to have an approach for each client (Jackson, 2003). Beels (2002) suggested that Erickson was one of a long line of American pragmatists who provided as much impetus for the development of 'family therapy' as the original Bateson group. To practise pragmatically, we need pluralism in psychotherapy. Therapists would need to be able to draw upon as wide a range of ideas as possible. Family therapy is clearly a useful tool to have at one's disposal when working with children and young people or looking at client problems that have a systemic flavour.

There is a clear way forward here—(1) turn down the positivistic rhetoric, (2) adopt a sceptical attitude to the claims of evidence-based practice proponents, and (3) offer solid pragmatic data in support of our discipline.

Conclusion

The evidence as it stands suggests that no one type of psychotherapy is generally superior to any other. CBT and medication do not appear to be superior technologies. Thus, we have numerous valid approaches through which to assist distressed persons. In the main, the positivistic paradigm in psychotherapy research has not produced many profound insights, but certain common-sense aspects of psychotherapy appear to be very important. Taking a pragmatic approach to therapy and research is a way forward for family therapists.

All references for articles included in *Taking Sides: Clashing Views on Psychological Issues, 17/e* can be found on the Web at **http://www.mhhe.com/cls.**

Jedidiah Siev, Jonathan D. Huppert,
and Dianne L. Chambless

The Dodo Bird, Treatment Technique, and Disseminating Empirically Supported Treatments

In a recent presidential column in *the Behavior Therapist*, Raymond DiGiuseppe observed that efforts to disseminate empirically supported treatments (ESTs), and especially cognitive-behavioral treatments, have been limited by perceptions "that all psychotherapies are equally effective [the Dodo Bird verdict], and . . . that common factors, therapist, and relationship variables account for the majority of the variance in therapy outcome studies" (2007, p. 118). He called for dialogue with proponents of those views, in an effort to understand their perspective and convey the alternative. Ultimately, "either we rebut these conclusions, conduct new research to show they are wrong, or we accept them and change our message" (p. 119). The aim of this article is to provide some historical context in terms of previous attempts to respond to these contentions and to present an update on recent research bearing directly on the Dodo Bird verdict and the assertions regarding variance accounted for by active ingredients (e.g., technique).

Aggregation

Evidence for the claim that all psychotherapies are equally efficacious derives from meta-analyses that combine various treatments for various disorders (e.g., Luborsky et al., 2002; Wampold et al., 1997). At most, these meta-analyses yield small effect sizes for average between-condition comparisons (e.g., $d = 0.21$; Wampold et al.), and the authors infer that, overall, no two psychotherapies are differentially efficacious for treating a disorder. Such a conclusion, however, is based on the fallacious reasoning that because all treatments for all disorders do not differ on average, no particular treatment is superior to another for a specific disorder (see Beutler, 2002; Chambless, 2002; Crits-Christoph, 1997; Hunsley & Di Giulio, 2002; and many others who have argued this point). Even operating with this reasoning, most meta-analyses have found differences between treatment orientations (Luborsky et al.; Shapiro & Shapiro, 1982; Smith & Glass, 1977; Wampold et al.), even when taking into account allegiance. Furthermore, in response to Wampold et al.'s meta-analysis, Crits-Christoph suggested that aggregating various populations, disorders, and treatments would likely obscure real differences in treatment outcomes. Moreover, half of the studies examined

From *The Behavioral Therapist*, vol. 32, no. 4, April 2009, pp. 32, 69–75. Copyright © 2009 by Association for the Advancement of Behavioral and Cognitive Therapies. Reprinted by permission.

by Wampold and colleagues evaluated the treatment of anxiety, and nearly 70% compared cognitive to behavioral therapies, characteristics of the studies that may minimize the likelihood of finding substantial treatment differences. Crits-Christoph demonstrated that 14 of the 29 studies that Wampold and colleagues included that compared two treatments for specific disorders grounded in different orientations yielded large effect sizes. Similarly, Beutler, Chambless, and others (Chambless & Ollendick, 2001; Hunsley & Di Giulio, 2002) have cited multiple studies and reviews that question the Dodo Bird verdict.

As a further challenge to the Dodo Bird verdict, Siev and Chambless (2007) recently conducted meta-analyses comparing CBT and relaxation (two bona fide treatments for anxiety disorders) for panic disorder (PD) and generalized anxiety disorder (GAD). In so doing, we compared two specific cognitive-behavioral interventions in the treatment of two anxiety disorders. The results revealed that for PD, CBT outperformed relaxation at posttreatment on all panic-related measures and indices of clinically significant change. In contrast, for GAD, the two treatments were equivalent on all measures. Furthermore, therapists in all studies were crossed with treatment condition, and most authors assessed client expectations and ratings of treatment credibility, which were high and never differed by treatment group. These methodological strengths bolster the likelihood that treatment techniques affected treatment effects.

In addition to combining various treatments and disorders, many meta-analyses in which the Dodo Bird verdict is advanced do not distinguish between primary and secondary outcome measures (Wampold et al., 1997). Rather, they derive a single effect size for each between-condition comparison by averaging all outcome measures. Their logic for doing so is:

> Given the assumption that researchers choose outcome measures that are germane to the psychological functioning of the patients involved in the study, it is the effect of the treatment on the set of outcome measures that is important. . . . Focusing on a few of many outcome measures to establish superiority causes fishing and error rate problems (Cook & Campbell, 1979) and distracts the researcher from examining the set of outcome measures, which might have produced a negligible effect size. (Wampold et al., 1997, p. 210)

However, the average of all outcome measures does not accurately capture the efficacy of the treatment for individuals suffering from a specific disorder, and is likely artificially to attenuate the magnitude of the effect size. The extent to which a treatment for a disorder (e.g., PD) affects domains of common comorbidity (e.g., depression) is critical information, but is not of equal import in evaluating the treatment's efficacy as is the extent to which it affects core symptoms of the disorder (e.g., panic symptoms and diagnostic status). Although it is true that researchers should articulate a priori the primary dependent measures, reasonable concerns about post hoc reporting biases (e.g., selectively emphasizing significant findings from a large set of mostly nonsignificant findings) ought not preclude researchers from investigating secondary outcomes. Combining measures of primary and secondary outcomes forces can obscure or mask entirely meaningful differences in treatment effects (see Crits-Christoph, 1997).

Meta-analytic data comparing CBT and relaxation for PD and GAD that were not published in Siev and Chambless (2007) illustrate the importance of considering not only disorders separately, but primary and secondary outcome measures separately, as well. . . .

Rather, in conducting or interpreting these data, one must consider a fundamental issue: What is the question? It is our contention that rarely does the researcher, clinician, or consumer care whether, on average, treatments for all disorders across all domains do not differ. Rather, the consumer (to take one, for example) wishes to know what treatment will best alleviate the distress caused by his or her symptoms (cf. the fundamental psychotherapy question of Paul, who articulated the importance of asking not only whether psychotherapy works, but "What treatment, by whom, is most effective for this individual with that specific problem, and under which set of circumstances?" [1967, p. 111; emphasis in the original]). When the presenting problem is PD, the best answer to that question (if the options are CBT and relaxation) is that CBT is likely to reduce primary panic-related symptoms by approximately half a standard deviation more than is relaxation. Cast as a binomial effect size display,[1] this represents an increase in the rate of success from 38% to 62%. The wise consumer suffering from PD will choose CBT.

Bona Fide Treatments

Even advocates of a common factors approach to psychotherapy acknowledge that not all conceivable interventions are efficacious. Instead, the Dodo Bird verdict extends only to bona fide treatments, meaning those "intended to be therapeutic" (Wampold et al., 1997, p. 205). This distinction between bona fide and sham treatments in evaluating the relative efficacy of different treatments, while having appeal, also introduces a number of theoretical and conceptual difficulties.

Wampold and colleagues (e.g., Ahn & Wampold, 2001; Messer & Wampold, 2002) conclude that treatment outcome studies are futile because comparisons between bona fide treatments yield clinically insignificant differences and those between bona fide treatments and controls yield uninteresting differences. This contention is somewhat circular, however, because categorization as a bona fide treatment is both a criterion for inclusion in, and an implication of, the results of clinical experience and treatment outcome research (and meta-analyses that synthesize multiple such studies). To illustrate, consider the history of behavioral treatments for obsessive-compulsive disorder (OCD). Forty years ago, behavioral therapists treated OCD with relaxation. As exposure and response prevention (ERP) was developed, clinicians discovered that it was far more efficacious than relaxation, which is now considered a placebo in the treatment of OCD. Does the discovery that one treatment outperforms a second render that very comparison invalid? In fact, in a recent survey of psychologists who treat anxiety disorders and who predominantly favor a CBT approach, more clinicians endorsed using relaxation to treat OCD, than endorsed using ERP (Freiheit, Vye, Swan, & Cady, 2004). Surely those clinicians consider relaxation to be a bona fide treatment. How can it then become something other than a bona fide treatment when a researcher uses it? Wampold and colleagues' concern that comparisons between bona fide treatments and shams are rigged and sometimes uninformative is well taken. Certainly treatments should be compared to real treatments and not trimmed down, three-legged horses. At the same time, to conduct component analyses that evaluate particular techniques often presented together as parts of a larger treatment package, certain treatment elements must be excluded. This is part of the bind.

A related complication stems from the study- or disorder-specific classification of a treatment as bona fide. Although Wampold et al. (1997) formulate an operational definition of bona fide to identify particular studies for inclusion in their meta-analysis, there is little conceptual justification for some resultant distinctions. For example, according to Wampold et al.'s guidelines, whereas relaxation is now considered a placebo for OCD, it is a bona fide treatment for GAD because studies have demonstrated that relaxation works as well as other treatments for GAD (and therefore therapists expect relaxation to be therapeutic), but not for OCD (and therefore [study] therapists now do not expect relaxation to be therapeutic). In other words, researchers expect some treatments to work because they have found them to do so, and others to work less well because they have found them to do so. Herein lies another difficulty with Wampold et al.'s classification of treatments as bona fide: It is circular to discount the superior efficacy of a treatment on the grounds that "I knew it would work better," if that assumption derived from observation of the same superior efficacy. Moreover, if this reasoning is correct, on what other grounds is relaxation a bona fide treatment for one anxiety disorder and not another? Considering that Wampold et al. aggregate across disorders and treatments, this poses a particular theoretical difficulty. Is it reasonable to include comparisons of CBT and relaxation for GAD (as they do), but not for OCD? Wampold et al. use the notion of bona fide treatment to ensure that the patient and the therapist have positive expectancies about outcomes, as expectancies are proposed to be an essential common factor related to outcome. However, if a therapist and a patient expect ERP to work better than relaxation for OCD, for example, then they are correct in their expectation, but it does not mean that expectancy is driving the treatment effect. Are the effects caused by expectancy, or do people expect more from treatments that work better? Finally, Wampold et al.'s criterion of bona fide treatment comparisons creates the potential trap that if consensus were reached that exposure-based CBT is the treatment of choice for OCD, then one could not establish its efficacy, as there could not be a bona fide treatment with which to compare exposure-based CBT.

Relationship and Therapist Variables, Common Factors, and Technique

The notion that the therapeutic relationship, therapist, and/or common factors contribute significantly more to treatment outcomes than do specific techniques has been stated by many (e.g., Levant, 2004; Messer & Wampold, 2002; Wampold, 2001), although with voices of opposition (Beutler, 2004; Huppert, Fabbro, & Barlow, 2006). The claim that technique accounts for approximately 10% to 15% of the variance of therapy outcome, whereas expectancy, relationship factors, and common factors account for closer to 40%, is frequently dem-onstrated in a pie chart (e.g., Lambert & Barley, 2001; 2002). However, the history of this chart may give the reader pause. Originally published in 1986 by Lambert, Shapiro, and Bergin in the *Handbook of Psychotherapy and Behavior Change* (3rd edition), the pie chart represented a summary of Lambert's read-ing of the literature from the previous 20+ years; it was not an empirical deter-mination. One would hope that some progress has been made in the 20 years since, especially with regard to understanding mediators, moderators, and processes in therapy, and in CBT in particular. To take one study as exceptional in terms of such progress, Clark et al. (2006) showed that CBT targeting core cognitions and concerns of individuals with social anxiety disorder was more effective than exposure therapy (with a purely behavioral rationale of habitu-ation) plus relaxation. Clark et al. report the effects of technique, alliance, and expectancy (see pie chart in Figure 1). Not only were therapist effects not large or significant, but there were no differences between the two treatment conditions in ratings of alliance ($p = .57$), credibility ($p = .26$), or expectancy ($p = .22$), suggesting that these mechanisms were not responsible for the dif-ferential treatment outcome between CBT and exposure. Similar data from another research group suggest that these CBT techniques for social anxiety disorder may be more effective than exposure alone (Huppert, Ledley, & Foa, 2007). At the same time, treatment technique did not account for 70% or 80% of the variance, and it is unlikely that any treatment will reach such a threshold.

How large are technique effects likely to be? Even Lambert's pie chart indicates that up to 15% of treatment effects may be due to technique, whereas Wampold (2001) suggests 8%. Before speculating about their magnitude, one needs to consider how best to determine technique effects. One method may be to compare active therapy to placebo. Overall, CBT for anxiety disorders has in fact shown significant superiority to placebo (cf. Hofmann & Smits, 2008), with an average effect size for the magnitude of the difference of 0.33 for intent-to-treat and 0.73 for completer analyses. However, there is variability in these

Figure 1

Breakdown of Clark et al.'s (2006) Data by Technique, Therapist Effects, and Unknown

CBT vs. Exposure Alone Effects

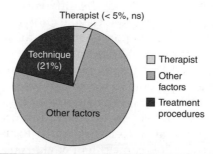

effects, with the strongest evident in the treatment of acute stress disorder and OCD, and the weakest in the treatment of PD. Why might this be? It has been shown previously that OCD is less placebo responsive than is PD or social anxiety disorder (Huppert et al., 2004; Khan et al., 2005), and technique effects are most demonstrable in the disorders that have the smallest placebo effects. In fact, for some disorders (e.g., major depression), significant technique effects are somewhat difficult to demonstrate by comparing placebo to CBT (DeRubeis et al., 2005), although such effects are more prominent when examining follow-up data (e.g., Hollon et al., 2005). Similarly, in the case of PD, for which the magnitude of placebo response also appears to be high (Huppert et al.; Khan et al.), significant between-treatment effects are more evident at long-term follow-up (Barlow, Gorman, Shear, & Woods, 2000). In sum, it is difficult to determine the overall effect of technique without considering disorder and population, a conclusion reinforced by our discussion of the Dodo Bird verdict.

There are other methods by which one may examine technique effects. For example, Ablon and Jones (2002) showed that cognitive therapy techniques accounted for a significant amount of change in depressive symptoms in the NIMH Treatment of Depression Collaborative Research Program in both CBT and interpersonal psychotherapy treatment conditions. In addition, Cukrowicz et al. (2005) reported data suggesting that when a clinic changed its policy to conduct only ESTs, there was significant improvement in patient outcomes. Howard (1999) noted that individuals in a managed care environment who had specialty training in CBT for anxiety disorders were more likely to retain their patients, and those patients were also less likely to receive further treatment 1 year later. It is important to note that studies that simply examine orientation are unlikely to find such effects, as many practitioners who identify their primary orientation as cognitive-behavioral continue to use relaxation as a treatment of choice for OCD and PD (e.g., Freiheit et al., 2004).

But what about the contribution of alliance, common factors, and therapist effects? On average, studies yield a correlation of .22 between measures of alliance and outcome (Martin, Garske, & Davis, 2000), demonstrating that the former accounts for 5% of the variance in the latter. Note that this effect size derives from data aggregated across studies of a range of therapies and treatments, similar to the effect sizes calculated by Wampold and colleagues, and Luborsky and colleagues. Again, looking at specific therapies and specific populations, the verdict is much less clear. For example, Lindsay, Crino, and Andrews (1997) showed that the alliance in ERP and the alliance in relaxation were equal for patients with OCD, but the differences in efficacy were substantial. Similarly, Carroll, Nich, and Rounsaville (1997) showed that alliance was correlated with outcome in a supportive therapy for substance abuse, but not CBT. In CBT for depression, the data from DeRubeis and colleagues' studies have consistently showed that the therapeutic alliance is better for patients whose symptoms and cognitions have already changed for the better (e.g., Tang & DeRubeis, 1999); that is, early improvement in treatment leads to a more positive alliance. However, in Cognitive Behavioral Analysis System of Psychotherapy, where the alliance is an explicit focus of treatment, alliance appears to be predictive of outcome (Klein et al., 2003). Overall, alliance may have the greatest relationship to outcome if the therapist makes it a central focus of treatment. However, in such treatments, the distinction between alliance and technique is blurred. As others have noted (Beutler, 2002; Crits-Christoph et al., 2006), if one addresses alliance directly in treatment sessions, the very focus on alliance becomes a treatment technique. There is only one pilot study to date that attempts to improve alliance by using specific alliance-enhancing techniques (Crits-Christoph et al.), and the results are equivocal. The effects of alliance-enhancing techniques in certain areas (e.g., change in alliance and improvement in quality of life) are large, but the impact on symptoms is small, and the results are difficult to interpret without a comparison group of new trainees who may have learned to improve alliance without additional techniques. However, the study is seminal in its attempt directly to improve alliance, and further such studies are needed to evaluate the causal impact of alliance on outcome.

Therapist effects have been discussed on and off for over 30 years. More recently, some have shown that differences between therapists in treatment outcome may be decreased with manualized treatments (Crits-Christoph et al., 1991), although not eliminated (e.g., Huppert et al., 2001). How large are therapist effects? Overall, they seem to range from 5% to 15% (see also Crits-Christoph & Gallop, 2006; Lutz, Leon, Martinovitch, Lyons, & Stiles, 2007). However, the question of what makes therapists different from each other remains, and one answer may be technique. Some therapists are likely more adept than others at using some techniques, formulating treatment plans, encouraging their patients to do difficult exposures, etc., even within CBT. Of course, therapists also differ on ability to form an alliance, but the therapist who is able to articulate a strong treatment rationale tailored to the patient's specific presentation and to explain why the treatment can help (or the therapist who is able to provide an example of an imaginal exposure that directly taps into an OCD patient's fears) will likely be experienced by the patient as empathic and understanding. Thus, techniques may be part of therapist effects (or vice versa), and not something that can be truly separated from them.

Just as alliance and therapist effects sometimes may be accounted for by technique, so may other putative common factors (consider, for example, how data on outcome provided during psychoeducation probably influence both therapist and patient expectancy). Indeed, the notion of common factors itself has broadened to the point that some would include the technique of exposure as a common factor (Lambert & Ogles, 2004). However, as Weinberger (1995) noted, common factors may not be so common after all. The extent of focus on alliance differs between treatments, and so does the amount, type, or quality of exposure. And if the goal of psychotherapy research is to determine the best ways to relieve suffering for the most people, researchers need to continue to focus on the areas that are most manipulable, such as technique. In fact, Lambert's latest research is an excellent example of high-quality research that integrates the arguments for the importance of technique, alliance, and therapist factors. In brief, Lambert has improved the quality of treatment outcome in therapy by providing therapists with feedback on patient progress and whether therapists are off track with their patients' predicted trajectories

(Lambert, 2007). Notably, the feedback includes specific techniques that may help put them back on track. One may wonder aloud whether use of other types of disorder-specific information could further enhance the efficacy of such interventions.

Overall, many researchers—ourselves included—attempt to quantify the relative contributions of technique and other effects. Frequently such data are presented so as to support the exclusive role of one of the aforementioned effects (e.g., alliance, therapist, common factors, technique) in influencing treatment outcome. It is equally important, however, to demonstrate how such partisan divisions are not reflected in the real world, where all of these effects meet in a complex series of interactions. In fact, the patient's contribution to outcome (including diagnosis, insight, motivation, severity, psychosocial background, etc.) is likely the greatest. One may conclude that effective techniques are likely to positively influence not only treatment outcomes, but also therapy relationships. Few would argue that one should conduct therapy in the context of a hostile or negative therapeutic relationship. However, techniques are ubiquitous and need to be studied in order to determine how to best improve them and, thereby, patient outcomes.

DiGiuseppe (2007) suggested that unless the Dodo Bird verdict and contentions regarding greater effects of therapist, alliance, and common factors are addressed empirically, psychologists who value scientific inquiry must accept the implications of those assertions. In fact, these notions have been argued against for years, and many continue to examine the data. In this review, we have attempted to convey the following. First, the Dodo Bird verdict is predicated on meta-analyses that aggregate data across treatments, disorders, and outcome measures, and such aggregation likely masks or attenuate treatment differences between particular treatments for particular disorders on primary outcomes, even though such differences have the most direct implications for treatment. Second, there are numerous logical difficulties with the classification of treatments as bona fide, a requisite criterion for inclusion in some of the aforementioned meta-analyses. Third, there is empirical evidence that technique effects are sometimes greater than effects of common factors. More generally, the magnitude of technique effects depends on disorder and population, bolstering the assertion that broad judgments about the relative importance of technique and common factors are insufficient and can be misleading. Instead, more nuanced accounts that do not aggregate across moderating variables are necessary to conduct and evaluate psychotherapy outcome research. Finally, putative common factors such as therapist skill, the therapeutic alliance, and treatment expectancy are likely influenced by technique. Hence, their effects are not easily separable from those of active ingredients, but instead are explained by series of complex interactions. Nevertheless, there will always be others who critique the analyses, draw different conclusions, and advocate for those stances, and efforts to disseminate ESTs are limited in part because opponents of ESTs have presented their perspective more aggressively to wide-spread audiences. We must continue to address their arguments with empirically based data and logic and make our voices heard in the broad court of professional opinion.

Note

1. The binomial effect size display is a means of depicting an effect size as a relative success rate. Based on the assumption that the rate of treatment success is 50% overall, the binomial effect size display is used to translate an association between treatment and outcome into the proportion of successes in one treatment group relative to another.

All references for articles included in *Taking Sides: Clashing Views on Psychological Issues, 17/e* can be found on the Web at **http://www.mhhe.com/cls.**

CHALLENGE QUESTIONS

Are All Psychotherapies Equally Effective?

1. Assuming that the Dodo hypothesis is correct, would *any* technique—perhaps even a nonsensical or an evil technique—produce equivalent results? Why or why not?
2. How would you know if one technique was superior to another? How do you think the authors of the readings would know?
3. From the perspective of the authors of the NO reading, why is it important to consider whether one technique or therapy is more effective than another?
4. Would the authors of the NO reading say that technique alone is sufficient to produce desired results in psychotherapy? What if the therapist is unskilled or inexperienced? Explain your answer.
5. Assuming that the Dodo hypothesis has been tested and found to be valid, how might it have advantages for the treatment of psychological disorders?

ISSUE 15

Should Therapists Be Eclectic?

YES: Jean A. Carter, from "Theoretical Pluralism and Technical Eclecticism," in Carol D. Goodheart, Alan E. Kazdin, Robert J. Sternberg, eds., *Evidence-Based Psychotherapy: Where Practice and Research Meet* (APA, 2006)

NO: Don MacDonald and Marcia Webb, from "Toward Conceptual Clarity with Psychotherapeutic Theories," *Journal of Psychology and Christianity* (Spring 2006)

ISSUE SUMMARY

YES: Counseling psychologist Jean Carter insists that the continued improvement and effectiveness of psychotherapy requires that techniques and theories include the different approaches of psychological theory and practice through an eclectic approach.

NO: Professors of psychotherapy Don MacDonald and Marcia Webb contend that eclecticism creates an unsystematic theoretical center for psychological ideas and methods that ultimately limits overall therapeutic effectiveness.

Most psychotherapists acknowledge that they need a good theory or theories to help guide their treatment of clients. If you were a psychotherapist, how would you use these ideas? Would you try to find the *single* best or most favorite theory, or would you pick and choose various parts from among *all* the theories? Some psychotherapists choose the single-theory approach because it seems more systematic and less fragmented. Other psychotherapists choose to work with many theories, because they see it as a way to create comprehensive therapies that are capable of addressing a variety of client situations.

The second approach is usually considered *eclectic* because psychotherapists select or employ individual elements from a variety of sources, systems, and styles. The word "eclectic" is derived from the ancient Greek and literally means "to choose the best." For example, some eclectic psychotherapists choose to subscribe to theories from humanistic psychology for their view of human nature, while practicing techniques derived from the cognitive psychology movement. Eclecticism is a popular way to resolve the varied problems of therapy. Surveys report that roughly two-thirds of all psychotherapists endorse some form of eclecticism. Still, its merit and validity as a guiding framework for psychological endeavors continues to generate debate.

Counselor Jean Carter is a prominent example of one side of this debate. In the YES reading, she argues that patients and their problems rarely fall into well-defined categories. As such, she believes that psychotherapists must embrace a variety of theories and associated techniques to overcome this challenge—eclecticism. She contends that real-world applications of an eclectic approach is a better treatment model, especially in comparison to single-theory approaches, because it is tailored for each patient and therefore adaptive and flexible across various scenarios. For this reason, she maintains that therapists should add diverse perspectives to their theoretical framework and avoid committing to any one conceptual approach.

Psychotherapists Don MacDonald and Marcia Webb oppose eclectic approaches because they sacrifice clarity in the process of psychotherapy. They argue that many psychotherapists opt for an eclectic approach just to avoid the difficult task of finding a single theory to guide their therapy. However, by sidestepping the process of committing to and thus understanding thoroughly a particular theory, eclectics unknowingly run the risk of understanding very little about the theories they employ. Indeed, this course of action eventually leads to a type of eclectic approach that is called *syncretism*. Syncretism occurs when psychotherapists try to unite aspects of theories and methods that are often contrary to one another. Don MacDonald and Marcia Webb conclude that a return to traditional single-theory approaches is required to achieve better clarity and effectiveness within psychotherapeutic practice.

POINT

- Therapy based on eclectic theories and techniques can manage diversion situations more readily.

- Eclectic systems allow therapists to choose the best methods and ideas for use.

- Therapy becomes more practical because therapists have all the theories and techniques they need.

- Therapists are better able to focus on therapeutic relationship because they do not have to focus on rigid single-theory concepts.

COUNTERPOINT

- Eclectic approaches have weak conceptual bases that fail to create a cogent rationale for clients to understand and trust.

- Without a guiding framework, therapists are less knowledgeable about theories overall.

- Access to a wide variety of theories and techniques does not necessarily ensure that the best option is selected.

- Single-theory therapists are well-versed in the techniques and conceptual basis that guide how they form the therapeutic relationship.

YES

Jean A. Carter

Theoretical Pluralism and Technical Eclecticism

The real world of psychotherapy practice is complex, requiring moment-by-moment decisions about the treatment plan, the techniques being used, the working diagnosis, and even the goals. Patients rarely can be put into neat diagnostic boxes, and there is a great deal about their lives that psychotherapists cannot control. Clinicians know that psychotherapy occurs within a relationship that is personal and interpersonal, deeply textured, and responsive to the patient. Psychologists are trained in both the science and the practice of psychology, and they firmly believe in the value of evidence and the science base for their practice. The integration of these factors in recent calls for greater accountability and quality improvement in health care practice creates important challenges for both the scientists and the practitioners within psychology. Although the two groups share the goals of improving the effectiveness of psychotherapy and enhancing outcomes for patients, the tools and methods each uses to approach these goals may reflect quite different viewpoints. Like the blind men exploring an elephant, the part of psychotherapy one touches shapes how one understands the nature of the endeavor.

Although psychology has been committed to the integration of science and practice throughout its history, current initiatives to articulate and implement evidence-based practice principles highlight both that commitment and the difficulties inherent in integrating disparate views (American Psychological Association [APA], 2005). From a scientific perspective, psychologists seek greater control of variables, clarity of questions and methods, and general principles that are valid and reliable. From a practice perspective, they are committed to enhancing the lives of patients, drawing on general psychological principles, treatment-oriented research, and their experience in the multilayered world of practice.

Inevitably, divergent perspectives result in conflicts as psychologists attempt to bring together different approaches to the same shared goal of more effective practice. The significance of these conflicts, and the tension surrounding them, rises as funding and policy implications are increasingly based on demonstrable effectiveness and its evidence base. Practitioners are concerned about the limitations required by scientific methodologies and the direct application of research findings to any particular individual or treatment, as well as funding and treatment constraints arising out of misapplications of methodologies and results. . . .

Clinicians know the impact of psychotherapy; they experience it as they sit with their patients hour after hour, struggling with the anguish and difficulties patients bring into their offices. A long history of evidence supports the effectiveness and durability of psychotherapy (Ahn & Wampold, 2001; Barlow, 2004; Elkin et al., 1989; Lambert & Barley, 2002; Lambert & Bergin, 1994; Lipsey & Wilson, 1993; Roth & Fonagy, 1996; Sloane, Staples, Cristol, Yorkston, & Whipple, 1975; Smith, Glass, & Miller, 1980; Wampold et al., 1997). These reports include psychotherapy studies, literature reviews, and meta-analyses and represent many theoretical perspectives, patient and treatment types, and a variety of outcome measures. The picture is clear—psychotherapy works, and works well, much of the time.

At the same time, no particular form or model of therapy has been found to consistently work better than others (Wampold, 2001). In recent research designed to evaluate psychological interventions to relieve specific target problems in well-defined treatment populations using controlled treatment protocols (Barlow, 2004), the data support the efficacy of specific treatments but do not clearly support differential treatment effects (Wampold, 2001; Westen, Novotny, & Thompson-Brenner, 2004). In addition, questions about the applicability of the results of these studies to the general treatment population and therapeutic realities abound. One cannot conclude that particular treatments are clearly better than other treatments or clearly better than treatment as usual in the community. The research literature thus supports clinicians' experiential knowledge that psychotherapy works but does not offer them specific information about what to do when or with whom to provide effective psychotherapy.

Practitioners value the grounding of practice within evidence, including the evidence that they collect and draw on as they engage in a version of science within the hour (Carter, 2002; Strieker & Trierweiler, 1995). They continually ask questions about what is or is not working and why, and they attempt to understand how to enhance the multilayered practice that occurs within a specific interpersonal context (Samstag, 2002) and with its own unique demands. . . . Within this continually changing world of practice, clinicians rely on the therapeutic relationship; a broad knowledge of individual differences, psychological principles, and change processes; a theoretical grounding that offers cogent explanations; and techniques that provide the necessary tools for change.

This chapter offers a perspective on the importance of maintaining multiple theoretical formulations for effective psychological practice and on the role of related techniques in the psychotherapy process. Evidence-based practice in psychology has as its background the complex factors that affect the psychotherapy process and the history of research demonstrating the effectiveness of psychotherapy. It reflects an understanding of the contextual model of psychotherapy with its emphasis on common factors. I propose the essential integration of theoretical pluralism and technical eclecticism as significant components of real-world applications of evidence-based practice in psychology.

The Multilayered Real World of Psychotherapy

Psychotherapy is complex and requires continual responsiveness. Many factors operate at any given moment, all of which may call for the clinician's attention, and many of which are not within his or her control. Clinicians look for ways to understand psychological distress and to effect change in a way that takes into account this complexity. Although this chapter does not primarily address the wide range of presentations and problem types or specific treatments designed to be effective with the variety of clients clinicians face, it is important that the reader understand the psychotherapy process as an ongoing complex interplay of factors in which the clinician makes frequent decisions within an uncertain context, using their own clinical expertise and probabilistic research evidence to guide them in the moment. . . .

[P]atients present dramatically different pictures, even those who meet the same diagnostic criteria from the *Diagnostic and Statistical Manual of Mental Disorders* (American Psychiatric Association, 1994). Clinicians attend to disorder-related issues, including presenting problem, level of distress, level of function, co-occurring problems, and attachment style (see Norcross, 2002). They attend to life circumstances (e.g., available resources and support systems, medical concerns, social skills), individual and group characteristics (APA, 2002, 2003; Sue, 2003; Sue & Lam, 2002), and values. These factors are what patients bring into treatment and what influences their lives outside of treatment as well as the treatment itself (see Miller, Duncan, & Hubble, 1997). In addition, these patient factors do not remain static and do not follow neat lines of development or change and may be affected by happenstance, or things that occur in people's lives that may not be under their control but that significantly affect their lives and the treatment.

In addition to patient factors, there are a number of factors related specifically to the therapist that operate throughout treatment (see Norcross, 2002, for a discussion of clinician factors). Clinicians vary in interpersonal skills and abilities, experience, training, values, personal characteristics, knowledge base, and worldview, as well as other factors. Just as no two patients are exactly the same, clinicians are not interchangeable.

Structural aspects of the clinical situation affect what can or does occur within treatment. These factors may include the resources available and costs related to engaging in treatment (Yates, 1994, 1995, 2000). The payer or agency may impose session or treatment limits. Moves, job changes, and other life events may affect the length or nature of treatment independent of patient preference or clinician recommendation.

Theoretical models also play a significant role in psychotherapy. Clinicians may rely on theory to explain change processes, and in the contextual model (Wampold, 2001) theories are valuable because they provide rationales for treatment, help organize it, and guide appropriate therapeutic goals for the particular clinical context. Clinicians also rely on a range of techniques drawn from multiple theoretical perspectives that research has found to be effective for particular symptom pictures or particular patient types and that the clinicians have found to be effective through their own experience and expertise (e.g., Arnkoff, Glass, & Shapiro, 2002; Beutler, Alomohamed, Moleiro, & Romanelli, 2002; Norcross, 2002).

The Contextual Model of Psychotherapy

Psychotherapy practice is inextricable from the context in which it occurs. Psychotherapy is an interpersonal experience, with a patient who is in distress and a treatment based on psychological principles and offered by a therapist. Wampold (2001), in *The Great Psychotherapy Debate,* presented a compelling differentiation between the medical model of psychotherapy and the contextual model of psychotherapy and described the research foundation on which the contextual model rests. Although not all clinicians or researchers see this model as a more accurate fit for psychotherapy process and outcomes data, the presentation closely matches the lived experience of many clinicians. It also provides the foundation for the remainder of this chapter. . . .

The Therapeutic Relationship

The therapeutic relationship is foundational to the psychotherapy endeavor. Just as psychotherapy cannot proceed without patients, it cannot proceed without a clinician,[1] and the therapeutic relationship is built by the two participants. The therapeutic relationship accounts for 30% of the variance in outcome in psychotherapy, second only to patient factors, which represent 40% of the variance (Assay & Lambert, 1999; Lambert, 1992; Lambert & Barley, 2002). . . .

The Working Alliance

The *therapeutic relationship* and the *working alliance* are often referred to synonymously, particularly in the research literature. The working alliance (originally conceptualized by Bordin, 1975) includes a bond between patient and therapist, agreement on goals, and consensus on therapeutic tasks. The alliance has repeatedly been found to be significantly related to outcome; Wampold (2001) and Horvath and Bedi (2002) provided summaries of this research. Given the large proportion of variance in outcome accounted for by the alliance, it is clearly important for clinicians and researchers to be continually attentive to the role and impact of the alliance and to the ways in which the alliance as a relationship can be enhanced.

The agreement on tasks and consensus on goals that are components of the alliance are significant in any consideration of the role of theory in evidence-based practice in psychology. Although well-designed research supports the effectiveness of psychotherapy, it does not offer clear support for relative effectiveness—that is, of one form of treatment over another, including treatment as usual in the community (Westen et al., 2004). . . .

The working alliance includes clinician and patient agreement on goals and tasks as major components of a successful alliance, and positive working alliance is related to better outcomes. The question may arise, however, about which goals and tasks the clinician and patient may agree on and how they come to the definition and the agreement. There are many possible goals and expected or desirable outcomes from psychotherapy, and it sometimes appears that there are as many measures of goals and outcomes as there are possible outcomes. Some examples included in studies of outcomes are self-esteem, premature termination, global change, symptom severity, interpersonal functioning, addiction severity, change in distress, drug use, alleviation of depressive symptoms, social adjustment, specific symptoms, social relationships, indecision, personal growth, relations with others, social or sexual adjustment, interpersonal problems, defense style, employment status, legal status, self-concept, anxiety symptoms, medication compliance, quality of life, hospitalization, productivity, and satisfaction with treatment (Horvath & Bedi, 2002). It is clear that the range of possible outcomes is huge. At the same time, the clinician and patient must identify outcomes they believe to be desirable and goals to be achieved and must reach agreement on these goals as an essential part of the alliance. The definition of outcomes arises from a shared perspective held by the clinician and patient.

Typically, the desirable goals for any particular psychotherapy are derived from patient need and problem type and patient and clinician worldviews. They are consistent with the theoretical framework from which the treatment was developed. Thus, agreement on goals implies agreement (whether implicit or explicit) on the theoretical framework (cogent and coherent explanation or rationale) from which the clinician operates. Therefore, the theoretical framework provides an important structure within which psychotherapy occurs and is significantly related to one of the components of psychotherapy outcome (agreement on goals as part of the alliance).

Patient Belief in the Treatment

According to Frank (1973; Frank & Frank, 1991) and Wampold (2001), the patient's belief in the treatment, its context, and the clinician is a component shared by all psychotherapy approaches. Indeed, it is hard to imagine how a patient without some belief and hope in the effectiveness of treatment could be an active participant in psychotherapy or could share an agreement on goals or outcome with the clinician. The participation of patients is essential, of course. Duncan (2002) described patients as the heroes of the treatment; it is the patient's therapy, and he or she makes whatever changes are to be made. Successful collaboration between clinician and patient (Tryon & Winograd, 2002) and lower levels of resistance (Beutler, Moleiro, & Talebi, 2002) are related to positive outcomes. Patient factors such as positive expectation, motivation, and openness to treatment (Grencavage & Norcross, 1990) account for 40% of the variance (Assay & Lambert, 1999). These factors, which are central to the patient's belief in the treatment, make patient characteristics and values the most potent component of successful treatment. These findings support the importance of agreement on goals and consensus on tasks, which are part of the alliance and part of the patient's belief in the healing benefit of psychotherapy. When there are difficulties in collaboration and resistance to the treatment is high (both reflect difficulties in the alliance), existing evidence suggests that acknowledging the patient's concerns, attending to the relationship, and renegotiating goals and roles may be effective in ameliorating problems in the alliance (Beutler & Harwood, 2002; Beutler, Moleiro, et al., 2002; Safran & Muran, 2002).

The Value of Flexible Theoretical Frameworks

Effective treatment clearly needs a cogent rationale, and clinician and patient need to agree on goals and tasks based on that rationale. At the same time, the complexity of psychotherapy may require renegotiating goals and roles to better align patient and clinician and to better match patient characteristics and worldview. Renegotiation and realignment call for flexibility in the theoretical framework guiding the treatment designed for the specific patient and his or her situation, as well as flexibility in the use of techniques derived from various theoretical approaches. The clinician needs to be adaptive and conversant with multiple theoretical perspectives that may guide his or her ability to integrate clinician worldview and patient worldview to match the particular patient. The clinician must be prepared to incorporate additional or different theoretical components to achieve better fit for the patient. In other words, the clinician's effectiveness rests in part on maintaining theoretical pluralism and the ability to be integrative in those theories.

A Conceptual Scheme

Rosenzweig (1936/2002) and Frank (Frank & Frank, 1991) supported the importance of an ideology or rationale provided by the clinician that presents a cogent, coherent, and plausible explanation for both the patient's distress and the approach the clinician will take to help the patient. This ideology engages the patient. It offers the patient hope and expectation (remoralization through positive expectation) in the treatment, as well as a way to understand the goals and tasks of treatment, which in turn enhance outcomes. Ideology, rationale, and coherent and cogent explanation are all different words for the *theoretical formulation* that guides the clinician in the treatment.

Patient Expectancy

Patient expectancy and hope are potent contributors to positive outcomes. Assay and Lambert (1999) suggested that the accumulation of research puts the contribution of patient expectancy for outcomes at about 15% of the variance. Expectation is typically cast as a placebo effect in medical model approaches, but the contextual model includes it as a central component of effective treatment. Placebo effects are essentially psychological effects and thus are undesirable in a model that attempts to minimize extrinsic factors through tight control and adherence to the treatment as defined. However, increased psychological effects as a result of psychological treatments seem desirable—not undesirable—outcomes and should be supported, and factors that increase positive expectations should be promoted. For example, a patient who moves into a hopeful state and no longer exhibits hopelessness (one of the primary symptoms of depression) because of his or her belief in the treatment demonstrates the effectiveness of nonspecific psychological factors in the treatment. The clinician wants to enhance the patient's belief in what he or she is offering to enhance expectancy effects. Therefore, the clinician would promote the importance of the theoretical framework to engage and encourage patients and heighten expectancy effects, as well as to take advantage of the positive contribution theory makes to agreement on goals and tasks.

Allegiance

Trust is a significant part of therapy; patient belief in and openness to treatment and the patient-clinician bond component of the alliance rely on trust (Horvath & Bedi, 2002). Clinicians' belief in their therapeutic models or theories is related to outcomes through its impact on clinician—patient agreement on goals and desirable outcomes and the extent to which it engages the patient. Therefore, the clinician must believe in his or her own treatment model, just as the patient does. The theoretical framework must therefore be cogent, coherent, and explanatory for the clinician as well as for the patient. Theory also provides the clinician with an underlying organization for the large amounts of information that are relevant to psychotherapy and that must be available for the clinician's use in the treatment.

To the extent that the clinician believes the theory to be explanatory for the patient's distress and to provide a rationale for the treatment plan and its implementation, one would expect the clinician to have considerable allegiance to the theoretical model he or she is using. Wampold (2001) offered extensive evidence regarding clinician allegiance to an espoused theoretical model and its strong positive relationship to outcomes.

It is important to note that the relationship between allegiance and outcomes appears to hold regardless of the truth value of the theory. One might think that this would lead to rampant development of a vast array of untested and untestable theoretical models. Despite frequent counts of theoretical models that number several hundred (e.g., Bergin & Garfield, 1994), the major models remain largely consistent categories.[2] At the same time, consistent with the importance of the theoretical model to both clinician and patient, clinicians would be expected to do one of two things: either endorse one of the existing general theoretical models or endorse an approach that draws from more than one model. Both seem to occur simultaneously, however. Clinicians choose one model as primary (often with a secondary choice when that is an alternative) and may also espouse an integrative perspective (drawing on multiple models) or eclecticism as their theoretical perspective (Garfield & Bergin, 1994; Jensen & Bergin, 1990; Norcross, Prochaska, & Farber, 1993; Wampold, 2001). Typically, *eclectic* draws the largest endorsement as a single category. Norcross et al. (1993) found that 40% of the members of the Division of Psychotherapy of the APA who responded to a survey of theoretical orientation chose *eclectic,* reflecting individualized versions based on experience, training in multiple models, and alterations in response to patient need. Clinicians' choice of eclectic as a theoretical perspective needs attention to understand its meaning, impact, and role as an explanatory system and the extent to which it is a well-developed individualized model versus a process for integrating multiple models (Carter, 2002).

Currently, theoretical integration, technical eclecticism, and common factors are receiving considerable attention, reflecting dissatisfaction with individual theoretical approaches and attempts to develop more flexible approaches. Theoretical integration is problematic if it becomes its own model, because it then has all of the problems that are associated with a single theoretical model (Feixas & Botella, 2004; O'Brien, 2004). However, it provides a useful framework if it provides procedures for integrating diverse perspectives into a system that is applicable for the particular clinician-patient pair, to the particular patient problems, and in the particular context (Feixas & Botella, 2004).

Technical eclecticism alone as a response to the poor fit of theoretical models is limited, because it takes only interventions into account and ignores the relevance and role of theoretical models. From an integrative or theoretically eclectic perspective, however, it is important for clinicians to be skilled in techniques drawn from the multiple theories from which their own theoretical perspective is derived. Because allegiance to a cogent rationale is important and clinicians and patients rely on theories to organize and guide their work, clinicians are expected to modify models as needed to be responsive to patients. Thus, psychologists must continue to develop and teach multiple models, to understand the components of the theories as explanatory tools, and to understand and effectively implement the techniques derived from the models.

Rituals and Procedures (Otherwise Known as Techniques)

Frank and Frank (1991), drawing on Rosenzweig's formulation (1936/2002), focused on the importance of rituals and procedures that are consistent with the rationale given for the treatment. The rituals and procedures that Frank and Frank suggested may best be understood as the interventions or techniques that are logically derived from the theoretical formulation of the causes of the patient's distress and the approach to ameliorating the dysfunction. Clinicians design techniques, then, to have a specific impact on symptoms, behaviors, or other components as defined by the theory from which they arise and with which they are consistent. Rosenzweig believed that an impact on any subsystem (or aspect) of personality affects all of the personality, suggesting that effective treatment may occur with any one of multiple symptoms as the target of interventions. If Rosenzweig was correct, techniques should have a positive impact on outcomes, but the impact should account for a relatively small portion of the variance. According to Assay and Lambert (1999), techniques overall account for only 15% of the variance, and specific techniques appear to make little additive difference in outcome (Wampold, 2001). Valuable research using designs that offer well-controlled and targeted interventions for specific symptom pictures demonstrates their effectiveness in both absolute and relative terms (Barlow, 2004). Although application of these results may call for adaptation to the particular treatment picture, these are useful tools for the clinician to have readily available. It is interesting to note that Westen et al. (2004), in a review of the current status of what have been known as empirically supported treatments, offered a hypothesis on the role of negative diatheses as an underlying principle that may be common to all psychological disorders and explanatory for varied presentations and comorbidity. The relationship between specific techniques for specific symptoms and the complex symptom picture in a typical clinical practice offers great opportunities for collaboration between research and practice.

Nevertheless, techniques do matter. Interventions are the tools through which psychotherapy occurs within the context previously described. They are the expression of the belief system arising from theoretical models. They operationalize the therapeutic tasks that are part of the alliance. They are the medium by which the relationship is developed and maintained. They build hope in the patient through active engagement in the tasks of therapy. They effectively alter specific symptoms. Hence, it is essential for clinicians to be technically eclectic and prepared with a wide range of tools to address the needs of patients in the continually changing world of psychotherapy. The contextual model, which reflects the deeply complex interpersonal world of psychotherapy, supports the importance of techniques as tools in trade (Wampold, 2001), with clinicians having the ability to apply multiple techniques in the service of an individually tailored psychotherapy.

Conclusion

Most clinicians strongly support models of psychotherapy that are context centered, that place a strong value on the relationship and alliance, and that are embedded in theoretical models. At the same time, clinicians rely on eclectic or integrative models, and their work reflects theoretical pluralism. In addition, experienced clinicians from different theoretical perspectives are more similar than different within the psychotherapy hour, using techniques drawn from a variety of theoretical approaches and reflecting technical eclecticism in the application of psychotherapy.

Psychological scientists and psychological practitioners have a number of areas of agreement about the evidence base underlying practice. The therapeutic relationship, a central component to practice, has strong evidentiary support as an essential factor in successful outcomes. Therefore, clinicians should devote considerable attention to building and maintaining a strong therapeutic relationship in the implementation of evidence-based practice. Evidence drawn from research on psychotherapy supports the importance of coherent and cogent explanations for distress, dysfunction, and treatment to positive outcomes. Therefore, clinicians who engage in evidence-based practice should devote time, energy, and attention to strengthening the cogency and clarity of their theoretical formulations, including both the major theoretical perspectives and the variants that are consistent with their own worldviews and psychology's scientific base. Theoretical pluralism is an important part of evidence-based practice.

The therapeutic alliance (which is part of the relationship) rests on agreement on goals and tasks and is positively related to outcomes. Agreement on goals and tasks is drawn from agreement on and belief in the explanations for and implementation of the treatment (the theoretical model the clinician uses and the techniques drawn from that model). The alliance necessarily takes into account the therapist's role, the patient's role, and the relationship between them. Clinicians who integrate principles of evidence-based practice devote energy to learning techniques that emanate from their own theoretical model. In addition, they should maintain openness to techniques that may complement or supplement those derived from their model, that may enhance the relationship, and that may fit the patient's desired goals, problems, and characteristics.

Placebo or expectancy effects are essentially belief in or hope for the treatment that rests on the patient's and the therapist's belief that the explanation is valid and that it will work—again, the important role of theory. Clinicians demonstrating evidence-based practice should support patients' hopes and beliefs, as well as their own, which requires a somewhat different approach to the evidence foundation for psychotherapy that draws on a context of discovery rather than a context of justification for the scientific thinking occurring within the hour.

Skill with a range of techniques is important as an expression of the theory (agreement on tasks), as a way to effectively manage the alliance and relationship, as rituals, and as ways to accommodate multiple problems, worldviews, and expected outcomes. Technical eclecticism is an important component of evidence-based practice in psychology.

Psychological research underlying evidence-based practice in psychology

- supports the use of theoretical pluralism and technical eclecticism to enhance the alliance and strengthen the therapeutic relationship;
- supports a coherent, cogent, and organized explanation for patient distress and its amelioration;
- fosters patient hope; and
- uses a range of techniques to maximize effectiveness.

Evidence-based practice in psychology has at its core an effort to enhance patient involvement and choice, as well as participation in his or her own health care. Implementing evidence-based practice requires the continuous and deliberate incorporation of both a scientific attitude and empirical research into an understanding and appreciation for the unique demands of psychotherapy practice. Commitment to evidence-based practice continues a strong belief in the integration of science and practice in psychology. Embracing it reflects psychology's past and supports its future.

Notes

1. Some computer models of intervention do not require the active participation of a clinician. However, psychotherapy is commonly understood
   to be an interpersonal process between a patient and a therapist.

2. The major models are behavioral and cognitive-behavioral, psychodynamic, humanistic or experiential, systems theory, and feminist theory.
   All of them have multiple variants that reflect shifts in perspective or incorporation of new knowledge drawn from general psychological principles or research on the treatment model itself.

**All references for articles included in *Taking Sides: Clashing Views on Psycho-
logical Issues, 17/e* can be found on the Web at http://www.mhhe.com/cls.**

Don MacDonald and Marcia Webb  **NO**

Toward Conceptual Clarity with Psychotherapeutic Theories

T he proliferation of theories for conducting psychotherapy makes it easy for a therapist to become lost in the welter of ideas. In particular, clarity about the criteria for and the evaluation of theories lags. The present article discriminates between syncretism and eclecticism. As part of the discrimination, it provides 14 interrelated criteria by which to assess a theory. It also distinguishes between theories and treatment models. Finally, it presents a proposal for the reciprocal development of both. These 14 criteria come from a broad array of professional literature, and provide an approximation of a holistic perspective of humanity. They also describe theories in a complex and comprehensive manner, and offer therapists the opportunity to make indepth attempts toward the integration of one's personal faith commitments and one's professional identity. Even with responsible efforts toward conceptual clarity, the authors describe the high potential for syncretism, due to the multitude of theories, models, and criteria currently available to psychotherapists. The authors further propose strategies to prevent the conceptual compromises associated with a syncretistic approach to the conceptualization and conduct of psychotherapy.

Psychotherapists look to theories to help them develop treatment goals, assessments, methods, and evaluations of processes and outcomes. Theory is a map and, as such, is an indispensable tool. Cherry, Messenger, and Jacoby (2000) and Striker (2002) identified psychotherapy as an important professional function, regardless of the preparation orientation of the therapist, viz., clinical scientist, scientist-practitioner, and practitioner-evaluator. Psychotherapeutic theories as maps, however, are only as helpful as their clarity permits. This article explores major sources of compromise for theoretical clarity and discusses means for fostering clarity. It makes no claims for achieving clarity. Rather the article proposes criteria that will hopefully stimulate discussion about the intentional development of theory. Thus, it is meant to be heuristic.

Theories of psychotherapy abound. Literally hundreds of theories exist and the number is growing (Corsini, 2000; Miller, Duncan, & Hubble, 1997). Naturally, it is impossible for a psychotherapist to know all or even most of them. Given that meta-analyses on the comparative effectiveness of many different therapeutic approaches indicate most are similar in being generally helpful (Shadish, Matt, Navarro, & Phillips, 2000; Smith & Glass, 1977;

Wampoldet al., 1997), it is unnecessary for psychotherapists to know multiple theories in order to work effectively. Rather, it seems that the therapist must be thoroughly grounded in the concepts and methods that he or she uses.

While knowledge of multiple theories may be unnecessary, it is nevertheless essential for effective psychotherapists to understand at least one theory well in order to apply it. On a continuum for comprehension of theory (McBride & Martin, 1990), one end entails understanding one or more theories thoroughly while the opposite end of the continuum entails understanding very little about even one theory. Limited understanding of even one theory relegates psychotherapists to adding a method here and an idea there, without a systematic conceptual basis to hold those methods and ideas together; this is conceptual *syncretism*. In the worst cases, psychotherapists operate out of syncretism, wherein they unsuccessfully attempt to synthesize different, perhaps contradictory, ideas and methods, with little or no awareness of their inherent incongruities. A cogent conceptual system, though, would solve this difficulty. . . .

The conceptual formation that psychotherapists go through is tantamount to the development of philosophies of science and practice. It may be a personal philosophy or one shared by colleagues in a department, school, or professional organization. It is nevertheless a conceptual guide to conducting and understanding research as well as clinical practice (Kendall, Butcher, & Holmbeck, 1999; Polkinghorne, 1986).

Arriving at a place of conceptual clarity vis-à-vis psychotherapeutic theories and a Christianity-theories relationship is far from an exact or predictable process. However, the process need not be hopeless or haphazard. We propose three broad approaches to intentionally enhance conceptual clarity. One, a common factors approach, is well established. The second, a rubric for theoretical criteria, is a proposal to establish descriptive criteria for theories of psychotherapy. Third, discriminating between theories and treatment models, is an established issue that is still seldom addressed. Admittedly all are exploratory efforts and will hopefully be heuristic. All are meant to stimulate discussion around how Christian psychotherapists and psychotherapy students can develop clear understandings of the profession and of themselves as persons and professionals.

Common Factors

Some researchers have suggested that common factors across all therapeutic modalities are responsible for treatment effectiveness, more than effects of any particular therapeutic approach (Carkhuff & Berenson, 1967; Corrigan, Dell, Lewis, & Schmidt, 1980; Hubble, Duncan, & Miller, 1999; Weinberger, 2002). Multiple studies confirm, for example, that a psychotherapist's warmth, regardless of the treatment modality employed in sessions, is associated with positive client outcomes. A placebo effect of treatment, or the client's simple expectation of progress, has also been demonstrated to be a catalyst of positive change in therapy, again regardless of the specific treatment approach.

Given the proliferation of multiple treatment modalities from which to choose for positive therapeutic outcomes and the evidence for common factors across various modalities, it is perhaps not surprising that in the last 40 years, movements for psychotherapeutic eclecticism or integration, have developed. Writers proposing the integration[1] of psychotherapies argue that no single theoretical system can account for, and meet, all therapeutic needs. They suggest instead that the use of flexible, varied treatment approaches is necessary to accommodate the multifaceted nature of human experience, rather than strict adherence to one narrowly defined, limited psychotherapeutic modality (Brammer, Shostrom, & Abrego, 1993; Carter, 2002; Prochaska & Norcross, 1999).

The prevalence of these ideas is evident in surveys of psychotherapists. Norcross and his colleagues undertook surveys in 1981, 1991, and 2001 (Norcross, Hedges, & Castle, 2002). Across the three surveys, more than one-third of the psychotherapists who practiced psychotherapy described themselves as eclectic; eclecticism was the by far the largest group. Jensen, Bergin, and Greaves (1990) obtained a broad sampling of psychotherapists, including psychologists and psychiatrists. Jensen et al. found that 59% (psychiatrists) to 70% (clinical psychologists) of the groups sampled regarded themselves as eclectic. While the figures vary, it is clear that a substantial number of psychotherapists, including psychologists, draw upon multiple theories to inform their clinical practices. Such a strategy, however, is no solution for syncretism; indeed, it may increase the risk of syncretism.

Eclecticism need not be de facto syncretistic. One of the more widely respected attempts at a form of eclecticism, known as Therapeutic Integration, is found in the writing of Paul Wachtel (1977). Wachtel provides a model for the harmonious interaction among diverse theories of treatment. His efforts toward integration of psychotherapeutic theories helped establish the potential and validity of the integration movement (Prochaska & Norcross, 1999). More recently, he reworked his original formulation to include further developments in psychotherapy, such as general system theory (Wachtel, 1997).

Even with prototypes such as Wachtel (1977, 1997), the task of psychotherapeutic integration is not for the faint of heart; it is more complex than assumed by perhaps too many psychotherapists. Given that the pluralistic praxis of daily experiences for psychotherapists is often complicated and challenging, conceptual clarity is a sine qua non. Unfortunately, more than one observer has noted that attempts at theoretical integration are often haphazard, unsystematic, internally conflicted, and arbitrary (Ginter, 1988; Norcross, 1986; Patterson, 1990). In other words, many psychotherapists function in a syncretistic manner.

The worst results of syncretism are conceptual confusion and ineffectiveness in treatment (McBride & Martin, 1990; Smith, 1982; Travis, 2003). In syncretism, the psychotherapist lacks overall organizing principles to guide treatment—the map is flawed or incomplete. As the descriptions of mental health and goals of therapy can vary across theories of psychotherapy, the syncretistic psychotherapist may unknowingly drift amidst competing, and potentially contradictory, notions of treatment plans and methods.

Understanding theoretical constructs is often difficult. Yet application of theory is even more difficult. Psychotherapy students often complain it is hard to put a theory into practice, as it ideally appears in a text or video. Even an experienced psychotherapist may have trouble clearly describing the theory drawn upon and its appearance in clinical situations. Conceptual clarity is essential, though, if psychotherapy is to fulfill its claim and potential to provide scientifically based services (Deegear & Lawson, 2003; McPherson, 1992; Striker, 2002). . . .

Distinctions Between Theories and Models

A major detraction from theoretical clarity exists around use of the term "theory." It is typically used inaccurately, with vague definitions and criteria (Blocher, 1987). As applied here, a theory is a formally organized collection of facts, definitions, constructs, and testable propositions that are meaningfully interrelated (Kendall et al., 1999; Mullins, 1971; Wallsten et al, 2000).

Few of the hundreds of "theories" meet most of the rubric's fourteen criteria. Probably none fulfill all of the criteria. Most of what are called theories are more accurately called treatment models. They develop in a process parallel to theories and share some features with theories (see Figure 1). A treatment model usually identifies therapy goals, processes, and methods thought to be helpful, but lack clarity about specific, foundational theses and hypotheses that support the use of certain treatment strategies. Instead, the assessment of helpfulness usually follows from clinical experiences of the person(s) who developed the model. While possibly useful and immediately applicable, a treatment model lacks the formal organization and verification of a theory (Blocher, 1987). It is possible for a treatment model to develop into a theory (Figure 1), however few do so.

Figure 1 traces major pieces in the development of theories and models. While a two-dimensional illustration suggests this development is linear and sequential, the actual process is more like a hologram: a three-dimensional sphere with worldviews . . . in the center and the other pieces arranged around the center, linked to each other through reciprocal feedback loops. Ideally, the process is open to new information on a selective basis (i.e., based on theory construction criteria), which balances change with organization and stability (Bertalanffy, 1968; Keeney & Ross, 1985).

Worldviews pervade all other theory development processes, as discussed in the section on theory development criteria. These cognitions directly affect the assumptions and beliefs a psychotherapist applies to creating, interpreting, and applying a theory or model. Insofar as they influence all aspects of theory, conceptual neutrality is impossible (MacDonald, 1991; Sue & Sue, 2003). A psychotherapist, for example, who holds the belief that the world is basically a safe place may tend to draw attention to instances of safety in the life of a client who was physically abused as a child and overlook the client's own view of the world as essentially a dangerous place.

Worldviews relate reciprocally with general life data. Worldviews are influenced by learning experiences and, in turn, affect what people perceive and how they interpret their perceptions. While genetically transmitted temperaments provide broad parameters for worldviews, daily life experiences

Figure 1

Major Pieces in the Development of Theories and Models

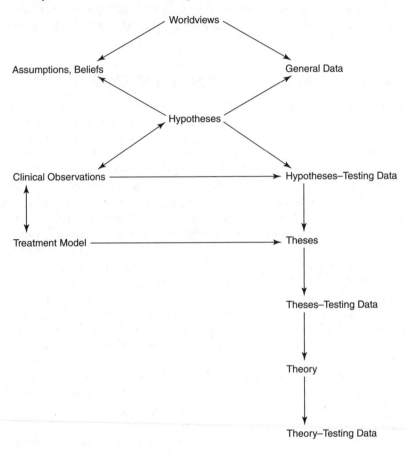

affect the particular manifestations of these temperaments (Kristal, 2005). Say, for instance, both the psychotherapist and client in the previous paragraph are born with a temperament of approach to human relations or sociability. The psychotherapist's overall life experiences of trust and security in relationships, . . . builds on this inherent tendency. The client's experiences of pain and betrayal in significant relationships, however, prompt an approach-avoidance conflict around relationships (i.e., temperament plus positive experiences prompt formation of relationships, while potent negative experiences signal danger in human relations).

Assumptions and beliefs and general life data, with their worldviews substrate, combine to foster hypotheses about psychotherapy in general and about specific clients (Figure 1). Thus, the personal life of the psychotherapist is an active participant in the conceptualization and execution of treatment processes (Corey, Corey, & Callanan, 2003; Tjeltveit, 1986). Hypotheses, then, have a recursive relationship with clinical observations, wherein the psycho-therapist notes how clients act vis-à-vis their personalities, therapeutic issues, and the therapeutic setting (including the psychotherapist), while the person-alities, issues, and setting influence the psychotherapist.

Psychotherapy hypotheses are also tested as to their veracity. That is, the psychotherapist checks the validity and reliability of conceptualizations about an individual or a group of clients (e.g., those diagnosed with bulimia). The psychotherapist systematically collects and tests data pertinent to thera-peutic hypotheses. This is where the criteria of the rubric may be especially useful. Testing usually involves a few clients and may consist of parametric, nonparametric, or qualitative research designs and statistics (Beutler, 2000; Striker, 2002).

The hypothesis-testing of therapeutic data demarcates the divergence of theory development from treatment model development (Figure 1). With the latter, clinical observations and inferences from them remain the primary data. The treatment model might be a valid and reliable representation of clients and psychotherapy, but subjectivity precludes such determinations (Campbell & Stanley, 1966). Data that are systematically collected and analyzed, plus clinical observations and inferences, afford a broader platform upon which to build theoretical constructs (Kendall et al., 1999). . . .

Well developed and tested hypotheses allow for thesis construction. The-ses, of course, guide formal data collection and analyses. From theses-testing, the psychotherapist has a clear data-based foundation for theory building. Theoretical constructions, in turn, are tested, retained, rejected, or modified (Carter, 2002; Mullins, 1971; Persons, 1991). Theory development through theses-testing does not guarantee unambiguous results, eliminate subjectivity, or partition out worldviews, but effects of these factors are easier to identify and explain when referenced to specific data.

Discussion in this section summarized general conceptual development of psychotherapeutic treatment models and theories. Even though most psy-chotherapists do not develop a formal theory or model, they either adopt an existing approach to psychotherapy or create a personal one (Corsini, 2000). This process yields optimal conceptual clarity when the psychotherapist man-ages it in the intentional, explicit manner of theory development.

Choosing a Theory or Model

At some point the psychotherapist chooses one or more theories or models as a means to work with people. This choice typically occurs in a preparation pro-gram (Capuzzi & Gross, 1995), although it is not limited to this period of time and the psychotherapist may subsequently add to the choice or even change entirely. Regardless of the timing, psychotherapists often experience direct or de facto pressure to make one of three choices: (a) align with one theory or model, (b) take an intentional eclectic or integration stance, or (c) do not think about it, thereby opening the door to syncretism. The preferred professional route, as discussed shortly, is either aligning with one theory or taking an intentionally eclectic stance. Both of these preferred choices are deliberate, systematic, and have their respective benefits and limitations. Unfortunately, some research suggests that psychotherapists who choose the third option of not thinking about it can be unaware of the degree to which they have adopted a de facto syncretistic approach to treatment.

Researchers have distinguished, for example, between those practitioners who are *explicitly eclectic,* who are aware of and intentional regarding their modalities of preference, and those who do not endorse an eclectic approach, but who nevertheless employ terminology and techniques from a variety of theories. This latter group has been described as *implicitly eclectic* (Hollanders, 1999). Findings surrounding the phenomenon of implicit eclecticism suggest that some practitioners in the process of theory adoption opt for the not-think-about-it stance, as listed above, or invest so little intellectual energy in a single theory or in an eclectic stance that it is almost the same as not thinking about the process altogether (Omer & Dar, 1992). It is this choice that fosters syncretism.

Selecting and staying with one theory or model has a number of benefits. Psychotherapists who commit themselves to the study and application of one theory or model have the potential to achieve a type of professional integrity in their practice of psychotherapy. They may be less prone to alteration by vacillations within the profession arising from, for example, treatment fads or pressures from external sources, such as insurance companies or public opinion (Prochaska & Norcross, 1999). These psychotherapists may be more likely to offer a consistent, balanced vision of treatment via their given modalities of intervention. In addition, adherence to a single theory or model allows for an enriched dialogue among similarly committed professionals who share the common knowledge of its language, ideas and history. This shared dialogue further augments the possibilities for development of the theory or model within professional societies over time. Finally, commitment to one theory or model may foster an appreciation not only of its unique advantages and limitations in psychotherapy, but also of its differences from other theories and models.

Syncretism, with its hodge-podge of multiple treatment elements, increases the possibility for the distinctiveness and organization of each theory or model, with its particular terminology and application, to be lost. This may result, paradoxically, in the lack of appreciation for, or even awareness of, the genuine diversity that exists across conceptual and treatment approaches.

Part of the difficulty in selecting and employing "theories," however, is that many of them are actually treatment models (ref. Figure 1), which are often less articulated than many psychotherapists find useful. The less articulated a model is, of course, the harder a psychotherapist must work to make sense of the model and to apply it. The assumption here is that no treatment strategy optimally coheres outside of the more comprehensive, schematic system afforded by a theory (Kendall et al., 1999). Perhaps the psychotherapist works out a personal resolution to the unexplained parts of a treatment model, creating individual theses and hypotheses where none have been formally articulated by proponents of the model. It is also possible, though, that the psychotherapist remains unclear about what the model means and how to implement it.

While this lack of comprehensiveness in models is problematic for psychotherapists, the adoption of a personal resolution surrounding the missing elements of a model may create other difficulties. This strategy unwittingly encourages the formation by multiple psychotherapists of idiosyncratic conceptualizations around a single model, each of which is tailor-made for and by the therapist in question, yet each of which bears the same name, and is promoted as reflecting the original model upon which it was based. This in itself may serve as a catalyst for some degree of confusion, rather than clear communication, among psychotherapists and consumers of therapeutic services.

Despite these difficulties, going the route of a treatment model has definite appeal. For one, it has fewer steps and is a faster route than theory-building (Omer & Dar, 1992) (Figure 1). Second, the usual datum of proof, "clinical observations," has a way of supporting existing hypotheses (Travis, 2003). That is, the subjectivity and arbitrariness of these observations makes it very difficult to validate their accuracy between observers. The observations are what Campbell and Stanley (1966) called case studies or crude correlations. Case studies or crude correlations may provide nominal data that are helpful in stimulating further research, but neither is sufficient in the long-term for inferring causality or systemic relational patterns.

Research in cognition identifies a tendency to focus upon and recall selectively that information which supports original ideas, a reasoning fallacy known as *confirmation bias. Belief perseverance,* a reasoning fallacy similar to confirmation bias, further complicates the problem. According to research examining belief perseverance, people tend to adhere to their original ideas, regardless of the presence of disconfirming evidence. While these studies in cognition considered the problematic reasoning of the average individual in everyday situations, anecdotal evidence also exists to support the existence of these fallacies in academic and scientific reasoning as well (Eysenck & Keane, 2000; Howard, 1985; Reisberg, 1997). As Tjeltveit (1986) demonstrated, psychotherapists also succumb to reasoning fallacies in their practical, daily work with clients and in how they think about working with clients. Theories, with their inherent processes of verification that are involved in their establishment and development, allow for greater challenges to reasoning fallacies such as confirmation bias and belief perseverance.

Knowing What to Believe: Strategies Toward the Prevention of Syncretism

Unfortunately, preparation programs may inadvertently encourage the development of syncretism among students. This implicit encouragement comes about when programs feel appropriately obligated to present students with the widest possible exposure to various treatment theories and models. The syncretistic effect compounds where faculty teach no differentiation between theories and models. At the same time, constraints on programs (e.g., administrative budget, faculty experience) may make it impossible to teach each of these approaches at sufficient depth or breadth to foster conceptual sophistication. Given this challenge, how might preparation programs provide opportunities for students both to grasp the diversity of theories and models available to psychotherapists today, while steering clear of the conceptual compromises accompanying syncretism?

Many programs offer at least one survey course in multiple therapeutic modalities (APA, 2003). In addition to its presentation of various approaches to treatment, this course could also include sections examining the broad distinctions between theories and models, and the relative benefits and challenges of each. Examining and applying the 14 criteria for a theory may help students comprehend significant issues involved when selecting a theory or model, or when considering some form of eclecticism or integration (MacDonald, 1991). Current research on common factors might be included as a topic for this course, allowing the student as well to consider the importance of factors beyond modality that impact treatment efficacy. In addition, this course might examine the movement for therapeutic integration, with its more sophisticated exemplars (e.g., Watchel, 1977, 1997). Finally, explicit discussion regarding the problems of syncretism might be included in a survey course covering multiple approaches to treatment. Faculty could describe examples of syncretistic analyses in class as an effort to illuminate their limitations.

It might be essential to cover philosophies of science and practice in a preparation program. These broad topics would provide students general worldviews through which they could evaluate theories and models. . . . Inasmuch as psychology and allied professions prematurely truncated the close relationship with its parent discipline, philosophy (MacDonald, 1991, 1996; Miller, 2005), the helping professions have unknowingly suffered from a lack of conceptual breadth and perspective. Addressing philosophy of science in a course or courses should help speak to this lack. . . .

Philosophies of science and practice in psychotherapy courses might consider the strengths and the limitations of the scientific enterprise in general, as well as the many variables which impact the development and application of psychotherapy over time. Such perspectives may allow the Christian therapist greater understanding when examining various psychotherapeutic theories or models. . . .

Following a preliminary course introducing several theories and models, students might be encouraged to focus upon one or two for the remainder of their preparation. This choice would hopefully impact the focus and themes of various papers they construct in classes. . . .

Supervision of therapy is another opportunity for preparation to focus upon one modality (Matarozzo & Garner, 1992). For individual supervision, programs could intentionally assign students to supervisors based on that supervisor's preferred treatment theory or model, allowing the student an extended opportunity to observe the elements of that approach in a mentoring relationship. Supervisors might also assign to supervisees readings composed by the major contributors to the theory or model under consideration. Supervisees could be taught to prepare in their client progress notes a written summary of the components of sessions, specifically utilizing the language and ideas of the specific model, to bring each time to supervision. In group supervision, supervisors might distribute information about one case to supervisees, with each supervisee assigned to describe that case from the perspective of a distinct theory or model before the group.

Fundamental to each of these suggestions is the need to be more intentional with the preparation of psychotherapists in order to foster greater conceptual clarity and to reduce the likelihood of syncretistism. The rapid proliferation of new therapies has created a situation in which the explicit discussion of the choice for therapeutic stance becomes all the more important. A student's eventual clinical efficacy as a psychotherapist, and thus even the future direction of psychotherapy as a valid resource for the community, necessitates clarity about communication and choices regarding therapeutic modalities.

Note

1. We realize that some authors distinguish between eclecticism and the more recent term of integration. To complicate matters further, the term integration has been used for several decades to denote efforts to bring Christian faith and psychology together. It is beyond the scope of our article to discern between eclecticism and integration. Since the terms overlap substantially, we use them interchangeably. We also assume that most psychotherapists who are Christians wish to integrate their faith and their craft, understanding that some differ on this point.

All references for articles included in *Taking Sides: Clashing Views on Psychological Issues, 17/e* can be found on the Web at http://www.mhhe.com/cls.

CHALLENGE QUESTIONS

Should Therapists Be Eclectic?

1. What are the advantages and disadvantages inherent in an eclectic approach and a single-theory approach?
2. Consider how you would go about selecting a theoretical orientation. What factors would be most important in deciding whether to adhere to one theory over another and why?
3. What hidden biases motivate the authors of the YES and NO articles to promote either an eclectic or a single-theory approach?
4. Are eclectic approaches ever truly capable of being systematic if they are created from diverse theories and techniques? State your own position on this issue and describe your justification for endorsing it.
5. Are there instances where a single-theory approach can draw from ideas and techniques that are not traditionally a part of that system?

Internet References . . .

Psychiatry Online

This site supplies a helpful article that outlines the ethical stance of the American Psychological Association on coercive interrogations.

http://pn.psychiatryonline.org/content/40/16/34.full

Evolutionary Psychology Journal

This is the site for a respected journal on evolutionary psychology.

http://www.epjournal.net/

Stanford Encyclopedia of Philosophy

This reference source, the *Stanford Encyclopedia of Philosophy*, is an excellent and balanced source for evolutionary psychology and its critique.

http://plato.stanford.edu/entries/evolutionary-psychology/

Medicinenet.com

This is an authoritative, general-topic Web site for sexual addiction.

http://www.medicinenet.com/sexual_addiction/article.htm

Psychcentral.com

This site has more of a psychological slant on the issue of sexual addiction.

http://psychcentral.com/lib/2006/what-is-sexual-addiction/

Social Issues

*S*ocial psychology is the study of humans in their social environments. For example, a social psychologist might ask how the social environment of torture affects a prisoner. Is coercive interrogation (possibly torture) a good method of gaining important information, or is it a waste of time that only does psychological harm? What can psychologists contribute to these questions? How much are social environments responsible for female mating preferences? Might mating preferences be more influenced by innate genetic and thus evolutionary factors? What about the relatively recent changes in our social environment? Some psychologists have pointed to the recent upsurge of sexually explicit "societal and cultural messages" on the Internet and other media. Could this upsurge lead to problems, such as pornography and sexual addictions in general? Do such addictions even exist?

- Should Psychologists Abstain from Involvement in Coercive Interrogations?
- Does the Evidence Support Evolutionary Accounts of Female Mating Preferences?
- Can Sex Be Addictive?

ISSUE 16

Should Psychologists Abstain from Involvement in Coercive Interrogations?

YES: Mark Costanza, Ellen Gerrity, and M. Brinton Lykes, from "Psychologists and the Use of Torture in Interrogations." *Analyses of Social Issues and Public Policy* (December 2007)

NO: Kirk M. Hubbard, from "Psychologists and Interrogations: What's Torture Got to Do with It?" *Analyses of Social Issues and Public Policy* (December 2007)

ISSUE SUMMARY

YES: Psychologists Mark Costanzo, Ellen Gerrity, and M. Brinton Lykes assert that all psychologists should be banned from any involvement in interrogations that involve torture or other unethical forms of coercion.

NO: Psychologist and intelligence consultant Kirk M. Hubbard argues that a ban on a psychologist's involvement in coercive interrogations would overly restrict the ways in which psychologists can ethically contribute to their country's intelligence needs.

Psychologists have long been noted for their productive interviews. This skill is, in some sense, the root of psychotherapy. In recent years, however, an ethical dilemma has emerged regarding particular interviews—"coercive interrogations." As reports of prisoner abuse at Abu Ghraib and Guantanamo Bay emerged, many Americans became concerned about the way the government was treating detainees. Many in the psychological community were concerned that psychologists were serving as consultants and perhaps even participating in coercive interrogations, recommending or using techniques that many considered to be torture. They called for the American Psychological Association (APA) to prohibit member psychologists from any involvement in coercive interrogations, claiming that such involvement would violate a psychologist's ethical commitment to "first do no harm."

Other psychologists, however, have worried that the APA barring members from such interrogations would be a hasty move. These psychologists have argued that APA members should be involved in planning interrogations precisely because their expertise can guide interrogators to use coercion ethically. Moreover, the ethical commitment to "first do no harm" could be applied to keeping the United States from harm. Indeed, some psychologists have argued that their primary duty is to prevent harm to their country and that they do not have the same duty to protect their country's enemies.

In the first article, psychologists Mark Costanzo, Ellen Gerrity, and M. Brinton Lykes make the case for prohibiting psychologists from involvement in coercive interrogations. They explain that coercive interrogation techniques, such as torture, are banned by professional organizations like the APA and are violations of US and international law. Further, they argue the research literature shows that coercion is not an effective interrogation technique and its poor results cannot justify its harmful impact. Costanzo and colleagues describe how "torture has long-term negative consequences for the mental health of both survivors and perpetrators of torture." They argue that the harmful nature and ineffectiveness of coercive interrogations require an explicit ban of psychologists' involvement in such practices.

In the second article, psychologist and intelligence consultant Kirk M. Hubbard argues that a ban on psychologists' involvement in torture is unnecessary, because torture is illegal and thus is already prohibited. Indeed, there is no evidence, according to Hubbard, that psychologists have been involved in torture. Hubbard asserts that providing formal restrictions on psychologists' involvement in interrogations will hamper what psychologists can legitimately lend to legal interrogations. He asks, "how is psychology accountable to society—should it withhold information about ways in which to protect our population or to influence terrorists to disclose information?" Because terrorists "do not care if they live or die and have no fear of prison," they "have little or no incentive to work with interrogators." Hubbard calls upon psychologists to become *more* involved in research and consultation about interrogating terrorists to develop effective and humane methods for obtaining information that will protect their country.

POINT

- "Psychologists should be expressly prohibited from using their expertise to participate in interrogations that make use of torture."
- "Torture is ineffective as a means of extracting reliable information and likely leads to faulty intelligence."
- The "ticking time bomb scenario" gives a false air of justification to coercive interrogation methods.
- Psychologists have a duty to do no harm at all costs, even to detainees who potentially threaten their country.

COUNTERPOINT

- Because torture is illegal, psychologists are already barred from participation.
- Legal coercion may be necessary for interrogating terrorists, given their decreased motivation to comply.
- The "ticking time bomb scenario" is real and has already occurred.
- Psychologists have a duty to provide their expertise where it might be instrumental in defending their country.

YES

Mark Costanzo, Ellen Gerrity, and M. Brinton Lykes

Psychologists and the Use of Torture in Interrogations

This article argues that psychologists should not be involved in interrogations that make use of torture or other forms of cruel, inhumane, or degrading treatment. The use of torture is first evaluated in light of professional ethics codes and international law. Next, research on interrogations and false confessions is reviewed and its relevance for torture-based interrogations is explored. Finally, research on the negative mental health consequences of torture for survivors and perpetrators is summarized. Based on our review, we conclude that psychologists' involvement in designing, assisting with, or participating in interrogations that make use of torture or other forms of cruel, inhumane, or degrading treatment is a violation of fundamental ethical principles, a violation of international and domestic law, and an ineffective means of extracting reliable information. Torture produces severe and lasting trauma as well as other negative consequences for individuals and for the societies that support it. The article concludes with several recommendations about how APA and other professional organizations should respond to the involvement of psychologists in interrogations that make use of torture or other forms of cruel, inhumane, or degrading treatment.

The United States and its military should immediately ban the use of torture, and psychologists should be expressly prohibited from using their expertise to plan, design, assist, or participate in interrogations that make use of torture and other forms of cruel, inhumane, or degrading treatment. The use of torture as an interrogation device is contrary to ethical standards of conduct for psychologists and is in violation of international law. Torture is ineffective as a means of extracting reliable information, and likely leads to faulty intelligence. Torture has long-term negative consequences for the mental health of both survivors and perpetrators of torture. The use of torture has far-reaching consequences for American citizens: it damages the reputation of the United States, creates hostility toward our troops, provides a pretext for cruelty against U.S. soldiers and citizens, places the United States in the company of some of the most oppressive regimes in the world, and undermines the credibility of the United States when it argues for international human rights.

From *Analyses of Social Issues and Public Policy,* 7(1), December 2007, pp. 7–16. Copyright © 2007 by The Society for the Psychological Study of Social Issues. Reprinted by permission of Wiley-Blackwell.

1. Torture as a Violation of Professional Codes of Conduct

The American Psychological Association's *Ethical Principles of Psychologists and Code of Conduct* encourages psychologists to, ". . . strive to benefit those with whom they work and take care to do no harm." These guidelines incorporate *basic principles* or *moral imperatives* that guide behavior as well as specific *codes of conduct* describing what psychologists *can* or *cannot* do and are, therefore, directly applicable to the participation of psychologists in torture or in inter- rogation situations involving harm. Psychologists, physicians, and other health and mental health professionals are also guided by international and inter- professional codes of ethics and organizational resolutions, such as the 1985 joint statement against torture issued by the American Psychiatric Association and the American Psychological Association. In 1986, the American Psychologi- cal Association passed a *Resolution against Torture and Other Cruel, Inhuman, or Degrading Treatment*. Both statements "condemn torture wherever it occurs."

The International Union of Psychological Science (IUPsyS), the Inter- national Association of Applied Psychology (IAAP), and the International Association for Cross-Cultural Psychology (IACCP) are collaborating in the development of a Universal Declaration of Ethical Principles for Psycholo- gists. They have identified "principles and values that provide a common moral framework . . . [to] "guide the development of differing standards as appropriate for differing cultural contexts" (www.am.org/iupsys/ethintro). An analysis of eight current ethical codes identified across multiple continents revealed five cross-cutting principles: (1) respect for the dignity and rights of persons, (2) caring for others and concern for their welfare, (3) competence, (4) integrity, and (5) professional, scientific, and social responsibility. Sin- clair traced the origins of these eight codes to 12 documents including the Code of Hammurabi (Babylon, circa 1795–1750 BC), the Ayurvedic Instruc- tion (India, circa 500–300 BC), the Hippocratic Oath (Greece, circa 400 BC), the (First) American Medical Association Code of Ethics (1847 AD), and the Nuremberg Code of Ethics in Medical Research (1948 AD). Among the ethi- cal principles proposed as universal for all psychologists is that they "uphold the value of taking care to do no harm to individuals, families, groups, and communities."

A wide range of declarations, conventions, and principles govern the conduct of doctors and all health professionals in the context of torture (e.g., the World Medical Association's (1975) Tokyo Declaration), including the establishment of international standards for medical assessments of allega- tions of torture (e.g., the *Manual on the Effective Investigation and Documentation of Torture and Other Cruel, Inhuman or Degrading Treatment or Punishment (Istanbul Protocol)*, United Nations, 1999). Specific restrictions prohibiting the participa- tion of medical personnel in torture and degrading interrogation practices were established in the 1982 United Nations' "*Principles of Medical Ethics* (United Nations, 1982)." The World Medical Association has also established that it is not ethically appropriate for physicians or other health professionals to serve as consultants or advisors in interrogation.

Psychologists can find themselves in contexts where expected professional and ethical conduct and the protection of human rights conflict with compliance with government policies and practices. A 2002 report of Physicians for Human Rights described this "dual loyalty" now confronting a growing number of health professionals within and outside of the Armed Forces. This tension is particularly acute when such policies and practices run counter to international declarations, laws, and conventions that protect human rights (see, for example, the report of Army Regulation-15, 2005).

2. Torture as a Violation of Law

As citizens, psychologists in the United States are required to observe a wide range of international and national treaties, conventions, and laws that prohibit torture. The *Universal Declaration of Human Rights* (United Nations, 1948) and the *International Covenant on Civil and Political Rights* (United Nations, adopted in 1966, entered into force, 1976), alongside six other core international human rights treaties, constitute an international "bill of human rights" that guarantees freedom from torture and cruel, inhuman, or degrading treatment (see Article 5 of the Universal Declaration on Human Rights).

Article 1 of the UN *Convention against Torture and other Cruel, Inhuman or Degrading Treatment (CAT)*, (United Nations, 1984, 1987), which was signed by the United States in 1988 and ratified in 1994, defines torture during interrogation as:

> Any act by which severe pain or suffering, whether physical or mental, is intentionally inflicted on a person for such purposes as obtaining from him or a third person information or a confession . . . when such pain or suffering is inflicted by or at the instigation of or with the consent or acquiescence of a public official or other person acting in an official capacity.

Article 2 (2) of the Convention outlines specific additional prohibitions and obligations of states that: "No exceptional circumstances whatsoever, whether a state of war or a threat of war, internal political instability or any other public emergency, may be invoked as a justification of torture". . . .

Multiple U.S. laws and resolutions, including the U.S. Bill of Rights, the U.S. Constitution, and the joint congressional resolution opposing torture that was signed into law by President Reagan on October 4, 1984 (United States Congress, 1984), prohibit cruel, inhuman, or degrading treatment or torture. Other conventions to which the United States subscribes prohibit any form of torture as a means of gathering information in times of war (see, for example, the *Geneva Conventions* (1949) and the *European Convention (1989)* relative to the treatment of prisoners of war and to the prevention of torture. In this tradition, Senator John McCain's Amendment (section 1403 of H.R. 1815), approved by the U.S. Congress and signed by President Bush at the end of 2005, prohibits torture and cruel, inhumane, and degrading treatment. However, President Bush's less widely publicized accompanying "signing statement" indicated that he would interpret the law in a manner consistent with his presidential powers, re-igniting debate in many circles within and beyond government. The inconclusiveness of debates among branches of government, and the condemnation of the United States's treatment of prisoners at Guantánamo and Abu Ghraib by foreign governments as well as the UN Committee Against Torture, underscore the urgent need to clarify ethical guidelines for psychologists.

3. Research on Interrogations and the Utility of Torture as an Interrogation Tool

Although the primary purpose of torture is to terrorize a group and break the resistance of an enemy, the use of torture is frequently justified as an interrogation device. However, there is no evidence that torture is an effective means of gathering reliable information. Many survivors of torture report that they would have said anything to "make the torture stop." Those who make the claim that "torture works" offer as evidence only unverifiable anecdotal accounts. Even if there are cases where torture may have preceded the disclosure of useful information, it is impossible to know whether less coercive forms of interrogation might have yielded the same or even better results.

Because torture-based interrogations are generally conducted in secret, there is no systematic research on the relationship between torture and false confessions. However, there is irrefutable evidence from the civilian criminal justice system that techniques *less coercive* than torture have produced verifiably false confessions in a surprising number of cases. An analysis of DNA exonerations of innocent but wrongly convicted criminal suspects revealed that false confessions are the second most frequent cause of wrongful convictions, accounting for 24% of the total (see www.innocenceproject.org). In a recent large-scale study, Drizin and Leo identified 125 proven false confessions over a 30-year period. Two characteristics of these known false confessions are notable. First, they tended to occur in the most serious cases—81% confessed to the crime of murder, and another 9% confessed to the crime of rape. Second, because only *proven* false confessions were included (e.g., cases where the confessor was exonerated by DNA evidence or cases where the alleged crime never occurred), the actual number of false confessions is likely to be substantially higher. Military action based on false information extracted through the use of torture has the potential to jeopardize the lives of military personnel and civilians.

The defining feature of an interrogation is the presumption that a suspect is lying or withholding vital information. If torture is an available option, interrogators are likely to resort to torture when they believe a suspect is lying about what he or she knows or does not know. However, there is no reason to believe that interrogators are able to tell whether or not a suspect is lying. Indeed, there is considerable research demonstrating that trained interrogators are *not* accurate in judging the truthfulness of the suspects they interrogate. Overall, people with relevant professional training (e.g., interrogators, polygraphers, customs officers) are able to detect deception at a level only slightly above chance. Moreover, some researchers have identified a troubling perceptual bias among people who have received interrogation training—an increased tendency to believe that others are lying to them. In addition, although specialized training in interrogation techniques does not improve the ability to discern lying, it does increase the confidence of interrogators in their ability to tell whether a suspect is lying or withholding information. The presumption that a suspect is lying, in combination with the overconfidence produced by interrogation training, leads to a biased style of questioning which seeks to confirm guilt while ignoring or discounting information that suggests that a suspect is being truthful. There is also evidence that interrogators become most coercive when questioning innocent suspects, because truthful suspects are regarded as resistant and defiant. Thus, interrogators may be especially likely to resort to torture when faced with persistent denials by innocent suspects. Under such conditions, torture may be used to punish a suspect or as an expression of frustration and desperation on the part of the interrogator. More broadly, there is substantial evidence that judgments about others are influenced by conscious and nonconscious stereotyping and prejudice. Prejudice may lead interrogators to target suspects for torture based on physical appearance, ethnicity, or erroneous stereotypes about behavioral cues.

Unless local authorities (e.g., commanders in charge of a military detention facility) explicitly prohibit the use of torture in interrogations, the risk of torture will be unacceptably high. Decades of research by social psychologists has demonstrated that strong situational forces can overwhelm people's better impulses and cause good people to treat others cruelly. These forces include the presence of an authority figure who appears to sanction the use of cruelty, and a large power disparity between groups, such as the disparity that exists between prisoners and guards. In addition, the dehumanization and demonization of the enemy that occurs during times of intense group conflict—particularly during times of war—reduce inhibitions against cruelty. All of these conditions, combined with the stresses of long-term confinement, appear to have been present at Abu Ghraib. The well-documented reports of torture at the Abu Ghraib and Guantanamo Bay facilities serve as disturbing reminders that it is essential for military authorities to issue clear directives about unacceptable practices in the interrogation of prisoners. These directives need to be combined with effective monitoring of military detention facilities, especially during times of war.

In an effort to circumvent ethical concerns and the lack of evidence about the effectiveness of torture, advocates of the use of torture often resort to hypothetical arguments such as the "ticking time bomb scenario." This frequently used justification for the use of torture as an interrogation tactic presupposes that the United States has in its custody a terrorist who has knowledge of the location of a time bomb that will soon explode and kill thousands of innocent people. Embedded in this implausible scenario are several questionable assumptions: that it is known for certain that the suspect possesses specific "actionable" knowledge that would avert the disaster; that the threat is imminent; that only torture would lead to the disclosure of the information; and that torture is the fastest means of extracting valid, actionable information. Of course, this scenario also recasts the person who tortures as a principled, heroic figure who reluctantly uses torture to save innocent lives. While this scenario might provide a useful stimulus for discussion in college ethics courses, or an interesting plot device for a television drama, we can find no evidence that it has ever occurred and it appears highly improbable.

4. The Effects of Torture on Survivors and Perpetrators

Torture is one of the most extreme forms of human violence, resulting in both physical and psychological consequences. It is also widespread and occurs throughout much of the world. Despite potentially confounding variables, including related stressors (such as refugee experiences or traumatic bereavement), and comorbid conditions (such as anxiety, depression, or physical injury), torture itself has been shown to be directly linked to post-traumatic stress disorder (PTSD) and other symptoms and disabilities. The findings from both uncontrolled and controlled studies have produced substantial evidence that for some individuals, torture has serious and long-lasting psychological consequences.

Most trauma experts—including survivors of torture, mental health researchers, and therapists—agree that the psychiatric diagnosis of PTSD is relevant for torture survivors. However, these same experts emphasize that the consequences of torture go beyond psychiatric diagnoses. Turner and Gorst-Unsworth highlighted four common themes in the complex picture of torture and its consequences: (1) PTSD as a result of specific torture experiences; (2) depression as a result of multiple losses associated with torture; (3) physical symptoms resulting from the specific forms of torture; and (4) the "existential dilemma" of surviving in a world in which torture is a reality. The 10th revision of the *International Classification of Diseases* includes a diagnosis of "Enduring Personality Change after Catastrophic Experience" as one effort to capture the long-term existential consequences of the tearing up of a social world caused by torture. The profound psychological and physical consequences of torture are also evident in several carefully written personal accounts of the experience of torture.

Comprehensive reviews of the psychological effects of torture have systematically evaluated research with torture survivors, examining the unique consequences associated with torture and the complex interaction of social, environmental, and justice-related issues. As noted in these reviews, the psychological problems most commonly reported by torture survivors in research studies include (a) psychological symptoms (anxiety, depression, irritability or aggressiveness, emotional instability, self-isolation or social withdrawal); (b) cognitive symptoms (confusion or disorientation, impaired memory and concentration); and (c) neurovegetative symptoms (insomnia, nightmares, sexual dysfunction). Other findings reported in studies of torture survivors include abnormal sleep patterns, brain damage, and personality changes. The effects of torture can extend throughout the life of the survivor affecting his or her psychological, familial, and economic functioning. Such consequences have also been shown to be transmitted across generations in studies of various victim/survivor populations and across trauma types.

Studies conducted over the past 15 years strongly suggest that people who develop PTSD may also experience serious neurobiological changes, including changes in the body's ability to respond to stress (through alterations in stress hormones), and changes in the hippocampus, an area in the brain related to contextual memory. Thus, the development of PTSD has direct and long-term implications for the functioning of numerous biological systems essential to human functioning.

For survivors, having "healers" participating in their torture by supporting interrogators or providing medical treatment in order to prolong torture can erode future recovery by damaging the legitimate role that physicians or therapists could provide in offering treatment or social support, essential components in the recovery of trauma survivors. For these reasons, numerous medical associations, including the American Psychiatric Association and the World Medical Association, include as part of their ethical and professional standards a complete prohibition against participation of their members in interrogation, torture, or other forms of ill treatment. Similarly, the South African Truth and Reconciliation Commission documented how health providers were at times complicit in human rights abuses under apartheid, and through their report, hoped to shed light on this worldwide phenomenon and work toward an international effort to prevent such abuses from occurring.

Research that focuses directly on the participation of health professionals in torture and interrogation has documented important contextual issues for understanding how such participation can occur. Robert Lifton interviewed Nazi doctors who participated in human experimentation and killings, and found them to be "normal professionals" who offered medical justifications for their actions. In studies of physicians and other health providers who are involved in forms of military interrogation, Lifton elaborates on "atrocity-producing" environments in which normal individuals may forsake personal or professional values in an environment where torture is the norm. Furthermore, these same health care professionals may, through their actions, transfer legitimacy to a situation, supporting an illusion for all participants that some form of therapy or medical purpose is involved.

Other studies of those who torture have provided details about the step-by-step training that can transform ordinary people into people who can and will torture others, by systematically providing justifications for actions, professional or role authority, and secrecy. Participation in torture and other atrocities has been shown to have long-term negative psychological consequences for perpetrators, even in situations where professional or environmental justifications were offered to them in the context of their actions. . . .

Therefore, we urge APA and other scholarly and professional associations of psychologists to:

1. Unambiguously condemn the use of torture and other forms of cruel, inhuman, or degrading treatment as interrogation devices and call upon the U.S. government and its military to explicitly ban the use of such treatment and enforce all laws and regulations prohibiting its use.

2. Conduct an independent investigation of the extent to which psychologists have been involved in using torture or other cruel, inhuman, or degrading treatment as interrogation tools. If psychologists are found to have participated in the design or conduct of interrogations that have made use of torture, they should be appropriately sanctioned by APA and other professional organizations.
3. Expressly forbid psychologists from planning, designing, assisting, or participating in interrogations that involve the use of torture and any form of cruel, inhuman, or degrading treatment of human beings.
4. Develop specific guidelines and explicit codes of conduct for psychologists working in contexts of war and imprisonment. These guidelines should be consistent with international treaties and human rights covenants as well as guidelines developed for health professionals. Such guidelines should include meaningful enforcement, processes for the investigation of violations, and professional and legal consequences for violations.

Kirk M. Hubbard  **NO**

Psychologists and Interrogations: What's Torture Got to Do with It?

In an article that has been endorsed by SPSSI, Costanzo, Gerrity, and Lykes (2007) argue that "psychologists should not be involved in interrogations that make use of torture or other forms of cruel, inhumane, or degrading treatment" (doi: 10.1111/j.1530-2415.2007.00118.x). Their statement is ironic, for torture is illegal in the United States. But even more importantly, it seems to come from and apply to a world that no longer exists, and that simplifies issues so that they can be as one might like them to be. As recent events in England illustrate (August 2006), Islamic militants seek to kill us and undermine if not destroy our way of life. We have only to listen to what they say and watch their actions in order to know that regardless of how we would like things to be, they mean us harm. We also know from findings of the 9/11 commission that this problem did not start, nor will it likely finish, with the current presidential administration. An important point that is illustrated is that we no longer live in a world where people agree on what is ethical or even acceptable, and where concern for other humans transcends familial ties. When adolescents carry bombs on their bodies and plan suicides that will kill others, we know that shared values no longer exist. In the words of Scottish comedian Billy Connolly, "It seems to me that Islam and Christianity and Judaism all have the same god, and he's telling them all different things."

A prominent challenge for psychologists is determining how narrowly or broadly the field should prescribe what is acceptable behavior for professionals working with diverse populations, for increasingly psychologists come from differing backgrounds and hold varying beliefs. Effective practice with one population may be totally ineffective with another; we as a profession have not yet thoughtfully addressed how we balance what one culture defines as ethical against what another could view as necessary to be successful. The comment by Costanzo et al., and its rejoinders, provide a good illustration, namely, how does one balance standards of behaviors against results. What if, hypothetically, Middle Eastern psychologists told us that in order to successfully obtain information from suspected terrorists we would have to use approaches that we found inappropriate or unethical? I reject the idea that it is somehow unfair to use what we know about psychological science to protect our families and defend our lives and culture. Many areas of psychology owe their advancement in large

From *Analyses of Social Issues and Public Policy,* 7(1), December 2007, pp. 29–33. Copyright © 2007 by The Society for the Psychological Study of Social Issues. Reprinted by permission of Wiley-Blackwell.

part to research conducted under the auspices of the military and supported by it. Clinical psychology has roots in the military and the OSS, and many psychologists have proudly defended their country with honor. In this context, the SPSSI policy statement by Costanzo et al. is both unnecessary and gratuitous. It is unnecessary because torture is already illegal in the United States. It is gratuitous because it feeds the egos of those who endorse it. It gives the illusion of possessing a higher moral ground, when in fact what is left unsaid and readable between the lines reveals it to be ideological and political. As parallels, SPSSI might put out policy statements against rape and murder, for those also are illegal, and we would not want our members participating in such behaviors. But murder and rape occur despite being illegal, and similarly, behaviors that are classified as torture may periodically occur. But that does not mean that torture is a government-sanctioned tool for conducting interrogations or even acceptable to use. There are specific and strict federal guidelines regarding what constitutes a legal and acceptable interrogation. I submit that there is no evidence that psychologists were involved in cases of torture—certainly not at Abu Ghraib prison.

A second issue of import is whether or not psychologists should be involved in legal interrogations. Again, the position of the authors is too simplistic. I take exception to the suggestion that all psychologists should be banned from assisting in legal interrogations. It is one thing to "ban" psychologists who are members of APA from engaging in torture, but quite another to prohibit them from consulting or advising during legal interrogations. First, there are many types of psychologists (social psychologist, industrial/organizational psychologists, and experimental psychologists, for example) who are not licensed mental health professionals and therefore should not be bound by the doctor/patient relationship code of ethics. Yet they bring information from their fields that help exert influence. Second, I object to the "psychocentric" and seemingly arrogant position that receiving training in psychology trumps all other roles a person may choose to pursue, or because of circumstances, are obliged to fulfill. Is it not possible for someone to receive training in psychology and then decide to pursue a career in law enforcement and engage in legal interrogations? Should being a psychologist as well as a law enforcement agent prohibit their participation if psychologists are prohibited? And, third, how is psychology accountable to society—should it withhold information about ways in which to protect our population or to influence terrorists to disclose information? What does psychology owe society? Should we focus exclusively on individuals with whom psychologists come in contact? What about helping to protect communities from terrorism? I simply do not believe that at a policy level we should decide that the "rights" of an individual count more than the rights and safety of society. APA and SPSSI should do something positive to fight terrorism rather than merely sit on the sidelines and criticize others who are trying to protect the United States from another senseless 9/11 attack. Honorable men and women are at war with those who seek to harm us, and the rest of us are at risk from terrorists. If psychology wants to make a positive contribution, the profession should accept that it is sometimes necessary to get information from those who would harm us and are intentionally withholding information that could stop attacks. If we as a profession do not like the use of coercion to obtain actionable information, then we as a profession should be willing to step up to the plate and suggest reliable and effective alternatives that do not rely on psychological or physical coercion. Have we as professional organizations of psychologists committed resources to develop ethical, non-punishing approaches that improve the quality of information that we can extract from individuals who are not willing to share it?

I also find it ironic that SPSSI can so readily become exercised about cruel and degrading treatment of suspected terrorists, yet conduct only limited research on similar behaviors that are manifested all too frequently in military boot camps, in legal police interrogations, in U.S. prisons, and government psychiatric hospitals. Indeed, even college fraternities and schoolyard bullies engage in cruel and degrading behavior. Why is it so easy for SPSSI to react so adamantly about illegal interrogations, yet do so little about domestic kinds of cruel and degrading treatment?

I also wonder how Costanzo et al. would feel if the "ticking time bomb scenario" that they attempt to render as "implausible" were to occur. Would they feel responsible for telling U.S. citizens that it won't ever happen? The "ticking bomb" scenario may be implausible for many APA members, but it was very real for those individuals interrogating Khalid Sheik Mohammed or Abu Zubayadh. Instead of focusing on decades old research that may no longer be relevant, Costanzo et al. might have cited the Jose Padilla case that was covered by the press. As readers may recall, Jose Padilla was a trained al Qaeda operative who was arrested as he tried to enter the United States in Chicago on May 8, 2002. He had accepted an assignment to destroy apartment buildings and had planned to detonate a radiological device commonly referred to as a "dirty bomb." As reported by CNN (June 11, 2002) and *Time* (June 16, 2002), Padilla was arrested directly as a result of an interrogation of captured senior al Qaeda member Abu Zubaydah. The Padilla case is a prime example of how a legal interrogation of a known terrorist led to the prevention of another terrorist attack.

Similarly, imagine that al Qaeda leader Abu Mussib al Zarqawri has been captured alive in Iraq rather than killed by bombings. Is there anyone who believes that he would have no potentially worthwhile knowledge of attacks planned to occur in the days following his capture? Costanzo et al. create a scenario that is not grounded in current knowledge of terrorism in general and terrorists in particular when they attempt to (mis)lead us into thinking legal interrogations do not yield actionable intelligence.

The prototypical "expert" on interrogation asserts that information is more reliable when voluntarily given rather than coerced. Well, of course it is. The expert then may assert that the way to elicit voluntary provision of information is to build a relationship with the terrorist so that the terrorist likes you or to appeal to common values so the terrorist sees your interests as converging with his/hers, and then the terrorist will tell you what you need to know. Such reasoning ignores the demand characteristics of both the prototypical law enforcement interrogation and the terrorist's values and operational intent. Are we to think the terrorist has the following thoughts: "You know, nobody has ever been as nice to me as these people—I'm going to turn my back on my

God and my life's work and tell them what they what to know." Alternatively, maybe the terrorist will think "What a clever way of asking that question. Now that they put it that way, I have no choice but to tell them what they need to know to disrupt my plans." Unfortunately, it is difficult to envision scenarios where useful information will be forthcoming.

For many Westerners caught after committing a crime, the psychological pressure of trying to influence whether or not they are charged, what they are charged with, and the kind of punishment they are likely to receive coerces them into working with the person who seems to understand them to make the best deal in a bad set of circumstances. The "experts'" assertion that rapport and liking are the keys to obtaining information, ignore the coercive pressures inherent in the circumstances. To pretend that these coercive pressures are not present does not make them go away. For terrorists who do not care if they live or die and have no fear of prison, there is little or no incentive to work with interrogators. And, to our discredit, we as psychologists have contributed little to increasing our understanding of circumstances like these and techniques of persuasion that might be effective.

Lastly, I found the call for an independent investigation of the extent to which psychologists have been involved in using torture or other cruel, inhuman, or degrading treatment during an interrogation unwarranted. Costanzo et al. present virtually no evidence that psychologists have been involved in even a single case. APA/SPSSI has no authority by which to sanction nonmembers. Many psychologists are choosing not to join APA or to allow their memberships to lapse, believing that as it does not represent their interests and values. In my opinion, APA and some of its divisions have drifted from a being a professional organization advancing the science of psychology and translating research to action and policy, to a point where they are promoting a social and political agenda.

I am opposed to torture. But I endorse the use of interrogation when used consistently with current federal law and conducted by trained interrogators. And I certainly see no reason why psychologists cannot assist in developing effective, lawful ways to obtain actionable intelligence in fighting terrorism. If the information can be obtained noncoercively, all the better. Social psychology taught us how to use social influence in getting people to do things they ordinarily would not do and buy things they often do not need or want. In my view, it is common sense that you would want psychologists involved in the interrogation of known terrorists. As psychologists, rather than decrying illegal use of cruel and inhumane treatment to obtain information, we should work to develop reliable noncoercive ways to get people to tell us about terrorist activity of which they have knowledge and are attempting to withhold. We need to take a proactive stance in saving lives and preventing acts of terror. The Costanzo et al. article does not appreciably help psychology to move forward, for it limits opportunities for psychologists to gain first-hand knowledge of the nature of the challenges interrogators face, and focuses on current approaches rather than on developing new ones that apply and improve current psychological knowledge.

CHALLENGE QUESTIONS

Should Psychologists Abstain from Involvement in Coercive Interrogations?

1. Costanzo, Gerrity, and Lykes argue that psychologists are acting harmfully by participating in coercive interrogations, whereas Hubbard argues that psychologists are potentially allowing harm to occur by not participating in interrogations. How do you think that psychologists should approach the issue of interrogation if they intend to "first do no harm"? Is it possible to do no harm in this scenario?
2. Hubbard seems to suggest that psychologists may be justified in causing enemy detainees a certain (legal) degree of harm if it produces life-saving information. Do you agree with this position? Why or why not?
3. Since, as both articles concede, torture is illegal and is officially condemned by the APA, why might it still be useful to expressly ban psychologists' involvement in coercive interrogations? Why might such a ban be problematic?
4. Is it possible for psychologists both to serve the interests of defending their country and to abstain from involvement in coercive interrogation? Why or why not?
5. Summarize the positions of the two articles on the "ticking time bomb scenario" and provide your own rationale for how you would act in this scenario.

ISSUE 17

Does the Evidence Support Evolutionary Accounts of Female Mating Preferences?

YES: **David M. Buss,** from *Evolutionary Psychology: The New Science of the Mind, 3rd Edition* (Allyn and Bacon, 2008)

NO: **David J. Buller,** from *Adapting Minds: Evolutionary Psychology and the Persistent Quest for Human Nature* (MIT Press, 2005)

ISSUE SUMMARY

YES: Professor of Psychology David M. Buss contends that the research data indicate an evolved female preference for high-status, resource-possessing males.

NO: Philosopher of Science David J. Buller argues that the research data support several alternative explanations for Buss's findings.

Have you ever wondered why women choose the partners they do? The relatively new field of Evolutionary Psychology has made some fascinating claims in answer to this question. One highly publicized claim is that women have an evolved preference for older men. Beginning with our Pleistocene ancestors, females who preferred older males were better able to protect and provide for their children, and thus were more likely to pass this preference onto the next generation. Evidence that this evolved preference remains today, according to evolutionary psychologists, can be seen in the behavior of several Hollywood celebrities, such as actress Catherine Zeta Jones marrying actor Michael Douglas, 25 years her senior.

While the general public seems to be intrigued by such evolutionary claims, some scholars have been critical. They believe that evolutionary accounts of human behavior reduce important aspects of our emotional lives, such as romantic and parental love, to an impersonal desire for reproductive success. These critics might sarcastically ask, "Is there really nothing more in Catherine Zeta Jones's choice to marry Michael Douglas than a desire to pass genes onto the next generation?" Evolutionary psychologists appear to have paid little heed to these criticisms, however, partly because they have been largely political or ideological, with little examination of the research behind evolutionary claims. To the authors' credit in the following articles, the question debated is whether or not the *research* provides real evidence of the evolutionary accounts of female mating preferences.

According to the author of the first selection, David Buss, the answer is a resounding "yes." In fact, he points to the study of human mating strategies as "one of the first empirical success stories of evolutionary psychology." In these passages from Buss's college textbook, *Evolutionary Psychology*, he cites findings from several studies that support his claim that females have an evolved preference for high-status, resource-possessing males, including women's responses to personal ads and demographic statistics of whom women actually marry. Finally, Buss recognizes that alternative hypotheses have been offered for women's preferences, such as the structural powerlessness hypothesis, but he ultimately argues that "this hypothesis receives no support from the existing empirical data."

On the other hand, David Buller argues against evolutionary accounts of female mating preferences based on the methodological problems of the studies cited by Buss and others. He begins by attacking the theoretical underpinnings of evolutionary psychology, stating that "given our lack of knowledge of our ancestors' lifestyles, we simply do not know whether selection would have favored and made universal a female preference for high-status males, resource-holding males." After a thorough examination of the research findings, Buller claims the data better explain a female preference for males of similar status than a robust universal preference for males of high-status. The supposed discovery of a female preference for high status males is "largely an illusion." As people let go of this illusion, he claims, "we will not be so convinced by impoverished evidence that human females prefer high-status males." Instead, we will see more clearly the complexities that are involved in female mate preferences.

POINT

- Women have an evolved universal preference for high-status, resource holding males.
- The data provide convincing evidence of a female preference for good financial prospects in males.
- The findings about high-SES women's mating preferences contradict the structural powerlessness hypothesis.

- Elder's findings provide evidence for a robust preference for men with status and resources.
- Buss's cross cultural studies provide evidence for a universal, evolved female preference for high-SES mates.

COUNTERPOINT

- We do not know the history of our ancestors well enough to know whether such preferences have evolved.
- The data better explain a preference for males of similar status.

- The findings of evolutionary psychology do not rule out alternative hypotheses such as the structural powerlessness hypothesis.
- Elder's findings are better understood as a correlation between high status and high attractiveness among men.
- Assortative mating by status cannot be ruled out as an alternative explanation of Buss's cross-cultural findings.

YES

David M. Buss

Evolutionary Psychology: The New Science of the Mind

Nowhere do people have an equal desire for all members of the opposite sex. Everywhere some potential mates are preferred, others shunned. Imagine living as our ancestors did long ago—struggling to keep warm by the fire; hunting meat for our kin; gathering nuts, berries, and herbs; and avoiding dangerous animals and hostile humans. If we were to select a mate who failed to deliver the resources promised, who had affairs, who was lazy, who lacked hunting skills, or who heaped physical abuse on us, our survival would be tenuous, our reproduction at risk. In contrast, a mate who provided abundant resources, who protected us and our children, and who devoted time, energy, and effort to our family would be a great asset. As a result of the powerful survival and reproductive advantages that were reaped by those of our ancestors who chose mates wisely, many specific desires evolved. As descendants of those winners in the evolutionary lottery, modern humans have inherited a specific set of mate preferences. . . .

Choosing a mate is a complex task, and so we do not expect to find simple answers to what women want. Perhaps no other topic has received as much research attention in evolutionary psychology, however, and so we have some reasonably firm answers to this long-standing question.

Preference for Economic Resources

The evolution of the female preference for males offering resources may be the most ancient and pervasive basis for female choice in the animal kingdom. Consider the gray shrike, a bird living in the Negev Desert of Israel (Yosef, 1991). Just before the start of the breeding season, male shrikes begin amassing caches of edible prey such as snails and useful objects such as feathers and pieces of cloth in numbers ranging from 90 to 120. They impale these items on thorns and other pointed projections within their territories. Females scan the available males and choose to mate with those with the largest caches. When Yosef arbitrarily removed portions of some males' stock and added edible objects to the supplies of others, females still preferred to mate with the males with the larger bounties. Females avoided entirely males without resources, consigning them to bachelorhood. Wherever females show a mating preference, the male's resources are often the key criterion.

Among humans the evolution of women's preference for a permanent mate with resources would have required two preconditions. First, resources would have to be accruable, defensible, and controllable by men during human evolutionary history. Second, men would have to differ from each other in their holdings and their willingness to invest those holdings in a woman and her children, because if all men possessed the same resources and showed an equal willingness to allocate them, there would be no need for women to develop such a preference for them.

These conditions are easily met in humans. Territory and tools, to name just two resources, are acquired, defended, monopolized, and controlled by men worldwide. Men vary tremendously in the quantity of resources they command—from the homeless to the jetsetters. Men also differ widely in how willing they are to invest their time and resources in long-term mateships. Some men prefer to mate with many women, investing little in each. Other men channel all their resources to one woman and her children (Belsky, Steinberg, & Draper, 1991).

Over the course of human evolutionary history women could often garner far more resources for their children through a single spouse than through several temporary sex partners. Men invest in their wives and children with provisions to an extent unprecedented among primates. In all other primates, females must rely solely on their own efforts to acquire food because males rarely share those resources with their mates (Smuts, 1995). Men, in contrast, provide food, find shelter, defend territory, and protect children. They tutor children in sports, hunting, fighting, hierarchy negotiation, friendship, and social influence. They transfer status, aiding offspring in forming reciprocal alliances later in life. These benefits are unlikely to be secured by a woman from a temporary sex partner.

So the stage was set for the evolution of women's preferences for men with resources. But women needed cues to signal a man's possession of those resources. These cues might be indirect, such as personality characteristics that signal a man's upward mobility. They might be physical, such as a man's athletic ability or health. They might include reputation, such as the esteem in which a man is held by his peers. The possession of economic resources, however, provides the most obvious cue.

Preference for Good Financial Prospects

Currently held mate preferences provide a window for viewing our mating past, just as our fears of snakes and heights provide a window for viewing ancestral hazards. Evidence from dozens of studies documents that modern U.S. women indeed value economic resources in mates substantially more than men do. In a study conducted in 1939, for example, U.S. men and women rated eighteen characteristics for their relative desirability in a marriage partner, ranging from irrelevant to indispensable. Women did not view good financial prospects as absolutely indispensable, but they did rate them as important, whereas men rated them as merely desirable but not very important. Women in 1939 valued good financial prospects in a mate about twice as highly as men did, a finding that was replicated in 1956 and again in 1967 (Buss, Shackelford, Kirkpatrick, & Larson, 2001).

The sexual revolution of the late 1960s and early 1970s failed to change this sex difference. In an attempt to replicate the studies from earlier decades, in the mid-1980s 1,491 people in the United States were surveyed using the same questionnaire (Buss, 1989a). Women and men from Massachusetts, Michigan, Texas, and California rated eighteen personal characteristics for their value in a marriage partner. As in the previous decades, women still valued good financial prospects in a mate roughly twice as much as did men. In 1939, for example, women judged "good financial prospect" to be 1.80 in importance on a scale ranging from 0 (irrelevant) to 3 (indispensable); men in 1939 judged "good financial prospect" to be only 0.90 in importance. By 1985 women judged this quality to be 1.90 in importance, whereas men judged it to be 1.02 in importance—still roughly a twofold difference between the sexes (Buss, Shackelford, Kirkpatrick, & Larsen, 2001).

The premium that women place on economic resources has been revealed in a diversity of contexts. Douglas Kenrick and his colleagues devised a useful method for revealing how much people value different attributes in a marriage partner by having men and women indicate the "minimum percentiles" of each characteristic they would find acceptable (Kenrick et al., 1990). The percentile concept was explained with such examples as the following: "A person at the 50th percentile would be above 50% of the other people on earning capacity, and below 49% of the people on this dimension" (p. 103). U.S. college women indicate that their minimum acceptable percentile for a husband on earning capacity is the seventieth percentile, or above 70 percent of all other men, whereas men's minimum acceptable percentile for a wife's earning capacity is only the fortieth. Women also show higher standards for economic capacity in a dating partner, in a sexual relationship, and in a steady dating context.

Personal ads in newspapers and magazines confirm that women actually on the marriage market desire strong financial resources. A study of 1,111 personal ads found that female advertisers seek financial resources roughly eleven times as often as male advertisers do (Wiederman, 1993). In short, sex differences in preference for resources are not limited to college students and are not bound by the method of inquiry.

Nor are these female preferences restricted to America, to Western societies, or to capitalist countries. A large cross-cultural study was conducted of thirty-seven cultures on six continents and five islands using populations ranging from coast-dwelling Australians to urban Brazilians to shantytown South African Zulus (Buss, Abbott, Angleitner, Asherian, Biaggio, et al., 1990). Some participants came from nations that practice *polygyny* (the mating or marriage of a single man with several women), such as Nigeria and Zambia. Other participants came from nations that are more *monogamous* (the mating of one man with one woman), such as Spain and Canada. The countries included those in which living together is as common as marriage, such as Sweden and Finland, as well as countries in which living together without marriage is frowned on, such as Bulgaria and Greece. The study sampled a total of 10,047 individuals in thirty-seven cultures (Buss, 1989a).

Male and female participants in the study rated the importance of eighteen characteristics in a potential mate or marriage partner, on a scale from unimportant to indispensable. Women across all continents, all political systems (including socialism and communism), all racial groups, all religious groups, and all systems of mating (from intense polygyny to presumptive monogamy) placed more value than men on good financial prospects. Overall, women valued financial resources about 100 percent more than men, or roughly twice as much. There are some cultural variations. Women from Nigeria, Zambia, India, Indonesia, Iran, Japan, Taiwan, Colombia, and Venezuela valued good financial prospects a bit higher than women from South Africa (Zulus), the Netherlands, and Finland. In Japan, for example, women valued good financial prospect roughly 150 percent more than men, whereas women from the Netherlands deem it only 36 percent more important than their male counterparts, less than women from any other country. Nonetheless, the sex difference remained invariant: Women worldwide desired financial resources in a marriage partner more than men.

These findings provided the first extensive cross-cultural evidence supporting the evolutionary basis for the psychology of human mating. Since that study, findings from other cultures continue to support the hypothesis that women have evolved preferences for men with resources. A study of mate selection in the country of Jordan found that women more than men valued economic ability, as well as qualities linked to economic ability such as status, ambition, and education (Khallad, 2005). Using a different method—analysis of folktales in forty-eight cultural areas including bands, tribes, preindustrial states, Pacific islands, and all the major continents—Jonathan Gottschall and colleagues found the same sex difference (Gottschall, Berkey, Cawson, Drown, Fleischner, et al., 2003). Substantially more female than male characters in the folktales from each culture placed a primary emphasis on wealth or status in their expressed mate preferences. Gottschall found similar results in a historical analysis of European literature (Gottschall, Martin, Quish, & Rea, 2004). A study of 500 Muslims living in the United States found that women sought financially secure, emotionally sensitive, and sincere partners, the latter likely being a signal of willingness to commit to a long-term relationship (Badahdah & Tiemann, 2005). Finally, an in-depth study of the Hadza of Tanzania, a hunter-gatherer society, found that women place a great importance on a man's foraging abilities—primarily his ability to hunt (Marlow, 2004).

This fundamental sex difference also appears prominently in modern forms of mating, such as speed dating and mail-order brides. In a study of speed dating, in which individuals engage in four-minute conversations to determine whether they are interested in meeting the other person again, women chose men who indicated that they had grown up in affluent neighborhoods (Fisman et al., 2006). A study of the mate preferences of mail-order brides from Colombia, the Philippines, and Russia found that these women sought husbands who had status and ambition—two key correlates of resource acquisition (Minervini & McAndrew, 2005). As the authors conclude, "women willing to become MOBs [mail-order brides] do not appear to have a different agenda than other mate-seeking women; they simply have discovered a novel way to expand their pool of prospective husbands" (p. 17).

The enormous body of empirical evidence across different methods, time periods, and cultures supports the hypothesis that women have evolved a powerful preference for long-term mates with the ability to provide resources. Because ancestral women faced the tremendous burdens of internal fertilization, a nine-month gestation, and lactation, they would have benefited tremendously by selecting mates who possessed resources. Today's women are the descendants of a long line of women who had these mate preferences— preferences that helped their ancestors solve the adaptive problems of survival and reproduction.

Preference for High Social Status

Traditional hunter-gatherer societies, which are our closest guide to what ancestral conditions were probably like, suggest that ancestral men had clearly defined status hierarchies, with resources flowing freely to those at the top and trickling slowly down to those at the bottom (Betzig, 1986; Brown & Chia-Yun, n.d.). Cross-culturally, groups such as the Melanesians, the early Egyptians, the Sumerians, the Japanese, and the Indonesians include people described as "head men" and "big men" who wield great power and enjoy the resource privileges of prestige. Among various South Asian languages, for example, the term "big man" is found in Sanskrit, Hindi, and several Dravidian languages. In Hindi, for example, *bara asami* means "great man, person of high position or rank" (Platts, 1960, pp. 151–152). In North America, north of Mexico, "big man" and similar terms are found among groups such as the Wappo, Dakota, Miwok, Natick, Choctaw, Kiowa, and Osage. In Mexico and South America "big man" and closely related terms are found among the Cayapa, Chatino, Mazahua, Mixe, Mixteco, Quiche, Terraba, Tzeltal, Totonaco, Tarahumara, Quechua, and Hahuatl. Linguistically, therefore, it seems that many cultures have found it important to invent words or phrases to describe men who are high in status. A man's social status, as indicated by these linguistic phrases, would provide a powerful cue to his possession of resources.

Women desire men who command a high position because social status is a universal cue to the control of resources. Along with status come better food, more abundant territory, and superior health care. Greater social status bestows on children social opportunities missed by the children of lower-ranking males. For male children worldwide, access to more and better quality mates typically accompanies families of higher social status. In one study of 186 societies ranging from the Mbuti Pygmies of Africa to the Aleut Eskimos, high-status men invariably had greater wealth and more wives and provided better nourishment for their children (Betzig, 1986).

One study examined short-term and long-term mating to discover which characteristics people especially valued in potential spouses, as contrasted with potential sex partners (Buss & Schmitt, 1993). Several hundred individuals evaluated sixty-seven characteristics for their desirability or undesirability in the short or long term, rating them on a scale ranging from -3 (extremely undesirable) to $+3$ (extremely desirable). Women judged the likelihood of success in a profession and the possession of a promising career to be highly desirable in a spouse, giving average ratings of $+2.60$ and $+2.70$, respectively. Significantly, these cues to future status are seen by women as more desirable in spouses than in casual sex partners, with the latter ratings reaching only $+1.10$ and $+0.40$, respectively. U.S. women also place great value on education and professional degrees in mates—characteristics that are strongly linked with social status.

The importance that women grant to social status in mates is not limited to the United States or even to capitalist countries. In the vast majority of the thirty-seven cultures considered in the international study on choosing a mate, women valued social status in a prospective mate more than men in both communist and socialist countries, among Africans and Asians, among Catholics and Jews, in the southern tropics and the northern climes (Buss, 1989a). In Taiwan, for example, women valued status 63 percent more than men, in Zambia women valued it 30 percent more, in West Germany women valued it 38 percent more, and in Brazil women valued it 40 percent more.

Hierarchies are universal features among human groups, and resources tend to accumulate to those who rise in the hierarchy. Women historically appear to have solved the adaptive problem of acquiring resources in part by preferring men who are high in status. . . .

Effects of Women's Personal Resources on Mate Preferences

An alternative explanation to the evolutionary psychological theory has been offered for the preferences of women for men with resources—the structural powerlessness hypothesis (Buss & Barnes, 1986; Eagly & Wood, 1999). According to this view, because women are typically excluded from power and access to resources, which are largely controlled by men, women seek mates who have power, status, and earning capacity. Women try to marry upward in socioeconomic status because this provides their primary channel for gaining access to resources. Men do not value economic resources in a mate as much as women do because they already have control over these resources and because women have fewer resources anyway.

The society of Bakweri, from Cameroon in West Africa, casts doubt on this theory by illustrating what happens when women have real power (Ardener, Ardener, & Warmington, 1960). Bakweri women hold greater personal and economic power because they have more resources and are in scarcer supply than men. Women secure resources through their own labors on plantations but also from casual sex, which is a lucrative source of income. There are roughly 236 men for every hundred women, an imbalance that results from the continual influx of men from other areas of the country to work on the plantations. Because of the extreme imbalance in numbers of the sexes, women have considerable latitude to exercise their choice in a mate. Women thus have more money than men and more potential mates to choose from. Yet Bakweri women persist in preferring mates with resources. Wives often complain about receiving insufficient support from their husbands. Indeed, lack of sufficient economic provisioning is the reason for divorce most frequently cited by women. Bakweri women change husbands if they find a man who can offer them more money and pay a larger bride-price. When women are in a position to fulfill their evolved preference for a man with resources, they do so. Having dominant control of economic resources apparently does not negate this mate preference.

Professionally and economically successful women in the United States also value resources in men. A study of married couples identified women who were financially successful, as measured by their salary and income, and contrasted their preferences in a mate with those of women with lower salaries and income (Buss, 1989a). The financially successful women were well educated, tended to hold professional degrees, and had high self-esteem. The study showed that successful women place an even greater value than less professionally successful women on mates who have professional degrees, high social status, and greater intelligence and who are tall, independent, and self-confident. Women's personal income was positively correlated with the income they wanted in an ideal mate (+.31), the desire for a mate who is a college graduate (+.29), and the desire for a mate with a professional degree (+.35). Contrary to the structural powerlessness hypothesis, these women expressed an even stronger preference for high-earning men than did women who are less financially successful.

In a separate study psychologists Michael Wiederman and Elizabeth Allgeier found that college women who expect to earn the most after college put more weight on the promising financial prospects of a potential husband than do women who expect to earn less. Professionally successful women, such as medical and law students, also place heavy importance on a mate's earning capacity (Wiederman & Allgeier, 1992).

Cross-cultural studies consistently find small but positive relationships between women's personal access to economic resources and preferences for mates with resources. A study of 1,670 Spanish women seeking mates through personal advertisements found that women who have more resources and status were more likely to seek men with resources and status (Gil-Burmann, Pelaez, & Sanchez, 2002). A study of 288 Jordanians found that both women and men with high socioeconomic status place more, not less, value on the mate characteristics of having a college graduate degree and being ambitious-industrious (Khallad, 2005). A study of 127 individuals from Serbia concluded that "The high status of women correlated positively with their concern with a potential mate's potential socio-economic status, contrary to the prediction of the socio-structural model" (Todosijevic, Ljubinkovic, & Arancic, 2003, p. 116). An Internet study of 1,851 women found that *attitudes* toward financial and career independence, including items such as "How important is having a career to you?" found that women who endorsed these attitudes valued physical attractiveness more than good financial prospects in a mate (Moore et al., 2006). However, in examining the effects of women's actual income, this study found that "wealthier women prefer good financial prospects over physical attractiveness"

(Moore, Cassidy, Smith, & Perrett, 2006, p. 201). Taken together, these results not only fail to support the structural powerlessness hypothesis, they directly contradict it. . . .

How Women's Mate Preferences Affect Actual Mating Behavior

For preferences to evolve, they must affect actual mating decisions because it is those decisions that have reproductive consequences. For a number of reasons, however, preferences should not show a *perfect* correspondence with actual mating behavior. People can't always get what they want for a variety of reasons. First, there is a limited number of highly desirable potential mates. Second, one's own mate value limits access to those who are highly desirable. In general only the most desirable women are in a position to attract the most desirable men, and vice versa. Third, parents and other kin sometimes influence one's mating decisions, regardless of personal preferences. Despite these factors, women's mate preferences must have affected their actual mating decisions some of the time over the course of human evolutionary history or they would not have evolved. Following are several sources of evidence that preferences do affect mating decisions.

Women's Responses to Men's Personal Ads

One source of evidence comes from women's responses to personal ads posted by men in newspapers. If women's preferences affected their mating decisions, then they would be predicted to respond more often to men who indicate that they are financially well off. Baize and Schroeder (1995) tested this prediction using a sample of 120 personal ads placed in two different newspapers, one from the West Coast and the other from the Midwest. The authors mailed a questionnaire to those who posted the ads, asking for information about personal status, response rate, and personality characteristics.

Several variables significantly predicted the number of letters men received in response to their ads. First, *age* was a significant predictor, with women responding more often to older men than to younger men ($r = +.43$). Second, *income* and *education* were also significant predictors, with women responding more to men with ads indicating higher salaries ($r = +.30$) and more years of education ($r = +.37$). Baize and Schroeder ended their article on a humorous note by recalling the question posed by Tim Hardin in his famous folk song: "If I were a carpenter and you were a lady, would you marry me anyway, would you have my baby?" Given the cumulative research findings, the most likely answer is: No.

Similar results have now been found in Poland in a study of response rates to ads placed by 551 men (Pawlowski & Koziel, 2002). Men with higher levels of education, men who were somewhat older, men who were taller, and men who offered more resources all received a larger number of responses from women than did men who lacked these qualities.

Women's Marriages to Men High in Occupational Status

A second source of findings pertains to women who are in a position to get what they want—women who have the qualities that men desire in a mate such as physical attractiveness (see Chapter 5). What are the mate choices of these women? In three separate sociological studies, researchers discovered that physically attractive women in fact marry men who are higher in social status and financial holdings than do women who are less attractive (Elder, 1969; Taylor & Glenn, 1976; Udry & Ekland, 1984). In one study, the physical attractiveness of women was correlated with the occupational prestige of their husbands (Taylor and Glenn, 1976). For different groups the correlations were all positive, ranging between +.23 and +.37.

A longitudinal study was conducted at the Institute of Human Development in Berkeley, California (Elder, 1969). Physical attractiveness ratings were made by staff members of then unmarried women when they were adolescents. This sample of women was then followed up in adulthood after they had married, and the occupational statuses of their husbands were assessed.

The results were examined separately for working-class and middle-class women. The correlations between a woman's attractiveness in adolescence and her husband's occupational status roughly a decade later was +.46 for women with working-class backgrounds and +.35 for women coming from middle-class backgrounds. For the sample as a whole, a woman's physical attractiveness correlated more strongly with her husband's status (+.43) than did other women's variables such as class of origin (+.27) or IQ (+.14). In sum, attractiveness in women appears to be an important path to upward mobility; women who are most in a position to get what they want appear to select men who have the qualities that most women desire—men with status and resources. . . .

Summary

We now have the outlines of an answer to the mystery of women's long-term mate preferences. Modern women have inherited from their successful ancestors wisdom about the men they consent to mate with. Ancestral women who mated indiscriminately were likely to have been less reproductively successful than those who exercised choice. Long-term mates bring with them a treasure trove of assets. Selecting a long-term mate who has the relevant assets is clearly an extraordinarily complex endeavor. It involves a number of distinctive preferences, each corresponding to a resource that helps women solve critical adaptive problems.

That women seek resources in a marriage partner might seem obvious. Because resources cannot always be directly discerned, however, women's mating preferences are keyed to other qualities that signal the likely possession, or future acquisition, of resources. Indeed, women may be less influenced by money per se than by qualities that lead to resources, such as ambition, intelligence, and older age. Women scrutinize these personal qualities carefully because they reveal a man's potential. . . .

According to the structural powerlessness hypothesis, women who have a lot of personal access to resources are predicted not to value resources in a mate as much as women lacking resources. This hypothesis receives no support from the existing empirical data, however. Indeed, women with high incomes value a potential mate's income and education more, not less, than women with lower incomes. . . .

David J. Buller

 **NO**

Adapting Minds: Evolutionary Psychology and the Persistent Quest for Human Nature

Women Seeking Men

"Choosing a mate is a complex task," David Buss says, "and so we do not expect to find simple answers to what women want. Perhaps no other topic has received as much research attention in evolutionary psychology, however, and so we have some reasonably firm answers to this longstanding question." Indeed, female mate preferences have been the focus of roughly twice as many studies in Evolutionary Psychology as male mate preferences. But, despite the efforts on this front, Evolutionary Psychology's answer to the question of what women want is not exactly firm.

As we have seen, Evolutionary Psychologists claim that women have an evolved preference for high-status men because, "in general, the higher a male is in status . . . the greater his ability to control resources across many situations" and to invest those resources in his mate and their offspring. This pre-supposes that, throughout our evolutionary history as hunter-gatherers, males have been the primary providers of food and other resources to their mates and their offspring and that, as a consequence, females evolved to prefer the males who excelled in this role.

. . . However, there is significant variation among hunter-gatherer populations with respect to male contributions to the diets of their young. In some hunter-gatherer populations female foraging provides a full 67 percent of the total daily caloric intake. And Kristen Hawkes found that a Hadza woman and her children receive more food from her mother than from her mate. As I argued, it's not clear which of the various hunter-gatherer populations we are to take as representative of our Pleistocene ancestors, or even whether Pleistocene hunter-gatherers led a uniform lifestyle.

This fact poses a problem for the claim that females have evolved a universal preference for males who show signs of being able providers. For, if ancestral hunter-gatherer populations were just as variable as contemporary hunter-gatherer populations with respect to the degree of male provisioning, then a preference for high-status males may have evolved in populations with high

From *Adapting Minds: Evolutionary Psychology and the Persistent Quest for Human Nature* by David J. Buller (MIT Press, 2005), 228–229, 232–244, 247–250. Copyright © 2005 by Massachusetts Institute of Technology. Reprinted by permission of MIT Press.

male provisioning, but not in populations where males provided relatively little in the way of essential resources. Given our lack of knowledge of our ancestors' lifestyles . . . we simply don't know whether selection would have favored and made universal a female preference for high-status, resource-holding males.

In keeping with this skepticism, a number of researchers—for example, Linnda Caporael, Alice Eagly, and Sarah Blaffer Hrdy—have challenged Evolutionary Psychology's account of female mate preferences. They argue that female preference for high-status males results from current economic inequality, not past selection. In this view, a preference for males with resources is a rational response to a social situation in which males control economic resources, since in such circumstances a female can gain access to economic resources only through her choice of mate.

Evolutionary Psychologists have dubbed this view the "structural (or economic) powerlessness hypothesis." They argue that this hypothesis entails the prediction that women in high-paying professions should place less emphasis on status in mate choice than unemployed women or women in low-paying jobs. Evolutionary Psychologists claim to have shown this prediction to be false. Thus, they claim, the evidence favors the evolutionary hypothesis over the structural powerlessness hypothesis.

What's at stake here is whether female preference for high-status males is an adaptation. Evolutionary Psychologists claim it is, and the structural powerlessness hypothesis claims it isn't. As I mentioned earlier, this debate is not my central concern. For, despite their disagreement with Evolutionary Psychology, advocates of the structural powerlessness hypothesis still accept that there is a robust female preference for high-status males. But, in what follows, I will argue that there is no good evidence of such a robust preference among women. . . .

The most fun studies purporting to demonstrate that females prefer high-SES males were conducted by the anthropologist John Marshall Townsend and the psychologist Gary Levy. The procedures and results of these studies were almost identical, so I will focus primarily on one of them, since it is representative of the others and discussion of it applies equally to the others.

In Townsend and Levy's study, 112 white female undergraduates from Syracuse University were shown photographs of two male models, who were selected for this purpose because an independent group had rated one as very handsome and the other as very homely. In the photographs, each male model was dressed in each of three different "costumes." One was the uniform of a Burger King employee, intended to depict low SES. Another was a plain off-white shirt, to depict medium SES. And the third was "a white dress shirt with a designer paisley tie, a navy blazer thrown over the left shoulder, and a Rolex wristwatch showing on the left wrist," to depict high SES.

The female subjects were asked to indicate their degree of willingness to enter six types of relationship, ranging from very casual to very serious, with "someone like" the models. The six types of relationship were described as "coffee and conversation," "date," "sex only," "serious involvement, marriage potential," "sexual and serious, marriage potential," and "marriage." Subjects were instructed to indicate their degree of willingness on the following five-point scale: (1) very willing, (2) willing, (3) undecided, (4) unwilling, and (5) very unwilling.

Table 1

Average Female Willingness to Enter a Relationship as a Function of Male "Costume"

Handsome model

Level of involvement	Costume		
	High SES	**Medium SES**	**Low SES**
Date	2.16	1.94	2.82
Serious involvement	2.58	2.74	3.87
Marriage	2.53	2.77	3.84

Homely model

Level of involvement	Costume		
	High SES	**Medium SES**	**Low SES**
Date	2.57	4.00	3.69
Serious involvement	3.20	4.35	4.13
Marriage	3.17	4.38	4.18

To simplify discussion, I'll focus on three representative relationship types: "date," "serious involvement, marriage potential," and "marriage." The average ratings from the female subjects for these three relationship types are presented in table 1.

Townsend and Levy found two aspects of the results in table 1 to be significant. First, at each level of involvement (from date to marriage), each model got better ratings in the high-SES costume than in the other costumes. The sole exception was that the handsome model was a slightly more desirable date in the medium-SES costume than in the high-SES costume. As the level of involvement became more serious, however, even the handsome model scored better in the high-SES costume than in either of the other costumes. Second, high status appears to compensate for homeliness, since the high-SES costume raised the homely model's acceptability at every level of involvement over that of the handsome model in the low-SES costume. Townsend and Levy conclude that females prefer high-status mates. And the Evolutionary Psychologist Bruce Ellis interprets the experiment as showing that "status and economic achievement are highly relevant barometers of male attractiveness, more so than physical attributes."

But, if we look at the data in a different way, we see a different barometer. For, at every level of involvement and at every status level, the handsome male is preferred over the homely male. In fact, the handsome male in the medium-SES costume scored better than the homely male in the high-SES costume, despite the fact that the latter can presumably provide more resources than the former. So the results could equally well be interpreted as showing that physical attributes are "highly relevant barometers of male attractiveness," more so than male status.

In addition, although Townsend and Levy claim that status compensates for homeliness, since the homely model in the high-SES costume scored higher than the handsome model in the low-SES costume, the homely model scored 3.20 and 3.17 for serious involvement and marriage respectively. Both of these scores lie between "undecided" and "unwilling" in the scale used to indicate degree of willingness to enter a relationship with someone like the model. So high SES doesn't appear to make females *willing* to enter a serious relationship with someone they find homely. (Also, the homely model inexplicably scored better in the low-SES costume than in the medium-SES costume, despite the fact that medium-SES males can provide resources that low-SES males can't. There is no doubt some fashion advice lurking here about who should wear plain off-white shirts.)

While Evolutionary Psychologists typically deemphasize the role of male physical attractiveness in female mate preferences, both of these objections could easily be accommodated simply by claiming that women weigh both physical attractiveness and status in choosing a mate. The data, it could be claimed, demonstrate that both have significant effects on female mate preferences. Thus, the data don't have to be a perfect fit to the prediction that females prefer high-status males, they only need to show that status plays a role in female mate preferences. And the data do seem to demonstrate this.

But there is a problem with the data nonetheless, which is due to the fact that Townsend and Levy's subjects were all university students. As we have seen, homogamy is the most robust mating phenomenon, and status homogamy is second only to race homogamy in the strength of its effect on mate choice. There are two possible explanations for this. First, it may be that everyone competes for high-status mates, but only high-status individuals succeed in attracting high-status mates. This effect could trickle down to other status levels, with the result that everyone ends up with a mate of comparable status. Second, it may be that people actually prefer mates of comparable status, and status homogamy results from this preference. The sociological evidence actually favors the second explanation. People mate with those of comparable status primarily out of preference, rather than settling for a mate of comparable status because of an inability to get a mate of higher status.

But why would anyone prefer to mate with a fellow medium-status individual, say, rather than a high-status individual? The reason could well be the one that Kenrick and Keefe give for why age similarity is important in mate choice. Recall that Kenrick and Keefe argued that *all forms* of similarity between mates may facilitate long-term parental cooperation, since homogamously mated individuals have "similar expectations, values, activity levels, and habits." Consequently, they suggested, selection may have favored homogamous mating—a "birds of a feather mate together" principle—among our ancestors. If this is right, then we should expect people to prefer mates of comparable status in addition to mates of similar age. As a consequence, assortative mating by status would be fairly robust, which in fact it is.

Studies of status homogamy have considered four different dimensions of status: education level, cultural status of occupation, income level, and social-class origins. Of these, educational homogamy is the most robust. Overwhelmingly, people select mates who have achieved (or will achieve) a comparable level of education. Indeed, one of the boundaries that is very rarely crossed in mating relationships is the boundary between those who have some college education (like Townsend and Levy's female subjects) and those who have only a high-school education (presumably like Townsend and Levy's Burger King employee). Consequently, the fact that Townsend and Levy's subjects preferred medium- to high-SES males over low-SES males could simply be an artifact of assortative mating by status. The results could simply be due to the fact that the female subjects perceived the low-SES model as uneducated and tended to consider only males of probable comparable education level as prospective mates.

This explains why the models would score so low in the low-SES costumes, but why would they score higher in the high-SES costumes than in the medium-SES costumes? Is this also the effect of status homogamy, or does it reveal a genuine preference for high-SES males?

To know for sure, we would need status information about Townsend and Levy's female subjects, and Townsend and Levy don't report having gathered such information. But recall that status involves social-class origins and cultural status of occupation in addition to level of education. The relevant information about respondent status would thus include information about social-class origins. Respondents with higher class origins should be expected to favor the high-SES models. Relevant information would also include not simply education level achieved at the time of response (which was sufficient to already place a social barrier between the respondents and the low-SES models), but also *anticipated* achieved level of education. Similarly, it would include anticipated occupation. Status homogamy should lead us to expect that all of these factors would influence female preference. And, if more of Townsend and Levy's female respondents were themselves high SES than medium SES, and if all respondents gave the highest score to the models from their own SES, then the average ratings of the high-SES models would be higher than the medium-SES models, even if all medium-SES respondents rated the medium-SES models highest.

There is reason to think that Townsend and Levy's sample *was* composed predominantly of high-SES females (or at least females who were toward the upper end of the SES continuum). For all the female subjects were white female undergraduates at one of the nation's most expensive private universities, and at least half of them belonged to sororities (half were interviewed in sororities). So it is highly probable that females with upper-middle-class origins were overrepresented in the sample. Further, there should be a correlation between these class origins and higher levels of anticipated educational achievement and anticipated occupational status. And females who are high-SES along these dimensions would prefer the high-SES models on the basis of status homogamy alone. Since the sample was no doubt composed predominantly of high-SES females, then, it should be expected that the average ratings of the high-SES models would exceed those of the medium-SES models.

Interestingly, Townsend repeated this experiment with 82 female law students, this time supplementing the pictures with descriptions. The model in the Burger King uniform was described as training to be a waiter who would earn a starting salary of $15,000 a year, the model in the off-white shirt as training to be a teacher who would earn $22,000 a year, and the model in the Rolex as training to be a doctor who would earn $80,000 a year. Guess what. The female law students preferred the doctor. But this doesn't necessarily indicate a preference for high SES per se. For this preference is precisely what we should expect if female law students were choosing mates of comparable education level, comparable cultural status of occupation, and comparable projected income level.

Further, the female law students rated the high-SES models higher than the college students had. This is also precisely what we should expect from assortative mating by status, since the law students form a more homogeneously high-status sample than the undergraduates. Because the undergraduate sample was less status homogeneous, containing a higher ratio of medium-SES respondents, they gave a lower average score to the high-SES model. In short, the Townsend and Levy data fit the preference ratings that would result from status homogamy alone.

Thus, given the composition of the subject groups in these experiments, none of the experiments can distinguish whether female respondents were indicating a genuine preference for a mate with high SES or whether their ratings were a product of simple assortative mating by status. Given the independently documented robustness of status homogamy, we already know that, if you ask medium- and high-SES females what they want in a mate, they will show a preference bias against low-SES males. In order to distinguish a genuine preference for high status from assortative mating by status, we would need data on the preferences of low-SES females. We would also need a subgroup analysis by status of female preferences; that is, we would need to see female preference orderings broken down by SES of female respondent. Evolutionary Psychologists have provided no such data, but it would be needed to substantiate their claim that females desire high-SES males. For without this data, there is no evidence that medium-SES females don't prefer the medium-SES model over the ostentatious high-SES model, or that low-SES females don't find the handsome model in the Burger King uniform most desirable of all. Only if low-SES females systematically indicate a preference for high-status males can we infer a real preference for high status. However, the independent evidence of status homogamy suggests that the latter preference pattern would not be found.

Of course, it is entirely possible that women actually have an evolved preference for high-status men, but that the experiments conducted by Evolutionary Psychologists have simply failed to reveal that fact because their results are confounded by status homogamy. This could be the case, for example, if dominance and high SES, as those are articulated in the experimental instruments used by Evolutionary Psychologists, are poor measures of the kind of status that women have evolved to prefer. After all, this preference is supposed to have evolved long before people had education levels and incomes or had careers as doctors and lawyers. . . . So maybe Evolutionary Psychologists have simply used experimental procedures that are incapable of detecting female preference for high-status mates, though it is there waiting to be detected.

Although this is a possibility, I doubt it's true. As Evolutionary Psychologists standardly define the concept, status "refers to an individual's *relative position in a social group;* it is a measure of where one stands among one's peers and competitors." If selecting a high-status mate had, and continues to have, significant fitness consequences for women, as Evolutionary Psychologists claim, we should expect women to have evolved techniques of detecting *social relations* among males. They should have evolved to be sensitive to the structural features of male interactions, detecting how males form a hierarchy in their interactions with one another, regardless of which particular intrinsic male qualities are correlated with high or low status. And, if women have evolved to be sensitive in this way to where a male stands in relation to other males, and to prefer those who are in the upper strata of male hierarchies, the kinds of experiment we've discussed should detect that preference. So, the fact that the results of these experiments are confounded by status homogamy probably isn't due to the experiments' making use of cues that didn't indicate status in the Pleistocene.

At this point Evolutionary Psychologists could respond that assortative mating by status cannot explain the sex differences they consistently find. For studies of mate preferences consistently find that women place a greater emphasis on a potential mate's status than do men. If female preferences for high status are simply a by-product of the fact that the female experimental subjects are relatively high status themselves and are merely indicating a preference for males of comparable status, then we should expect male experimental subjects (who tend to be from the same social classes as female subjects) to place a comparable emphasis on a potential mate's status. For, if people prefer mates of similar status, that should be evident not only in female preferences, but in male preferences as well. But study after study finds that a potential mate's status doesn't matter to men in the way that it matters to women.

The studies showing a sex difference with respect to preferences for high-status mates have focused on the income dimension of status, finding that women care more about a potential mate's earning capacity than men do. In Buss one such study was conducted by Douglas Kenrick in collaboration with the psychologists Edward Sadalla, Gary Groth, and Melanie Trost. Kenrick and his collaborators provided 64 female and 29 male undergraduates with a list of characteristics and asked them how they would weigh those characteristics in choosing a partner for a date, for steady exclusive dating, and for marriage. "Participants were asked to give the minimum and maximum percentiles of each characteristic that they would find acceptable in a partner at each level of involvement. Several examples were given to clarify any questions about the percentile concept, e.g., 'A person at the 50th percentile would be above 50%

Table 2

Average Minimum Acceptable Earning Capacity of a Potential Partner

	Earning capacity (expressed as percentile)	
Level of involvement	Female respondents	Male respondents
Date	44.58	23.79
Steady dating	61.08	36.86
Marriage	67.17	42.21

of other people on [the characteristic] kind and understanding, and below 49% of the people on this dimension.'"

The primary evidence supporting the claim that females desire high-status mates came from responses regarding *minimum acceptable earning capacity.* With respect to this characteristic, average responses for each sex were as presented in table 2, and these results do appear to show that male earning capacity plays a strong role in female mate choice. Indeed, in accordance with Evolutionary Psychologists' expectations, as the level of involvement becomes more serious, and consequently a male's ability to provide resources becomes increasingly important, females appear to place increasing weight on earning capacity. And this result appears to confirm that women prefer high-SES males.

Again, however, the female subjects were all American undergraduates, hence, on average, of medium SES or higher. (Education level alone would make them of medium SES, but some may be higher because of higher social-class origins, anticipated high-status occupations, or anticipated high income levels after college.) Thus, again, it is not clear whether the results actually demonstrate a preference for high status per se, or whether they merely reflect status homogamy. For, again, if the subjects are predominantly from the upper half of the socioeconomic continuum, and if they express preferences for same-status males, their average preference rating will fall in the upper half of the socioeconomic continuum.

But what about the sex difference in the results? Males clearly placed much less emphasis than females on earning capacity, although males did, like females, place greater emphasis on earning capacity as the level of involvement increased. If the results are a product of assortative mating by status, we should expect males to express the same preferences as females: Medium- to high-SES males should indicate a preference for females whose earning capacities fall in the medium- to high-SES range. But, in fact, the average minimum acceptable earning percentiles preferred by males run a full 20 to 25 percentile points lower than female averages. Doesn't this show that the results are not an artifact of status homogamy and that females have a genuine preference for high status per se in a mate?

In short, no. Recall that status has four dimensions: education level, cultural prestige of occupation, social-class origins, and income level. In

American society (from which the subjects in this experiment were drawn), earning capacity is a cue to, or a predictor of, other dimensions of a male's status in a way that it is not for a female. In American society, women hold only about one-quarter of the jobs in professions paying over $40,000 a year. And, in professions and trades where women hold a larger fraction of the jobs, women earn only about three-quarters as much as men performing the same job. Given this significant economic inequality between the sexes, a medium-SES male seeking a medium-SES female can expect his prospective mate to earn significantly less than he does, even if they are perfectly matched on other dimensions of status. Consequently, even if upper-SES subjects chose mates by employing the criterion of similar status alone, females should specify significantly higher minimum acceptable earning percentiles for prospective mates than males, since income is a better predictor of other dimensions of male status than it is of other dimensions of female status.

If people select mates of comparable status because people of comparable status have "similar expectations, values, activity levels, and habits," and these similarities facilitate parental cooperation (as per Kenrick and Keefe's argument), surely education level, occupation, and social-class origins are better indicators of one's values and so on than income level alone. Social-class origins and the education level one achieves play a role in shaping personality, expectations, and values, and chosen occupation is a reflection of one's values and expectations in life. One's income, in itself, is much less a reflection of one's values and character than the other dimensions of status. So, education level, occupation, and social-class origins should be more important factors in mate choice than income level. And the sociological evidence of status homogamy does show these factors to have a stronger effect on mate choice than income level. Since economic inequality between the sexes makes income level a better predictor among males than females of these other dimensions of status, if subjects are asked specifically to rate the importance of income level in mate choice, we should expect females to accord it greater weight than males. Thus, under conditions of economic inequality between the sexes, a sex difference in the importance attached to a potential mate's earning capacity is fully consistent with simple assortative mating by status.

In addition, if you reread the instructions given to participants in Kenrick's study, which I quoted above, you'll see that subjects were instructed to provide percentile rankings for each characteristic *relative to the whole population* ("50th percentile would be above 50% of other people"), not just relative to the sex of a potential mate. So males indicated a preference to marry a woman whose income is in the 42nd percentile of all Americans, not just in the 42nd percentile of American women. Similarly, females indicated a preference to marry a man whose income is in the 67th percentile of all Americans, which includes the lower-earning female half of the population. Thus, if the earning-capacity percentile rankings were adjusted to accommodate the economic inequality between the sexes, the sex difference in the rankings would virtually disappear.

My argument sounds suspiciously like the structural powerlessness hypothesis, but it's not exactly the same. According to the structural powerlessness hypothesis, women desire high-SES mates because, under conditions of economic inequality between the sexes, the only way a woman can gain access to economic resources is through her mate. The suggestion I'm making is that, in the results obtained by Kenrick and his collaborators (and in similar studies), women only *appear* to desire high-SES mates because only upper-SES women have been asked about their preferences, and the economic inequality between the sexes results in a sex difference in the percentiles assigned to the characteristic *minimum acceptable earning capacity*. The structural powerlessness hypothesis takes the reality of a female preference for high earning capacity for granted, and I'm suggesting that females merely appear to prefer high earning capacity, but that the data don't provide good evidence that they in fact do. Nonetheless, my suggestion is similar enough to the structural powerlessness hypothesis to warrant examining the evidence that Evolutionary Psychologists present against the latter.

Evolutionary Psychologists contend that the structural powerlessness hypothesis entails that female preference for high earning capacity should vary with a female's own economic power, so that women with a high earning capacity should place less emphasis on earning capacity in choosing a mate than do women with a low earning capacity. Evolutionary Psychologists claim that two studies have shown this to be false. First, from his large survey, Buss had data on personal income and class background for 100 of the female respondents from his United States sample. Among this group, he found that "women who make *more* money tend to value monetary and professional status of mates *more* than those who make less money." Second, the Evolutionary Psychologists Michael Wiederman and Elizabeth Allgeier asked 637 female undergraduates and 167 women in two Ohio communities to rate the importance of several characteristics in the selection of a husband, one of which was *good financial prospect*. They also asked them to indicate the annual income they expected to earn in the following year or in the years immediately after finishing college. They found that "the more personal income the women in the sample expected to earn, the more likely they were to value good financial prospects in a mate." Evolutionary Psychologists claim that both results directly contradict the prediction entailed by the structural powerlessness hypothesis and support their evolutionary hypothesis.

But there are a few problems with this claim. First, it's not clear that the structural powerlessness hypothesis in fact entails the prediction tested. The structural powerlessness hypothesis claims only that females will prefer high-income mates under conditions of economic inequality, in which women gain access to economic resources primarily through their mates. One way that a preference for high-income mates could become prevalent among women under such conditions is through "socialization" during formative childhood and teen years. Women could be encouraged by their family members, friends, or other advisors to select high-SES mates (doctors, lawyers, or the like). There is no reason why a preference formed through twenty or so years of such socialization should disappear simply because a woman finds herself earning a good salary. So, the structural powerlessness hypothesis doesn't actually entail that high-paid women will not share a preference for high-SES mates with other women.

Second, it's not at all clear how the data support Evolutionary Psychology's hypothesis. If women have an evolved preference for high-status males, which translates into a preference for high-income males in contemporary societies, they should prefer as high an income as they can get in a mate, regardless of their own income. Evolutionary Psychology's hypothesis doesn't entail that medium-SES women should have lower standards for income in a potential mate than high-SES women.

However, third, if women prefer males in their own socioeconomic group, then medium-SES women will, on average, exhibit a preference for medium-SES males, which will appear as a preference for a moderate ability to provide resources. High-SES women, on the other hand, will exhibit a preference for high-SES men, which will make them appear to desire an even greater ability to provide resources than is desired by medium-SES women. Such preference patterns are precisely those that assortative mating by status should lead us to expect. So, again, the data are unable to demonstrate a female preference for high status per se rather than simple assortative mating by status.

Of course, all the studies so far considered have involved only American female subjects. So perhaps the results of these studies are confounded by status homogamy simply because the studies made use of unrepresentative samples. If so, a much larger, cross-cultural study should be able to provide results that are not confounded by status homogamy.

This larger study would obviously be Buss's cross-cultural study, in which he had his male and female respondents rate the importance of eighteen characteristics in choosing a mate. Respondents used a four-point scale, ranging from 0 (irrelevant or unimportant) to 3 (indispensable). In thirty-six of Buss's thirty-seven samples, females valued the characteristic *good financial prospect* significantly more than did males. In the remaining sample (Spain), females valued it more than males, but the difference was not significant. In the entire study, the average female rating of *good financial prospect* was 1.76 and the average male rating was 1.51. This appears to show that female preference for high-SES mates is not an artifact of unrepresentative American samples, but is in fact a robust universal preference.

Despite the size of Buss's sample, however, and despite the number of cultures sampled, the sample is still not representative in the way that would be needed to distinguish a preference for high SES per se from simple assortative mating by status. As Buss himself admits: "The samples obtained cannot be viewed as representative of the populations in each country. In general, rural, less-educated, and lower levels of socioeconomic status are underrepresented." But these underrepresented groups are precisely those who might, on average, place much less emphasis on earning capacity because of status homogamy. In fact, the preference ratings of these groups could significantly lower the average rating of *good financial prospect* and thereby remove the appearance of a female preference for high-SES mates. For, as we have seen, in samples that are skewed toward the upper half of the socioeconomic continuum, assortative mating by status biases preference ratings in favor of males in the upper half, and against males in the lower half, of the socioeconomic continuum.

Further, the psychologists Alice Eagly and Wendy Wood reanalyzed Buss's data and compared it with transnational data on economic inequality between the sexes gathered by the United Nations. They found that the sex difference in ratings of *good financial prospect* by Buss's subjects was greater in societies with greater economic inequality between the sexes. Where there was less economic inequality between the sexes, the sex difference in ratings of *good financial prospect* was smaller.

If, as I have argued, income is a better predictor of other dimensions of status among males than among females under conditions of economic inequality between the sexes, this is precisely the result we should expect. For, under conditions of strict economic equality between the sexes, income will be as good a predictor of other dimensions of status for one sex as for the other, and the sex difference in emphasis on earning power will disappear. The fact that Eagly and Wood found a correlation between degree of economic inequality across societies and the strength of the sex difference in emphasis on *good financial prospect* is thus fully consistent with assortative mating by status. Therefore, since low-SES groups are strongly underrepresented in Buss's study, and since the sex difference in emphasis placed on *good financial prospect* diminishes as economic inequality between the sexes diminishes, even Buss's study fails to demonstrate a female preference for high-SES mates per se. . . .

Another study sometimes cited by Evolutionary Psychologists as indirect evidence of a female preference for high-status mates was conducted by the sociologist Glen Elder. Published in 1969, Elder's study was based on an "exchange theory" of human mating, according to which women offer what males desire in exchange for the male characteristics they desire. Elder took for granted that males desire youth and attractiveness in a mate and that females desire high status in a mate, so he expected to find very attractive women mated to higher-status men. Among 76 married women he studied, he found a correlation between female attractiveness and husband's status. Indeed, he concluded that very attractive lower-class women were often able to use their attractiveness to "marry up" and secure a high-status husband.

Commenting on this study, Buss says: "High-status men, such as the aging rock stars Rod Stewart and Mick Jagger and the movie stars Warren Beatty and Jack Nicholson, frequently select women two or three decades younger. . . . Men who are high in occupational status are able to marry women who are considerably more physically attractive than are men who are low in occupational status." Presumably, the attractive young women are in very high demand, so the greater ability of high-status men to marry them attests to the fact that women desire them more. Indeed, women with the attractiveness that men desire appear to use it to bag the high-status husbands that every woman wants.

There is, however, a problem with this argument. For Elder's study obtained attractiveness ratings for the female subjects, but not for their husbands. Indeed, the only measure of the husbands' desirability that Elder used was status level. This raises the possibility that Elder's findings were confounded by male physical attractiveness. To test this idea, the sociologists Gillian Stevens, Dawn Owens, and Eric Schaefer analyzed the wedding announcements of 129 couples that appeared in the major daily newspaper of a small city. Each wedding announcement contained information about the education levels and occupations of the bride and groom, plus a wedding photograph. The images of bride and groom in these photographs were separated, so that spouses didn't appear together, and a mixed-sex panel rated each bride and each groom for physical attractiveness. Since all couples were dressed in formal wedding attire in the photographs, differences in attractiveness judgments weren't affected by differences in the everyday attire of the brides and grooms. So there were no "Burger King uniform" effects in the attractiveness judgments.

Stevens and her colleagues found a strong correlation between the attractiveness ratings of spouses. Very attractive females married very attractive males, average-looking females married average-looking males, and unattractive females married unattractive males. Indeed, there was a much stronger correlation between the attractiveness of spouses than between female attractiveness and male social status. They concluded that "physical attractiveness plays a large and an approximately equal role in marriage choices for men and for women." In short, mating is strongly assortative by degree of attractiveness.

Further, a number of independent sociological studies have demonstrated a strong positive correlation between attractiveness and both income level and occupational achievement. Highly attractive people have better jobs and make more money, on average, than do average-looking people, who in turn have better jobs and make more money than people who are judged to be homely. Perhaps contrary to what you'd expect, this effect is even stronger among men than among women. Thus, Elder's finding that higher-status men tended to be married to more attractive women may simply be a by-product of a correlation between high status and high attractiveness among men. Attractive women marry attractive men, who incidentally tend to be more successful than less attractive men. Thus, Elder's study doesn't actually provide the support that Buss claims it does for the idea that women prefer high-status men.

Finally, there is significant evidence from a much larger sample that directly contradicts Evolutionary Psychologists' claim that high-status males enjoy greater mating success (as a result of female preference for high-status males). The sexologists Martin Weinberg and Colin Williams analyzed the data collected by Alfred Kinsey from 5,460 white males in the United States between 1938 and 1963, which remain the most comprehensive data ever collected on sexual behavior. Analyzing sexual behavior by social class of male respondents in the Kinsey data, Weinberg and Williams found a *negative correlation* between social status and mating success (that is, the higher one's social status, the lower one's mating success). They found that low-SES males had coitus at a significantly younger age than high-SES males and that they had more coital partners than high-SES males. The averages, broken down by three social classes, are presented in table 3. Weinberg and Williams subsequently conducted a study, in 1969–1970, of 284 white males, that replicated these findings. . . . These larger, more representative samples present a picture of the relation between status and mating success that is directly at odds with Evolutionary Psychology's claim that females preferentially mate with high-status males. Indeed, this evidence seems to indicate that sexual activity is greater

Table 3

Mating Success of Males by Class

	Social class		
	Low SES	Medium SES	High SES
Age at first coitus	17.3	17.8	20.5
Number of partners	18.9	10.5	9.6

among low-status males than among high-status males. *Somebody* must like low-status males. . . .

Although we have long been held captive by a picture in which high-status primate males are the preferred mates of primate females, there are reasons for thinking that the picture has been largely an illusion. If we let go of that picture, we will also let go of the reflexive expectation that the link between male high status and female preference exists in us, too. And, if we let go of that reflexive expectation, we will not be so easily convinced by impoverished evidence that human females prefer high-status males. We will then be able to look at the evidence with eyes unclouded by an antecedent conviction regarding what we'll find. When we do, as I have argued, we will see that there is no convincing evidence of a robust female preference for high-status males. Just as male mate preferences will turn out to be more complex than Evolutionary Psychologists have claimed, female mate preferences will no doubt turn out to be more strongly tied to physical attributes of males (physical attractiveness, bodily symmetry, or chemical signaling of histocompatibility) than Evolutionary Psychologists have claimed. Indeed, evidence of this association is already beginning to accumulate. . . .

CHALLENGE QUESTIONS

Does the Evidence Support Evolutionary Accounts of Female Mating Preferences?

1. Both Buss and Buller are considered to be rigorous scholars who are pro-evolution, and yet each has a different interpretation of the same data. How can we account for this different interpretation, and what does this say about evolutionary psychology?
2. If Buss's research findings on female and male mate preferences are correct, what implications do they have for you and your relationships?
3. Buller argues that many of the findings for an evolved female mate preference could be accounted for by societal influences. How might society influence a person's mate selections?
4. What about lesbian sexual orientation? How might evolution account for same-sex orientation when it does not accommodate reproductive success?
5. Read the sections on the evolution of male mating preferences in Buss's and Buller's books. Do you feel there is an inherent double standard in evolutionary accounts of male and female mate preferences? Why or why not?
6. Evolutionary accounts of human mating assume that male and female mate preferences are determined by reproductive success. If this is true, how might this explain to whom you are attracted and whom you choose to date or marry?

ISSUE 18

Can Sex Be Addictive?

YES: Patrick Carnes, from "Understanding Sexual Addiction," *SIECUS Report* (June/July 2003)

NO: Lawrence A. Siegel and Richard M. Siegel, from "Sex Addiction: Recovering from a Shady Concept," An Original Essay Written for *Taking Sides: Human Sexuality*, 10th edition (2007)

ISSUE SUMMARY

YES: Sexual addiction expert Patrick J. Carnes argues not only that sex can be addictive but that sex can be as addictive as drugs, alcohol, or any other chemical substance.

NO: Sex therapists Lawrence A. Siegel and Richard M. Siegel believe that while some sexual behaviors might be dysfunctional, calling those behaviors "addictive" confuses a moralistic ideology with a scientific fact.

Addiction has become a pervasive feature of modern societies. Of the $666 billion spent for health care in the United States, 25% was spent on health-care problems related to addiction (Kinney, 2003; American Medical Association, 2003). Of the 11 million victims of the violent crimes that are committed each year in the United States, nearly 3 million reported that the offender had been drinking prior to the crime (Greenfield, 1998). Research also suggests that between 6 and 15 million Americans have compulsive shopping behaviors that result in unmanageable debt, bankruptcy, and damaged relationships (Stanford University, 2005). These varied examples demonstrate not only the damage addiction does but also the widely varying meanings it has—from drug addiction to shopping addiction.

Should we add "sex addiction" to the list? Few would dispute that certain chemicals, such as cocaine and even alcohol, merit the addiction label, but is it taking the label too far to consider sexual practices that lead to dysfunction an addiction? The term "addiction" is thought to be derived from the Latin word *addicere*, meaning to adore or to surrender oneself to a master (White, 1998). From this perspective, the term might seem to fit because some people appear to "surrender" themselves to the "master" of sexual games, sexual banter, and sexual intercourse. Indeed, sexuality seems to consume our popular culture.

On the other hand, would not many adolescents (and even our popular culture itself) be considered "addicts" in this sense? What meaning does addiction have if everyone is addicted? Would not everyone be addicted to food in the same sense? Obviously, such questions have great importance for whether something should be treated in psychotherapy.

Widely regarded as an expert on sexual addiction, Patrick J. Carnes has been at the forefront of sexual addiction therapy. Carnes firmly believes that sex can be addictive and dysfunctional sexual practices ought to be treated in therapy. In fact, he promotes the use of a 12-step program, not unlike Alcoholics Anonymous, to help overcome sexual addiction on his Web site, www.sexhelp.com. He justifies this parallel with chemical dependency and treatment because sexual intercourse has a clear physiological component—sexual pleasure. Carnes claims that compulsively seeking sexual stimulation can lead to many negative consequences in an addict's life.

Sex therapists Lawrence A. Siegel and Richard M. Siegel disagree sharply with Carnes's position. In the second article they argue that those who want to call sex addictive have a hidden agenda. Their agenda is to extend society's fairly clear moral condemnation of drug abuse to sexual behaviors. The Siegels ask whether sexual behaviors are not in a different category altogether than drug abuse. If they are, then the unacceptability of drug-related abuse should not be extended to sexual behaviors, at least not in the same way. The Siegels go on to argue that the term "addiction" itself has difficulties. They contend that psychology cannot decide what it means, either to be addicted to something or to have an addictive nature. They conclude by reviewing some of Carnes's early work in sexual addiction, and then they respond to it by attempting to show his moral bias toward any sexual practice other than monogamous intimacy in marriage.

POINT

- Sex can be addictive.

- Sex addiction has physical and chemical components.

- Many deviant sexual behaviors fit the definition of what makes something addictive.

- Sex addicts, like those with eating disorders or alcoholism, cannot control their destructive behavior and need help.

COUNTERPOINT

- Addiction is merely a term for any behavior that falls outside of social norms.

- Chemical dependency should not be confused with mechanisms that drive sexual appetite.

- A consistent clinical definition of "addiction" has not been agreed upon.

- Sexual behavior is an issue of personal responsibility, not personal physiology.

YES

Patrick Carnes

Understanding Sexual Addiction

During the past three decades, professionals have acknowledged that some people use sex to manage their internal distress. These people are similar to compulsive gamblers, compulsive overeaters, or alcoholics in that they are not able to contain their impulses—and with destructive results.

Definition

To facilitate classification and understanding of psychological disorders, mental health professionals rely on the *Diagnostic and Statistical Manual of Mental Disorders* (DSM) published by the American Psychiatric Association and now in its fourth edition.

Each edition of this book represents a consensus at the time of publication about what constitutes mental disorders. Each subsequent edition has reflected changes in understanding. The *DSM's* system is, therefore, best viewed as a "work in progress" rather than the "bible."

The term *sexual addiction* does not appear in *DSM-IV*. In fact, the word *addiction* itself does not appear. It condenses the criteria for addictive disorders—such as substance abuse and pathologic gambling—into three elements:

- *Loss of control (compulsivity).* "There is a persistent desire or unsuccessful efforts to cut down or control substance abuse." "Has persistent unsuccessful efforts to control, cut back, or stop gambling."
- *Continuation despite adverse consequences.* "The substance use is continued despite knowledge of having a persistent or recurrent physical or psychological problem that is likely to have been caused or exacerbated by the substance use." "Has committed illegal acts such as forgery, fraud, theft, or embezzlement to finance gambling."
- *Obsession or preoccupation.* "A great deal of time is spent in activities necessary to obtain the substance, use the substance, or recover from its effects." "Is preoccupied with gambling."[1]

Complex Problem

Typically, individuals in trouble for their sexual behavior are not candid about whatever incident has come to light, nor are they likely to reveal that the specific behavior actually is a part of a consistent, self-destructive pattern. The nature of this illness causes patients to hide the severity of the problem from others, to

From *SIECUS Report*, vol. 31, no. 5, June/July 2003, pp. 5–7. Copyright © 2003 by Sexuality Information and Education Council of the United States. Reprinted by permission of SIECUS.

delude themselves about their ability to control their behavior, and to minimize their impact on others.

Often some event will precipitate a visit to the primary care provider. Sexual excess of some type will create a physical problem. Sexually transmitted diseases, damage to genitals, unwanted pregnancies: all are among the reasons for such a visit. Most patients will say that the event is a unique situation.

The primary care provider will often treat the physical problem without probing for more information. If, however, there is sexual addiction, the problem will not disappear. A wide range of behaviors can be problematic, including compulsive masturbation, affairs, use of pornography, voyeurism, exhibitionism, sexual harassment, and sex offending.

Health care providers must understand that underneath what appears to be an isolated event may be a more complex pathologic problem with a host of related factors such as the following:

- A high incidence of depression and suicide
- The presence of high-risk and dangerous behaviors including self-harm designed to escalate sexual experiences
- The high probability of other addictive behaviors including alcoholism, drug abuse, and pathologic gambling
- Extreme disruption of the family, including battering, sexual abuse, and financial distress

Behaviors

Clinicians should remember that the discovery of something sexual does not make an addictive illness. A long-term affair, for example, would be a problem for a spouse but would not be a compulsive pattern. Likewise, a person with exploitive or violent behavior does not necessarily have an addictive illness.

I have been gathering data on sexual addiction since 1985. In the process, I have found that sexually addictive behavior clusters into 10 distinct types. Patients often will be active in more than one cluster. That is one of the most important lessons of sexual addiction: Patterns exist among behaviors.

The 10 distinctive types of behaviors are:

- *Fantasy sex.* Arousal depends on sexual possibility. The individual neglects responsibilities to engage in fantasy and/or prepare for the next sexual episode.
- *Seductive role sex.* Arousal is based on conquest and diminishes rapidly after the initial contact. It can be heightened by increasing risk and/or number of partners.
- *Voyeuristic sex.* Visual stimulation is used to escape into an obsessive trance. Arousal may be heightened by masturbation or risk (peeping), or violation of boundaries (voyeuristic rape).
- *Exhibitionistic sex.* The individual attracts attention to the body or its sexual parts. Arousal stems from the shock or the interest of the viewer.
- *Paying for sex.* Arousal is connected to payment for sex and, with time, it actually becomes connected to money itself. Payment creates an

entitlement and a sense of power over meeting needs. The arousal starts with "having money" and the search for someone in "the business."

- *Trading sex.* Arousal is based on gaining control of others by using sex as leverage.
- *Intrusive sex.* Arousal occurs by violating boundaries with no repercussions.
- *Anonymous sex.* Arousal involves no seduction or cost and is immediate. It has no entanglements or obligations associated with it and often is accelerated by unsafe or high-risk environments such as parks and restrooms.
- *Pain-exchange sex.* Arousal is built around specific scenarios or narratives of humiliation and shame.
- *Exploitive sex.* Arousal is based on target "types" of vulnerability. Certain types of vulnerable people (such as clients/patients) become the focus.

In addition, in recent years people have begun to use cybersex in unexpected numbers, and many are finding themselves accessing sex in problematic ways.

Individuals suffering from sexual addiction have found sex on the Internet a natural extension of what they are already doing. They can act out any of the previously mentioned 10 types of sexual behavior on the Internet. They can find sex partners, be voyeuristic, start affairs, and swap partners, among other things.

There are also many individuals who never would have experienced sexual compulsive behavior had it not been for the Internet. Consider this:

- About 200 sex-related Web sites are added each day, and there are more than 100,000 existing sites.
- Sex on the Internet constitutes the third largest economic sector on the Web (software and computers rank first and second), generating one billion dollars annually.
- A total of 65 million unique visitors use free porn sites, and 19 million unique visitors use pay porn sites each month.
- Approximately one percent of Internet users have a severe problem that focuses almost exclusively on cybersex, with major neglect of the rest of their life's activities.[2]

Successful Treatment

A number of key factors are involved in successful recovery from sexual addition. They include:

- *A good addiction-oriented primary therapist.* Most successful recoveries involve a relationship with a therapist over a three- to five-year period, the first two years of which are very intense.
- *A 12-step sexual addiction group.* The probability of relapse is extremely high if the addict does not attend meetings.
- *A 12-step program for other addictions.* If the addict has other addictions, a 12-step program is necessary for those as well. A suggestion that

makes things easier is to find a sponsor or sponsors who attends all of the same meetings your patient does. This way, there is a consolidation of relationships.

- *Program work, not just attendance.* Completing step work, finding a sponsor, and doing service are all key elements of recovery. Individuals should become actively involved in the program's activities. In a recent outcome study of an inpatient program for sexual addiction, researchers discovered that only 23 percent actually complete the first nine of the 12 steps in 18 months. However, of those who did, recidivism was rare.[3]
- *Early family involvement.* Family participation in the patient's therapy improves the chance for success.
- *Spiritual support.* Addicts report that the spiritual work started in their 12-step communities and continued in various spiritual communities was critical to the changes they needed to make.
- *Exercise along with good nutrition and a healthy lifestyle.* Addicts who reduce their stress, start an exercise program, and eat more healthfully do better in their recovery.

In discussing what had helped them in their recovery, over 190 sex addicts indicated that these treatments were the most helpful (in order from most to least): a higher power (87 percent); couples 12-step group based on sexual addiction (85 percent); a friend's support (69 percent); individual therapy (65 percent); a celibacy period (64 percent); a sponsor (61 percent); exercise/nutrition (58 percent); a 12-step group based on subjects other than sexual addiction (55 percent); partner support (36 percent); inpatient treatment (35 percent); outpatient group (27 percent); therapy (21 percent); family therapy (11 percent); and after care (hospital) (9 percent).[4]

Healthy Sexuality

The goal of treatment is healthy sexuality. Some therapists insist on a period of celibacy, which does help to reduce chaos and make patients available for therapy. But recovery from sexual addiction does not mean sexual abstinence.

The objective of treatment is to help individuals develop a healthy, strong sexual life. One of the risks is that the patients may slip to a position of sexual aversion, in which they think all sex is bad. Sexual aversion, or "sexual anorexia," is simply another variant of sexual compulsive behavior.

Patients will sometimes bounce from one extreme to the other. True recovery involves a clear understanding about abstaining from certain sexual behaviors combined with an active plan for enhancing sexuality.

Recovery from sexual addiction is likened to recovery from eating disorders. Food is a necessary part of life, and recovery from eating disorders requires defining what is healthy eating and what is not. Similarly, the goal of recovery from sexual addiction is learning what is healthy sexuality for the individual.

Healthy sexuality for most sexually addicted individuals involves not only a change in behavior but also an avoidance of fantasizing about behaviors that are unhealthy. Sexual fantasizing can be healthy, particularly for a reasonably healthy couple that uses their increased excitement to move toward rather than away from the partner. However, sexual imagery that is not respectful of other human beings increases objectification, depersonalization, and destructive bonding based on hostility rather than affection. Asking patients about his or her "sobriety" definition and about the content of fantasies provides clues to help with treatment and recovery.

Keeping Up

To determine how well the patient is doing in establishing a healthy lifestyle, clinicians can ask some simple questions. Does the patient have tools for avoiding relapse during times of hunger, anger, loneliness, and tiredness? Is the patient attending 12-step self-help meetings? If not, what are the obstacles preventing the patient from doing so? What are the patient's perceptions of what goes on at a meeting? Does he or she have a sponsor (a person longer in recovery who can guide the newer member)?

Is the patient seeking a counselor or therapist who is knowledgeable in addiction recovery? Is there balance between work and recreation? Is the patient exercising or engaging in any sports? Is the patient actively working to improve his or her relationship with a spouse or significant other? Is the spouse also attending a self-help meeting? These are all indicators to determine if the individual is fully engaged in building a healthier lifestyle.

Conclusion

The treatment of sexual addiction has taken a long time to gain recognition and respect as an area of medical specialty.

As with other disorders, such as alcoholism or anorexia, clinicians face many challenges in learning about sexual addiction. Most who take time to learn find patients who are profoundly grateful.

In many ways, the field of sexual addiction lags behind both professional and lay awareness of alcoholism or anorexia. Yet, important strides are being made in both understanding and awareness.

Appreciating the issues and challenges of sexual addiction will help clinicians when their patients' behaviors cross the line from problems of judgment to symptoms of a clinical disorder.

All references for articles included in *Taking Sides: Clashing Views on Psychological Issues, 17/e* can be found on the Web at http://www.mhhe.com/cls.

**Lawrence A. Siegel and
Richard M. Siegel**

Sex Addiction: Recovering
from a Shady Concept

It seems, more than ever, that many Americans are more comfortable keeping sex in the dark or, as sex addiction advocates might actually prefer, *in* the shadows. We seem to have gotten no further than the Puritan claims of sex being evil and pleasure being threatening. "The Devil made me do it" seems to be something of a battle cry, especially when someone gets caught cheating on their spouse, having inappropriate dalliances with congressional pages, or visiting prostitutes. Even those not in relationships are easily targeted. We constantly hear about the "dangers" of internet porn and how every internet chat room is just teeming with predators just waiting to devour our children. Daily masturbation is considered by these folks as being unhealthy and a marked pathology. As a society, we seem able to be comfortable with sex only as long as we make it uncomfortable. As one of the leading sexologists, Marty Klein, once wrote:

> "If mass murderer Ted Bundy had announced that watching Cosby Show reruns had motivated his awful crimes, he would have been dismissed as a deranged sociopath. Instead, Bundy proclaimed that his 'pornography addiction' made him do it, and many Right-wing feminists and conservatives treated this as the conclusion of a thoughtful social scientist. Why?"[1]

The whole idea of "sex addiction" is borne out of a moralistic ideology masquerading as science. It is a concept that seems to serve no other purpose than to relegate sexual expression to the level of shameful acts, except within the extremely narrow and myopic scope of a monogamous, heterosexual marriage. Sexual diversity? Interests in unusual forms or frequency of sexual expression? Choosing not to be monogamous? Advocates of "sex addiction" would likely see these as the uncontrollable acts of a sexually pathological individual; one who needs curing.

To be clear, we do not deny the fact that, for some people, sexual behavior can become problematic, even dysfunctional or unmanageable. Our objection is with the use of the term "sexual addiction" to describe a virtually unlimited array of—in fact, practically ANY—aspect of sexual expression that falls outside of the typically Christian view of marriage. We believe that the term contributes to a generally sex-negative, pleasure-phobic tone in American society, and it also tends to "pathologize" most forms of sexual expression that fall outside of a narrow view of what "normal" sex is supposed to look like. This is a point made clear by sex addiction advocates' own rhetoric. Three of the guiding principles of Sexaholics Anonymous include the notion that (1) sex is most healthy in the context of a monogamous, heterosexual relationship; (2) sexual expression has "obvious" limits; and (3) it is unhealthy to engage in any sexual activity for the sole purpose of feeling better, either emotionally or to escape one's problems. These principles do not represent either science or most people's experience. They, in fact, represent a restrictive and repressive view of sex and sexuality and reflect an arrogance that sex addiction proponents are the keepers of the scepter of morality and normalcy. Moreover, the concept of "sex addiction" comes out of a shame-based, arbitrarily judgmental addiction model and does not speak to the wide range of sexual diversity; both in and outside the context of a committed relationship.

A primary objection to the use of the term "sex addiction," an objection shared with regard to other supposed behavioral "addictions," is that the term *addiction* has long ago been discredited. Back in 1964, the World Health Organization (WHO) declared the term "addiction" to be clinically invalid and recommended in favor of dependence, which can exist in varying degrees of severity, as opposed to an all-or-nothing disease entity (as it is still commonly perceived).[2] This is when we began to see the terms *chemical dependency* and *substance abuse*, terms considered to be much more appropriate and clinically useful. This, however, did not sit well with the addiction industry. Another objection to the concept of "sex addiction" is that it is a misnomer whose very foundation as a clinically significant diagnosis is built on flawed and faulty premises. For example, a common assertion put forth by proponents of sex addiction states that the chemical actions in the brain during sexual activity are the same as the chemical activity involved in alcohol and drug use. They, therefore, claim that both sexual activity and substance abuse share reward and reinforcement mechanisms that produce the "craving" and "addictive" behaviors. This assertion is flawed on several levels, not the least of which is that it is based on drawing conclusions from brain scan imaging that are devoid of any real interpretive foundation; a "leap of faith," so to speak. Furthermore, it is somewhat of a stretch to equate the neurophysiological mechanisms which underlie chemical dependency, tolerance, and withdrawal with the underlying mechanisms of what is most often obsessive-compulsive or anxiety-reducing behaviors like gambling, shopping, and sex. Another example often cited by sex addiction proponents is the assertion that, like alcohol and drugs, the "sex addict" is completely incapable of controlling his or her self-destructive behavior. Of course, this begs the question of how, then, can one change behavior they are incapable of controlling? More importantly, however, is the unique excuse this "disease" model provides for abdicating personal responsibility. "It's not my fault, I have a disease." Finally, a major assertion put out by sex addiction advocates is that anyone who is hypersexual in any way (e.g., frequent masturbation, anonymous "hook ups," infidelity, and cybersex) must have been abused as children or adolescents. Again, the flaws here are obvious and serve to continue to relegate any type of frequent sexual engagement to the pathological and unseemly.

Every clinician knows that "addiction" is not a word that appears any-where in the *Diagnostic and Statistical Manual,* or "DSM," the diagnostic guide-book used by psychiatrists and psychologists to make any psychopathological diagnosis. Nor does it appear in any of the International Classification of Diseases (ICD-10), codes used for classifying medical diagnoses. "Abuse" and "dependence" do appear in the DSM, relevant only to substance use patterns, but "addiction" does not. Similarly, there is an ICD-10 code for "substance dependence," but not addiction. Why? Perhaps because the word means different things to differ-ent people, especially when used in so many different contexts. Even without acknowledging the many trivial uses of the addiction concept, such as bumper stickers that proclaim, *"addicted to sports, not drugs,"* cookies that claim to be *"deli-ciously addicting,"* Garfield coffee mugs that warn *"don't talk to me until after my first cup,"* or T-shirts that say *"chocoholic,"* there aren't even consistent *clinical* definitions for the concept of addiction. A 1993 study, published in the *American Journal of Drug and Alcohol Abuse,* compared the diagnostic criteria for substance abuse and dependence between the DSM and ICD-10. The results showed very little agreement between the two.[3]

Pharmacologists, researchers who study the effects of drugs, define addic-tion primarily based on the presence of tolerance and withdrawal. Both of these phenomena are based on pharmacological and toxicological concepts of "cellular adaptation," wherein the body, at the very cellular level, becomes accustomed to the constant presence of a substance, and readjusts for "nor-mal" function; in other words, whatever the "normal" response was before regular use of the substance began returns. This adaptation first accounts for tolerance, wherein an increasing dose of the substance to which the system has adapted is needed to maintain the same level of "normal." Then it results in withdrawal, wherein any discontinuation of the substance disrupts the "new" equilibrium the system has achieved and symptoms of "withdrawal sickness" ensue. This is probably most often attributed to addiction to opiates, such as heroin, because of its comparison to "having a monkey on one's back," with a constantly growing appetite, and its notorious "cold turkey" withdrawal. But perhaps it is most commonly observed with the chronic use of drugs with less sinister reputations, such as caffeine, nicotine or alcohol.

Traditional psychotherapists may typically define addiction as a faulty coping mechanism, or more accurately, the *result* of using a faulty coping mechanism to deal with some underlying issue. Another way to consider this is to see addiction as the symptom, rather than the disease, which is why the traditional therapist, of any theoretical orientation, is likely to want to find the causative issue or issues, and either teach the patient more effective coping mechanisms or resolve the unresolved issue(s) altogether.

Another definition of addiction has emerged, and seems to have taken center-stage, since the development of a pseudo-medical specialty known as "addictionology" within the last twenty or so years. Made up primarily of physicians, but including a variety of "addiction professionals," this field has helped to forge a treatment industry based on the disease model of addiction that is at the core of 12-Step "fellowships," such as Alcoholics Anonymous and Narcotics Anonymous. Ironically, despite the resistance to medical or psychiatric treatment historically expressed in AA or NA, their philosophy has become the mainstay of the addictionological paradigm.

If the concept of chemical addictions, which have a neurophysiological basis that can be measured and observed, yields no clinical consensus, how, then, can we legitimize the much vaguer notion that individuals can be "addicted" to behavior, people, emotions, or even one's own brain chemistry? Other than to undermine responsibility and self-determination, we really can't. It does a tremendous disservice to our clients and patients to brand them with a label so full of judgment, arbitrary opinion, and fatuous science. It robs individuals of the ability to find their own levels of comfort and, ultimately, be the determining force in directing their own lives. There is a significant and qualitative difference between the person who acts because he or she can't (not a choice, but a position of default) and the person who is empowered to choose not to. As clinicians, we should be loathe to send our clients and patients down such a fearful, shameful road.

In 1989, Patrick Carnes, founder of the sex addiction movement, wrote a book entitled *"Contrary to Love."* The book is rife with rhetoric and personal ideology that reveals Carnes's lack of training, knowledge, and understanding of sexuality and sexual expression; not surprising for someone whose background is solely in the disease model of alcoholism. This, while seemingly a harsh judgment, is clearly reflected in his Sex Addiction Screening Test (SAST). Even a cursory glance at the items on the SAST show a deep-seeded bias against most forms of sexual expression. Unlike other legitimate screening and assessment tools, there is no scientific foundation that would show this tool to be credible (i.e., tests of reliability and validity). Instead, Carnes developed this "test" by simply culling his own ideas from his book. Annie Sprinkle, America's first adult-film-star-turned-PhD-Sexologist, has written a very good web article on the myth of sex addiction. In it, she also describes some of the shortcomings of the SAST. While not describing the complete test here, a listing of some of the assessment questions are listed below, along with commentary.[4]

1. *Have you subscribed to sexually explicit magazines like* Playboy *or* Penthouse? This question is based on the assumption that it is unhealthy to view images of naked bodies. Does that mean that the millions of people who subscribe to or buy adult magazines are sex addicts? Are adolescent boys who look at the *Sports Illustrated* Swim Suit edition budding sex addicts? By extension, if looking at Playboy or Penthouse is unhealthy and pathological, then those millions of people who look at hardcore magazines or Internet porn should be hospitalized!

2. *Do you often find yourself preoccupied with sexual thoughts?* This is totally nebulous. What does "preoccupied" mean? How often does one have to think about sex in order to constitute preoccupation? Research has shown that men, on average, think about sex every eight seconds; does that mean that men are inherently sex addicts?

3. *Do you feel that your sexual behavior is not normal?* What is normal? What do they use as a comparison? As sexologists, we can state unequivocally that the majority of people's sexual concerns relate, in one way or another, to the question "Am I normal?" This is incredibly vague, nebulous, and laughably unscientific.

4. *Are any of your sexual activities against the law?* This question is also steeped in a bias that there is only a narrowly acceptable realm of sexual expression. It assumes that any sexual behavior that is against the law is bad. Is being or engaging a prostitute a sign of pathology? What about the fact that oral sex, anal sex, and woman on top are illegal in several states?

5. *Have you ever felt degraded by your sexual behavior?* Again, there is a serious lack of quantification here. Does regretting a sexual encounter constitute feeling degraded? Does performing oral sex for your partner, even though you think it's degrading, constitute a pathology or compromise? What if one's partner does something during sex play that is unexpected and perceived as degrading (like ejaculating on someone's face or body)? What if someone enjoys feeling degraded? This question pathologizes at least half of the S/M and B/D communities. Moreover, anyone who has had a long and active sexual life may likely, at one point, have felt degraded. It is important to note that this question does not ask if one consistently puts oneself in a position of being degraded but, rather, have you ever felt degraded. We suspect that most people can lay claim to that.

6. *Has sex been a way for you to escape your problems?* Is there a better way to escape one's problems temporarily? This is a common bias used against both sex and alcohol use: using sex or alcohol to provide relief from anxieties or problems is inherently problematic. It also begs the question: why are things like sex and alcohol not appropriate to change how one is feeling but Zoloft, Paxil, Xanax, and Klonopin are? The truth of the matter is that sex is often an excellent and healthy way to occasionally experience relief from life's stressors and problems.

7. *When you have sex, do you feel depressed afterwards?* Sex is often a great way to get in touch with one's feelings. Oftentimes, people do feel depressed after a sexual experience, for any number of reasons. Furthermore, this doesn't mean that sex was the depressing part! Perhaps people feel depressed because they had dashed expectations of the person they were involved with. Unfulfilled expectations, lack of communication, and inattentiveness to one's needs and desires often result in post-coital feelings of sadness and disappointment. In addition, asking someone if they "feel depressed" is arbitrary, subjective, and clinically invalid.

8. *Do you feel controlled by your sexual desire?* Again, we are being asked to make an arbitrary, subjective, and clinically invalid assessment. There is an undercurrent here that seems to imply that a strong sexual desire is somehow not normal. Human beings are biologically programmed to strongly desire sex. Our clients and patients might be better served if we addressed not their desires, but how and when they act upon them.

Again, it needs noting that the concept of "sex addiction" is one with very little clinical relevance or usefulness, despite it's popularity. Healthy sexual expression encompasses a wide array of forms, functions, and frequency, as well as myriad emotional dynamics and personal experiences. Healthy behavior, in general, and sexual behavior, in particular, exists on a continuum rather than a quantifiable point. Using the addiction model to describe sexual behavior simply adds to the shame and stigma that is already too often attached to various forms of sexual expression. Can sexual behaviors become problematic? Most certainly. However, we must be careful to not overpathologize even problematic sexual behaviors because, most often, they are symptomatic expressions rather than primary problems.

For many years, sexologists have described compulsive sexual behavior, where sexual obsessions and compulsions are recurrent, distressing, and interfere with daily functioning. The actual number of people suffering from this type of sexual problem is relatively small. Compulsive sexual behaviors are generally divided into two broad categories: *paraphilic* and *non-paraphilic*.[5] Paraphilias are defined as recurrent, intensely arousing fantasies, sexual urges, or behaviors involving non-human objects, pain and humiliation, or children.[6] Paraphilic behaviors are usually non-conventional forms of sexual expression that, in the extreme, can be harmful to relationships and individuals. Some examples of paraphilias listed in the DSM are pedophilia (sexual attraction to children), exhibitionism (exposing one's genitals in public), voyeurism (sexual excitement from watching an unsuspecting person), sexual sadism (sexual excitement from dominating or inflicting pain), sexual masochism (sexual excitement from being dominated or receiving pain), transvestic fetishism (sexual excitement from wearing clothes of the other sex), and frotteurism (sexual excitement from rubbing up against or fondling an unsuspecting person). All of these behaviors exist on a continuum of healthy fantasy play to dangerous, abusive, and illegal acts. A sexologist is able to view these behaviors in varying degrees, knowing the difference between teacher-student fantasy role play and cruising a playground for victims; between provocative exhibitionist displays (including public displays of affection) and illegal, abusive public exposure. For those with a "sex addiction" perspective, simply having paraphilic thoughts or desires of any kind is reason to brand the individual a "sex addict."

The other category of compulsive sexual behavior is non-paraphilic, and generally involves more conventional sexual behaviors which, when taken to the extreme, cause marked distress and interference with daily functioning. This category includes a fixation on an unattainable partner, compulsive masturbation, compulsive love relationships, and compulsive sexuality in a relationship. The most vocal criticism of the idea of compulsive sexual behavior as a clinical disorder appears to center on the overpathologizing of these behaviors. Unless specifically trained in sexuality, most clinicians are either uncomfortable or unfamiliar with the wide range of "normal" sexual behavior and fail to distinguish between individuals who experience conflict between their values and sexual behavior, and those with obsessive sexual behavior.[7] When diagnosing compulsive sexual behavior overall, there is little consensus even among sexologists. However, it still provides a more useful clinical framework for the professional trained in sexuality and sexual health.

To recognize that sexual behavior can be problematic is not the same as labeling the behaviors as "sexually compulsive" or "sexual addiction." The reality is that sexual problems are quite common and are usually due to non-pathological factors. Quite simply, people make mistakes (some more than others). People also act impulsively. People don't always make good sexual choices. When people do make mistakes, act impulsively, and make bad decisions, it often negatively impacts their relationships; sometimes even their lives. Moreover, people do often use sex as a coping mechanism or, to borrow from addiction language, medicating behavior that can become problematic. However, this is qualitatively different from the concept that problematic sexual behavior means the individual is a "sexual addict" with uncontrollable urges and potentially dangerous intent. Most problematic sexual behavior can be effectively redirected (and cured) through psycho-sexual education, counseling, and experience. According to proponents of "sex addiction," problematic sexual behavior cannot be cured. Rather, the "sex addict" is destined for a life of maintaining a constant vigil to prevent the behavior from reoccurring, often to the point of obsession, and will be engaged in a lifelong process of recovery. Unfortunately, this view often causes people to live in fear of the "demon" lurking around every corner: themselves.

All references for articles included in *Taking Sides: Clashing Views on Psychological Issues, 17/e* can be found on the Web at http://www.mhhe.com/cls.

CHALLENGE QUESTIONS

Can Sex Be Addictive?

1. The Siegels see the "diagnosis" of sexual addiction as having a moral basis. Are there other, more conventional diagnoses in the *DSM-IV* that might also be viewed in this manner? If so, what implications would this have for those diagnoses?
2. Examine some of the addiction literature and see what other definitions of "addiction" there might be. What might those definitions imply about the possibility of a sexual addiction? Support your answer.
3. Imagine you are working with a couple in therapy and the husband frequently views pornography. What possible dangers could his behavior present? Should his habit be considered a sexual addiction? Support your answer.
4. What is involved in the process of a 12-step program? How well do these programs address the specific issues involved in sex addiction? What might the Siegels criticize about the application of the Alcoholics Anonymous model to sex?
5. Compare and contrast the physiological mechanisms underlying chemical addiction with the physiological mechanisms underlying sexual stimulation. Are they similar as Carnes seems to believe?
6. What is "healthy sex"? Who should get to define it? Would what is considered "healthy" sexual practices be different for a (recovering) sex addict?

ISSUE 19

Does Birth Order Predict Intelligence?

YES: R. B. Zajonc and Frank J. Sulloway, from "The Confluence Model: Birth Order as a Within-Family or Between-Family Dynamic?" *Personality and Social Psychology Bulletin* (vol. 33, no. 9, pp. 1187–1194, 2007)

NO: Aaron L. Wichman, Joseph Lee Rodgers, and Robert C. MacCallum, from "Birth Order Has No Effect on Intelligence: A Reply and Extension of Previous Findings," *Personality and Social Psychology Bulletin* (vol. 33, no. 9, pp. 1195–1200, 2007)

ISSUE SUMMARY

YES: R. B. Zajonc (deceased), professor of psychology at Stanford University, and Frank J. Sulloway, adjunct professor in the Department of Psychology at the University of California, Berkeley, maintain that due to available resources, earlier-born children have higher IQ.

NO: Aaron L. Wichman, assistant professor of psychology at Western Kentucky University, Joseph Lee Rodgers, professor of psychology at the University of Oklahoma, and Robert C. MacCallum, professor of psychology at the University of North Carolina–Chapel Hill, argue that the birth-order effect on intelligence does not hold when comparing siblings within a single family.

Ever wonder how much the order of your birth has affected you? In case you've never heard of the birth-order phenomenon, there are many psychologists who contend that your chronological placement among your siblings may even influence whether you win the Nobel Prize. Researchers have claimed that firstborns are more likely to be conscientious and dutiful than their younger siblings (Badger & Reddy, 2009), less likely to be arrested (Zweigenhaft & Von Ammon, 2000), and likely to have more conflict with their parents (Whiteman, McHale, & Crouter, 2003). The problem, however, is that these claims are not always supported by studies of birth order and its effects. As strong as the birth-order phenomenon seems to be in some studies, it appears to wash out or not show up in other studies. In other words, some-times the association of high achievement with earlier birth order is quite clear, and other times there is no association (Burton, 1968; Paulhus, Trapnell, & Chen, 1999). What is going on?

Many of the recent studies and discussions have focused on what factors could answer this question. The findings are puzzling, because they are both inconsistent and persistent. Explanations of the birth-order phenomenon have focused on the constraints that more children place on family resources, such as money and time. Raising one child takes less money and less time than raising two. Could differences in these resources explain the inconsisten-cies in research results? Other factors are also considered to mediate the birth-order effect on intelligence. Researchers have examined socioeconomic status, family size, maternal age and educational attainment, social ranking within the family, and gestational factors (Kristensen & Bjerkedal, 2007). Perhaps the most prominently cited reason for the discrepancy between birth-order claims is that the studies themselves are afflicted with problems, such as investigator bias or lack of experimental control (Adams, 1972). The YES and NO selections represent what many psychological researchers view as the major disagree-ment about the way birth-order studies are conducted and the consequential disparity in their results.

Zajonc and Sulloway clearly consider the birth-order effect to be real. They claim that even after controlling for other factors, such as family size and socioeconomic status, birth order makes a meaningful contribution to intelligence. Their "confluence model" attributes this effect to family dynamics, which provide an advantageous intellectual environment for the first-born in terms of parental attention and opportunities to tutor younger siblings. Arguing that the analyses of nearly all the large datasets support the birth-order effect on intelligence, they illustrate the problems with smaller datasets, such as those from an earlier study conducted by Wichman, Rodgers, and MacCallum (2006). For example, Zajonc and Sulloway claim that the Wichman et al. sample is heavily skewed toward younger children where the birth-order effect is least likely to show up. They also claim that a more balanced sample may have been the difference between statistical significance and nonsignificance, the criterion that determines disciplinary credibility.

Wichman, Rodgers, and MacCallum—the authors of the study originally criticized by Zajonc and Sulloway—argue in the NO selection that a host of misleading research studies have fostered the misconception of the birth-order phenomenon. They contend that the problem is due to analyzing the relation-ship between birth order and IQ without considering the effect of factors that vary from family to family. They illustrate this point by first analyzing family data without considering any factors that vary across families. This analysis produces a significant birth order/intelligence correlation, which is a miscon-ception from their perspective. They next analyze the same data but include a factor that varies from family to family, the mother's IQ. Including this factor, they contend, changes the relationship between birth order and intelligence so that no significant correlation is found. Wichman et al. then argue not only that this re-analysis is the more appropriate analysis but also that the first analysis is completely misleading birth-order researchers such as Zajonc and Sulloway.

References

Adams, B. N. (1972). Birth order: A critical review. *Sociometry, 35*(3), 411–439. doi: 10.2307/2786503

Badger, J., & Reddy, P. (2009). The effects of birth order on personality traits and feelings of academic sibling rivalry. *Psychology Teaching Review, 15*(1), 45–54.

Burton, D. (1968). Birth order and intelligence. *The Journal of Social Psychology, 76*(2), 199–206.

Kristensen, P., & Bjerkedal, T. (2007). Explaining the relation between birth order and intelligence. *Science, 316*(5832). doi: 10.1126/science.1141493

Paulhus, D. L., Trapnell, P. D., & Chen, D. (1999). Birth order effects on personality and achievement within families. *Psychological Science, 10*(6), 482–488. doi: 10.1111/1467-9280.00193

Whiteman, S. D., McHale, S. M., & Crouter, A. C. (2003). What parents learn from experience: The first child as a first draft? *Journal of Marriage and Family, 65*(3), 608–621. doi: 10.1111/j.1741-3737.2003.00608.x

Wichman, A. L., Rodgers, J., & MacCallum, R. C. (2006). A multilevel approach to the relationship between birth order and intelligence. *Personality and Social Psychology Bulletin, 32*(1), 117–127. doi: 10.1177/0146167205279581

Zweigenhaft, R. L., & Von Ammon, J. (2000). Birth order and civil disobedience: A test of Sulloway's "born to rebel" hypothesis. *The Journal of Social Psychology, 140*(5), 624–627. doi: 10.1080/00224540009600502

POINT	COUNTERPOINT
• Multiple studies show that earlier-born children have higher intelligence.	• These studies do not differentiate between within-family and between-family variables.
• Even when controlling for variables between families, nearly all large data-sets support the birth-order effect.	• Regardless of sample size, analyses that control for between-family variables reduce the supposed birth-order effect.
• The Wichman et al. study sample is skewed so that the birth-order effect is less likely to appear.	• The skewness of the Wichman et al. sample is representative of the actual U.S. population, not a problem of study design.
• Even the data from the Wichman et al. study nearly support the birth-order effect.	• The birth-order effect is a proxy for many other variables existing between families.

YES

R. B. Zajonc and
Frank J. Sulloway

The Confluence Model: Birth Order as a Within-Family or Between-Family Dynamic?

Arecent article by Wichman, Rodgers, and MacCallum (2006) claims to have decisively shown that the typical birth-order effects on intellectual performance found in hundreds of studies are not a function of within-family factors but are the consequence of between-family influences. They argue that:

> If the birth order effect is primarily a within-family . . . phenomenon, then accounting for between-family . . . variance should have little influence on the effect. However, if the birth order effect is primarily due to factors varying between families, then the addition of a *between-*family variable could reduce or even eliminate the effect. (p. 124)

That between-family variable is mother's age at birth of the first child. The authors ran three regression analyses on 3,671 children. In two analyses—one without external controls and another with a partial control of participants' age—Wichman et al. did obtain significant birth-order differences on three measures of cognitive performance. In a third, "critical" (Wichman et al., 2006, p. 124) analysis, mother's age at birth of the first child enters into the regression equation. That analysis renders birth-order effects not significant on all three measures, although two of these measures remain near significance.

There is nothing wrong with the logic of this argument, and Wichman et al.'s (2006) efforts to devise an innovative within-family methodology represent a useful addition to existing research. Wichman et al., however, are virtually unique in having mitigated birth-order effects by adding a between-family control. Nearly all other large datasets (which are mostly uncited by these authors) retain their typical birth-order patterns even when exogenous between-family factors are introduced. Thus, the pioneering study by Belmont and Marolla (1973), with an *N* of 386,114, divided its population of Dutch 19-year-old individuals into nonmanual, manual, and farm subgroups. Significant birth-order effects remained, as they also did when these data were stratified by the number of children in the family. Because the number of children in the family is closely related to the age of the mother at first birth, one would expect, according to the Wichman et al. thesis, that birth-order effects would

Zajonc, R. B.; Sulloway, Frank J. From *Personality and Social Psychology Bulletin*, vol. 33, no. 9, 2007, pp. 1187–1194. Copyright © 2007 by Sage Publications—JOURNALS. Reprinted by permission via Rightslink.

be substantially diluted when controlled for family size. The literature shows that they are not (Belmont and Marolla, 1973; Breland, 1974; Claudy, Gross, & Strause, 1974; Davis, Cahan, & Bashi, 1977; Zajonc, 1983). The same result is true of a large dataset published by the French Institute of Demographic Studies (Gille et al., 1954, pp. 55–58). Their sample of 65,250 children, 6 to 14 years old, consisted of professional and executive levels ($N = 1,325$), small businesses ($N = 7,289$), clerical ($N = 14,527$), skilled workers ($N = 17,160$), farmers ($N = 3,733$), special workers ($N = 8,255$), and farm workers ($N = 12,961$). Overall intellectual performance declined with lower socioeconomic status (SES) levels, but within each SES level, intellectual performance also systematically declined with birth order and family size. Adding a significant between-family control therefore had no effect on birth-order differences. A similar pattern of results was obtained by Claudy et al. (1974). These researchers stratified their project talent sample of American 12-year-old students ($N = 81,175$) into five socioeconomic categories. Data from each SES group showed identical patterns of declining scores by birth order.

There are also 41,482 data points from Scotland (Scottish Council for Research on Education, 1949), 3,418 from England (Douglas, 1964), and 36,000 from Columbia (Velandia, Grandon, & Page, 1978) that conform to these patterns. All of these results are extensively discussed by Zajonc (1983) but are ignored by Wichman et al. (2006). Also ignored by them is the classic within-family study by Tabah and Sutter (1954a, pp. 97–138) that obtained birth-order effects on 1,244 sibling pairs.

A particularly impressive study examined 127,902 Norwegian 18- and 19-year-olds from the same families (Bjerkedal, Kristensen, Skjeret, and Bervik, in press). In this study, IQ declined significantly with increasing birth rank. The reported disparity between firstborns and secondborns was 2.3 IQ points. These findings were nearly identical to those obtained by the same researchers in a large between-family analysis ($N = 112,799$). In another study based on this same Norwegian sample, Kristensen and Bjerkedal (2007) found that IQ corresponded with how subjects were raised—taking into account the early death of older siblings—rather than with how subjects were born, and these results also appear to rule out a biological (gestational) explanation. Such findings are scarcely compatible with the hypothesis that birth order effects are spurious and derive from uncontrolled differences between families (Sulloway, 2007b).

Now, why did Wichman et al. (2006) fail to find birth-order effects when they introduced mother's age at the birth of her first offspring into their regression equation? Maternal age does influence family size, and it is also correlated with SES. But how exactly would these factors dilute within-family differences in birth order? Wichman et al. asserted that they "expected that maternal age values would be positively associated with child intelligence" (p. 121), given that older mothers are more likely to be career oriented, to value education, and to foster educational achievement in their children. Women in their sample who have a first child at a later age, Wichman et al. implied, are likely to raise the intelligence scores of firstborns relative to children of higher birth orders because such women tend to have smaller families than do other women and perhaps also value education more highly. This argument rests partly on the premise that birth-order patterns vary substantially with family size—a premise that the vast birth-order literature does not support.

Wichman et al.'s (2006) failure to obtain birth-order effects when maternal age is introduced into the equation can also be attributed to their problematic study design. First, the participant population sample in Wichman et al.'s analysis is seriously skewed by family size. Second, the number of mothers (and their within-family offspring) is perfectly correlated with this skew in family size. In the younger cohort, there are 1,329 mothers with one child in the study, 259 mothers with two children, 17 mothers with three children, and, *nota bene*, just 1 mother with four children. Among the older participants, there is also just 1 mother of four offspring. At the level of participants, rather than mothers, 50% of the sample are firstborns but only 14% are thirdborns and 4% are fourthborns. In addition, owing to the peculiar distribution of the sample, only 34% of the participants constitute a within-family comparison.

The more critical methodological issue, however, is why the mean scores by birth order are not statistically significant when Wichman et al. (2006) introduced maternal age at first birth as a control. A closer look at the data indicates that the search for statistical significance is obscuring a much more important conclusion from this study, namely, that the mean differences between birth ranks in the controlled data are close to what would be expected given the nature of the sample and the specific cognitive tests included in their study. Table 5 of Wichman et al.'s study shows that differences in reading recognition involve a mean decrease of 0.85 points per increase in birth rank, from 103.17 to 100.61. Similarly, the mean decrease in reading comprehension scores by birth rank is 0.72, from 104.35 to 102.19. (To put these differences in perspective, they represent 62% of the highly significant differences observed in the magnitude of the β_{1-4} scores reported in Wichman et al.'s Table 3 before controlling for cohort effects and for mother's age at the birth of her first child.) Only the scores in mathematics exhibit a trend in the opposite direction (there is a negligible increase of 0.12 points in the mean scores by birth rank, from 99.11 to 99.46).

Typically, however, larger differences by birth order and family size are found in language-related tests than in mathematics tests (Ernst & Angst, 1983). These aggregate findings reflect the richer verbal environment that, according to the confluence model, older children are expected to experience within the family. Also important to note is that birth-order differences in most intellectual test scores involve a decline of about one IQ point per birth rank. In the study by Wichman et al. (2006), the mean decrease by birth rank in the two reading scores is 0.79 points, or a total of 2.4 points between the firstborn and the fourthborn after controlling for mother's age at the birth of her first child. In addition, it can be seen from Wichman et al.'s Table 5 that these differences are nearly statistically significant, suggesting that these findings reflect inadequate statistical power to test the expected results rather than a refutation of the confluence model. This lack of statistical power is aggravated, moreover, by the skewed distribution of the data, which underrepresents precisely those birth ranks that are expected to exert the greatest influence on the statistical results. (There are only 158 fourthborns and 507 thirdborns in Wichman et al.'s sample, compared with 1,162 secondborns and 1,844 firstborns.)

In addition, in analyses that are controlled for the critical role of the mother's age at the birth of her first offspring, Wichman et al. (2006) tested the rather uninteresting hypothesis that scores by birth order would differ from one another in some indeterminate way. This test is decidedly not a test of the confluence model, and it is also not the recommended way to test any hypothesis about predicted trends (Rosenthal, Rosnow, & Rubin, 2000). Instead, Wichman et al. should have employed focused comparisons to test the expected results, namely, that scores by birth rank would be successively different. . . .

As we have noted, the sample sizes in Wichman et al.'s (2006) study diminish in direct proportion to the observed birth-order differences, thereby underestimating the effects that might have been observed in a more balanced sample with the same means and variances. For reading comprehension scores, the resulting power loss is a substantial 66% (Rosenthal et al., 2003, Equation 3.25) had the sample sizes for each birth-order group been equal (keeping the total N unchanged), $t_{contrast}$ would have been 4.82, $p = .00001$, yielding $r_{contrast} = .09$—nearly twice the effect size obtained from the unbalanced sample ($r_{contrast} = .05$). In short, Wichman et al.'s (2006) unbalanced study design appears to substantially underestimate the effect sizes and hence the statistical significance of the birth-order trends inherent in their data.

We have performed the same series of contrast analyses for reading recognition scores. To summarize these results, all of the values for Z and $t_{contrast}$ are statistically significant, and the effect sizes computed using these differing methods agree closely. In addition, the results derived from a balanced research design would have yielded a substantially larger effect compared with the unbalanced sample ($r_{contrast} = .08$ versus $r_{contrast} = .05$). Hence, when analyzed by the method of contrasts, the scores for both reading tests yield significant differences by birth order and also exhibit effect sizes similar to those found in other large, between-family studies. Although these findings are consistent with the confluence model's predictions about intellectual performance, they are also consonant with other explanations of how birth order affects intellectual ability, including theories based on sibling differences in family niches and differences in parental investment (Hertwig, Davis, & Sulloway, 2002).

There are at least three other reasons why the Wichman et al. (2006) study fails to document statistically significant birth-order effects. First, their study appears to include an unknown number of only children, who are not expected to exhibit as high scores on intelligence tests as are firstborns with younger siblings, owing to the teaching function that a younger sibling provides for the firstborn in the family (Zajonc, 1976) as well as higher rates of single-parent households among families with only children (Ernst & Angst, 1983). Second, the sample is limited to children up to the age of 14, around the point where the confluence model predicts that the scores of firstborns have begun to outstrip those of laterborns, owing to the dynamics of how the confluence model actually relates to the family's intellectual environment. If children are tested for birth-order effects at the same age, then necessarily the younger child in a two-child family will experience a more favorable intellectual environment at that age than the older child had. Thus, for example, when two siblings born 3 years apart are both tested at 7 years of age, the environment of the younger will encompass a 10-year-old sibling, whereas the environment of the older will encompass a less mature 4-year-old sibling (Zajonc, Markus, & Markus, 1979, pp. 1333–1336). According to the confluence model, it is only as children approach adulthood that the intellectual superiority of higher birth ranks finally manifests itself in a distinct manner as older children finally achieve maximum benefit from their efforts at teaching what they have learned to younger siblings. The confluence model is also consistent with the argument that older siblings act as surrogate parents within the family system and thereby attempt to increase parental investment by occupying a responsible and adult-like family niche, which typically includes efforts to do well in scholastic pursuits (Sulloway, 1996, 2007a, 2007b). These two complementary family dynamics also explain why only children generally score at a lower level than do firstborns of two. The cumulative benefits of teaching and surrogate parenting more generally are presumably why the data analyzed by Belmont and Marolla (1973), which included only 19-year-old individuals, produced such clear and consistent patterns of birth-order and family-size differences for nearly 400,000 individuals. They reported a significance level at $p < 10^{-15}$, controlled for sibship size and social class. If such differences were merely artifacts of uncontrolled maternal age, one would not have expected the extensive data published by Belmont and Marolla to have produced such systematic birth-order differences, after being controlled for sibship size and socioeconomic status, given that these two variables are consistently correlated with mother's age at first birth.

This prediction about the reversal of birth-order effects with age, which is made by the confluence model, brings up a third important point. A number of studies have failed to obtain the typical birth-order effects (reviewed in Zajonc, 2001; Zajonc et al., 1979). These studies are almost all conducted on children under the age of 12 and are thus congruent with the predictions of the confluence model.

Bearing in mind this information about the ages of the subjects in Wichman et al.'s (2006) study and how age relates to the confluence model, it is now relevant to note that Wichman et al. combined their two samples (of 7- and 8-year-old and 13- and 14-year-old children) in all of their statistical analyses, thereby obscuring the important fact that laterborns are expected to have slightly higher test scores than are firstborns at the younger age. Given the mean age of their combined sample (10.4 years), their results closely match the trends observed in other studies. That is to say, in younger samples laterborns tend to outstrip firstborns, and in older samples firstborns tend to outstrip laterborns. In general, the crossover age is predicted to be 11 ±2 years (Zajonc & Mullally, 1997). It should be noted, however, that exactly when this crossover point is reached in any given dataset depends on the age spacing between offspring as well as family size—matters that are not addressed by Wichman et al. (Zajonc, 1983; Zajonc et al., 1979).

[B]ased on 51 samples involving more than 150,000 observations, it can . . . be seen that Wichman et al. (2006) could hardly have picked a more inappropriate set of subjects with which to conduct their "critical" tests of the confluence model. For a sample with an average age of 10.4 years, laterborns are actually expected to have slightly higher scores than are firstborns by about 0.07 standard deviation units, although additional data on age spacing and family size would be required to make an accurate prediction for this particular dataset. More to the point, Wichman et al.'s results are close to the regression line for the overall trend, which is statistically significant for the 51 samples ($r = .63$, $p < .001$).

Significant also are previously published one- and two-child family data (Zajonc, 2001; Zajonc et al., 1979) for a large sample ($N = 33,339$) collected by the Institut National d'Études Démographiques (1973). This is quite clear in demonstrating three important features of family dynamics, predicted by the confluence model, as they change with age. First, at an early age, the secondborn is ahead of the firstborn in intellectual performance. Second, beginning at ages 8 and 9, the firstborn starts surpassing the younger sibling. Third, the only child does not benefit from the teaching function. Hence, he or she has a lower score than either of the children in two-child families except at the very youngest age, when there is less opportunity for instructing siblings. (This only-child disparity may also reflect a higher rate of single-parent households among people with one child.)

Of even greater relevance are within-family sibling data published by Tabah and Sutter (1954b). Using a sample of 1,244 two-child families, they found second-born children 9 years and younger to score higher than first-borns on the French intellectual performance test (standard scores of −.175 vs. −.003 for firstborn and secondborn children, respectively). Siblings older than 9 years, however, manifested the opposite trend. The scores of the firstborns were higher than those of the secondborns (.048 vs. .036). Zajonc et al. (1979) found the above interaction to be significant ($F[1, 2476] = 6.65$, $p < .01$). This age-dependence of birth-order effects found in within-family data is parallel to the aggregate two-child family data. Although Wichman et al. (2006) alluded to a small number of other within-family studies that show no significant birth-order effects, these other studies, like that by Wichman et al., involve modest sample sizes (especially for children of high birth rank) and also fail to adopt adequate controls for the changing patterns of birth-order results that are expected for children of differing ages.

These patterns of differences replicate the results of the large between-family datasets of Belmont and Marolla (1973), Breland (1974), and Claudy et al. (1974)—each based on many thousands of data points. In addition, the study by Bjerkedal et al. (in press) offers clear evidence that IQ declines with increasing birth rank among 127,902 Norwegian siblings raised in the same families. Such collective findings from both between-family and within-family studies, spanning the ages from 6 to early adulthood, are entirely consistent with the changes in family circumstances that involve the relatively poor early environment of a young firstborn with siblings, the tendency for older siblings to benefit from a teaching function over time, and associated niche partitioning among siblings.

One additional methodological point bears emphasizing. Critics of birth-order theories about intellectual ability, and about human behavior more generally, have often dismissed such reported differences as being negligible because they typically explain only 1% or less of the variance in test or survey data (Ernst & Angst, 1983). One must keep in mind that error variance substantially reduces reported effect sizes. Even ignoring this important methodological fact, a relationship that explains just 1% of the variance in any test outcome (which is equivalent to an odds ratio of 1.38) is much more substantial than most people realize. For example, one well-known drug study whose results explained substantially less than 1% of the variance in therapeutic outcomes was terminated early because researchers considered it unethical to further withhold such lifesaving medications either from the untreated control population or from the public at large. Even more notably, the much acclaimed results of the 1954 Salk vaccine trial for polio explained only 1/100th of 1% of the variance in treatment outcomes (Rosnow & Rosenthal, 2003). In a world in which intelligence and human behavior are influenced by innumerable factors, it is noteworthy whenever one can isolate a single influence that explains just 1% of the variance in test scores. We are not, therefore, arguing that birth order is a major determinant of intellectual ability—only that it makes a modest and meaningful contribution after being controlled for other influences.

In sum, the study by Wichman et al. (2006) blends two different datasets with two different birth-order trends that are expected to cancel each other out. Given other problems in their study—such as their skewed sample distributions, the presumed mixing of only children with firstborns having younger siblings, and age distributions that are not in fact expected to produce large birth-order effects (especially after being blended together, in violation of the confluence model)—it is noteworthy that their controlled results were nearly statistically significant for two of the three tests (and are significant when tests entailing the proper contrasts are conducted). It is even more noteworthy that these results produced almost the same effect sizes that have been reported for birth order and verbal ability in other studies conducted on participants of similar ages. The problem of Wichman et al.'s study is thus one of inadequate statistical power compounded by multiple methodological limitations all tending to reduce the reported effect sizes as well as to deprive them of statistical significance.

Despite its methodological limitations in design, sampling, and analysis, the study by Wichman et al. (2006) actually adds to rather than subtracts from the extensive and compelling published record of birth-order effects that support the confluence model. Indeed, given the age of their subjects, Wichman et al.'s findings are almost as predicted by the confluence model. The fact that the authors themselves fail to assert this conclusion needs to be understood in terms of the various methodological problems associated with their study and their failure to specify clearly what the confluence model actually predicts about birth order and intellectual ability.

References

Altus, W. D. (1965). Birth order and scholastic aptitude. *Journal of Consulting Psychology, 29,* 202–205.

Arthur, W. D. (1926). The relation of IQ to position in family. *Journal of Educational Psychology, 17,* 541–550.

Belmont, L., & Marolla, F. A. (1973). Birth order, family size, and intelligence. *Science, 182,* 1096–1101.

Bjerkedal, T., Kristensen, P., Skjeret, G. A., & Brevik, J. I. (in press). Intelligence test scores and birth order among young Norwegian men (conscripts) analyzed within and between families. *Intelligence,* DOI:10.1016/j.intell.2007.01.004.

Breland, H. M. (1974). Birth order, family configuration, and verbal achievement. *Child Development, 45,* 1011–1019.

Burton, D. (1968). Birth order and intelligence. *Journal of Social Psychology, 76,* 199–206.

Cicirelli, V. G. (1977). Children's school grades and sibling structure. *Psychological Reports, 41,* 1055–1058.

Claudy, J. G., Gross, D., & Strause, R. (1974). *Family size, birth order, and characteristics of young adults* [Final Report AIR-41900-10/74-FR]. Palo Alto, CA: American Institute for Research.

Davis, D., Cahan, S., & Bashi, J. (1977). Birth order and intellectual development: The confluence model in the light of cross-cultural evidence. *Science, 196,* 1470–1472.

Douglas, J. W. B. (1964). *The home and the school: A study of ability and attainment in the primary school.* London: Macgibbon & Kee.

Ernst, C., & Angst, J. (1983). *Birth order: Its influence on personality.* Berlin: Springer-Verlag.

Eysenck, H. J., & Cookson. D. (1970). Personality in primary school children: 3. Family background. *British Journal of Educational Psychology, 40,* 117–131.

Galbraith, R. C. (1982). Sibling spacing and intellectual development: A closer look at the confluence models. *Developmental Psychology, 18,* 181–191.

Gille, R., Henry, L., Tabah, L., Sutter, J., Bergues, H., Girard, A., & Bastide, H. (1954). *Le niveau intellectuel des enfant d'age scolaire: Cahier No. 23. La détermination des aptitudes, l'influence des facteurs constitutionnels, familiaux et sociaux. Institut National d'Études Démographiques.* Paris: Presses Universitaire de France.

Hertwig, R., Davis, J. N., & Sulloway, F. J. (2002). Parental investment: How an equity motive can produce inequality. *Psychological Bulletin, 128,* 728–745.

Hsiao, H. H. (1931). The status of the first-born with special reference to intelligence. *Genetic Psychology Monographs, 9,* 43–115.

Institut National d'Études Démographiques. (1973). *Enquête nationale sur le niveau intellectuel des enfants d'âge scolaire* [National survey of intellectual level of school-age children]. Paris: Presses Universitaire de France.

Koch, H. L. (1954). The relation of "primary mental abilities" in five- and six-year-olds to sex of child and characteristics of his sibling. *Child Development, 25,* 209–223.

Kristensen, P., & Bjerkedal, T. (2007). Explaining the relation between birth order and intelligence. *Science, 317,* 1717.

Kunz, P. R., & Peterson, E. T. (1977). Family size, birth order, and academic achievement. *Social Biology, 24,* 144–148.

Page, E. B., & Grandon, G. M. (1979). Family configuration and mental ability: Two theories contrasted with U.S. data. *American Educational Research Journal, 16,* 257–272.

Richardson, S. K. (1936). The correlation of intelligence quotients of siblings at the same chronological age levels. *Journal of Juvenile Research, 20,* 186–197.

Rosenberg, B. G., & Sutton-Smith, B. (1969). Sibling age spacing effects upon cognition. *Journal of Developmental Psychology, 1,* 661–668.

Rosenthal, R., Rosnow, R. L., & Rubin, D. B. (2000). *Contrasts and effect sizes in behavioral research: A correlational approach.* Cambridge, UK: Cambridge University Press.

Rosenthal, R., & Rubin, D. (2003). $r_{equivalent}$: A simple effect size indicator. *Psychological Methods, 8,* 492–496.

Rosnow, R. L., & Rosenthal, R. (2003). Effect sizes for experimenting psychologists. *Canadian Journal of Experimental Psychology, 57,* 221–237.

Schachter, S. (1963). Birth order, eminence and higher education. *American Sociological Review, 28,* 757–768.

Scottish Council for Research on Education. (1949). *The trend of Scottish intelligence.* London: University of London Press.

Steckel, M. L. (1930). Intelligence and birth order. *Journal of Social Psychology, 1,* 329–344.

Steelman, L. C., & Mercy, J. A. (1980). Unconfounding the confluence model: A test of sibship size and birth order effects on intelligence. *American Sociological Review, 45,* 571–582.

Sulloway, F. J. (1996). *Born to rebel: Birth order, family dynamics, and creative lives.* New York: Pantheon.

Sulloway, F. J. (2007a). Birth order and sibling competition. In R. Dunbar & L. Barrett (Eds.), *Handbook of evolutionary psychology* (pp. 297–311). Oxford, UK: Oxford University Press.

Sulloway, F. J. (2007b). Birth order and intelligence. *Science, 317,* 1711–1712.

Svanum, S., & Bringle, R. G. (1980). Evaluation of confluence model variables on IQ and achievement test scores in a sample of 6- to 11-year-old children. *Journal of Educational Psychology, 72,* 427–436.

Tabah, L., & Sutter, L. (1954a). Le niveau intellectuel des enfants d'une même famille [The intellectual level of children of the same family]. In R. Gille, L. Henry, L. Tabah, J. Sutter, H. Bergues, A. Girard, & H. Bastide, *Le niveau intellectuel des enfants d'âge scolaire: Cahier No. 23. La détermination des aptitudes, l'influence des facteurs constitutionnels, familiaux et sociaux. Institut National d'Études Démographiques* (pp. 97–138). Paris: Presses Universitaire de France.

Tabah, L., & Sutter, J. (1954b). Le niveau intellectuel des enfants d'une meme famille. *Annals of Human Genetics, 19,* 120–150.

Velandia, W., Grandon, G. M., & Page, E. B. (1978). Family size, birth order, and intelligence in a large South American sample. *American Educational Research Journal, 15,* 399–416.

Wichman, A. L., Rodgers, J. L., & MacCallum, R. C. (2006). A multilevel approach to the relationship between birth order and intelligence. *Personality and Social Psychology Bulletin, 32,* 117–127.

Zajonc, R. B. (1976). Family configuration and intelligence. *Science, 192,* 227–236.

Zajonc, R. B. (1983). Validating the confluence model. *Psychological Bulletin, 93,* 457–480.

Zajonc, R. B. (2001). The family dynamics of intellectual development. *American Psychologist, 56,* 490–496.

Zajonc, R. B., & Bargh, J. (1980). Birth order, family size, and decline of SAT scores. *American Psychologist, 35,* 662–668.

Zajonc, R. B., Markus, H., & Markus, G. B. (1979). The birth order puzzle. *Journal of Personality and Social Psychology, 37,* 1325–1341.

Zajonc, R. B., & Mullally, P. R. (1997). Birth order: Reconciling conflicting effects. *American Psychologist, 52,* 685–699.

Aaron L. Wichman, Joseph Lee
Rodgers, and Robert C. MacCallum

 **NO**

Birth Order Has No Effect on Intelligence: A Reply and Extension of Previous Findings

We recently published findings (Wichman, Rodgers, & MacCallum, 2006) showing that when the hierarchical nature of birth order is taken into account (i.e., children are nested within families) with modern statistical techniques, birth order is not related to intelligence. This finding is at odds with some studies done using less sophisticated approaches, and it is consistent with others. Given its significance, one would expect that this finding would invite criticism, which in turn provides an opportunity for further clarification of its conceptual underpinnings. We thank Zajonc and Sulloway (2007 [this issue]) for providing this opportunity. Some of their questions and criticisms may be shared by other researchers, and should be addressed. We believe that their criticisms are not warranted or defensible. In this response, we elaborate this position in ten paragraphs. We subsequently present two empirical extensions of our earlier work.

Ten Responses

First, Zajonc and Sulloway (2007) suggested that we ignored relevant evidence, and they spent much of their response reviewing cross-sectional data to argue for the existence of birth-order effects. Unfortunately, these cross-sectional data, showing significant declines in means on relevant outcome variables for later birth orders, tell us nothing about the true existence of such effects *within* the family. Zajonc and Sulloway's Figure 1 shows the patterns that hold in these (overwhelmingly) cross-sectional data. In this type of data, although birth order could potentially be the cause of the patterns, birth order is also a proxy variable, standing in and measuring potentially dozens or hundreds of other real causal factors, the majority of which occur at the between-family level (see Rodgers, Cleveland, van den Oord, & Rowe, 2000, for a more complete explanation). True birth-order effects can be studied only by using data that maintain information about family membership along with statistical models that can differentiate within-family from between-family effects. Our study did this. Virtually all of the evidence cited by Zajonc and Sulloway is drawn from studies that did not.

Wichman, Aaron L.; Rodgers, Joseph Lee; MacCallum, Robert C. From *Personality and Social Psychology Bulletin,* vol. 33, no. 9, 2007, pp. 1195–1200. Copyright © 2007 by Sage Publications—JOURNALS. Reprinted by permission via Rightslink.

Second, Zajonc and Sulloway (2007) suggested that we treated birth order "as a linear phenomenon" and thus ignored differential age patterns. This is incorrect. The method we used to represent birth order using dummy variables allowed for both nonlinear and linear patterns. A significant additional misunderstanding concerns the way cohort age was treated in our models. Zajonc and Sulloway suggested that we collapsed across cohorts to analyze our data. This also is incorrect. As explained in Wichman et al. (2006), we coded birth order as a series of dummy variables in a no-intercept model (Model 1) and then included dummy-coded cohorts by introducing its interactions with each dummy-coded birth order (Model 2). Rather than collapsing, our models simultaneously analyze IQ–birth order patterns separately for both cohorts. Furthermore, differential nonlinear patterns in the two cohorts can be identified by this modeling approach. Results showed a difference in level between cohorts but not a major difference in the pattern of the apparent birth-order effect. Both cohorts also can be separately plotted using this coding approach.

Third, Zajonc and Sulloway (2007) suggested that we used a "problematic study design," resulting in data "seriously skewed by family size." They noted later that "there are only 158 fourthborns and 507 thirdborns in Wichman et al.'s sample, compared with 1,162 secondborns and 1,844 firstborns." The data we used—the National Longitudinal Survey of Youth—came from a probability sample. Up to attrition and nonresponse, they are representative of the 1979 U.S. population of households that contained adolescents. Any skewness reflects the structure of the U.S. population. We fail to see how our use of national data from a probability sample constitutes a problematic study design.

Fourth, they suggested that some of our results almost were significant and would have been so with a larger sample size. This comment seems to discount the large sample size that we did have; few within-family studies with thousands of respondents exist. However, this criticism also fails on a more critical point: We reduced the often-found cross-sectional pattern of significant birth-order effects (which we found in our Models 1 and 2 before controls for between-family variance were added) to nonsignificance using only *one* between-family covariate. We did not come close to using the full power of the multilevel approach in this demonstration. There are dozens of other between-family control variables that should reduce the within-family variance in children's intelligence even further. Contenders include family income, neighborhood characteristics (e.g., library support, school quality), mother's IQ, parental education, and so forth. Any or all of these between-family variables, if included within the analysis, likely would absorb more of the overall variance into the between-family part of the design. After further reducing the birth-order effect in this manner, enormous increases in sample size would then be required to again make it significant. Regardless of the ultimate sample size, though, the fact that between-family variables reduce a supposedly within-family effect is damning evidence against cross-sectional approaches to the study of birth-order effects.

Fifth, regardless of whether the sample size is a dozen or 400,000, using cross-sectional data to infer within-family processes is an example of the ecological fallacy (see Rodgers, 1988). This error in reasoning involves making inferences about individual-level phenomena based on group-level data. So long as cross-sectional, or between-family, data are used to infer within-family birth-order effects, this fallacy persists. We note that many others have pointed out this issue in relation to birth-order research and the confluence model (e.g., Berbaum & Moreland, 1980; McCall, 1985). As Sulloway himself (1996) noted, "More research needs to be done on siblings who have grown up together in the same family." Wichman et al. (2006) is an example of such research.

Sixth, the ecological fallacy can lead to inappropriate analyses. As one example, consider the use of alerting correlations (Rosnow & Rosenthal, 2002) to analyze birth-order data (see Zajonc & Sulloway, 2007). Alerting correlations do not take into consideration within-family variance. In this context, they deliver results based only on between-family observations. Consider that "the special characteristic of $r_{alerting}$ is that it regards as noise or error *only* the disagreement between the predicted and obtained values of the means. That is, the level of noise or error found within conditions is simply set aside" (Rosnow & Rosenthal, 2002, p. 60). Of course, our own results also show these between-family patterns before we control for between-family variance (e.g., Model 1). Our point is that it is a critical mistake to infer that alerting correlations measure within-family birth-order effects. As noted by Rosnow and Rosenthal (2002), such within-family effects are considered "error" by the alerting correlation. We consider overlooking these (nonsignificant) within-family effects to be the primary error in studying birth order.

Seventh, another example of inappropriate analyses involves Zajonc and Sulloway's (2007) use of nonhierarchical methods to reanalyze our patterns of birth-order means; they tested planned contrasts between different pairs of birth-order levels. Typically, this type of contrast analysis follows a significant overall result across all of the birth orders (but our overall test was nonsignificant). Even granting this approach, however, we are surprised that such a method would be chosen over multilevel modeling (MLM) as a preferred analysis technique. MLM is a modern improvement over such methods, one that explicitly accounts for the different sources of variance that underlie hierarchically structured data like birth order nested within families. The contrasts used by Zajonc and Sulloway in no way separate these sources of variance, nor do they model their interrelationship. It is hard to understand how these contrasts are valid in this context.

Eighth, Zajonc and Sulloway (2007) suggested that the confluence model can make null predictions like those found in our analyses. Their response suggests slippage in the confluence age crossover previously identified in cross-sectional analyses as being somewhere around age 12 (Zajonc, Markus, & Markus, 1979). Now, Zajonc and Sulloway suggest that our age 13 to 14 results may not have picked up this crossover. Regardless of how much the crossover age is shifted to try to explain our results, this shift does nothing to explain our significant birth-order results before we controlled between-family variance. We know of no other highly parameterized nonlinear mathematical models whose developers would argue they were supported by null results. Complex mathematical models are unnecessary to explain effects that do not exist (see also Rodgers, 1984).

Ninth, contrary to Zajonc and Sulloway's (2007) claims, we note that Wichman et al. (2006) provided substantial information on properly done within-family studies of birth order as well as information on improperly done studies. We see only two studies that Zajonc and Sulloway mentioned that contain within-family patterns; the Tabah and Sutter (1955) study and the data from Zajonc et al. (1979). Each has weaknesses, but rather than debate those, we will simply grant their existence. In contrast, there are more than a dozen within-family studies that unequivocally fail to support birth-order effects on intelligence. Zajonc and Sulloway failed to acknowledge these within-family studies, studies that raise deep and fundamental issues regarding the legitimacy of the confluence model. This unfortunate pattern of overlooking results inconsistent with the confluence model has been noted before: "Zajonc's citation of (at most) one half of the opinions regarding the model's efficacy leave the naïve reader (at most) half informed" (Rodgers, 1988, p. 476).

Tenth, we urge readers to recognize that the literature contains numerous previous criticisms of the confluence model. Shortly after the publication of the model in the mid-1970s, the criticism began in earnest (Page & Grandon, 1979; Valencia, Grandon, & Page, 1978), peaked in the early 1980s (Brackbill & Nichols, 1982; Galbraith, 1982; Pfouts, 1980; Price, Walsh, & Vilberg, 1984; Steelman & Mercy, 1980), and has continued more recently (Guo & VanWey, 1999; Retherford & Sewell, 1991). Virtually all of these criticisms still stand as originally stated. The standard and often-repeated defense of the model is the same as that offered now by Zajonc and Sulloway: The model seems able to capture patterns in cross-sectional data. This explanation has been refuted many times. Rodgers et al. (2000), Rodgers (2001), and Wichman et al. (2006) are the most recent articles to do so. In the face of such evidence against birth-order effects, confluence model advocates have not been able to explain why patterns in cross-sectional and within-family data are incompatible. Nor have they been able to explain why simple models perform better than the more complex confluence model, or why a large body of empirical data from exactly the domain the model describes does not match the predictions of the model. When the hierarchical nature of birth-order data is taken into account, birth order has no effect on intelligence. The existence of the confluence model hinges on avoiding recognition of this fact.

Two Empirical Extensions

To be sure, the general ideas in the ten preceding paragraphs are not new. The fragility of birth order as an explanatory variable is known. For example, we agree with the following quote written about birth order as an explanation of radical thinking:

> Birth order is not the *real* cause . . . , even though it is strongly correlated with it. But birth order can be seen as a proxy for differences in age, size, power, and status within the family. Common sense tells us that causation probably lies in those other variables, not in birth order *per se.* (Sulloway, 1996, p. 373)

From a multilevel perspective, proxies logically can lie within the family, as this quote suggests. But they exist outside the family as well. Our findings show that birth order is confounded with between-family influences on intelligence and that, when these are controlled, birth order ceases to be associated with IQ. It follows that no matter what their size, cross-sectional samples have no internal validity for assessing birth order.

There is nothing unique about the particular between-family control variable we chose, nor the outcome measures we used, nor the within-family data-set we used. Our analyses reflect the general principle of taking the hierarchical nature of birth-order data into account. To better demonstrate just how general this principle is and to respond to the earlier-raised concerns about the skewed distribution of birth order in our sample, we conducted two new analyses.

First, we reanalyzed birth orders 1 and 2 in both cohorts (i.e., deleting all birth orders 3 and 4, which were used in our earlier analysis), using data and models from our original publication. The first model separately estimated the birth-order effect in both cohorts (7- to 8-year-olds and 13- to 14-year-olds) without controlling for between-family variance in the relationship between birth order and intelligence. . . . The second model added to the first model a partial control for between-family variance in this relationship. The partial control was mother's age at birth of first child. . . . If the skewed distribution of birth order present in our original sample were responsible for our effects, as Zajonc and Sulloway (2007) suggested, this reanalysis should show very different effects than our original analysis did. This reanalysis provides additional evidence for the value of the MLM approach and for the internal validity of the previous findings.

However, the generalizability of our approach logically should not be limited merely to reanalyses of subsets of our original data. To test this principle, we conducted new analyses that extend the findings from Wichman et al. (2006). As before, data from the National Longitudinal Survey of Youth–Children (NLSY-Children) survey were used. This sample contains all biological children ever born to the women in the original NLSY 1979 survey. In comparison to our previous approach, the new analyses used a different outcome variable, a different covariate, and a series of simple linear multilevel models. We used data from the beginning of the child data collection program from 1986 to 1998. . . .

We specified our models as follows. In Model 1, we represented the outcome variable as a linear function of birth order, with birth order coded 0 to 4. We did not yet control for between-family influences on intelligence. On average, earlier born children showed higher scores for digit span than did later born children. We then introduced two different between-family covariates in separate models. . . . In both models, the coefficient representing the effect of birth order became nonsignificant. The within-family MLM approach yields generalizable, replicable results showing that birth order has no effect on intelligence.

In sum, we do not believe that *any* of the criticisms levied against our original article are valid. Our original sample had more than 2,000 families and was approximately representative of the household structure of the United States. Furthermore, we first replicated apparent birth-order effects on IQ before adding between-family control variables. This pattern suggests it is unlikely that our results were because of lack of power. When we reanalyzed our original data to test for potential problems with the skewed birth-order distribution, our results were even clearer than before. Finally, when we conducted another test of the possibility that uncontrolled between-family variance was responsible for our results, using another cognitive measure (digit span) as an outcome variable and a new control variable (mother's IQ), we again found that what appeared to be a birth-order effect disappeared into the between-family variance.

Reflecting on the simplicity of the within–between explanation, one might ask why it is that some researchers still believe that birth order influences intelligence—or, even more puzzling, why cross-sectional designs are still considered by some to be legitimate in evaluating birth-order effects. This is a complex issue, but we have some ideas. One is that researchers are people, too. People like simple explanations, and birth order is simple. Everyone has a birth order, it does not change, and lay theories abound to suggest its systematic influence on outcomes from intelligence to personality. This is a simple statement of the "birth order trap" (see Rodgers, 2000). These qualities make birth-order effects alluring, although deceptive. For too long, a simple oversight (in retrospect) has deceived both researchers and the public about birth order's real "effects."

There are a number of reasons that help explain why the truth has been so long in coming. One is that birth order is hard to study, and that the data's complexity encourages such mistakes as the ecological fallacy. Another is that within-family and longitudinal data are considerably harder to collect than are between-family or cross-sectional data. These two factors have led to a great number of studies that unfortunately have little to say about the true influences on children's intelligence. A multilevel approach to the research questions and the data structure helps explain both the apparent findings of previous between-family studies and the null effects of birth order within the family. We prefer this parsimonious explanation.

References

Berbaum, M. L., & Moreland, R. I. (1980). Intellectual development within the family: A new application of the confluence model. *Developmental Psychology, 16,* 500–515.

Brackbill, Y., & Nichols, P. L. (1982). A test of the confluence model of intellectual development. *Developmental Psychology, 18,* 192–198.

Center for Human Resource Research. (1999). *The 1998 NLSY79 child assessments: Selected tables.* Columbus: The Ohio State University, CHRR User Services.

Galbraith, R. C. (1982). Sibling spacing and intellectual development: A closer look at the confluence models. *Developmental Psychology, 18,* 151–173.

Guo, G., & VanWey, L. K. (1999). Sibship size and intellectual developmental: Is the relationship causal? *American Sociological Review, 64,* 169–187.

McCall, R. B. (1985). The confluence model and theory. *Child Development, 56,* 217–218.

Page, E. G., & Grandon, G. (1979). Family configuration and mental ability: Two theories contrasted with U.S. data. *American Educational Research Journal, 16,* 257–272.

Pfouts, J. H. (1980). Birth order, age-spacing, IQ differences, and family relations. *Journal of Marriage and the Family, 42,* 517–531.

Price, G. G., Walsh, D. J., & Vilberg, W. R. (1984). The confluence models' good predictions of mental age beg the question. *Psychological Bulletin, 96,* 195–200.

Retherford, R. D., & Sewell, W. H. (1991). Birth order and intelligence: Further tests of the confluence model. *American Sociological Review, 56,* 141–158.

Rodgers, J. L. (1984). Confluence effects: Not here, not now! *Developmental Psychology, 20,* 321–331.

Rodgers, J. L. (1988). Birth order, SAT, and confluence: Spurious correlations and no causality. *American Psychologist, 43,* 476–477.

Rodgers, J. L. (2000). The birth order trap. *Politics and the Life Sciences, 19,* 167–170.

Rodgers, J. L. (2001). What causes birth order–intelligence patterns? The admixture hypothesis, revived. *American Psychologist, 56,* 505–510.

Rodgers, J. L., Cleveland, H. H., van den Oord, E., & Rowe, D. C. (2000). Resolving the debate over birth order, family size, and intelligence. *American Psychologist, 55,* 599–612.

Rosnow, R. L., & Rosenthal, R. (2002). Contrasts and correlations in theory assessment. *Journal of Pediatric Psychology, 27,* 59–66.

Steelman, L. C., & Mercy, J. A. (1980). Unconfounding the confluence model: A test of sibship size and birth-order effects on intelligence. *American Sociological Review, 45,* 571–782.

Sulloway, F. J. (1996). *Born to rebel.* New York: Vintage.

Tabah, L., & Sutter, J. (1955). Le niveau intellectuel des enfants d'une meme famille. *Annals of Human Genetics, 19,* 120–150.

U.S. Department of Defense. (1982). *Profile of American youth: 1980 nationwide administration of the Armed Services Vocational Aptitude Battery.* Washington, DC: Author.

Valendia, W., Grandon, G., & Page, E. G. (1978). Family size, birth order, and intelligence in a large South American sample. *American Educational Research Journal, 15,* 399–416.

Wechsler, D. (1974). *Wechsler Intelligence Scales for Children–Revised.* New York: Psychological Corporation.

Wichman, A. L., Rodgers, J. L., & MacCallum, R. C. (2006). A multilevel approach to the relationship between birth order and intelligence. *Personality and Social Psychology Bulletin, 32,* 117–127.

Zajonc, R. B., Markus, H., & Markus, G. B. (1979). The birth order puzzle. *Journal of Personality and Social Psychology, 37,* 1325–1341.

Zajonc, R. B., & Sulloway, F. J. (2007). The confluence model: Birth order as a within-family or between-family dynamic? *Personality and Social Psychology Bulletin, 33,* 1187–1194.

CHALLENGE QUESTIONS

Does Birth Order Predict Intelligence?

1. Choose one of the above positions and consider it to be the "correct" viewpoint on birth order. What are some decisions families might make as a result?
2. What is the reason for Wichman et al.'s insistence that cross-sectional studies are not legitimate for evaluating birth-order effects?
3. If a study finds significant results supporting the birth-order effect even after controlling for a between-family variable such as the mother's age at the birth of the first child, what plausible reasons (other than birth order itself) might account for the results?
4. The last paragraph of the YES selection says the Wichman study actually supports the confluence model. What do they mean by this?
5. What do Wichman et al. mean when they say (last paragraph) they prefer the parsimonious explanation?

ISSUE 20

Is the Need for Social Enhancement Universal Across Cultures?

YES: Constantine Sedikides, Lowell Gaertner, and Jack L. Vevea, from "Inclusion of Theory-Relevant Moderators Yield the Same Conclusions as Sedikides, Gaertner, and Vevea (2005): A Meta-analytical Reply to Heine, Kitayama, and Hamamura (2007)," *Asian Journal of Social Psychology* (vol. 10, no. 2, pp. 59–67, 2007). doi: 10.1111/j.1467-839X.2007.00212.x

NO: Steven J. Heine, Shinobu Kitayama, and Takeshi Hamamura, from "Inclusion of Additional Studies Yields Different Conclusions: Comment on Sedikides, Gaertner, and Vevea (2005), *Journal of Personality and Social Psychology*," *Asian Journal of Social Psychology* (vol. 10, no. 2, pp. 49–58, 2007). doi: 10:1111/j.1467-839X.2007.00211.x

ISSUE SUMMARY

YES: Constantine Sedikides, director of the Center for Research on Self and Identity at the University of Southampton, England; Lowell Gaertner, professor of psychology at the University of Tennessee, Knoxville; and Jack L. Vevea, associate professor of quantitative psychology at the University of California, Merced, maintain that all people, regardless of culture, positively inflate self-ratings on dimensions important to themselves.

NO: Steven J. Heine, professor of psychology at the University of British Columbia; Shinobu Kitayama, professor of psychology at the University of Michigan; and Takeshi Hamamura, assistant professor of psychology at the Chinese University of Hong Kong, argue that people of interdependent cultures inflate positive self-ratings less than those of independent cultures.

The humorist Dave Barry may have been on to something when he said "the one thing that unites all human beings . . . is . . . we ALL believe that we are above average drivers." Could Barry have discovered a universal psychological principle? One social science theory has named this more general tendency *self-enhancement*, the notion that people generally inflate ratings of themselves, especially on dimensions they consider important. In fact, research suggests that self-enhancement may be an important component of mental health, because it is positively correlated with one's ability to care about others, be happy, and work productively (Taylor & Brown, 1999). If Barry is right about the unity of "all human beings," then the need for social enhancement might be universal across all cultures.

Psychological researchers disagree on this issue. Some would likely agree with Barry that some degree of universality is probably correct, especially if self-enhancement is part of universal mental health. Others, however, point to evidence that indicates only individualist cultures, such as the United States, have this tendency. They contend that your friend from a collectivist culture would not automatically consider herself to be an "above average driver"—or an above average anything. A universal need to self-enhance also seems to fly in the face of research showing that accurate self-perceptions are essential for good mental health (Kim, 2012). In this sense, research has supported both ideas—self-enhancement is universal *and* it is unique to modern Western societies. The articles chosen for this issue represent sophisticated defenses of each of these positions.

Sedikides, Gaertner, and Vevea assert the universality of self-enhancement, citing studies that correlate self-esteem with psychological well-being in both Eastern and Western cultures. They theorize that even though people from Eastern cultures have more interdependent values than do Westerners, they still try to view themselves in a better light on those dimensions important to them. Sedikides et al. also conduct a thorough analysis of the opposing article by Heine Kitayama, and Hamamura. They argue that self-enhancement theory states that people will enhance on those factors specifically important to them. However, some of the methods reported in the opposing article do not have factors that were scientifically shown to be uniquely important to people of Eastern cultures. Consequently, Sedikides et al. exclude these studies from their analysis and conclude that self-enhancement is universal.

By contrast, Heine, Kitayama, and Hamamura argue that self-enhancement is a uniquely Western phenomenon. They assert that while Western cultures' value standing out from the crowd, Eastern cultures' value adjusting one's self to fit the high standards set by society. These researchers contend that the methods of a previous study by authors of the opposing article (Sedikides et al., 2005) are likely to confuse self-enhancement data and inflate self-ratings. Heine et al. claim that their own broader study allows for more meaningful conclusions and shows how particular methods influence results. Their results support the idea that self-enhancement is not inherent in all people, but is rather a cultural phenomenon.

References

Kim, Y. H. (2012). *Know thyself: Misperceptions of actual performance undermine subjective well-being, future performance, and achievement motivation.* 72, ProQuest Information & Learning, US.

Sedikides, C., Gaertner, L., & Vevea, J. L. (2005). Pancultural self-enhancement reloaded: A meta-analytic reply to Heine (2005). *Journal of Personality and Social Psychology, 89*(4), 539–551. doi: 10.1037/0022-3514.89.4.539

Taylor, S. E., & Brown, J. D. (1999). Illusion and well-being: A social psychological perspective on mental health. In R. F. Baumeister (Ed.), *The self in social psychology* (pp. 43–68). New York, NY: Psychology Press.

POINT

- Western and Eastern self-enhancement differs tactically, not fundamentally.

- Easterners self-enhance on collectivist characteristics important to their culture.

- Heine et al. include studies that do not empirically validate comparisons.

- Using studies with criteria outside the domain of inquiry results in misleading conclusions.

COUNTERPOINT

- Many studies confirm that Eastern cultures self-enhance much less than Western cultures.

- Eastern cultures place less importance on standing out and more on fitting in.

- The Sedikides et al. meta-analysis omits a substantial number of relevant studies.

- The Sedikides et al. study is confounded by the better-than-average effect, which is likely to produce inflated self-enhancement data.

YES

Constantine Sedikides, Lowell Gaertner, and Jack L. Vevea

Inclusion of Theory-Relevant Moderators Yield the Same Conclusions as Sedikides, Gaertner, and Vevea (2005): A Meta-analytical Reply to Heine, Kitayama, and Hamamura (2007)

Introduction

Heine, Lehman, Markus, and Kitayama (1999) concluded that self-esteem is culturally specific. In their own words, 'The empirical literature provides scant evidence for a need for positive self-regard among Japanese', 'the need for self-regard must be culturally variant', and 'the need for self-regard . . . is not a universal, but rather is rooted in significant aspects of North American culture' (p. 766). Easterners (East Asians, and Japanese in particular) not only lack high self-esteem, but they do not even have a need for self-esteem. Only Westerners (e.g. Americans, Canadians, Northern Europeans) have high self-esteem and a need for it. By implication, only Westerners self-enhance.

We (Sedikides, Gaertner, & Toguchi, 2003) argued that their claim was implausible, given the evidence: (i) in favour of the genetic underpinnings (Neiss *et al.*, 2005) and existential relevance (Pyszczynski, Greenberg, Solomon, Arndt, & Schimel, 2004) of self-esteem; (ii) that positive implicit self-esteem is universal (Yamaguchi *et al.*, in press); and (iii) that self-enhancement is a marker of good mental health both in the West (Taylor, Lerner, Sherman, Sage, & McDowell, 2003) and the East (Kobayashi & Brown, 2003). Instead, we offered an alternative hypothesis.

We hypothesized that both Easterners and Westerners self-enhance on domains that are personally important. It so happens that these domains are different for the two cultural groups. The collectivistic domain is more personally important to Easterners, the individualistic domain to Westerners. Hence, Easterners will self-enhance on collectivistic domains, Westerners on individualistic domains. Self-enhancement is a universal esteem-seeking strategy. Our

Sedikides, Constantine.; Gaertner, Lowell; Vevea, Jack L. From *Asian Journal of Social Psychology*, vol. 10, no. 2, 2007, pp. 59–67. Copyright © 2007 by John Wiley & Sons, Ltd. Reprinted by permission via Rightslink.

hypothesis was supported in two primary experiments (Sedikides *et al.*, 2003). Challenged by Heine (2005), we accumulated further support for our hypothesis in a meta-analysis (Sedikides, Gaertner, & Vevea, 2005). Heine, Kitayama, and Hamamura (2007) provided another challenge to our hypothesis.

Clarifying the Exclusion Criteria

In a previously published paper, Heine *et al.* (2007) argued that Sedikides *et al.* (2005) did not include 'six previously published papers that also tested the Hypothesis but yielded findings directly counter to the claims of Sedikides *et al.* (2003)'. They further stated that 'we are unclear as to the rationale of Sedikides *et al.* for excluding these studies, as the only mention of these studies in their 2005 paper is in a footnote on page 540 which reads "These criteria identify a subset of studies that are relevant to our framing of the research question. There are other studies on this general topic that are not included, such as Heine and Lehman (1995), Heine *et al.* (2001), and Kitayama *et al.* (1997)"' (Heine *et al.*, 2007).

We believe that we (Sedikides *et al.*, 2005) mentioned the broad exclusion grounds in our p. 540 footnote, and we also detailed exclusion reasons for Heine and Renshaw (2002) in our footnote 6 on p. 546. Regardless, we submit that a meta-analysis is under scholarly constraints to: (i) propose a theoretical formulation; (ii) set theory-testing parameters by defining the domain of empirical inquiry; and (iii) select studies that fit that domain (Johnson & Eagly, 2000). We followed these principles in our meta-analysis (Sedikides *et al.*, 2005), and this resulted in our exclusion criteria. What were these criteria? They were as follows (Sedikides *et al.*, 2005, p. 540):

> First, studies had to sample either members of Western or Eastern culture. Such studies identified cultural membership on the basis of nationality (e.g. Japan, United States), ethnicity (e.g. Asian), or self-construal (Singelis, 1994). Second, studies had to provide a measure of one's perception of self relative to others. Participants in such studies (a) performed a distribution task in which they estimated the percentage of the population from which they are better in terms of a given attribute (b) rated separately self and other . . . , or (c) rated simultaneously self and other on a bipolar scale anchored at the extremes by self and other. Finally, studies had to assess explicitly the self-other comparison on attributes associated with individualism versus collectivism. Participants in such studies compared self and other in regard to individualistic traits or behaviors or collectivistic traits or behaviors.

Our New Meta-analysis

The purpose of the rationale is not merely retrospective. Instead, the rationale is relevant to a new meta-analysis that we undertook as a response to Heine *et al.* (2007). In the present article, we heeded Heine *et al.*'s call to expand the scope or criteria of the meta-analysis by including the six papers. We incorporated two of these papers (Markus & Kitayama, 1991; Heine & Lehman, 1995) in Investigation 1, and the remaining four papers (Kitayama, Markus, Matsumoto, & Norasakkunkit, 1997; Heine & Lehman, 1999; Heine *et al.*, 2001; Heine & Renshaw, 2002) in Investigation.

More to the point, the empirical viability of our hypothesis rests on two theory-relevant moderators, which Heine *et al.* (2007) did not include in their meta-analysis. The first moderator is the empirical validation of the comparison dimension (i.e. individualistic *vs* collectivistic). Our theoretical formulation predicts that pancultural self-enhancement will be manifested on dimensions that are empirically validated as either individualistic (i.e. Western self-enhancement) or collectivistic (i.e. Eastern self-enhancement). Unvalidated dimensions are non-diagnostic and, thus, incapable of providing a test of the theory. Unfortunately, Heine *et al.* (2007) ignored this distinction and aggregated across effects from validated and unvalidated studies. The second moderator is personal importance of the dimension (i.e. important *vs* unimportant). Our theoretical formulation predicts that pancultural self-enhancement will be manifested by both Westerners and Easterners on dimensions of high (rather than low) personal importance. Heine *et al.* (2007) obscured assessment of this possibility by considering what we regard as irrelevant effects from our perspective. Omitting the validation issue and including irrelevant effects results in misspecified meta-analyses, which leads to two inevitable, if not grave, consequences: inappropriate theory-testing and misleading conclusions.

Investigation 1

This investigation addressed Heine *et al.*'s (2007) failure to take into consideration that some effect sizes originated from studies which did not empirically validate the comparison dimensions. Our investigation includes this vital and theory-relevant moderator: samples varied on whether the researchers empirically validated the individualistic and collectivistic dimensions of comparison. Is pancultural self-enhancement observed on validated (rather than unvalidated) comparison dimensions, as Sedikides *et al.* (2005; Investigation 1) proposed and found?

Method

Data sources. Data were obtained from: (i) the eight studies included in Investigation 1 of Sedikides *et al.*'s (2005) meta-analysis, which yielded 15 effect sizes from 15 samples; (ii) the three additional studies included in Investigation 1 of Heine *et al.*'s meta-analysis (2007), which yielded eight effect sizes from six samples; and (iii) a recently completed study (Gaertner, Sedikides, & Chang, 2006), which yielded one effect size from one sample. . . .

Participants in each sample rated self and other on individualistic and collectivistic comparison dimensions. [E]ach sample represented either Eastern or Western culture. Also, samples varied as to whether the researchers empirically validated the individualistic and collectivistic dimensions.

Calculation of effect sizes.   The effect of interest examines whether individuals more favourably compare self with other on individualistic versus collectivistic comparison dimensions. Following Sedikides *et al.* (2005), we calculated an effect size by: (i) subtracting the mean self-other rating on the collectivistic dimension from the mean self-other rating on the individualistic dimension; and (ii) standardizing that difference by the sample standard deviation of the within-subject difference score. The standard deviation of the difference score is appropriate, because the effect of interest conceptually is a within-subject effect and each sample assessed that effect with a within-subject method.

A positive effect size indicates that the self-other comparison was more favourable to self on the individualistic dimension. A negative effect size indicates that the self-other comparison was more favourable to self on the collectivistic dimension. An effect size of zero indicates that the self-other comparison was equally favourable to self on the individualistic and collectivistic dimensions.

Results and Discussion

We created 12 data sets to address three issues. The first issue was raised by Heine *et al.* (2007). They were concerned that the Eastern and Western effect sizes from Sedikides *et al.* (2003; Study 2) biased the results, because participants were Americans who were identified as having either an independent or interdependent self-construal. Consequently, half of our data sets included those effect sizes, whereas the other half excluded them.

The second issue was introduced by the studies that Heine *et al.* (2007) included in their meta-analysis. [T]he two Eastern effect sizes . . . from Heine and Lehman (1995) were derived from the same samples of participants. Inclusion of these samples in the same analysis violates the independence assumption. We satisfied that assumption with data sets that varied which nonindependent samples were excluded. Half of the data sets excluded the second Western and Eastern effect size from Heine and Lehman (1995; i.e. effect sizes = 0.41 and 0.87), whereas the other half excluded the first Western and Eastern effect size from that study (i.e. effect sizes = −0.47 and 0.33). . . .

We planned to approach the analysis with a mixed-effects model, because: (i) it enables a broader context of generalization; and (ii) data typically violate the homogeneity assumption of the fixed-effects model Research Council, 1992; Hedges & Vevea, 1998; Hunter & Schmidt, 2000; Field, 2001, 2003). We regressed effect sizes on culture, validate and the Culture–Validate interaction, and proceeded to estimate parameters with unconditional maximum likelihood using a program developed for that purpose (Vevea & Hedges, 1995; Vevea & Woods, 2005). Each analysis evidenced a significant Q-test of the fixed-effects model's homogeneity assumption, which bolsters our choice for the mixed-effects model.

[A]ll data sets yielded the same conclusion. Consistently with Sedikides *et al.* (Investigation 1), each analysis evidenced a Culture–Validate interaction. For studies that validated the comparison dimensions, there was a significant effect of culture. Westerns evidenced a more self-favouring social comparison on the individualistic than collectivistic dimension, whereas Easterners evidenced a more self-favouring social comparison on the collectivistic than on the individualistic dimension. For studies that did not validate the comparison dimensions, however, there was no effect of culture. Both Westerners and Easterners evidenced social comparisons that were no more self-favouring on what was ostensibly an individualistic than a collectivistic dimension of comparison. The methodologically superior studies substantiate the argument that both Westerners and Easterners strategically self-enhance on comparison dimensions that are uniquely infused by their culture.

Investigation 2

Although Western and Eastern cultures self-enhance on different comparison dimensions (i.e. individualistic *vs* collectivistic), the pancultural self-enhancement formulation anticipates that the same process underlies the differential expression: people self-enhance on personally important comparison dimensions. Such was the pattern reported by Sedikides *et al.* (2005; Investigation 2). Will the present Investigation 2 replicate this pattern?

As a reminder, Heine *et al.* (2007) added several effect sizes to their meta-analytical Investigation 2. [E]ach of the added effect sizes is irrelevant to the question of whether self-other comparisons become more favourable to self with increasing importance of the comparison dimension. Nonetheless, we did code and include in the factorial design whether effect sizes from primary studies are relevant or not.

Method

Data sources. Data were obtained from: (i) the seven studies included in Investigation 2 of Sedikides *et al.*'s (2005) meta-analysis, which yielded 12 effect sizes from 12 samples; (ii) the six additional studies included in Investigation 2 of Heine *et al.*'s (2007) meta-analysis, which yielded 12 effect sizes from 12 samples; and (iii) two studies by Hamamura, Heine, and Takemoto (2006), which yielded four effect sizes from four samples, as well as one study by Gaertner *et al.* (2006), which yielded one effect size from one sample. . . .

Participants from Western or Eastern samples ostensibly rated self and other on a series of attributes and rated the personal importance of each attribute. [T]he 12 effect sizes introduced by . . . Heine *et al.* (2007) used alternative procedures and are irrelevant to the issue of whether self-other comparison becomes increasingly self-favouring as a function of personal importance of the comparison dimension.

Calculation of effect sizes. Authors of the primary studies graciously provided for each sample the average within-person correlation between the self-other rating and the importance rating. A positive correlation indicates that the self-other comparison became more favourable to self as the importance of the comparison dimension increased. A negative correlation indicates that the self-other comparison became more favourable to self as the importance comparison dimension decreased. A correlation of zero indicates the absence of a linear relationship between the self-other rating and the importance of the comparison dimension.

It is unclear, however, how to interpret correlations from the 12 irrelevant effect sizes. The components of those correlations vary and are consistent only in the fact that they do not involve a self-other comparison and subjective importance rating. . . .

Results and Discussion

We created eight data sets to address two issues. As in Investigation 1, half of the data sets included the two effect sizes from Sedikides *et al.* (2003; Study 2), whereas the other half excluded them. We further varied those data sets to avoid violating the independence assumption. We implemented two strategies to form data sets. The first strategy was to bracket the best approximation of the effect by excluding from Set 1 the two smallest non-independent effect sizes (i.e. 0.0393 and −0.039) and excluding from Set 2 the two largest non-independent effect sizes (i.e. 0.0566 and 0.1). The second strategy was to exclude non-independent effect sizes based on whether they were coded as being relevant to the issue. Set 3 excluded the two effect sizes coded as irrelevant (i.e. 0.1 and −0.039), and Set 4 excluded the two effect sizes coded as relevant (i.e. 0.0393 and 0.0566).

We regressed effect sizes on culture, relevant and Culture × Relevant. We planned to use a mixed-effects model. However, analysis of each data set evidenced a non-significant Q-test of the homogeneity assumption. Consequently, we report results of the fixed-effects model. . . .

In particular, analysis of each data set yielded a Culture–Relevant interaction. Studies yielding effect sizes relevant to whether self-other comparison varies with the importance of the comparison dimension did not produce an effect of culture. Both cultures evidenced significantly positive correlations of equivalent magnitude indicating that Westerners and Easterners manifested self-other comparisons that increasingly favoured the self to the extent that the comparison dimension was personally important. In contrast, studies yielding effect sizes irrelevant to the issue produced an effect of culture. Westerners evidenced a significantly positive correlation, Easterners a significantly negative correlation. Unfortunately, those correlations are uninterpretable, given the inconsistency across effect sizes in the components of the correlation (i.e. each effect size addresses a different question).

Finally, readers might note the elevated *p*-values from analyses excluding Sedikides *et al.* (2003; Study 2). Importantly, those analyses yielded estimated effects equivalent to those that included Sedikides *et al.* The elevated *p*-values are due to the reduction in power incurred by the exclusion of additional effect sizes, rather than the values of those effect sizes.

In summary, the relevant studies boost the thesis of pancultural self-enhancement. Members of Western and Eastern culture self-enhance to the extent to which they subjectively deem as important the dimension of comparison. These findings replicate those of Sedikides *et al.* (2005; Investigation 2).

As an aside, Heine *et al.* (2007) argued that the better-than-average effect 'artificially inflates estimates of the correlations between self-enhancement and importance for people of both cultures'. Even if this is the case, the point is inconsequential for our meta-analytical findings. The effect was significant for both cultural groups, and it was manifested selectively: For Westerners, the better-than-average judgement was correlated with individualistic dimensions, for Easterners with collectivistic dimensions.

General Discussion

Heine *et al.* (2007) suggested that the exclusion of six papers compromised the meta-analytical conclusion Sedikides *et al.* (2005) reached, namely that self-enhancement is pancultural. Furthermore, Heine *et al.* maintained that their meta-analysis, which included the six papers, demonstrated that self-enhancement is a Western motive because: (i) Easterners and Westerners did not differentially enhance on individualistic and collectivistic dimensions; and (ii) only Westerners enhanced to the extent to which the comparison attribute was important.

In response to Heine *et al.*'s (2007) challenge, we carried out a new meta-analysis, in which we included those six papers. We identified several faults in their meta-analytical procedure, as described in the Results and Discussion sections of our Investigations 1 and 2. More importantly, we noted a serious omission: their meta-analysis was misspecified. In particular, Heine *et al.* failed to take into account two moderators central to the theory. These are: (i) whether the comparison dimensions were validated or not; and (ii) whether effect sizes were relevant to the self-enhancement by personal importance association. Our theoretical formulation predicts that pancultural self-enhancement will be observed in the case of validated and personally important dimensions.

We addressed the Heine *et al.* (2007) procedural faults and omissions in two investigations. In Investigation 1, we demonstrated that Westerners self-enhance on individualistic dimensions, whereas Easterners self-enhance on collectivistic dimensions. This finding replicates that of Sedikides *et al.* (2005; Investigation 1). In Investigation 2, we demonstrated that both Westerners and Easterners self-enhance on personally important dimensions. This finding also replicates that of Sedikides *et al.* (2005; Investigation 2). In summary, the existing evidence is consistent with the view that tactical self-enhancement is pancultural.

References

Becker, B. J. (2006). The meaning and suitability of various effect sizes for structured rater X ratee designs. *Psychological Methods, 11,* 72–86.

*Brown, J. D. & Kobayashi, C. (2002). Self-enhancement in Japan and America. *Asian Journal of Social Psychology, 5,* 145–167.

Field, A. P. (2001). Meta-analysis of correlation coefficients: A Monte Carlo comparison of fixed- and random-effects methods. *Psychological Methods, 6,* 161–180.

Field, A. P. (2003). The problems using fixed-effects models of meta-analysis on real-world data. *Understanding Statistics, 2,* 77–96.

*Gaertner, L., Sedikides, C. & Chang, K. (2006). *Tactical Self-Enhancement in Taiwan: Implications for Psychological Health.* Unpublished manuscript. Knoxville, TN: University of Tennessee.

*Hamamura, T., Heine, S. J. & Takemoto, T. (2006). *Why the Better-Than-Average Effect Is a Worse-Than-Average Measure of Self-Enhancement.* Unpublished manuscript. Vancouver, BC: University of British Columbia.

Hedges, L. V. & Vevea, J. L. (1998). Fixed- and random-effects models in meta-analysis. *Psychological Methods, 3,* 486–504.

Heine, S. J. (2005). Where is the evidence for pancultural self-enhancement?: A reply to Sedikides, Gaertner, and Toguchi (2003). *Journal of Personality and Social Psychology, 89,* 531–538.

*Heine, S. J. & Lehman, D. R. (1995). Cultural variation in unrealistic optimism: Does the West feel more vulnerable than the East? *Journal of Personality and Social Psychology, 72,* 1268–1283.

*Heine, S. J. & Lehman, D. R. (1997). Culture, dissonance, and self-affirmation. *Personality and Social Psychology Bulletin, 23,* 389–400.

*Heine, S. J. & Lehman, D. R. (1999). Culture, self-discrepancies, and self-satisfaction. *Personality and Social Psychology Bulletin, 25,* 915–925.

*Heine, S. J. & Renshaw, K. (2002). Interjudge agreement, self-enhancement, and liking: Cross-cultural divergences. *Personality and Social Psychology Bulletin, 28,* 578–587.

Heine, S. J., Kitayama, S. & Hamamura, T. (2007). Inclusion of additional studies yields different conclusions: Comment on Sedikides, Gaertner & Vevea (2005), *Journal of Personality and Social Psychology. Asian Journal of Social Psychology, 10,* 49–58.

*Heine, S. J., Kitayama, S., Lehman, D. R., *et al.* (2001). Divergent consequences of success and failure in Japan and North America: An investigation of self-improving motivations and malleable selves. *Journal of Personality and Social Psychology, 81,* 599–615.

Heine, S. J., Lehman, D. R., Markus, H. R. & Kitayama, S. (1999). Is there a universal need for positive self-regard? *Psychological Review, 106,* 766–794.

Hornsey, M. J. & Jetten, J. (2005). Loyalty without conformity: Tailoring self-perception as a means of balancing belonging and differentiation. *Self and Identity, 4,* 81–95.

Hunter, J. E. & Schmidt, F. L. (2000). Fixed effects *vs* random effects meta-analysis models: Implications for cumulative knowledge in psychology. *International Journal of Selection and Assessment, 8,* 275–292.

Johnson, B. T. & Eagly, A. H. (2000). Quantitative synthesis in social psychological research. In: H. T. Reise & C. M. Judd, eds. *Handbook of Research Methods in Social and Personality Psychology,* pp. 496–528. New York: Cambridge University Press.

*Kitayama, S., Markus, H. R., Matsumoto, H. & Norasakkunkit, V. (1997). Individual and collective processes in the construction of the self: Self-enhancement in the United States and self-criticism in Japan. *Journal of Personality and Social Psychology, 72,* 1245–1267.

*Kobayashi, C. & Brown, J. D. (2003). Self-esteem and self-enhancement in Japan and America. *Journal of Cross-Cultural Psychology, 34,* 567–580.

*Kurman, J. (2001). Self-enhancement: Is it restricted to individualistic cultures? *Personality and Social Psychology Bulletin, 12,* 1705–1716.

*Markus, H. R. & Kitayama, S. (1991). Cultural variation in the self-concept. In: G. R. Goethals & J. Strauss, eds. *Multidisciplinary Perspectives on the Self,* pp. 18–48. New York: Springer-Verlag.

Morris, S. B. & DeShon, R. P. (2002). Combining effect size estimates in meta-analysis with repeated measures and independent-groups designs. *Psychological Methods, 7,* 105–125.

National Research Council (1992). *Combining Information: Statistical Issues and Opportunities for Research.* Washington, DC: National Academy Press.

Neiss, M. B., Stevenson, J., Sedikides, C., Kumashiro, M., Finkel, E. J. & Rusbult, C. E. (2005). Executive self, self-esteem, and negative affectivity: Relations at the phenotypic and genotypic level. *Journal of Personality and Social Psychology, 89,* 593–606.

*Norasakkunkit, V. & Kalick, S. M. (2002). Culture, ethnicity, and emotional distress measures: The role of self-construal and self-enhancement. *Journal of Cross-Cultural Psychology, 33,* 56–70.

Pyszczynski, T., Greenberg, J., Solomon, S., Arndt, J. & Schimel, J. (2004). Why do people need self-esteem?: A theoretical and empirical review. *Psychological Bulletin, 130,* 435–468.

*Ross, M. Heine, S. J. Wilson, A. E. & Sugimori, S. (2005). Cross-cultural discrepancies in self-appraisals. *Personality and Social Psychology Bulletin, 31,* 1175–1188.

*Sedikides, C. Gaertner, L. & Toguchi, Y. (2003). Pancultural self-enhancement. *Journal of Personality and Social Psychology, 84,* 60–70.

Sedikides, C. Gaertner, L. & Vevea, J. L. (2005). Pancultural self-enhancement reloaded: A meta-analytic reply to Heine (2005). *Journal of Personality and Social Psychology, 89,* 539–551.

Singelis, T. M. (1994). The measurement of independent and interdependent self-construals. *Personality and Social Psychology Bulletin, 20,* 580–591.

Taylor, S. E. Lerner, J. S. Sherman, D. K. Sage, R. M. & McDowell, N. K. (2003). Portrait of the self-enhancer: Well-adjusted and well-liked or maladjusted and friendless? *Journal of Personality and Social Psychology, 84,* 165–176.

Vevea, J. L. & Hedges, L. V. (1995). A general linear model for estimating effect size in the presence of publication bias. *Psychometrika, 60,* 419–435.

Vevea, J. L. & Woods, C. M. (2005). Publication bias in research synthesis: Sensitivity analysis using a priori weight functions. *Psychological Methods, 10,* 428–443.

Yamaguchi, S. Greenwald, A. G. Banaji, M. R., *et al.* (in press). Apparent universality of positive implicit self-esteem. *Psychological Science.*

References accompanied by an asterisk include studies that were used in the meta-analysis.

Steven J. Heine, Shinobu Kitayama,
and Takeshi Hamamura

 **NO**

Inclusion of Additional Studies Yields Different Conclusions: Comment on Sedikides, Gaertner, & Vevea (2005), *Journal of Personality and Social Psychology*

Introduction

In a number of publications, we have argued that in Western cultures 'to be a good person' implies standing out, confirming, expressing, and actualizing positive interpersonal attributes of the self, but in Eastern cultures it means something else (Markus & Kitayama, 1991; Kitayama, Markus, Matsumoto, & Norasakkunkit, 1997; Heine, Lehman, Markus, & Kitayama, 1999; Heine, 2005a). Specifically, 'to be a good person' in the latter cultures entails fitting in and actively adjusting to pertinent social contexts and improving the self vis-à-vis high standards shared in the society by identifying one's shortcomings.

At the centre of this theoretical claim is an important cross-cultural difference in self-enhancement tendencies. In support of our theoretical characterization of Western versus Eastern cultures, a number of papers have argued that East Asians have weaker self-enhancement tendencies than Westerners (Kitayama *et al.*, 1997; Heine *et al.*, 1999). Given its theoretical significance, however, it should not come as any surprise that this particular cross-cultural difference has sparked a considerable amount of controversy, with some questioning whether the cultural difference can be accepted at face value.

In particular, some theorists have argued that Westerners and Easterners self-enhance to an equal extent as long as they evaluate themselves in domains that matter to them (Brown & Kobayashi, 2002; Sedikides, Gaertner, & Toguchi, 2003; Sedikides, Gaertner, & Vevea, 2005). These theorists would suggest that the existing evidence for cross-cultural differences in self-enhancement is an artifact caused by inadvertent variation in the perceived importance of the domains tested in this literature, with these domains being far more important for Westerners than for Easterners. It is quite timely therefore that several researchers have examined whether East Asians might self-enhance more for traits that they view to be especially important compared with those that

Heine, Steven J.; Kitayama, Shinobu; Hamamura, Takeshi From *Asian Journal of Social Psychology*, vol. 10, no. 2, 2007, pp. 49–58. Copyright © 2007 by John Wiley & Sons, Ltd. Reprinted by permission via Rightslink.

they view to be less important. Throughout the current paper, we refer to this question as 'the Hypothesis.'

Although we do not know of any studies that have investigated whether the traits used in cross-cultural studies differ in their perceived importance for Westerners and East Asians (which would seem to be a critical point to demonstrate in order to accept this alternative account), there have been a number of recent papers that have investigated the Hypothesis (Kitayama et al., 1997; Heine & Lehman, 1999; Heine et al., 1999; Brown & Kobayashi, 2002). In particular, Sedikides et al. (2003) argued that the self-enhancement motivation was universal because they found evidence that Japanese students self-enhanced more for interdependent traits than independent ones, whereas American students enhanced more for independent than interdependent ones, and that Americans who scored high on a measure of interdependence self-enhanced more for interdependent traits than did those who scored high on a measure of independence.

In a rejoinder to that paper, Heine (2005b) highlighted six previously published papers that also tested the Hypothesis but yielded findings directly counter to the claims of Sedikides et al. (2003). These six papers, which used a variety of different methods, also compared the degree to which East Asian and North American participants self-enhanced in independent and interdependent domains, and the degree to which East Asian and North American participants self-enhanced in domains that varied in their importance. Those papers, and relevant page numbers for the analyses, are: Heine et al. (2001, pp. 604, 606); Heine and Lehman (1995, pp. 602–3); Heine and Lehman (1999, p. 923); Heine and Renshaw (2002, pp. 581–2); Kitayama et al. (1997, pp. 1251–2, 1258); Markus and Kitayama (1991, p. 39).

Sedikides et al. (2005) responded to Heine's rejoinder by conducting two meta-analyses of studies that have investigated the Hypothesis. First, they conducted a meta-analysis of studies of self-enhancement that included traits categorized as independent or interdependent. Their reasoning was that, to the extent that self-enhancement is a pan-cultural motivation, people from primarily independent cultural contexts should direct their self-enhancing motivations towards the independent self and people from largely interdependent cultural contexts should self-enhance more for interdependent aspects of the self. In that meta-analysis, the most direct test of the Hypothesis is a calculation of the effect size (g) indicating the extent to which people self-enhance more for independent traits than they do for interdependent traits in the five papers that met their inclusion criteria (see table 3 from Sedikides et al., 2005, p. 542). Consistent with the Hypothesis, Sedikides et al. found that Westerners overall showed more self-enhancement for independent traits than interdependent ones (point estimate of $g = 0.23$), whereas East Asians showed more self-enhancement for interdependent traits than independent ones (point estimate of $g = -0.56$).

Second, Sedikides et al. conducted a meta-analysis of studies that investigated the relations between degrees of self-enhancement for particular traits and the importance of those traits. If self-enhancement were a universal motivation, it follows that people everywhere would self-enhance in those domains that were of special importance to them. This reasoning suggests that previously identified cross-cultural differences in self-enhancement between Westerners and East Asians (for a review see Heine & Hamamura in press) exist because those studies did not include traits that were of sufficient importance to East Asians. This second meta-analysis summarized the correlations (r) between self-enhancement and trait importance in the five papers that met their inclusion criteria. Consistent with the Hypothesis, Sedikides *et al.* found that both Westerners and East Asians showed a significant correlation between self-enhancement and importance ($r_s = 0.26$ and 0.22, respectively), and these correlations did not differ across cultures.

The result of these two meta-analyses thus largely supported the Hypothesis. However, for reasons that are not specified in Sedikides *et al.* (2005), the data from the six papers highlighted by Heine's comment were not included in the two meta-analyses, despite the fact that these analyses were conducted in response to his comment (Sedikides *et al.*, 2005). Given that the two original meta-analyses by Sedikides *et al.* (2005) only included eight papers total, the omission of those six papers could greatly impact the conclusions that could be drawn. We summarize here how the two meta-analyses conducted by Sedikides *et al.* (2005) appear when all of the relevant studies that investigate the Hypothesis are included.

Investigation 1

Methods

The first investigation conducted by Sedikides *et al.* (2005) investigated whether Westerners tended to self-enhance more in independent domains and whether East Asians tended to self-enhance more in interdependent domains. The results of their investigation suggested that this was the case. We searched PsycINFO with the identical inclusion criteria used by Sedikides *et al.* (2005). That is, we searched PsycINFO from 1872 to November 2005 using 'culture' and 'self' as joint search terms. Studies were selected that: (i) sampled members of Western or Eastern cultures; (ii) included a measure of one's perception of self relative to others; and (iii) the studies explicitly assessed self-other comparisons on attributes associated with individualism and collectivism. That search revealed the same five papers identified by Sedikides *et al.* (2005; we use the effect sizes that they calculated), as well as one additional paper (Heine & Lehman, 1995). We have also included another study that meets the selection criteria (Markus & Kitayama, 1991), and is well known as the first study to investigate the Hypothesis, although it is puzzlingly not listed in PsycINFO. Last, one additional paper emerged that was not published at the time that Sedikides *et al.* conducted their meta-analysis (Ross, Heine, Wilson, & Sugimori, 2005). We summarize the procedure for calculating the effect sizes from each individual study in the Appendix. The effect sizes (gs) reflect the number of standard deviations that people self-enhanced more for independent traits than for interdependent ones.

As in the analyses by Sedikides *et al.* (2005), effect sizes here were weighted and aggregated by a random effect model. . . . With a random effect model, each study in the meta-analysis is treated as a random observation of a population of studies. Hence, a random effect model allows one to generalize the findings of the meta-analysis not just to those studies that are included in the meta-analysis but to any studies that are drawn from the same population of studies (Rosenthal, 1995). These analyses also weight the observations by a function of their sample sizes. . . .

Results

. . . We exclude the study that identified cultural membership by people's responses to a trait measure of interdependence, as cultural membership is clearly not something that is determined by a personality measure. Such a definition of culture is at odds with virtually any of the dozens of definitions of culture that have been proposed by anthropologists (e.g. Kroeber & Kluckholn, 1952/1963). Furthermore, in this particular case, identifying cultural membership by how much one identifies with interdependence is tautological with the self-enhancement dependent measure which evaluates how much one possesses interdependent traits and engages in interdependent behaviours (Heine, 2005b). Indeed, this tautology is evident in the unusually large size of the effects from this one study (gs = 1.76 and 1.33 for East Asians and Westerners, respectively). . . .

The Hypothesis predicts that Easterners would self-enhance more on interdependent traits than independent ones (i.e. negative values of g) and that Westerners would self-enhance more on independent traits than interdependent ones (i.e. positive values of g). . . . East Asians self-enhanced significantly more for interdependent than independent traits ($p < 0.01$), whereas Westerners showed a non-significant tendency to self-enhance more for independent than interdependent traits ($p > 0.30$), and this cultural difference was significant (Qb = 7.10, $p < 0.01$). That is, people from the two cultural groups self-enhanced to different degrees depending on the domains of the traits under study. In contrast, . . . people from both cultures self-enhance non-significantly more for interdependent than independent traits (both $ps > 0.20$). Furthermore, a test of heterogeneity reveals that the point estimates of the effects do not differ across cultures, Qb = 0.53, ns. In sum, once all cross-cultural studies available in the literature are admitted into the meta-analysis, the domain of the traits does not affect the degree of self-enhancement for either culture and thus the Hypothesis is not supported. East Asians do not self-enhance significantly more for interdependent traits than independent ones (although the trend is in the right direction), and Westerners do not self-enhance significantly more for independent traits than interdependent ones (and the trend is in the opposite direction).

Investigation 2

Methods

The second investigation by Sedikides *et al.* (2005) tested the Hypothesis by examining whether people tend to self-enhance more for traits or domains that they view to be especially important. We conducted the same investigation by searching PsycINFO with the search terms 'culture' and 'self-enhancement' or 'self-enhancing biases; 'the terms most germane to the hypothesis.' We included those papers that contrasted people from Western and Eastern cultures and included a measure or manipulation of the importance of the domains under study. This search revealed the same five papers identified by Sedikides *et al.* (2005; we again use the effect sizes they calculated) plus four additional papers that were not in their meta-analysis: Heine *et al.* (2001), Heine and Lehman (1999), Heine and Renshaw (2002), Kitayama *et al.* (1997). . . .

Results

. . . The Hypothesis predicts that both East Asians and Westerners would show a positive correlation between self-enhancement and domain importance, and that there would be no cultural difference in the magnitude of those correlations. East Asians do not show a correlation between self-enhancement and trait importance, whereas Westerners do ($p < 0.001$). Furthermore, the magnitude of the Western correlation is significantly larger than that of the East Asian correlation, $Qb = 6.14$, $p < 0.05$. In sum, an analysis of all cross-cultural studies is inconsistent with the Hypothesis. Westerners do self-enhance more in especially important traits, but East Asians do not.

The studies in Investigation 2 used a variety of different methods. The most commonly used method was the 'better-than-average effect', in which participants rate themselves compared to the 'average' other, or to 'most others'. Looking at the magnitude of the correlations for each of the studies, there appears to be a pattern regarding which methods tend to yield more positive correlations between self-enhancement and importance. Studies which used the better-than-average effect ($k = 10$) revealed marginally more pronounced positive correlations between trait importance and self-enhancement than the other studies ($k = 14$), $Qb = 3.05$, $p < 0.09$. The better-than-average effect studies revealed an average correlation between self-enhancement and importance of $r = 0.20$, which is significant, $Z = 2.87$, $p < 0.001$. In contrast, all of the other studies revealed an average correlation of $r = 0.05$, which is not significant, $Z < 1$. Apparently, the method that one chooses influences the likelihood that one will detect a positive correlation between these two variables. We shall argue below that this is likely to be due to a methodological artifact.

Discussion

The question of whether people are motivated to self-enhance in domains that are especially important to them is a key question for understanding cultural differences in self-enhancement. It is necessary to consider because it is possible that cross-cultural studies on self-enhancement may have systematically underestimated the extent of East Asian self-enhancement by only including traits or domains that were important to Westerners, but were not important to East Asians.

The two investigations presented here provide strong evidence to challenge this alternative account. An examination of all of the relevant published studies that have investigated self-enhancing motivations across culture by domain (independent *vs* interdependent) and by importance, is not in support of the Hypothesis. In Investigation 1, the domain of the traits (independent *vs* interdependent) had no consistent impact on self-enhancement for either East Asians or Westerners. Likewise, in Investigation 2, although Westerners exhibited a significant correlation between self-enhancement and domain importance, there was no such correlation for East Asians. In sum, when all of the relevant studies are considered, the two investigations do not support the Hypothesis. Sedikides *et al.*'s two investigations yielded a very different conclusion because a number of relevant studies were not included in their analyses.

The correlation between self-enhancement and importance can be seen as an additional measure of self-enhancement (Sedikides *et al.*, 2003), as it is indicating that people view themselves especially positively in the domains that matter the most to them. That the Western correlation is significant provides further evidence that self-enhancing motivations are pronounced among people in Western cultures. The lack of a correlation for East Asians is additional evidence that self-enhancing motivations are more elusive in that cultural group.

Contrasting the Better-than-average Effect with Other Methods

We note that meta-analyses are often more informative in the pattern of results that they yield across methods. Although in meta-analyses that include only a small number of studies, particularly in the present case where there are occasionally only one or two studies per method, any observed patterns must be interpreted cautiously. With this caveat in mind, we note that one striking pattern emerges here. In Investigation 2, the better-than-average effect was the method that most consistently revealed a significant correlation between self-enhancement and importance. Overall, the other studies did not reveal a significant correlation between self-enhancement and importance. Because the second investigation conducted by Sedikides *et al.* (2005) only included studies of the better-than-average effect, plus the one unpublished analysis of the false uniqueness effect by Heine and Lehman (1997), their analysis only included studies that showed strong positive correlations between self-enhancement and importance.

Why might the better-than-average effect yield a more positive correlation between self-enhancement and importance? We have argued elsewhere (Heine, 2005b; Hamamura, Heine, & Takemoto, 2006; Heine & Hamamura in press) that this method uniquely inflates estimates of this correlation due to a methodological artifact, known as the 'everyone is better-than-average-effect' (EBTA; Klar & Giladi, 1997). Specifically, people have a tendency to evaluate any specific person as better-than-average, which inflates estimates of self-enhancement when people are asked to compare themselves with the average other. Prior research suggests that the better-than-average effect does not exclusively measure self-enhancing motivations per se but, in addition, reveals an independent cognitive bias that emerges when people process singular versus distributional information (cf. Kahneman & Tversky, 1973). Klar and Giladi (Klar & Giladi, 1997, 1999; Giladi & Klar, 2002) have suggested that when making a comparative judgment between a singular target (e.g. the self, a friend, a stranger) and a distributional target (e.g. most other students in my university, most of my friends, the average person), people fail to adequately consider the qualities of the group, and the comparison comes to only reflect their absolute evaluations of the singular target. Thus, if people are comparing a fictitious target (e.g. 'Miwa') with most other members of a positively evaluated group (e.g. university students), participants have a mildly favourable attitude towards Miwa as a member of this positive group, and they express this favourability by concluding that Miwa is 'better than average.' Viewing a random other as better than average is a finding parallel to what is seen in the better-than-average effect design, yet it could not be driven by self-enhancing motivations as it has nothing to do with the self. Importantly, our argument is not that Western self-enhancement in the better-than-average effect is solely due to the EBTA effect—we argue that the EBTA effect inflates the magnitude of apparent self-enhancement. To the extent that Westerners contrast themselves to specific others, a comparison which circumvents the EBTA effect, they may still evaluate themselves especially positively because of self-enhancing motivations (Alicke, Klotz, Breitenbecher, Yurak, & Vredenburg, 1995; Chang & Asakawa, 2003; Hamamura et al., 2006); however, the magnitude of those effects are less than what they are when they contrast themselves to an unspecified 'average' other. In the case of East Asians, their self-enhancing motivations are weak enough that they do not evaluate themselves more positively than a specific other (Chang & Asakawa, 2003; Hamamura et al., 2006).

If people are especially prone to view specific others as better than average because of the EBTA effect, it follows that they may rate specific others as better than average especially for those traits that are most important. Favourable evaluations of people are most afforded by traits that are especially valued. For example, if a person evaluated a target extremely positively on strongly valued traits, such as warm, intelligent, or trustworthy, they would likely have an overall positive view of that target. In contrast, extremely positive evaluations on less valued traits such as punctual, impulsive, or cautious, would not necessarily translate into an overall positive view of the target. Positive evaluations of people and objects are most afforded by traits that are especially valued, and this suggests an alternative explanation to the correlations between self-enhancement and importance that have been found in studies of the better-than-average effect. This is a relation analogous with that identified in expectancy-value theory (Fishbein, 1963). In support of this, Hamamura et al. (2006) found that the positive correlation among East Asians between importance and self-enhancement in a better-than-average effect design was no longer significant once the EBTA effect was controlled for. In sum, we suggest that the better-than-average effect artificially inflates estimates of the correlations between self-enhancement and importance for people of both cultures. If this artifact was controlled for, we predict that the average correlations in Investigation 2 would be even lower (or more negative) for people of both cultures.

Contrasting the Inclusion Criteria of the Present Paper and Those of Sedikides *et al.* (2005)

The selection criteria of Sedikides *et al.* (2005) resulted in the inclusion of only studies that used the better-than-average effect and the false uniqueness effect (with the exception of the missing study by Markus & Kitayama, 1991). Their analyses did not include studies of absolute and relative-likelihood estimates of unrealistic optimism, self-discrepancies, self-peer evaluations, situation sampling, or studies that manipulated success and failure. We are unclear as to the rationale of Sedikides *et al.* for excluding these studies, as the only mention of these studies in their 2005 paper is in a footnote on page 540 which reads 'These criteria identify a subset of studies that are relevant to our framing of the research question. There are other studies on this general topic that are not included, such as Heine and Lehman (1995), Heine *et al.* (2001), and Kitayama *et al.* (1997).' We suggest that, in general, broader inclusion criteria in meta-analyses allow for researchers to draw more confident and meaningful conclusions. In this case, broader criteria not only yielded very different overall effects than a narrower set of criteria, but they also highlighted how the effects appear to be greatly influenced by the particular method that is used.

Which set of inclusion criteria is most appropriate for answering the question of whether East Asians self-enhance in domains that are of special importance to them? If the question that the meta-analyses were to address was 'Are the better-than-average effect and the false-uniqueness effect pancultural?', we would agree that the inclusion criteria used by Sedikides *et al.* (2005) were the most appropriate. However, the question that was addressed in both Sedikides *et al.* (2003) and Sedikides *et al.* (2005) was 'Is self-enhancement pancultural?' Indeed, the conclusion that they draw from their meta-analyses in their abstract is that the 'self-enhancement motivation is universal' (p. 539). We submit that to address the question of whether self-enhancement is universal a meta-analysis must include all relevant studies that have investigated self-enhancement. We originally conducted our various studies that investigated the Hypothesis with several different methods precisely to obtain the most convergent evidence with respect to testing it. We suggest that convergent evidence across methods will always be more compelling than evidence from a limited set of methods.

In sum, the Hypothesis is supported by the two investigations only when some relevant studies are not included in the analysis. When all the relevant cross-cultural studies are examined, there is not support for the notion of pancultural self-enhancement. Rather, the results demonstrate that East Asians do not self-enhance more for domains that they view to be especially important.

References

Alicke, M. D., Klotz, M. L., Breitenbecher, D. L., Yurak, T. J. & Vredenburg, D. S. (1995). Personal contact, individuation, and the better-than-average effect. *Journal of Personality and Social Psychology, 68,* 804–825.

Borenstein, M. & Rothstein, H. (1999). *Comprehensive Meta-Analysis: a Computer Program for Research Synthesis* [Computer software]. Englewood, NJ: Biostat.

*Brown, J. D. & Kobayashi, C. (2002). Self-enhancement in Japan and America. *Asian Journal of Social Psychology, 5,* 145–167.

Chang, E. C. & Asakawa, K. (2003). Cultural variations on optimistic and pessimistic bias for self versus a sibling: Is there evidence for self-enhancement in the West and for self-criticism in the East when the referent group is specified? *Journal of Personality and Social Psychology, 84,* 569–581.

Fishbein, M. (1963). An investigation of the relationship between beliefs about an object and the attitude toward that object. *Human Relations, 16,* 233–240.

Giladi, E. E. & Klar, Y. (2002). When standards are wide of the mark: Nonselective superiority and bias in comparative judgments of objects and concepts. *Journal of Experimental Psychology: General, 131,* 538–551.

Hamamura, T., Heine, S. J. & Takemoto, T. (2006). *Why the Better-Than-Average Effect Is a Worse-Than-Average Measure of Self-Enhancement.* Unpublished manuscript. Vancouver, BC: University of British Columbia.

Hedges, L. V. & Becker, B. J. (1986). Statistical methods in the meta-analysis of research in gender differences. In: J. S. Hyde & M. C. Linn, eds. *The Psychology of Gender: Advances Through Meta-Analysis,* pp. 14–50. Baltimore: Johns Hopkins University Press.

Heine, S. J. (2005a). Constructing good selves in Japan and North America. In: R. M. Sorrentino, D. Cohen, J. M. Olson & M. P. Zanna, eds. *Culture and Social Behavior: The Tenth Ontario Symposium,* pp. 115–143. Hillsdale, NJ: Lawrence Erlbaum.

Heine, S. J. (2005b). Where is the evidence for pancultural self-enhancement? A reply to Sedikides, Gaertner & Toguchi. *Journal of Personality and Social Psychology, 89,* 531–538.

Heine, S. J. & Hamamura, T. (2007). In search of East Asian self-enhancement. *Personality and Social Psychology Review, 11,* 1–24.

*Heine, S. J. & Lehman, D. R. (1995). Cultural variation in unrealistic optimism: Does the West feel more invulnerable than the East? *Journal of Personality and Social Psychology, 68,* 595–607.

*Heine, S. J. & Lehman, D. R. (1997). The cultural construction of self-enhancement: An examination of group-serving biases. *Journal of Personality and Social Psychology, 72,* 1268–1283.

*Heine, S. J. & Lehman, D. R. (1999). Culture, self-discrepancies, and self-satisfaction. *Personality and Social Psychology Bulletin, 25,* 915–925.

*Heine, S. J. & Renshaw, K. (2002). Interjudge agreement, self-enhancement, and liking: Cross-cultural divergences. *Personality and Social Psychology Bulletin, 28,* 578–587.

*Heine, S. J., Kitayama, S., Lehman, D. R., *et al.* (2001). Divergent consequences of success and failure in Japan and North America: An investigation of self-improving motivations and malleable selves. *Journal of Personality and Social Psychology, 81,* 599–615.

Heine, S. J., Lehman, D. R., Markus, H. R., & Kitayama, S. (1999). Is there a universal need for positive self-regard? *Psychological Review, 106,* 766–794.

*Hornsey, M. J. & Jetten, J. (2005). Loyalty without conformity: Tailoring self-perception as a means of balancing belonging and differentiation. *Self and Identity, 4,* 81–95.

Kahneman, D. & Tversky, A. (1973). On the psychology of prediction. *Psychological Review, 80,* 237–251.

*Kitayama, S., Markus, H. R., Matsumoto, H. & Norasakkunkit, V. (1997). Individual and collective processes in the construction of the self: Self-enhancement in the United States and self-criticism in Japan. *Journal of Personality and Social Psychology, 72,* 1245–1267.

Klar, Y. & Giladi, E. E. (1997). No one in my group can be below the group's average A robust positivity bias in favor of anonymous peers. *Journal of Personality and Social Psychology, 73,* 885–901.

Klar, Y. & Giladi, E. E. (1999). Are most people happier than their peers, or are they just happy? *Personality and Social Psychology Bulletin, 25,* 585–594.

*Kobayashi, C. & Brown, J. D. (2003). Self-esteem and self-enhancement in Japan and America. *Journal of Cross-Cultural Psychology, 34,* 567–580.

Kroeber, A. L. & Kluckholn, C. (1952/1963). *Culture: A Critical Review of Concepts and Definitions.* Cambridge, MA: Harvard University.

*Kurman, J. (2001). Self-enhancement: Is it restricted to individualistic cultures? *Personality and Social Psychology Bulletin, 12,* 1705–1716.

*Markus, H. R. & Kitayama, S. (1991). Cultural variation in the self-concept. In: G. R. Goethals & J. Strauss, eds. *Multidisciplinary Perspectives on the Self,* pp. 18–48. New York: Springer-Verlag.

*Norasakkunkit, V. & Kalick, S. M. (2002). Culture, ethnicity, and emotional distress measures: The role of self-construal and self-enhancement. *Journal of Cross-Cultural Psychology, 33,* 56–70.

Rosenthal, R. (1995). Writing meta-analytic reviews. *Psychological Bulletin, 118,* 183–192.

*Ross, M., Heine, S. J., Wilson, A. E. & Sugimori, S. (2005). Cross-cultural discrepancies in self-appraisals. *Personality and Social Psychology Bulletin, 31,* 1175–1188.

*Sedikides, C., Gaertner, L. & Toguchi, Y. (2003). Pancultural self-enhancement. *Journal of Personality and Social Psychology, 84,* 60–79.

Sedikides, C., Gaertner, L. & Vevea, J. (2005). Pancultural self-enhancement reloaded: A meta-analytic reply to Heine (2005). *Journal of Personality and Social Psychology, 89,* 539–551.

References with an asterisk indicate studies included in the meta-analysis.

Appendix

Procedures for Calculating Effect Sizes from the Individual Studies

The effect sizes from all studies included in meta-analyses by Sedikides *et al.* (2005) were based on their calculations.

Heine and Lehman (1995). Relative likelihood measure of unrealistic optimism.

Magnitude of the optimism bias on a 7-point Likert scale was compared between independent and interdependent traits divided by the pooled standard deviation of those two variables.

Heine and Lehman (1995). Absolute likelihood measure of unrealistic optimism.

The optimism bias was calculated by the difference between percentage estimates for self and others. This bias was compared between independent and interdependent traits divided by the pooled standard deviation of the four variables (i.e. independent self-estimates, interdependent self-estimates, independent other estimates, interdependent other estimates).

Markus and Kitayama (1991). False uniqueness effect.

Percentage estimates of others superior to oneself were compared between independent and interdependent domains. The standard deviations and Ns are no longer available for this study. The standard deviations for these analyses are based on those found from Heine and Lehman (1997; Study 1), which used the same design. The sample sizes are the average of the Ns used from all of the other studies in Investigation 1.

Heine *et al.* (2001) (Studies 1 and 2). Manipulations of success and failure.

Compared the importance ratings for task following success or failure feedback divided by the pooled standard deviation of those two variables to calculate d. d was then converted to an r.

Heine and Lehman (1999). Actual-ideal self-discrepancies.

Magnitude of self-discrepancies were correlated with rated importance of the trait within participants.

Heine and Renshaw (2002). Self-peer biases.

For each trait, a bias was calculated by the difference score between self-evaluations and evaluations by peers. The magnitudes of these biases were correlated within-participants with the average rated importance of the traits conducted by an independent sample.

Kitayama *et al.* (1997) (Studies 1 and 2). Situation sampling.

Magnitude of self-esteem increases and decreases were compared between situations generated within one's own culture and situations generated within the comparison culture, divided by the pooled standard deviation of these four variables (i.e. self-esteem increasing situations in own culture, self-esteem decreasing situations in own culture, self-esteem increasing situations in other culture, self-esteem decreasing situations in other culture) to calculate d. d was then converted to an r.

Ross *et al.* (2005) (Study 1).

The weighted average of positive and negative statements about the self were calculated ((positive − negative)/(positive + negative)) and compared between independent and interdependent domains.

CHALLENGE QUESTIONS

Is the Need for Social Enhancement Universal Across Cultures?

1. Consider the self-reports used to quantify self-enhancement in these studies. What other methods might be used to measure self-enhancement?
2. Compare the reasons Sedikides et al. give for omitting a number of studies on self-enhancement and the reasons Heine et al. give for including them. Who do you think makes the better case, and why?
3. If studies in both Eastern and Western countries support the hypothesis that people self-enhance, do you think it justifies a claim that self-enhancement is a global phenomenon? Support your answer.
4. Imagine you are a leader in a culture that values interdependence. If self-enhancement were shown scientifically to be a universal need for human psychological well-being, what changes, if any, would you try to implement in society?
5. What other variables might affect the results of self-report studies on self-enhancement?

Contributors to This Volume

EDITOR

DR. BRENT SLIFE is currently professor of psychology at Brigham Young University, where he chairs the doctoral program in theoretical and philosophical psychology and serves as a member of the doctoral program in clinical psychology. He has been honored recently with several awards for his scholarship and teaching, including the Eliza R. Snow Award (for research on the interface of science and religion), the Karl G. Maeser Award (top researcher at BYU), Circle of Honor Award (Student Honor Association), and both Teacher of the Year by the university and Most Outstanding Professor by the psychology student honorary, Psi Chi.

Professor Slife moved from Baylor University, where he served as director of clinical training for many years and was honored there as Outstanding Research Professor. He also received the Circle of Achievement award for his teaching. The recipient of numerous grants (e.g., NSF, NEH), he is also listed in *Who's Who in the World, America, Science and Engineering,* and *Health and Medicine.* As a fellow of several professional organizations, including the American Psychological Association, he recently served as the president of the Society of Theoretical and Philosophical Psychology and serves currently on the editorial boards of six journals: *Journal of Mind and Behavior, Journal of Theoretical and Philosophical Psychology, Humanistic Psychologist, Qualitative Research in Psychology, International Journal of Existential Psychology and Psychotherapy,* and *Terrorism Research.*

He has authored over 120 articles and six books, including *Taking Sides: Clashing Views on Psychological Issues* (2011, McGraw-Hill), *Critical Thinking About Psychology: Hidden Assumptions and Plausible Alternatives* (2005, APA Books), *Critical Issues in Psychotherapy: Translating New Ideas into Practice* (2001, Sage), *What's Behind the Research? Hidden Assumptions in the Behavioral Sciences* (1995, Sage), and *Time and Psychological Explanation* (1993, SUNY Press). Dr. Slife also continues his psychotherapy practice of over 25 years, where he specializes in marital and family therapies. Please check his Web site, www.brentdslife.com, for downloadable articles and links to his books.

AUTHORS

JEFFREY J. ARNETT is a psychological research professor at the Department of Psychology at Clark University. Dr. Arnett is the author of several books on adolescents.

JULIA K. BOEHM is a postdoctoral research fellow at Harvard School of Public Health. She received her BA from Lewis & Clark College and her MA and PhD from University of California, Riverside, where she also received the Chancellor's Dissertation Fellowship. Her research focuses on mental and physical well-being.

DAVID J. BULLER is a professor in the Department of Philosophy at Northern Illinois University. He has published numerous articles and books on evolutionary psychology.

DAVID M. BUSS is a professor of psychology at the University of Texas at Austin and is well known for his evolutionary psychology research on human mating strategies. He is the author of over 200 scientific articles and has won several awards for his work such as the APA Distinguished Scientific Award for Early Career Contribution to Psychology and the APA G. Stanley Hall Lectureship.

PATRICK J. CARNES is a nationally known speaker on sex addiction and recovery issues and is currently the executive director of the Gentle Path program at Pine Grove Behavioral Center in Hattiesburg, Mississippi.

JEAN A. CARTER is currently a member of the board of directors of the American Psychological Association. She began a psychotherapy practice in Washington, D.C., after receiving her PhD in counseling psychology from the University of Maryland in 1980 and continues her practice. At the Washington Psychological Center, she focuses on psychotherapy with individuals and couples, emphasizing aspects of serious trauma, relationship issues, depression, and work stress/vocational adjustment. Other areas of interest for her include grief and loss and issues related to sexual orientation for both individuals and couples. She also serves as an adjunct faculty member at the University of Maryland in counseling psychology.

DAVID CARUSO is a research affiliate in the Department of Psychology at Yale University and the coauthor of the Mayer, Salovey, Caruso Emotional Intelligence Test (MSCEIT). He was a National Institute of Child Health and Human Development predoctoral fellow and received a PhD in psychology from Case Western Reserve University. He was then awarded a National Institute of Mental Health fellowship and spent two years as a postdoctoral fellow in Developmental Psychology at Yale University.

DIANNE L. CHAMBLESS is a Merriam Term Professor of Psychology at the University of Pennsylvania. She is also the director of clinical training for the Department of Psychology. Her areas of research include anxiety disorders, expressed emotion, and empirically supported treatments.

KATHLEEN CLARKE-PEARSON is an assistant professor in the department of pediatrics at University of North Carolina at Chapel Hill. Her research focuses on pediatric and adolescent medicine and adolescent risk behaviors; attention-deficit hyperactivity disorder; behavioral/developmental problems in toddlers and children; emotional and mental health; medical effects on toddlers, children, teens, and families; and obesity.

PRISCILLA K. COLEMAN is an associate professor in the School of Family and Consumer Sciences at Bowling Green State University. Dr. Coleman's research interests include the development, expression, and effects of individual differences in parenting, socioemotional development in early childhood, and postabortion emotional sequelae.

MARK COSTANZO is a professor of psychology and the codirector of the Center for Applied Psychological Research at Claremont McKenna College. He has published research on a variety of law-related topics. He frequently serves as an expert witness and has appeared in the national media to discuss the applications of psychological science to the legal system.

LAUREN DONCHI has a bachelor's degree with honors from Swinburne University in Melbourne, Australia. She is a registered psychologist with a strong background in schools and education and is currently employed by the Department of Education and Training to provide psychology services within a network of schools in outer eastern Melbourne.

BRENT DONNELLAN is a professor of psychology at Michigan State University. He received his PhD from the University of California, Davis. His research interests include personality development, self-esteem, and narcissism.

LOWELL GAERTNER is professor of psychology at University of Tennessee, Knoxville and past director of its graduate program in experimental psychology. He has served on editorial boards including the *Journal of Personality and Social Psychology*, where he is a past associate editor. He is the author of numerous publications and received a PhD from University of North Carolina, Chapel Hill.

EDWIN E. GANTT is a professor of psychology at Brigham Young University. He received his PhD from Duquesne University. Dr. Gantt is interested in theory and philosophy of psychology and coedited *Psychology for the Other: Levinas, Ethics and the Practice of Psychology.*

GLENN GEHER is professor and Director of Evolutionary Studies in the Department of Psychology at SUNY New Paltz. He received his PhD in social and personality psychology.

ELLEN GERRITY is the associate director of the UCLA-Duke University National Center for Child Traumatic Stress and is on the faculty of the Duke University Department of Psychiatry and the Duke University Sanford Institute of Policy Studies. She has worked in the field of trauma and violence for more than 25 years and is the senior editor of *Mental Health Consequences of Torture.*

AMY L. GONZALES is a Robert Wood Johnson Health and Society Scholar at the University of Pennsylvania. Her research explores the effects of social media and mobile technology on the individual, particularly as it relates to mental and physical health.

GERALD J. HAEFFEL is an assistant professor of psychology at Notre Dame. His program of research is devoted to understanding the cognitive processes and products that contribute to risk and resilience for depression.

TAKESHI HAMAMURA is assistant professor of psychology at the Chinese University of Hong Kong, where he received the Faculty of Social Science Exemplary Teaching Award. Author of numerous publications, his research is in social relations across cultures. He received a PhD from the University of British Columbia.

JEFFREY T. HANCOCK is an associate professor at Cornell University. His research has focused on two types of language, verbal irony and deception, and on a number of cognitive and social psychological factors affected by online communication.

BENJAMIN HANSEN is a psychologist and the team leader of the Mackay District Child and Youth Mental Health Service in Queensland, Australia. He provides assistance to children and adolescents through development and coordination of a range of early identification, assessment, treatment, and support plans for emotional and behavioral disturbances and/or emerging mental health issues. He also does tutoring work with James Cook University and dabbles in private practice.

STEVEN J. HEINE is professor of psychology at University of British Columbia. He researches the role of culture in motivation and is the author of more than 30 articles and nine book chapters. He is recipient of the Distinguished Scientist Early Career Award for Social Psychology from the American Psychological Association and is a fellow of the Association for Psychological Science. He received a PhD in from UBC.

KIRK M. HUBBARD received his doctorate from the University of Minnesota, Minneapolis, and has served in both administrative and clinical positions in the Veterans Administration Medical Center in Hampton, VA. He has also held adjunct faculty positions at the Eastern Virginia Medical School and the College of William & Mary. Dr. Hubbard served as a psychologist supporting field operations for the Central Intelligence Agency for 10 years and served as the Director of Behavioral Sciences Research at the CIA. Dr. Hubbard is now president of Porter Judson, LLC, a private consulting firm involved in the application of psychology to operational and field settings.

JONATHAN D. HUPPERT is a professor of psychology at The Hebrew University of Jerusalem. His research efforts are aimed at developing the optimal psychosocial treatments for anxiety and related disorders. He conducts studies on the process and outcomes of cognitive-behavioral treatments for anxiety disorders. He also examines the impact of the co-occurrence for other types of psychopathology such as depression or psychosis on anxiety and their impact on treatment outcomes and processes.

STANTON L. JONES is a professor of psychology and provost at Wheaton College. He received his PhD in clinical psychology at Arizona State University and is the author of over 50 articles and book chapters.

SHINOBU KITAYAMA is professor of psychology and director of the Culture and Cognition Program at University of Michigan. He was elected a Guggenheim fellow, a fellow of the American Psychological Association, and named a fellow at the Center for Advanced Study in the Behavioral Sciences. Editor of *Personality and Social Psychology Bulletin,* he is the author of numerous book chapters and articles on cultural differences and similarities. He received a PhD from the University of Michigan.

ALEX W. KWEE is a licensed clinical psychologist and cofounder and president of Harmony Pacific Clinical Consultants (HPCC). He has published and presented internationally on various facets of cross-cultural psychology, values, and addiction.

RANDY J. LARSEN is Chairman of the Psychology Department at Washington University and the William R. Stuckenberg Professor of Human Values and Moral Development. He received his MA from Duquesne University and a PhD from University of Illinois. He was elected a Fellow of the American Psychological Association and the Association for Psychological Science.

SCOTT O. LILIENFELD is a professor of psychology at Emory University and a clinical psychologist. He conducts research on the causes and assessment of personality disorders (especially psychopathic personality), scientific thinking and its application to psychology, and philosophical psychology.

EDWIN A. LOCKE is Dean's Professor of Leadership and Motivation (Emeritus) at the R. H. Smith School of Business at the University of Maryland, College Park. He received his BA from Harvard in 1960 and his PhD in industrial psychology from Cornell University in 1964. He has published more than 240 chapters, notes, and articles in professional journals. Dr. Locke has been elected a fellow of the American Psychological Association, of the American Psychological Society, and of the Academy of Management. He is interested in the application of the philosophy of objectivism to the behavioral sciences.

M. BRINTON LYKES is a professor of community-cultural psychology in the Lynch School of Education and the associate director of the Boston College Center for Human Rights and International Justice. She has contributed chapters on participatory action research in the Handbooks of Feminist Research and Action Research II and a chapter on reparations and psychosocial interventions in the Handbook on Reparations, a project of the International Center of Transitional Justice. She is the 2007 recipient of the American Orthopsychiatric Association's Marion Langer Award for distinction in social advocacy and the pursuit of human rights.

SONJA LYUBOMIRSKY is a professor of psychology at University of California, Riverside, and associate editor of *The Journal of Positive Psychology*. She received a BA from Harvard and a PhD from Stanford. Her research on happiness has been widely featured in journals and the popular media.

ROBERT C. MacCALLUM is professor of psychology at University of North Carolina, Chapel Hill, where he is director of the L. L. Thurstone Psychometric Laboratory. He was elected a member of the Society of Multivariate Experimental Psychology (1990). His research involves multilevel models and methods for analyzing correlational data. He received a PhD in quantitative psychology from the University of Illinois, Urbana-Champaign.

DON MacDONALD is a professor of marriage and family therapy in the psychology department at Seattle Pacific University. He received his PhD in counseling psychology at Michigan State University in 1984. His interests include the theological, philosophical, and historical influences of Christianity and psychology.

JOHN D. MAYER is professor of psychology at the University of New Hampshire. He received his PhD and MA in psychology at Case Western Reserve University and his BA from the University of Michigan. Dr. Mayer has served on the editorial boards of *Psychological Bulletin,* the *Journal of Personality and Social Psychology,* and the *Journal of Personality,* among others, and has been an Individual National Institute of Mental Health Postdoctoral Scholar at Stanford University. He has published extensively in emotional intelligence, integrative models of personality, and the effects of personality on an individual's life.

BRENT MELLING is a doctoral candidate in theoretical and philosophical psychology at Brigham Young University. He holds a BS in bioinformatics.

SUSAN MOORE is a professor in the department of life and social sciences at the University of Swinburne. She has more than 30 years, teaching and research experience in universities, in psychology and education, as well as experience as a school psychologist.

EDDY NAHMIAS is an associate professor in the philosophy department and the Neuroscience Institute at Georgia State University. His research is devoted to the study of human agency: what it is, how it is possible, and how it accords with scientific accounts of human nature. He is working on a book project, *Rediscovering Free Will,* which is contracted with Oxford University Press and funded by a Wisdom Grant (2008–2010) from the University of Chicago's Arete Initiative and the John Templeton Foundation.

NATIONAL INSTITUTE ON DRUG ABUSE (NIDA) was established in 1974 and became part of the National Institutes of Health, Department of Health and Human Services, in October 1992. Since then, it has been a federal focal point for research on drug abuse and addiction. NIDA's aim is to use the power of science to analyze drug abuse and addiction. NIDA addresses the most fundamental and essential questions about drug abuse, from detecting and responding to emerging drug abuse trends, and understanding how drugs work in the brain and body, to developing and testing new treatment and prevention approaches.

THE NATIONAL INSTITUTE OF MENTAL HEALTH has the mission to transform the understanding and treatment of mental illnesses through basic and clinical research, paving the way for prevention, recovery, and cure.

LAUREL C. NEWMAN is an assistant professor and director of psychology at Fontbonne University in St. Louis. She received a BA from Lindenwood University in Missouri and her MS and PhD from Washington University. She conducts research on the influence of self-perceptions, values, and goals.

GWENN SCHURGIN O'KEEFFE is a board-certified pediatrician and a very active member of the American Academy of Pediatrics (AAP) as an official national media spokesperson and as an Executive Committee member of the Council on Communications and Media. She founded PediatricsNow.

JOCHEN PETER is an associate professor in the Amsterdam School of Communications Research at the University of Amsterdam. He received a Veni award for talented junior researchers from the Dutch National Science Foundation. His research focuses on the consequences of adolescents' Internet use for their sexual socialization and psychosocial development.

QAZI RAHMAN is a cognitive biologist at Queen Mary, University of London. His research interests focus on the biological origin of sexual orientation in humans.

RICHARD W. ROBINS is a professor in the Department of Psychology at the University of California, Davis. He received his PhD from the University of California, Berkeley. He has received the APA's Distinguished Scientific Award for Early Career Contribution and the Theoretical Innovation Prize from the Society for Personality and Social Psychology.

JOSEPH LEE RODGERS is professor of quantitative psychology at the University of Oklahoma, where he has been named a George Lynn Cross Research Professor and a Robert Glenn Rapp Foundation Presidential Professor. His research is on multidimensional data analysis, adolescent development, and fertility decision-making. He received a PhD in psychology from University of North Carolina, Chapel Hill.

NANCY F. RUSSO, PhD, Regents Professor of Psychology and Women and Gender Studies, Arizona State University, is editor or author of more than 200 publications related to gender and the psychology of women. Former editor of the *Psychology of Women Quarterly,* she has received the American Psychological Association's (APA) award for Distinguished Contributions to Psychology in the Public Interest, and is a fellow of the APA, the Association for Psychological Science, and the New York Academy of Sciences.

PETER SALOVEY, provost at Yale University, is the Chris Argyris Professor of Psychology and a professor of management and of epidemiology and public health at Yale University. He directs the Health, Emotion and Behavior Laboratory. He also has affiliations with the Yale Cancer Center and the Institution for Social and Policy Studies. Dr. Salovey received an AB in psychology and a coterminal MA in sociology from Stanford University in 1980. He holds three Yale degrees in psychology: an MS (1983), an MPhil (1984), and a PhD (1986). He was president of the Graduate and Professional Student Senate at Yale in 1983–1984. He joined the Yale faculty as an assistant professor in 1986 and has been a full professor since 1995.

SALLY SATEL is a practicing psychiatrist and lecturer at the Yale University School of Medicine as well as a resident scholar for the American Enterprise for Public Policy Research. She examines mental health policy as well as political trends in medicine. Some of her publications include *The Health Disparities Myth* and *One Nation under Therapy*, which she coauthored with Christina Hoff Sommers.

JONATHAN W. SCHOOLER is a professor of psychology. He pursues research on consciousness, memory, the relationship between language and thought, problem solving, and decision making. A fellow of the Association for Psychological Science, he was also an Osher Fellow at the Exploratorium Science Museum in San Francisco. His work has been supported by the National Institute of Mental Health, the Unilever Corporation, the Center for Consciousness Studies, the Office of Educational Research, the Canada Foundation for Innovation, Canada's Social Sciences and Humanities Research Council, the National Sciences and Engineering Research Council of Canada, the Canadian Institute for Health Research, the Bial Foundation, and the Bower Foundation. He currently is on the editorial boards of *Consciousness and Cognition* and *Social Cognitive and Affective Neuroscience*. Dr. Schooler is the author or coauthor of more than 100 papers published in scientific journals or edited volumes and was the editor (with J. C. Cohen) of *Scientific Approaches to Consciousness*, which was published in 1997 by Lawrence Erlbaum.

CONSTANTINE SEDIKIDES is director of the Center for Research on Self and Identity at University of Southampton, England. He is a fellow of the American Psychological Association and past president of the International Society for Self and Identity, serving on international grant panels and many journal editorial boards. He received his PhD in social psychology from The Ohio State University.

LAWRENCE A. SIEGEL practices forensic psychiatry and psychiatry in Valhalla, NY.

RICHARD M. SIEGEL is a Florida-licensed Mental Health Counselor, Board-Certified Sex Therapist, and Certified Addictions Professional.

JEDIDIAH SIEV is a clinical fellow in psychology (psychiatry) at the Massachusetts General Hospital/Harvard Medical School. While completing his graduate studies at the University of Pennsylvania, he specialized in empirically supported treatments for obsessive-compulsive disorder and related disorders, as well as other anxiety and internalizing disorders. He is interested in cognitive factors that contribute to the development and maintenance of obsessive-compulsive disorder and related disorders. He also investigates the relationship between psychotherapy outcomes in regard to active ingredients and common factors.

JULIA RENEE STEINBERG, PhD, is a postdoctoral fellow in the Department of Obstetrics, Gynecology and Reproductive Sciences at the University of California, San Francisco. Her research interests are in gender and the psychology of women.

FRANK J. SULLOWAY is visiting/adjunct professor of psychology and a member of the Institute of Personality and Social Research at the University of California, Berkeley. Recipient of the MacArthur Fellowship and the Golden Plate Award of the American Academy of Achievement, he is also a fellow of the American Association for the Advancement of Science, the Association for Psychological Science, and the Linnean Society of London. He received a PhD from Harvard in the history of science.

KALI H. TRZESNIEWSKI is a professor of psychology at the University of Western Ontario. Having received a PhD from the University of California, Davis, Dr. Trzesniewski's research interests include self-esteem and academic achievement.

JEAN M. TWENGE is a professor of psychology at San Diego State University. She has published extensive research on narcissism and young people. She received her PhD from the University of Michigan.

PATTI M. VALKENBURG is a professor in the Amsterdam School of Communications Research and director of the Center for Research on Children, Adolescents, and the Media. She received her PhD from Leiden University, the Netherlands. She received a Vici award for top researchers from the Dutch National Science Foundation. Her research interests include children's and adolescents' likes and dislikes of entertainment, their development as consumers, and the cognitive, emotional, and social effects of media contents and technologies on young people.

JACK L. VEVEA is associate professor of quantitative psychology at University of California, Merced. He is the author of numerous publications and technical reports. His research is in meta-analysis, item response theory, and mathematical models of memory. He received a PhD in educational statistics from the University of Chicago.

KATHLEEN D. VOHS is a professor of marketing, McKnight Presidential Fellow, and Land O'Lakes Professor of Excellence in Marketing. She has authored more than 130 scholarly publications and served as the editor of six books. She has written extensively on self-regulation, intrapersonal and interpersonal processes, the objective consequences of self-esteem, bulimic symptoms, and consequences of self-control failure on impulsive behavior. She was named a McKnight Land-Grant Professor (2007–2009), and a McKnight

Presidential Fellow at the University of Minnesota (2008), and received the 2008 International Society for Self and Identity Early Career Award.

MARCIA WEBB is an associate professor in the Department of Clinical Psychology at Seattle Pacific University. She is involved in the Living Well Initiative, a multidisciplinary program providing education and conducting research about severe and persistent mental illnesses. Her research emphasizes forgiveness, the self-conscious emotions of shame and guilt, the integration of psychology and theology, and the psychology of religion.

AARON L. WICHMAN is assistant professor of psychology at Western Kentucky University at Bowling Green, where he was awarded the Pressey Grant for honors program teaching in 2009. His research is in social cognition and responses to uncertainty. He received a PhD from and was a postdoctoral teaching and research fellow at The Ohio State University.

ROGERS H. WRIGHT is a past president of Division 12 and founding president of Division 31 of the APA. He cofounded and was founding president of the Council for the Advancement of the Psychological Professions and Sciences.

R. B. ZAJONC (1923–2008) was professor of psychology at Stanford University and recipient of many awards, including the APS William James Fellow Award, the APA Distinguished Scientific Contributions Award, and the SESP Distinguished Scientist Award. He was an APS fellow and charter member, serving on the APS Social Science Research Council. He received a PhD in social psychology from the University of Michigan.